BEST PLACES®

NORTHERN CALIFORNIA

The Locals' Guide to the Best Restaurants, Lodgings, Sights, Shopping, and More!

Edited by
MATTHEW RICHARD POOLE
& KRISTIN LUNA

6 EDITION

SASQUATCH BOOKS
SEATTLE

Printed in the United States of America
Published by Sasquatch Books
Distributed by PGW/Perseus

Sixth edition
15 14 13 12 11 10 10 9 8 7 6 5 4 3 2 1

ISBN-13: 978-1-57061-601-3
ISBN-10: 1-57061-601-9
ISSN 1533-3981

Cover design: Sasquatch Books
Interior design: Scott Taylor/FILTER/Talent
Interior composition: Sarah Plein
Interior maps: Lisa Brower/GreenEye Design
Indexer: Michael Ferreira
Project editors: Rachelle Longé, Tara Spicer, and Kurt Stephan

SPECIAL SALES

Best Places guidebooks are available at special discounts on bulk purchases for corporate, club, or organization sales promotions, premiums, and gifts. For more information, contact your local bookseller or Special Sales, Best Places Guidebooks, 119 South Main Street, Suite 400, Seattle, Washington, 98104, 800/775-0817.

SASQUATCH BOOKS
119 South Main Street, Suite 400
Seattle, Washington 98104
206/467-4300
www.sasquatchbooks.com
custserv@sasquatchbooks.com

CONTENTS

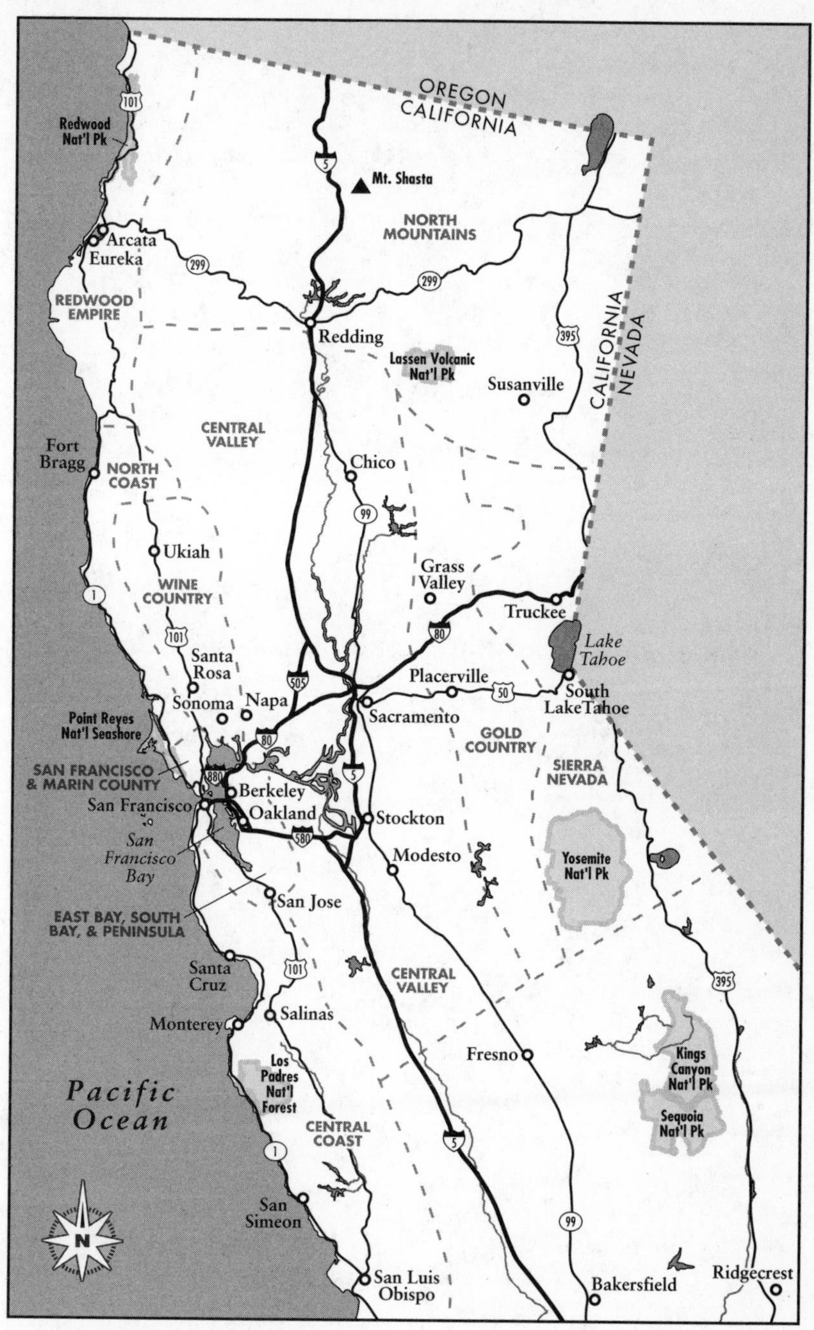

Northern California Overview

Contributors

MATTHEW RICHARD POOLE, a native Northern Californian, has authored more than two dozen travel guides to California and abroad, including *Best Places San Francisco*, *ACCESS Hawaii*, *Berlitz Las Vegas*, and the Frommer's guidebooks to California, San Francisco, and Los Angeles. Before becoming a full-time travel writer and photographer, he worked as an English tutor in Prague, a ski instructor in the Swiss Alps, and a scuba instructor in Maui and Thailand. Matthew currently lives in Mill Valley and is the co-founder of a local travel company called LocalGetaways.com, which offers expert hotel recommendations and travel advice for great getaways throughout Northern California.

KRISTIN LUNA bounced around the globe—from her birthplace in Tennessee to New York City, Scotland, Denmark, Holland, and back again—before finding a permanent home in San Francisco. An adventurist and avid scuba diver, there's not much Kristin won't try, whether its swimming cageless with sharks in the South Pacific, jumping out of a plane over the Pyrenees, or abseiling 100 feet into a glow-worm-lit cave in New Zealand. She has contributed to various Frommer's guides and has written for *Newsweek*, *Forbes Traveler*, *Sherman's Travel*, *Real Simple*, *People*, *Entertainment Weekly*, *InStyle*, *Glamour*, *San Francisco Chronicle*, and more.

SCOTT VAN VELSOR is a Bay Area native and closeted foodie. A Navy vet with a journalism degree and a panache for photography, Scott has written for many of the local news outlets like *SF Weekly*, *Oakland Tribune*, KALW, and *Contra-Costa Times*, as well as authored his own guide, *Newcomer's Handbook for San Francisco*. He's most at home when crashing into inanimate objects on his motorcycle in California's Mojave Desert.

About Best Places® Guidebooks

People trust us. Best Places guidebooks, which have been published continuously since 1975, represent one of the most respected regional travel series in the country. Our reviewers know their territory, and seek out the very best a city or region has to offer. We provide tough, candid reports about places that have rested too long on their laurels, and delight in new places that deserve recognition. We describe the true strengths, foibles, and unique characteristics of each establishment listed.

Best Places Northern California is written by and for locals, and is therefore coveted by travelers. It's written for people who live here and who enjoy exploring the region's bounty and its out-of-the-way places of high character and individualism. It's these very characteristics that make *Best Places Northern California* ideal for tourists, too. The best places in and around the region are the ones that denizens favor: independently owned establishments of good value, touched with local history, run by lively individuals, and graced with natural beauty. With this sixth edition of *Best Places Northern California*, travelers will find the information they need: where to go and when; what to order; which rooms to request (and which to avoid); where the best skiing, hiking, wilderness getaways, and local attractions are; and how to find the region's hidden secrets.

NOTE: *The reviews in this edition are based on information available at press time and are subject to change. Readers are advised that places listed in previous editions may have closed or changed management or may no longer be recommended by this series. The editors welcome information conveyed by users of this book. A report form is provided at the end of the book, and feedback is also welcome via e-mail: BPFeedback@sasquatchbooks.com.*

How to Use This Book

This book is divided into 20 regional chapters covering a wide range of establishments, destinations, and activities. All evaluations are based on numerous reports from local and traveling inspectors. Final judgments are made by Sasquatch editors. **EVERY PLACE FEATURED IN THIS BOOK IS RECOMMENDED.**

STAR RATINGS (*for restaurants and lodgings only*) Restaurants and lodgings are rated on a scale of one to four stars (with half stars in between), based on uniqueness, loyalty of local clientele, performance measured against the establishment's goals, excellence of cooking, cleanliness, value, and professionalism of service. Reviews are listed alphabetically by region, and every place is recommended.

★★★★ The very best in the region

★★★ Distinguished; many outstanding features

★★ Excellent; some wonderful qualities

★ A good place

(For more on how we rate places, see "Best Places Star Ratings" on page xiv.)

PRICE RANGE (*for restaurants and lodgings only*) Prices for restaurants are based primarily on dinner for two, including dessert and tip, but not alcohol. Prices for lodgings are based on peak season rates for one night's lodging for two people (i.e., double occupancy). Peak season is typically Memorial Day to Labor Day for summer destinations, or November through March for winter destinations; off-season rates vary but often can be significantly less. Call ahead to verify, as all prices are subject to change.

- $$$$ Very expensive (more than $100 for dinner for two; more than $200 for one night's lodging for two)
- $$$ Expensive (between $65 and $100 for dinner for two; between $120 and $200 for one night's lodging for two)
- $$ Moderate (between $35 and $65 for dinner for two; between $80 and $120 for one night's lodging for two)
- $ Inexpensive (less than $35 for dinner for two; less than $80 for one night's lodging for two)

RESERVATIONS (*for restaurants only*) For each dining establishment listed in the book, we used one of the following terms for its reservations policy: reservations required, reservations recommended, or no reservations.

ADDRESSES AND PHONE NUMBERS Every attempt has been made to provide accurate information on an establishment's location and phone number, but it's always a good idea to call ahead and confirm.

WEB SITE/E-MAIL ADDRESSES Web site or e-mail addresses have been included where available. Please note that the Web is a fluid and evolving medium, and that Web pages are often "under construction" or, as with all time-sensitive information, may no longer be valid.

CHECKS AND CREDIT CARDS Many establishments that accept checks also require a major credit card for identification. Note that some accept only local checks. Credit cards are abbreviated in this book as follows: American Express (AE), Carte Blanche (CB), Diners Club (DC), Discover (DIS), Enroute (E), Japanese credit card (JCB), MasterCard (MC), Visa (V).

ACCESS AND INFORMATION At the beginning of each chapter, you'll find general guidelines about how to get to a particular region and what types of transportation are available, as well as basic sources for any additional tourist information. Also check individual town listings for specifics about visiting those places.

MAPS AND DIRECTIONS Each chapter in the book begins with a regional map that shows the general area being covered. Throughout the book, basic directions are provided with each entry. Whenever possible, call ahead to confirm hours and location.

THREE-DAY TOURS In every chapter, we've included a quick-reference, three-day itinerary designed for travelers with a short amount of time. Perfect for weekend

BEST PLACES® STAR RATINGS

Any travel guide that rates establishments is inherently subjective—and Best Places is no exception. We rely on our professional experience, yes, but also on a gut feeling. And, occasionally, we even give in to a soft spot for a favorite neighborhood hangout. Our star-rating system is not simply a checklist; it's judgmental, critical, sometimes fickle, and highly personal.

For each new edition, we send local food and travel experts out to review restaurants and lodgings, and then to rate them on a scale of one to four, based on uniqueness, loyalty of local clientele, performance measured against the establishment's goals, excellence of cooking, cleanliness, value, and professionalism of service. That doesn't mean a one-star establishment isn't worth dining or sleeping at. Far from it! When we say that all the places listed in our books are recommended, we mean it. That one-star pizza joint may be just the ticket for the end of a whirlwind day of shopping with the kids. But if you're planning something more special, the star ratings can help you choose an eatery or hotel that will wow your new clients or be a

getaways, these tours outline the highlights of a region or town; each of the establishments or attractions that appear in boldface within the tour are discussed in greater detail elsewhere in the chapter.

THE DETAILS Most bed and breakfasts don't allow children, or have age limits. Most don't allow pets, either. Some places require two-night stays during weekends or busy seasons. Ask about these topics when you make reservations.

HELPFUL ICONS Watch for these quick-reference symbols throughout the book:

FAMILY FUN Places that are fun, easy, and great for kids.

GOOD VALUE While not necessarily cheap, these places offer a good deal within the context of the region.

ROMANTIC These spots offer candlelight, atmosphere, intimacy, or other romantic qualities—kisses and proposals are encouraged!

EDITORS' CHOICE These are places we especially love.

Appears after listings for establishments that have wheelchair-accessible facilities.

stunning, romantic place to celebrate an anniversary or impress a first date.

We award four-star ratings sparingly, reserving them for what we consider truly the best. And once an establishment has earned our highest rating, everyone's expectations seem to rise. Readers often write us specifically to point out the faults in four-star establishments. With changes in chefs, management, styles, and trends, it's always easier to get knocked off the pedestal than to ascend it. Three-star establishments, on the other hand, seem to generate healthy praise. They exhibit outstanding qualities, and we get lots of love letters about them. The difference between two and three stars can sometimes be a very fine line. Two-star establishments are doing a good, solid job and are gaining attention, while one-star places are often dependable spots that have been around forever.

The restaurants and lodgings described in *Best Places Northern California* have earned their stars from hard work and good service (and good food). They're proud to be included in this book: look for our Best Places sticker in their windows. And we're proud to honor them in this, the sixth edition of *Best Places Northern California*.

INDEX All restaurants, lodgings, town names, and major tourist attractions are listed alphabetically at the back of the book.

READER REPORTS At the end of the book is a report form. We receive hundreds of reports from readers suggesting new places or agreeing or disagreeing with our assessments. They greatly help in our evaluations, and we encourage you to respond.

SAN FRANCISCO AND THE NORTH BAY

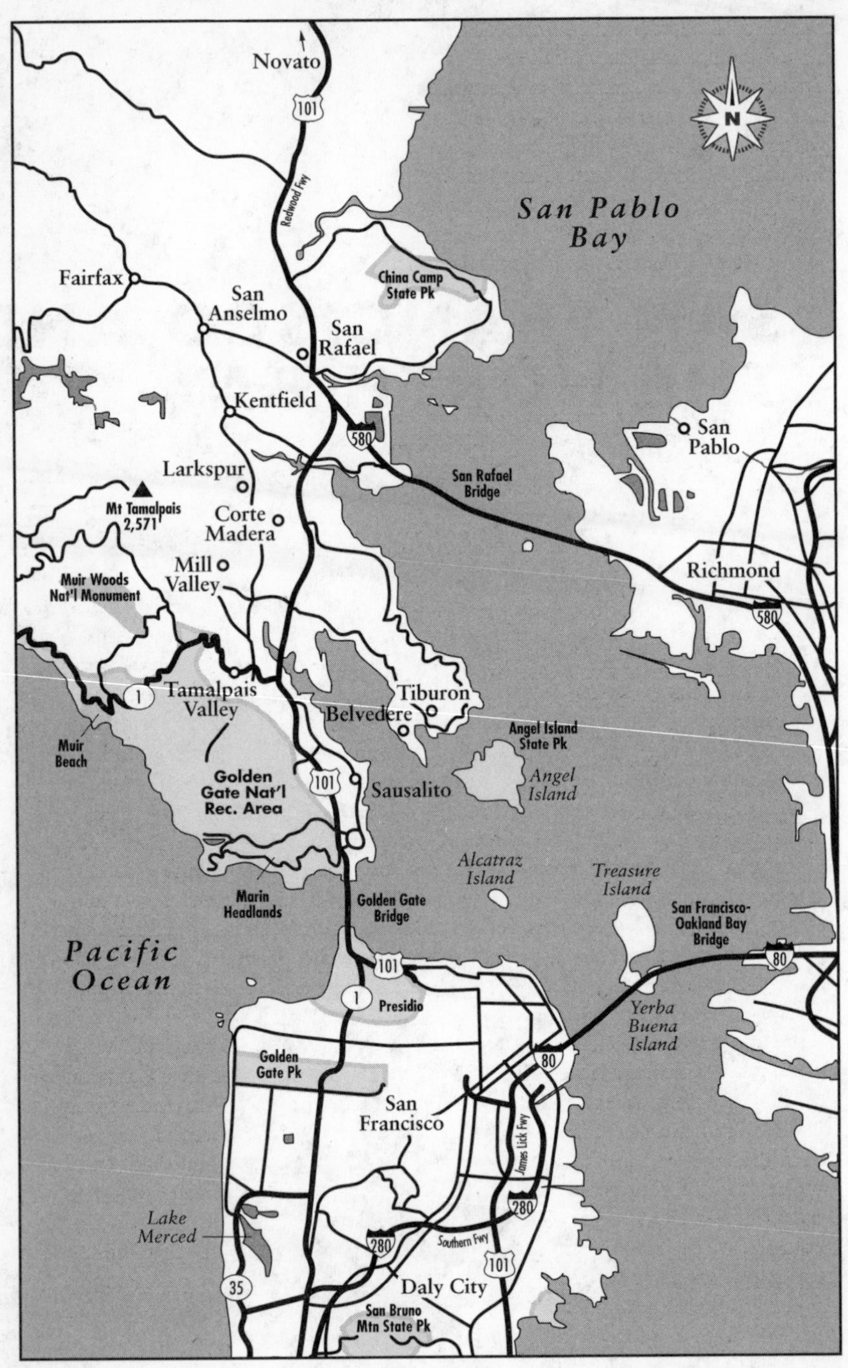

Novato
101
Redwood Fwy
N
San Pablo Bay
China Camp State Pk
Fairfax
San Anselmo
San Rafael
Kentfield
580
San Pablo
Larkspur
San Rafael Bridge
Mt Tamalpais 2,571
Corte Madera
Mill Valley
Richmond
Muir Woods Nat'l Monument
580
1
Tamalpais Valley
Tiburon
Belvedere
Angel Island State Pk
Muir Beach
Golden Gate Nat'l Rec. Area
101
Sausalito
Angel Island
Alcatraz Island
Treasure Island
Marin Headlands
Golden Gate Bridge
San Francisco-Oakland Bay Bridge
Pacific Ocean
101
80
1
Presidio
Yerba Buena Island
Golden Gate Pk
80
San Francisco
James Lick Fwy
Lake Merced
280
280
Southern Fwy
101
35
Daly City
San Bruno Mtn State Pk

SAN FRANCISCO AND THE NORTH BAY

San Francisco

Being a San Francisco resident carries a certain kind of clout. Travel anywhere in the world, and you'll be met with oohs and aahs when you reveal the place in which you've made your home. Trite adjectives—"alluring," "majestic," "awe-inspiring"—don't even begin to describe the lure that has cast a spell over millions. San Francisco is proud yet progressive, vintage but shining with freshly installed glass and steel, and ultrarich bastions like the Seacliff and Gold Coast neighborhoods. The city itself is a curious mix of the uber-wealthy and their needs, which brings along with it the boot-strapping community that has continued to thrive since the 1960s.

Because of rent control and a solid, community-oriented board of supervisors, San Francisco has escaped from becoming a concrete, skyscraper-scattered jungle like Manhattan. The area offers something for everyone, from the curious hipster fresh off the plane from Wisconsin to the founders of global empires who view the city as their playground. This said, expect to find an interesting amalgamation of natives who have seen it evolve through the decades and newcomers eager to add "Bay Area resident" to their repertoire of achievements (we've determined it takes a good five years of residency before one can truthfully claim to be "from San Francisco"). Many will live the rest of their days among the misty maze; others see it simply as an experiment, a stepping stone to the next big thing.

Whatever you do, though, please don't call it Frisco. It's San Francisco to you. Spouting off loathed nicknames like Frisco will label you a tourist—or even worse, a bright-eyed import—before you've even stepped foot outside the airport. Locals use the shorthand terms San Fran, "the city," or simply SF with confidence because they know they have something special: In no other place in the country is the meeting of land and sea so spectacular or the combination of nature and culture so enticing. Surrounded by ocean and bay, crinkled into hill after hill, the city rests under a downy layer of fog one moment and sparkles in the clear Northern California sunlight the next.

But the attraction isn't just the setting: San Francisco's neighborhoods exude a personality that makes this place much more than a pretty collection of natural gifts. The neighborhoods are as varied as the topography. A trendy albeit yuppie energy radiates from the Marina on summer days, with joggers, cyclers, and inline skaters gliding along the Marina Green. The alternative lifestyle is alive and thriving in the Haight, among the colorful, bohemian shops. The Haight's edgy neighbor, the Castro, serves as the epicenter for gays worldwide: rainbow flags adorn many establishments along Market Street in this part of town, with unabashed volition.

The Mission District moves to a multiethnic beat, stirring the cultural pot in its eateries and public artwork. SoMa (South of Market) is a new haven for financial execs, accompanied by the city's foodies, as lower rent and industrial spaces are just begging to be filled with some of California's finest dining. The gritty Tenderloin, once feared for its ubiquitous homeless population and high drug use, has bled into trendy Nob Hill, creating the newly dubbed Tender Nob area. In fact, you'll find the areas of San Francisco change like the tides: New 'hoods are constantly popping up, while corners where certain districts meet are revamped and renamed at the drop of a hat. And while it's true that on some days the fog never clears, it's a small price to pay to play in one of the world's greatest cities.

ACCESS AND INFORMATION

Two major airports serve the city—**SAN FRANCISCO INTERNATIONAL AIRPORT (SFO)** (650/821-8211; www.flysfo.com) and **OAKLAND INTERNATIONAL AIRPORT (OAK)** (510/563-3300; www.oaklandairport.com). Most travelers use SFO, which is located 14 miles south of downtown San Francisco via Highways 101 or 280. Fares to either airport are often identical, so if a flight to SFO is sold out, there may still be available seats on flights to OAK. Trips to or from SFO are easy with one of the fast, reliable **SHUTTLE SERVICES**, such as SuperShuttle (415/558-8500; www.supershuttle.com) or Quake City (415/255-4899; www.quakecityshuttle.com); fares are around $14. Bayporter Express (877/467-1800 in the Bay Area or 415/467-1800 elsewhere; www.bayporter.com) is a popular Oakland Airport shuttle service that charges $29 per person for rides to San Francisco. **BAY AREA RAPID TRANSIT (BART)** (510/464-6000; www.bart.gov) trains run daily from the SFO terminal to downtown San Francisco and cost about $5 one way; BART also services OAK, but you'll need to take a free shuttle from the airport. **TAXIS** wait at each SFO terminal's arrival area and will relieve you of $35 for the 20-minute trip downtown.

PARKING in San Francisco can be an ordeal; many neighborhoods limit nonresidents to only 2 hours, and most downtown meters have a maddening maximum time limit of 30 minutes. To make things even more frustrating, traffic cops are quick, ruthless, and in abundance (almost 30 percent of all parking tickets issued statewide are issued in San Francisco). If you see a tow-away warning, take it seriously. Public parking garages abound, and if you look hard enough, you can find some garages or park-and-pay lots that don't charge Manhattan rates. If you park in a disabled zone, the violation alone will cost $275, not to mention the towing fees and hassle of getting the car back.

Major hotels have taxi stands; otherwise, telephone for a cab, since taxis usually cruise along only the most populated streets.

Public transportation reaches every neighborhood but grows sparse after midnight. **MUNI**, the **SAN FRANCISCO MUNICIPAL RAILWAY** (415/673-6864; www.sfmuni.com), includes buses, above-ground/underground streetcars, and cable cars. Exact change is required ($1 bills are OK), and free transfers (except for cable cars) grant two more rides within the next 1½ hours (be sure to ask for a transfer as soon as you board the bus). Short-term (one-, three-, and seven-day) and monthly Muni passes allowing unlimited rides are available at the

Visitor Information Center and at City Hall during weekday business hours. (For information on cable cars, see the Major Attractions section.)

BART (510/464-6000; www.bart.gov) is a clean, reliable, high-speed underground commuter train system that runs through the southeastern side of the city, with routes to Daly City and the East Bay, including Berkeley and Oakland.

San Franciscans have become masters at dressing in layers, never sure exactly what the day's **WEATHER** holds. Sunny afternoons can be warm and spectacular, but are often preceded by foggy mornings or followed by cool evenings. The climate is mild, rarely rising above 80°F or falling below 40°F, but bring a sweater or coat—chances are you'll need it. Spring and fall months are warmest, as the fog makes its most frequent appearances in summer.

For more details on San Francisco sites and attractions, visit the helpful staff at the Convention and Visitors Bureau's **VISITOR INFORMATION CENTER** (lower level of Hallidie Plaza at Market and Powell sts; 415/391-2000; www.sfvisitor.org; open 9am–5pm Mon–Fri, 9am–3pm Sat–Sun). Visit the Web site to order a free visitor kit. The bureau's **HOTEL RESERVATION SERVICE** (888/782-9673; www.sfvisitor.org) provides photos, descriptions, and features of more than 200 Bay Area hotels.

MAJOR ATTRACTIONS

San Francisco, like so many of its European sister cities, is a great walking town, and one of the most spectacular scenic walks is along the **GOLDEN GATE PROMENADE**, a 4-mile stretch from **AQUATIC PARK** in front of the Cannery through the beautiful **MARINA GREEN** and **CRISSY FIELD** to historic **FORT POINT**, a fortification built in 1861 that's nestled under the south end of the Golden Gate Bridge. If you have the energy, continue your tour with a walk across the bridge for a breathtaking view of the Bay Area and the Pacific. Another gorgeous waterfront stroll follows the Embarcadero north from Market Street. Stop in the newly restored Ferry Building Marketplace—tenants within this historic landmark include several cafés, wine shops, and some of Northern California's finest artisan food producers, including Cowgirl Creamery, Ricchiuti Confections, and Scharffen Berger Chocolate. At Pier 7, you'll get a good look at **TREASURE ISLAND** and the yachts and freighters sailing beneath the San Francisco–Oakland Bay Bridge. A hop on the **F LINE**, which runs vintage trolleys up the palm-filled center of the Embarcadero, takes you to touristy Pier 39. There you can watch hundreds of barking **SEA LIONS** playing and basking in the sun on the west side of the pier.

The third-most-visited amusement attraction in the nation, **PIER 39** (415/981-PIER; www.pier39.com) is packed with kitschy shops and overpriced, touristy restaurants, but it boasts beautiful views of Angel Island, Alcatraz, and the bay. It has great entertainment for kids with its **VENETIAN CAROUSEL**, jugglers, mimes, big-screen **CINEMAX THEATER**, and an arcade stocked with every gizmo and quarter-sucking machine the young-at-heart could dream of. Once you've had your fill of the tourist-packed pier, jump aboard the ferry for the **ISLAND HOP TOUR** and make your way around

SAN FRANCISCO THREE-DAY TOUR

DAY ONE: *The streets of San Francisco.* Strap on your walking shoes because you're going to attempt to see the majority of San Francisco's most famous attractions in a single day. Start the day off in high style with a light breakfast of tea and scones at the **GARDEN COURT** within the **PALACE HOTEL**, one of the most elaborate and beautiful dining rooms ever built. Since you're in the neighborhood, it's time to do a little window shopping at **UNION SQUARE**—with a mandatory stop at **NEIMAN MARCUS** to chuckle at the absurd price tags and then a stroll through the gilded lobby of the **WESTIN ST. FRANCIS**. Next, hop on either the **POWELL-MASON** or **POWELL-HYDE CABLE CAR** to **FISHERMAN'S WHARF** and head to Pier 41 to catch the fantastic **ALCATRAZ ISLAND TOUR**; be sure to make a reservation far in advance and ask for the headphone tour. After the prison tour, walk west along the water near Fisherman's Wharf to the intersection of Jefferson and Taylor streets and buy a fresh **DUNGENESS CRAB COCKTAIL** from the boisterous street vendors. Continue west along the wharf, making a few optional side trips to the **CANNERY**, **GHIRARDELLI SQUARE**, and the **SAN FRANCISCO MARITIME NATIONAL HISTORICAL PARK** (2905 Hyde St; 415/447-5000), a museum and fleet of historic vessels at Hyde Street Pier. You're probably in need of a picker-upper by now, so head for the intersection of Beach and Hyde streets to have a world-famous Irish coffee at the **BUENA VISTA CAFE**. If you don't mind the long but beautiful walk (if you do, take the number 28 or 29 bus, or hail a taxi), continue west along the shoreline, past **AQUATIC PARK**, along the **GOLDEN GATE PROMENADE** to the **GOLDEN GATE BRIDGE** for an at-least-once-in-your-lifetime stroll across the world's most famous bridge. OK, you've walked the bridge and now you're starving. Take a bus or taxi back to **NORTH BEACH** and head for **ENRICO'S** (504 Broadway St, San Francisco; 415/ 982-6223; www.enricossf.com). It's not the best restaurant in the city, but it has one of the best San Francisco vibes and live jazz nightly. Get

both Angel Island and Alcatraz (make advance reservations), or take a **SAN FRANCISCO BAY CRUISE** or a scenic trip to the pretty towns across the bay, **SAUSALITO** and **TIBURON**. For tour information and ferry schedules, call the Blue & Gold Fleet (415/705-5555; www.blueandgoldfleet.com).

Just a short jaunt west of Pier 39 are world-famous **FISHERMAN'S WHARF**, **THE CANNERY**, and **GHIRARDELLI SQUARE**. They're always mobbed with tourists, but they offer some interesting shops. It's also still a working waterfront—stroll along the north side of Jefferson Street, between Taylor and Jones streets, to see the colorful fishing boat fleet. And from mid-November through a patio seat and order the burger and a rum-and-mint-infused *mojito* (very tasty). Afterward, cruise northwest up **COLUMBUS AVENUE**, soaking up the sights and smells and stopping in at classic San Francisco haunts such as **SPECS' TWELVE ADLER MUSEUM CAFE**, **VESUVIO** (255 Columbus Ave; 415/ 362-3370; www.vesuvio.com), and **CAFFE TRIESTE** (601 Vallejo St; 415/392-6739; www.caffetrieste.com). By now it's probably time for the second showing of **BEACH BLANKET BABYLON** at **CLUB FUGAZI**, San Francisco's best and longest-running comedic musical (buy your tickets well in advance). If you're still up for more after the show, head back to **UNION SQUARE** to the **SIR FRANCIS DRAKE HOTEL** and finish the night off in style with some drinking and dancing at the rooftop **HARRY DENTON'S STARLIGHT ROOM**. Now go back to your hotel, take two aspirin, and recover.

DAY TWO: *From pastries to Postrio.* There are still plenty more quintessential San Francisco sights to see. Even if you have a car, you might want to pick up a bus map and purchase a day pass from a Muni driver because you'll be adventuring all over the city today. Start the day European-style with a pastry and cappuccino at **CAFÉ DE LA PRESSE** (352 Grant Ave at Bush St; 415/398-2680). Next, spend a few hours wandering through San Francisco's world-famous **CHINATOWN**, exploring all the funky shops and back alleys; or take a guided **WOK WIZ CHINATOWN WALKING TOUR** (650/355-9657; www.wokwiz.com). This should work up enough of an appetite for lunch at **HOUSE OF NANKING** (919 Kearny St at Columbus Ave; 415/421-1429), another San Francisco landmark. Now that you're refueled on pot stickers and Chinese greens, break out the map and head for **COIT TOWER** on the top of Telegraph Hill for a breathtaking view of the city (and some serious stair climbing). Catch your breath, take out your camera, and head west to the famous winding block of **LOMBARD STREET** between Hyde and Leavenworth streets (car or no car, it's still worth a visit). Next, head to the fantastic **SAN FRANCISCO CABLE CAR MUSEUM** (1201 Mason St; 415/474-1887; www.cablecarmuseum.org) to see how those amazing machines work in real

June, this is where you'll see the city's highly touted (and delicious) **DUNGENESS CRABS** boiling in large metal pots on the sidewalks lining the wharf.

While tourists flock to Fisherman's Wharf and Pier 39, locals often take their kids in the other direction to the **EXPLORATORIUM** (415/561-0360; www.exploratorium.edu), a unique interactive museum that brings scientific concepts to vivid life. The Exploratorium's marvelous **TACTILE DOME**, where visitors feel their way through a maze of hurdles in total darkness, requires a certain amount of nerve. The Exploratorium is housed within the magnificent **PALACE OF FINE ARTS THEATRE** (3601 Lyon St, between Jefferson and Bay sts;

time. Afterward, take the **POWELL-MASON** or **POWELL-HYDE CABLE CAR** back to **UNION SQUARE**. By now you're probably ready for some well-deserved R & R, so treat yourself to a blowout dinner at **FARALLON**, **POSTRIO**, or the **GRAND CAFE** in the Hotel Monaco, three of the best "big-city" restaurants in San Francisco. Order a triple espresso for dessert and walk to **BISCUITS & BLUES** for some toe-tappin' blues or, if you prefer a quieter evening, sip a cocktail high above the city in the lounge of the **CARNELIAN ROOM**. Back to the hotel, more aspirin.

DAY THREE: *Dim sum and then some*. You've seen a lot of the big-name attractions; now it's time to do what you really came to San Francisco for—eat, drink, shop, and repeat. Sleep in late and have a very light breakfast because for lunch you'll be stuffing your face at **YANK SING**, the most popular dim sum restaurant in the city (you can't go to San Francisco and not have a dim sum experience). Since you're already downtown, spend an hour shopping at **EMBARCADERO CENTER** or walking around the **FINANCIAL DISTRICT** marveling at the numerous skyscrapers. Now take a bus, taxi, or long walk to San Francisco's SoMa District. Three must-stops here are the **SAN FRANCISCO MUSEUM OF MODERN ART** and the adjoining **MUSEUMSTORE** for great souvenirs and gifts, the beautiful **YERBA BUENA GARDENS**, and, especially if you have kids tagging along, the **METREON** megaplex entertainment center—all right next to each other. This should take you well into the evening, so now it's time for dinner. If you want small, intimate, and French, make a reservation right now for **FRINGALE**. If you prefer a high-energy, big city–style dining experience, then either walk or take a taxi to the foot of Mission Street to **BOULEVARD**, one of the city's most popular restaurants. When dinner is over, do something really romantic: hail a taxi and ask the driver to take you to the top of **TWIN PEAKS** for a breathtaking view of the city lights. Or, if you're in the mood to party, walk south along the Embarcadero to **PIER 23** for a stiff Long Island Iced Tea and dancing. Now *that's* a San Francisco vacation.

415/567-6642; www.palaceoffinearts.org), designed by renowned architect Bernard Maybeck for the 1915 Panama-Pacific International Exposition. Surrounded by a natural lagoon, the Palace is an ideal spot for a picnic.

In the southwest corner of the city, near the ocean and Lake Merced, is the popular **SAN FRANCISCO ZOO** (1 Zoo Rd, 45th Ave and Sloat Blvd; 415/753-7080; www.sfzoo.org). Don't miss the famed Primate Discovery Center, where several species of apes and monkeys live in glass-walled condos. The zoo also has rare Sumatran and Siberian tigers, African lions (visit during their mealtimes), a children's petting zoo, and even an insect zoo.

On the other side of the Golden Gate Bridge, in Sausalito, is the **BAY AREA DISCOVERY MUSEUM** (East Fort Baker; 415/487-4398; www.badm.org), a wonderland of hands-on science, art, and multimedia exhibits designed for kids. Go north across the bridge, exit at Alexander Avenue, and follow the signs.

For a sweeping view of the Pacific Ocean, visit the historic **CLIFF HOUSE** (415/386-3330; www.cliffhouse.com) and sip a cocktail at a window-side table, then climb around the neighboring ruins of the once-spectacular **SUTRO BATHS** (1090 Point Lobos Ave).

To explore some of the city's multiethnic neighborhoods and architectural masterpieces, strap on your heavy-duty walking shoes and hike around the **RUSSIAN HILL** neighborhood, starting at the top of the crookedest street in the world, **LOMBARD STREET** (at Hyde St). Wind your way down Lombard's many flower-lined curves and continue east until Lombard intersects with Columbus Avenue, then turn right and stay on Columbus for a tour of charming **NORTH BEACH**—a predominantly Italian and Chinese neighborhood where residents practice tai chi in **WASHINGTON SQUARE** on weekend mornings or sip espresso as they peruse Proust or the San Francisco *Bay Guardian*'s racy personal ads (guaranteed to make you blush). You can extend this tour by turning right off Columbus onto Grant Avenue, which will take you through the heart of the ever-bustling and fascinating **CHINATOWN**—the only part of the city where vendors sell live, 3-foot-long slippery eels next to X-rated fortune cookies and herbs meant to cure whatever ails you.

For an aerobic workout, take a different tour: instead of turning off Lombard onto Columbus, keep following Lombard Street east all the way up to **COIT TOWER** (415/362-0808) on the top of **TELEGRAPH HILL**, then reward yourself for making the steep ascent (gasp, gasp) with an elevator trip to the top of the tower for a panoramic view of the Bay Area.

If you'd rather ride than walk the hills of San Francisco, an outside perch on one of the city's famed **CABLE CARS** is always a kick. The three cable car routes are named after the streets on which they run (you can take them in either direction), operate daily from 6:30am to 12:30am, rain or shine, and cost only $3 one-way. Unlimited one-, three-, and seven-day passes are available for $9, $15, and $20, respectively. The Powell-Mason line starts at Powell and Market streets and terminates at Bay Street near Fisherman's Wharf; the Powell-Hyde line also begins at Powell and Market streets but ends at Victorian Park near Aquatic Park and the bay, making it the most scenic route; and the California line runs from California and Market streets through Chinatown to Van Ness Avenue. Expect very long lines during peak travel times, especially when the weather is warm. For more information, call Muni or visit the cable car Web site (415/673-6864; www.sfcablecar.com).

MUSEUMS

The **SAN FRANCISCO MUSEUM OF MODERN ART** (151 3rd St, between Mission and Howard sts; 415/357-4000; www.sfmoma.org), housed in a dramatic modernist building designed by Swiss architect Mario Botta, offers works by Picasso, Matisse, O'Keeffe, Rivera, Pollock, Warhol, Klee,

DeForest, and Lichtenstein, among others. The **ASIAN ART MUSEUM** (415/581-3500; www.asianart.org) is the largest museum outside of Asia devoted exclusively to Asian art, housed in a new 165,000-square-foot home in the 1917 Beaux Arts building that used to be the city's main library.

The **CALIFORNIA PALACE OF THE LEGION OF HONOR** (in Lincoln Park near 34th Ave and Clement St; 415/863-3330 or 415/750-3600; www.legionofhonor.com), a three-quarter-scale replica of Paris's grand Palais de la Légion d'Honneur, features European paintings (including works by Monet, Cézanne, and Rembrandt), sculptures (a large collection of Rodin), and decorative art. It also houses a small collection of ancient art and hosts a constant stream of interesting international exhibits. Galleries for established San Francisco artists are located primarily on lower Grant Avenue and near Union Square; up-and-coming artists tend to exhibit in SoMa (the South of Market Street area).

Fantastic **MURALS** decorate many public spaces in the city, particularly in the **MISSION DISTRICT**, a vibrant, primarily Hispanic neighborhood; for maps outlining self-guided walks or for very good two-hour guided tours, contact the **PRECITA EYES MURAL ARTS CENTER** (2981 24th St at Harrison St; 415/285-2287; www.precitaeyes.org). If you don't have time for a tour, at least stroll down narrow **BALMY ALLEY** (near Harrison and 25th sts), which is lined with about 30 incredibly colorful murals displayed on garages and fences and is the birthplace of mural painting in San Francisco.

SHOPPING AND BOOKSTORES

The famous and oh-so-trendy **UNION SQUARE** area and the nearby **SAN FRANCISCO SHOPPING CENTRE** (Market and 5th sts) together boast many major department stores (including Macy's, Nordstrom, Saks Fifth Avenue, and Neiman Marcus) and more specialty shops than you can shake a credit card at. A short walk away is the chichi **CROCKER GALLERIA** (bounded by Post, Kearny, Sutter, and Montgomery sts), a 70-foot-high, glass-domed, three-level shopping mall with Ralph Lauren, Versace, and similar boutiques, which was modeled after Milan's 1867 Galleria Vittoria Emmanuelle II. The vast **EMBARCADERO CENTER** (between Clay, Sacramento, Battery, and Drumm sts) is a sophisticated three-level, open-air neo-mall also well worth a spree.

Stroll down **SACRAMENTO STREET** (between Lyon and Spruce sts) for elegant clothing and furnishings. For vintage, cutting-edge, and folksy fashions and crafts, shop on **24TH STREET** (between Castro and Church sts) and **HAIGHT STREET** (between Masonic Ave and Shrader St). Hip, eclectic, and classic items abound on **CASTRO STREET** (between Market and 19th sts), **FILLMORE STREET** (between Jackson and Sutter sts), and **UNION STREET** (between Gough and Steiner sts). The 5-acre **JAPAN CENTER** (Post St, between Laguna and Fillmore sts) houses several shops selling Japanese crafts, housewares, and books, with numerous sushi bars and other Japanese-style eateries sandwiched in between.

Cosmopolitan cooks can stock up on Asian foodstuffs in **CHINATOWN** along Stockton Street (between California and Broadway sts) or in **NEW CHINATOWN** on Clement Street (between Arguello Blvd and 10th Ave, and 18th

SAGE ADVICE FOR PARKING IN SAN FRANCISCO

Driving around San Francisco presents a formidable challenge. The combination of hills, traffic, aggressive drivers, and a notable lack of parking will tax your driving skills and patience. To avoid runaway cars on steep hills, *curb your wheels*! Turn the tires *away* from the curb and toward the street when facing uphill, and *toward* the curb when facing downhill—otherwise your car may find itself on a surprise journey or, at best, slapped with a parking ticket (yes, oddly enough, curbing is a law in SF, and one that often catches tourists off guard). Also, tow-away zones and time limits proliferate, and parking regulations (particularly on street-cleaning days) are strictly enforced. The best way to chalk up tickets is to either ignore parking signs or assume any degree of flexibility. In fact, the city relies on parking citations to augment the government coffers (we're talking *millions* of dollars annually).

As for all those multicolored curbs, here's what the parking department is trying to tell you: A *red* curb means no stopping or parking ever, not even for a second; a *blue* curb is reserved for drivers with disabilities who have a California-issued disabled plate or a placard; a *white* curb means there's a five-minute limit *if* the business it fronts is open; a *green* curb indicates a 10-minute limit during business hours; and *yellow* and *yellow-black* curbs are for commercial vehicles only during the day.

Ultimately, the best way to see the city is by walking or using public transportation. Taxis are few and far between; locals even joke that there are only four or five cabs in the whole city—which doesn't seem so far-fetched when you try to find a free one on a Friday night. Instead of relying on taxis, buy a bus map and a day pass and take **MUNI**, the sometimes-unreliable-but-essential public transport system of buses, streetcars, and cable cars. For information about the Muni system, including rates and routes, call 415/673-6864 or visit www.sfmuni.com.

and 25th aves). Shops along **COLUMBUS AVENUE** (between Broadway and Bay sts) in North Beach sell Italian treats, while **MISSION DISTRICT** stores offer Latin specialties on 24th Street (between Guerrero St and Potrero Ave).

Good bookstores include **CITY LIGHTS** (261 Columbus Ave at Broadway; 415/362-8193; www.citylights.com), still Beat after all these years, and **STACEY'S BOOKSTORE** (581 Market St at 2nd St; 415/421-4687; www.staceys.com). **GET LOST TRAVEL BOOKS** (1825 Market St at Guerrero St; 415/437-0529; www.getlostbooks.com) and **RAND MCNALLY MAP & TRAVEL STORE** (595 Market St at 2nd St; 415/777-3131; store.randmcnally.com) are great stops for any traveler.

PERFORMING ARTS

San Franciscans' love of the arts is evident not only in the number of artsy goings-on but also in the number of ways to discover them. For up-to-the-moment information, surf to the **SAN FRANCISCO ARTS MONTHLY** Web site (www.sfarts.org) or check the *San Francisco Chronicle*'s Datebook (more commonly known as "the pink section") in the Sunday paper.

TIX BAY AREA (251 Stockton St, on the east side of Union Square; 415/433-7827; www.theatrebayarea.org) sells half-price tickets to many of San Francisco's dance, music, and theater events on the day of the performance only, beginning at 11am (tickets for Monday events are sold on Sunday). You must purchase the tickets in person and can pay with cash, credit card (AE, DIS, MC, V), or travelers checks. Advance full-price tickets are sold here, too. Tickets to most dance and theater events are also sold by phone through the **CITY BOX OFFICE** (415/392-4400; www.cityboxoffice.com) and **BASS TICKETMASTER** (510/762-2277; www.tickets.com).

Music

San Francisco's music scene has a 24-hours-a-day tempo. The accordion is the city's official musical instrument, but don't look for the squeezebox in the venues below. It makes most of its appearances in street performances.

The world-class **SAN FRANCISCO OPERA** (415/864-3330, box office, or 415/861-4008, general information; www.sfopera.com) alternates warhorses with rarities from September through January at the War Memorial Opera House. This beloved Beaux Arts beauty was modeled on Garnier's Paris Opéra. Subscribers grab up most of the red velvet seats, but fans with smaller bankrolls can stand in line early on performance mornings to buy one of the 200 $10 standing-room tickets, which go on sale at 10am (50 of these inexpensive tickets are held until two hours before the performance). The **SAN FRANCISCO SYMPHONY** (415/864-6000; www.sfsymphony.org), under the heralded baton of music director Michael Tilson Thomas, performs from September through July at the modern Louise M. Davies Symphony Hall (201 Van Ness Ave at Grove St), a gorgeous building with a wraparound glass facade.

On summer Sundays, families and couples tote blankets and picnic baskets to free outdoor performances (everything from jazz to opera to symphony) at the pretty **STERN GROVE** (Sloat Blvd and 19th Ave; 415/252-6252; www.sterngrove.org). The **SAN FRANCISCO JAZZ FESTIVAL** (415/398-5655; www.sfjazz.org), one of the largest in the country, toots its horn every fall with concerts, dances, films, and lectures. (For the scoop on the city's best nightclubs, see the Nightlife section.)

Theater and Comedy

AMERICAN CONSERVATORY THEATER (415/749-2ACT; www.act-sfbay.org), the city's best-known theater company, presents solid productions of new works and classics under the artistic direction of Carey Perloff from September through July in the Geary Theater (415 Geary St). Broadway shows on tour are performed at the **GOLDEN GATE**, **CURRAN**, and **ORPHEUM THEATERS** (415/551-2075; www.shnsf.com). **THEATRE ON THE SQUARE** (450 Post St, between Powell and Mason sts; 415/433-9500) and **MARINES MEMORIAL THEATRE** (609 Sutter St at Mason St; 415/771-6900; www.unionsquaretheatres.com) showcase off-Broadway acts.

Among the small local theater companies offering wonderful performances are the **LORRAINE HANSBERRY THEATRE** (777 Jones St; 415/345-3980; www.lhtsf.org); the **LAMPLIGHTERS MUSIC THEATER** (415/227-4797; www.lamplighters.org), which performs primarily Gilbert and Sullivan comic operas at Yerba Buena Gardens' Center for the Arts (701 Mission St at 3rd St) and the Ira & Lenore S. Gershwin Theater (2350 Turk St at Masonic St); and the **MAGIC THEATRE** (Fort Mason Center, Building D, off Marina Blvd at Buchanan St; 415/441-8822; www.magictheatre.org). **THEATRE RHINOCEROS** (2926 16th St at S Van Ness Ave; 415/861-5079; www.therhino.org) specializes in gay and lesbian drama. Summer and early autumn bring free outdoor performances at various venues by America's oldest political musical-comedy theater group, the Tony award–winning **SAN FRANCISCO MIME TROUPE** (415/285-1717; www.sfmt.org). The more serious **SHAKESPEARE IN THE PARK** (415/558-0888; www.sfshakes.org) theater group also performs for free in the summer in Golden Gate Park. **BEACH BLANKET BABYLON**, the longest-running musical revue in the world, is a cabaret-style show full of silly jokes that's famous for its wild costumes and humongous hats. It remains a favorite of residents and visitors alike, so be sure to reserve seats in advance at Club Fugazi (678 Green St near Powell St; 415/421-4222; www.beachblanketbabylon.com).

San Francisco has launched the careers of many comedians, including Robin Williams and Whoopi Goldberg. See the latest talents at the **PUNCHLINE** (444 Battery St, 2nd Fl, between Clay and Washington sts; 415/397-4337 or 415/397-7573 for recorded information; www.punchlinecomedyclub.com).

Dance

The internationally renowned **SAN FRANCISCO BALLET** (415/861-5600; www.sfballet.org), led by artistic director Helgi Tomasson, leaps into its season in December with the classic Nutcracker and begins its repertory season in February; performances take place at the beautiful War Memorial Opera House (401 Van Ness Ave at Grove St). For modern and contemporary performances, see the **ODC/SAN FRANCISCO** dance troupe (415/863-6606; www.odcdance.org); for contemporary ballet, **LINES** (415/863-3040; www.linesballet.org) is a local favorite and often performs at Yerba Buena Gardens' Center for the Arts (701 Mission St at 3rd St). Modern dance recitals are also frequently held at **THEATER ARTAUD** (450 Florida St at 17th St; 415/626-DOME; www.artaud.org).

Film

The **SAN FRANCISCO INTERNATIONAL FILM FESTIVAL** (415/931-FILM; www.sfiff.org) attracts film fanatics for a fortnight every spring; screenings

SAN FRANCISCO'S SUNDAY MORNING SENSATION

Ever since the Reverend Cecil Williams took the helm of the **GLIDE MEMORIAL CHURCH** in 1963, San Franciscans of every color, tax bracket, and lifestyle have joined together on Sunday mornings to celebrate life in one of the most high-energy, roof-raising renditions you'll ever witness. As Glide's new reverend, Williams first removed all overt religious icons in order to establish a nondenominational setting. He then assembled a 120-member choir accompanied by a blues-style band and opened the doors to every type of person—poor, famous, homeless, wealthy, crazy—of every religion and raised their spirits with uplifting sermons and songs about hope and love.

The Reverend Williams's efforts to help the homeless and poor of the Tenderloin District (one of the city's most poverty-stricken neighborhoods) have attracted nationwide attention and inspired regular appearances by San Francisco local Sharon Stone. Other luminaries either on the stage or in the audience have included Bobby McFerrin, Robin Williams, Maya Angelou, Oprah Winfrey, and Bill Clinton. Even if you've never set foot in a church before, go: you'll be glad you did. Just be sure to arrive a little early to get a first-floor seat (the balcony's view is limited). The church is located at 330 Ellis Street at Taylor Street, west of Union Square (415/771-6300; www.glide.org). Services take place every Sunday at 9am and 11am.

happen at various venues in San Francisco, Berkeley, and Marin County. Another popular event is the **SAN FRANCISCO INTERNATIONAL LESBIAN AND GAY FILM FESTIVAL** (415/703-8650; www.frameline.org), which takes place in June. For rare revivals and premieres, check out the palatial **CASTRO THEATRE** (429 Castro St off Market St; 415/621-6120; www.castrotheatre.com), a flamboyant Spanish baroque–style movie palace designed by Timothy Pflueger in 1923; the funky (but finely programmed) **ROXIE CINEMA** (3117 16th St at Valencia St; 415/863-1087; www.roxie.com); and the homey **RED VIC MOVIE HOUSE** (1727 Haight St, between Cole and Shrader sts; 415/668-3994; www.redvicmoviehouse.com).

PARKS, GARDENS, AND BEACHES

GOLDEN GATE PARK, encompassing 1,017 acres of lush grounds dotted with magnificent museums, lakes, and gardens, is a masterpiece of park design. For a good introduction to its attractions, join one of the **FREE GUIDED WALKING TOURS** offered by Friends of Recreation and Parks (415/263-0991 or 415/750-5105) every weekend from May through October. Plant enthusiasts mustn't miss the **STRYBING ARBORETUM AND BOTANICAL GARDENS** (near 9th Ave and Lincoln Wy; 415/661-1316; www.strybing.org), home to more than 7,000 plant and tree varieties. Free guided walks are given daily at 1:30pm. A somewhat more Zen-like experience is offered by the lovely **JAPANESE TEA GARDEN**, the oldest Japanese-style park in the United States, which always attracts crowds but particularly when the cherry blossoms and azaleas bloom in March and April (pssst . . . to avoid the hordes, visit when it's raining). In the northeast corner of the park is the spectacular **CONSERVATORY OF FLOWERS** (John F. Kennedy Dr, near Conservatory Dr; 415/831-2700; www.conservatoryofflowers.org), an 1879 Victorian fairyland hothouse full of tropical flora. It's an architectural beauty worth admiring both inside and out. In the middle of the park, serene **STOW LAKE** compels you to rent a rowboat, paddleboat, or electric boat (415/752-0347) and circle the 430-foot-high artificial island known as **STRAWBERRY HILL**, the highest peak in the park. Look for the hill's waterfall and Chinese moon-watching pavilion as well as the many turtles and ducks that live on the lake. If you have youngsters in tow, don't skip the **CHILDREN'S PLAYGROUND** (off Kezar Dr), which has a dazzling Golden Age 1912 carousel (the oldest one in a public park) that's guaranteed to make every child's heart go pitter-patter. Every Sunday, Golden Gate Park's main drag is closed to auto traffic so skaters and joggers can let loose on the tree-lined street. **SKATE RENTALS** are readily available on Fulton and Haight streets.

The city's entire northwest corner is part of the **GOLDEN GATE NATIONAL RECREATION AREA (GGNRA)**, the largest urban park in the world. Take a hike along its gorgeous wildflower-laced **COASTAL TRAIL**, which hugs the headlands for more than 10 miles and offers fantastic views of the Pacific Ocean; start at Point Lobos (at the end of Point Lobos Ave, near the Sutro Baths) and wind your way to the Golden Gate Bridge. **THE PRESIDIO**, a lush 1,480-acre former military base, has become part of the GGNRA and offers superb views to hikers (and drivers) as well as historic buildings, a scenic golf course, walking and biking tours, and a national cemetery. Also part of the GGNRA are **CRISSY FIELD**, a fabulous windsurfing spot, and the **MARINA GREEN**, prime kite-flying and jogging territory; both are located off Marina Boulevard, near the on-ramp to the Golden Gate Bridge. For maps and more details on the GGNRA, call the National Park Information Center (415/556-0560).

In the heart of the city, across from the Museum of Modern Art, is **YERBA BUENA GARDENS** (Mission St between 3rd and 4th sts), San Francisco's 5-acre urban park featuring a walk-through waterfall enclosing a beautiful memorial for Martin Luther King Jr., a sculpture garden, and terrace cafés. The Yerba Buena **CHILDREN'S CENTER**, cleverly situated on the roof of the Moscone Convention Center, has plenty of diversions for little tykes, including a carousel, an ice-skating rink, a bowling alley, an arts and technology center, and a children's garden. For consumers of all ages, **SONY'S METREON ENTERTAINMENT COMPLEX** has shops, restaurants, a 15-screen cinema, an IMAX theater, and a children's play center designed by author-illustrator Maurice Sendak.

Riptide-ridden and blustery **OCEAN BEACH** is a haven for seasoned surfers as well as for families, dog walkers, joggers, and lovers who enjoy the long,

GET PLUGGED IN

With such close ties to Silicon Valley, it doesn't come as a surprise that wireless Internet access is easy to come by in San Francisco. Many independent coffee shops are going a step further and offering free wireless access to patrons. Still, instead of trying to hunt it down when you're in a time crunch, hit up one of these beloved cafés.

BEAN BAG CAFE (601 Divisadero St at Hayes St; 415/563-3634)

This cutesy Bohemian joint in Hayes Valley isn't the best place to get actual work done, as an interesting mix of music is usually blaring at top volume. But the staff is friendly and the Internet free. Plus, the chalkboard menu of sweet and savory crepes is so enticing, you might spend more time eating than checking your e-mail.

CAFE FLORE (2298 Market St at Noe St; 415/621-8579)

This Castro café—restaurant by day, hopping night club by night—is perfect for people watching (the scene is half of the appeal of this gay-friendly bistro-esque bar) while catching up on your correspondence. The wait's a bit lengthy, so if you're planning on setting up shop for the afternoon, schedule your visit around prime dining hours.

NANI'S COFFEE (2739 Geary Blvd between Masonic and Wood sts; 415/928-8817)

Owned and operated by the same family since it opened in 2002, Nani's oozes charm and genuineness and boasts an impressive selection of fancy brews. Just try to find someone who will say a bad word about this neighborhood hangout that straddles Pacific Heights and the Western Addition neighborhood.

NOOK (1500 Hyde St at Jackson St; 415/447-4100)

With nearly as many outlets as it has seats, Nook is a favorite spot with writers and other independent entrepreneurs in the Russian and Nob Hills, as they can stay hooked up all day long without a hitch. It doesn't hurt that the menu of gourmet salads and sandwiches is nothing short of spectacular.

ON THE CORNER (359 Divisadero St at Oak St; 415/522-1101)

There's nothing particularly special about this Hayes Valley spot, but it's popular among the computer-toting crowd and offers a decent selection of coffee and basic lunch items.

sandy beach located off the Great Highway (the main street that flanks the western side of the city). On warm days, sun worshippers prefer to bask at **BAKER BEACH** (at the south end of Lincoln Blvd) while gazing at the stupendous view of the Golden Gate (as at most of the city's beaches, however, swimming is unsafe here). The east side of the beach is a popular gay hangout, where sunbathers wear nothing but sunscreen. Other scenic spots include **GLEN CANYON PARK** (Bosworth St and O'Shaughnessy Blvd), which has a playground; the lush **STERN GROVE** (Sloat Blvd at 19th Ave); and **LAKE MERCED** (off Harding Dr between Hwy 35 and Sloat Blvd, near the zoo).

NIGHTLIFE

Bars

San Franciscans need something to cut the chill of those long, foggy nights, so many head to North Beach, which has more than its fair share of popular watering holes, including the funky **SPECS' TWELVE ADLER MUSEUM CAFE** (12 Saroyan Pl; 415/421-4112), an old Beat generation hangout; the charming but rough-around-the-edges **SAVOY TIVOLI** (1434 Grant Ave, between Union and Green sts; 415/362-7023); and **TOSCA CAFE** (242 Columbus Ave, between Pacific Ave and Broadway; 415/986-9651), where locals hang out (and celebs hide in the back room) sipping the house specialty: coffeeless cappuccinos made with brandy, milk, and chocolate.

When the fog burns off and the weather heats up, grab a chair on the patio of **CAFE FLORE** (2298 Market St at Noe St; 415/621-8579; www.cafeflore.com) in the Castro District and order a glass of white wine or a latte. Or get the full array of spirits on the outdoor decks of such local favorites as the **RAMP** (855 Terry Francois St off 3rd St; 415/621-2378; www.ramprestaurant.com) and **PIER 23** (the Embarcadero, between Broadway and Bay sts; 415/362-5125; www.pier23cafe.com).

For a more romantic retreat, make your toasts at the lounge of the **CARNELIAN ROOM** restaurant at the top of the 52-story Bank of America building (555 California St, between Kearny and Montgomery sts; 415/433-7500; www.carnelianroom.com), which offers a dizzying view of the city when the sky is clear; the plush **CROWN ROOM** in the Fairmont Hotel & Tower (950 Mason St at California St, 24th Fl; 415/772-5131; www.fairmont.com/sanfrancisco); or the scenic, glass-walled **TOP OF THE MARK** lounge in the InterContinental Mark Hopkins (999 California St at Mason St; 415/392-3434; www.ichotelsgroup.com), with dancing to live music after 8:30pm.

Union Square's best bustling bars are at **KULETO'S** restaurant (221 Powell St, between Geary and O'Farrell sts; 415/397-7720; www.kuletos.com) and the **COMPASS ROSE** in the Westin St. Francis Hotel (335 Powell St, between Post and Geary sts; 415/397-7000; www.westinstfrancis.com), which boasts the largest martini in the city. For the best Irish coffee in town, the **BUENA VISTA** (2765 Hyde St at the corner of Beach St; 415/474-5044; www.thebuenavista.com) takes top honors.

Clubs

Great clubs abound in San Francisco, the city that never seems to sleep. Most of San Francisco's clubs present an ever-changing lineup of bands or recorded music, so call ahead for up-to-date recorded listings at each venue. The **BE-AT LINE** (415/626-4087) recorded hotline will also tell you where you can find the night's hot musical acts. Locals tend to pick up a copy of the free *San Francisco Bay Guardian* weekly newspaper (available at cafés and most major street corners) for the straight scoop on the city's wild and ever-changing club scene.

For live blues, jazz, and rock, **SLIM'S** (333 11th St, between Folsom and Harrison sts; 415/522-0333; www.slims-sf.com) can't be beat. The famous **FILLMORE** (1805 Geary Blvd at Fillmore St; 415/346-6000; www.thefillmore.com) always books top talents, and **BRUNO'S** (2389 Mission St at 20th St; 415/643-5200; www.brunossf.com) is boffo. If you just want to dance and don't care about what to wear or the color of your hair, show up after 10pm at **NICKIES** (466 Haight St, between Webster and Fillmore sts; 415/255-0300; www.nickies.com). If dancin' among the teeming masses is more your thing, go to **TEN 15** (1015 Folsom St at 6th St; 415/730-1015; www.1015.com). For a mix of live music, the trendy set kicks up its heels at **CAFE DU NORD** (2170 Market St, between Church and Sanchez sts; 415/861-5016; www.cafedunord.com). If you want to shake, rattle, and roll with the high-fashion crowd, put on your best dancing shoes and go to **HARRY DENTON'S STARLIGHT ROOM** at the top of the Sir Francis Drake Hotel (450 Powell St, between Sutter and Post sts; 415/392-7755; www.harrydenton.com).

To hear the sounds of the city's new bands, stroll Haight Street. Numerous venues line both sides of this famous strip, still populated by dazed youth, the homeless, and various eccentrics. Great cocktails and live swing bands will get you out of your seat and onto the dance floor at **CLUB DELUXE** (1511 Haight St at Ashbury St; 415/552-6949; www.liveatdeluxe.com). Elsewhere, the ornate **GREAT AMERICAN MUSIC HALL** (859 O'Farrell St, between Polk and Larkin sts; 415/885-0750; www.musichallsf.com) hosts hundreds of concerts a year, ranging from Motown, rock, and jazz to bluegrass, folk, and zydeco. For a blast of the blues, go to the candlelit **BISCUITS & BLUES** (401 Mason St at Geary St; 415/292-2583; www.biscuitsandblues.com), or enjoy a night of jumpin' jazz at **BUTTERFLY** (Pier 33 at the Embarcadero; 415/864-8899; www.butterflysf.com).

SPORTS AND RECREATION

Bay Area sports buffs are proud of their **SAN FRANCISCO 49ERS** football team (www.sf49ers.com), which plays home games at **MONSTER PARK** (previously named 3Com Candlestick Park and still called "the Stick" by Bay Area residents; www.monsterpark.com). The **SAN FRANCISCO GIANTS** (www.sfgiants.com) play at the home-run-friendly **AT&T PARK.** It's of the "new" intimate ballpark genre, so there are good views of the field even from on high. Perhaps more enticing, depending on the game, are views of the bay and downtown San Francisco. True to the foodie spirit of the city, regular ballpark fare is enhanced by concession stands and bistros serving pan-Latin and Asian cuisine as well as *bazurros*, salads rolled into fresh flat bread. If none of that appeals, restaurants are springing up all around the park. (Fans of the **OAKLAND A'S** and the **GOLDEN STATE WARRIORS** should turn to the Oakland section in the next chapter.)

The **SAN FRANCISCO MARATHON** (800/698-8699; http://runsfm.com) is usually run in late July or early August, but if you'd rather race against two-legged Brillo boxes, centipedes, Snow White and the Seven Dwarfs, and a Whitney Houston clone in drag, sign up for the wild-and-wacky 7½-mile **BAY TO BREAKERS** race and walk (415/359-2800; www.baytobreakers.com), held in mid-May.

FESTIVALS

Every winter, the two-week-long **CHINESE NEW YEAR** (415/982-3000; www.chineseparade.com) celebration culminates explosively with an electrifying parade that winds through downtown, Union Square, and Chinatown. In spring and summer, neighborhood **STREET FAIRS** pop up (from upscale Union Street to the still-hairy Haight). Japantown launches its **CHERRY BLOSSOM FESTIVAL** with a parade in April; the Mission District draws crowds with its **CINCO DE MAYO PARADE**; and the **SAN FRANCISCO LESBIAN, GAY, BISEXUAL, TRANSGENDER PRIDE CELEBRATION PARADE** (415/864-3733; www.sfpride.org) attracts thousands of revelers on the last weekend of June.

All heads turn skyward when the U.S. Navy flaunts its amazing acrobatic flight team—the **BLUE ANGELS**—during **FLEET WEEK CELEBRATION** (near Fisherman's Wharf and Pier 39; 415/705-5500; www.fleetweek.com) in early October. Bands, boat rides, and a parade of ships and submarines on the bay round out the festivities.

RESTAURANTS AND LODGINGS BY NEIGHBORHOOD

The city's restaurant scene keeps food reviewers busy inventing new adjectives and diners tottering on the verge of gluttony.

North Beach

Long a neighborhood of immigrants, North Beach is famous for its Italian food and sidewalk cafés. So charismatic is the area that few notice there isn't even a beach here. There was one about a hundred years ago, until it was filled in to make room for factories and waterfront activity. Shopkeepers still stand on their stoops chatting with friends in Italian while cafés and restaurants send up aromatic espresso, focaccia, and saucy pasta greetings. These days, Chinatown—just to the west—also exerts an influence on the community. **SAINTS PETER AND PAUL ROMAN CATHOLIC CHURCH**, the neighborhood's spiritual anchor, now offers services in English, Italian, and Chinese. Tai chi is as ubiquitous in **WASHINGTON SQUARE PARK** as sunbathing. Always a haven for bohemian society, North Beach attracts residents who treasure a literary history that embraces Beat writers like Allen Ginsberg, Lawrence Ferlinghetti, and Jack Kerouac, and local bars and bookstores still celebrate them.

RESTAURANTS

L'Osteria del Forno / ★★½

519 COLUMBUS AVE, SAN FRANCISCO; 415/982-1124

Don't let the touristy Columbus Avenue location fool you: This small 10-table café attracts legions of locals who brave lousy parking for anything that comes out of the brick-lined oven, such as fantastic focaccia sandwiches, freshly made pizzas and pastas, kick-butt cipolline, and a wondrously succulent roast pork braised in milk (everyone's all-time favorite). Small baskets of warm focaccia bread and Italian wine served by the glass tide you over until the entrée arrives. The kitchen is run by two charming Italian women who have successfully combined good food with a homey Italian-bistro atmosphere. Ergo, expect a warm welcome and authentic Italian food at low prices. Darn good espresso, too. *$–$$; cash only; travelers checks OK; lunch, dinner Wed–Mon; full bar; no reservations; www.losteriadelforno.com; between Green and Union sts.* ♿

Mo's Grill / ★★

1322 GRANT AVE, SAN FRANCISCO; 415/788-3779

How do you make the perfect hamburger? If you're a grillmaster at Mo's, you use only the best-quality center-cut chuck ground fresh daily and hand-formed into big, thick patties. Next, ignite the volcanic rock underneath the custom-made rotating grill, slap those puppies on, grill 'em exactly to the customer's liking, cover 'em with soft-yet-crusty buns, and serve with a host of accoutrements. Voilà! Mo's "Best Burger." Other variations include the BBQ, Bacon, Mushroom, Tex-Mex, California (with avocado), Western (with apple-smoked bacon), Belly Buster, and Alpine (with Swiss Gruyère cheese). Steaks, pork chops, chicken, and a few vegetarian dishes are also on the menu, but it's the burgers that draw carnivores in from all around the city. Oh, and don't pass up the mocha shake, served thick and tall in a shimmering steel container. *$; MC, V; no checks; breakfast, lunch, dinner every day; beer and wine; no reservations; www.mosgrill.com; between Vallejo and Green sts.* ♿

Peña Pachamama / ★★½

1630 POWELL ST, SAN FRANCISCO; 415/646-0018

The moment you walk past the neon-orange-clad figure of Kusillo at the door, you are folded into the musical family of Sukay. This Andean ensemble, which has been performing together for more than 20 years, opened Peña Pachamama (Mother Earth in the ancient Quechua language) to create a center for Bolivian food and music in San Francisco. The Nuevo Latino cuisine—a fusion of traditional Bolivian dishes with the lighter, organic California sensibility—is the perfect opening act for the show; Friday and Saturday nights, the group plays an invigorating, nonamplified set of traditional and Bolivian music on a stage next to the dining room. Peña Pachamama's engaging warmth gives it the feel of a neighbor's house, but the kitchen creates

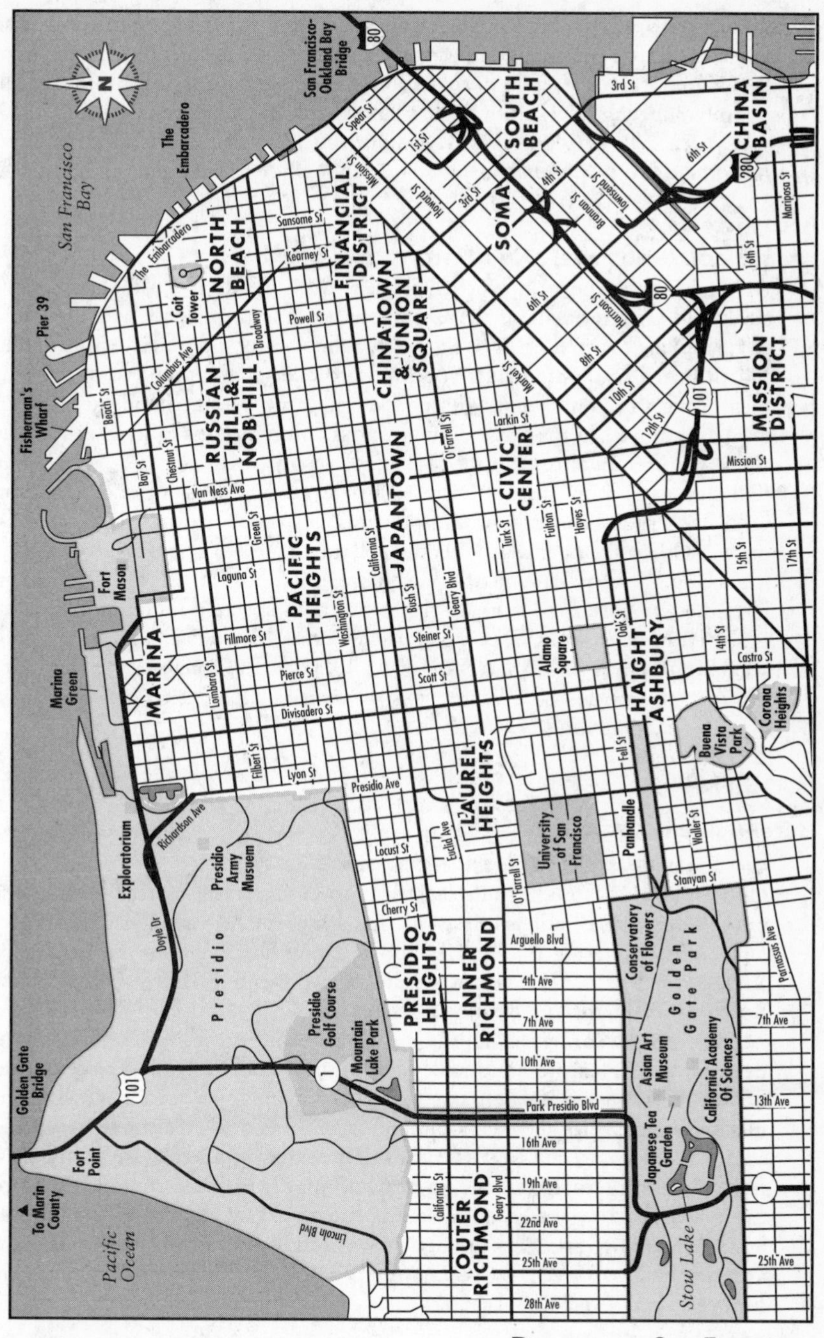

Downtown San Francisco

savory concoctions that your next-door neighbor might never imagine. The Pacha Pollo is a succulent pan-seared chicken with Andean spices, a purée of Peruvian potatoes (they're purple!), and organic greens. Vegetable lovers can happily put themselves in the chef's hands with his vegetarian selections. *$$; AE, MC, V; checks OK; dinner Wed–Sun, brunch Sat–Sun; full bar; reservations recommended; www.penapachamama.com; between Union and Green sts.* ♿

Rose Pistola / ★★★

532 COLUMBUS AVE, SAN FRANCISCO; 415/399-0499

A star has been born in North Beach, and her name is Rose Pistola. This sleek and sexy resident of the Columbus Avenue promenade is as pleasing to behold as it is to dine in (it's actually named after a popular octogenarian North Beach restaurateur). If you prefer to oversee the preparation of your meal, sit at the counter overlooking the grill; however, the family-style meals are best enjoyed in the large dining room's comfy booths (and tables on the sidewalk offer an alfresco option). The food is rustic Italian with a California flair (less fats, more flavors) inspired by the cuisine of Liguria: roast rabbit with fresh shell-bean ragout and polenta, asparagus risotto, or petrale sole grilled with white beans, arugula, fennel, and lemon. The pastas, wood-fired pizzas, and antipasti are also very well prepared, but the fish dishes (particularly the whole roasted fish) are the restaurant's specialty. A late-night menu is served until 1am on weekends, at which time patrons can mellow out to some soulful jazz. *$$–$$$; AE, DC, MC, V; no checks; lunch, dinner every day, brunch Sat–Sun; full bar; reservations recommended; www.rosepistolasf.com; between Union and Green sts.* ♿

LODGINGS

Hotel Bohème / ★★

444 COLUMBUS AVE, SAN FRANCISCO; 415/433-9111

Hopelessly chic is perhaps the best way to describe the Hotel Bohème, one of the sexiest small hotels in the city and a favorite retreat of visiting writers and poets. Hovering two stories above Columbus Avenue—the Boulevard Saint-Michel of San Francisco streets—the Bohème artfully reflects North Beach's bohemian flair dating from the late 1950s and early '60s. Sixteen guest rooms, decorated in soothing shades of sage green, cantaloupe, lavender, and black, feature handmade light fixtures crafted from glazed collages of jazz sheet music, Ginsberg poetry, and old menus and headlines, as well as black iron beds with sheer canopies, European armoires, bistro tables, wicker chairs, and Picasso and Matisse prints. Amenities include private baths, TVs, free wireless Internet, and telephones with modem jacks. A couple of minor caveats: most rooms are quite small, and those facing Columbus Avenue aren't kind to light sleepers (though views of the ever-bustling cafés and shops are entrancing). *$$; AE, DC, DIS, MC, V; no checks; www.hotelboheme.com; between Vallejo and Green sts.*

Chinatown

Chinatown has long been a blend of tacky and traditional. As early as 1893, *Baedeker's Guide to the United States* was advising travelers that "the Chinese Quarter is one of the most interesting and characteristic features of San Francisco and no one should leave the city without visiting it." Today, San Francisco has one of the largest communities of Chinese in the United States (about 20 percent of the city's population is Chinese), and Chinatown spreads from Union Square toward North Beach and the Financial District. More than 100,000 people live in Chinatown, making it one of the most densely packed neighborhoods in the country—second only to Harlem. Stores crammed full of poorly made luggage and trinkets rub elbows with those selling elegant jade jewelry. The sidewalks are packed with tourists and locals alike, all moving at a snail's pace past lively fishmongers and produce markets bursting with durian, Asian pears, lychees, Chinese broccoli, and baby bok choy. Other markets specialize in packaged goods like dried shiitake mushrooms, jasmine tea, and crispy rice snacks. Stop by a shop and watch as a merchant measures out a gnarled ginseng root or haggles over the price of fresh armadillo meat. Though not on Stockton Street, another must-see is the **GOLDEN GATE FORTUNE COOKIES** factory (56 Ross Alley at Washington St; 415/781-3956), which sits amid cloistered sweatshops on Ross Alley. Said to be the birthplace of the fortune cookie, the factory is open to tourists.

RESTAURANTS

Great Eastern / ★★

649 JACKSON ST, SAN FRANCISCO; 415/986-2500

If you love seafood and Chinese food and have an adventurous palate, have we got a restaurant for you. The venerable Great Eastern restaurant in Chinatown is renowned for its hard-to-find seafood, yanked fresh from the myriad huge fish tanks that line the back wall. If it swims, hops, slithers, or crawls, it's probably on the menu. Frogs, sea bass, soft-shell turtles, abalone, sea conch, steelhead, and Lord only knows what else are served sizzling on large, round family-style tables. Check the neon board in back to peruse the day's catch, which is sold by the pound. Our advice: Unless you're savvy at translating an authentic Hong Kong menu, order one of the set dinners (the crab version is fantastic) or point to another table and say, "I want that." (Don't expect much help from the harried servers.) *$$; AE, MC, V; no checks; lunch, dinner every day; beer and wine; reservations recommended; between Kearny St and Grant Ave.* ♿

R&G Lounge / ★

631 KEARNY ST, SAN FRANCISCO; 415/982-7877

Situated in limbo between Chinatown and the Financial District, the two-story R&G Lounge attracts a mixed crowd of tourists, business people, and local Chinese residents. The restaurant's loyal following champion the fresh

Cantonese seafood dishes and good prices. The main downstairs dining room has all the charm of a cafeteria, with glaring fluorescent lights and Formica tables. It's harder to get a table in the formal upstairs dining room, where the lighting is a little easier on the eyes. Each dining room offers the same menu, half in English, half in Chinese. But not every item is on the menu, so ask your server for recommendations, or order what we order every time: the very greasy but rich deep-fried salt and pepper crab, the tangy R&G Special Beef, the savory roast duck, the seafood in a clay pot, and for dessert the adzuki bean pudding. R&G offers an added luxury: Free two-hour parking in a garage just a block away. *$$; AE, DC, MC, V; no checks; lunch, dinner every day; full bar; no reservations; www.rnglounge.com; between Clay and Commercial sts.*

Financial District/Downtown

More than 200,000 people make the pilgrimage to the Financial District's sea of glass and steel skyscrapers every Monday through Friday to work, work, work. They come from as far away as Sacramento and Sebastopol and arrive by bridge, BART, Muni, ferry, train, bike, or on foot. From seven in the morning to six at night the streets are filled with people, cars, and buses, and the air is filled with a cacophony of horns, the clanging of construction equipment, and the tell-tale bells of the cable cars. Among the towering skyscrapers are two little-known downtown museums that celebrate the city's chaotic growth during the 19th century: the **WELLS FARGO HISTORY MUSEUM** (415/396-2619; www.wellsfargohistory.com) at 420 Montgomery Street (at California St), which has hundreds of genuine vestiges from the company's Wild West days—pistols, posters, photographs, and mining equipment—and the **MUSEUM OF THE MONEY OF THE AMERICAN WEST** in the massive Bank of California building at 400 California Street (at Kearny St). Both museums are free of charge. Before you leave the Financial District, be sure to visit the lively **FARMERS MARKET** held in front of the Ferry Building on Saturday mornings. Local restaurants offer breakfast snacks and coffee, but the real stars here are the Northern California farmers and ranchers who fill the market with fabulous fresh produce, organic meats, local oysters, and olive oils.

RESTAURANTS

Aqua / ★★★

252 CALIFORNIA ST, SAN FRANCISCO; 415/956-9662

When it opened in 1991, Aqua was the first restaurant in the city to elevate the humble seafood house to a temple of haute cuisine. Huge towering flower arrangements punctuate its spacious high-ceilinged dining room, where slipcovers on the chairs change with the seasons and the large mirrors and dramatic lighting reflect a well-heeled Financial District crowd. You're bound to overhear a lot of oohing and aahing when the artfully presented dishes arrive. Though Aqua's chefs seem to rotate in and out on a regular basis, everyone's favorite dishes still remain on the menu (and for good reason). The ahi tartare, mixed table-side with pears, pine nuts, quail egg, and spices, is the best we've ever had. As is the melt-in-your-mouth glazed Chilean sea bass with mushrooms, scallops, shiso tortellini, and miso broth. Oh, what the heck—we'll have the grilled medallions of ahi tuna with foie gras in pinot sauce as well. *$$$–$$$$; AE, DC, DIS, MC, V; no checks; lunch Mon–Fri, dinner every day; full bar; reservations recommended; www.aqua-sf.com; between Battery and Front sts.* ♿

Bix / ★★½

56 GOLD ST, SAN FRANCISCO; 415/433-6300

One of the sexiest and most sophisticated supper clubs in the city (and consistently voted best bar in *San Francisco* magazine's readers' poll), Bix never seems to go out of fashion. Modeled after a 1920s "New American" supper club, complete with massive silver columns, art deco–style lighting, and oodles of hand-carved Honduran mahogany (it's truly a beautiful room), the restaurant's raison d'être is the top-notch martinis that really sneak up on you. If you manage to make it to a dinner table (the ones on the intimate mezzanine are the best), it's de rigueur to order the crispy chicken hash, a Bix best seller for more than a decade. Other popular choices include the crisp potato pancake with smoked salmon and caviar, classic steak tartare prepared table-side, and day-boat scallops with black Périgord truffles pomme purée. *$$–$$$; AE, CB, DC, DIS, MC, V; no checks; lunch Fri, dinner every day; full bar; reservations recommended; www.bixrestaurant.com; between Sansome and Montgomery sts.* ♿

Boulevard / ★★★½

1 MISSION ST, SAN FRANCISCO; 415/543-6084

Nancy Oakes, a self-taught chef whose cooking career began in 1977 at a scruffy San Francisco saloon, teamed up with nationally renowned restaurant designer Pat Kuleto in 1993 and created this glittering jewel that sits squarely in the center of the city's culinary crown. Previously hailed as one of the nation's best chefs by *Food & Wine* magazine, Oakes has come a long way from her days of dishing out pub grub to an audience of longshoremen. These days her patrons tend to be well-heeled gastronomes who have been fans ever since she opened her first restaurant, L'Avenue, in 1988. At big, bustling Boulevard she serves hearty American-style cuisine with French and Italian influences. On the seasonal menu you'll find a well-chosen mix of dishes. Oysters, giant beluga caviar, and fresh sautéed Sonoma foie gras served on an apple and fig strudel top the extensive appetizer list. Main courses might include a boneless rabbit stuffed with fresh chicken-and-sun-dried-tomato sausages, roasted to perfection in the wood-fired oven; asparagus risotto accompanied by roasted prawns and shiitake mushrooms filled with herbed goat cheese; and oven-roasted northern halibut resting on a large bed of wilted baby spinach sprinkled with chanterelle mushrooms and a side of buttery potato-chive fritters. For dessert, the ganache-mousse tart with fresh raspberries or pecan

LET THEM EAT CAKE

Ever since that little-known HBO television series *Sex and the City* popularized the childhood treat prevalent at birthday parties and holiday soirees, people everywhere have gone wild over cupcakes. The craze started in New York City and quickly spread west to invade the culinary conscience of many San Franciscans, as well—particularly bake-shop owners looking to capitalize on the trend that shows no signs of slowing down. Here's where to go the next time your cupcake craving bites.

AMERICAN CUPCAKE (415/244-7650; www.americancupcake.com)

If bubblegum cake doesn't sound appetizing to you (what, you didn't even know such creations existed?), then you obviously haven't sampled the wonderful inventions of American Cupcake, one of the city's most beloved cupcakeries. Still not feeling very adventurous? Start out slow with the cotton candy, lemon drop, black and white, or banana pudding varieties. Call for the new store location (previously, American Cupcake only took phone orders).

MIETTE (1 Ferry Bldg, Shop 10; 415/837-0300; www.miettecakes.com)

Miette's masterpieces are often described as "too pretty to eat" (though you'd have more willpower than most if you could actually resist the sugary goodness). Favorites include gingerbread with cream cheese, hazelnut, and chocolate with lavender or raspberry buttercream frosting. Miette Confiserie, traditionally a candy store that also sells cupcakes, is located at 449 Octavia St.

THAT TAKES THE CAKE (2271 Union St, between Filmore and Steiner sts; 415/567-8050; www.that-takes-the-cake.com)

With a rotating menu varying by the day, That Takes the Cake keeps a line out the door with its standard and mini cupcakes in scrumptious flavors and creative names like Sleepless in San Francisco (double chocolate devil's food cake with espresso buttercream frosting), Snow Balls (coconut-almond buttermilk cake with lemon curd filling and flaked coconut on top), and Prom Queen (strawberry with strawberry buttercream frosting).

pie topped with vanilla ice cream and chocolate sauce push the sated diner over a blissful edge. *$$$; AE, DC, DIS, MC, V; no checks; lunch Mon–Fri, dinner every day; full bar; reservations recommended; www.boulevardrestaurant.com; between Steuart St and the Embarcadero.* ♿

Kokkari Estiatorio / ★★★☆

200 JACKSON ST, SAN FRANCISCO; 415/981-0983

Kokkari's owners have done their best to invent a new category—upscale Greek with a California twist. And why not? It worked for Italian food.

Indeed, Kokkari (pronounced koh-CAR-ee) works on many levels: it's a beautiful, lavishly decorated restaurant with a ritzy country-house ambience, thanks to the fire crackling in the oversize fireplace, the ornate rugs and plush chairs suitable for royalty, and the large windows and sun-bleached walls. This is a place to relax, soak up the atmosphere, and revel in the California-style contemporary Hellenic cuisine. Besides the luxurious front dining room there's a second, larger dining room with an open kitchen and cushy booths. The usual Greek suspects play well here: avgolemono, the lemony egg, rice, and chicken soup; moussaka, the divinely spiced casserole of eggplant, lamb, and potato; and the quintessential Greek salad—no lettuce, just tomato, olive, red onion, and cucumber. Presentations are stunning, and the flavors are fresh and bright. For starters, don't miss the whole crispy smelt and the octopus salad. The grilled lamb chops with fried potatoes are classic, as is the whole grilled fish. Thick Greek coffee is made in a multiple-step process that involves an elaborate urn of sand (you can even ask the waitstaff for a demo). *$$$; AE, DC, DIS, MC, V; no checks; lunch Mon–Fri, dinner Mon–Sat; full bar; reservations recommended; www.kokkari.com; at Front St.* ♿

One Market / ★★★

1 MARKET ST, SAN FRANCISCO; 415/777-5577

When it first opened, One Market turned out surprisingly inconsistent fare, bringing both bravos and boos from major restaurant critics. But the ratings improved rapidly and the restaurant now boasts a Michelin star thanks to an ever-changing menu that makes the most of California's abundance of farm-fresh products. Executive chef Mark Dommen describes his cuisine as contemporary American. Entrées might include Yukon gold potato and portobello mushroom terrine, with Tuscan kale, black trumpet mushrooms, and red wine–shallot purée; Alaskan halibut *sous vide* with bamboo rice, peanuts, shiitake mushrooms, and shrimp-coconut *nage*; or roasted duck breast with duck leg confit, rhubarb, vanilla–sweet potato purée, and five spice jus. Desserts often incorporate the freshest in seasonal fruits, like the lemon cream–blueberry tart brûlée with an organic blueberry mascarpone ice cream shake, or a crepe stack of organic strawberries, muscat caramel, and cinnamon swirl–sour cream ice cream. The 400-plus list of American wine selections is one of the city's best, and live jazz piano music filters through the cavernous dining room every evening. *$$$; AE, DC, MC, V; no checks; lunch Mon–Fri, dinner Mon–Sat; full bar; reservations recommended; www.onemarket.com; at Steuart St.* ♿

Rubicon / ★★★

558 SACRAMENTO ST, SAN FRANCISCO; 415/434-4100

Thanks to Rubicon's star-studded cast of financial backers—Robert De Niro, Robin Williams, and Francis Ford Coppola—this Financial District restaurant received so much advance publicity that San Franciscans were setting dates to eat here long before the seismic reinforcements were bolted to the floorboards. Chances are slim that you'll see any Tinseltown talent at the table next to you, but one bite of the foie gras with caramelized rhubarb compote and you couldn't care less who walks in. Other highlights on the monthly changing menu might include butter-poached Alaskan halibut, seared scallops in a sweet onion purée, venison chops over barley, and roulades of steelhead under a crisp herbal crust. The excellent, extensive, and expensive wine list is literally one of the nation's best. *$$$; AE, DC, MC, V; no checks; lunch Wed, dinner Mon–Sat; full bar; reservations recommended; www.sfrubicon.com; between Sansome and Montgomery sts.* ♿

The Slanted Door / ★★★

1 FERRY BLDG, SAN FRANCISCO; 415/861-8032

Chef Charles Phan and his large extended family first opened their restaurant—specializing in country Vietnamese food—in a vacant space on a slightly run-down stretch of Valencia Street in 1995. But Phan's creative cooking and design talents (he's a former UC Berkeley architecture student) eventually made his humble restaurant a nationwide sensation, attracting celebrities like Mick Jagger and former President Clinton. He had no choice but to move it to a larger location in the nicely renovated Ferry Building. Phan's unique fare, based on his mother's recipes, attracts droves of diners for lunch and dinner. The menu changes weekly to reflect the market's offerings, but look for the favored spring rolls stuffed with fresh shrimp and pork, crab and asparagus soup, caramelized shrimp, curried chicken cooked with yams, "shaking" beef sautéed with onion and garlic, any of the terrific clay pot dishes, and, of course, Phan's special Vietnamese crepes. There's also an eclectic collection of teas, which come by the pot for $3 to $5. For dessert, the hands-down favorite is the all-American chocolate cake. Go figure. *$$–$$$; AE, DC, DIS, MC, V; no checks; lunch, dinner every day; full bar; reservations recommended; www.slanteddoor.com; at the Embarcadero and Market St.* ♿

Yank Sing / ★★★

101 SPEAR ST, SAN FRANCISCO; 415/957-9300

Living on the edge of the Pacific Rim has its advantages. For example, the best dim sum in the United States is probably served in the Bay Area at places like Ton Kiang and Yank Sing. Yank Sing serves more than 90 varieties of dim sum, including such standards as pot stickers, spring rolls, plump shrimp dumplings (dee-licious!), stuffed crab claws, fried eggplant, and *bao* (steamed buns stuffed with aromatically seasoned minced meat). The barbecued chicken is a house specialty, although some find it too sweet; other favorites are Peking duck (served by the slice), minced squab in lettuce cups, and soft-shell crab. Make reservations or prepare to wait and wait and wait, especially for a weekend brunch. Takeout is available, too, and it costs much less. A second location has opened at 49 Stevenson Street (between 1st and 2nd sts.). *$$–$$$; AE, DC, MC, V; no checks; lunch every day, brunch Sat–Sun; beer and wine; reservations recommended; www.yanksing.com; between Mission and Howard sts (inside 1 Rincon Center).* ♿

LODGINGS

Mandarin Oriental / ★★★★

222 SANSOME ST, SAN FRANCISCO; 415/276-9888 OR 800/622-0404

The rooms at the Mandarin Oriental offer some of the most remarkable views in the city. Because it's perched high in the sky (on the top 11 floors of the 48-story 345 California Center Building, San Francisco's third-tallest skyscraper), you're guaranteed a bird's-eye view not only of the city but also of the entire Bay Area, including the Golden Gate Bridge, Alcatraz, and Coit Tower. The 158 guest rooms are comfortable and deceptively austere. Well hidden among the simple blond-wood furniture and fine Asian artwork are deluxe amenities: three two-line speakerphones with fax hookups, cordless phones, Internet access, remote-control televisions with access to videos and DVDs, fully stocked minibars, binoculars, and CD players, as well as jumbo marble bathrooms with stall showers and extra-deep soaking tubs. (If you request a Signature Room, you can even admire the city's skyline from floor-to-ceiling windows next to the tubs.) Once settled in your room, you'll be treated to complimentary jasmine tea service and your choice of either Thai silk or terry-cloth slippers. Contrary to the policy of many other hotels, the room rates at the Mandarin don't vary according to scenery, so request one of the corner rooms (numbers ending with 6 or 11) or the Signature rooms (04 or 14) for the best views. Additional perks include access to numerous business services, valet parking, continental breakfast and afternoon tea served in the lounge, complimentary shoe shines, concierge, 24-hour room service, and a state-of-the-art fitness center. The hotel's award-winning restaurant, Silks, may be the Maytag repairman of luxury restaurants: it's all gussied up and anxious to serve, but a tad lonely and underappreciated. *$$$–$$$$; AE, DC, DIS, MC, V; checks OK; www.mandarinoriental.com/sanfrancisco; between Pine and California sts.* ♿

Omni San Francisco Hotel / ★★★

500 CALIFORNIA ST, SAN FRANCISCO; 415/677-9494 OR 800/788-6664

After a $100 million renovation, the city's historic 1926 Financial Center Building now houses one of San Francisco's most luxurious hotels, replete with twinkling crystal chandeliers and an elaborate iron staircase in the lobby that evokes an old-world ambience. There are just two room types in the 17-story hotel, each featuring classic 1920s decor with mahogany and cherry-wood furniture, warm sunset tones, and green-and-gold color schemes. All the standard luxuries are here: in-room high-speed Internet access, safes, minibars, and 27-inch televisions, as well as a fitness center and complimentary luxury car transportation within the downtown area. Kids Fantasy Suites are outfitted with bean bags, bunk beds, and games and toys galore to keep little ones occupied. The Get Fit guest rooms come with portable treadmills, yoga mats, dumbbells, and even healthy snacks—all for just a few extra dollars per day. The best rooms are the corner suites; each has six huge windows, a large living room, and a king-size bed. Major financial deals are cut over 28-ounce slabs of beef at Bob's Steak and Chop House just off the lobby, and the adjoining bar has been packed with lively locals since the day it opened. *$$$$; AE, DC, DIS, MC, V; checks OK; www.omnisanfrancisco.com; at Montgomery St.* ♿

Orchard Garden Hotel / ★★★

466 BUSH ST, SAN FRANCISCO; 415/399-9807 OR 888/717-2881

If you're looking for a personalized bed-and-breakfast-type stay, but don't want to sacrifice location, the downtown eco-chic Orchard Garden Hotel is the perfect choice. California's first LEED-certified hotel and the third of its kind in the nation, the Orchard Garden began welcoming visitors in 2006 after its $25 million construction. The bright and airy rooms sport light wood furnishings and a cheery color scheme of pale yellow and—what else?—seafoam green. Book a room on the ninth floor, the only quarters you'll find with sprawling balconies and lounge chairs. The Orchard Garden has a more business-y sister property, the Orchard Hotel, located just down the street, and Roots, a top-notch restaurant. *$$$–$$$$; AE, MC, V; www.theorchardgardenhotel.com; between Kearny and Grant sts.* ♿

The Palace Hotel / ★★★

2 NEW MONTGOMERY ST, SAN FRANCISCO;
415/512-1111 OR 888/627-7196 (RESERVATIONS)

This opulent hotel, originally built in 1875, underwent a hefty restoration in 1989, restoring it to its original splendor. The downstairs decor is truly breathtaking, from the multiple sparkling Austrian-crystal chandeliers, the double row of white Italian marble Ionic columns, and the stained-glass dome of the Garden Court, to the three grand ballrooms and early 19th-century French tapestry gracing the walls. Unfortunately, all this impressive glitz comes to a screeching halt when you open the door to one of the 552 guest rooms. Although comfortable and attractive, the rooms are more akin to gussied-up generic hotel rooms than to any palace chamber. However, this place does offer all the perks you'd look for in a luxury hotel, including a concierge, 24-hour room service, valet parking, and an elaborate business center, plus a palm-embellished health club with an exercise room, a co-ed sauna, a whirlpool, and a stunning white-tiled lap pool capped by a dome of clear glass. Restaurants include the Garden Court, famous for its elaborate breakfast buffet and elegant afternoon tea; Kyo-ya, a rather austere Japanese dining room serving the best (and most expensive) sushi and sashimi in town; and the Pied Piper Bar. Even if you don't have the resources to recline or dine here, this place, like most palaces, is worth a self-guided tour. *$$$$; AE, DC, DIS, MC, V; checks OK (for lodging only); www.sfpalace.com; at Market St.* ♿

Union Square

For shopping fanatics, this is the heart of it all, the sine qua non for credit card aerobics. But don't despair if Saks Fifth Avenue, Neiman Marcus, Macy's, Gump's, and Tiffany & Co. are not on your top-10 list of vacation destinations. The **THEATER DISTRICT** is right around the corner, and a "French Quarter" hides on Bush Street between Grant and Montgomery streets, and down tiny Claude and Belden lanes. Dining options range from relaxed bistros to some of the most elegant restaurants in town. Union Square is named for the fiery pro-Union rallies that took place here during the Civil War; today it provides plenty of free space so you can take a break from power shopping, have a snack at the corner café, and watch the street performers. The number and quality of the hotels in this area make it the ideal launching pad for excursions into other neighborhoods.

RESTAURANTS

Farallon / ★★★

450 POST ST, SAN FRANCISCO; 415/956-6969

In 1997, chef Mark Franz (of Stars restaurant fame) and master designer Pat Kuleto opened this dazzling $4 million, 160-seat restaurant, offering seafood dishes as innovative as the elegant aquatic-themed decor. For starters, consider delectable asparagus bisque with cardamom cream; truffled mashed potatoes with crab and salmon caviar artfully stuffed into a real sea-urchin shell; Maine lobster and wild-mushroom gnocchi with a leek, tarragon, and champagne lobster sauce; or giant tiger prawns—the best thing on the menu. Entrées change daily and might include ginger-steamed salmon and sea-scallop pillows with a prawn mousse or sautéed gulf prawns with potato risotto, English peas, pearl onions, and truffle portobello coulis. While Franz's forte is fish, he also has a flair for meat dishes such as a juicy grilled fillet of beef served with a portobello mushroom and potato galette, haricot verts, and black truffle aioli. The 300-item wine list fits in swimmingly with the menu (though prices are high), and about two dozen wines are available by the glass. The attentive staff helps make Farallon a deep-sea dine to remember. *$$$; AE, DC, DIS, MC, V; travelers checks OK; lunch Tues–Sat, dinner every day; full bar; reservations recommended; www.farallonrestaurant.com; between Mason and Powell sts.* ♿

Le Colonial / ★★½

20 COSMO PL, SAN FRANCISCO; 415/931-3600

This hideaway, tucked-away on a side street near the Tenderloin and Union Square, serves excellent Vietnamese food that is much more expensive than what you'll find at the usual Asian restaurants around town. But this is no typical Asian restaurant: it's a place to be seen with the other pretty people who arrive here after work to schmooze and flirt. Fashioned after a 1920s Vietnamese plantation, complete with wicker, fans, and rich wood, Le Colonial offers a blend of French and Vietnamese cooking. Upstairs in the lounge, relax with a drink on the cozy couches and choose from an extensive list of appetizers. The dinner menu also offers a tantalizing blend of sweet, spicy, sour, and aromatic dishes, which can be ordered individually as entrées or served family-style. Some good choices include the steamed sea bass wrapped in a banana leaf (their best dish), coconut curry prawns with mango and eggplant, wok-seared beef tenderloin with watercress and onion salad, cold beef salad with tender chunks marinated in lime, ginger roast duck, and the crispy Vietnamese spring rolls. *$$$; AE, DC, MC, V; no checks; dinner every day; full bar; reservations recommended; www.lecolonialsf.com; off Taylor St, between Post and Sutter sts.* ♿

Postrio / ★★★

545 POST ST (THE PRESCOTT HOTEL), SAN FRANCISCO; 415/776-7825

Owned by Southern California superstar chef Wolfgang Puck and the Kimpton Hotel & Restaurant Group, Postrio is a splashy slice of Hollywood set in the heart of San Francisco, with superglitzy decor à la restaurant designer Pat Kuleto, delightful culinary combinations, and the perpetual hope of a celebrity sighting. It's a lovely, sophisticated setting for some terrific food, prepared by chefs Mitchell and Steven Rosenthal. Working closely with Puck, the brothers Rosenthal have crafted an exciting hybrid of California-Asian-Mediterranean cuisine that includes such creations as grilled quail accompanied by spinach and a soft egg ravioli with port wine glaze; sautéed salmon with plum glaze, wasabi mashed potatoes, and miso vinaigrette; Chinese duck with mango sauce; and roasted leg of lamb with garlic potato purée and niçoise olives. The dessert menu boasts its own array of showstoppers—from the potato-pecan pie to the caramel pear tart with Grand Marnier crème fraîche. The wine list is excellent, the service professional, and reservations are essential—make them several weeks in advance. *$$$; AE, DC, DIS, MC, V; no checks; dinner every day; full bar; reservations recommended; www.postrio.com; between Mason and Taylor sts, in the Prescott Hotel.* ♿

LODGINGS

Campton Place Hotel / ★★★½

340 STOCKTON ST, SAN FRANCISCO; 415/781-5555 OR 800/235-4300

Almost as soon as Campton Place reopened after an extensive restoration in 1983, its posh surroundings, stunning objets d'art, superlative service, and elegant accommodations began swaying the patrons of the carriage trade away from traditional San Francisco hotels. The 110 guest rooms are very comfortable, and the custom-built chairs and handsome desks help create a pervasive air of luxury. For the best views, ask for one of the larger deluxe corner rooms on the upper floors. The view from room 1501, which overlooks Union Square, is particularly stunning. For help with your laundry, dry cleaning, shoe shining, or even babysitting, just pick up the phone and you'll be accommodated, tout de suite. The concierge will make any and all of your arrangements (a reservation for the hotel's limo, perhaps?), and 24-hour room service will deliver whatever you're craving from the menu at the well-regarded Campton Place restaurant, one of the city's prettiest—and priciest—dining establishments. *$$$–$$$$; AE, DC, MC, V; checks OK (for lodging only); www.camptonplace.com; between Fillmore and Steiner sts.* ♿

The Clift / ★★★★

495 GEARY ST, SAN FRANCISCO; 415/775-4700 OR 800/652-5438

San Francisco's opulent turn-of-the-19th-century hotel has been given a decidedly 21st century makeover by celebrity hotelier Ian Schrager, the man behind L.A.'s Mondrian, Miami's Delano, and New York City's Royalton and Paramount. It is the hippest, most trendsetting hotel in the city and will likely remain so for years to come. With the help of designer Philippe Starck, Schrager has transformed this stately old gal into functional modern art. Each of the 375 guest rooms includes such luxuries as a massive sleigh bed made from English sycamore on a polished chrome base, 400-thread-count Italian percale bedding, an oversize bathroom with dressing area and vanity table, custom cabinetry housing a state-of-the-art entertainment center, vivid orange Plexiglas night tables, and enormous floor-to-ceiling mirrors. But wait, there's more: the stodgy old Redwood Room cocktail lounge has been transformed into a monochromatic masterpiece, where the city's dig-me crowd watches flat-screen TVs playing digital works by avant garde artists, and the same lavish theme is carried over to the hotel's Asian-Cuban restaurant, Asia de Cuba. Other basic amenities for all guests include a 24-hour business center with computer workstations, 24-hour concierge service, and a 24-hour gym with private trainers and fitness classes. *$$$$; AE, DC, MC, V; checks OK; www.clifthotel.com; at Taylor St.* ♿

Golden Gate Hotel / ★☆

775 BUSH ST, SAN FRANCISCO; 415/392-3702 OR 800/835-1118

The Union Square area has a slew of small, reasonably priced European-style hotels housed in turn-of-the-century buildings, and the Golden Gate Hotel is one of the best. It's a family-run affair, owned by John and Renate Kenaston and managed by their daughter, and these kind folks will bend over backward to make sure you enjoy your stay. The 25 guest rooms are individually decorated with antique and wicker furnishings, quilted bedspreads, and sweet-smelling fresh flowers; all have phones and TVs as well. If you like a good soak, request a room with a claw-foot tub. A complimentary afternoon tea is served daily from 4 to 7pm. *$–$$; AE, CB, DC, MC, V; no checks; www.goldengatehotel.com; between Powell and Mason sts.*

Hotel California / ★★

580 GEARY ST, SAN FRANCISCO; 415/441-2700 OR 800/227-4223

Originally built in 1913 for the Panama-Pacific International Exposition and formerly the popular Savoy Hotel, this seven-story building is a posh French country–style inn with a gorgeous facade of richly veined black marble, beveled glass, mahogany, and polished brass. The 83 guest rooms and suites are small—don't be surprised if you overhear your neighbors in the next room—but beautifully appointed, with reams of toile de Jouy fabrics, heavy French cotton bedspreads, imported Provençal furnishings, plump feather beds, goose-down pillows, two-line telephones with modem jacks, and minibars. A few of the suites come with Jacuzzi tubs. The most tranquil rooms are on the northeast corner (farthest from the traffic noise), facing a rear courtyard. Guests are nurtured with an afternoon wine and cheese; a full breakfast is also available every morning for just $9. And how's this for first-class service: guests are generously served a frosted shot of tequila upon check-in. The adjoining restaurant, Millennium, comes highly praised for its fine vegan fare. *$$; AE, DC, DIS, MC, V; no checks; www.thesavoyhotel.com; between Taylor and Jones sts.* ♿

Hotel Diva / ★★

440 GEARY ST, SAN FRANCISCO; 415/885-0200 OR 800/553-1900

Ever since it opened in 1985, Hotel Diva has been the prima donna of San Francisco's modern hotels, winning a design award from *Interiors* magazine for its suave, ultrasleek design. The 116 guest rooms are all works of art, decorated with cobalt blue carpets, sculptured steel furnishings, and haute-design metal headboards fashioned after ocean waves. Each room has invigorating bath products, designer bathrobes, a flat-screen TV, a DVD player, an iPod dock, a CD player, and a cordless phone with voice mail. Guest services include valet parking, room delivery from adjacent Colibri restaurant, concierge, free wireless Internet throughout the hotel, a 24-hour cardio workout room, four 24-hour lounges with Internet access, and a business center offering free use of computers, software, and a laser printer. Insider tips: Rooms ending in 09 have extra-large bathrooms with vanity mirrors and makeup tables; rooms on the Salon Floor offer upgraded amenities like down feather beds and comforters, votive candles, complimentary breakfast, and Voss bottled water. The Little Divas Kids Suites are outfitted by Design Within Reach and spruced up for the pint-size traveler with modern bunk beds, colorful cushions, and drawing tables. The suites give children their own space, which is connected to their parents' room. Before you hit the town, ask the concierge for Diva's "SF Hot Spots" checklist. *$$$; AE, DC, DIS, MC, V; checks OK; www.hoteldiva.com; between Mason and Taylor sts.* ♿

Hotel Monaco / ★★★☆

501 GEARY ST, SAN FRANCISCO; 415/292-0100 OR 800/214-4220

"Wow!" is a common exclamation from first-time guests at Hotel Monaco, one of the hottest hotels in a city brimming with top-notch accommodations. Expect a melding of modern European fashion with flourishes of the American Beaux Arts era—the trademark of award-winning designer Cheryl Rowley, who envisioned the 201-room hotel as a "great ship traveling to the farthest reaches of the world, collecting exotic, precious treasures and antiquities." Hence the guest rooms—replete with canopy beds, Chinese-inspired armoires, bamboo writing desks, old-fashioned decorative luggage, and a profusion of bold stripes and vibrant colors. The entire hotel is truly a feast for the eyes, particularly the Grand Cafe with its 30-foot ceilings, cascading chandeliers, stately columns, and many art nouveau frills—all vestiges of its former incarnation as the hotel's grand ballroom. And, of course, there are the requisite hotel toys (health club, steam room, whirlpool spa, sauna), services (massages, manicures, valet parking, business and room service), and complimentary perks (newspaper delivery, morning coffee, afternoon tea and cookies, evening wine reception). *$$$–$$$$; AE, DC, DIS, MC, V; no checks; www.monaco-sf.com; at Taylor St.* ♿

Hotel Rex / ★★★

562 SUTTER ST, SAN FRANCISCO; 415/433-4434 OR 800/433-4434

The Joie de Vivre hotel company has created a winner with the 94-room Hotel Rex, yet another addition to its cadre of fashionable yet affordable accommodations. The hotel's sophisticated and sensuous lobby lounge is cleverly modeled after a 1920s library, which functions as a stylish sanctuary for San Francisco's arts and literary community (hence the adjoining antiquarian bookstore). All of the spacious (for a downtown hotel) guest rooms feature CD players, two-line cordless telephones with voice mail, and free wireless Internet. The rooms in the back are quieter and overlook a tranquil, shaded courtyard. Perks include room service, same-day laundry and dry cleaning, complimentary newspaper, an evening wine hour, concierge service, and morning car service to the Financial District. *$$$; AE, DC, MC, V; no checks; www.thehotelrex.com; between Powell and Mason sts.* ♿

Hotel Triton / ★★★

342 GRANT AVE, SAN FRANCISCO; 415/394-0500 OR 800/800-1299

The Hotel Triton has been described as modern, whimsical, sophisticated, chic, vogue, neobaroque, ultrahip, and retro-futuristic—but words just don't do justice to this unique hostelry-cum-art-gallery that you'll simply have to see to appreciate. The entire hotel, from the bellhop's inverted pyramid–shaped podium to the iridescent throw pillows on the beds and the ashtrays ringed with faux pearls, is the original work of four imaginative (some might say wacky) San Francisco artisans. For a preview of what's behind the bedroom doors, peek in to the lobby, where you'll see curvaceous chairs shimmering in gold silk taffeta; an imposing duo of floor-to-ceiling pillars sheathed in teal, purple, and gold leaf; and a pastel mural portraying mythic images of sea life, triton shells, and human figures. Add to this visual extravaganza all the amenities you'd find in any luxury hotel, including a concierge, valet parking (essential in this part of town), room service, complimentary wine and coffee, business and limousine services, and even a fitness center. The 140 guest rooms and designer suites continue the modern wonderland theme: walls are splashed with giant, hand-painted yellow and blue diamonds; king-size beds feature navy-and-khaki-striped camelback headboards; and armoires that hide remote-control TVs are topped with golden crowns. *$$$; AE, DC, DIS, MC, V; checks OK; www.hoteltriton.com; at Bush St.* ♿

A VIEW FROM THE TOP

One big-city perk is riding one of those lighting-fast elevators to the top of a hotel skyscraper and hanging out for a while in the bar, feigning importance. Sure, the drinks are overpriced, but for $8 (or $9, or $12 . . .) you get a million-dollar view of the city and the bay. Here's a list of our favorites; a few have a cover charge at night, but most are free during the day.

CARNELIAN ROOM (555 California St, between Kearny and Montgomery sts; 415/433-7500)

Located on the 52nd floor of the Bank of America Building, the Carnelian Room is a swanky reservations-only restaurant, but the adjoining cocktail lounge is open to everyone, and the view looking north toward the Golden Gate Bridge is phenomenal.

CITYSCAPE (333 O'Farrell St at Mason St; 415/923-5002)

OK, so it's a hokey Hilton hotel, but they can't corporatize the amazing views from high atop the 46th floor. Sit under the glass roof, knock down a few Long Islands, and ponder your existence among the stars.

CROWN ROOM (950 Mason St at California St; 415/772-5131)

Half the fun of getting here is riding in the glass elevator Willy Wonka–style. The panoramic 360-degree view from the 24th floor of the Fairmont Hotel & Tower—the highest observation point in the city—is well worth that $10 Manhattan you're carrying around; in fact, it's widely considered *the* best view in the city.

Hotel Union Square / ★☆

114 POWELL ST, SAN FRANCISCO; 415/397-3000

If you love to be in the heartbeat of the city, there's nary a better place to lay your head than the Hotel Union Square. In fact, upon first look, you might not even spot it among the storefronts and bodegas crammed along the streets surrounding Union Square. A favorite among European travelers—on any given stay, you could hear a multitude of languages on your ride up the building's sole elevator—this budget-friendly option is surely lighter on your wallet than any of its neighboring accommodations. Yet, it still boasts all of the same comforts: flat-screen TVs, complimentary wireless Internet, feather beds, pay-per-view movies, Nintendo games, and more. The penthouse suites are accessed by private stairwells and have their own rooftop patios with views of the San Francisco skyline. Elements like splashy hues of red and gold, artistic light fixtures, and exposed-brick walls are other unique touches. Other amenities include same-day laundry and dry cleaning service, on-site parking, discounted admission to nearby Club One Fitness center, currency exchange, and complimentary coffee and tea service. It's one of a handful of

GRANDVIEWS (345 Stockton, between Sutter and Post sts; 415/398-1234)
It may not be the Equinox—the famed spinning restaurant at the Hyatt Regency that recently shut its doors—but this 36th-floor eatery at the Grand Hyatt serves three meals a day, with a hearty portion of scenery for dessert.

HARRY DENTON'S STARLIGHT ROOM (450 Powell St at Sutter St; 415/395-8595)

On the 21st floor of the Sir Francis Drake Hotel is a 1930s-style club complete with chandeliers, red velvet banquettes, and glittering views of the city streets far below. A Sunday drag show brunch is wildly popular, as is the youthful indulgence party every Wednesday, but it's the nightly dig-me-and-dance scene and live music on Tuesdays, Fridays, and Saturdays that bring out the masses.

TOP OF THE MARK (1 Nob Hill at California and Mason sts; 415/616-6916)
"Meet me at the Mark" is the slogan of one of the most famous cocktail lounges in the world. During World War II, Pacific-bound servicemen toasted their good-byes to the States here, and you can kiss a Hamilton (or several) good-bye as you sip your cocktail and enjoy the magnificent 19th-floor view atop the InterContinental Mark Hopkins.

THE VIEW LOUNGE (55 4th St, between Market and Mission sts; 415/896-1600)
The name says it all: this cocktail lounge on the top floor of the San Francisco Marriott hotel offers some of the best views in (and of) the city. Only thick glass windows separate you from one helluva first step. It's a very casual place where you can linger all day in your shorts and nobody will care.

pet-friendly hotels, so feel free to bring your pooch along. *$$; AE, DC, DIS, MC, V; checks OK; www.hotelunionsquare.com; at Ellis St.* ♿

The Prescott Hotel / ★★★

545 POST ST, SAN FRANCISCO; 415/563-0303 OR 866/271-3632
Opened in 1989 by the late San Francisco hotel magnate Bill Kimpton, the Prescott has put pressure on Union Square's neighboring luxury hotels by offering first-rate accommodations at a fairly reasonable price. This, combined with dining privileges at one of the city's most popular restaurants (the adjoining Postrio; see review), superlative service from an intelligent, youthful staff, and a prime location in the heart of San Francisco, places the Prescott at the top of the Union Square hotel list. The rooms, decorated with custom-made cherry-wood furnishings, black granite–topped nightstands and dressers, and silk wallpaper, have rich color schemes of hunter green, deep purple, cerise, taupe, and gold. The Prescott offers 164 rooms, including numerous suites and a wildly posh penthouse complete with a grand piano, a rooftop Jacuzzi, a formal dining room, and twin fireplaces. Standard perks include

limo service to the Financial District, wireless Internet, overnight shoe shine, valet parking, laundry service, a daily newspaper delivered to your room, and access to the adjacent fitness facility. *$$$; AE, DC, DIS, MC, V; checks OK (for lodging only); www.prescotthotel.com; between Mason and Taylor sts.* ♿

Serrano Hotel / ★★★

405 TAYLOR ST, SAN FRANCISCO; 415/885-2500 OR 866/289-6561

The staff at the Serrano Hotel like to play games. Literally. Guests arriving at this Theater District hotel sense the tongue-in-cheek fun immediately when invited to play Check-in Challenge and go up against the house in blackjack for free upgrades and other perks. This theme is carried throughout the hotel, from the residential-style lobby featuring ancient Egyptian games in front of the fireplace to the mini board games for sale in the honor bars. A 1999 restoration has completely transformed this 1920s historic landmark; the 236 guest rooms are decorated in a sophisticated yet whimsical style with an eclectic charm, including intricately painted ceiling beams and Moroccan-style carvings. If you're a theater buff, ask for the ACT Suite—the nearby American Conservatory Theater regularly updates its decor, and the headboard in the master suite is a replica of their stage. Guests are invited to an evening wine hour, and the hotel even brings in a chair masseuse and tarot card reader. The hotel restaurant, Ponzu, is a sexy, curvaceous velvet-draped space with huge glass aquariums and dazzling lighting. The menu is best described as Asian-fusion comfort food (think hoisin sauce sticky ribs). The location is an easy 2½-block walk to Union Square and the Powell Street cable-car line. *$$$$; AE, DC, DIS, MC, V; no checks; www.serranohotel.com; at O'Farrell St.* ♿

Sir Francis Drake Hotel / ★★½

450 POWELL ST, SAN FRANCISCO; 415/392-7755 OR 800/795-7129

While nowhere near as resplendent as the nearby Westin St. Francis (see review), the 21-story Sir Francis Drake gives us ordinary folks a reasonably priced opportunity to stay in one of San Francisco's grande dames. A $5 million renovation in 1999 spruced up the 416 rooms a bit, but there's still a little wear around the edges. No matter—it's the experience of listening to the sounds of Union Square wafting through your window that makes staying here an enjoyable experience. Then there's Tom Sweeny, the legendary and ever-jovial beefeater doorman who has graced more snapshots than any other San Franciscan; the top-floor Harry Denton's Starlight Room, one of the most fun and fashionable cocktail-dance lounges in the city; Scala's Bistro, an upscale yet affordable restaurant we guarantee you'll enjoy; and all the requisite big-hotel amenities such as room service, newspaper delivery, business services, babysitting, in-room massage, and laundry service. So considering that you can get a standard room here for about half the price of rooms at the St. Francis—and with far better eating, drinking, and dancing—the Drake is definitely worth looking in to. *$$$–$$$$; AE, DC, DIS, MC, V; no checks; www.sirfrancisdrake.com; at Sutter St.* ♿

Westin St. Francis / ★★★½

335 POWELL ST, SAN FRANCISCO; 415/397-7000 OR 800/WESTIN-1

San Francisco's first world-class hotel still attracts a legion of admirers; most of them can't afford the steep room rates but are content with lounging in the lobby just to soak up the heady, majestic aura of this historic hotel. The who's who of the world have all checked in at one time or another, including all the U.S. presidents since Taft. To keep up with the times, the adjacent 32-story Tower was added in 1972, which doubled the capacity (1,194 guest rooms total) and provided the requisite banquet and conference centers. A recent $40 million renovation transformed the old-world guest rooms in the main building into modern works of art, while still maintaining the original charm. The Tower rooms, however, have better views of the city from the 18th floor and above. If there's one thing you must do while visiting San Francisco, it's high tea (3–5pm) at the hotel's Compass Rose café and lounge, one of San Francisco's most enduring and pleasurable traditions. *$$$$; AE, DC, DIS, JCB, MC, V; checks OK; www.westin.com; between Geary and Post sts.* ♿

Nob Hill

The staggering wealth of railroad and silver barons had a significant impact on the history and development of San Francisco. The Big Four, as they were called, left their personal marks all over the city in the last half of the 1800s, particularly on the peak called Nob Hill, where the city's first cable car started operating in 1873. Sacramento power brokers Leland Stanford, Collis Huntington, Charles Crocker, and Mark Hopkins joined forces to create the Central Pacific Railroad, which connected the rest of the country to California. These "nabobs" (Urdu for "very rich men") amassed an amazing fortune in the bustling days before the earthquake and fire, and they sank their money into ostentatious mansions high atop Nob Hill. Only the **FLOOD MANSION** (1000 California St at Mason St), now the exclusive Pacific Union Club, remains. Although the original architecture was destroyed in the 1906 earthquake and fires, the summit of Nob Hill still reflects that golden era of unbridled wealth. The Fairmont, Mark Hopkins, Stanford Court, and Huntington hotels are bastions of antique opulence. The manicured lawns, sandbox, swings, and central Tortoise Fountain attract tourists and locals alike to **HUNTINGTON PARK**, donated to the city in 1915 by the widow of Collis Huntington. **GRACE CATHEDRAL**'s 20th-century Gothic architecture creates an impressive profile on the corner of California and Taylor streets. With its popular meditative labyrinth, stained-glass windows, and formidable bronze doors, this house of worship offers something for even the most ardent atheist.

RESTAURANTS

The Dining Room at the Ritz-Carlton / ★★★★

600 STOCKTON ST (THE RITZ-CARLTON), SAN FRANCISCO; 415/773-6198

For those special occasions (or when the other person is buying), few restaurants go the extra distance to spoil you rotten like the Dining Room at the Ritz-Carlton hotel. No less than five tuxedoed waitstaff are at your beck and call, surreptitiously attending to your needs as you bask in your evening of opulence. The setting is, as one would expect, sumptuous and regal, dripping with old-world charm but with modern art touches that add interest and vibrancy. Chef Ron Siegel (America's first Iron Chef) continues the Ritz-Carlton tradition of using only the finest, freshest ingredients from around the world with a regional focus, and he brings a very modern style of French cooking with an Asian twist. The seasonal menu is largely prix fixe, with a choice of multicourse dinners; optional wine pairings per course—chosen from one of most extensive wine lists in the country—are offered for a hefty additional fee. The menu changes seasonally, offering such decadent dishes as coveted kindai tuna tartare (very hard to find in the United States), baby lamb ravioli with morel mushrooms, lobster risotto with snap peas and lemon sauce, troll-caught King salmon with squash blossoms stuffed with provençal vegetables, Alaskan halibut with suckling pig, and Devil's Gulch Ranch pork chop with crispy skin and blackberry gastrique. For the finale, indulge in the ultimate French dessert: chocolate Manjari caramel cake with white chocolate ice cream. *$$$–$$$$; AE, DC, DIS, MC, V; no checks; dinner Mon–Sat; full bar; reservations required; www.ritzcarlton.com; at California St.* ♿

Fleur de Lys / ★★★

777 SUTTER ST, SAN FRANCISCO; 415/673-7779

Fleur de Lys is definitely a Grand Occasion restaurant, with fantastic food, formal service, breathtaking decor, and a superb wine list. Trained by such French superstars as Paul Bocuse and Roger Vergé, chef and co-owner Hubert Keller displays a formidable technique—beautifully prepared ingredients accompanied by surprising garnishes and subtle sauces—and many of his contemporary French dishes are near-miracles. And unlike a lot of celebrity chefs, Keller's probably in the kitchen preparing your meal (he's also a really nice guy). Standouts include the choucroute-crusted veal loin wrapped in apple wood–smoked bacon, fresh Atlantic salmon baked in a tender corn pancake topped with imperial caviar and a watercress sauce, marinated loin of venison with a mustard seed sabayon, and a four-course vegetarian feast. Critics sometimes sniff that particular dishes are too complex, portions small, and prices large, but these are small dents in Fleur de Lys's mighty armor. Fleur de Lys isn't always crowded, but reservations are required. *$$$–$$$$; AE, DC, MC, V; no checks; dinner Mon–Sat; full bar; reservations required; www.fleurdelyssf.com; between Jones and Taylor sts.* ♿

Masa's / ★★★★

648 BUSH ST (HOTEL VINTAGE COURT), SAN FRANCISCO; 415/989-7154

No one just drops in for dinner at Masa's. Not only do you have to make a reservation weeks, sometimes months, in advance, but also you may need that much time to arrange the financing, as this is one of San Francisco's most expensive restaurants. That said, the prices accurately reflect the precious ingredients, generous portions, stunning presentations, and labor-intensive nature of the elegant French-California cuisine invented by the late Masataka Kobayashi. Former French Laundry culinary star–cum–Masa's executive chef, Gregory Short, helps bring a fresh, trendy look to pair with the $100 six- and $105 nine-course tasting menus (which must be prepared for the whole table). By all accounts Masa's continues to impress a cultivated clientele with its inviting atmosphere (neither glitzy nor snobbish), professional service (never intimidating), and unremittingly stellar cuisine. Offerings from a typical *ménu dégustation* include salt-and-pepper-grilled ahi, accompanied by Hawaiian hearts of palm, red radish, edamame, and tsume glaze; lamb Navarin Printanier with young carrots, haricots verts, sweet turnips, baby leeks, *pommes noisette*, and roasted lamb jus; and foie gras mousse napoleon red plout tartare, served with toasted phyllo, vanilla bean gastrique, and baby greens. The 9,000-bottle wine collection, comprising more than 900 selections, is remarkable to say the least, but if you want to bring a special bottle of your own, you should know that the corkage fee is equal to the retail value of a top-flight chardonnay. *$$$$; AE, DC, DIS, MC, V; checks OK; dinner Tues–Sat; full bar; reservations required; www.masasrestaurant.com; between Powell and Stockton sts, in the Hotel Vintage Court.* ♿

Swan Oyster Depot / ★★

1517 POLK ST, SAN FRANCISCO; 415/673-1101

You won't find white linen tablecloths at this oyster bar—in fact, you won't even find any tables. Since 1912, loyal patrons have balanced themselves on the 19 hard, rickety stools lining the long, narrow marble counter cluttered with bowls of oyster crackers, fresh-cut lemons, napkin holders, Tabasco sauce, and other seasonings. On the opposite side stands a quick-shucking team of some of the most congenial men in town, always ready and eager to serve. Lunch specialties include Boston clam chowder, sizable salads (crab, shrimp, prawn, or a combo), seafood cocktails, cracked Dungeness crab, Maine lobster, and smoked salmon and trout. If you want to take home some fish for supper, take a gander in the display case: fresh salmon, swordfish, delta crawfish, red snapper, trout, shrimp, lingcod, and whatever else the boat brought in that day. Truly, this is a classic San Francisco experience that you shouldn't miss, even if the line's long (it moves fast). *$$; no credit cards; checks OK; lunch Mon–Sat; beer and wine; no reservations; between California and Sacramento sts.* ♿

LODGINGS

Fairmont Hotel & Tower / ★★★½

950 MASON ST, SAN FRANCISCO; 415/772-5000 OR 800/527-4727

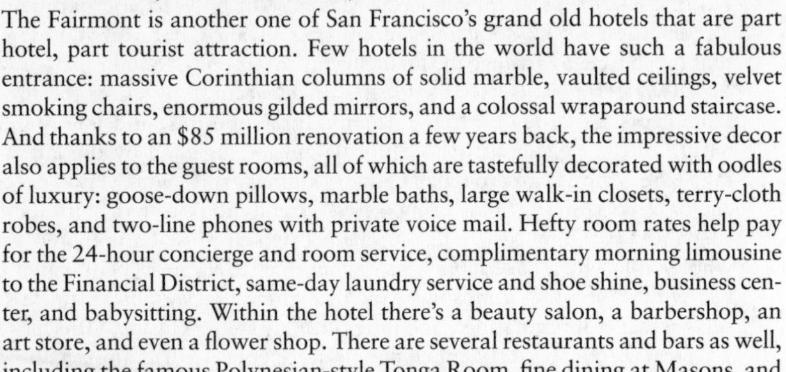

The Fairmont is another one of San Francisco's grand old hotels that are part hotel, part tourist attraction. Few hotels in the world have such a fabulous entrance: massive Corinthian columns of solid marble, vaulted ceilings, velvet smoking chairs, enormous gilded mirrors, and a colossal wraparound staircase. And thanks to an $85 million renovation a few years back, the impressive decor also applies to the guest rooms, all of which are tastefully decorated with oodles of luxury: goose-down pillows, marble baths, large walk-in closets, terry-cloth robes, and two-line phones with private voice mail. Hefty room rates help pay for the 24-hour concierge and room service, complimentary morning limousine to the Financial District, same-day laundry service and shoe shine, business center, and babysitting. Within the hotel there's a beauty salon, a barbershop, an art store, and even a flower shop. There are several restaurants and bars as well, including the famous Polynesian-style Tonga Room, fine dining at Masons, and the top-floor Crown Room restaurant and bar, which has a spectacular panoramic view of the city (see "A View from the Top"). *$$$$; AE, CB, DC, DIS, MC, V; checks OK; www.fairmont.com/sanfrancisco; at California St.* ♿

Huntington Hotel / ★★★

1075 CALIFORNIA ST, SAN FRANCISCO; 415/474-5400 OR 800/227-4683

The small, modest lobby of this imposing Nob Hill landmark belies its lavish interiors. The Huntington is graced with a remarkable array of antiques, plush sofas, and museum-quality objets d'art. The 12-story hotel's 136 rooms are spacious and lavish, with imported silks, 17th-century paintings, and stunning views of the city and the bay. The rooms are individually decorated, and some are so handsome they have been featured in *Architectural Digest*. Guests are treated to a formal afternoon tea and complimentary sherry, a nightly turndown service, and a morning paper. At the 5th floor Nob Hill Spa, guests can enjoy manicures, pedicures, aromatherapy, and facials, as well as more creative specials like the alchemy transformation massage. The Premier Spa Suite is perfect for bachelorette parties, bridal showers, birthday soirees, or corporate events: it accommodates 5 to 10 people, and you can rent it for up to five hours, with all the regular spa options on tap, plus access to the pool and fitness facilities, in-room dining, and beverage services. *$$$$; AE, DC, DIS, MC, V; checks OK; www.huntingtonhotel.com; between Mason and Taylor sts.* ♿

The Ritz-Carlton / ★★★★

600 STOCKTON ST, SAN FRANCISCO; 415/296-7465 OR 800/542-8680

In 1991, after a four-year, multimillion-dollar renovation, this 1909 17-columned neoclassical beauty—formerly the Metropolitan Life Insurance Company building—reopened as the Ritz-Carlton hotel. Since then, it's been stacking up heady accolades, including *Condé Nast Traveler*'s Gold List for 13 consecutive years and Mobil Five Star ratings for both the hotel and its

Dining Room. The hotel's lobby is breathtaking, with a series of enormous, high-ceilinged lounges, gigantic floral arrangements, an abundance of museum-quality paintings and antiques, and crystal chandeliers at every turn. The spectacular Lobby Lounge is the place to mingle over afternoon tea or sushi, and live piano performances perk up the scene every day. The 336 guest rooms are also luxury personified and were fully renovated in 2006: sinfully plush and loaded with high-society amenities such as spiffy Italian-marble bathrooms, 300-thread-count sheets, flat-screen televisions, fully stocked honor bars, thick terry-cloth robes, high-speed Internet access, and in-room safes. Some (though not many) have wonderful views of the city and the bay, but your best bets are the quieter rooms overlooking the landscaped courtyard. Business travelers should book one of the upper-floor club rooms, which come with a dedicated concierge, elevator-key access, and complimentary meals throughout the day. The hotel's ritzy fitness center has an indoor lap pool, a whirlpool, a sauna, a fully equipped training room, and massage services. Two restaurants are located in the hotel: the formal Dining Room at the Ritz-Carlton (see review), and the more casual Terrace, serving excellent Mediterranean fare and sensational desserts. *$$$$; AE, DC, DIS, MC, V; no checks; www.ritzcarlton.com; between Pine and California sts.*

Russian Hill

Russian Hill earned its name from the Russian explorers and trappers who arrived in the early 1800s to trade with the Spanish and Native Americans in the San Francisco Bay area. The rough voyage from Fort Ross up north, combined with exposure to the New World diseases, proved too much for many sailors, who didn't live to make the journey home. They were buried high atop the hill that overlooked the harbor, their graves marked by black crosses with Russian inscriptions. For years the gravestones were all that distinguished this uninhabited hill. Today, tombs are long covered over, and even the literati who once populated the summit of the knoll—Mark Twain, Jack London, Ambrose Bierce, and Jack Kerouac, among them—could barely afford an apartment in this high-rent district. Polk Street is the neighborhood commercial center, with shops, cafés, and restaurants that keep locals fed and happy, and draw those brave enough to try to find parking. Hyde Street has several excellent little restaurants tucked between apartment buildings and grocery stores. Oh, and if you're in search of that famous steep, crooked street, it's here—on Lombard between Hyde and Leavenworth streets.

RESTAURANTS

Antica Trattoria / ★★☆

2400 POLK ST, SAN FRANCISCO; 415/928-5797

Soon after Antica Trattoria opened its doors in 1996, the surrounding Russian Hill neighborhood was abuzz with talk of how incredible the Italian fare is here. Occupying a moderately busy corner on Polk and Union streets, this simply decorated restaurant with dark wood floors and cream-colored walls has developed a deserved reputation as one of the city's best Italian trattorias. Appetizers might include asparagus with black pepper, pecorino zabaglione, and tomato confit, or delicate (and divine) slices of beef carpaccio enhanced with capers, arugula, mustard, and Parmesan shavings. Main dishes span from a savory monkfish wrapped in pancetta, potatoes, and wild mushrooms, to a risotto spruced up with dandelion, cherry tomatoes, prosciutto, and scamorze. It's not the most surprising Italian fare in the city, but it's some of the best prepared and reasonably priced. Top it off with the terrific tiramisu, a restaurant staple. *$$; AE, DC, MC, V; no checks; dinner Tues–Sun; beer and wine; reservations recommended; www.anticasf.com; at Union St.* ♿

Gary Danko / ★★★★

800 NORTH POINT, SAN FRANCISCO; 415/749-2060

Call them the dynamic duo if you will—the culinary team of award-winning chef Gary Danko (of San Francisco's Ritz-Carlton fame) and well-connected maître d' Nick Peyton created quite a stir when they opened this highly anticipated restaurant. The concept sounds simple but is surprisingly difficult to achieve: fine French–New American cuisine combined with impeccable service. At Gary Danko, it seems to be working like a well-oiled machine, so much so that it was rated the number-one restaurant in *San Francisco* magazine's readers' poll when it opened in 2001. The namesake chef fashions a seasonally changing menu rooted in the classical school. His signature dishes include glazed oysters; seared foie gras with peaches, caramelized onions, and verjuice sauce; roast lobster with chanterelle mushrooms; and an amazing herb-crusted lamb loin. Dinners are served in three tasting-menu formats: you choose either the three-, four-, or five-course meal. A meal now includes a tea service from Rishi Tea Company, served in traditional Asian style, and Danko recently acquired a property in Napa Valley's Yountville, which will be used to grow herbs and produce for the restaurant. *$$$; AE, DC, MC, V; no checks; dinner every day; full bar; reservations recommended; www.garydanko.com; at Hyde St.*

Harris' / ★★

2100 VAN NESS AVE, SAN FRANCISCO; 415/673-1888

Not just another steak house, Harris' is a living monument to the not-quite-bygone joys of guiltless beef eating. The hushed, formal club setting boasts dark wood paneling, plush carpets, large brown tufted booths, well-spaced white-draped tables, and roomy chairs. Jackets are appreciated (though no longer required). Harris's choice midwestern beef, impeccably dry-aged for three weeks on the premises, bears the same relation to supermarket beef as foie gras bears to chicken liver; the tender steaks, grilled to order, can even be chosen by cut and by size. The larger bone-in cuts (such as the Harris Steak and the T-bone) have the finest flavor, but the pepper steak and the rare prime rib are great, too. Those who prefer calf brains to these sanguine beauties will find a flawless version here. You might want to skip the usual steak-house appetizers in favor of Harris's excellent Caesar salad. For true-blue traditionalists, the exemplary martini—served in a carafe placed in a bucket of shaved ice—makes an excellent starter. *$$$; AE, DC, DIS, MC, V; no checks; dinner every day; full bar; reservations recommended; www.harrisrestaurant.com; at Pacific Ave.* ♿

La Folie / ★★★½

2316 POLK ST, SAN FRANCISCO; 415/776-5577

After a stingy San Francisco restaurateur fired him for spending too much on ingredients and serving overly generous portions, French-born chef Roland Passot decided to open his own restaurant where he could spend as much as he liked to make the food perfect. The paradisiacal result is the charming, small, family-run La Folie. The whimsical, theatrical dining room sets an appropriate stage for Passot's creative, exuberant, but disciplined menu. His Roquefort soufflé with grapes, herbs, and walnut bread alone is worthy of four stars. Other recent dishes have included a roti of quail, squab stuffed with wild mushrooms and wrapped in crispy potato strings, and tournedos of roasted salmon served with a purée of sweet onions and pinot noir sauce. To accommodate vegetable lovers, Passot thoughtfully offers a separate Menu Jardinière. And for those who can't make up their minds, there are the tasting menus, which allow you to choose three, four, or five courses (though it's pricey at $70, $80, and $90, respectively). The wine list is extensive, but the prices are steep. *$$$–$$$$; AE, DC, DIS, MC, V; no checks; dinner Mon–Sat; full bar; reservations recommended; www.lafolie.com; near Union St.* ♿

Marina/Cow Hollow

With spectacular views of the Golden Gate Bridge, Alcatraz, and the bay, the Marina is desirable real estate for the young and affluent (it's also where you'll find a big bulk of the city's yuppies, who assuredly think they're better than you unless you share the same zip code). A middle-class Italian neighborhood until the 1960s, the Marina now houses some of that community's wealthiest families, who live in the elegant homes that line the waterfront. Cozy art deco flats and stucco houses with Mediterranean-tiled roofs sit on quiet streets only steps away from waterfront activities. At the turn of the century, the Marina was virtually under water. The marshland was filled in when it was chosen as the site of the 1915 Panama-Pacific International Exposition, which celebrated the opening of the Panama Canal. Today, the Palace of Fine Arts building, located at Baker and Beach streets, serves as a beautiful reminder of that festive event. Within a few blocks of home, Marina residents often spend their weekends at the **EXPLORATORIUM** and **PALACE OF FINE ARTS**, the historic Presidio (now a national park featuring attractions like Crissy Field, a former airfield turned wetland and bird refuge), and the Marina Green, popular with joggers, in-line skaters, sunbathers, kite flyers, and outdoor sports enthusiasts of all kinds. The heart of the Marina is **CHESTNUT STREET** between

Fillmore and Divisadero streets. Once a quaint shopping district, the area was permanently altered by the 1989 earthquake. Extensive damage forced a number of small businesses to close. It was only a matter of months before big-name chains and high-end boutiques set up shop (an unwelcome citywide trend that sticks in the gullet of most every San Franciscan). Today, it's an uppity shopping haven—particularly on Union Street between Gough and Buchanan streets—with designers ranging from Nine West to BCBG having set up shop between independent boutiques like Ambiance and bridal store Forget Me Knot.

RESTAURANTS

Betelnut / ★★

2030 UNION ST, SAN FRANCISCO; 415/929-8855

A member of the Real Restaurants company (which includes such successes as Tra Vigne and Bix), this sumptuously decorated Asian "beer house" has the ever-so-slightly tarty feel of an exotic 1930s Shanghai brothel. Named after a popular seed that is chewed throughout Asia for its intoxicating side effects, Betelnut became a huge success in a short time, and it's still on everyone's list of places to try (though, alas, the namesake nut is not offered here). The mixed menu is pan-Asian, with an array of authentic dishes from Vietnam, Singapore, China, Thailand, Indonesia, and Japan. While the unusual concept entices diners, the reality is not always up to par. With more than a dozen cooks in the kitchen on busy nights, results can vary. Some dishes consistently get raves, including the spicy coconut chicken with eggplant, lemongrass, and basil; the crunchy tea-smoked duck; the succulent short ribs; and the sun-dried anchovies with peanuts, chiles, and garlic. But the green papaya salad gets mixed reviews, and Betelnut's dumplings can be downright disappointing. *$$; DC, DIS, MC, V; no checks; lunch, dinner every day; full bar; reservations recommended; www.betelnutrestaurant.com; between Buchanan and Webster sts.* ♿

Greens / ★★½

FORT MASON CENTER, BLDG A, SAN FRANCISCO; 415/771-6222

As Le Tour d'Argent in Paris is to the dedicated duck fancier and the Savoy Grill in London is to the roast beef connoisseur, so is Greens at Fort Mason to the vegetarian aesthete. Not only is the food politically correct here, but it's also often so good that even carnivores find it irresistible. Located in a converted barracks in the historic Fort Mason Center, the enormous, airy dining room is surrounded by huge windows with a spectacular view of the bay and the Golden Gate Bridge, and a gigantic sculpted redwood burl is a Buddhist-inspired centerpiece in the waiting area. Yes, Greens is owned and operated by the Zen Center—but this is a restaurant, not a monastery. The menu changes often: expect to see such dishes as mesquite-grilled polenta; phyllo turnovers filled with mushrooms, spinach, and Parmesan; pizza sprinkled with onion confit, goat cheese, and basil; and fettuccine with mushrooms, peas, goat cheese, and crème fraîche. Greens to Go, a take-out counter inside the restaurant, also sells baked goods, savory soups, sandwiches, and black bean chili. An à la carte dinner menu is offered Sunday through Friday; guests may order from the $49 prix-fixe five-course dinner menu only on Saturday. *$$–$$$; DIS, MC, V; local checks only; lunch Tues–Sat, dinner Sun–Fri (prix fixe only on Sat), brunch Sun; beer and wine; reservations recommended; www.greensrestaurant.com; off Marina Blvd at Buchanan St.* ♿

Isa / ★★★

3324 STEINER ST, SAN FRANCISCO; 415/567-9588

This modest Marina restaurant has the locals raving about the tapas-style French dishes emanating from the tiny kitchen. At this family-run affair named for the couple's daughter, the staff puts heart and soul into both the service and the à la carte–size dishes. Typical of Marina restaurants, the long, narrow building has a few tables up front, but most everyone requests a table in the tent-covered and heated outdoor patio in back (très romantique). Many of the menu's 20-something enticing dishes are carefully crafted using fresh, seasonal ingredients (and would cost twice as much at a fancy French restaurant). Try the potato-wrapped halibut with capers, tomato confit, and lemon, or the roasted lamb tenderloin, artichokes, fava beans, and red peppers. Other dishes range from lemon dill cured salmon to morel and shiitake mushroom risotto. Monday through Thursday are prix-fixe nights, where you get a choice of two courses for just $22. *$$; AE, DC, MC, V; no checks; dinner Mon–Sat; full bar; reservations recommended; www.isarestaurant.com; between Chestnut and Lombard sts.* ♿

Pane e Vino / ★★★

1715 UNION ST, SAN FRANCISCO; 415/346-2111

Well hidden on the outskirts of posh Pacific Heights, this dark-wood-trimmed trattoria framed by a cream-colored awning is a local favorite. The simply furnished dining room and patio with small white-clothed tables fill up fast. Do yourself a favor and indulge in the amazing chilled artichoke appetizer, stuffed with bread and tomatoes and served with a vinaigrette. Follow that lead with one of the perfectly prepared pastas, ranging from the simple but savory capellini tossed with fresh tomatoes, basil, garlic, and extra-virgin olive oil to the zesty bucatini (hollow straw pasta) smothered with pancetta, hot peppers, and tomato sauce. The excellent entrées vary from rack of lamb marinated in sage and rosemary to the whole roasted fresh fish of the day. Before you raise your napkin to your lips for the last time, dive into the delightful dolci: a luscious crème caramel, assorted gelati, and a terrific tiramisu are the standouts. *$$; AE, MC, V; no checks; dinner every day; beer and wine; reservations recommended; www.paneevinotrattoria.com; between Gough and Octavia sts.* ♿

PlumpJack Cafe / ★★★

3127 FILLMORE ST, SAN FRANCISCO; 415/563-4755

Co-owned by Bill Getty (son of billionaire Gordon Getty) and wine-connoisseur-cum-mayor Gavin Newsom, this exotic California–Mediterranean bistro is one of San Francisco's leading restaurants, with consistently excellent food and (thanks to its companion wine store a few doors away) a surprisingly extensive wine list featuring fine bottles offered at near-retail prices. Executive chef Rick Edge has a passion for seasonal menus that combine classical and modern techniques. The appetizers are often the highlight of the menu, particularly the bruschetta, topped with roasted beets, goat cheese, and garlic one night, and eggplant, sweet peppers, and chèvre the next. Don't miss the remarkable risottos, richly flavored with artichokes, apple wood–smoked bacon, and goat cheese, or perhaps smoked salmon and shiitake mushrooms. Other recommended dishes include the superbly executed roast herb chicken breast with foie gras, hedgehog mushrooms, and spinach, and the roast duck breast and leg confit with French green lentils, barley, parsnip chips, and a sour cherry jus. *$$$; AE, MC, V; no checks; lunch Mon–Fri, dinner Mon–Sat; full bar; reservations recommended; www.plumpjack.com; between Filbert and Greenwich sts.* ♿

LODGINGS

Marina Inn / ★★☆

3110 OCTAVIA ST, SAN FRANCISCO; 415/928-1000 OR 800/274-1420

If you don't really care where you stay in San Francisco and you want the most for your money, book a room here; we checked out all the inexpensive lodgings in the city and none have come close to offering as good a deal. The building, located on busy Lombard Street (the only caveat; expect noise depending on where your room faces), is a handsome 1924 four-story Victorian, and the guest rooms are equally impressive: two-poster beds with cozy comforters and mattresses; rustic pine-wood furnishings; attractive wallpaper; and a pleasant color scheme of rose, hunter green, and pale yellow. You'll especially appreciate the high-class touches that many of the city's expensive hotels don't include, such as full bathtubs with showers, remote-control televisions discreetly hidden in pine cabinetry, and nightly turndown service à la chocolates on your pillow. How much for all these creature comforts? As little as $40 a night during off-peak times (though on average, rooms run around $95), with complimentary continental breakfast and afternoon sherry. Hotel services include a 24-hour concierge, wireless Internet access, a barber shop, and an on-site nail salon. Marina Inn's in a good location as well—within easy walking distance of the shops and restaurants along Chestnut and Union streets, and right on the bus route to downtown. Another bonus: You can check in as early as 2pm and out as late as noon—a rarity in a city full of stingy hotels. *$–$$; AE, MC, V; no checks; www.marinainn.com; at Lombard St.* ♿

Pacific Heights

Pacific Heights is one of San Francisco's most exclusive neighborhoods. When transportation extended to the outer districts of the city, the elite moved west away from the noise of downtown, seeking quieter streets and bigger lots on which to build their grand mansions. Whether your architectural tastes lean toward Victorians, over-the-top neoclassical manors, or something elegantly in between, there are jaw-dropping buildings for you to admire and many to tour. The views from the higher intersections are stunning, particularly at sunset. Two beautiful parks offer greenery in this otherwise cramped neighborhood. Landscape architect John McLaren, who designed Golden Gate Park, also left his mark on **ALTA PLAZA PARK**, a small patch of land bordered by Clay, Steiner, Jackson, and Scott streets. The park's terraced landscape was modeled after the Grand Casino in Monte Carlo. The uppermost level affords spectacular vistas in all directions. A few blocks to the east, **LAFAYETTE PARK** sits at the corner of Laguna and Sacramento streets. The four square blocks of open space offer views of Twin Peaks and the bay to the north.

RESTAURANTS

Cafe Kati / ★★★

1963 SUTTER ST, SAN FRANCISCO; 415/775-7313

Cafe Kati may not have the elbow room of some of San Francisco's other top restaurants, but there are few chefs on the West Coast who can match Kirk Webber—a California Culinary Academy graduate—when it comes to culinary artistry. Obscurely located on a residential block off Fillmore Street, this tiny, modest, 60-seat café has garnered a monsoon of kudos for Webber's weird and wonderful cuisine. Even something as mundane as a Caesar salad is transformed into a towering monument of lovely romaine arranged upright on the plate and held in place by a ribbon of thinly sliced cucumber. Fortunately, it tastes as good as it looks. Though the menu changes monthly, it always spans the globe: miso-marinated Chilean sea bass topped with tempura kabocha squash; pancetta-wrapped pork tenderloin bathed in a ragout of baby artichokes and chanterelle mushrooms; walnut-crusted chicken with Gorgonzola; and crispy duck confit with sweet potato polenta and wild mushrooms. Complete the gustatory experience with the to-die-for butterscotch pudding. When making a reservation, request a table in the front room—and don't make any plans after dinner, because the kitchen takes its sweet time preparing your work of art. *$$; AE, MC, V; no checks; dinner Mon–Sat; beer and wine; reservations recommended; www.cafekati.com; between Fillmore and Webster sts.*

Eliza's / ★★★

2877 CALIFORNIA ST, SAN FRANCISCO; 415/621-4819

Eliza's is not only one of our favorite Chinese restaurants in San Francisco, but it's also one of our favorite San Francisco restaurants, period. Where else can you get such fresh, high-quality cuisine in an artistic setting for less than $10 a dish? You'll either love or be confused by the decidedly anti-typical-Chinese-restaurant decor—oodles of gorgeous handblown glassware, orchids, and modern accents create a rather curious ambience that works for some and appalls others. The menu offers classic Hunan and Mandarin dishes, all served on beautiful Italian plates. Start with the assorted appetizer dish, which is practically a meal in itself. Three other recommended dishes are the kung pao chicken (a marvelous mixture of tender chicken, peanuts, chile peppers, hot sauce, and fresh vegetables), the sea bass in black bean sauce, and the vegetable mu shu (with sweet plum sauce). Regardless of what you order you're likely to be impressed, and the lunch specials are a steal. The only drawback is the line out the door that often forms around 7pm (they don't take reservations). *$; MC, V; no checks; lunch Mon–Fri, dinner every day; beer and wine; no reservations; at Broderick St.* ♿

Garibaldis / ★★☆

347 PRESIDIO AVE, SAN FRANCISCO; 415/563-8841

Evocative of the great neighborhood-type restaurants in New York's Greenwich Village and SoHo, Garibaldis seems like a place where every diner has just walked over from his or her home around the corner. The place is small and the tables are jammed so close together that at times you feel like reaching over and trying something from your neighbor's plate. So it's a good thing the atmosphere is friendly and lively, if at times decidedly loud. The staff, polished yet down-to-earth, makes everyone feel like a regular. The dishes are sophisticated without being highfalutin. The risottos (there are usually two on the menu) are quite good. If you are looking to eat light but don't want to forsake robust flavor, try one of the entrée salads, such as the signature Garibaldis salad, combining mixed greens, Gorgonzola, nectarines, spicy pecans, and white balsamic vinaigrette. Among the entrée highlights are a steamed wild Alaskan halibut and a generous cut of tender filet mignon. And don't miss the rich desserts, like the chocolate budino, with praline, espresso gelato, and caramel sauce. *$$; AE, MC, V; local checks only; lunch Mon–Fri, dinner every day; full bar; reservations recommended; www.garibaldisrestaurant.com; between Sacramento and Clay sts.* ♿

LODGINGS

Hotel Drisco / ★★★

2901 PACIFIC AVE, SAN FRANCISCO; 415/346-2880 OR 800/634-7277

If you're a fan of San Francisco's Ritz-Carlton, you'll adore Hotel Drisco. The five-story structure, perched on one of the most coveted blocks in the city, was built in 1903 as a boardinghouse for neighborhood servants. After surviving the great fire of 1906, it was converted into a hotel in the mid-1920s but eventually fell into major disrepair. Combining the financial might of hotelier Tom Callinan (Meadowood, the Inn at Southbridge) and the interior design skills of Glenn Texeira (Ritz-Carlton, Manila), Hotel Drisco's proprietors transformed years of blood, sweat, and greenbacks into one of the finest small hotels in the city. The 48 rooms are bathed in soothing shades of alabaster, celadon, and buttercup yellow and feature rich fabrics, quality antiques, and superior mattresses. Standard amenities include complimentary Internet access, a two-line phone with a modem hookup, a CD player, a discreetly hidden TV with a VCR, and a minibar; each suite includes a handsome sofa bed, an additional phone and TV, and a terrific view. Added features are a 24-hour coffee and tea service, overnight shoe shine, evening wine apéritif service, morning newspaper, complimentary use of nearby fitness facilities, and turndown service. Room 404A—a corner suite with an extraordinary view of Pacific Heights mansions and the surrounding neighborhood—is a favorite. An extended continental breakfast is served in one of the three quiet, comfortable common rooms. *$$$; AE, DC, DIS, MC, V; no checks; www.hoteldrisco.com; at Broderick St.* ♿

Civic Center

Politics, highbrow culture, and homelessness all mingle at the Civic Center. The mayor's office and the board of supervisors' chambers are housed in the beautiful Beaux Arts **CITY HALL** designed in 1916 by Arthur Brown. Its magnificent dome measures 308 feet tall, a full 16 feet higher than the Capitol dome in Washington, D.C., and is a visible landmark from many points in the city. The **WAR MEMORIAL OPERA HOUSE**—another Arthur Brown design—stretches along Van Ness Avenue, the city's widest thoroughfare. **LOUISE M. DAVIES SYMPHONY HALL**, built in 1981 on the corner of Van Ness Avenue and Gough Street, houses the largest concert-hall organ in North America—so massive that the instrument's 9,235 pipes are played with the aid of a computer. The **SAN FRANCISCO PUBLIC LIBRARY** (100 Larkin St at Grove St; 415/557-4400) opened in 1996 to mostly rave reviews and more than a few boos for its less-than-inviting exterior. On Grove Street across from the main library, the **BILL GRAHAM CIVIC AUDITORIUM**, named after the late rock impresario, is used as a convention hall and music venue. The Civic Center borders the city's infamous red-light district, the **TENDERLOIN**, where many homeless live on the streets. While this has long been a neighborhood to avoid, an influx of Vietnamese, Laotian, and Cambodian families has changed the neighborhood over the years. And while it's still not for the fainthearted, it now has a number of good ethnic markets and many excellent—though bare-bones—eateries. If you're looking for kaffir lime leaves or galangal (and who isn't?), this is the place to come.

RESTAURANTS

Absinthe Brasserie and Bar / ★★

398 HAYES ST, SAN FRANCISCO; 415/551-1590

Stylish Absinthe, named for the green herbal liqueur so potent it was banned in turn-of-the-century France, re-creates the romance and mystery of the bygone Belle Epoque. With the appointment of executive chef and *Top Chef* contestant Jamie Lauren in 2007, the brasserie-style French and Italian eatery's menu got rejuvenated with a hearty dose of organic, locally grown, seasonal ingredients. Such dishes include grilled day boat scallops with sautéed summer squash, sugar snap peas, baby tomatoes, pea tendrils, and nepitella; slow-cooked pork confit with creamed corn, Benton's bacon, fingerling potatoes, and watercress salad; and saffron and cinnamon braised beef cheeks with smashed potatoes, English peas, and roasted baby vegetables. And with absinthe finally legalized in 2007, the Absinthe bar now can serve its namesake. *$$; AE, DC, DIS, MC, V; no checks; lunch Tues–Fri, dinner Tues–Sun, brunch Sat–Sun; full bar; reservations recommended; www.absinthe.com; at Gough St.* ♿

Jardinière / ★★★½

300 GROVE ST, SAN FRANCISCO; 415/861-5555

A native Californian and James Beard recipient, chef Traci Des Jardins worked in many notable restaurants in France, New York, and Los Angeles before co-opening Rubicon in San Francisco, which launched her culinary reputation nationwide. With Pat Kuleto as her business partner, Des Jardins was assured of an impressive setting for her French-California cuisine when she opened Jardinière in 2007. Formerly home to a jazz club, the two-story interior is elegantly framed with violet velvet drapes, and the focal point is the central oval mahogany and marble bar, frequently mobbed with local politicos and patrons of the arts (the symphony hall and opera house are across the street). Appetizers are Des Jardins's strong point, especially the flavor-packed lobster, leek, and chanterelle strudel and the delicate kabocha squash ravioli with chestnuts and sage brown butter. Some of the best entrées have included the crisp chicken with chanterelles and apple wood–smoked bacon; herbed lamb loin with cranberry beans and tomato confit; and pan-roasted salmon with lentils, celery root salad, and red wine sauce. A chef's tasting menu is available for $125 and a sommelier wine pairing for $65. After your meal, consider the selection of domestic and imported cheeses, which are visible in the temperature-controlled cheese room. The live entertainment makes this restaurant ideal for a special night on the town. *$$$$; AE, DC, DIS, MC, V; no checks; dinner every day; full bar; reservations recommended; www.jardiniere.com; at Franklin St.* ♿

Zuni Café / ★★★

1658 MARKET ST, SAN FRANCISCO; 415/552-2522

Before it got famous, Zuni was a tiny Southwestern-style lunch spot in a low-class neighborhood. When Chez Panisse alumna Judy Rodgers came on board as chef and co-owner, the café became so popular it had to more than double in size. Today, with its roaring copper-topped bar, grand piano, and exposed-brick dining room, it's nearly as quintessential a San Francisco institution as Dungeness crab and sourdough bread. Zuni's Mediterranean-influenced upscale food is as divinely simple as only the supremely sophisticated can be. Picture a plate of mild house-cured anchovies sprinkled with olives, celery, and Parmesan cheese; polenta with delicate mascarpone; a terrific Caesar salad; a small, perfectly roasted chicken for two on a delicious bed of Tuscan bread salad (perhaps the best chicken you've ever tasted); and a grilled rib-eye steak accompanied by sweet white corn seasoned with fresh basil. At lunchtime and after 10pm, you can order some of the best burgers in town here, too, served on focaccia with aioli and house pickles (and be sure to add a side of the shoestring potatoes). Service is first-rate for regulars and those who resemble them. Tip: Dinner is served until midnight Tuesday through Saturday. *$$$; AE, MC, V; no checks; lunch, dinner Tues–Sun; full bar; reservations recommended; www.zunicafe.com; at Franklin St.* ♿

LODGINGS

Chateau Tivoli / ★★★

1057 STEINER ST, SAN FRANCISCO; 415/776-5462 OR 800/228-1647
A bed-and-breakfast occupying a corner building that dates back to 1892, Chateau Tivoli has all the traditional makings of an old-fashioned Victorian home: hand-carved woodwork, oriental carpets, crystal chandeliers, antique furniture, and stained glass windows, to name a few. Many bed-and-breakfast aficionados might even say that it's the best of its kind in the City by the Bay. Expect to find accents like wallpapered ceilings; renaissance furniture; mirrored canopy beds; antique cameras; and an odd amalgamation of landmark, entertainer, and taxidermy photos mixed in the quirky decor. Some of the spacious digs—which include five standard rooms and four suites—feature curiosities like a secret room and murals painted on the ceilings. Tivoli is lauded for its tasty continental breakfast and equally impressive staff, and the B and B, situated right around the corner from Alamo Square's famed Painted Ladies row of houses, even hosts a daily two-hour wine and cheese reception for guests. *$$; AE, MC, V; no checks; www.chateautivoli.com; between Golden Gate Ave and Steiner St.*

The Richmond District

The Richmond District neighborhood, which sits at the western end of the city and stretches from Arguello Boulevard out to the ocean, is known as "the avenues" (as opposed to SoMa and the Mission District, which are referred to as "the streets"). This area first became popular at the end of the 19th century when Adolph Sutro created two crowd-pleasing attractions in the city's western reaches. The first and foremost in the city's memory was the seven-story Victorian masterpiece called the **CLIFF HOUSE** (Sutro was responsible for its second and most splendid incarnation). The second was the ambitious **SUTRO BATHS**, a compilation of a half dozen indoor ocean-water swimming pools. Sadly, neither attraction remains standing today—at least not as conceived by Sutro—but in their heyday they helped to bring the growing city out west.

Many present-day landmarks still attract tourists and San Franciscans alike to the Richmond District. Perhaps the most dramatic are the rocky cliffs that loom over the pounding surf at Land's End. At the end of Clement Street and 34th Avenue, Lincoln Park is home to the **CALIFORNIA PALACE OF THE LEGION OF HONOR** art museum. In recent decades, thousands of Russian, Irish, and Chinese immigrants have landed in the Richmond District. They've settled in the bland stucco-covered houses that stretch from just past Pacific Heights to the Pacific Ocean, making this one of the most international neighborhoods in the city.

RESTAURANTS

Khan Toke Thai House / ★★½

5937 GEARY BLVD, SAN FRANCISCO; 415/668-6654

If you're in the mood for an exotic dining experience (or if you just want to impress the heck out of your date), dine at the Khan Toke Thai House, the loveliest Thai restaurant in San Francisco. Following Thai tradition, you'll be asked to remove your shoes at the entrance, so be sure to wear clean (and hole-free) socks. You'll then be escorted through the lavishly decorated dining room—replete with carved teak, Thai statues, and hand-woven Thai tapestries—and seated on large pillows at one of the many sunken tables (or, if you prefer, at a table in the garden out back). Start with the appetizing *tom yam gong*, lemongrass shrimp with mushroom, tomato, and cilantro soup. Other delicious dishes include the prawns with hot chiles, mint leaves, lime juice, lemongrass, and onions; the chicken with cashew nuts, crispy chiles, and onions; and the ground pork with fresh ginger, green onion, peanuts, and lemon juice. For those dining family-style, be sure to order the exquisite deep-fried pompano topped with sautéed ginger, onions, peppers, pickled garlic, and yellow-bean sauce. If the vast menu bewilders you, opt for the multicourse dinner: appetizer, soup, salad, two main courses, dessert, and coffee. And if you're feeling frivolous after sipping a Singha beer or two, you might want to engage your tablemate in a game of shoeless footsie—after all, how often do you get a chance to do that in public? *$$; AE, MC, V; no checks; dinner every day; beer and wine; reservations recommended; between 23rd and 24th aves.*

Ton Kiang / ★★½

5821 GEARY BLVD, SAN FRANCISCO; 415/387-8273

Ton Kiang has established a solid reputation as one of the best Chinese restaurants in the city, particularly when it comes to dim sum and Hakka cuisine (a mixture of Chinese cuisines sometimes referred to as "China's soul food," developed by a nomadic Chinese tribe). Ton Kiang's dim sum is phenomenal—fresh, flavorful, and not the least bit greasy. (Tip: On weekends, ask for a table by the kitchen door to get first dibs from the dim sum carts.) Other proven dishes on the regular menu are the ethereal steamed dumplings, chicken wonton soup, house special beef and fish-ball soup (better than it sounds), fried spring rolls, steamed salt-baked chicken with a scallion and ginger sauce (a famous though quite salty Hakka dish), and any of the stuffed tofu or clay pot dishes (a.k.a. Hakka casseroles). Seriously, this place is worth the drive and the wait. *$$; AE, DC, DIS, MC, V; no checks; lunch, dinner every day; beer and wine; reservations recommended; www.tonkiang.net; between 22nd and 23rd aves.* ♿

Haight-Ashbury

The Summer of Love lasted a mere three months, but 30 years later tourists and nostalgic San Franciscans still flock to the Haight to experience the flavor of the late '60s. Once home to Janis Joplin, the Grateful Dead, and myriad hippies, Haight-Ashbury has long since lost the uplifting spirit of that infamous summer, but drugs, alcohol, and tie-dye remain. A new generation of street urchins zones out along the storefronts of the neighborhood, playing guitars, stringing beads, or mumbling "Kind bud" (translation: "Want to buy some pot?") to random passersby. Economically, Haight-Ashbury, or the Upper Haight as it is also known, has cashed in on its illustrious past: stores dedicated to the hippie legacy sell psychedelic posters, incense, pot paraphernalia, and used records. The **RED VICTORIAN BED & BREAKFAST PEACE CENTER** (see review) dedicates its entire lower level to '60s and '70s memorabilia. Tattoo parlors and pipe shops draw alternative crowds, but the majority of people parading down Haight Street are tourists. Hundreds flock here each day to witness the nonstop freak show this street has become. When Jerry Garcia died in 1995, the neighborhood became a meeting place for the bereaved. His former home at 710 Ashbury (at Waller St) has long been part of the Haight pilgrimage. As a sign of the times, the Gap now holds down the fort at the infamous corner of Haight and Ashbury; across the street is the hippie-capitalist bastion Ben & Jerry's.

RESTAURANTS

Cha Cha Cha / ★★☆

1801 HAIGHT ST, SAN FRANCISCO; 415/386-7670
2327 MISSION ST, SAN FRANCISCO; 415/824-1502

When we're asked which San Francisco restaurants are our favorites (and we're asked all the time), one of the first we mention is Cha Cha Cha. It's fun, it's festive, the Caribbean food is very good, the prices are reasonable, the sangría is addictive, and every meal ends with a free Tootsie Roll. What's not to like? The café is wildly decorated with Santeria altars and such, which blend in perfectly with the mix of pumped-up patrons quaffing pitchers of sangría while waiting for a table (which often takes up to an hour on weekends). We always start with these tapas-style dishes: sautéed mushrooms, fried calamari, fried new potatoes (dig the spicy sauce), Cajun shrimp, mussels in saffron (order more bread for the sauce), and plantains with black bean sauce. Check the specials board for outstanding seafood dishes, but skip the so-so steak. A second branch in the Mission District serves exactly the same food in a much larger space; not only is the wait shorter (or nonexistent), but there's also a full bar. Still, the original is our favorite simply for its only-in-SF ambience. *$; MC, V; no checks; lunch, dinner every day; beer and wine; no reservations; www.cha3.com; Haight St location at Shrader St; Mission St location between 19th and 20th sts.* ♿

Eos Restaurant & Wine Bar / ★★★

901 COLE ST, SAN FRANCISCO; 415/566-3063

One of the most-talked-about restaurants in the city, Eos has the tourists asking, "Where is Cole Valley?" It's not so much the menu—the Euro-Asian fusion theme is hardly original—as it is the portions (generous) and presentations (brilliant) that have enticed throngs of visitors and residents to this once-little-known San Francisco neighborhood nestled near the southeast corner of Golden Gate Park. It's a desecration simply to dig in to the culinary artwork composed by executive chef Daniel Guerrini, though one's guilt is soon assuaged, particularly when dining upon the tender breast of Peking duck, smoked in ginger-peach tea leaves and served with a plum-kumquat chutney. Other notable dishes are the almond-encrusted soft-shell crab appetizer dipped in spicy plum ponzu sauce, shiitake mushroom dumplings, blackened Asian catfish atop a bed of lemongrass risotto, five-pepper calamari; and the red curry–marinated rack of lamb. A quiet, romantic dinner is out of the question here, since the stark deco-industrial decor merely amplifies the nightly cacophony. After dinner, adjourn to the restaurant's popular wine bar, which stocks more than 200 selections—many at reasonable prices—from around the globe. Nearly 50 red and white wines are available by the glass, too. *$$$; AE, MC, V; no checks; dinner every day; beer and wine; reservations recommended; www.eossf.com; at Carl St.* ♿

Kan Zaman / ★★

1793 HAIGHT ST, SAN FRANCISCO; 415/751-9656

Glass-beaded curtains lead into Kan Zaman, a favorite destination for grunge types who populate the Haight. Shed your shoes and gather around knee-high tables under a canopy tent—or snag the premier window seat—and recline on pillows while sampling the tasty, inexpensive hot and cold Middle Eastern meze. Before long, you'll think you've been transported to (as Kan Zaman literally translates) "a long time ago." Traditional menu items include hummus, baba ghanoush, *kibbeh* (cracked wheat with spiced lamb) meat pies, and various kebabs. Sample platters offering tastes of a little bit of everything are ideal for large parties. For a novel and truly exotic finish, puff on an *argeeleh* (hookah pipe) filled with fruity honey or apricot tobacco. Wine, beer, and spiced wine round out the beverage offerings. Another plus: Kan Zaman serves till midnight—a real find in this town. On the weekends, a pair of belly dancers—male and female—entertain at the joint, but take note: Wait time on these nights is usually long, even if you have a reservation. *$; MC, V; no checks; lunch Sat–Sun, dinner every day; full bar; reservations recommended; www.hookahbargrill.com; at Shrader St.* ♿

Thep Phanom / ★★★

400 WALLER ST, SAN FRANCISCO; 415/431-2526

San Francisco boasts dozens of Thai restaurants; most of them are good, and many (including Khan Toke Thai House and Bang San Thai) are excellent. Why, then, has Thep Phanom alone had a permanent line out its front door for the last 20 years even though it takes reservations? At this restaurant, housed in a grand Victorian, a creative touch of California enters the cultural mix, resulting in sophisticated preparations that have a special sparkle. The signature dish, *ped swan*, is a boneless duck in light honey sauce served on a bed of spinach—and it ranks with the city's greatest entrées. Tart, minty, spicy *yum plamuk* (calamari salad), *larb ped* (minced duck salad), coconut chicken soup, and the velvety basil-spiked seafood curry served on banana leaves are superb choices, too. Service is charming and efficient; the tasteful decor, informal atmosphere, eclectic crowd, and discerning wine list are all very San Francisco. *$$; AE, DC, DIS, MC, V; no checks; dinner every day; beer and wine; reservations recommended; www.thepphanom.com; at Fillmore St.* ♿

LODGINGS

Red Victorian Bed & Breakfast Peace Center / ★☆

1665 HAIGHT ST, SAN FRANCISCO; 415/864-1978

The Red Vic, located smack-dab on an exciting stretch of Haight Street, is one of the most eclectic and groovy lodgings in the city. Don't be deterred by its garish facade: you'll have the quintessential Haight-Ashbury experience staying in any of the 18 colorfully decorated rooms, each with its own '60s Summer of Love theme. For example, the luxury Peacock Suite features stained-glass windows, a canopied king bed, and a bathtub in a mirrored window alcove. Economy double rooms include the Earth Charter Room and Summer of Love Room. Eight of the guest rooms have private baths, while the remaining rooms share five bathrooms. In fact, owner Sami Sunchild will suggest that you take the time to explore the shared Aquarium Bathroom (where goldfish swim in the toilet tank), the Starlight Bathroom, the Love Bathroom, the Infinity Bathroom, and the Bird's Nest Bathroom. A complimentary "breakfast conversation" is served family-style in the salon at 9 o'clock each morning. *$–$$$; AE, DIS, MC, V; checks OK; www.redvic.com; between Clayton and Cole sts.*

SoMa (South of Market Street)

The area south of Market Street, known by the acronym SoMa, is many things to many people: cutting-edge arts mecca, club-hopping heaven, and over-development hell. The multiple-personality syndrome is not surprising, considering that SoMa encompasses a huge amount of real estate that continues to retain value despite its close proximity to San Francisco's Skid Row.

Until the last decade or so, much of SoMa had long been a bastion of affordable—albeit ramshackle—housing; even in the early days of the gold rush, it was home to a tent city for newly arrived immigrant forty-niners. As San Franciscans prospered on gold rush fever, the area around South Park evolved into a gated community surrounded by opulent mansions. The mansions have since vanished, but a bit of old-world charm remains: at 615 Third

Street, a plaque marks the site where Jack London was born in 1876 (the original structure was destroyed in the 1906 quake). Though the **MOSCONE CONVENTION CENTER**—completed in 1981 and named after the mayor who was slain in 1978—was the first major development to inject tourist money into the area, it was the 1995 unveiling of Swiss architect Mario Botta's **SAN FRANCISCO MUSEUM OF MODERN ART** that solidified SoMa's reputation as the artistic heart of the city, attracting visitors from all over the world. On the heels of the museum's completion came the **YERBA BUENA CENTER FOR THE ARTS**, which hosts exhibitions ranging from avant-garde video and installation art to the more conventional "Impressionists in Winter." Surrounding the center is **YERBA BUENA GARDEN**, a 5-acre public oasis that includes a Martin Luther King Jr. memorial—etched glass panels displayed behind a long, shimmering cascade of water—and other sculptures.

One thing's for sure, you won't go hungry should you choose to lodge in this mecca for financial types and foodies alike. In recent years, many top-notch restaurants have taken advantage of low rent and lots of space and moved into the industrial warehouses.

RESTAURANTS

Azie / ★★★

826 FOLSOM ST, SAN FRANCISCO; 415/538-0918

Chef-restaurateur Jody Denton wants to corner the culinary market in the up-and-coming scene on Folsom Street. By the looks of Azie, wedged in next door to his wildly popular Restaurant LuLu, he's well on his way. This stylish restaurant bears its SoMa surroundings in mind, with 22-foot vaulted ceilings supported by four huge columns. The dining room is split-level; in the booths on the main level, you can draw a set of curtains for a truly exclusive feel. The main level is also home to the exhibition kitchen, where Asian-inspired French cuisine such as roulade of monkfish, grilled veal medallions with sea urchin–wasabi butter, and aromatic oxtail bundles are beautifully arranged. Some of the most popular dishes are the boneless short ribs, roasted lobster in scallion-ginger cream, and braised duck in red curry; if you can't decide, opt for the nightly tasting menu. Dining is also available at the bar, where a DJ plays oh-so-cool music nightly. *$$$; AE, DC, MC, V; no checks; dinner Mon–Sat; full bar; reservations recommended; www.azierestaurant.com; at 4th St.*

bacar / ★★½

448 BRANNAN ST, SAN FRANCISCO; 415/904-4100

You don't even want to know how much money was poured into this three-decker restaurant. The exposed-brick-and-timber warehouse-size restaurant consists of a lower-level jazz lounge (which has a list of specialty cocktails created by famous mixologist Dominic Venegas), a high-energy (and loud) mezzanine bar, and somewhat quieter seating upstairs. Dishes like Alaskan king salmon with morel mushrooms, new potatoes, and pickled ramps; bacon-wrapped Sonoma rabbit loin with chantenay carrots and polenta; and mesquite-grilled butcher's steak with heirloom squash, romano beans, and potato purée are expertly paired with wines. In fact, no other restaurant in the city pays such careful attention to pairing wines with each dish: wine director and general manager Mickey Clevenger's mind-melting 1,200-bottle wine list includes 65 selections by the glass, as a 2-ounce sampler, or via a decanter. Tip: bacar offers free live jazz on Friday and Saturday from 8:30pm to midnight, and the kitchen stays open until 11pm on weekends. *$$$; AE, DC, DIS, MC, V; no checks; dinner every day; full bar; reservations recommended; www.bacarsf.com; between 3rd and 4th sts.* ♿

COCO500 / ★★½

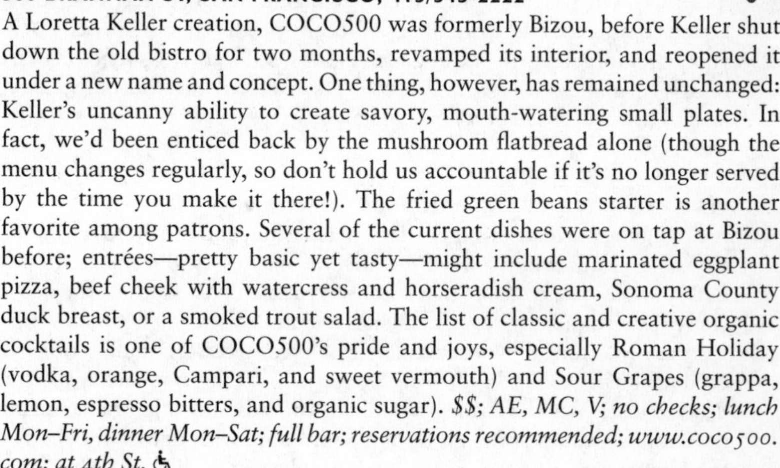

500 BRANNAN ST, SAN FRANCISCO; 415/543-2222

A Loretta Keller creation, COCO500 was formerly Bizou, before Keller shut down the old bistro for two months, revamped its interior, and reopened it under a new name and concept. One thing, however, has remained unchanged: Keller's uncanny ability to create savory, mouth-watering small plates. In fact, we'd been enticed back by the mushroom flatbread alone (though the menu changes regularly, so don't hold us accountable if it's no longer served by the time you make it there!). The fried green beans starter is another favorite among patrons. Several of the current dishes were on tap at Bizou before; entrées—pretty basic yet tasty—might include marinated eggplant pizza, beef cheek with watercress and horseradish cream, Sonoma County duck breast, or a smoked trout salad. The list of classic and creative organic cocktails is one of COCO500's pride and joys, especially Roman Holiday (vodka, orange, Campari, and sweet vermouth) and Sour Grapes (grappa, lemon, espresso bitters, and organic sugar). *$$; AE, MC, V; no checks; lunch Mon–Fri, dinner Mon–Sat; full bar; reservations recommended; www.coco500.com; at 4th St.* ♿

Fringale / ★★★½

570 4TH ST, SAN FRANCISCO; 415/543-0573

Once you've achieved excellence, it's tough to triumph over all the hype. But Fringale has done just that for more than 18 years, consistently garnering press accolades and drawing crowds to this tiny, boisterous 50-seat French restaurant tucked away in a charmless section of the city. Behind this restaurant's cheery yellow facade, however, there's plenty of charm emanating from the casual, blond-wood-trimmed interior, petite curved bar, and friendly, largely French waitstaff. Chef and owner Jean-Marie Legendre creates outstanding takes on classic dishes like a frisée salad topped with a poached egg and warm bacon dressing, steamed mussels sprinkled with garlic and parsley, wild mushroom ravioli, rack of lamb, and his signature (and meltingly tender) pork tenderloin confit with onion and apple marmalade. Fringale—French for "a sudden pang of hunger"—is perpetually packed at dinnertime, so expect a noisy crowd and a wait for a table, even if you've made a reservation. *$$; AE, MC, V; no checks; lunch Tues–Fri, dinner Tues–Sun; full bar; reservations recommended; www.fringalesf.com; between Brannan and Bryant sts.* ♿

Jack Falstaff / ★★★★

598 2ND ST, SAN FRANCISCO; 415/836-9239

Servers who could double as characters from the *Matrix* breeze through the plush, olive-toned interior that comprises the dark, clean-cut addition to the PlumpJack suite of restaurants (this one's owned by Mayor Gavin Newsom). The restaurant's staff and executive chef Jonnatan Leiva have it burned into their DNA to accommodate your wish for a memorable dining experience. The modern art on the plate in front of you includes delectable starters such as ahi tuna flirting with slowly melting jalapeno and onion raspado; Liberty Farms duck rillettes with buttery foie gras, huckleberry sauce, and homemade pancakes; and the pan-seared Sonoma free-range quail resting on a bed of locally grown peaches. The rapidly changing menu reflects both the chef's eclectic nature and the availability of locally produced ingredients. For a meal you won't forget, try the tasting menu ($85). *$$$; AE, MC, V; no checks; lunch Mon–Fri, dinner Mon–Sat; full bar; reservations recommended; www.jackfalstaff.com; at Brannan St.* ♿

Koh Samui & The Monkey / ★★☆

415 BRANNAN ST, SAN FRANCISCO; 415/369-0007

Asian joints, particularly of the Thai persuasion, abound in this cosmopolitan city, so it's important to weed through the masses. And it's nice, for once, to find suitable Asian cuisine that's not served in a dive. Much of the decor here was procured directly from Thailand, including the chairs, which were made for the restaurant out of recycled sugar palm trees. Yet unlike other dining establishments of its kind, Koh Samui is anything but tacky; instead, the decor is tasteful and soothing with shades of reds, mood lighting, and authentic Buddha statues sprucing up the joint. Start with one of the many street food appetizers, like the crispy imperial rolls or the chicken or beef saté. For entrées, choose mango salad, with juicy mango, prawn, ground dried shrimp, and onion tossed in spicy lime juice; the hearty Phuket seafood, with sticky rice noodles, shrimp, crab meat, squid, mussels, fish balls, and broccoli; or the festive pumpkin chicken curry, served with red curry sauce inside a carved-out gourd. Order the coconut rice to accompany any dish; Koh Samui prepares this particularly well. *$$; AE, MC, V; no checks; lunch Mon–Sat, dinner every day; full bar; reservations recommended; www.kohsamuiandthemonkey.com; between 3rd and 4th sts.* ♿

Local Restaurant & Wine Merchant / ★★☆

330 1ST ST, SAN FRANCISCO; 415/777-4200

While wine is this Rincon Hill restaurant's forte (you may have guessed that by its name) and accordingly the drinks list is more extensive than the food menu, this is a one-stop evening out, as you can nosh on shared plates while getting happily buzzed on the 250-plus selections the sommelier recommends. Executive chef and one of the partners—the other brains behind the operation include sommelier Mark Bright and general manager Maria Hilario-Fendert—Ola Fendert kick-started his culinary career peeling potatoes in

Stockholm, Sweden, before relocating to San Francisco two decades ago and helming both Local and Oola (see review). The restaurant's mission is to source ingredients from local operations; thus, the menu features dishes like a bay shrimp and hard-boiled egg sandwich; pan-seared blue-nose sea bass with *pepperonatta agro dulce*, tapenade, and mâche; and scallop and pesto risotto. *$$–$$$; AE, MC, V; no checks; lunch, dinner every day, brunch Sat–Sun; beer and wine; reservations recommended; www.sf-local.com; between Folsom and Harrison sts.* ♿

Luce / ★★★

888 HOWARD ST (INTERCONTINENTAL SAN FRANCISCO), SAN FRANCISCO; 888/811-4273

Cool, yet inviting, Italian restaurant Luce has a cosmopolitan, loungelike vibe, with its gold-tinged palette and silk-draped windows. The eatery (pronounced LOO-chay) offers its eponymous wine—a Frescobaldi and Mondavi product—and the chef boldly takes chances, creating original dishes like celery cappuccino soup; *acquerello canaroli* rice with wild mushroom, truffle, and grana padano cheese; and venison served with vanilla crust, parsnip-celeriac, blackberry compote, asparagus, and spiced chocolate. Luce's breakfast and brunch, too, are divine, spanning more simple plates (with a flair) like lemon ricotta pancakes and steelcut oatmeal with mascarpone and cider poached apples to masterpieces such as Niman Ranch short-ribs hash with organic poached egg, root vegetable, and fingerling potatoes, and smoked salmon benedict with spinach, hollandaise, and cucumber fennel salad. In summer months, five- and eight-course tastings are offered for $65 and $95, and a spring vegetable menu is available upon request. Before dinner, be sure and sip the house specialty, grappa, at adjoining Bar 888. *$$–$$$; AE, DC, DIS, MC, V; no checks; breakfast, lunch, dinner every day, brunch Sat–Sun; full bar; reservations recommended; www.lucewinerestaurant.com; between 4th and 5th sts.* ♿

Oola / ★★

860 FOLSOM ST, SAN FRANCISCO; 415/995-2061

An enterprise of Ola Fendert—who is also executive chef at Local Restaurant & Wine Merchant (see review)—this bilevel restaurant is promoted as an American bistro with some of the best "San Francisco food" around, which essentially translates to a menu offering classics like spicy ahi tuna and baby back ribs in an artful presentation. Don't let the "bistro" part fool you—Oola is anything but casual and quick (though you can get by in smart casualwear). A perfect meal might begin with roasted beet and watermelon salad, accompanied by watercress, pistachios, goat cheese, and thyme vinaigrette; followed by bacon-wrapped monkfish with baby artichokes, fava beans, and a sage–brown butter sauce; and topped off by a cake of white chocolate with a peppermint ganache center, dark chocolate sauce, and mint–chocolate chip gelato. Clearly a fan of truffles, Fendert adds this delicacy to many of the menu items. The atmosphere is sexy and dark, with gauzy accents and candlelit tables—the perfect setting to woo or be wooed. The cocktails, in particular, are divine. Overall, the place is a bit loud, but if you request a second-floor table, the noise won't be quite as daunting. *$$–$$$; AE, MC, V; no checks; dinner every day; full bar; reservations recommended; www.oola-sf.com; between 4th and 5th sts.* ♿

Restaurant Lulu / ★★

816 FOLSOM ST, SAN FRANCISCO; 415/495-5775

Restaurant LuLu may not enjoy the legendary status it once commanded, but it's still one of the most energetic and popular restaurants in San Francisco and yet another feather in the chef's cap of Reed Hearon (who has since gone on to fry bigger fish). It's easy to see why LuLu was and *is* a hit. As soon as you enter, you're pleasantly assaulted with divine aromas emanating from the massive open kitchen, which overlooks the cavernous-yet-stylish dining room where a hundred or more diners are feasting family-style and creating such a din that the kitchen staff has to wear two-way headsets (it's quite a scene). The sine qua non starter is the sputtering iron-skillet-roasted mussels served with drawn butter. Everything that comes from the twin wood-burning ovens is superb, particularly the pork loin rubbed with fennel, garlic, and olive oil and served with mashed potatoes; the rosemary-infused chicken served with warm potato salad; and the thin, crisp pizzas topped with first-rate prosciutto, pancetta, and other savory toppings. Everything is served on a large platter for sharing. For dessert, go for the gooey chocolate cake served with a scoop of gourmet ice cream. *$$; AE, DC, MC, V; no checks; lunch, dinner every day; full bar; reservations recommended; www.restaurantlulu.com; at 4th St.* ♿

Salt House / ★★☆

545 MISSION ST, SAN FRANCISCO; 415/543-8900

This often loud, rail-car-style industrial space creates a mildly pleasing mix of intimacy and publicity among the smartly dressed clientele and kitchen staff, who studiously prepare the food in an open kitchen. The rough-hewn interior is complemented by bare brick walls and 1920s light fixtures hanging from the ceiling like arachnids on fire. An oversize mural by local dark artist Freya Prowe dominates the back wall and hangs over a—perhaps unsurprisingly—salty menu with items such as petrale sole in a celery root, lemon, and shrimp jus; wild striped bass, red cabbage, and chorizo jumble; baked oysters with bacon and leeks; day boat scallops in a cider and black pepper sauce; and, as a nice starter, pieces of suckling pig with lentils and garlic. Creatively filled martini glasses and a full-page wine list make this a good place to meet and lush it up with strangers. If you're not feeling that hungry, feel free to just sample the dessert menu, which can include a divine cookie plate, an ice cream sandwich, or the scandalous-to-the-senses chocolate malt Bavarian. *$$–$$$; AE, MC, V; no checks; lunch Mon–Fri, dinner every day; full bar; reservations recommended; www.salthousesf.com; between 2nd and 3rd sts.* ♿

Tres Agaves / ★★

130 TOWNSEND ST, SAN FRANCISCO; 415/227-0500

Mexican joints aren't hard to come by in the Bay Area, which could more or less be dubbed Little Mexico in certain parts. Thus, it's important to weed through the options. For food alone, Tres Agaves is hardly at the top of the pack in its genre—you'll likely find better tacos at most neighborhood taquerias—but it's definitely the wide selection of tequila that keeps this classy Mexican restaurant hopping. Tres Agaves features a distillery of the month, and prides itself on serving all tequilas in the appropriate barware, not a shot glass (which is implied as amateur). And the food really isn't bad at all: start with the *albóndigas*, Mexican meatballs in tomato habanero sauce; for mains try the *chiles rellenos con huitlacoche*, poblano chiles stuffed with cheese, corn, zucchini, mushroom, and Mexican truffle, or the *carnitas*, slow-roasted pork rubbed with Mexican oregano, sea salt, and arbol chile. The restaurant's snarky disclaimer is that it doesn't "wrap everything in tortillas, smother everything in cheese, offer 'combination plate #2,' and serve lame drinks" (just so you don't go in expecting any ol' Mexican experience). *$$–$$$; AE, DIS, MC, V; no checks; lunch Mon–Fri, dinner every day, brunch Sat–Sun; full bar; reservations recommended; www.tresagaves.com; at 2nd St.* ♿

LODGINGS

Harbor Court Hotel / ★★★

165 STEUART ST, SAN FRANCISCO; 415/882-1300 OR 866/792-6283

On the southwest edge of the Financial District, this low-key, high-style hotel caters mainly to business travelers, but will equally impress the weekend vacationer. It was once a YMCA, but don't let that dissuade you: the high-quality accommodations, gorgeous bay views, and complimentary use of the adjoining fitness club—complete with indoor Olympic-size swimming pool—add up to one sweet deal. Each of the 131 guest rooms is nicely equipped with soundproof windows, a half-canopy bed, a large armoire, Aveda bath products, a flat-screen television, and a writing desk. Amenities include room service, free wireless, laundry and dry cleaning, evening wine reception, newspaper delivery, valet service, and car service to the Financial District. When the sun drops, slip on down to the bar at Boulevard (see review), one of the hippest downtown restaurants, and mingle with the swinging singles. *$$$–$$$$; AE, DC, MC, V; no checks; www.harborcourthotel.com; between Mission and Howard sts.* ♿

InterContinental San Francisco / ★★★

888 HOWARD ST, SAN FRANCISCO; 888/811-4273

Opened in 2008, the eco-friendly InterContinental, with its turquoise aquariumlike facade, is a prime example of the city's progressive art attitude. The interior is minimal yet inviting with a neo-Japanese style, contemporary art, dark polished wood walls, and marble floors. The 550 accommodations are distributed among 32 stories and feature floor-to-ceiling windows with sweeping views of the city, not to mention sensors that detect body heat and adjust each room's temperature accordingly, to conserve energy. Each room is equipped with wireless Internet, a high-definition television, an iPod dock, a minibar, and fluffy robes and slippers. Spanning two floors, the 2,000-square-foot penthouse suite provides the best panorama, with two private terraces (complete with fire pit), a banquet table for eight, a master bedroom with a piano, a fireplace, two bathrooms, and a Jacuzzi. While you're here, visit Luce (see review), the lobby restaurant with an inventive menu and wine options galore, and the adjoining Bar 888, where a sampling of the grappa is an absolute must. The luxurious iSpa, a 24-hour fitness center, and a lap pool illuminated by skylights complete the package. Only one drawback: Like at many of the downtown hotels, parking is ridiculously pricey (starting at $46 a night); it might be wiser to leave your car in one of the nearby public lots. *$$$–$$$$; AE, DIS, MC, V; checks OK; www.intercontinentalsanfrancisco.com; at 5th St.* ♿

W Hotel / ★★★

181 3RD ST, SAN FRANCISCO; 415/777-5300 OR 877/822-0000

Art, technology, service, and sex appeal are all applied in force from the moment you walk into the lobby of this hip hotel chain, a favorite of business travelers. In fact, at first you don't even realize you're in a 31-story hotel, because the first person to greet you is the bartender (brilliant). To your right is a gaggle of hip, young, beautiful people lounging in the ever-so-chic lobby, and to the left is XYZ, a popular SoMa restaurant. The decor of each guest room mimics the overall theme—bold colors, soft fabrics, sensual curves, mirrors galore—almost enough to make you *not* notice how small the rooms are. No matter: dive onto the thick, luscious goose-down comforter and you won't ever want to leave. Every room comes with high-tech toys, including a plasma television, CD and DVD player, and DVD library; high-speed Internet; Bliss spa products; a minibar and munchie box; and a pillow menu (how's that for being spoiled?). Located smack-dab in the center of the smoking-hot SoMa District, the hotel literally shares real estate with the beautiful San Francisco Museum of Modern Art and Yerba Buena Gardens. If you want to play with San Francisco's "in" crowd, W is the place to be (at least for now). *$$$$; AE, DC, JCB, MC, V; checks OK; www.whotels.com; between Mission and Howard sts.* ♿

Potrero Hill

Sitting between two freeways and on a rise directly south of downtown, Potrero Hill flutters between industrial chic and leafy residential. Sometimes the lines cross, and the results are brightly hued, high-tech abodes in the middle of sleepy old streets. Once called Goat Hill and now overlapping with the loft-ridden Dogpatch neighborhood, this former home to ungulates is now an up-and-coming residential area, shedding its former incarnation as a site for affordable housing "projects." Interior design heaven (furniture and antique shops as well as design studios) lies at its base, in the area between 16th and Division streets. Climb the hill for expansive views of downtown and the bay. On 18th Street, a little commercial area (between Arkansas and Texas streets) features several charming restaurants.

RESTAURANTS

Just for You Cafe / ★

732 22ND ST, SAN FRANCISCO; 415/647-3033

As you round the corner of 3rd Street and onto 22nd, you'll wonder what all of those people are doing lined up ahead. If it's a weekend, no matter the time, you can be sure they're waiting to brunch at this neighborhood hot spot, so be among the first to arrive when the doors open at 8am to ensure a table sooner rather than later. Outdoor and bar seating are also available if you're more concerned with time than dining location. Honestly, the food is nothing spectacular at this cute and cozy (read: small) café near the Giants ballpark, though portion sizes are generous and the menu has a good, down-home Southern quality (many dishes come with a side of grits). Menu items might include the Frittata of the Decade, an omelet with zucchini, mushrooms, garlic, and cheddar; Creole crab cakes over poached eggs; or wheat-free, sugar-free (still tasty) oatmeal pancakes. Filling specials like eggs Benedict with a twist (maybe roast beef, crab, or roasted tomatoes) or the scramble of the day will keep the hunger at bay. Failing to order a plate of the house favorite, the beignets, is simply a faux pas. *$–$$; cash and local checks only; breakfast, lunch every day, brunch Sat–Sun; beer and wine; no reservations; www.justforyoucafe.com; between 3rd and Tennessee sts.*

Mission District

The site of San Francisco's original Spanish settlement, Mission Dolores, the Mission District owes much to the Mexican ranchers who bought up large tracts of land during the pre–gold rush days when Alta California belonged to Mexico. During the early 1900s, a large number of immigrants settled here. But the Mission isn't merely a home to recent arrivals. For decades artists, students, and blue-collar workers of all stripes have flocked here for sunshine and affordable housing. The heart and namesake of the neighborhood, **MISSION DOLORES**, sits on Dolores Street at 16th Street. The newer basilica's spires tower above the much-smaller mission next door, which was dedicated in 1791 and still has original adobe walls and roof tiles. Cruise Valencia and 16th streets for interesting shopping and good restaurants, 24th Street between Guerrero and South Van Ness for the epicenter of the Mission's Latino culture, and the entire neighborhood for ethnic markets, inexpensive taquerias, and vibrant murals.

RESTAURANTS

Blowfish Sushi to Die For / ★★

2170 BRYANT ST, SAN FRANCISCO; 415/285-3848

Japanese anime plays on two suspended TVs for the young and the hip who pack this place, lounging against a backdrop of velvet walls, techno dance music, and acid jazz. Located in the industrial northeast Mission District, the restaurant offers a combination of traditional and more adventurous sushi. If you're intent on trying the infamously deadly blowfish, the Japanese delicacy otherwise known as puffer fish, expect to fork over about $30 if it's in season, and be prepared for a letdown: it's fairly bland. Move on to the mavericks: Maui Maki (tuna, mango, and macadamia nuts); double crab salad with soft-shell crab; tempura-battered asparagus maki wrapped in rice; and the restaurant's namesake, Blowfish Maki (a roll of yellowtail, scallions, and tobiko, draped with salmon—but, ironically, no blowfish). Non-fish-eaters also have choices: filet mignon with rosemary garlic butter, chicken pot stickers, or asparagus spring rolls with duck. Chef Ritsuo Tsuchida likes to tempt his regular customers with unusual creations: seared ostrich on portobello mushroom tempura, anyone? Service is friendly and efficient. *$$–$$$; AE, DC, DIS, MC, V; no checks; lunch Mon–Fri, dinner every day; full bar; reservations recommended; www.blowfishsushi.com; between 19th and 20th sts.* ♿

Delfina / ★★★

3621 18TH ST, SAN FRANCISCO; 415/552-4055

Opening to rave reviews just over a decade ago, this tiny Mission District neighborhood restaurant with a clean, modern design and pea-green walls has been packed ever since. Partners Anne and Craig Stoll have extensive pedigrees at other Bay Area restaurants, and chef Stoll's daily changing creations showcase his skills for cooking Italian regional cuisine. Top-notch starters have included nettles-and-ricotta ravioli; a salad studded with fresh cracked crab, fennel, and grapefruit segments; and the far-from-ordinary fried Ribollita da Delfina minestrone. Entrées are hearty and include rich, braised meat dishes, excellent pastas, and fish. Pancetta-wrapped rabbit loin bursts with flavor, as do the buttermilk-battered fried onions with polenta served on the side. Desserts are simply delicious: profiteroles stuffed with coffee ice cream, creamy buttermilk panna cotta (baked custard), and Gorgonzola with chestnut honey. The wine list is a well-edited one, with many moderately priced bottles among the offerings. As Delfina has garnered quite the reputation, you often need to book a table well in advance, though a dining room that seats 70 and an outdoor heated patio that accommodates an additional 25 allow more people the chance to experience the magic of this Mission favorite. *$$; MC, V; no checks; dinner every day; beer and wine; reservations recommended; www.delfinasf.com; between Dolores and Guerrero sts.* ♿

Foreign Cinema / ★★

2534 MISSION ST, SAN FRANCISCO; 415/648-7600

The concept behind this contemporary California-Mediterranean restaurant is to combine dinner and a movie in a single location. Accessed through an unassuming door along Mission Street, the restaurant has an industrial-chic appearance, with deliberately unfinished walls, exposed mechanics in the ceiling, a stark open kitchen, and hard surfaces throughout. On one wall in a center courtyard, classic foreign and indie films are projected in all their grainy black-and-white glory. Drive-in-movie–type speaker boxes are placed at each table so you can listen along as you dine—sort of like a movie-and-dinner-date all rolled into one. But mostly the films are just an imaginative distraction from the main attraction: the food. The lobster and monkfish bouillabaisse is rich and decadent, the roasted Sonoma duck breast is tender and bursting with flavor, the rosemary-marinated lamb melts in your mouth, and for dessert it's the chocolate pot de crème. It's all quite a production, enough so that you may not even notice that some of the dishes seem a bit rushed and decidedly subpar (go with the waitstaff's suggestions). *$$–$$$; AE, MC, V; no checks; dinner every day, brunch Sat–Sun; full bar; reservations recommended; www.foreigncinema.com; between 21st and 22nd sts.* ♿

La Taqueria / ★★

2889 MISSION ST, SAN FRANCISCO; 415/285-7117

Among the colorful fruit stands, thrift shops, and greasy panhandlers lining bustling Mission Street sits La Taqueria, the Bay Area's best burrito factory. Its lackluster interior is brightened only by a vibrant mural depicting south-of-the-border scenes and a shiny CD jukebox pumping out merry Mexican music, all of which could mean only one thing: people come here for the food. Don't expect a wide variety, for the folks behind the counter just churn out what they do best: burritos, tacos, and quesadillas. The moist, meaty fillings include excellent *carnitas* (braised pork), grilled beef, sausage, beef tongue, and chicken (you won't find any rice in these burritos); and the *bebidas* vary from beer and soda to cantaloupe juice and even *horchatas*. Stand in line to place your order and pay, then take a seat at one of the shared, long wooden tables and wait for someone to bellow out your number (somehow they just know whether to say it in Spanish or English). *$; no credit cards; local checks only; lunch, dinner every day; beer only; no reservations; between 24th and 25th sts.* ♿

Ti Couz / ★★☆

3108 16TH ST, SAN FRANCISCO; 415/252-7373

Other restaurants offer crepes, but none compare to what this popular Mission District establishment does with the beloved French pancake. Ti Couz (French for the Old House and pronounced "TEE cooz") serves delectable Brittany-style sweet and savory crepes in a homey setting that feels very much like an old French inn. Don't be overwhelmed: though the menu lists countless ingredients (in French and English) so you can create your own *crêpe bretonne*, it also includes several suggestions. Entrée recommendations include ham and cheese, mushroom-almond, and fresh tomato. A ratatouille-and-cheese creation bursts with flavor, and the hearty sausage-filled pancake won't disappoint. But be forewarned: The large buckwheat crepes are très énormes. And you must leave room for dessert. The sweet wheat-flour crepes, fluffier than the savory buckwheat versions, are ideal for luscious fillings such as apple, ice cream, and caramel, or fresh berries à la mode. Complete the meal with a choice of several hard ciders served in bowls. You can also choose from a list of French wines or Celtic beers, as well as French-style coffees and cocktails. *$; MC, V; no checks; lunch, dinner every day; full bar; no reservations; at Valencia St.* ♿

The Castro

Once part of the 4,000-acre ranch belonging to Jose de Jesus Noe, former alcalde of Mexican San Francisco, the Castro area underwent a huge transformation when the Yankees moved into town. The 1920s were boom years for the newly developed neighborhood. Built in 1922, the Castro Theatre stood as the elegant centerpiece of this growing community (and still does). In the 1970s, a large number of gay men moved into the area, renovated weathered Victorians, and gave the neighborhood a general face-lift. The Castro came alive again, this time as the epicenter of gay pride. The neighborhood rejoiced in 1977 when local camera-store owner Harvey Milk was elected to the city council, becoming the nation's first openly gay elected city official. A year later, the community suffered a devastating blow when Supervisor Milk and Mayor George Moscone were gunned down in City Hall by former supervisor Dan White. Today, **HARVEY MILK PLAZA** at Castro and Market streets is a popular gathering place for marches and political rallies. The Spanish Renaissance–style **CASTRO THEATRE** (429 Castro St near Market St; 415/621-6120) draws crowds for its innovative and retro movie offerings as well as its landmark architecture. Another attraction is the restored Wurlitzer on which an organist plays "San Francisco, Open Your Golden Gate" before each show (it then sinks into the floor by way of a hydraulic lift—very cool). Market, Castro, and 18th streets are lined with eclectic purveyors of clothing and housewares, bookstores, gift shops, and cafés such as the **METRO** (3600 16th St at Market St; 415/703-9750), a great place to sit on the balcony and watch the locals stroll by.

RESTAURANTS

2223 Restaurant & Bar / ★★½

2223 MARKET ST, SAN FRANCISCO; 415/431-0692

Also known as the No Name, this popular Castro District spot has been packing in the crowds because it was one of the first upscale restaurants in the area to offer serious food, friendly and professional service, and a terrific bar scene. You'll see only the restaurant's address on the outside of the building, so look for a red exterior and a lively crowd visible through large storefront windows. The menu is eclectic—mostly American-Mediterranean, with Southwestern and Southeast Asian touches. The romaine salad is a great Caesar variation, with capers, thinly sliced cornichons, and smoky onions. Try one of the pizzas, such as the pancetta, onion confit, Teleme cheese, marjoram, and sun-dried tomato pesto version. For entrées, the kitchen serves generous portions of comfort food: juicy pan-roasted chicken with garlic mashed potatoes, a double-cut pork chop served with a side of chayote squash, grilled salmon with lemon-caviar fondue, and sliced lamb sirloin fanned on a ragout of fava beans and fresh artichoke hearts. Indulge in the Louisiana crème brûlée with pecan pralines for dessert. Despite the noise from the bar, 2223 Market is a terrific neighborhood spot—especially if you can find a nearby parking place. *$$; AE, DC, MC, V; local checks only; dinner every day, brunch Sun; full bar; reservations recommended; www.2223restaurant.com; between Sanchez and Noe sts.* ♿

LODGINGS

Inn on Castro / ★☆

321 CASTRO ST, SAN FRANCISCO; 415/861-0321

This convivial bed-and-breakfast, catering to the gay and lesbian community for 25 years, has developed an ardent following. The restored Edwardian exterior is painted in a pleasing medley of blue, rose, and green, with gilded details and dentils. The interior is equally festive, with contemporary furnishings, original modern art, exotic plants, and elaborate flower arrangements. Eight individually decorated guest rooms range from a small single to a suite with a deck; each room has a private bath, a TV, and wireless Internet. Avoid the sunny but noisy rooms facing Castro Street. An elaborate breakfast, served in the dining room, may feature a fresh fruit salad, house-made muffins, fruit juice, and scrambled eggs, French toast, or pancakes. After your repast, relax in the cozy living room with fireplace and deeply tufted Italian couches, or head out for a stroll in the colorful, ever-bustling Castro. Note: For longer stays, the inn also rents corporate apartments. *$$; MC, V; checks OK; www.innoncastro.com; at Market St.*

Noe Valley

Sunny Noe Valley sits west of wide, palm-lined Dolores Street and below Twin Peaks. Twenty-fourth Street is the bustling commercial center for this mostly residential neighborhood, with plenty of places to grab a bagel or ice cream, as well as some great restaurants. The street's shops reflect the surrounding demographics (largely young families and couples): organic produce and groceries, children's clothing and supplies, shoes, and body and bath sundries. Primarily residential Church Street has restaurants for every palate—from American to German to Japanese to Thai to vegetarian—in the stretch between 24th and 30th streets.

RESTAURANTS

Firefly / ★★☆

4288 24TH ST, SAN FRANCISCO; 415/821-7652

Hidden in a cluster of homes on the west end of 24th Street is Noe Valley's best restaurant—just look for a giant metal sculpture of its namesake nocturnal insect perched above a lime green and sizzling yellow door. Inside, eclectic modern art surrounds small tables laden with an equally eclectic display of food, which might include steaming bowls of bouillabaisse de Marseilles bubbling over with monkfish, prawns, scallops, and bass; shrimp-and-scallop pot stickers served with a spicy sesame-soy dipping sauce (Firefly's signature appetizer); and a portobello mushroom Wellington served with linguine that's swirled with fresh vegetables. Chef/co-owner Brad Levy and co-owner Veva Edelson, both formerly of Embarko, dub it "home cooking with few ethnic boundaries." They also proudly announce that their meat comes from the well-known Niman Ranch, home of "happy, drug-free animals with an ocean view." The changing roster of desserts is as good as it looks, especially the not-too-sweet strawberry shortcake and the banana bread pudding with caramel à l'anglaise. *$$–$$$; AE, MC, V; checks OK; dinner every day; beer and wine; reservations recommended; www.fireflyrestaurant.com; at Douglas St.*

Incanto / ★★★

1550 CHURCH ST, SAN FRANCISCO; 415/641-4500

The valley's edgy Incanto has made waves for its bold use of ingredients not typically found in gourmet meals (e.g., green peaches and acorns). In keeping with San Francisco's environment-friendly approach to everything, the Italian eatery has a "waste not, want not" sort of philosophy and was one of the original restaurants to offer a five-course head-to-heel menu. Simply put, innovative executive chef Chris Cosentino, formerly a part of the Aqua Restaurant Group, dares to be different. The result: A delightful experience for your taste buds. Appetizers include pig's trotter with foie gras, bacon, and roasted figs; entrées such as raw venison liver sound unlikely to woo the palate, yet are surprisingly successful at doing just that. The menu changes nightly, but expect appetizers like roasted grapes and baby turnips with almonds or a watermelon, olive, and ricotta salad; entrées such as sweet corn gnocchi, opal basil, and popcorn shoots, or local albacore shank, chickpeas, tomato, and mint; and desserts including stout cake, Irish cream à l'anglaise, and malt-chip ice cream or a very tart lemon verbena *sorbetto* with candied lemon zest. Many of the restaurant's herbs are grown on the rooftop garden. *$$–$$$; AE, MC, V; no checks; dinner Tues–Sun; beer and wine; reservations recommended; www.incanto.biz; at Duncan St.* ♿

Marin County

When you consider that the San Francisco Bay Area has more people than the entire state of Oregon, and that Marin County has the highest per-capita income in the nation, you would expect Marin to be brimming with four-star resorts and restaurants. Well, that's not the case. The third-smallest county in California, this little package is full of natural wonders, picturesque towns, and attractions, but nary a Spago or megaresort. It's no wonder that weary urbanites seeking respite and recreation stream across the Golden Gate Bridge to visit Marin's secluded beaches, pristine mountain lakes, and virgin redwood forests. In fact, the Marin coast is just short of Eden for the outdoor adventurer, a veritable organic playground for nature lovers in search of a patch of green or a square of sand to call their own for a day.

ACCESS AND INFORMATION

Two major airports provide access to Marin County. **SAN FRANCISCO INTERNATIONAL AIRPORT (SFO)** (650/821-8211; www.flysfo.com) is 34 miles away, and **OAKLAND INTERNATIONAL AIRPORT (OAK)** (510/563-3300; www.oaklandairport.com) is 19 miles from Marin. **SHUTTLE SERVICE** to and from SFO is provided throughout the day by two carriers: **MARIN AIRPORTER** (415/461-4222; www.marinairporter.com) and **MARIN DOOR TO DOOR** (415/457-2717; www.marindoortodoor.com) pick up and deliver in Marin. Marin Door to Door also offers service to Oakland International Airport. **RADIO CAB** (415/485-1234) services all of Marin County. Marin Door to Door is the only company that provides daily 24-hour service to San Francisco, Oakland, and San Jose airports.

Bus and ferry service is offered by the **GOLDEN GATE TRANSIT SYSTEM** (415/455-2000; www.goldengate.org). Ferries run daily between the Larkspur Landing Terminal and Sausalito to San Francisco's Ferry Building and Fisherman's Wharf. The **BLUE & GOLD FLEET** (Pier 41, Fisherman's Wharf; 415/705-8200; www.blueandgoldfleet.com) runs to and from Sausalito and Tiburon. The **ANGEL ISLAND–TIBURON FERRY** (415/435-2131; www.angelislandferry.com) provides service between downtown Tiburon and Angel Island.

Buses connect to the terminals and run daily throughout the county. However, it is generally not convenient to get around Marin on the bus. Schedules are focused on the commute to and from San Francisco. The service to West Marin is infrequent.

Two major bridges connect Marin to the greater Bay Area. The **GOLDEN GATE BRIDGE** provides access to and from San Francisco (pedestrians and bicyclists can use bridge sidewalks); the southbound toll is $5. The **RICHMOND–SAN RAFAEL BRIDGE** connects the county to the East Bay; the westbound toll is $4. Most Marin visitors travel north to south using Highway 101 (the central artery) or coastal Highway 1, with its near-legendary grades, narrow winding roads, and gorgeous views. Sir Francis Drake Boulevard, the longest east-west artery in the county, extends from Interstate 580

(Richmond–San Rafael Bridge) to the Point Reyes Lighthouse. This route runs through the heart of scenic West Marin; it features pastoral settings and rolling hills. Highway 1 and Sir Francis Drake intersect at Olema.

Although Marin enjoys a temperate climate all year round, the weather changes quickly from one location to the next. Expect cool, foggy mornings close to the bay and the ocean. The central part of the county is located in a sun belt. Spring and fall can be the best seasons of the year along the coast: southern Marin can be socked in with fog, but the sun will be shining brightly over West Marin beaches. Layers of clothing are recommended, along with comfortable walking shoes.

The **MARIN COUNTY CONVENTION & VISITORS BUREAU** (1 Mitchell Blvd, San Rafael; 415/925-2060; www.visitmarin.org) is an excellent county resource.

Sausalito

Nestled on the east side of Marin County is the pretty little Mediterranean-style town of Sausalito, a former Portuguese fishing village that's now home to about 7,500 residents, including several well-heeled owners of spectacular hillside mansions. It's hard to imagine Rosie the Riveter here, much less victory ships rolling off assembly lines, but Sausalito was a major shipbuilding site during World War II. Today most folks are browsing the upscale boutiques or popular art galleries between gourmet dining and wine tasting. If you're driving to Sausalito from the city, immediately after crossing the Golden Gate Bridge, turn right on Alexander Avenue, which after about a mile turns into Bridgeway, the main drag through the center of town. Pricey boutiques and waterfront restaurants line this street, and a paved promenade offers a truly breathtaking, unobstructed view of Angel Island, Alcatraz, and the San Francisco skyline. For more information contact the **SAUSALITO VISITOR CENTER** (10 Liberty Ship Way, Bay 2, Ste 250, Sausalito; 415/332-0505; www.sausalito.org).

RESTAURANTS

Hamburgers / ★

737 BRIDGEWAY, SAUSALITO; 415/332-9471

One of the best places to eat in Sausalito also happens to be one of the cheapest: a narrow little hamburger stand with a sign outside that says simply "Hamburgers." Look for the flat rotating grill in the window off Bridgeway, then stand in line. For $5 and some change, you'll get a homemade burger, just like the ones Dad used to flip off the grill. Order a side of crispy fries, grab a bunch of napkins, and then head over to the park down the street. Hot dogs, meatball sandwiches, and steak sandwiches are also served here. *$; cash only; lunch every day; no alcohol; no reservations; downtown Sausalito, north of Princess St.*

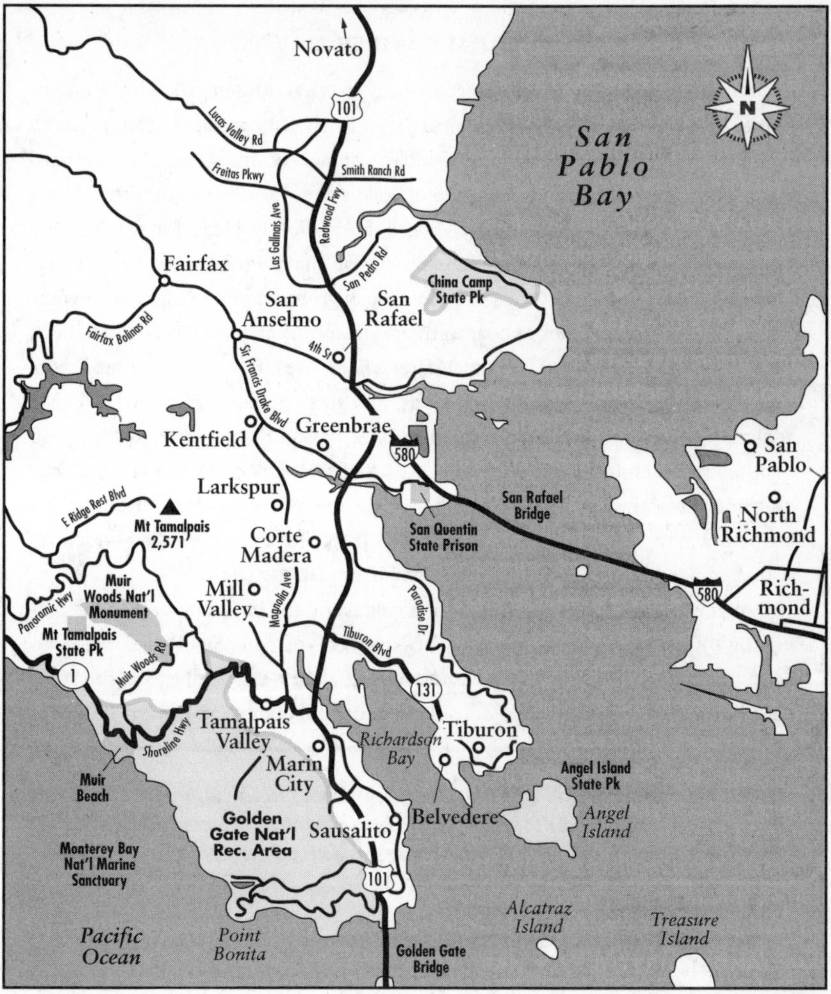

Marin County

Horizons / ★★

558 BRIDGEWAY, SAUSALITO; 415/331-3232

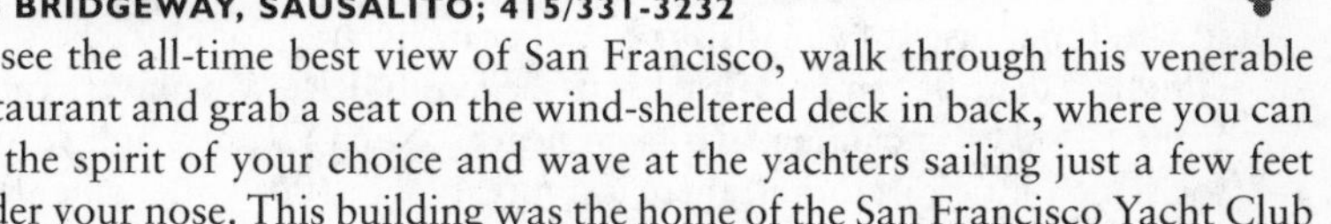

To see the all-time best view of San Francisco, walk through this venerable restaurant and grab a seat on the wind-sheltered deck in back, where you can sip the spirit of your choice and wave at the yachters sailing just a few feet under your nose. This building was the home of the San Francisco Yacht Club until 1925. Horizons is a great place to stop for a Bloody Mary and a snack, and is an easy, casual place to find a seat for lunch during the week. The servings are bountiful and the menu is typical American—shrimp or crab salads, hamburgers, broiled steaks, roast chicken, or grilled or sautéed fish entrées.

MARIN COUNTY THREE-DAY TOUR

DAY ONE: *Indulge yourself.* Start the day in **SAN ANSELMO** with a down-home breakfast at **BUBBA'S DINER**. Browse the shops along San Anselmo Avenue. You'll find antiques and collectibles, vintage clothing, home and gardening delights, new and used books, and upscale attire. Stock up with picnic fixings at **COMFORT'S** (335 San Anselmo Ave; 415/454-9840). Head for the hills and points west via Sir Francis Drake Boulevard. You'll know the season by the ever-changing colors in the pastoral landscape—lush greens come with a rainy winter and spring; golden browns appear in the dry summer and fall. Make **SAMUEL P. TAYLOR STATE PARK** (off Sir Francis Drake Blvd; 415/488-9897) your next stop. Picnic under a canopy of giant redwoods, and stretch your legs on the 1¼-mile self-guiding Pioneer Trail before heading back to San Rafael. It'll take about 30 minutes to reach the inviting **GERSTLE PARK INN**. Check in and enjoy a late-afternoon refreshment. How about dinner? Sausalito here we come, because the best sushi in the entire Bay Area is at **SUSHI RAN**. Toast the end of a perfect day with a cocktail while admiring the city view from **HORIZONS**.

DAY TWO: *Past perfect.* Linger over breakfast on the inn's sunporch, anticipating the discovery of nearby hidden places. While you're in San Rafael, step into the past at **MISSION SAN RAFAEL ARCANGEL**, Marin's oldest historic site. Your next destination is North San Pedro Road and a beautiful loop drive around San

$–$$; AE, DC, DIS, MC, V; no checks; brunch, lunch, dinner every day; full bar; reservations recommended; www.horizonssausalito.com; on the strand, 1 block south of the intersection of Bridgeway and Princess St.

Sushi Ran / ★★★☆

107 CALEDONIA, SAUSALITO; 415/332-3620

The sushi served at this southern Marin culinary landmark is impeccable, prepared with aplomb and served with a flourish by highly trained sushi chefs and an amiable waitstaff. The fish is glisteningly fresh, and the daily specials are invariably fantastic. Start with the miso-marinated cod or sea bass, along with a seaweed salad and miso soup. The kamikaze roll is stuffed with yellowfin tuna, bright flying-fish roe, and crunchy green onions; the spider roll enfolds a delicate tempura-fried soft-shell crab. Rice-wine lovers can choose from 17 sakes, including two from nearby Napa County, and surprisingly, for such a little restaurant, there is a mighty fine 100-bottle wine list. If you can't wait for a table in the main restaurant, the adjoining wine and sake bar serves a wide variety of appetizers. *$$$; AE, DIS, MC, V; no checks; lunch Mon–Fri, dinner every day; beer, wine, and sake; reservations recommended; www.sushiran.com; next to the Marin Theater.* ♿

Pablo Bay. Stop at the Frank Lloyd Wright–designed **MARIN COUNTY CIVIC CENTER** and stroll around the peaceful lagoon. Next, head for lunch at the **BUCK-EYE ROADHOUSE**, then drive south to the **SAN FRANCISCO BAY–DELTA MODEL** (2100 Bridgeway Blvd, Sausalito; 415/332-3871). In addition to the amazing half-acre scale model operated by the U.S. Army Corps of Engineers, you'll enjoy exploring the world-class visitor center and Marinship, an exhibit on a World War II shipbuilding facility. Relax back at the **GERSTLE PARK INN** and top off the evening with dinner at **INSALATA'S** or **LEFT BANK** (507 Magnolia Ave, Larkspur; 415/927-3331).

DAY THREE: *Lazy does it.* Be sure to take a peek at neighboring **GERSTLE PARK** before leaving. Make your way to Tiburon and **BLACKIE'S PASTURE** park (located off Tiburon Blvd), where you'll access the popular multiuse path that traces the former railroad right-of-way. Join the local runners, bikers, walkers, and rollerbladers headed for downtown (it'll take about an hour to walk there). You'll think this waterfront setting is postcard-perfect, but wait until you arrive at **SAM'S ANCHOR CAFÉ**. Head for the deck and order a margarita and bowl of spicy cioppino. Time permitting, you might want to visit **MILL VALLEY**. Tool around the plaza for a while, then have an early dinner at **PIAZZA D'ANGELO** to complete your Mill Valley experience before checking into **CASA MADRONA HOTEL & SPA** on the Sausalito waterfront for the night.

LODGINGS

Casa Madrona Hotel & Spa / ★★★½

801 BRIDGEWAY, SAUSALITO; 415/332-0502 OR 800/567-9524

There are two Sausalitos—the tourist-trampled waterfront area and the exclusive residential region in the hills—and the Casa Madrona is where they meet. The entrance to this unique hotel complex is on boutique-lined Bridgeway, where natives never venture and visitors love to shop. Step onto the Madrona property and you'll quickly be transported into Sausalito's enclave of multimillion-dollar mansions and panoramic bay views. The hotel offers everything you could possibly desire: sweeping bay vistas, an outdoor Jacuzzi, a full-service spa, a fine restaurant, and all the amenities of a citified hotel. Casa Madrona's 63 rooms are spread throughout the landscaped hillside. A newer wing of 31 contemporary guest rooms and suites all have sunken tubs and most are equipped with private balconies overlooking the Sausalito waterfront. The rates depend on the view: the garden and courtyard rooms are the least expensive, followed by the bay-view rooms and the one-bedroom suites. For greater privacy, choose one of the charming Victorian cottages. *$$$$; AE, DC, DIS, MC, V; no checks; 3-night minimum stay May–Oct; www.casamadrona.com; downtown.* ♿

The Inn Above Tide / ★★★★

30 EL PORTAL, SAUSALITO; 415/332-9535 OR 800/893-8433

The soothing ebb and flow of gentle tides is a natural attraction at this idyllic hideaway, the only hotel in the Bay Area built over the water. Every room faces the bay, and nearly all of the 29 rooms have balconies that you could literally drop a line and fish from. Airy and spacious interiors, awash with soft aquatic blues and misty greens, enhance the sense of serenity. Check out the Vista Suite, a private world of luxury featuring a romantic king-size canopied bed, wet bar, wood-burning fireplace, and spa tub (for a mere $925 a night). Water and views, the best that Sausalito has to offer, are always beckoning. There's plenty to look forward to at this comfortably elegant inn: complimentary wine and cheese at sunset, evening turndown service, overnight shoe shine, wireless Internet, fluffy robes, LCD television and DVD player, morning newspaper delivery, and an elaborate continental breakfast, delivered to your room on request. *$$$$; AE, DC, MC, V; no checks; www.innabovetide.com; El Portal is off Bridgeway, turn toward the water at downtown plaza.* ♿

Tiburon and Belvedere

Priceless views, waterfront dining, and interesting shops make Tiburon a popular destination for explorers arriving by ferry, car, or tour bus. Formerly a railroad town—until 1963 it was the terminus of the Northwestern Pacific Railroad—Tiburon (Spanish for "shark") is now a quaint New England–style coastal village. Its short Main Street is packed with expensive antique and specialty shops, as well as restaurants with incredible bay views. You can leave your car on the outskirts and walk to the village, or park in the large pay lot off Main Street. An even better way to get here is by bicycle or by ferry from San Francisco; it drops off passengers at the edge of town.

Past the Yacht Club, the road continues around the protected bay—this is where Tiburon blends into Belvedere (Italian for "beautiful view"), an ultra-exclusive community. The entire city consists of only half a square mile of land, but this is one tony piece of real estate. To get a better view of Belvedere, reclaim your car and drive up the tiny town's steep, narrow roads for a glimpse of the highly protected, well-shielded multimillion-dollar homes where international celebrities such as Elton John have been known to hide out.

RESTAURANTS

Guaymas / ★★

5 MAIN ST, TIBURON; 415/435-6300

Mexican food is as elaborate and nuanced as any of the world's great cuisines, with its mixture of indigenous, Spanish, and French flavors. Guaymas's kitchen offers superb versions of Mexican classics such as posole, a hearty stew from Jalisco, as well as California-inspired variations like the *sopes con*

BLACKIE'S PASTURE

In an urbanized area, it isn't often that a patch of land becomes so well known that locals give directions with it as a landmark. Blackie, a sweet-natured sway-backed horse, lived 28 of his 40 years in Tiburon, standing in a pasture off Tiburon Boulevard. A woman who grew up in Tiburon said that many local children stopped by the pasture on the way to school to offer apples and carrots to the old fellow; when he died in 1968, the nearby elementary school proclaimed a half-day of mourning. Blackie still stands in his pasture, in the form of a life-size bronze statue by sculptor Albert Guibara. As you drive along Tiburon Boulevard toward Tiburon, look to your right—you can't miss him.

pato, crisp, deep-fried corn shells filled with braised duck, pasilla peppers, onions, and garlic. The piping-hot white-corn tortillas are served with three sauces: a tangy salsa verde; a sweet and tantalizing salsa chipotle with smoked jalapeños, pineapples, and carrots; and a more pedestrian salsa *cruda* with tomatoes, onions, cilantro, and garlic. For an appetizer, try the Petrale sole ceviche marinated in fresh lime juice with avocado, chopped onions, tomatoes, Serrano chiles, and cilantro, or else the tamalitos filled with chicken and pumpkin seed sauce and accompanied by pork with guajillo chile sauce. Once your palate is warmed up, move on to the spicy tamales, the marinated shrimp, or the seafood platter of grilled octopus, squid, shrimp, and salmon. When the weather is favorable, dine on the deck and take in the incredible view of the bay, Angel Island, and the San Francisco skyline as you sip one of the mighty margaritas. *$$$; AE, DC, MC, V; no checks; lunch, dinner every day; full bar; reservations recommended; www.guaymasrestaurant.com; on Tiburon Harbor at the ferry landing.* ♿

Sam's Anchor Cafe / ★★

27 MAIN ST, TIBURON; 415/435-4527

It's another marvelous day in Marin. You want to relax with friends on a sun-drenched deck, enjoy a burger and fries, and relish views of neighboring San Francisco—so it's time to rally the troops and head for Sam's and a quintessential Marin experience. The classic bar is a great spot to eavesdrop, spin your own tale, or ask about Sam, a bootlegger and colorful character. Seafood is a popular choice; try the house specialty, cioppino, or stay with the tried-and-true oysters on the half shell. Or how about cracked Dungeness crab or a grilled halibut sandwich with pesto on focaccia? Weekend brunches feature eggs Benedict and a longtime favorite, Ramos gin fizzes. *$$; AE, DC, DIS, MC, V; no checks; lunch, dinner every day, brunch Sat–Sun; full bar; no reservations for outside seating (reservations recommended for inside dining Sat–Sun); www.samscafe.com; downtown.* ♿

Mill Valley

Everything in Mill Valley is either on or near Mount Tamalpais, the focal point of Marin County. Today's residents, including a bevy of famous musicians, writers, and actors, wouldn't dream of living anywhere else. The **MILL VALLEY BOOK DEPOT AND CAFE** (87 Throckmorton Ave; 415/383-2665), site of the town's last railway depot, is a favorite spot for locals to meet and greet. Brightly garbed bikers, hikers, and runners headed for the mountain add pops of color. Annual claims to fame include the **DIPSEA**, the oldest cross-country foot race on the West Coast, in June, and the **MILL VALLEY FILM FESTIVAL** in the fall. You never know who will be jamming at **SWEETWATER** (153 Throckmorton Ave; 415/388-2820; www.sweetwatersaloon.com) or enjoying a soothing massage at **TEA GARDEN SPRINGS** (38 Miller Ave; 415/389-7123; www.teagardensprings.com). For more information, contact the **MILL VALLEY CHAMBER OF COMMERCE** (85 Throckmorton Ave; 415/388-9700; www.millvalley.org).

RESTAURANTS

Buckeye Roadhouse / ★★½

15 SHORELINE HWY, MILL VALLEY; 415/331-2600

The decor at the Buckeye Roadhouse combines a reserved elegance with over-the-top Marin kitsch—lofty ceilings, mahogany beams, glass chandeliers and sconces, a massive stone fireplace, a huge stuffed yellowfin tuna, and a moose head. The cuisine, likewise, is both classic and eclectic. For an appetizer, try local oysters on the half shell; Buckeye's memorable Caesar salad; a tangled mound of thin, sweet onion rings cooked in a feathery batter and served with house-made ketchup; or the house-smoked Atlantic salmon. The most popular entrées are the barbecued baby back ribs served with coleslaw; smoked Sonoma duck with wild rice and huckleberry sauce; and a sweet, tender, marinated grilled pork chop with to-die-for garlic mashed potatoes. Top off your meal with one of the old-time desserts such as warm gingerbread cake with Meyer lemon curd and whipped cream. *$$$; DC, DIS, MC, V; no checks; lunch Mon–Sat, dinner every day, brunch Sun; full bar; reservations recommended; www.buckeyeroadhouse.com; from Hwy 101 take the Stinson Beach–Mill Valley exit.* ♿

Dipsea Cafe / ★★

200 SHORELINE HWY/HWY 1, MILL VALLEY; 415/381-0298

At the Dipsea—a local favorite for big breakfasts—the cooks flip huge, delicious buttermilk and whole-wheat blueberry pancakes every day of the week. Other well-loved standbys include eggs Benedict big enough for two, eggless tofu-vegetable scramble, and excellent house-made corned-beef hash. The lunch plates, especially the salade niçoise and special pasta entrées (chorizo sausage in a thick tomato base over fettuccine, for example), are equally hearty. Expect a wait on weekends for both breakfast and lunch as the locals and tourists fuel up for a day of hiking around Mount Tam. *$; MC, V; no checks; breakfast, lunch every day, dinner Wed–Sun; beer and wine; no reservations; www.dipseacafe.com; 200 yards south of Tam Junction (where Shoreline Hwy/Hwy 1 meets Almonte Blvd on the south side of town).* ♿

Joe's Taco Lounge & Salsa / ★

382 MILLER AVE, MILL VALLEY; 415/383-8164

This exuberant Mill Valley hole-in-the-wall taqueria with cherry-red counters and festive decor is where the locals go to feast on gordo soft tacos as big as your forearm. Joe's specialty is grilled Pacific snapper tacos with salsa fresca and habanero mayonnaise; a close second are the *carnitas*—shredded pork braised in orange juice and molasses, served with *cebolla* (onion) salsa. A painted penguin on the window proclaims Cool Inside, and we couldn't agree more. *$; MC, V; no checks; lunch, dinner every day; beer and wine; no reservations; at Montford and La Goma sts.* ♿

Piazza D'Angelo Ristorante / ★½

22 MILLER AVE, MILL VALLEY; 415/388-2000

When owners Paolo and Domenico Petrone renovated this restaurant in 1990, Piazza D'Angelo became one of Mill Valley's most popular restaurants—and it still is, with large (often noisy) crowds of Marinites packing the pleasant, airy bar. They don't necessarily come for the food, mind you, but for the charged atmosphere. D'Angelo's Italian menu abounds with familiar though not always well-executed fare, including numerous pasta plates—spaghetti sautéed with kalamata olives, chile peppers, baby spinach, onions, sun-dried tomatoes, white wine, and pecorino cheese is one of the better choices—and several juicy meat dishes from the rotisserie. The calzone, stuffed with fresh ingredients like ricotta, spinach, caramelized onions, mozzarella, and sausage, comes out of the pizza oven puffy and light. Desserts are made fresh daily, and if there's a crème brûlée on the tray, oh yeah. The extensive wine list features a respectable selection of California and Italian labels (about 150 bottles). *$$; AE, DC, MC, V; no checks; lunch, dinner every day, brunch Sat–Sun; full bar; reservations recommended; www.piazzadangelo.com; located on the downtown square.* ♿

LODGINGS

Mill Valley Inn / ★★★

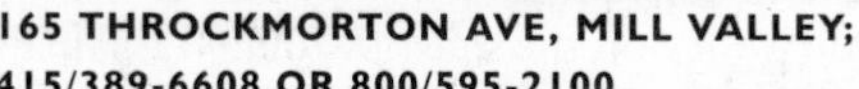

165 THROCKMORTON AVE, MILL VALLEY; 415/389-6608 OR 800/595-2100

Smack in the heart of trendy Mill Valley, you'll discover towering redwoods and a babbling creek just beyond the small reception area at this European-style inn. Accommodations, all designed with convenience, comfort, and California charm in mind, are secluded and quiet. There are 25 rooms, including one executive suite and two creek-side cottages, each with a private bath, a king- or queen-size bed, and French doors that open onto views of redwood

CHINA CAMP STATE PARK

CHINA CAMP STATE PARK, featuring 1,640 acres of natural watershed, is one of Marin's best-kept secrets. A hundred years ago a quaint fishing village thrived on its quiet shores, just 4 miles east of what is today downtown San Rafael. Most of the residents came from the Kwangtung province of China and brought with them a heritage of fishing methods dating back thousands of years. Their first stop was San Francisco. Good fortune smiled on these hardworking immigrants, who carved out a new life doing what they knew best. Business flourished, thanks in part to the gold rush frenzy and bounty from the bay (daily catches were as much as 3,000 pounds). By 1852 the enterprising immigrants were peddling fresh fish door to door, but times were changing. Some resented the success of these first commercial fishermen. In 1860 the state legislature placed a heavy tax on commercial Chinese fishing. The Chinese, eager to avoid the tax collector and discrimination, relocated to Marin. Fishing camps, where residents lived and worked in isolation, soon dotted the shoreline along San Pablo Bay.

By 1887 China Camp had become a prosperous shrimp-fishing village. Shrimp

trees or downtown Mill Valley. Room service is available from Piazza D'Angelo Ristorante (see review). A complimentary continental breakfast, along with the morning paper, is served on the flower-filled sun terrace. Would you like a double latte with low-fat milk and a sprinkling of chocolate to go with your assortment of pastries, breads, cereals, and fresh fruits? Make your request at the espresso bar before you head for the east peak of Mount Tam, test your lung capacity on the famous Dipsea Trail, or enjoy a picnic at Muir Beach. *$$$; AE, DC, MC, V; no checks; www.millvalleyinn.com; downtown.* ♿

Mountain Home Inn / ★★

810 PANORAMIC HWY, MILL VALLEY; 415/381-9000

Much has changed at the remote Mountain Home Inn since it opened in 1912 as a Bavarian restaurant, but what has stayed constant through the years is the stunning view. On clear days you can see the Marin hills, San Francisco Bay, the East Bay hills, and even Mount Diablo at the edge of the Central Valley. Perched high above Mill Valley on the side of Mount Tamalpais, the inn now has 10 guest rooms decorated in what might best be described as Marin modern, with plush carpeting and wood-paneled walls. All of the rooms have private baths. The TV-less guest rooms come with a wide variety of amenities—the most deluxe rooms have wood-burning fireplaces, decks, king-size beds, and oversize tubs with Jacuzzi jets. Wireless Internet is available. The New American cuisine served for lunch and dinner (Wed–Sun) in the dining room is adequate, but you'd be better off bringing a picnic or making caught in the bay were dried and then exported to Hawaii, Japan, and China, where they were used to flavor and garnish traditional Asian dishes. Discarded shells were sold as fertilizer and feed for farm animals. The lucrative shrimp industry supported the community of 3,000 until 1910, when the State of California introduced sea bass into San Pablo Bay. New regulations forced the Chinese to abandon their trap nets. The village population dwindled. Finally, only the well-known Quan family remained at China Camp.

Leave it to Hollywood to capture the lovely cove setting and lasting impressions of China Camp on celluloid. *Blood Alley*, starring Lauren Bacall and John Wayne, was filmed there in 1955. Like a deserted movie set, remnants of the past greet visitors today. The old fan mill formerly used to winnow shrimp is displayed in a wooden building, along with a replica of a sampan used by Chinese fishermen, and haunting photographs of early settlers.

China Camp State Park also features extensive intertidal, salt marsh, meadow, and oak habitats that are home to a variety of wildlife, including deer and red-tailed hawks. Visitors enjoy camping, hiking, swimming, boating, and windsurfing. Call for more information (415/388-2070).

the winding 15-minute drive down the mountain to a restaurant in one of the neighboring towns. Mountain Home Inn becomes a madhouse on sunny weekends, when hikers and mountain bikers descend for après-trek drinks and snacks or a late brunch on the deck. A full breakfast is included with your stay. *$$$–$$$$; AE, MC, V; no checks; www.mtnhomeinn.com.* ♿

Larkspur

Larkspur got its name from the blue flowers that grew on nearby hillsides in the late 1800s. Today white larkspurs grow in the historic downtown village, adorning the blue banners that hang from the old-fashioned lampposts lining Magnolia Avenue. There's a lot to discover within four short blocks: boutiques, restaurants, and splashes of European influence.

RESTAURANTS

Marin Brewing Company / ★

1809 LARKSPUR LANDING CIRCLE, LARKSPUR; 415/461-4677

Noisy, fun, and crowded, this brewery produces excellent ales and beers—Mount Tam Pale Ale and the unfiltered-wheat Hefeweizen are favorites—and hearty pub food (the Mount Tam burger with a side of onion rings is the bomb). Specials include Monday night's $2 tacos (after 5pm), Tuesday's

$3 pints (always fills the place), and summer oyster barbecues ($1.50 each on Wednesday). This is a good place to meet and greet, too; the crowd often includes quite a few brew-and-pizza lovers from the nearby gym, and seating outside during warm days is a real pleasure. *$; AE, MC, V; no checks; lunch, dinner every day; beer and wine; no reservations; www.marinbrewing.com; in Larkspur Landing Circle shopping center off Sir Francis Drake Blvd, across from the ferry landing.* ♿

Kentfield

RESTAURANTS

Half Day Café / ★★

848 COLLEGE AVE, KENTFIELD; 415/459-0291

Breakfast in this beautifully renovated, plant-filled mechanic's garage features a number of first-rate dishes, including fluffy omelets stuffed with a variety of fresh fillings, jumbo orange-currant scones, and fine, dark espresso. One complaint: you may have to wait a stomach-growling hour for a table on a busy weekend morning, and even longer if you have your eye on the sunny patio. At lunchtime, the College of Marin's ravenous crowds pack the place for fresh salads, hearty sandwiches, and grilled specials. *$; MC, V; local checks only; breakfast, lunch every day; beer and wine; no reservations; www.halfdaycafe.com; across from the College of Marin.* ♿

San Anselmo

Most people don't set out for San Anselmo; they pass through it on their way to West Marin, via Sir Francis Drake Boulevard. The smart rows of **ANTIQUE STORES** situated along the boulevard are eye-catching enough, but they're only a preview of downtown attractions. You'll discover a diminutive version of a sophisticated city, a blending of old and new, on **SAN ANSELMO AVENUE**.

RESTAURANTS

Bistro 330 / ★★

330 SAN ANSELMO AVE, SAN ANSELMO; 415/460-6330

The fresh French dishes here are delicious, and the origins of the ingredients couldn't be better: local ranch-raised beef, lamb, and chicken (no antibiotics or hormones), produce from local farmers, and farmed seafood. The restaurant uses organic and humane resources, and the menu—including such dishes as *coquelet rôti au balsam* (pan-roasted young chicken in rosemary balsamic reduction) and *côtes d'agneau grillées provençale* (grilled Atkins Ranch lamb chops with provençal sauce)—is consistently a winner. The sleek, modern interior is made user-friendly by the judicious use of warm reds and golds in the decor. This is a true bistro—patrons don't have to wrestle with floor-length tablecloths or pretentious waiters; the service is efficient and friendly. *$$; MC, V; no checks; dinner Tues–Sun; beer and wine; reservations recommended; downtown San Anselmo.* ♿

Bubba's Diner / ★★

566 SAN ANSELMO AVE, SAN ANSELMO; 415/459-6862

There's probably nothing on the menu at Bubba's that you couldn't make at home, but chances are you just couldn't make it as well. Bubba's offers classic diner food with decor to match: red Naugahyde booths, a black-and-white tile floor, a big Bubba's clock, and a daily special board. People stand in line for the hearty breakfast offerings, including chunky corned beef hash, honey whole-wheat flapjacks, and eggs prepared however you like 'em with home fries and a big, delicious, freshly baked biscuit. For lunch or dinner choose from a selection of salads, or order from an equally delicious, if slightly less health conscious, list of sandwiches, such as the burger slathered with Swiss cheese or the terrific meatloaf sandwich smothered in barbecue sauce. After 5:30pm you can indulge in chicken-fried steak with red-eye gravy, pot roast and mashed potatoes, crisp fried chicken, and similar fare. And since you've totally blown your diet by now, celebrate your newfound freedom with a real milk shake or malt, tapioca pudding, or a slice of banana-butterscotch pie. *$$; MC, V; no checks; breakfast, lunch, dinner Wed–Sun; beer and wine; reservations recommended for 6 or more; www.bubbas-diner.net; downtown.* ♿

Insalata's / ★★☆

120 SIR FRANCIS DRAKE BLVD, SAN ANSELMO; 415/457-7700

In a handsome, mustard-colored building large enough to house a car showroom, chef-owner Heidi "Her Lusciousness" Insalata Krahling (formerly of Square One in San Francisco and Butler's in Mill Valley) showcases her dazzling Mediterranean fare behind her restaurant's floor-to-ceiling windows. At tables cloaked in white linen, diners bask in the spaciousness while noshing on the seven-vegetable Tunisian *tagine* served on a bed of fluffy couscous, or the savory Genovese fish and shellfish stew simmering in a prosciutto broth seasoned with sage. You'll have no problem finding the perfect wine to accompany your meal from Insalata's list, and don't hesitate to ask the staff for suggestions. Service is quite friendly and attentive. After dinner head to the back of the restaurant, where goodies-to-go are sold (11am–7:30pm Mon–Sat), and pick up a little bag of biscotti studded with plump golden raisins—a great treat for the drive home. *$$$; MC, V; no checks; lunch, dinner every day; beer and wine; reservations recommended; www.insalatas.com; at Barber St.* ♿

I ONLY HAVE EYES FOR YOU

In north San Rafael, **GUIDE DOGS FOR THE BLIND** has been breeding and training Labrador retrievers, German shepherds, and golden retrievers to act as eyes for the blind since 1942. At that time, founder Lois Mayhew realized a dream and became the first female guide dog trainer in the United States, creating the school that would move permanently to San Rafael in 1947. After the dogs go through a rigorous four- to five-month training (you'll often see them on the streets of San Rafael with their trainers), they're introduced to their new owners, who then go through another few weeks of training with their canine companions. The dogs are provided free of charge. Visitors may watch a graduation ceremony (one takes place monthly at 1:30pm on a specified Saturday), tour the kennels, and see a demonstration of the dogs' skills. *350 Los Ranchitos Rd; 800/295-4050; www.guidedogs.com; drop-in tours of the campus 10:30am and 2pm Mon–Sat.*

San Rafael

San Rafael wins the prize for being the oldest, largest, and most culturally diverse city in Marin. **SAN RAFAEL ARCANGEL** (1104 5th Ave; 415/454-8141), the second-to-last in the California mission chain, was founded here in 1817. Masses in Haitian and Vietnamese are conducted regularly at the mission chapel. Every second weekend in June, the **ITALIAN STREET PAINTING FESTIVAL** (415/457-4878; www.youthinarts.org) takes place on Fifth Avenue and A Street in front of the mission. Scores of professional and student artists create chalk reproductions of old masterpieces or vivid original works.

The **MARIN COUNTY CIVIC CENTER** (3501 Civic Center Dr; 415/499-6400; www.marincenter.org) was the last design on Frank Lloyd Wright's famous drawing board. Completed in 1969, the center is the seat of county government and has been designated a state and national historic landmark. Its 74-foot golden spire, rising above the azure roof, is a familiar beacon for those traveling north on Highway 101.

Fourth Street coffeehouses, trendy microbreweries, and restaurants with international cuisine offer popular choices night and day. Movie buffs will enjoy the **SAN RAFAEL FILM CENTER** (1118 4th St; 415/454-1222; www.cafilm.org), a vintage art deco theater restored to perfection in 1998. Independent and art films from all over the world are showcased year-round.

RESTAURANTS

Royal Thai / ★★

610 3RD ST, SAN RAFAEL; 415/485-1074

Now that Thai restaurants have sprouted up all over the Bay Area, it takes something special to lure people away from their neighborhood favorites.

Royal Thai, housed in a restored Victorian frame house underneath Highway 101, brings in Thai aficionados from far and wide. Chef-owner Jamie and co-owner Pat Disyamonthon's dishes are expertly prepared and beautifully presented, but what really distinguishes this restaurant is its range. In addition to thick coconut-milk curries and perfect pad thai, it turns out a kaleidoscope of beef and chicken saté sparkling with ginger paste, chile oil, nuts, fresh mint, basil, and garlic. Other favorites are the salmon in red curry sauce and the barbecued squid. *$; AE, DIS, MC, V; no checks; lunch Mon–Fri, dinner every day; full bar; reservations recommended on weekends; www.royalthaisanrafael.com; in the little French Quarter shopping area under Hwy 101 between 3rd and 4th sts.*

Yet Wah / ★★

1238 4TH ST, SAN RAFAEL; 415/460-9883

There are many Yet Wahs—the restaurant started in San Francisco in 1969 and has replicated itself throughout the Bay Area since then, for good reason. The menu is classic Chinese—glazed walnut prawns, Mandarin beef, barbecued spareribs—and the food is always plentiful, beautifully presented, and reliably good. The spring rolls are crunchy and the hot-and-sour soup is both. The Marin branch of Yet Wah began life as a classic Mandarin-style restaurant near Larkspur Landing and has been reborn downtown, warmly decorated in a modern theme—think upscale Hong Kong: a cross between elegant and trendy. The service is quick and quiet. Yet Wah offers lunch specials during the week and is often crowded. *$; AE, MC, V; no checks; lunch, dinner every day; full bar; reservations recommended; www.yetwahsanrafael.com; downtown.* ♿

LODGINGS

Gerstle Park Inn / ★★★

34 GROVE ST, SAN RAFAEL; 415/721-7611 OR 800/726-7611

One step onto the grounds of this inviting inn and you'll want to stay, return often, and share the experience with family and friends. Tucked away on a quiet street in the charming old Gerstle Park neighborhood in San Rafael, it's like no other place in Marin—or almost anywhere. Each of the unique suites in the wood-shingled main house has a private bath and an individual patio or deck; four suites have Jacuzzi tubs. The Lodge, or Honeymoon Suite, comes with a separate parlor, private outside entrance, and two-person Jacuzzi tub with shower. Families and long-term guests might prefer one of the two separate cottages, complete with living room, bedroom, and kitchen. Business travelers especially appreciate the high-tech amenities and the comfortable balance between a full-service hotel and a homelike environment. All guests enjoy the idyllic 1½-acre setting and proximity to beautiful Gerstle Park. A full breakfast is served either in the glassed-in sunporch, outside on the terrace, or in suites. The kitchen is open to guests at all hours for snacks and beverages. *$$$–$$$$; AE, DIS, MC, V; checks OK; www.gerstleparkinn.com; off San Rafael Ave.* ♿

EAST BAY, SOUTH BAY, AND THE PENINSULA

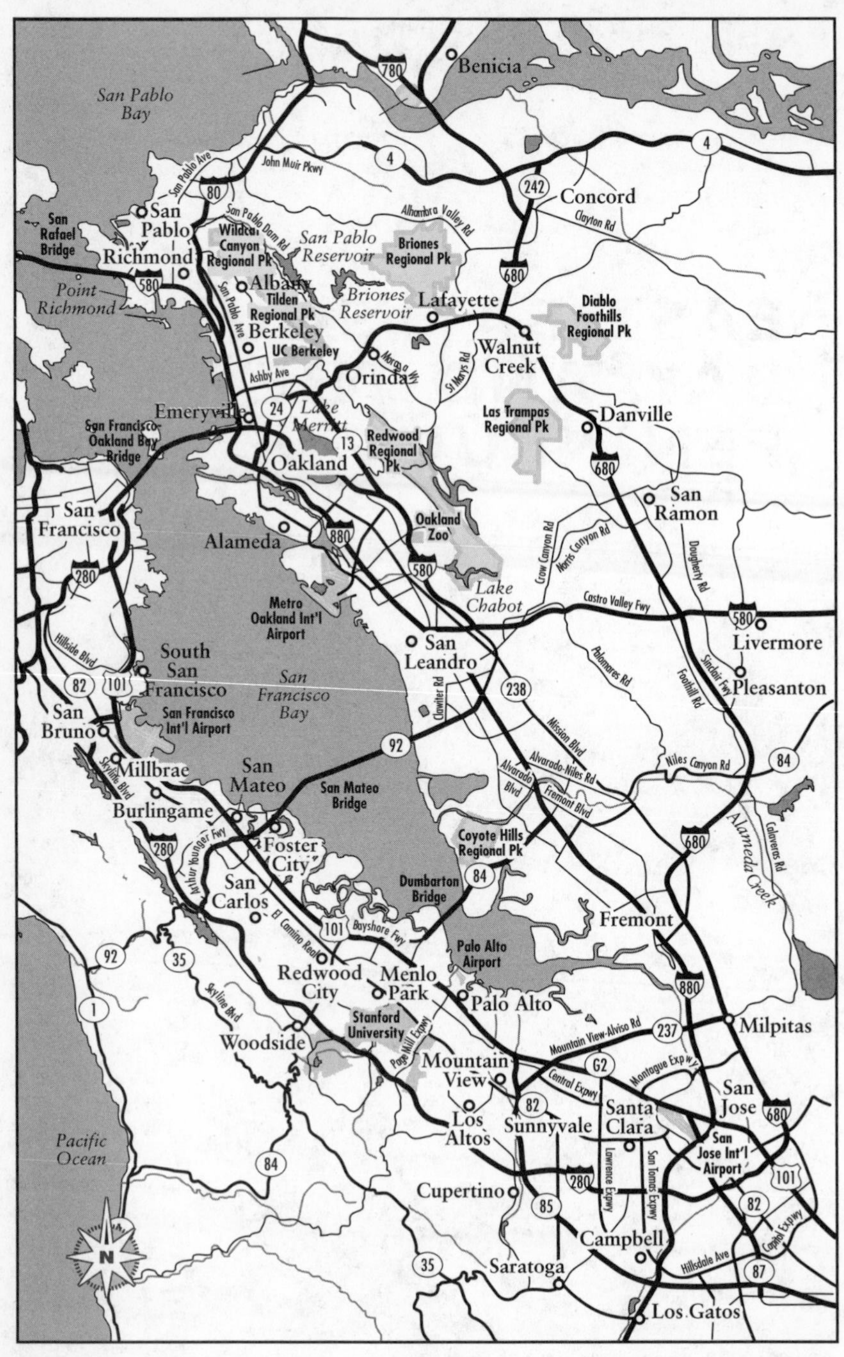
San Pablo Bay
Benicia
Concord
San Pablo
Richmond
San Rafael Bridge
Point Richmond
Albany
Berkeley
UC Berkeley
Wildcat Canyon Regional Pk
Tilden Regional Pk
San Pablo Reservoir
Briones Regional Pk
Briones Reservoir
Lafayette
Orinda
Walnut Creek
Diablo Foothills Regional Pk
Emeryville
Lake Merritt
Oakland
San Francisco-Oakland Bay Bridge
Redwood Regional Pk
Las Trampas Regional Pk
Danville
San Ramon
San Francisco
Alameda
Oakland Zoo
Lake Chabot
Metro Oakland Int'l Airport
San Leandro
Livermore
Pleasanton
South San Francisco
San Francisco Bay
San Bruno
San Francisco Int'l Airport
Millbrae
Burlingame
San Mateo
San Mateo Bridge
Foster City
San Carlos
Coyote Hills Regional Pk
Dumbarton Bridge
Fremont
Alameda Creek
Redwood City
Menlo Park
Palo Alto
Palo Alto Airport
Stanford University
Woodside
Milpitas
Mountain View
Los Altos
Sunnyvale
Santa Clara
San Jose
San Jose Int'l Airport
Cupertino
Campbell
Saratoga
Los Gatos
Pacific Ocean
N
San Pablo Ave
John Muir Pkwy
San Pablo Dam Rd
Alhambra Valley Rd
Clayton Rd
Ashby Ave
Moraga Wy
St Marys Rd
Crow Canyon Rd
Norris Canyon Rd
Dougherty Rd
Castro Valley Fwy
Palomares Rd
Foothill Rd
Sinclair Fwy
Hillside Blvd
Skyline Blvd
Clawiter Rd
Mission Blvd
Alvarado-Niles Rd
Alvarado Blvd
Fremont Blvd
Niles Canyon Rd
Calaveras Rd
Arthur Younger Fwy
El Camino Real
Bayshore Fwy
Page Mill Expwy
Mountain View-Alviso Rd
Central Expwy
Montague Expwy
Lawrence Expwy
San Tomas Expwy
Hillsdale Ave
Capitol Expwy
780
4
80
242
680
580
24
13
880
280
238
82
101
92
84
35
1
237
G2
85
87

EAST BAY, SOUTH BAY, AND THE PENINSULA

It's been a long time coming, but the Bay Area is finally growing out of the restrictive name "the San Francisco Bay Area." It's as if the once lesser-known municipalities of the Bay Area, like younger siblings paying due respect to an older one, are saying to San Francisco, "Thank you very much for all you've done for us, but we've got our own identities now and would prefer to be called by our own names."

To the south of San Francisco on a verdant stretch of land referred to as the Peninsula, with the Pacific Ocean on one side and a grand bay on the other, lie the posh communities of Burlingame, Redwood City, Woodside, and San Carlos. Posher still, if that's even possible, is Atherton, as well as Menlo Park and most of Palo Alto, situated farther south.

Beyond the Peninsula, capping the bottom tip of the bay, is that massive and sometimes ambiguous stretch of land known as Silicon Valley—perhaps the only instance on earth in which a business moniker has redefined geography. Silicon Valley is a valley, true, but where it stops and starts is difficult to track. It includes, at present, Santa Clara, Sunnyvale, Mountain View, and even Saratoga and Los Gatos, but keep an eye on it as it inches its way toward Morgan Hill to the south.

Working your way up the eastern side of the bay, banked by rolling hills, you'll find Milpitas—once the butt of Bay Area jokes because its only claim to fame was a sprawling dump site, but now a blossoming residential city rising from the compost of its former reputation. North of Milpitas are Fremont, Newark, Hayward, and San Leandro. Across the bay from San Francisco is Oakland; once considered the bad stepchild of the Bay Area, it's now in the throes of a renaissance. Baby boomers will remember Berkeley, to the north of Oakland, for its legacy of '60s radicalism. Farther north still are Albany, Richmond, Pinole, and the charming Benicia.

East Bay

You've heard the comments about Californians: "Oh, those Californians are weird," or "Oh, those sprout-eating, tree-hugging Californians." When tightly wound outsiders refer to Californians as too "granola" or "woo-woo" or just plain old "touchy-feely," they don't realize they are unwittingly complimenting the East Bay, from whence the perception came. There are good reasons for the perception.

First of all, the East Bay is cradled by the San Francisco Bay on one side and a range of beautifully undulating hills on the other—an enviable location for any segment of civilization. Who wouldn't feel a little "organic" living in such surroundings? The East Bay is also home to the largest regional park system in the United States. Founded in the 1930s, the system boasts 59 exquisitely maintained parks and untamed sanctuaries—each a haven for indigenous wildlife and plants as well as the East Bayers who cherish them.

EAST BAY AREA THREE-DAY TOUR

DAY ONE: *The historic hills of the East Bay*. Start your day with a hearty breakfast at beloved local establishment **CABRILLO PARK CAFÉ** (4673 Thornton Ave, Fremont; 510/792-2664). From there, it's off to **MISSION SAN JOSE**, (43300 Mission Blvd, Fremont; www.missionsanjose.org) one of the 21 world-famous Spanish missions in California. If you're feeling energetic, you can pack a picnic lunch, hike to the top of **MISSION PEAK** (E end of Stanford Ave, off Mission Blvd, Fremont; 510/562-7275), and enjoy a breathtaking view of the Bay Area. If, however, the mission has whetted your appetite for more history, including the kind you can purchase, drive down Mission Boulevard to **NILES** (Alvarado Niles Blvd, Fremont; 510/742-9868; www.niles.org). Originally intended to be the moviemaking capital of the world—where Charlie Chaplin was filmed in his early movies—it's now a charming, refurbished enclave of antique shops and restaurants. Stop by the **TYME FOR TEA & CO.** (37501 Niles Blvd, Fremont; 510/790-0944) for a light lunch and tea. After you've returned to your room and freshened up, walk across the street to **OLIVE HYDE ART GALLERY** (123 Washington Blvd, Fremont; 510/791-4357) and enjoy one of the many rotating exhibits featuring the first-rate work of local artists. For dinner and gourmet Italian, the best choice is **RISTORANTE IL PORCINO** (3339 Walnut Ave, Fremont; 510/791-7383). Drive 30 miles north to Berkeley and drag your bag-laden self to your luxurious room at the **CLAREMONT RESORT AND SPA**.

DAY TWO: *Shop-till-you-drop day*. After breakfast at the inn, put on comfortable shoes and drive up to Berkeley's famous **FOURTH STREET**. There you'll find an array of stores including the **GARDENER** (1836 Fourth St; 510/548-4545; www.thegardener.com), which features the finest in ethnic antiques, contemporary home decor, and an olfactory delight of a bed-and-bath department. Other gorgeous boutiques dot the narrow street, including **SUMMER HOUSE**, **SUR LA TABLE**, **GARDEN HOME**, and **MIKI'S PAPER** for beautiful handmade papers. There's even an exotic pet store on Fifth Street, **VIVARIUM** (1827-C Fifth St, Berkeley; 510/ 841-1400; www.eastbayvivarium.com)—almost as educational as a trip to the zoo. Enjoy lunch at **BETTE'S OCEANVIEW DINER**, but expect a wait and don't expect an ocean view because you won't be anywhere near the ocean.

Aside from being a topographical paradise, the region is also known for representing just about every ethnicity and major religion in the world. It's a place where Chinese, Ethiopian, Cambodian, and Brazilian cuisine is readily available; where a mosque and a church can be happy neighbors; where you can hear the

However, if you want to see the bay and distant San Francisco, go to the nearby **BERKELEY MARINA** (510/981-6740) for an after-lunch walk. Then, assuming you haven't had your fill of shopping, wander through **IKEA** in Emeryville. The Swedish home store opened in April 2000 to a crowd of approximately 15,000 and still attracts throngs of people on a daily basis. Return to the Claremont and collapse poolside or schedule an afternoon massage to loosen your limbs. Then, having made your dinner reservations in advance, head over to **CHEZ PANISSE**, the most notoriously divine restaurant in Northern California, for a meal you'll never forget.

DAY THREE: *Park-yourself-someplace day*. After a luxurious breakfast and equally luxurious view at **JORDAN'S**, located in the Claremont Resort, you're pretty much on your own. The only requirement is that you choose one of the East Bay's 59 regional parks to visit—one cannot experience the East Bay without enjoying the natural beauty that comprises over 91,000 acres of its total mass. **LAKE CHABOT** (17930 Lake Chabot Rd, Castro Valley) is nestled in the hills and features boating and incredibly scenic walks. Before you head out, pack a picnic lunch of delectables from **WHOLE FOODS MARKET** (3000 Telegraph Ave; 510/649-1333) in Berkeley.

MOUNT DIABLO (96 Mitchell Canyon Rd, Clayton; 925/837-2525) is one of the most bucolic spots and, with its spectacular views, one of the most awe-inspiring. This, after all, is the point from which much of the Bay Area's early survey work was done because it was and is the highest peak for miles. **DIABLO FOOTHILLS PARK** (1700 Castle Rock Rd, Walnut Creek; 510-562-7275), entrée to Mount Diablo, has no developed facilities but is perfect for hiking and wildlife watching. If you decide on Diablo, leave for the mountain early. **TILDEN PARK** (2501 Grizzly Peak Blvd, Berkeley; 510/ 843-2137) is thought of as the jewel of the East Bay park system. Some of its many attractions are the Botanic Garden, Lake Anza, and the Herschell Spillman merry-go-round, complete with intricately carved antique horses. After communing with nature, end the day by indulging in a romantic dinner at **BAY WOLF RESTAURANT** in Oakland. Before you settle in for a night at the Claremont Resort, stop by the famous **FENTON'S CREAMERY** (4226 Piedmont Ave, Oakland; 510/658-7000) for some memorable homemade ice cream—or, better yet, pick up a pint to go.

exuberant harmonies of a gospel choir on one corner, then cross the street and be mesmerized by chanting coming from an ashram. And, not to refute the rumors, it's a place where words like karma, chakras, channeling, aromatherapy, Reiki, and feng shui are part of everyday mainstream vocabulary.

ACCESS AND INFORMATION

The influx of people into the Bay Area has turned its freeway and bridge system into a bay-wide web. On these highways, there are only a few precious hours on a weekday—sometimes even on a weekend—when you actually get up to the speed limit. So if your destination is the East Bay, it's advisable to fly directly into **OAKLAND INTERNATIONAL AIRPORT (OAK)** (1 Airport Dr; 510/563-3300; www.oaklandairport.com) rather than its San Francisco or San Jose counterparts. Shuttle services such as **DOOR TO DOOR** (888/806-8463) or **BAYPORTER EXPRESS** (415/467-1800 or 877/467-1800) abound. Taxis are available, though not in unending streams, and charge a flat rate of $30 from the airport to downtown Oakland.

The Bay Area's public transit crown jewel is still **BAY AREA RAPID TRANSIT**, or **BART** (510/465-2278), but even though locals would agree it's in the Bay Area and it's transit, they'd likely take issue with the "rapid" part. Consider yourself warned. Occasional delays aside, it's still a relatively stress free, quiet way to travel the greater part of the Bay Area. BART now has six lines, including a San Francisco International Airport line. Hours of operation are weekdays 4am–midnight, Saturday 6am–midnight, and Sunday 8am–midnight. **AC TRANSIT** (Alameda/Contra Costa Transit; 510/817-1717 or 511 and say "AC Transit") is the bus system covering Alameda and western Contra Costa counties and also provides trans-bay service from those areas to San Francisco. If your travels take you into San Francisco from the East Bay, try slicing the waters of the bay via ferry; it's the most scenic and enjoyable way to get there. Just make sure you wear a jacket, as it's always several degrees colder than on land. The **OAKLAND/ALAMEDA FERRY** (510/522-3300) runs between Alameda, Oakland, and San Francisco on a daily basis, and the **HARBOR BAY MARITIME** (510/769-5500) provides commuter service from Harbor Bay Isle in Alameda to San Francisco.

Unlike its politics, the Bay Area's weather is moderate most of the year, but there are several microclimates that vary by a few degrees. The Peninsula, like San Francisco, is generally the coolest because it's closest to the ocean; the East Bay is often two to four degrees warmer; and San Jose can run a couple of degrees warmer still. Savvy residents whose agendas will take them to more than one locale in the course of a day will not leave the house unlayered—ready to strip or cloak themselves at a moment's notice. Of course, the El Niño and La Niña cycles have made the weather a bit unpredictable over the past few years, but it's still safe to say that in winter and spring you can expect some rain, and summer will be temperate. The real treat comes in early fall, and it goes by the name Indian summer. Then you can expect temperatures to rise as if summer is offering everyone one last hurrah before disappearing into a mellow autumn.

The staff at the office of the **OAKLAND CONVENTION AND VISITORS BUREAU** (463 11th St, near Broadway; 510/839-9000; www.oaklandcvb.com) is cordial and helpful. The **BERKELEY CONVENTION AND VISITORS BUREAU AND FILM COMMISSION** (510/549-7040) is at 2015 Center Street, between Shattuck and Milvia (www.visitberkeley.com).

Benicia

RESTAURANTS

Camellia Tea Room / ★★

828 1ST ST, BENICIA; 707/746-5293

If you've fallen under the spell of the ubiquitous tea trend, but are put off by the formality of the English ritual, you'll appreciate the Camellia Tea Room. Located in historic Benicia in a sunflower-yellow Victorian storefront, this minute establishment pays homage to the afternoon tea tradition with a decidedly California-esque nod. Try the Traditional Tea, which includes finger sandwiches, scones, wickedly rich Devon cream, chocolate cookies, and other sweets. Of course, the featured act is tea, and the 42-tea menu doesn't disappoint. If the three-tiered sandwich and cake presentations aren't your cup of tea, consider the reasonably priced, though minimal, lunch menu and follow with a decadent dessert like chocolate-orange cloud cake. *$$; DC, MC, V; checks OK; lunch, tea service Tues–Sun; champagne only; reservations recommended; www.camelliatearoom.com; near the corner of 1st and Military sts.* ♿

Walnut Creek

RESTAURANTS

Prima / ★★

1520 N MAIN ST, WALNUT CREEK; 925/945-1800

When Italophiles Michael and Janet Verlander first offered sidewalk dining outside their restaurant on Walnut Creek's tree-lined Main Street, the city had laws against it. City politicos soon wised up, however, so now you can people watch to your heart's content while savoring chef Peter Chastain's fine repertoire of northern Italian specialties. If you've opted for dining alfresco, start with a refreshing watermelon cocktail of mint, chives, and aged balsamico. Then try a perfectly al dente tagliolini with fresh seafood and house-dried organic tomatoes sautéed in a white wine sauce, or sample the risotto of the day. The roasted loin of rabbit wrapped in pancetta with fresh morels and mashed potatoes or the grilled pork rib chop smothered with braised fennel are just a couple of the well-executed entrées prepared nightly. The wine list is encyclopedic—more than 1,500 California, Italian, and French bottles, with several available by the taste or the glass. Some can even be purchased in the adjacent wine shop. Prima's patrons are treated to live jazz on the grand piano starting at 7pm Thursday through Saturday. *$$; AE, DIS, MC, V; no checks; lunch Mon–Sat, dinner every day; full bar; reservations recommended; www.primaristorante.com; downtown, near Lincoln St.* ♿

Lafayette

LODGINGS

Lafayette Park Hotel / ★★

3287 MOUNT DIABLO BLVD, LAFAYETTE; 925/283-3700

Set at the end of a cobblestone drive on a hill on the east side of town, this golden ersatz French château is a briskly efficient operation catering to the booming Contra Costa corporate scene. In keeping with its upscale image, rates are steep for this part of the Bay Area (about $175 to $400). But the 139 rooms—all of which are designated nonsmoking—are suitably commodious. Wood-burning fireplaces and vaulted ceilings adorn the more luxurious rooms and suites. Bathrooms are equipped with Italian granite counters, hair dryers, ironing boards, and telephones. An inviting 50-foot heated lap pool, a Jacuzzi, a redwood sauna, and a fitness center are also available to guests 24 hours a day. The hotel's cushy Duck Club Restaurant offers a small, pricey menu featuring filet mignon, fresh fish, pasta, and, of course, plenty of duck, including a light crepe topped with crème fraîche and a succulent roasted duckling with orange-raspberry sauce. A prix-fixe menu with well-selected, mostly California wine pairings is worth the splurge ($75 per person). The hotel's Bistro at the Park—reminiscent of an erudite men's club lounge—is a great place for a drink. *$$$; AE, DC, DIS, MC, V; checks OK; www.lafayetteparkhotel.com; from Hwy 24, take Pleasant Hill Rd S exit and turn right on Mount Diablo Blvd.*

Danville

RESTAURANTS

Blackhawk Grille / ★★

3540 BLACKHAWK PLAZA CIRCLE, DANVILLE; 925/736-4295

In the exclusive community of Blackhawk, this glamorous, offbeat 7,000-square-foot restaurant is a testament to California's adoration of the automobile. The Grille's exotic interior glows with brushed stainless steel, copper, and verdigris. Lighting fixtures are stylized hubcap sconces, and the bar is topped with etched glass. There's an eclectic but down-to-earth menu of wood-fired pizzas plus satisfying and competently prepared entrées, including the pan-seared Alaskan halibut with golden tomato gazpacho, bay shrimp, and sweet peppers. The wine list is vast and focuses on California vintners. Desserts, like everything else about this place, are excessive and fluctuate in quality: try the decadent Blackhawk peanut butter cup with roasted peanut fudge gelato and chocolate ganache or the blackberry-cassis granita with macerated berries and vanilla tuile. *$$$; AE, DC, DIS, MC, V; no checks; lunch Mon–Sat, dinner every day, brunch Sun; full bar; reservations recommended; www.calcafe.com; from I-680, take Crow Canyon exit, head east on Crow Canyon, drive 7 miles to Camino Tassajara, and bear right to Blackhawk Plaza.* ♿

Bridges / ★★★

44 CHURCH ST, DANVILLE; 925/820-7200

Japanese businessman Kazuo Sugitani was so happy with the education his son received at Danville's famed Athenian prep school that he wanted to give something back to the town. Blending the best of East and West cuisine, Bridges is a pretty nifty gift. Sugitani eventually passed the restaurant on to his son Ryoto, who wisely recruited executive chef Allen Vitti, previously of Fringale in San Francisco. Vitti has created a pared-down selection of superbly well-crafted dishes, including a delicate three-fish tartare of ahi, yellowfin tuna, and salmon with diced mangoes, tomatoes, and avocados; a seared lemongrass-rosemary marinated rack of lamb served with mashed sweet potatoes and a cherry port wine sauce; a melt-in-your-mouth spinach and mushroom ravioli; and spicy pan-seared sea scallops and prawns with a roasted pepper curry sauce. The respectable wine list includes an extensive collection of dessert wines to match such sweet delights as the Tahitian vanilla-bean crème brûlée, a berry pudding topped with lychee gelée, or the popular go-ahead-and-splurge dessert sampler for two. For those on a budget, step across the street to Bridges' latest offspring, Zensai, for a slightly more Pacific Rim experience at much slighter prices. *$$$; AE, DC, MC, V; no checks; dinner Tues–Sat; full bar; reservations recommended; www.bridges restaurant-bar.com; from I-680, take Diablo Rd exit, go west to Hartz Ave, turn left on Hartz, and drive 2 blocks to Church St.*

San Ramon

RESTAURANTS

Bighorn Grill / ★★

2410 SAN RAMON VALLEY BLVD, SAN RAMON; 925/838-5678

As the name suggests, this pleasant Western-themed restaurant attracts big beef eaters. They come for baby back pork ribs slathered with a watermelon barbecue sauce, meat loaf topped with country gravy and mashed sweet potatoes, and a 14-ounce garlic-roasted Black Angus New York steak, to name just a few of the meaty entrées. Freshly tossed salads and pasta and fish dishes are also on the menu. Designed by popular San Francisco Bay Area restaurateur Pat Kuleto (think Farallon, Kuleto's, and Boulevard), the Bighorn's large, airy, lodgelike dining room has antler chandeliers and horn-shaped hooks on the walls. A bronze bighorn sheep's head hangs over the long bar, where urban cowboys and business execs sip frosty beers or very large martinis. Families love the Bighorn, too, and a Just for Kids menu caters to the young buckaroo wannabes. *$$; AE, MC, V; no checks; lunch Mon–Fri, dinner every day; full bar; reservations recommended; www.bighorngrill.com; near Crow Canyon Rd.* ♿

Cafe Esin / ★★

750 CAMINO RAMON, DANVILLE; 925/314-0974

At first glance this nondescript little place in a suburban strip mall appears to be little more than a generic, run-of-the-mill restaurant. But looks can be deceiving, and when it comes to the food, Cafe Esin is neither generic nor run-of-the-mill. Husband-and-wife team Curtis and Esin DeCarion cook up simple, exceptionally well-prepared food for lucky Contra Costa residents. Look for Mediterranean-inspired dishes like creamy zucchini fritters with a tangy yogurt-dill sauce and grilled chicken breast salad with toasted pecans, blue cheese, and raisins. Nourishing entrées include a couple of fresh pastas daily (like fettuccine with rock shrimp and mushrooms in a light cream sauce); Niman Ranch pot roast with garlic mashed potatoes; and grilled pork tenderloin served with fruit chutney and fingerling potatoes. The exquisite dessert list might include up to 10 choices, like seasonal fruit tarts with winning combinations of raspberries and figs dabbed with whipped cream, classic crème brûlée, and the signature Esin's baklava. A substantial wine list features a range of mostly California wines, with several good choices available by the glass. *$$; AE, DC, MC, V; no checks; lunch Tues–Fri, dinner Tues–Sat; full bar; reservations recommended; www.cafeesin.com; near Crown Canyon Rd.* ♿

Livermore

RESTAURANTS

Wente Vineyards Restaurant / ★★★

5050 ARROYO RD, LIVERMORE; 925/456-2400

The Wente family couldn't have devised a better way to showcase its wines than with this exquisite neo-Spanish colonial restaurant set among the vineyards and rolling hills of the 1,200-acre Wente estate. Chef Kimball Jones's daily-changing menu is a pleasant blend of traditional and experimental, showcasing fresh Hog Island oysters on the half shell served with a sparkling wine mignonette and roasted butternut squash soup with crème fraîche and sage. House-smoked meats and fresh fish are presented with intriguing, tangy sauces and exotic chutneys, and Wente's trademark beef dishes, such as rib-eye steak with a fire-roasted onion and portobello mushroom relish, are delicious. While it's unfortunate that the Wente wines don't usually measure up to the food, the good news is that the restaurant sells other wines, too. *$$$; AE, DC, MC, V; checks OK; lunch Mon–Sat, dinner every day, brunch Sun; wine and wine-based spirits; reservations recommended; www.wentevineyards.com; follow L St until it turns into Arroyo Rd, about 4 miles south of town.* ♿

Point Richmond

LODGINGS

Hotel Mac / ★★

10 COTTAGE AVE, POINT RICHMOND; 510/235-0010

Who would have thought there'd be a handsome hotel nestled in the quaint village of Point Richmond, a remote hamlet straddling the edge of the city of Richmond? Built in 1911, this imposing three-story, red-brick edifice on the National Register of Historic Places was remodeled in 1995 and now offers 10 lovely guest rooms (including two deluxe suites) that cost half as much as similar rooms in San Francisco. Each unit is individually decorated with rich, colorful fabrics and brass light fixtures, and the windows are framed with handsome white plantation shutters. Every room also has a queen- or king-size bed, cable TV with a VCR, a small refrigerator, terry-cloth robes, and a safe for storing valuables; four rooms have gas fireplaces. Colorful stained-glass windows line the Hotel Mac's dining room, where a respectable mix of cuisine—ranging from risotto with Florida rock shrimp to rack of lamb and chicken cordon bleu—is served. But the hotel's highlight is the spacious, high-ceilinged oak and mahogany bar, an ideal place for an aperitif. A continental breakfast is included in the room rate. *$$; AE, MC, V; checks OK; www.hotelmac.net; at Washington Ave.*

Albany

RESTAURANTS

Britt-Marie's / ★★

1369 SOLANO AVE, ALBANY; 510/527-1314

As inviting as a pair of favorite slippers, Britt-Marie's offers comfort food from many corners of the globe. Partisans of the Portuguese sandwich—garlic-rubbed toast topped with salt cod and potatoes—would revolt if it were to disappear from the menu, as would avid fans of the cucumbers in garlicky sour cream, the roast chicken with herbs, and the pork schnitzel with buttered noodles. Sweet-toothed patrons can top off their meal with desserts like bourbon-pecan tart or chocolate cake with a thin layer of marzipan tucked under the chocolate frosting. *$$; no credit cards; checks OK; lunch Tues–Sat, dinner Tues–Sun; beer and wine; no reservations; between Ramona and Carmel sts.* ♿

Fonda / ★★

1501 SOLANO AVE, ALBANY; 510/559-9006

The team behind longtime favorite Lalime's in Berkeley has jumped on the tapas bandwagon to bring *antojitos*, or little Latin American plates, to Albany. Chef David Rosales, who once won the *San Francisco Chronicle*'s rising star of the year award, creates delicious flavor-packed dishes at this lively corner hot spot. If you want to be part of the action, opt for a seat at the bar or any of the downstairs tables that overlook the bustling kitchen; for a more intimate meal, head upstairs to the mezzanine. The menu features about 13 little plates, including a popular Veracruz-style cocktail brimming with scallops, sea bass, and crab; succulent duck tacos with sweet and smoky arbol salsa; unusual deep-fried quesadillas with mushrooms, epazote, and cream; and a grilled skirt steak with nopals (cactus), chayote, and an avocado salad. Be sure to try one of the specialty drinks like the eponymous Fonda—an exotic concoction of tequila and hibiscus infusion—or the fresh cucumber and vodka martini. *$$; AE, DC, MC, V; no checks; dinner every day; full bar; no reservations; www.fondasolana.com; at Curtis St.* ♿

Berkeley

The minds of Berkeley's residents are almost audible. Try walking down **TELEGRAPH AVENUE** and looking into the faces of pedestrians. You can almost hear what they're thinking. Some look pensive, nagged, as though they can't get that pesky Nietzsche quote out of their heads; others appear to be in the silent throes of planning activist strategies; while still others look as if they're communing with a presence invisible to mundane mortals. You'll conclude that Berkeley hasn't changed all that much since the '60s, when it was the earth's axis for social change—things have simply become a bit more introspective.

That's not to say Berkeleyites aren't vocal. In some respects, the action has moved from the campus and People's Park to **CITY HALL** (2180 Milvia St). There the town's residents—many of them former hippies, student intellectuals, and peace activists—seek to voice their opinions on issues from Columbus Day (Berkeley celebrates Indigenous People's Day instead) to the opening of a large video store downtown (too lowbrow and tacky). You can also find folks on a street corner or hovering near a retail establishment's door, passing out flyers and gathering petition signatures to defeat the latest unjust bill before the state senate. The *San Francisco Chronicle* once called Berkeley the "most contentious of cities," and it's a mantle most of its inhabitants either wear with pride or shrug off like an uncomfortable suit.

Don't draw conclusions just yet. Berkeley is dichotomous. It's also known for its overwhelming plethora of fine restaurants, hip boutiques, and the best furniture stores in the Bay Area. Arguably, that could be why its residents often wear looks of consternation or deep concentration—they might be trying to justify the coexistence of conspicuous consumption and heightened consciousness in the same city. Or maybe they're trying to decide where to eat.

MAJOR ATTRACTIONS

If you're a newcomer to Berkeley, start your tour of the town at the world-renowned **UC BERKELEY CAMPUS** (www.berkeley.edu), also known as Cal, the oldest and second largest of the nine campuses of the UC system. Driving

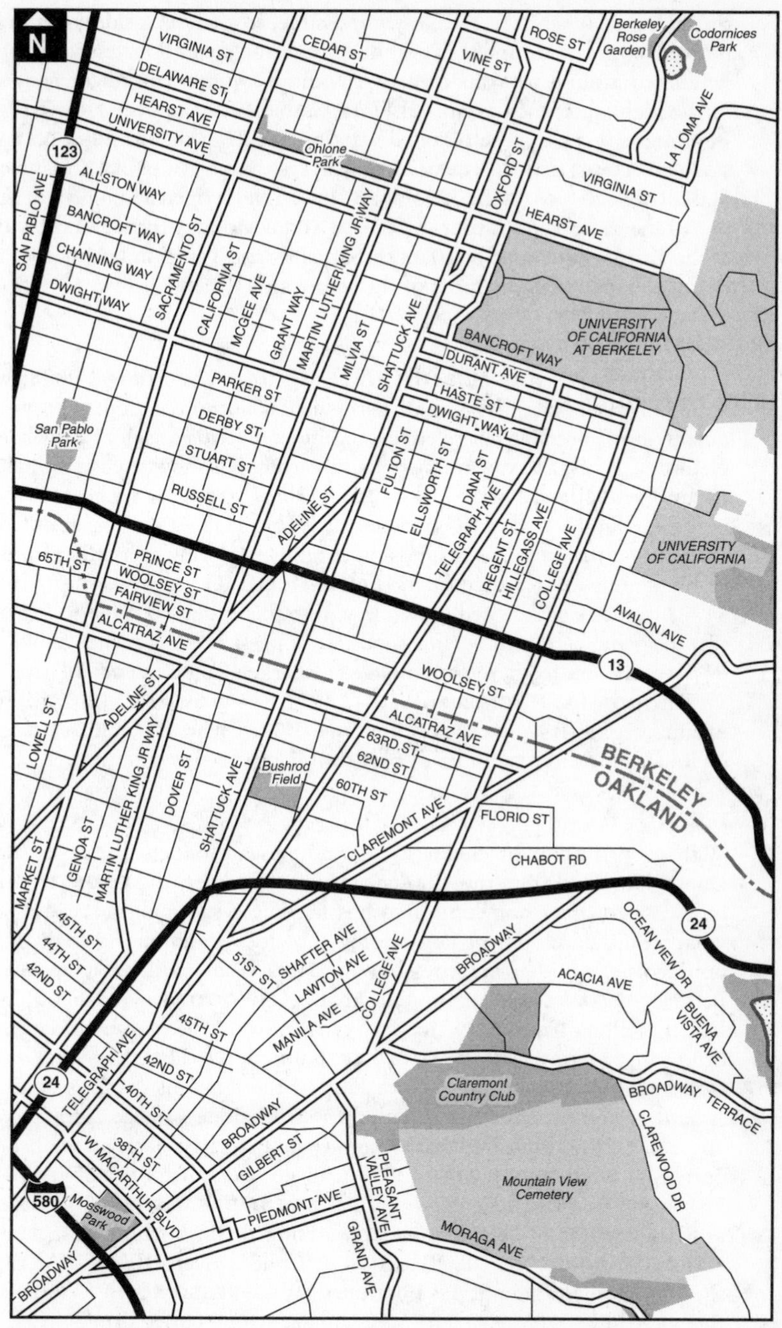

Berkeley and North Oakland

through the university is virtually impossible, so park on a side street and set out on foot. The campus isn't so huge that you'd get hopelessly lost if you wandered around on your own, but without a guide you might miss some of the highlights, such as Sproul Plaza, Sather Gate, and the Hearst Mining Building. So pick up a self-guided walking packet at the **UC BERKELEY VISITOR INFORMATION CENTER** (2200 University Ave at Oxford St, University Hall, Room 101; 510/642-5215 or 510/642-INFO; open Mon–Fri), or attend one of the free one-hour tours offered at 10am Monday through Friday (meet at the visitor center) and at 10am on Saturday and 1pm Sunday (meet in front of the Campanile in the heart of the campus).

MUSEUMS

The **UNIVERSITY ART MUSEUM** (2626 Bancroft Wy; 510/642-0808; www.bampfa.berkeley.edu) has a small, permanent collection of modern art and frequently hosts peculiar but riveting exhibitions by artists such as Robert Mapplethorpe. A vast array of anthropological artifacts is showcased at the **PHOEBE HEARST MUSEUM OF ANTHROPOLOGY** (510/643-7649; www.hearstmuseum.berkeley.edu), located in UC Berkeley's Kroeber Hall, at the corner of College Avenue and Bancroft Way. Hands-on exhibits exploring everything from bats to holograms are featured at the **LAWRENCE HALL OF SCIENCE** (510/642-5132; www.lhs.berkeley.edu). While you're there, duck outside to hear (and see) the giant, eerie wind chimes and take a peek at the Stonehenge-like solar observatory, located in the hills above UC Berkeley on Centennial Drive.

The **JUDAH L. MAGNES MUSEUM** (2911 Russel St; 510/549-6950; www.magnes.org) offers numerous exhibitions of Jewish art and culture, including a Holocaust memorial and a display of modern Jewish paintings.

SHOPPING

With its profusion of chichi stores and upscale outlets (Crate & Barrel, Dansk, Sur La Table, the Gardener, Sweet Potatoes, the **FOURTH STREET** (www.fourthstreetshop.com) area has become a shopping mecca—a somewhat ironic development considering the city's traditional disdain for the bourgeoisie. Another favorite shopping area is in south Berkeley, near the Berkeley-Oakland border, in the small **ELMWOOD** neighborhood, which stretches along College Avenue and crosses over Ashby Avenue. Poke your head into the tiny **TAIL OF THE YAK** boutique (2632 Ashby Ave, west of College Ave; 510/841-9891) for a look at the fabulous displays of Central American and other art treasures, then stroll along College Avenue, where you can pet the lop-eared baby bunnies and squawk back at the beautiful parrots at **YOUR BASIC BIRD** (2940 College Ave, north of Ashby; 510/841-7617); dip into the huge candy jars at **SWEET DREAMS** (2901 College Ave at Russell; 510/548-8697); munch on a fantastic fresh-fruit cheese danish at **NABOLOM BAKERY** (2708 Russell St at College Ave; 510/845-BAKE); and shop for clothes at numerous boutiques. At **ESPRESSO ROMA** (2960 College Ave at Ashby; 510/644-3773), you can sip strong coffee drinks, teas, fresh lemonade, beer on tap, or wine by the glass and eat some good calzones and sandwiches. On the other side of Berkeley, where the northwest border meets the little town of Albany, is Solano Avenue, a popular mile-long street lined with shops and cafés frequented by locals.

BLACK OAK BOOKS (1491 Shattuck Ave; 510/486-0698) is a popular purveyor of new and used books. The four-story **MOE'S BOOKS** (2476 Telegraph Ave; 510/849-2087) specializes in used tomes and remainders. And a **BARNES & NOBLE** megastore (5604 Bay St; 510/547-0905) offers discounts on *New York Times* best sellers and hardcover books, and stocks hundreds of periodicals.

For some of the best bread in the Bay Area, go to Steve Sullivan's famous **ACME BREAD COMPANY** (1601 San Pablo Ave; 510/524-1327) or the **CHEESE BOARD** (1504 Shattuck Ave; 510/549-3183), a collectively owned bakery and vast gourmet cheese shop. If you're a bagel lover, two Berkeley bagel shops rival Brooklyn's best: **NOAH'S BAGELS** (3170 College Ave, 510/654-0944; and 1883 Solano Ave, 510/525-4447) and **BOOGIE WOOGIE BAGEL BOY** (1281 Gilman St; 510/524-3104).

Like many university towns, this one seems to run on coffee. **PEET'S COFFEE & TEA** (2124 Vine St, 510/841-0564; 2916 Domingo Ave, 510/843-1434; 1825 Solano Ave, 510/526-9607), with its sizable selection of beans and teas, is the local favorite. For an outdoor latte beneath the trees, try **CAFFE STRADA** (2300 College Ave; 510/843-5282) or the hip, crowded, college-hangout **CAFE MILANO** (2522 Bancroft Wy; 510/644-3100). **CAFFE MEDITERRANEUM** (2475 Telegraph Ave; 510/549-1128) churns out excellent cappuccinos and captures the bohemian flavor of Telegraph Avenue, still a favorite of students, street people, runaways, hipsters, professors, tarot readers, and street vendors. Or check out the homemade pastries and tasty lunch fare at **INTERMEZZO CAFE** (2442 Telegraph Ave; 510/849-4592), another popular Berkeley haunt.

Some of the best beer in the Bay Area is brewed at the frat-packed **TRIPLE ROCK BREWERY** (1920 Shattuck Ave; 510/843-2739). In 1997, the **PYRAMID BREWERY & ALE HOUSE** (901 Gilman St; 510/528-9880) joined the fray with a state-of-the-art brewery and refined pub fare.

For something completely different, treat your taste buds to a tour of **TAKARA SAKE USA** (708 Addison St; 510/540-8250), a sake factory that provides tastings of sake and plum wine.

PERFORMING ARTS

Music

The Berkeley Symphony blends new and experimental music with the classics at **ZELLERBACH HALL** (510/841-2800) on the UC Berkeley campus. Modern rock, funk, and acid jazz are blasted at **BLAKE'S** (2367 Telegraph Ave; 510/848-0886). If you're feeling a bit more mellow, take a seat at the **FREIGHT & SALVAGE** coffeehouse (1111 Addison St; 510/548-1761), a prime Euro-folkie hangout. In the mood to dance? Drop in at **ASHKENAZ** (1317

San Pablo Ave; 510/525-5054). Live rock, jazz, folk, reggae, and other concerts are frequently held at UC Berkeley's intimate, open-air **GREEK THEATRE** (Gayley Rd off Hearst Ave; 510/642-9988), a particularly pleasant place for sitting beneath the stars and listening to music on warm summer nights. **CAL PERFORMANCES** (510/642-9988) presents up-and-coming and established artists of all kinds—from the Bulgarian Women's Chorus to superstar mezzo-soprano Cecilia Bartoli; the concerts are held at various sites on the UC Berkeley campus.

Theater and Film

The **BERKELEY REPERTORY THEATRE** (2025 Addison St; 510/647-2949) has a national reputation for experimental productions of the classics and innovative new works, and the **BLACK REPERTORY GROUP** (3201 Adeline St; 510/652-2120) offers a range of plays, dance performances, and art by African Americans. Every summer the **CALIFORNIA SHAKESPEARE FESTIVAL** (701 Heinz Ave; 510/548-9666) performs in an outdoor theater in the Berkeley hills near Orinda (bundle up 'cause it's usually freezing). **PACIFIC FILM ARCHIVE** (2625 Durant Ave; 510/642-1412) shows underground avant-garde movies as well as the classics. For up-to-date listings of cultural events, pick up a free copy of **THE EXPRESS**, the East Bay's alternative weekly, available at cafés and newsstands throughout the area.

PARKS AND GARDENS

For more pastoral diversions, stroll through the **BERKELEY ROSE GARDEN** (Euclid Ave, between Bay View and Eunice sts), a terraced park with hundreds of varieties of roses and a great view of San Francisco. Or visit the 30-acre **UNIVERSITY OF CALIFORNIA BOTANICAL GARDEN** (Strawberry Canyon on Centennial Dr; 510/643-2755), where you'll see a spectacular collection of cacti from around the world, a Mendocino pygmy forest, a Miocene-era redwood grove, and the giant corpse flower named Odoardo. The gigantic **TILDEN REGIONAL PARK** (off Wildcat Canyon Rd; 510/525-2233), set high in the hills above town, offers miles of hiking trails plus a steam train, a merry-go-round, and a farm and nature area for kids. Tilden also boasts a beautiful **BOTANICAL GARDEN** (510/841-8732) specializing in California native plants.

RESTAURANTS

Ajanta / ★★

1888 SOLANO AVE, BERKELEY; 510/526-4373

This brightly lit and attractive restaurant is one of the East Bay's best Indian restaurants. The dining room is a serene and exotic space, with intricate woodwork, golden fabrics, and graceful reproductions of murals found in India's Ajanta cave temples. The lamb rib chops, *murg ularthu* (boneless chicken simmered in a sauce made with onions, mustard seeds, fennel, garlic, and ginger), and prawn curry are a few of the standout dishes usually featured. There are always about half a dozen vegetarian dishes to choose from, including the wonderful *baigan ki boorani* (pan-fried eggplant slices topped with a garlic-lemon yogurt sauce). *$$; AE, DC, DIS, MC, V; local checks only; lunch, dinner every day; beer and wine; reservations recommended; www.ajantarestaurant.com; near the Alameda.*

Bette's Oceanview Diner / ★★

1807-A 4TH ST, BERKELEY; 510/644-3230

The charm of Bette's Oceanview Diner doesn't have anything to do with the ocean (there's not even a view here). What this small, nouveau-'40s diner does have is red booths, chrome stools, a checkerboard tile floor, a hip waitstaff, the best jukebox around, and darn good breakfasts. On weekends expect a 45-minute stomach-growling wait, but consider the payoff: enormous soufflé-style pancakes stuffed with pecans and ripe berries, farm-fresh eggs scrambled with prosciutto and Parmesan, outstanding omelets, corned beef hash, and the quintessential huevos rancheros with black beans. If you can't bear the wait, pop into Bette's-to-Go (BTG) next door for a prebreakfast snack. Later in the day, BTG offers superlative focaccia sandwiches and California pizzas. *$; MC, V; local checks only; breakfast, lunch every day; beer and wine; no reservations; www.worldpantry.com/bettes; between Virginia St and Hearst Ave.* ♿

Cafe Fanny / ★★

1603 SAN PABLO AVE, BERKELEY; 510/524-5447

Alice Waters's diminutive corner café can handle fewer than a dozen stand-up customers at once, but that doesn't deter anyone. On sunny Saturday mornings the adjacent parking lot fills with the overflow. Named after Waters's daughter, this popular spot recalls the neighborhood cafés so dear to the French, but Fanny's food is much better. Breakfast on crunchy Cafe Fanny granola, jam-filled buckwheat crepes, or perfect soft-boiled eggs served on sourdough toast with a side of house-made jam, and sip a cafe au lait from a big authentic French handleless bowl. The morning meal is served until 11am and all day on Sunday. For lunch, order one of the seductive sandwiches, such as egg salad on crunchy Levain bread with sun-dried tomatoes and anchovies or the simple but delicious grilled eggplant with olive paste. Many fans combine a visit here with a stop at Fanny's illustrious neighbors: Acme Bread Company on one side and Kermit Lynch Wine Merchant on the other. *$; MC, V; checks OK; breakfast, lunch every day; beer and wine; no reservations; www.cafefanny.com; between Cedar and Virginia sts.*

Cafe Rouge / ★★

1782 4TH ST, BERKELEY; 510/525-1440

Opened in 1996, this Fourth Street bistro offers everything from duck braised in white wine and smoked trout with frisée and leeks to hot dogs and cheeseburgers. Maybe it all makes a little more sense when one realizes that those aforementioned burgers and franks are the creations of Niman Ranch, so they're the most upscale versions you're likely to have. In fact, chef-owner

Marsha McBride, a Zuni Cafe alumna, insists on high quality in all the ingredients, so it's hard to go wrong with anything on the small but beguiling menu. Her passions are oysters and charcuterie, but there are also creative salads and pastas, great grilled steaks, and juicy spit-roasted chicken. Desserts are absolute knockouts, including a seasonal warm quince bread pudding and a Jonathan apple puff-pastry tartlet. Many of the house-smoked charcuterie items are available in the market in the back of the airy, bilevel restaurant, which boasts a long, curved zinc counter, skylights, and gold walls punctuated by red-paper wall sconces and modern artwork. *$$$; AE, MC, V; no checks; lunch every day, dinner Tues–Sun; full bar; reservations recommended; www.caferouge.net; between Hearst Ave and Delaware St.*

César / ★★★

1515 SHATTUCK AVE, BERKELEY; 510/883-0222

This perennially packed tapas bar has proven without a doubt that the small-plates trend is here to stay. Right next door to the acclaimed Chez Panisse (César happens to be owned by Alice Waters's ex-husband), this 65-seat restaurant with a large communal table in the center of the room serves up delicious Spanish-style tapas. The no-reservations policy doesn't keep diners from coming to enjoy chef Maggie Pond's food in a convivial setting more reminiscent of a local bar than a restaurant. Start with the salty roasted almonds and a cool cucumber gazpacho. You can't go wrong here, as most of the 20 or so items on the menu are superb—especially the salt cod and potato *cazuela* (the Spanish version of brandade), which is served with slices of crunchy baguette. The *papas fritas* (fried potatoes) seasoned with cumin and garlic are delicious, as is the ham with sweet grilled figs. Dessert selections include a honey-sweetened, creamy fromage blanc served with peaches; bread pudding; and a rich crema de chocolate. *$$; AE, MC, V; no checks; lunch, dinner every day; full bar; no reservations; www.barcesar.com; between Cedar and Vine sts.*

Chez Panisse / ★★★★

1517 SHATTUCK AVE, BERKELEY; 510/548-5525

In the heart of Berkeley's gourmet ghetto, the most famous restaurant in Northern California is almost invisible from the street. Chef-owner Alice Waters has been at the forefront of the California cuisine revolution since 1971, when she started cooking simple French-influenced meals for groups of friends, then opened her legendary restaurant. Chez Panisse is divided into a fantastic (albeit expensive) prix-fixe dining room downstairs and a lighthearted (and more reasonably priced) upstairs café. Downstairs, the daily-changing dinner menu might begin with a bowl of olives and warm Acme bread, followed by aromatic, seasonal dishes such as an appetizer of thin-sliced salmon flash-cooked on a hot plate and served with an herbed flower butter, or a smooth corn-and-garlic soup flavored with a subtle touch of leek. An entrée of boneless pigeon wrapped and grilled in vine leaves has a lovely smoky quality with a hint of mint and shallots; and a simple but sensational mixed-greens salad cleanses the palate before the appearance of a beautiful kirsch-infused Bavarian pudding. The warm, bustling upstairs café has a fine wine bar and seldom enough seats to go around. Its popular pizzas and calzones, baked in a wood-burning oven, often feature ingredients such as squid and roasted onion or simply mozzarella and the finest vine-ripened tomatoes in the state. Desserts include house-made ice creams and sherbets, fruit cobblers, tarts, and pies. *$$$; AE, DC, DIS, MC, V; local checks only; dinner Mon–Sat (restaurant); lunch, dinner Mon–Sat (café); beer and wine; reservations required; www.chezpanisse.com; between Cedar and Vine sts.*

Kirala / ★★

2100 WARD ST, BERKELEY; 510/549-3486

A no-reservations policy often means a long wait at this small restaurant with the down-at-the-heels facade and plain-Jane decor. It features an extensive sake bar—boasting more than 20 premium sakes from Japan—where you can enjoy a light meal. Once you snag a seat in the dining area or sushi bar, however, get ready to taste some of the best Japanese food in town. The sushi is fresh and ready in a flash of a knife; the *gyoza* and other appetizers are first rate; and the skewers of seafood, vegetables, and meats emerging from the robata grill are cooked to perfection and seasoned with a delicate hand. *$$; AE, MC, V; no checks; lunch Tues–Fri, dinner every day; beer and wine; no reservations; www.kiralaberkeley.com; near Shattuck Ave.*

Lalime's / ★★

1329 GILMAN ST, BERKELEY; 510/527-9838

It's hard to pass Lalime's at night without stopping to stare at the goings-on through its fishbowl front window: the radiant yellow dining room boasts high ceilings, colorful collages on the walls, and a crush of sleek patrons leaning intimately over candlelit, white-linen-cloaked tables. The menu changes monthly, but if they're serving the soup made with Finn potatoes, golden beets, and ginger, or the roast garlic and shiitake mushroom ravioli, don't hesitate—they're always delicious. Desserts, such as the creamy house-made anise ice cream, mango flan, and chocolate cake with brandied cherries, are equally splendid. Lalime's prix-fixe dinners are often a good bet: one might feature seared spearfish marinated in fresh lime and curry and served with a blood-orange and fennel salad, followed by grilled chicken breast accompanied by crisp polenta triangles and a sweet onion, red pepper, and raisin relish, and, for dessert, a candied pecan tart with a buttery crust. The witty, efficient, and exceptionally knowledgeable staff can direct you to the gems on Lalime's extensive beer and wine list. *$$$; AE, MC, V; no checks; dinner every day; beer and wine; reservations recommended; www.lalimes.com; between Neilson and Peralta sts.*

O Chamé / ★★★

1830 4TH ST, BERKELEY; 510/841-8783

Even jaded Berkeley food fanatics are bewitched by the fare in this exotic restaurant. Chef David Vardy spent years studying Buddhist-Taoist cooking in Taiwan, as well as Kansai and Kaiseki cuisine in Japan. (Kansai is the regional cuisine of Osaka; Kaiseki, created to complement the Japanese tea ceremony, consists of small dishes that can be consumed in a couple of bites.) An intriguing assortment of teas, bento box lunches, Vardy's popular Nambu tea cakes—thin, sesame-based biscuits flavored with nuts or seeds—and more elaborate works of culinary art are found at O Chamé, a soothing café crafted in the style of a rustic wayside inn from Japan's Meiji period. The à la carte menu changes often, but typical dishes include a very fresh vinegared wakame seaweed, cucumber, and crab salad; tofu dumplings with burdock and carrot; grilled river eel with endive and chayote; and soba noodles with shiitake mushrooms and daikon sprouts. O Chamé also offers a range of delicately flavored teas and sakes as well as several good beers. *$$; AE, DC, MC, V; no checks; lunch, dinner Mon–Sat; beer and wine; reservations recommended; near Hearst Ave.*

Rivoli / ★★★

1539 SOLANO AVE, BERKELEY; 510/526-2542

Chef Wendy Brucker first came to the attention of East Bay diners in 1992 when she took over the kitchen of the dining room at Berkeley's Shattuck Hotel. That venue was too stiff and formal for her California sensibilities—honed at places such as San Francisco's now-shuttered Square One and the eclectic City Restaurant in L.A.—so she transferred her talents to a much more suitable place: her own, where she could have the freedom to present her relaxed yet refined ideas about California-Mediterranean cuisine. Start your meal with bruschetta topped with goat cheese, sun-dried tomatoes, and basil (a cliché, perhaps, but a wonderfully tasty one) or the renowned and expertly fried portobello mushrooms with arugula and aioli (definitely not a cliché). The grilled sage brined porkloin with honey-roasted figs and baked eggplant and fennel is the essence of good country cooking. Along with her husband and partner, Roscoe Skipper, Brucker deserves kudos for assembling a tantalizing menu that changes every three weeks. The wine list offers several good choices under $20. *$$$; AE, DC, DIS, MC, V; local checks only; dinner every day; beer and wine; reservations recommended; www.rivolirestaurant.com; between Peralta Ave and Neilson St.*

Spenger's Fresh Fish Grotto / ★★

1919 4TH ST, BERKELEY; 510/845-7771

Weary of minimalist restaurants with painfully modern furniture, vying for the title "Most Tragically Hip Eating Establishment"? Spenger's Fresh Fish Grotto is confirmation that a classic never goes out of style. This unassuming restaurant is situated in Berkeley's famous Fourth Street shopping district and was there long before it was chic—since 1890, actually. The decor is restored rather than renovated and speaks to a seafaring time long gone. The waitstaff is equally charming, having been chosen for their knowledge and dedication rather than their looks. But naturally, it's the food in which you're most interested, and Spenger's will satisfy you on every level. The menu changes twice daily, based on fresh catch availability, but you can always expect simply prepared seafood with just the right amount of detail. Appetizers include tender fried calamari and stone crab claws with jalapeños, cilantro, and Key lime juice. Main courses may include such wonders as monchong blackened with Cajun spices, served with jasmine rice and Thai coconut-curry sauce, or mahimahi, pan seared with a macadamia nut crust, served with mashed potatoes and spicy Jamaican hot rum butter. *$$$$; AE, MC, V; checks OK; lunch, dinner every day; full bar; reservations recommended; www.spengers.com; off University Ave.* ♿

LODGINGS

The Berkeley City Club / ★

2315 DURANT AVE, BERKELEY; 510/848-7800

Architect Julia Morgan called this lovely edifice with the grand Moorish flourishes her "little castle" (her "big castle" was Hearst Castle in San Simeon, the crowning achievement of her architectural career). The 1927 building, with its hallways graced by soaring buttresses and its tall lead-paned windows, garden courtyards, and handsome sandstone-colored facade, was designed as a women's club. Today both genders are welcomed through its stately portals, not only as members who enjoy the club's fitness and social activities but also as bed-and-breakfast guests. The club's 40 rooms are simply appointed, small, and old-fashioned (if the rooms were as grand as the public areas, this would be a three-star hotel), but all have private baths and many boast views of the bay, the nearby UC campus, or the Berkeley hills. If you need a bit more elbow room, try to book one of the two suites. Overnight guests have access to the club's dining room and fitness facilities, including a 25-yard-long indoor pool. Daily rates include a buffet breakfast; weekly and monthly arrangements are available, too. *$$; MC, V; checks OK; berkeleycityclub.com; between Dana and Ellsworth sts.*

The Claremont Resort and Spa / ★★★

41 TUNNEL RD, BERKELEY; 510/843-3000 OR 800/551-7266

With its towers and cupolas gleaming white against the green and golden Berkeley hills, this proud prima donna of a hotel holds fast to its Edwardian roots. It's hard to hurry here: the posh lobby with its plush furniture and alabaster chandeliers is made for loitering and gaping, while the 22 acres of gorgeous grounds invite leisurely strolling. The only folks scurrying about are those rushing the net on the Claremont's 10 championship tennis courts or feeling the burn in one of the spa's aerobics classes. Amenities include everything you'd expect in a grand hotel, including concierge and room service, a fully equipped business center, and extensive spa facilities. Parking at the resort and transportation to the airports and San Francisco are available for a fee. In addition to the tennis courts, guests have access to fitness classes, spa treatments, two heated pools, saunas, and a hot tub. Three restaurants grace the premises: the Paragon Bar & Grill, which offers casual fare including burgers, pastas, and fresh fish along with live music and a hopping bar scene; the Bayview Cafe, which is located by the pool and serves sandwiches, salads, and grilled fare; and Jordan's, the Claremont's California–Pacific Rim flagship restaurant, which serves breakfast, lunch, and dinner in a casually elegant setting known for its stupendous views. *$$$; AE, DC, DIS, MC, V; checks OK; www.claremontresort.com; at the intersection of Ashby and Domingo aves.*

Rose Garden Inn / ★★

2740 TELEGRAPH AVE, BERKELEY; 510/549-2145

This attractive bed-and-breakfast surrounded by beautifully landscaped lawns started out as a restored Tudor-style mansion furnished with wonderful old furniture and period antiques. Then it swallowed the house next door and added a couple of cottages and a carriage house, giving the Rose Garden Inn's empire enough space for 40 guest rooms. The best rooms are in the Fay House, which has glowing hardwood walls and stunning stained-glass windows. All of the rooms in the Garden and Carriage houses have fireplaces and overlook the inviting English country garden in back (room 4 in the Carriage House is the best). Of course, the rooms facing away from Telegraph Avenue are the most tranquil. Each guest room has a private bath, a color TV, and a phone; some have balconies and views of San Francisco. *$$; AE, DC, DIS, MC, V; local checks only; www.rosegardeninn.com; between Ward and Stuart sts.*

Emeryville

This tiny town slivered between Oakland, Berkeley, and the bay was once a dowdy industrial area, but a dozen-plus years of manic redevelopment has turned it into one of the most intriguing urban centers in the Bay Area; computer jockeys, artists, and biotechies now abound here in their live-work spaces. Emeryville's town center is a nouveau ultramall called the **EMERYBAY PUBLIC MARKET**. The center offers great ethnic food stands, stores, and a 10-screen cinema; take the Powell Street exit from Interstate 80. Nearby is one of Emeryville's biggest attractions: the Swedish home store **IKEA** (4400 Shellmound; 510/420-4532). You really can't miss it. The bright blue behemoth seems to have engulfed every previously undeveloped lot in town.

RESTAURANTS

Bucci's / ★★

6121 HOLLIS ST, EMERYVILLE; 510/547-4725

Located in a beautifully restored former warehouse, Bucci's is all brick and glass, with soaring ceilings, an open kitchen, and a small patio garden. At lunch, biotech execs and multimedia artists nosh on rich focaccia sandwiches and crisp thin-crust pizzas topped with prosciutto, roasted peppers, provolone, mozzarella, and cherry tomatoes. Dinner offers more elaborate fare from a daily-changing menu, which might include a tender roast duck served with a rich butternut-squash risotto or delicate cannelloni stuffed with spinach, walnuts, roasted red peppers, and cheese and served in a lemon cream sauce. The desserts and espressos are topflight, and the full bar specializes in classic cocktails. *$$; MC, V; checks OK; lunch Mon–Fri, dinner Mon–Sat; full bar; reservations recommended; www.buccis.com; between 59th and 61st sts.*

Hong Kong East Ocean Seafood Restaurant / ★★★

3199 POWELL ST, EMERYVILLE; 510/655-3388

With its green pagoda-style tile roof topped with writhing gold dragons and its white imperial lions guarding the front door, Hong Kong East Ocean looks more like a temple than a restaurant. Indeed, its worshippers are legion, thanks in large part to its superior dim sum. Best bets are the crystal buns (delicate steamed dumplings filled with plump shrimp, chopped water chestnuts, cilantro, and ginger); crisp, baked *bao* (buns) filled with sweet red pork and topped with crunchy sesame seeds; and shrimp embedded in a noodle-dough crepe served in a savory sauce. Besides dim sum, Hong Kong East Ocean offers authentic and exquisitely prepared Cantonese-style lunches and dinners: try the whole black cod dressed in a satiny soy-ginger-garlic sauce; the addictive, peppery deep-fried squid topped with chopped chiles and scallions; or anything that includes the feathery egg noodles. *$$; AE, MC, V; no checks; lunch, dinner every day; full bar; reservations recommended; www.hongkongeastocean.com; at the end of the Emeryville Marina.*

Oakland

There's no question that Oakland has gotten a bad and, in many respects, undeserved rap. After all, it was once ranked 12th on *Money* magazine's Best Places to Live in the United States list and third by the *Wall Street Journal* for fastest-rising real estate prices in the nation. But just ask Oakland residents what they love about their city—where to shop, where to eat—and you'll get a prideful response. They'll likely point you in the direction of charming yet somewhat eccentric Rockridge. They might give you directions to Piedmont Avenue or Victorian Row. They'll tell you that if you follow Broadway to the bay, you'll hit Jack London Square. They may even let you know which neighborhoods boast some of the most amazing historic architecture in the Bay Area, or that the view from the Mormon Temple can't be bested. What they probably won't do is "dis" their city—Oaktown, as it is sometimes affectionately called.

With a resident celebrity list as diverse as its culture—Gertrude Stein, Maya Angelou, Bruce Lee, R & B group En Vogue, Amy Tan, and, of course, Jack London, all of whom either called Oakland home or were born there—this city seems to have something about it that fosters self-expression. Even Mayor Jerry Brown—yes, the former California governor—has recognized the creative spirit that seems to run through the city's veins. He once declared promotion of the arts part and parcel of a citywide renaissance and made it one of his primary focuses for his term in office. While the city hasn't changed much in outward appearance, there is still something quite gritty and artistic about the place.

In the book *Oakland: Story of a City* by Beth Bagwell, an anonymous Oaklander captured the mystique of the city best: "Oakland now is like a great old blues singer. She knows how to moan and cry, but the bad times behind her make her know how to savor the good times. The old-time Oaklanders, and the port, and the big corporations building new skyscrapers downtown are like instruments in a band, and all together now we're blowing some pretty good jazz."

MAJOR ATTRACTIONS

Oakland's premier tourist destination is **JACK LONDON SQUARE** (www. jacklondonsquare.com), a sophisticated seaside spread of boutiques, bookstores, restaurants, hotels, cinemas, and saloons that is refreshingly void of the touristy schlock that pervades San Francisco's Pier 39. Must-see stops along the promenade include **HEINOLD'S FIRST & LAST CHANCE SALOON** (56 Jack London Sq; 510/839-6761), a decidedly funky little bar crammed with faded seafaring souvenirs, and the overhauled **USS POTOMAC** (510/627-1215), the 165-foot presidential yacht that served as FDR's "floating White House."

The sunken building that holds the **OAKLAND MUSEUM** (1000 Oak St, between 10th and 12th sts; 510/238-6614), a spectacular specimen of modern architecture designed by Kevin Roche in 1969, features innovative displays of the art, history, and ecology of California and also boasts beautiful terraced gardens.

Tots will get a kick out of Lake Merritt's **CHILDREN'S FAIRYLAND** (699 Bellevue Ave; 510/238-6876), a kid-size amusement park that supposedly inspired Walt Disney to construct Disneyland. Kids will also thrill to the beasts at the **OAKLAND ZOO** (9777 Golf Links Rd; 510/632-9525).

SHOPPING

In genteel North Oakland, the Rockridge neighborhood running along College Avenue boasts numerous bookstores, cafés, antique stores, expensive clothing boutiques, and a gourmet's paradise that rivals North Berkeley. Stroll through the **ROCKRIDGE MARKET HALL** (5655 College Ave at Shafter Ave, across from the Rockridge BART station; 510/250-6000), a chic multivendor market offering fresh pastas, gourmet cheeses, chocolates, fresh-cut flowers, delicious deli sandwiches and salads, breads from the great Grace Baking Company, exquisite produce, and a wide selection of wine. Grittier but just as interesting is downtown Oakland's **CHINATOWN** (tour the area between 7th and 10th sts and Broadway and Harrison), which is not as congested (with cars or tourists) as San Francisco's Chinatown. An assortment of Mexican bakeries and taquerias tempt passersby along **E 14TH STREET**, between 2nd and 13th avenues. The **PACIFIC COAST BREWING COMPANY** (906 Washington St; 510/836-2739) offers a lively bar scene and good microbrews. On the

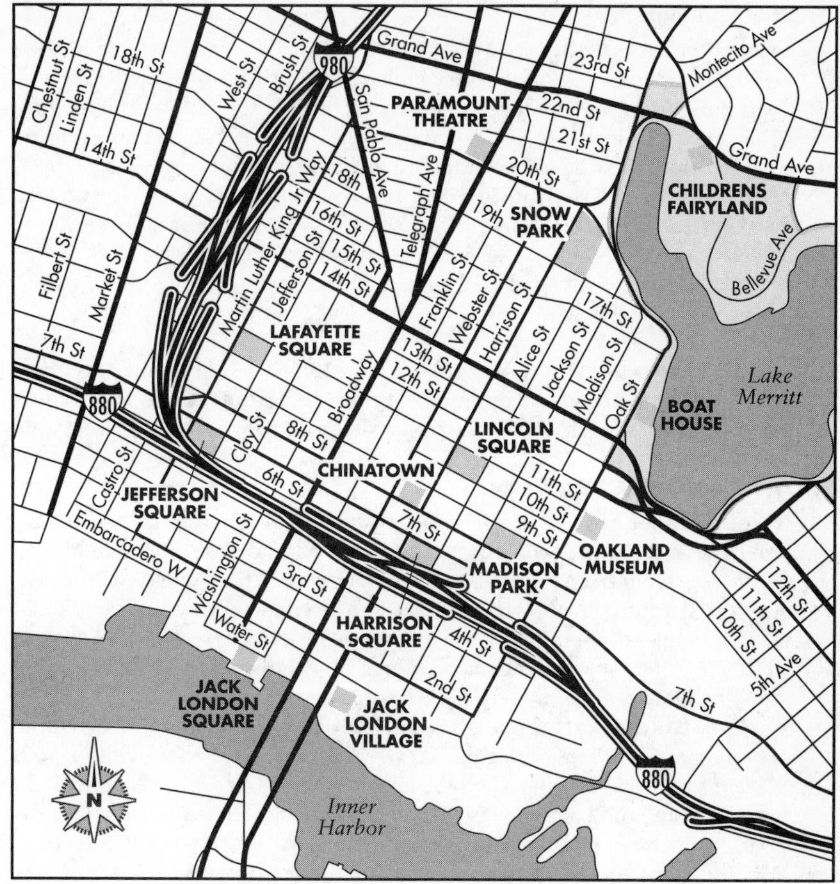

Downtown Oakland

other side of town are your best bets for books and coffee near Oakland's downtown: **WALDEN POND BOOKS** (3316 Grand Ave; 510/832-4438) and the **COFFEE MILL** (3363 Grand Ave; 510/465-4224).

PERFORMING ARTS

Music

The highly regarded **OAKLAND EAST BAY SYMPHONY** (2025 Broadway; 510/465-6400) offers classical and choral concerts at the Paramount Theatre and the Calvin Simmons Theatre. You can catch the hottest jazz in town at **YOSHI'S** (see review). Gospel acts abound in the East Bay, but often they're hard to find; try calling **REID'S RECORDS IN BERKELEY** (510/843-7282), which has a bulletin board where folks post the latest local musical events.

Theater and Film

Downtown's **PARAMOUNT THEATRE** (2025 Broadway at 21st St; 510/465-6400), an architectural masterpiece built in 1931 and restored in 1973, offers everything from organ concerts and rock concerts to plays and films from Hollywood's Golden Age. Guided tours of the 3,000-seat theater are given the first and third Saturday of each month, excluding holidays. No reservations are necessary—just show up at 10am at the box office entrance. The **GRAND LAKE THEATRE** (3200 Grand Ave; 510/452-3556), a beautifully restored Egypto deco movie palace, shows new films, which are kicked off on the weekends by a live organist's dazzling performance.

Dance

The **OAKLAND BALLET** (2025 Broadway; 510/465-6400) jumps and twirls at the beautiful art deco Paramount Theatre, and at many Oakland venues contemporary and African dance troupes kick up their heels.

SPORTS AND RECREATION

Those hot shot boys of summer, the **OAKLAND A'S**, are usually knocking 'em dead at the **OAKLAND COLISEUM** (from I-80 take the Coliseum exit or, better yet, avoid the freeway crawl by taking a BART train; 510/638-4900). And the sparkling **OAKLAND COLISEUM ARENA**—renovated to the tune of $102 million—is the home of the tall guys: the **GOLDEN STATE WARRIORS** (510/986-2200; www.nba.com/warriors). The building is currently sponsored by Oracle, a major software corporation.

Pretty **LAKE MERRITT**, one of the largest saltwater tidal lakes in the world, is home to flocks of migrating ducks, geese, and herons, and provides a great place for a leisurely stroll or jog; the lake is bounded by Grand Avenue, Lake Shore Avenue, and Lakeside Drive. For fun on the water, rent a sailboat, rowboat, paddleboat, or canoe at the lake's **SAILBOAT HOUSE** (510/238-3187). For the ultimate urban escape, head for the hills to **REDWOOD REGIONAL PARK** (off Joaquin Miller Rd; 510/636-1684), where miles of fern-trimmed trails wind through redwood groves and oak woodlands.

RESTAURANTS

Asmara Restaurant and Bar / ★

5020 TELEGRAPH AVE, OAKLAND; 510/547-5100

Asmara has a split personality: the comfortable restaurant is full of East African kitsch, while the adjacent bar—stark white and brightly lit—is a sterile jolt to the senses. Eritrean expatriates seem to prefer the bar, while locals enjoy the restaurant's African decor. Both groups, however, often get caught up in the communal spirit of the place, sharing their meals with fellow diners and using pieces of spongy injera bread to scoop up tasty *ziggni* (beef marinated in a surprisingly mild berbere sauce made with jalapeño and other chile peppers) and *yegomen alicha* (mustard greens simmered with spices). Make the most of this culinary adventure by getting one of

THE CALL OF THE NOT-SO-WILD

JACK LONDON SQUARE is like a luxury SUV or a sailor in drag: gussied up, baubled, and bangled, when what it really wants to do is to load cargo. Beneath its tartish paint job lies the tattooed soul of a salty dog.

Back in the 1800s, when Oakland was little more than a township, the area at the end of Broadway was singled out to become a port that would rival—even surpass—the port of San Francisco; there was money to be made in the estuary muck. Soon docks sprang up, whaling ships lurched into Oakland, riverboats churned the water, and the locale gained a reputation as a rough and rowdy seafarer's gathering spot.

Nowadays there are a few places in Jack London Square where its beard stubble pokes through the blush. A ride on the **JACK LONDON SQUARE WATER TAXI** or the **ALAMEDA/OAKLAND FERRY** (Alameda; 510/522-3300; www.eastbayferry.com) will take you past the real guts of the area: the docks. They were the places where, during the '40s, scores of women lent their hands to the wartime effort and where massive shipments from far-off lands are received to this day. A walk through the nearby produce district will reveal the grittier side of the area—the raw inner workings of a diminished though still vibrant industry. **HEINOLD'S FIRST & LAST CHANCE SALOON** still stands; this is the bar where a young Jack London sold newspapers from a barstool and bent his ear to sailors' woolly tales.

It may not look as wild as it once was, thanks to the industrious efforts of makeup-artist developers, but explore—answer the call, pull back the wig—and you'll find a weathered mariner, ready to hum a sea shanty.

the combination dinners. *$; AE, DIS, MC, V; no checks; lunch Fri–Sun, dinner Tues–Sun; full bar; reservations recommended; www.asmararestaurant.com; at 51st St.*

Bay Wolf Restaurant / ★★★

3853 PIEDMONT AVE, OAKLAND; 510/655-6004

Located in an attractive Victorian house with dark wood wainscoting and pale yellow walls, Bay Wolf first became a local favorite under the direction of co-owner and executive chef Michael Wild. More than 30 years old, this East Bay institution is beginning to show its age. Nevertheless, fresh ingredients and careful preparation of seasonal dishes keep Bay Wolf at the top of everyone's list of favorites. Typical first courses might include a spiced scallop and endive salad or a rich, smoky asparagus and hazelnut soup with lemon cream. Main courses vary from tender grilled duck with spiced nectarines, escarole, and shell bean ragout to a flavorful seafood stew bubbling with cracked Dungeness crab, prawns, rockfish, and mussels. Desserts change every two weeks, but a couple of summer offerings included an irresistible berry pudding chock-full of seasonal berries along with a warm chocolate pudding cake drizzled with crème anglaise and cocoa sauce. The carefully selected wine list offers a number of moderately priced vintages, and more than 10 wines are available by the glass. *$$$$; AE, MC, V; checks OK; lunch Mon–Fri, dinner every day; beer and wine; reservations recommended; www.baywolf.com; between 40th St and MacArthur Blvd.*

Caffe 817 / ★★

817 WASHINGTON ST, OAKLAND; 510/271-7965

Visit the downtown Oakland farmers market on Friday morning, then rest your weary bag-laden arms at Caffe 817. This tiny restaurant bears the stamp of its design-conscious owner, Sandro Rossi, an electrical engineer who saw potential in this high-ceilinged space and hired local craftspeople to fashion its avant-garde furnishings. Despite its lofty decor, the café has modest ambitions: cappuccino and pastries are mainstays in the morning, and Italian sandwiches, simple salads, and fresh soups and stews are on the midday menu. The sandwich fillings are what you might call contemporary Italian-American: roast beef with arugula, grilled mozzarella with artichokes, prosciutto with herb butter and pears. But the rice-and-borlotti-bean soup is a classic Tuscan dish. If all this good fare inspires you to make your own Italian classics at home, head next door to G. B. Ratto International Grocers, a favorite East Bay source for Arborio rice, olive oil, beans, and other imported foodstuffs. *$; AE, MC, V; checks OK; breakfast, lunch Mon–Sat; beer and wine; no reservations; www.cafe817.com; between 8th and 9th sts.*

Citron / ★★★

5484 COLLEGE AVE, OAKLAND; 510/653-5484

An immediate hit when it opened in 1992, Citron has settled in for the long run. The intimate dining room, which, true to its French name, is bathed in soothing shades of lemon yellow, sets the stage for chef Chris Rossi's equally small menu of contemporary French-Mediterranean fare. Rossi's menu changes every two weeks. Recent appetizers included a grilled corn and sorrel soup with soft-shell crab, as well as a yellowtail carpaccio with a citrus–red onion salad. One taste of the chicken with 40 garlic cloves and you'll think you've been transported to Provence. Then again, if it's Italian fare you're craving, look for Rossi's chanterelle mushroom soup and ricotta fritters, or the lamb osso buco served on a bed of flageolet-bean and sun-dried tomato ragout with a sprinkling of pistachio gremolata garnish. Sip your glass of viognier under vine-covered trellises on the patio. Or slip right next door to À Côté, which serves delicious French appetizers in a warm and beautifully lit dining room. *$$; AE, DC, DIS, MC, V; checks OK; dinner every day; full bar; reservations recommended; www.citron-acote.com; between Taft and Lawton sts.*

Jade Villa / ★★

800 BROADWAY, OAKLAND; 510/839-1688

Ever since Lantern restaurant closed, the title of Oakland's top dim sum house has been transferred to Jade Villa, a behemoth of a restaurant that takes up nearly a quarter block in Oakland's Chinatown. During the lunch hour the place is packed with Chinese families sitting at large, round tables. The ornate dining room offers a tempting array of dinners, but the real reason you should come here is for the dim sum, served from early morning to midafternoon. Sip a cup of aromatic tea as servers circulate through the room pushing carts laden with assorted delicacies. They'll pause by your table and lift the lids off tiered metal steamers to let you inspect the barbecued pork buns, stuffed dumplings, wedges of green pepper filled with shrimp, and lots of other tasty treats. Hold out for at least one order of the steamed prawns-in-shell, the best dish. You'll be charged by the plate, and you can afford to experiment here—two people can eat with abandon for about 30 bucks. *$$; AE, DC, DIS, MC, V; no checks; lunch, dinner every day; beer and wine; reservations recommended; at 8th St.*

Le Cheval / ★★

1007 CLAY ST, OAKLAND; 510/763-8496

With everyone in the restaurant shouting to be heard, the din in Le Cheval is impossible to ignore. The egg-carton acoustic material on the ceiling doesn't help since it's about 3 miles away from the dining room floor—it's like trying to sound-dampen a stadium with velvet curtains. Nevertheless, people still flock to Le Cheval for some of the best Vietnamese food in the Bay Area. The menu is mind-bogglingly long, the seasonings are exotic, and the family-style portions are beyond generous. You could really pick just about anything off the menu and experience gastronomic euphoria, but be sure to sample some of the range of appetizers, which include imperial rolls, roast quail, marinated beef in lemon, or "bun"—similar to imperial rolls but of the do-it-yourself variety. Whatever you choose from the main course menu—whether prawns stewed in a clay pot or chicken with bamboo shoots—you'll be so content it won't matter that you can't hear yourself chew. *$$; AE, MC, V; no checks; lunch, dinner every day; full bar; reservations recommended; www.lecheval.com; near 10th St.* ♿

Mama's Royal Café / ★

4012 BROADWAY, OAKLAND; 510/547-7600

Die-hard regulars don't even question the 40- to 60-minute wait required on weekends to get a seat at this 35-year-old Oakland landmark known simply as Mama's. A combination of good food served in large portions and a schizo decor (picture a '40s-style diner/noodle house with pagoda door frames and Rosie the Riveter–era ads on Formica tabletops) attracts the bohemian-boomer crowd in Doc Martens and Tevas for some of the heartiest breakfasts in the East Bay. Unfortunately, the prices are kinda high, the service is suh-loooow (leave the antsy kids at home), and the waiters sometimes serve up a little attitude with your home fries. But who cares when the menu includes 31 types of omelets and such breakfast specials as fresh fruit crepes and burritos with chipotle tortillas? *$; cash only; breakfast every day, lunch Mon–Fri; beer and wine; no reservations; www.mamasroyalcafeoakland.com; at 40th St.* ♿

Nan Yang Rockridge / ★★

6048 COLLEGE AVE, OAKLAND; 510/655-3298

When Nan Yang opened in 1983, restaurants offering a full spectrum of Burmese delights were virtually nonexistent. Chef-owner Philip Chu assembled the menu by tracking down recipes from monasteries, street vendors, festival food booths, and family homes to create the first Burmese restaurant in the Bay Area. His noble efforts have been rewarded with rave reviews and long lines of customers clamoring for his fare—especially his ginger salad, a crunchy, textural delight with 16 ingredients including split peas, fava beans, shredded cabbage, coconut slices, sun-dried shrimp, garlic oil, roasted peanuts, and shredded ginger. The generous curry dishes come with giant chunks of beef, chicken, or fish; there are also plenty of seductive vegetarian variations. On sunny days, opt for a table on the front patio. *$$; MC, V; no checks; lunch, dinner Tues–Sun; beer and wine; reservations recommended; www.nanyangrockridge.com; just south of Claremont Ave.*

Oliveto Cafe and Restaurant / ★★★

5655 COLLEGE AVE, OAKLAND; 510/547-5356

Oliveto has always been a top East Bay destination, thanks in part to chef Paul Canales and chef-owner Paul Bertolli's obvious passion for the Italian table and careful interpretations of Italy's rustic cuisine. Trimmed with granite, olive wood, and custom ironwork, the restaurant has the air of a Florentine trattoria, and the well-dressed, well-heeled stockbroker-and-filmmaker crowd cements the impression. House specialties include the fresh fish dishes, such as *petrale sole piccata* served on a bed of sautéed spinach and topped with a caper, white wine, and butter sauce. Meats from the wood-fired rotisserie and grill range from Watson Farm lamb to the house-made pork sausage and grilled rabbit. Downstairs, the more casual café draws a crowd of commuters (a BART station is across the street) and neighbors from morning till night. You'll see tense-but-chic workaholic singles sizing each other up over small, crisp pizzas and sophisticated salads like the panzanella with cherry tomatoes and fresh mozzarella. A wood-burning oven rotisserie and high-end liquor cabinet (i.e., hard alcohol and a few mixed drinks) only add to Oliveto's popularity. *$$$; AE, DC, MC, V; no checks; breakfast, lunch, dinner every day (café); lunch Mon–Fri, dinner every day (restaurant); beer and wine; reservations recommended; www.oliveto.com; at Shafter Ave, across from the Rockridge BART station.*

Pho Anh Dao / ★

280 E 18TH ST, OAKLAND; 510/836-1566

Essentially a one-dish restaurant, Pho Anh Dao specializes in pho, the Hanoi anise-scented beef and noodle soup that many Vietnamese eat almost every day. This aromatic meal-in-a-bowl has everything in its favor: it's cheap, delicious, plentiful, and healthful. The essential garnishes arrive on the side: Asian basil, sliced green chiles, a lime or lemon wedge, and bean sprouts. Add as much of them as you like and then, with chopsticks in one hand and a soup spoon in the other, dive in. Pho aficionados ask for raw beef so they can "cook" it in the hot broth a slice at a time. *$; cash only; breakfast, lunch, dinner every day; beer only; no reservations; between 2nd and 3rd aves.*

Pizza Rustica Café / ★

5422 COLLEGE AVE, OAKLAND; 510/654-1601

Housed in a salmon-colored postmodern building with blue Corinthian columns, this jazzy nouveau pizza joint has a cramped, noisy dining room with tiny, knee-bruising tables, bright pop art on the walls, and California pizzas made with a light, crunchy cornmeal crust or a traditional peasant-bread crust. The traditional Mediterranean-style pizzas are impeccable, but pizza adventurers should try one of the more exotic offerings, such as the Thai or Ambrosia pizzas. Check out the upstairs retro-tropical Conga Lounge, where you and 14 of your closest friends (minimum of 15 people) can nibble on pies in a kitschy Polynesian setting replete with fake palm trees. *$; AE, MC, V; no checks; lunch, dinner every day; beer and wine; no reservations; www.caferustica.com; between Kales and Manila sts.* ♿

Soizic Bistro-Cafe / ★★★

300 BROADWAY, OAKLAND; 510/251-8100

Just two blocks from Jack London Square in the produce and fishmonger districts, this handsome converted warehouse with 18-foot ceilings and a second-floor loft dining room is owned and operated by Hisuk and Sanju Dong, former owners of the now-closed (but it was wonderful) Cafe Pastoral in Berkeley. Hisuk is an architect, and Sanju is a painter and the head chef. They've created a Paris salon straight out of The Moderns, with warm, golden colors and rich details. Named after a French friend of the owners, Soizic (SWA-zik) offers a wonderful mix of Mediterranean-style cuisine: a terrific eggplant entrée is layered with sun-dried tomatoes, goat cheese, and mushrooms and is served on a bed of polenta topped with a balsamic-kissed tomato sauce; tender smoked-chicken sandwiches are dressed with sun-dried tomatoes, watercress aioli, and spinach; and a hefty bowl of fresh New Zealand mussels is served steaming in a savory saffron broth with diced tomatoes. The fare is quite memorable and reasonably priced, too. Celebrate the occasion with the bistro's legendary dessert: a creamy ginger custard. *$$$; MC, V; local checks only; lunch Tues–Fri, dinner Tues–Sun; full bar; reservations recommended; www.soizicbistro.com; near Jack London Sq.* ♿

Spettro / ★★

3355 LAKESHORE AVE, OAKLAND; 510/451-7738

Would you consider it creepy to savor pasta and pizza amid the dearly departed? Well, welcome to Spettro (Italian for "spirit"). This restaurant's otherworldly theme is a bit unsettling at first (there is an assortment of macabre gravestone photography gracing the walls), but your appetite will return once you get a whiff of the dishes being concocted in the kitchen. Run by the owners of the now-defunct Topless Pizza, Spettro has given rebirth to some of Topless's pies and added an ever-changing menu of international dishes for variety, such as a vegan peanut pigeon stew prepared with tofu instead of pigeon, smoked chicken and oyster gumbo, and Brazilian feijoada with black beans and linguiça on a bed of rice. The wait for a table can be as long as an hour on the weekend, but the chatty staff will ply you with cider and wine to raise your own spirits. *$$; cash or local checks only; dinner every day; beer and wine; reservations for parties of 6 or more; at Trestle Glen St.*

Yoshi's / ★★★

510 EMBARCADERO W, OAKLAND; 510/238-9200

This jazz-club-cum-Japanese-restaurant—once a premier destination for live jazz on the West Coast—after a $5.1 million relocation and makeover, paid for by the City of Oakland, now resides in a glitzy new spread at Jack London Square. Architect Hiroshi Morimoto has fused traditional Japanese materials and elements with a sleek, modern design, and the results are fantastic. Equal attention was paid to the separate 300-seat amphitheater, a semicircular room equipped with a state-of-the-art sound system—there's nary a bad seat in the house. And then there's the food: textbook Japanese all the way, including sukiyaki, tempura, seafood, vegetarian cuisine, and a sophisticated ash-wood sushi bar. Prices are reasonable, particularly for combo dinner specials that include rice, miso soup, and an entrée. But let's be honest: You've come to hear America's top jazz and blues bands, as well as occasional big-name talents such as Herbie Hancock and John Lee Hooker. There are typically two gigs every night at 8pm and 10pm, and ticket prices range from about $20 to $30. Monday-night headliners are local artists trying to hit the big time. Sunday matinees have been added to the lineup; tickets for these daytime gigs are a bargain. *$$$; AE, DC, DIS, MC, V; no checks; lunch, dinner every day; full bar; reservations recommended; www.yoshis.com; 1 block west of Broadway.* ♿

Zatis / ★★★

4027 PIEDMONT AVE, OAKLAND; 510/658-8210

Zatis is a real find, discreetly tucked into a narrow spot near a bagel shop and Peet's coffeehouse on Piedmont Avenue. It's hardly noticeable during the day; only at night does the elegant ice-blue neon light entice you to step through the doors, where the aroma of roasted garlic and olive oil will certainly convince you to take a seat and stay for a while. The light seduces, and the jazz soothes. Think intimate (about 15 tables), and think Valentine's Day. Got the picture? Start with the savory phyllo triangles stuffed with perfectly seasoned chicken and spinach, or dip into the roasted garlic with Gorgonzola and flatbread. Then try the vegetarian eggplant entrée stuffed with kalamata olives, jalapeños, and artichoke hearts and baked in a spicy tomato sauce; the grilled fillet of wild salmon served with red potatoes and fresh seasonal vegetables; or any of the chef's specialties of the day. The exceptionally professional waitstaff is welcoming and efficient. *$$$; AE, MC, V; no checks; lunch Mon–Sat, dinner every day; beer and wine; reservations recommended; www.zatisrestaurant.com; between 40th and 41st sts.* ♿

LODGINGS

Lake Merritt Hotel Clarion Suites / ★★

1800 MADISON ST, OAKLAND; 510/832-2300 OR 800/933-HOTEL

This art deco masterpiece standing right next to downtown Oakland looks out over Lake Merritt. Built in 1927, the vintage white stucco hotel was restored in 2000 to its original opulence with stunning light fixtures, richly patterned carpeting, plush furniture, and lush flower arrangements. Most of its 50 rooms are standard suites appointed in the charming manner of studio apartments circa 1930 (with a nod to modern-day microwaves and coffeemakers). Every room has satellite TV, an updated bathroom, a stocked minifridge, and a phone, and some units face the lake. Other amenities include a concierge, weekly wine tastings, and a continental breakfast served downstairs in the Terrace Room. If you're a business exec, you'll be happy to know the hotel provides fax and copy services, and a complimentary shuttle to whisk you to the nearby Oakland Financial District. *$$$$; AE, DC, DIS, MC, V; no checks; www.lakemerritthotel.com; at Lakeside Dr.* ♿

Waterfront Plaza Hotel / ★★

10 WASHINGTON ST, OAKLAND; 510/836-3800 OR 800/729-3638

This small luxury hotel perched on the water's edge at Jack London Square is not the fanciest hotel you'll ever stay in, but it comes with all the essential amenities at a reasonable price. Each of the 144 rooms is attractively outfitted with pine furnishings, pleasing prints, quilted comforters, and color schemes of beige, copper, and blue. Be sure to request a room with a deck and a view of the harbor (for an extra fee), and in the winter months ask for a unit with a fireplace. Additional perks include business and fax services, a fitness center, and a heated pool and sauna overlooking the harbor. Adjacent to the hotel is Jack's Bistro, where you can munch on wood-fired entreés in a dining room with a view of the marina. *$$$$; AE, DC, DIS, MC, V; no checks; www.waterfrontplaza.com; in Jack London Sq.* ♿

SAN JOSE, SOUTH BAY, AND THE PENINSULA THREE-DAY TOUR

DAY ONE: *Afterlife day*. Check in to your room at the predictably luxurious **FAIRMONT** hotel in San Jose. You'll be glad you did since you'll be spending the day at some of the most peculiar sites in the Bay Area. Your first stop is at the **EGYPTIAN MUSEUM AND PLANETARIUM**. This attraction features incredible mummies, Egyptian artifacts, scale models of temples, and accurate reproductions of tombs. But that's not the unusual part. The unusual part is that the museum is run by the Rosicrucian Order—not unlike the Theosophic Society—which takes rather seriously the mysterious tenets of ancient Egypt. Don't worry, you won't be converted. Drop in at **71 SAINT PETER** for lunch. From there, head on over to the **WINCHESTER MYSTERY HOUSE** for more otherworldly fun. After you've been thoroughly spooked, go back to your accommodations at the Fairmont—where the doors do open up to rooms—and relax for a bit before heading off to **ORLO'S** (200 Edenvale Ave, San Jose; 408/226-3200). Housed in a mansion built by faith healer Mary Hayes Chynoweth, it's the perfect place for an ethereal dinner.

DAY TWO: *Day of the cat*. Start your morning with breakfast at the hotel. No visit to the Silicon Valley would be complete without a side trip to Los Gatos. Located off Highway 17 just before the Santa Cruz Mountains, this enclave put both charming and chichi on the map. All you really need to do is find a place to park, which could take a while, as there is primarily on-street parking, and start walking. Brimming over with stylish boutiques, exclusive gift stores, and home accessory shops, this town will keep your credit card humming for some time. Try **I GATTI** (the cats) for

San Jose and the South Bay

Nowadays, the answer to Dionne Warwick's question "Do You Know the Way to San Jose?" might well be "Dionne, honey, you've been away too long."

The rolling fields and orchards and the small-town spirit of the South Bay memorialized in Warwick's '60s hit song are gone—swallowed up by office complexes and shopping malls. The bumper crops San Jose peddles now are measured in gigabytes. With skyscrapers and stadiums springing up in unlikely places over the past few decades, and traffic rerouted for construction, it's become somewhat the East Berlin of the Bay Area—constantly expanding its concrete girth—though nowhere near as bleak. There are a few undeveloped spots, rare and strangely beautiful against the backdrop of chrome and glass. And many of the ethnic neighborhoods—vibrant and alive with Latin rhythms or Asian austerity—remain intact.

lunch before sojourning through pesto-thick traffic to your room at the **GARDEN COURT HOTEL** in Palo Alto. After you've had a chance to unwind from the drive, treat yourself to an amazing dinner at **MANRESA**. You will have earned it.

DAY THREE: *The garden-variety day.* After a breakfast of Italian pastries at **IL FORNAIO** in the Garden Court Hotel, if you haven't yet done your share of shopping, you can start your day with more retail therapy in Palo Alto's **STANFORD SHOPPING CENTER**. This shopping experience is a cut above the rest—the center retains its original outdoor layout, and its gardens are meticulously tended. For lunch, indulge in the exceptional fare at **MAX'S OPERA CAFE** (650/323-6364), located in the shopping center. However, if gardens get your heart pumping, you could skip Stanford Shopping Center and go directly to **WOODSIDE AND FILOLI ESTATE AND GARDENS** (86 Canada Rd; 650/364-8300; open Feb–Oct). This palatial mansion on Canada (pronounced con-YA-da) Road was built in 1915 by the founders of the Empire Gold Mine. Filoli stands for "fight, love, live"—to fight for just cause, to love your fellow man, to live a good life—just in case you were wondering. Both the sprawling house and the spectacular gardens are open for tours, but take your time and journey back to a way of life long gone. A light, casual lunch at the **QUAIL'S NEST CAFE** on the Filoli grounds will be the perfect respite between tours and strolling. If all that fresh air has built you an appetite, head into downtown Woodside (you'll practically miss it if you blink) to dine at the recently revamped **VILLAGE PUB**. Don't let the name of the restaurant mislead you—a top-notch American-inspired menu is what you will find in this chic and luxurious establishment. Linger over an after-dinner cordial before heading back to your room at the Garden Court to relax.

ACCESS AND INFORMATION

Do yourself an enormous favor: fly into **SAN JOSE INTERNATIONAL AIRPORT (SJC)** (408/501-0979; www.sjc.org) if your final destination is anywhere near San Jose. While Silicon Valley's traffic problem is not as bad as it was, say, a decade ago, you can still find yourself languishing in the same spot for up to 30 minutes—especially during rush-hour traffic. Even if your final destination is downtown, it still may take you forever to get there from the airport, but you'll have shaved off another two or more hours if you've arrived at San Jose International Airport instead of San Francisco International or Oakland International. Shuttle services include **ON TIME AIRPORT SHUTTLE** (650/207-0221), **SAN JOSE EXPRESS** (408/370-0701), and **SILICON VALLEY AIRPORTER** (800/400-2365). There are plenty of taxis available and the airport is blanketed with free wireless access.

The **SANTA CLARA VALLEY TRANSPORTATION AUTHORITY (VTA)** (408/321-2300; www.vta.org) runs the buses as well as the 24-hour light rail system that serves San Jose, Santa Clara, Sunnyvale, and Mountain View. **CALTRAIN** (800/660-4287; www.caltrain.com) provides service from Silicon Valley to San Francisco.

San Jose enjoys the distinction of almost always being several degrees warmer than the rest of the Bay Area regardless of the season. Its valley location, with the Santa Cruz Mountains on the west and rolling hills to the east, locks in a temperate climate—and sometimes it's downright hot. You'd be safe dressing fairly lightly, even in winter, when the barometer drops to 64-or-so degrees. But be sure to bring a sweater or other layering piece any time of year, especially if your travels will take you to other parts of the Bay Area, as the evenings can be on the cool side.

The **SAN JOSE MCENERY CONVENTION CENTER** is affiliated with the **VISITOR INFORMATION BUREAU** (150 W San Carlos St and 333 W San Carlos St, Ste 1000; 408/977-0900; www.sanjose.org).

San Jose

While some San Jose residents mourn the continuing loss of open space and grittiness to the onslaughts of new construction and gentrification, others seem puffed up with understandable pride at the city's energetic new look and feel. First-class restaurants, an upscale state-of-the-art light rail system, a flourishing arts scene, a dazzling sports arena, and, most recently, an exquisitely designed multi-use shopping complex all contribute to the city's revitalization, furthering its emergence from the long cultural shadow cast by San Francisco, its cosmopolitan neighbor to the north.

MUSEUMS

The **SAN JOSE MUSEUM OF ART** (110 S Market St; 408/271-6840) provides a handsome setting for contemporary European and American art. The **EGYPTIAN MUSEUM AND PLANETARIUM** (1664 Park Ave; 408/947-3636), run by the mystical Rosicrucian order, presents a collection of Egyptian artifacts, mummies, and re-creations of tombs in a pyramidlike structure (the British Museum it's not, but it's educational, funky, and fun). The lively and ever-so-loud **CHILDREN'S DISCOVERY MUSEUM** (180 Woz Wy; 408/298-5437), painted in Easter-egg purple, offers kids the opportunity to explore exhibits of urban life: traffic lights, fire engines, a post office, a bank, and even a sewer (spanking clean and minus any errant rats or Ninja turtles). A Wells Fargo stagecoach, a farmhouse, and rural diversions such as corn-husk doll making help youngsters experience what the valley was like when it produced major crops instead of microchips. The **TECH MUSEUM OF INNOVATION** (201 S Market St; 408/294-8324) is a terrific hands-on science museum where adults and kids alike can play with robots, gain insight into genetic engineering, or design a high-tech bicycle; it's located across from the San Jose Museum of Art.

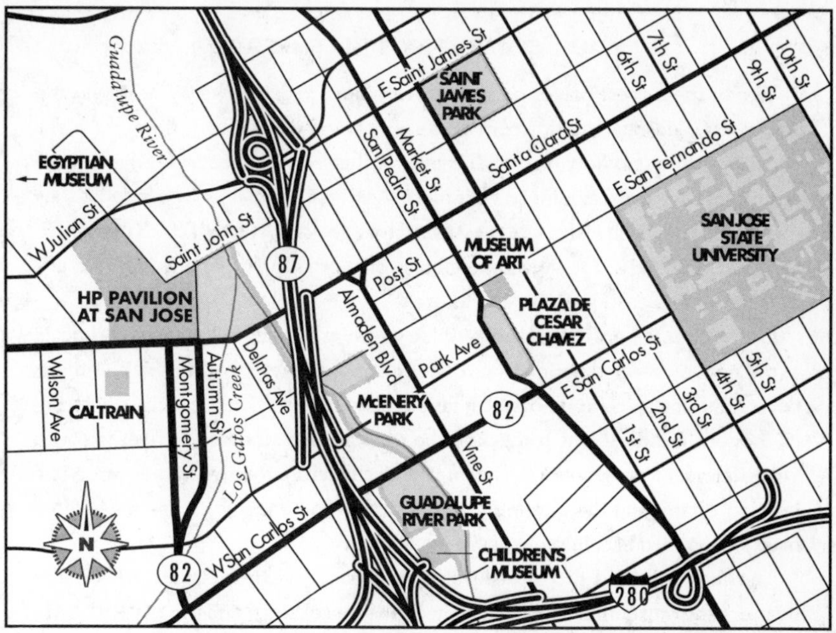

Downtown San Jose

Fans of the supernatural might enjoy a tour of the **WINCHESTER MYSTERY HOUSE** (525 S Winchester Blvd; 408/247-2101), an odd, rambling mansion with an intriguing history: After inheriting $20 million from her husband's repeating-rifle company, Sarah Winchester became convinced that the ghosts of people killed by Winchester rifles were coming back to haunt her. Her paranoia led her to continually have additions built onto her home over a period of 38 years to house their restless spirits. The lovely—if somewhat unorthodox—Victorian mansion is a 160-room labyrinth of crooked corridors, doors opening into space, and dead-end stairways.

SHOPPING

For anyone who loves to shop, the ritzy **SANTANA ROW** (400 S Winchester Blvd; 408/551-4600; www.santanarow.com) is not to be missed. Plopped down in an unlikely suburban locale, this ready-made European townscape boasts everything from Gucci and Escada to Pasta Pomodoro and Ann Taylor Loft. Along with well-known designers, numerous one-of-a-kind boutiques offer such chichi items as custom-made leather shoes and pricey handmade jewelry. Although you'll encounter droves of well-heeled shoppers with bags under their arms, there are plenty of other diversions with lower price tags. With countless restaurants, cafés, and even a Borders Books, you can avoid the retail temptation and simply people watch in the Spanish-style palazzo. When you've worked up an appetite, enjoy dining Parisian-style at the southern

YOUR COMPUTER'S BIRTHPLACE

Two of the biggest babies on record were born in Silicon Valley—Google and Apple—and despite the dot-com collapse nearly a decade ago, this area is still considered the unofficial high-tech capital of the world. Of course, where there are babies, there are albums to document their first steps, first words, what they might become. Such is the **TECH MUSEUM OF INNOVATION** (201 S Market St, San Jose; 408/294-8324; www.thetech.org) or, more simply, "The Tech"—a cache of technology's past, present, and future.

One look at the orange and cobalt-blue museum building will make you chuckle at the now outmoded notion that "techie" was synonymous with "geek"—this is not a gathering place for nerds with taped glasses and pocket protectors. Instead, its modern facade seems to beckon the tragically hip to enter and get in touch with their inner programmer. The interior architecture follows suit, drawing one in, then catapulting the attention upward via a dramatic curved staircase and a massive supporting column lathered in gold leaf.

The Tech is divided into three levels. The ground level features an IMAX dome theater—no museum is complete without one these days—and the **TECHSTORE**, as interesting as the museum itself. The upper level contains the Innovation

outpost of the celebrated **LEFT BANK** restaurant (377 Santana Row; 408/984-3500; www.leftbank.com). At night things continue to buzz at the **VBAR** (355 Santana Row; 408/551-0010) in the Valencia Hotel, and the hip **BLOWFISH SUSHI** (355 Santana Row; 408/345-3848; www.blowfishsushi.com) offers tempuras, fresh sushi, and premium sakes until late in the evening.

PERFORMING ARTS

San Jose has a thriving community of theater, ballet, and opera groups, most of which may be found at the **SAN JOSE CENTER FOR THE PERFORMING ARTS** (255 Almaden Blvd at Park Ave; 408/792-4145; www.sanjose.org). **OPERA SAN JOSE** (408/437-4450; www.operasj.org), the **BALLET SAN JOSE** (408/288-2800; www.balletsanjose.org), and the **SAN JOSE SYMPHONY ORCHESTRA** (408/286-2000; www.symphonysiliconvalley.org) offer more classical cultural enrichments. **LOS LUPEÑOS DE SAN JOSE DANCE COMPANY** (1700 Alum Rock Ave; 408/928-5564) reflects the Spanish heritage of the city. For drama, the **SAN JOSE REPERTORY THEATRE** (101 Paseo de Antonio St; 408/367-7255; www.sjrep.com) offers innovative productions of new works and classics. The **SAN JOSE STAGE COMPANY** (490 S 1st St; 408/283-7142; www.sanjose-stage.com) primarily showcases American contemporary drama and comedy, while the **CITY LIGHTS THEATRE** (529 S 2nd St; 408/295-4200; www.cltc.org) follows the more experimental route.

area, where you can, among other things, design and ride a virtual roller coaster or tour a computer chip lab, and the Life Tech area—an utterly fascinating look at technology's role in studying, diagnosing, and treating the human body. The squeamish and the recently lunched should avoid the video display that shows how a computer-generated image of the human body and all its internal organs is created by using a cadaver. The upper level also includes an interactive area called **IMAGINATION PLAYGROUND** that dispels the notion that high-tech endeavors are always sedentary. A Sneaks and Spies exhibit boasts hideouts armed with the latest and greatest surveillance equipment, so that visitors can be James Bond for a day. A Shadows and Sands display projects your movements on screen for an interactive media experience. The lower level is where you can catch a glimpse of technology's future. From robotic dogs with amazingly realistic movement—you can special-order one if the four-digit price tag doesn't intimidate you—and a robotic submarine you can pilot to a model Mars rover you can ride, it's a techie playground. Be sure to take a spin on the **SEGWAY HUMAN TRANSPORTER**—the stand-up scooter that is propelled by the way you shift your weight. Finally, the **CENTER OF THE EDGE** area showcases rotating exhibits of the newest state-of-the-art technology.

PARKS AND GARDENS

KELLEY PARK is a pleasant place for a picnic and a stroll around the **JAPANESE FRIENDSHIP GARDEN** (corner of Senter Rd and Keyes St; 408/277-3664), complete with a koi pond and a teahouse. If you have little ones in tow, they're sure to be beguiled by the old-fashioned, low-tech charms of **HAPPY HOLLOW** next door, a zoo and amusement park aimed at the toddler-through-early-grade-school set. **GUADALUPE RIVER PARK** is undergoing constant renovations as part of a master plan for both the park and garden; call the **SAN JOSE DEPARTMENT OF PARKS AND RECREATION** (408/535-3570) for more information.

NIGHTLIFE

Once the red-light district, the area around Market and First streets has gradually developed into a clean, hip home for many nightclubs and a slightly more alternative scene. If you gotta dance, you'll find live rock and recorded dance tunes in the **CACTUS CLUB** (417 S 1st St, two blocks south of the Fairmont hotel; 408/491-9300). For live jazz and a bit of alternative rock, head to **AGENDA LOUNGE** (at the northwest corner of S 1st St and E San Salvador St; 408/287-3991). Live rock, dance classics, and cheap draft beer are featured at **TOONS** (52 E Santa Clara St at 2nd St; 408/292-7464).

RESTAURANTS

Agenda Lounge / ★★★

399 S 1ST ST, SAN JOSE; 408/287-3991

At this chic and beautifully designed restaurant, stylish types sip cosmopolitans at the sculptured wood bar, Silicon Valley execs talk shop at tables flanked by arty souls, and jazz buffs check out the live (and very loud) band. Under executive chef Brad Kraten, the food has a decidedly American flavor. Look for offerings such as a cheeseburger on a house-made focaccia roll with apple wood–smoked bacon and white cheddar cheese. Eclectic combinations continue to reign on this inspired menu, with dishes ranging from spicy tuna tartare to delicate English pea–filled ravioli, from barn-burning pot stickers to comfort food like garlic mashed potatoes. Portions are generous, but try to save room for dessert; choices that seem passé on paper, such as chocolate mud pie and crème caramel, turn out to be retro revelations. Service is savvy but a bit slow, which gives you a chance to soak up the scene and consider the rest of the evening. *$$; AE, DC, MC, V; no checks; dinner Tues–Sat; full bar; reservations recommended; www.agendalounge.com; at San Salvador St.*

Chez Sovan Restaurant / ★★

923 OLD OAKLAND RD, SAN JOSE (AND BRANCHES); 408/287-7619

This restaurant specializes in Cambodian cuisine and exceptionally friendly service. For a full review, see the Restaurants section of Campbell. *$; AE, MC, V; no checks; lunch Mon–Fri; beer and wine; reservations recommended; www.chezsovan.com; between Berryessa Rd and E Hedding St.*

Gombei Restaurant / ★★

193 E JACKSON ST, SAN JOSE; 408/279-4311

Among the many worthy restaurants in San Jose's Japantown, tiny, lively Gombei stands out with its unparalleled noodle dishes and the near-volcanic energy of its devoted patrons and youthful staff. The menu offers everything from teriyaki and domburi to Gombei's renowned udon—the Japanese equivalent of Jewish chicken soup, which arrives in a huge ceramic bowl filled with fat wheat noodles, loads of tender strips of chicken, ribbons of egg, green onion, and a sheaf of dried seaweed. Be sure to check the specials board for such irresistible nibbles as deep-fried oysters or cold chicken salad served on buckwheat noodles. *$; cash only; lunch, dinner Mon–Sat; beer and wine; reservations recommended; between 4th and 5th sts.*

La Forêt French Restaurant / ★★★

21747 BERTRAM RD, SAN JOSE; 408/997-3458

Located in an old two-story hotel overlooking Los Alamedos Creek, this picturesque and pricey restaurant offers unusual wild game that's flown in daily. Chef Vazgen "Ken" Davoudi can always be counted on to create superb sauces for the day's special, which might be tender medallions of wild boar marinated in shallots, balsamic vinegar, brandy, and cumin and topped with an outstanding pink peppercorn sauce, paired with medallions of elk in an equally masterful tarragon cream sauce. Davoudi's prowess isn't limited to game; he also works well with seafood, including a perfectly poached salmon served with a port wine sauce. Appetizers might feature fusilli with olive oil, herbs, garlic, wild mushrooms, and Gouda cheese or escargot with garlic butter and Pernod. The dessert list features cakes, cheesecakes, and exotic soufflés. *$$$; AE, DC, DIS, MC, V; no checks; dinner Tues–Sun, brunch Sun; full bar; reservations recommended; www.laforetrestaurant.com; from the Almaden Expressway, take the Almaden Rd exit, go south for 3 miles, turn left at Almaden Wy, and cross the small bridge to Bertram Rd.*

Paolo's / ★★★

333 W SAN CARLOS ST, SAN JOSE; 408/294-2558

A longtime San Jose institution, Paolo's serves flavorful food and remains authentically Italian. Look for unexpected little flourishes that give even the most tried-and-true dishes an interesting twist: osso buco, for example, is served on a bed of saffron-infused farro, while Paolo's gnocchi is baked with black truffle butter. Other outstanding items include *ravioli con formaggio di pecora* (pasta stuffed with sheep's-milk ricotta, fava beans, and heirloom tomatoes); roasted quail with white raisins and grappa; and an intriguing appetizer of pan-seared foie gras with caramelized fennel, grilled strawberries, and a chestnut honey–infused duck sauce. Service can be a little brusque at times, especially if you're not a silver-haired CEO on his or her lunch hour, but it's always efficient. The wine list, a 50-page tome, encompasses an outstanding variety of domestic and European selections. *$$$; AE, DC, DIS, MC, V; no checks; lunch Mon–Fri, dinner Mon–Sat; full bar; reservations recommended; www.paolosrestaurant.com; between Woz Wy and Almaden Blvd.* ♿

71 Saint Peter / ★★

71 N SAN PEDRO ST, SAN JOSE; 408/971-8523

Chef/co-owner Mark Tabak has attracted a loyal following with this tiny and romantic Mediterranean bistro. The Spanish floor tiles, flowers, exposed brick walls, and crisp linens help create a feeling of rustic elegance, a theme echoed by Tabak's robust yet refined cuisine. Outstanding starters include steamed New Zealand clams simply seasoned with tomato, basil, and garlic, and a bevy of interesting salads. For your entrée, you'd do well to consider the roasted hazelnut pork loin cloaked in a zinfandel-mango au jus with pear chutney and spinach mashed potatoes, the seafood linguine in a spicy tomato broth, or any of the fresh fish dishes. Tabak is justly proud of his crème brûlée, which was once voted the best in Santa Clara Valley. The sensibly priced wine list includes French and Italian selections as well as the usual California suspects. *$$; AE, DC, DIS, MC, V; local checks only; lunch Mon–Fri, dinner Tues–Sat; beer and wine; reservations recommended; www.71saintpeter.com; between St John and Santa Clara sts.*

LODGINGS

The Fairmont / ★★★

170 S MARKET ST, SAN JOSE; 408/998-1900

Twenty stories high in the heart of downtown, the city's most luxurious hostelry has become one of the best-known features of the skyline. After a $67 million renovation in 2003, the Fairmont now features a grand 13-story tower that boasts 264 additional rooms and 74 luxurious suites, bringing the total capacity to 805 rooms. The guest rooms (as well as the public areas) have been refurbished and feature such niceties as marble bathrooms, plush robes, electric shoe polishers, desks, walk-in closets, custom-made mattresses, minibars, and nightly turndown service. In keeping with the Silicon Valley setting, they also contain an arsenal of tech toys such as high-speed modem links and interactive TVs that let a guest do everything from ordering up a movie to checking out of the hotel. During the summer months the cabana rooms that directly face the 58-foot-long swimming pool and feature small, private sundecks are especially popular. Three well-regarded restaurants stand ready to serve peckish travelers: the Pagoda serves Chinese food at lunch and dinner; the Fountain is a casual spot for breakfast, lunch, and dinner; the poolside Gazebo Bar and Grill offers cocktails and light fare in summer and fall, weather permitting. In addition, an elegant afternoon tea is served in the hotel's lobby on weekends. *$$$; AE, DC, DIS, V; checks OK; www.fairmonthotels.com; between San Fernando and San Carlos sts.* ♿

Hotel De Anza / ★★★

233 W SANTA CLARA ST, SAN JOSE; 408/286-1000

This 1931 grand dame's richly colored Moorish ceilings in the De Anza Room and the Hedley Club are art deco jewels, and the same design influence can be felt in the guest rooms. Each of the 101 rooms has a multiple-line desk phone with a data port, high-speed Internet access, an armoire with an honor bar, and a TV with a DVD player and VCR (you can check out movies gratis from the video library downstairs). Ask for one of the south-facing rooms to enjoy a sweeping view of downtown. The hotel's flagship restaurant, La Pastaia, serves some of the best Italian food in town, and the place is always packed with locals as well as hungry travelers. The stately Palm Court Terrace is a favorite place to meet for drinks in the warmer months, and a live jazz band performs in the Hedley Club on Wednesday through Saturday nights. *$$$; AE, DC, MC, V; checks OK; www.hoteldeanza.com; at Almaden Blvd.*

Hyatt Sainte Claire / ★★★

302 S MARKET ST, SAN JOSE; 408/295-2000

This gracious Spanish Revival–style hostelry was built in 1926 by the same architectural firm responsible for the design of the Mark Hopkins Hotel in San Francisco. The 170 refurbished guest rooms (including 14 one-bedroom suites and 1 grand suite boasting 2 fireplaces and a library) feature feather beds, dual phone lines with high-speed modems, safes, and minibars among the other usual first-class amenities. In addition, some of the rooms have whirlpool tubs and fireplaces, and 80 percent are equipped with laser printers and computers with Internet access. A small exercise room stands ready to help guests work out any knots or kinks resulting from sessions at those computers. And the Hyatt has a pleasant coffee shop, the Panetteria, serving Italian sandwiches and pastries, as well as a top-rated branch of Il Fornaio restaurant. *$$$; AE, DC, DIS, MC, V; checks OK; www.sanjose.hyatt.com; at San Carlos St.*

Santa Clara

RESTAURANTS

Birk's / ★★

3955 FREEDOM CIRCLE, SANTA CLARA; 408/980-6400

Despite its office-park setting and rather stern exterior, Birk's is a handsome American grill with a spirited atmosphere. Design features mark Birk's as a Pat Kuleto creation, and the hearty food reflects the vaguely men's-club feel of the place. Appetizers might include steak bits with béarnaise sauce, a grilled artichoke with garlic-lemon aioli, or oysters Rockefeller. For a main course, you can choose from all manner of grilled and smoked meat, fish, and fowl. Standouts include the popular smoked prime rib, peppered filet mignon topped with a Cognac–green peppercorn sauce, and grilled lamb chops marinated in oregano, lemon, garlic, and olive oil. Probably the most surprising item on the menu is a pasta paella loaded with prawns, crab, mussels, fresh fish, and sausage in a steaming saffron cream sauce. If you still have room for dessert, Birk's offers a dynamite chocolate cake, berry crisp à la mode, and other oh-I'll-diet-tomorrow temptations. The wine list reflects a good range of California vintners, and you'll find an excellent selection of single-malt scotches and beers on tap, many from local microbreweries. *$$$; AE, DC, DIS, MC, V; no checks; lunch Mon–Fri, dinner every day; full bar; reservations recommended; www.birksrestaurant.com; at Hwy 101 and Great America Pkwy.*

Campbell

RESTAURANTS

Chez Sovan Restaurant / ★★

2425 S BASCOM AVE, CAMPBELL; 408/371-7711

An upscale cousin of the San Jose original, Chez Sovan's Campbell branch features the same authentic Cambodian cuisine and exceptionally friendly service. The stars of the menu are the *samlaws*, Cambodian stews. *Samlaw korko* is a brothy concoction that combines tender chicken with an exotic array of vegetables. Several catfish dishes are offered, too, including a dynamite version with black beans, green onions, vinegar, and loads of fresh ginger.

PARAMOUNT'S GREAT AMERICA

Once the gleaming high-tech, dot-com center of the universe, Santa Clara and other cities in the Silicon Valley are still reeling from one of the most spectacular boom-bust economic cycles in history. With the dot-com meltdown, a steady stream of cutbacks in the high-tech industry, and massive job losses, the landscape has changed dramatically in this once high-powered tech universe. Alongside empty office buildings, though, is one of California's largest and most popular theme parks—**PARAMOUNT'S GREAT AMERICA** (Great America Pkwy between Hwys 101 and 237; 408/988-1776; www.cagreatamerica.com). If you have kids, it's a must-visit. With more than 50 rides, this park has some of the most thrilling roller coasters anywhere (with names like Delirium and Soar on Stealth). For the younger non-thrill-seeking set there is also the **NICKELODEON PARK** at Great America, filled with favorite characters from the network's popular television shows. An Australian-themed water park, **BOOMERANG BAY** (4701 Great America Pky, Santa Clara; 408/988-1776; www.pgathrills.com)—the size of five football fields!—features a variety of slides and kiddie splash areas. Be forewarned: It gets very hot during the summer, so pack the sunscreen, hats, and lots of water.

Skip the house specialty, *amok*—chicken or fish marinated in coconut milk and wrapped in a banana leaf (it may be a little too authentic for untutored Western palates). The fresh salads are packed with cilantro, mint, shredded Napa cabbage, bell peppers, and carrots, plus your choice of chicken, pork, or beef. *$; AE, DIS, MC, V; no checks; lunch, dinner Mon–Sat; beer and wine; reservations recommended; near Dry Creek Rd.*

Los Gatos

RESTAURANTS

I Gatti / ★★★

25 E MAIN ST, LOS GATOS; 408/399-5180

With its sponge-painted mustard and red-brown walls, weathered wooden shutters, and terra-cotta floor tiles, I Gatti evokes a Tuscan patio on a sunny afternoon. Terrific appetizers are *scampi al vino blanco*, goat-cheese ravioli with a rich chianti-wine glaze, and gnocchi (which can be a little doughy) with a first-rate creamy tomato-vodka sauce. There's a selection of both traditional and unusual salads (try the mixed greens with roasted walnuts, goat cheese, and caramelized onions drizzled with a balsamic pancetta dressing) and *secondi piatti* that include roasted filet mignon with a barolo wine and wild mushroom sauce, braised lamb shank, and *pollo modo mio* (lightly breaded breast of chicken served with a champagne, lemon-herb, and caper sauce). *$$$; AE, MC, V; checks OK; dinner every day; beer and wine; reservations recommended; www.igatti.com; near University Ave.*

Los Gatos Brewing Company / ★

130-G N SANTA CRUZ AVE, LOS GATOS; 408/395-9929

This cheery, upscale techno-barn of a restaurant has something for everyone: good house-made beers and ales for the thirsty, a lively singles scene for the action oriented, crayons and coloring books for the wee ones, and, of course, good pub fare for the hungry. Executive chef Jim Stump (who formerly graced Birk's in Santa Clara) has created an ambitious menu encompassing everything from pizzas and fresh oysters on the half shell to roasted chicken. You can indulge in a dainty seared ahi tuna salad or give your arteries a workout with the generously portioned pot roast accompanied by hearty root vegetables and mashed potatoes. In-house brewskis include special seasonal brews ranging from nut-brown ale to a German-style wheat beer. *$$; AE, DC, DIS, MC, V; no checks; lunch, dinner every day, brunch Sun; beer and wine; reservations recommended; www.lgbrewingco.com; at Grays Ln.* ♿

Manresa / ★★★★

320 VILLAGE LN, LOS GATOS; 408/354-4330

From the first bite of lychee nut, mint, and condensed milk granita, it's evident that it is all about the food here. The unusual combinations of savory and sweet in a less qualified chef's hands could be disastrous, but with owner David Kinch it works—magically. Select from one of three prix-fixe menu options, or try the "seasonal and spontaneous" chef's tasting menu for the ultimate splurge. A recent menu included crispy soft shell crab with yogurt, garden herbs, and green pesto; roast squab with crushed farro grain, fennel, and parsnips with argan oil was equally interesting and delicious. The perfect combinations continue through the dessert menu with hazlenut and cocoa tartines with bitter chocolate sorbet. The 17-page wine list can be intimidating, but a knowledgeable waitstaff is eager to make recommendations. Dinner can easily be a three-hour event here; just relax and savor every bite. *$$$$; MC, V; no checks; dinner every day; beer and wine; reservations recommended; www.manresarestaurant.com; near Santa Cruz Ave.* ♿

LODGINGS

Hotel Los Gatos / ★★

210 E MAIN ST, LOS GATOS; 408/335-1700 OR 866/335-1700

Joie de Vivre Hospitality, a San Francisco–based hotel group known for its stylish boutiques, has expanded its offerings to encompass many of the outlying towns in the Bay Area, such as Los Gatos. Unlike some of this company's ventures, Hotel Los Gatos was built from the ground up and was clearly tailor-made for this upscale suburb. The eclectic decor of old-world baroque meets sun-splashed Mediterranean works surprisingly well at this 72-room luxury hotel. Rich, deep-colored fabrics and custom furnishings adorn all of the rooms; a stone-tiled bathroom adjoins each room. The usual amenities are offered along with a heated pool, business services, high-speed Internet access, and a full-service day spa. Everything is clean and new, and the sophisticated courtyard design features fountains, gardens, and decorative ceramic tile that make you feel like you're in a private villa. Kuleto's Italian restaurant on the ground floor offers well-prepared northern Italian fare and boasts a spacious courtyard ideal for eating alfresco in the summer months. *$$$$; AE, DC, DIS, MC, V; checks OK; www.jdvhospitality.com; between Fiesta Wy and Jackson St.*

Sunnyvale

RESTAURANTS

Il Postale / ★★

127 WASHINGTON ST, SUNNYVALE; 408/733-9600

Set in Sunnyvale's old post office (hence the name), Il Postale is an airy, attractive trattoria with brick walls hung with large framed prints of Italian postal stamps, dark-wood bistro furniture set with white linens, and an open kitchen. Although owner Joe Antuzzi insists that his welcoming little restaurant serves Italian-American bistro food, that designation doesn't begin to describe the ambitious menu. Sure, there are plenty of Italian classics (spaghetti puttanesca, linguine with clams, veal braciola, cheese pizza), but the kitchen seems to delight in putting its own twist on some of the standards, tossing grilled boar sausage in wild mushroom risotto; serving veal scaloppini with a sun-dried tomato, caper, and black-olive sauce; even stuffing agnolotti with garlic mashed potatoes (yikes!). And then there are dishes like grilled prawns with soba noodles, defying inclusion on any Italian-American menu we've ever seen. Most of the time this iconoclastic approach works, resulting in a satisfying, interesting meal at a reasonable price. *$$; AE, DC, DIS, MC, V; no checks; lunch Mon–Fri, dinner every day; beer and wine; reservations recommended; www.ilpostale.com; near Murphy Ave.*

Kabul Afghan Cuisine / ★★

833 W EL CAMINO REAL, SUNNYVALE; 408/594-2840

This family-run establishment re-creates the Mediterranean to Southeast Asian tastes of Afghanistan's national cuisine. For a full review, see the Restaurants section of San Carlos. *$$; AE, MC, V; checks OK; lunch Mon–Fri, dinner every day; beer and wine; reservations recommended; www.kabulrestaurant.net; at Pastoira St.* ♿

Mountain View

RESTAURANTS

Amber India Restaurant / ★★

2290 EL CAMINO REAL, MOUNTAIN VIEW; 650/968-7511

Amber India offers an escape into a serene, exotic realm. The staff is solicitous and welcoming, and the food is a cut above the fare typically found in Bay Area Indian restaurants, in both quality and variety. The menu derives its inspiration from several regions of India, resulting in an adventurous selection of exceptionally flavorful yet well-balanced dishes. Appetizers include deep-fried fish pakora, *shami kabab* (lamb patties mixed with lentils and onions), and *reshmi tikka* (marinated and barbecued chicken morsels seasoned with saffron and topped with mint). A large variety of distinctively spiced curries, tandoori selections, and rice dishes rounds out the menu; come with a group so you can order enough items to sample the kitchen's impressive breadth. Intrepid diners can top off their meal with *kulfi* (saffron-flavored ice cream with pistachios) or *gulab jamun* (deep-fried cheese balls drizzled with honey). *$$; AE, DC, DIS, MC, V; no checks; lunch, dinner every day; full bar; reservations recommended; www.amber-india.com; between Rengstorff and Ortega aves.*

Hangen Szechuan Restaurant / ★★

134 CASTRO ST, MOUNTAIN VIEW; 650/964-8881

Mountain View's Castro Street is undeniably saturated with Asian restaurants of all descriptions, but chef Neng Wang's delicate and tasty Sichuan fare still has managed to carve out a distinctive niche. At lunch, Hangen caters to its workday crowd by offering multicourse menus entitled the Executive Lunch and the Business Lunch, both of which provide several choices. At dinner the chef spreads his culinary wings, and the far-ranging menu includes delights such as Emerald Shrimp (shrimp with a spinach-wine sauce perched on a bed of orange slices and lettuce), deep-fried whole fish in a spicy sauce, beef saté, conch salad, tea-smoked duck, and mushrooms in a tangerine-zest sauce. Some non-Asian customers grumble about being given a different, smaller menu than their Chinese counterparts, but they're still assured plenty of delicious options. *$$; AE, DC, MC, V; no checks; lunch, dinner every day; beer and wine; reservations recommended; just west of the Central Expressway.*

Los Altos

RESTAURANTS

Beauséjour / ★★★

170 STATE ST, LOS ALTOS; 650/948-1382

A downtown gem, Beauséjour (bow-zay-ZHUR, French for "a beautiful visit") presents French cuisine in a charming old building with a European country-house feel. The atmosphere may be a little prim, but the food is executed with rare skill and precision. Traditional favorites are well covered, including escargots in puff pastry and sautéed sweetbreads, but the menu also branches out into unusual, lighter fare. Starters might include pan-seared prawns on a bed of Parmesan mashed potatoes or duck mousse pâté with truffles. The soups are excellent, and the salads range from a very simple medley of mixed baby greens to a tiger prawn salad with grapefruit and red potatoes. The inviting entrées include roasted chicken served on marsala risotto and herbed carrots, calamari steak in a lemon-caper sauce, and filet mignon with a mushroom herb sauce. Beauséjour is also known for its duck with raspberry sauce and lamb with mint sauce and potato timbale. A reasonably priced prix-fixe dinner is offered daily and includes soup or salad, entrée, and dessert. *$$$; AE, DIS, MC, V; no checks; lunch Mon–Fri, dinner every day; full bar; reservations recommended; www.beausejourrestaurant.com; between 3rd and 4th sts.*

Chef Chu's / ★★

1067 N SAN ANTONIO RD, LOS ALTOS; 650/948-2696

Take a culinary tour of Mainland China without ever leaving your table. Feast on dim sum from Guangzhou, banquet dishes from Shanghai and Beijing, dumplings and stretched noodles from Xian, and spicy favorites from Sichuan and Hunan—all from the kitchen of Lawrence Chu, the chef-owner who's been expanding the culinary horizons of Los Altos for more than three decades. Chef Chu does all the standards well and offers some delicious innovations of his own, such as wok-seared scallops served in a spicy garlic sauce. Munch on jumbo prawns with candied pecans in a mild mustard sauce. The Peking duck, which must be ordered in advance, is crisp and flawless, with virtually all the fat melted away. *$$; AE, DC, DIS, MC, V; no checks; lunch, dinner every day; full bar; reservations recommended; www.chefchu.com; at El Camino Real.* ♿

The Peninsula

The Peninsula Q&A:

Q: Are there houses for sale on the Peninsula under $500,000?

A: Not unless you're looking for a one-bedroom fixer-upper barely standing on its last leg.

Q: Will I see one of those artsy, hand-painted VW vans driving the streets of the Peninsula?

A: Only if one is visiting from Berkeley.

Q: Will I be able to fly down Highway 101 at the speed limit anytime I like?

A: Not unless you're driving at midnight.

The Peninsula enjoys a prime location between cosmopolitan San Francisco and the Silicon Valley. As a result, living, eating, and playing here all come at a premium. From the stately mansions on University Avenue in Palo Alto to the sprawling ranch-style homes of Los Altos and the hillside estates of Woodside, the Peninsula wears its prosperity sometimes with restraint, other times with abandon, but always with pride.

With the tech explosion, the Peninsula catapulted past its already posh aura to an almost astronomical exclusivity. Since the dot-com collapse, housing prices have become slightly less prohibitive, but for most remain exorbitant.

ACCESS AND INFORMATION

SAN FRANCISCO INTERNATIONAL AIRPORT (SFO) (located off Hwy 101, just south of San Francisco; 650/821-8211; www.flysfo.com) services both the Peninsula and San Francisco (of course) handily. Well, as handily as can be expected with traffic being what it is. Plan your appointments to allow for jockeying through traffic delays to your final destination. In fact, if at all possible, it would be best not to plan anything of importance to attend to for several hours after you arrive.

Sometimes—OK, frequently—SFO can be blanketed in fog as thick and heavy as a down comforter, so don't be surprised if your takeoff or landing at SFO is delayed, especially if you're arriving on a morning when the white stuff is spilling over the Peninsula hills. Once you've landed, though, you'll find a user-friendly airport layout and plenty of taxis to spare. Shuttle services include **BAYPORTER EXPRESS** (415/467-1800; www.bayporter.com), **BAY SHUTTLE** (415/564-3400; www.bayshuttle.com), and **SUPER SHUTTLE** (415/558-8500; www.supershuttle.com). **CALTRAIN** (800/660-4287; www.caltrain.com) runs train service the length of the Peninsula from Silicon Valley to San Francisco, and **BART** (415/989-2278; www.bart.gov) has recently completed an airport connection making it much easier for travelers to visit San Francisco.

Temperatures on the Peninsula are among the coolest in the Bay Area, often by several degrees, due to its close proximity to the chilly Pacific Ocean, so it's advisable to bring a midweight jacket, even in summer; evenings can also be on the cool side.

Palo Alto

The home of **STANFORD UNIVERSITY** (www.stanford.edu), notable restaurants, fine-art galleries, foreign-movie houses, great bookstores, a thriving theater troupe, and some of the best shopping this side of heaven, Palo Alto is a beacon of cosmopolitan energy shining on the suburban sea. In spite of the fact that many of the Bay Area's rich-and-maybe-famous call Palo Alto home, much of the fuel for this cultural lighthouse comes from the university, which offers tours of its attractive campus on a fairly regular basis. Highlights of the university include the Main Quad, Hoover Tower (there are great views from its observation platform), the huge bookstore, and gorgeous Memorial Church; call the campus (650/723-2300) for more tour information. If

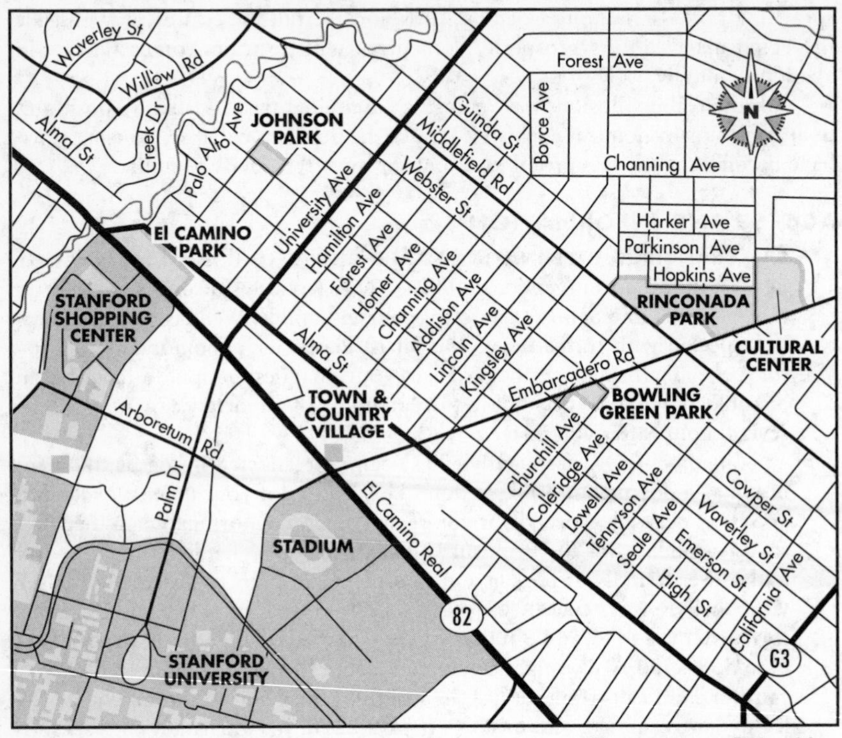

Downtown Palo Alto

you'd like to try to glimpse some atom smashing, visit the nearby **STANFORD LINEAR ACCELERATOR CENTER**; call 650/926-3300 to arrange a tour.

Moviegoers have a broad range of choices. The beautifully restored **STANFORD THEATRE** (221 University Ave; 650/324-3700; www.stanfordtheatre.org), which showcases classic flicks, is especially worth a visit. If you prefer your performances live, check out the **LIVELY ARTS SERIES** at Stanford University (650/725-2787) or the top-name talents currently appearing at the **SHORELINE AMPHITHEATER** (1 Amphitheater Pkwy, Mountain View; 650/967-4040).

If you have nothing to wear for the show (or, indeed, if you have any other shopping need), Palo Alto won't let you down. University Avenue and its side streets contain a plethora of interesting stores. The **STANFORD SHOPPING CENTER** (north of downtown on El Camino Real; 650/617-8200; www.stanfordshop.com) is a sprawling, beautifully landscaped temple of consumerism (stores include Bloomingdales, Macy's, Nordstrom, Ralph Lauren, the Gap, Crate & Barrel, and many more). Good places to eat in this shoppers' paradise include La Baguette, P. F. Chang's, Palo Alto Creamery Fountain & Grill, and Max's Opera Cafe (avoid the handsome but substandard branch of Piatti).

Although several locally owned bookstores have closed their doors, Palo Alto and its neighbors still offer some good outlets for bibliophiles. **KEPLER'S BOOKS AND MAGAZINES** (1010 El Camino Real, Menlo Park; 650/324-4321) is a wonderland for serious bookworms, and you'll find a healthy selection of mind food at **BORDERS BOOKS** (456 University Ave; 650/326-3670) and **BOOKS INC.** (at the Stanford Shopping Center, on El Camino Real near University Ave; 650/321-0600).

You'll probably need to follow that literary excursion with a cup of joe. Some of the bookstores, such as Borders, serve coffee and light snacks, but for authentic coffeehouse atmosphere and great espresso try **CAFE BORRONE** (1010 El Camino Real, Menlo Park; 650/327-0830), located right next to Kepler's.

RESTAURANTS

Bistro Elan / ★★★

448 CALIFORNIA AVE, PALO ALTO; 650/327-0284

This natty little bistro is one of the best and brightest in the California Avenue area. Although many of the offerings would be at home in any classic French bistro (duck confit, grilled pork tenderloin, lamb ragout), chef/co-owner Ambjörn Lindskog is not averse to taking cues from California cuisine. You'll find such seemingly disparate appetizers as sautéed Sonoma foie gras on brioche with oranges and arugula in hazelnut oil or fresh Maine crab with cucumber, mango, avocado, and a honey-and-coriander vinaigrette. Entrées might range from duck with English pea and Parmesan risotto to sautéed California swordfish with sweet corn, okra, and Yukon gold potatoes. Desserts include such diverse creations as a stellar warm orange chocolate cake with whipped cream, a trio of tropical fruit ice creams topped with vanilla-butter sauce, and fresh-baked cookies and cupcakes. *$$$; AE, DC, MC, V; no checks; lunch Tues–Fri, dinner Tues–Sat; beer and wine; reservations recommended; www.bistroelan.com; just off El Camino Real.* ♿

Calafia Café / ★★★

855 EL CAMINO REAL (IN TOWN & COUNTRY VILLAGE) PALO ALTO; 650/322-9200

In 1999, thousands of food fanatics showed up to try out for the coveted position of head chef at the Google campus; only Mark Ayres made the cut. And as Google rose to fame with its cutting-edge Web services, so did Ayres with his "slow food, served fast." He's now forayed this concept into a highly affordable (dishes start as low as $4.50), yet insanely tasty eatery, Calafia, which opened in 2009 in Palo Alto's Town & Country Village. Expect unique spins on classic dishes: A pizza, for example, might be topped off with spicy beef, jalapeños, and Oaxaca-style mozzarella; a braised pork shoulder mingles with citrus juices, black beans, brown rice and jicama jalapeño slaw to create the delectable Angry Pork Wrap. Desserts are scrumptious; try the Death by Chocolate or Warm Apple Galette. If you think you can't possibly fit anything more in your belly, ask for a box of gooey cookies (chocolate cinnamon, orange oatmeal raisin, peanut butter) to go. Calafia also has a quickie side, Market a Go Go, where diners on-the-go can pick up take-out orders, cafeteria-style. *$–$$; AE, DC, DIS, MC, V; no checks; breakfast, lunch, dinner every day; beer and wine; no reservations; www.calafiapaloalto.com; at Embarcadero Rd.* ♿

Evvia Estiatorio / ★★★

420 EMERSON ST, PALO ALTO; 650/326-0983

This warm and welcoming restaurant—sister to San Francisco gem, Kokkari—has a sun-drenched, Mediterranean feel. Colored bottles, ceramic plates, and copper pots line the walls and the mantel of an imposing fireplace; beaded light fixtures cast a golden glow; and wooden beams and a planked oak floor add handsome rustic accents. Traditional Greek dishes have succumbed to California's culinary charms here, resulting in an emphasis on fresh produce and interesting twists on traditional dishes such as moussaka and Greek salad. Fish and pasta dishes are other good choices, and if leg of lamb is offered as a special, order it—the meat is exceptionally tender and juicy and comes flanked by some fine roasted potatoes and vegetables. Good desserts include the baklava and the chocolate torte. Order a traditional Greek coffee to top off your meal. *$$$; AE, DC, DIS, MC, V; no checks; lunch Mon–Fri, dinner every day; full bar; reservations recommended; www.evvia.net; between Lytton and University aves.* ♿

Maddalena's Continental Restaurant / ★★★

544 EMERSON ST, PALO ALTO; 650/326-6082

If your mood is romantic, your culinary craving continental, and your wallet well padded, it's time to slip on your glad rags and head over to Maddalena's. This longtime favorite of Palo Alto's haves and have-mores is a splendid example of a dying breed: an unapologetically classic continental restaurant. The lush decor exudes an old-world formality, and waiters in tuxes hover about, ready to spring into service. Chef Jaime Maciel excels with veal dishes and such opulent fare as crisp duck with juniper berries and cassis, delicate poached salmon with a mustard-and-white-wine cream sauce, pheasant with Grand Marnier, and steak au poivre. If it's pasta you fancy, try the Fettuccine Chef Maciel (with smoked duck, spinach, and garlic in a light Roma tomato sauce) or fettuccine with lobster. The desserts, as rich and decadent as you'd expect, include a wonderful house-made cheesecake and a three-layer chocolate mousse cake. The wine list, tipped toward expensive vintages, offers mostly Italian and California selections. For a romantic surprise, book the beautifully appointed art deco private room for two upstairs. If you'd like to sample this Palo Alto classic but your bankroll is a little thin, try Cafe Fino, the less-expensive Italian bistro next door, which has the same management and shares Maddalena's kitchen. *$$$; AE, DC, MC, V; checks OK; lunch Tues–Fri, dinner Mon–Sat; full bar; reservations recommended; between University and Hamilton aves.*

Tamarine / ★★★

546 UNIVERSITY AVE, PALO ALTO; 650/325-8500

If you think the only way to enjoy Vietnamese food is at your favorite hole-in-the wall where you resort to pointing to menu items because you don't speak Vietnamese, think again. This hip, upscale Vietnamese restaurant in downtown Palo Alto is one of the best around. Owners Anne Le and Tammy Huyhn learned the trade at their family business, Vung Tau in San Jose and Milpitas, and have created an exciting concept that includes everything from a stunningly designed space showcasing the works of Vietnamese artists to exquisitely fresh, inventive food. The small plates are meant to be shared; some of the best include shrimp cupcakes made with crispy rice flour and coconut milk; juicy shaking beef served on a mound of watercress; perfectly seared ahi tuna salad over green papaya; and spicy mango and noodles topped with lemongrass sea bass. Several infused rices, such as ginger and garlic, coconut, or coriander, are available to mix and match with the wide range of flavors. For an unconventional dessert, try the chocolate-filled wontons. *$$; AE, DC, DIS, MC, V; no checks; lunch Mon–Fri, dinner every day; full bar; reservations recommended; www.tamarinerestaurant.com; between Webster and Cowper sts.*

LODGINGS

The Garden Court Hotel / ★★★

520 COWPER ST, PALO ALTO; 650/322-9000 OR 800/824-9028

If you like elegance, pampering, and a happening location (well, some people may not), this is a darn good place to stay. A flower-laden courtyard, providing the balcony view for most of the 62 rooms, is surrounded by Italianate architecture draped with arches and studded with colorful tile work and hand-wrought iron fixtures. The Mediterranean modern rooms are tinted in pastel shades of green, peach, and violet; most have four-poster beds, white faux-marble furniture, and thickly cushioned couches. The suites approach decadence; the penthouse, for example, has a fireplace, a whirlpool bath, and a wet bar. All the little details are covered in style, from an exercise room to terry-cloth robes to complimentary copies of the *Wall Street Journal*. Complimentary fresh Bing cherries and iced tea are offered to guests in the summer, and hot apple cider takes the chill off weary travelers in the winter. The hotel is in a good shopping and nightlife area, just off University Avenue, and room service is available from Il Fornaio restaurant, which shares the building. *$$$$; AE, DC, MC, V; checks OK; www.gardencourt.com; between University and Hamilton aves.* ♿

Menlo Park

RESTAURANTS

Carpaccio / ★★

1120 CRANE ST, MENLO PARK; 650/322-1211

Carpaccio was started by the same folks responsible for the wildly successful Osteria in Palo Alto, but a parting of the ways has left this restaurant to evolve along its own lines. Carpaccio holds tightly to its northern Italian roots, as evidenced by such dishes as the grilled polenta with tomatoes and pesto and the restaurant's namesake dish, served with onions, capers, lemon, and mustard, plus a grating of grana cheese and a drizzle of olive oil. The real treat here is the free-range veal: the scaloppine features veal medallions and mushrooms, but those in search of the platonic veal ideal should choose the simple grilled chop. Also keep an eye out for the prosciutto-wrapped grilled prawns with garlic and shallots in a smooth lemon-cream sauce. The wood-burning oven (with bricks imported from Italy) turns out divine pizzas with premium toppings laced together with fresh mozzarella, Gorgonzola, and fennel sausage on wonderful smoke-flavored crusts. *$$; AE, DC, MC, V; no checks; lunch Mon–Fri, dinner every day; full bar; reservations recommended; www.carpaccios.com; between Oak Grove and Santa Cruz aves.*

Marché / ★★★

898 SANTA CRUZ AVE, MENLO PARK; 650/324-9092

If you are looking for bizarre flights of food fancy, you won't find them here; Marché (market) offers refined, straightforward French-inspired food in a sophisticated and elegant setting. Chef-owner Howard Bulka's confident cooking style shines in his weekly changing menu that relies heavily on whatever is fresh at the market. Past starters included a crispy soft-shell crab with citrus slaw and chile dipping sauce; a very rich sweet corn soup with lobster garnish; and an heirloom tomato salad with house-made pita bread and hummus. Competent waitstaff seem to magically appear with impeccably prepared entrées, such as a juicy pan-roasted pork chop served with colorful spiced peach chutney. For dessert, the classic Paris-Brest of cream puff pastry and almond praline custard is downright dreamy, and the lemon tart is made with the sweetest, freshest lemon curd you will ever taste. Prices are high, but that doesn't seem to faze the predominately older clientele who frequent this upscale establishment. *$$$$; AE, DC, DIS, MC, V; no checks; dinner Tues–Sat; full bar; reservations recommended; www.restaurantmarche.com; at University Ave.*

LODGINGS

Stanford Park Hotel / ★★★

100 EL CAMINO REAL, MENLO PARK; 650/322-1234 OR 866/241-2431

Cedar shingles, dormer windows, serene courtyards, and a copper-clad gabled roof distinguish this gracious low-rise hotel near Stanford University. Some of the 163 rooms have fireplaces, balconies, vaulted ceilings, courtyard views, or parlors, and all are appointed with handsome English-style furniture and splashed with accents of green and mauve. The Stanford Park provides a fitness room, sauna, heated pool, and spa for its guests, as well as complimentary newspapers, morning coffee, turndown service, fresh-baked cookies, and shuttle service within the Menlo Park–Palo Alto area. High-speed Internet access is available. The Duck Club restaurant serves good American regional cuisine and, appropriately enough, duck is the specialty of the house. Guests can dine or enjoy an evening cocktail outside in the serene courtyard. *$$$$; AE, DC, DIS, MC, V; checks OK; www.stanfordparkhotel.com; just north of University Ave.* ♿

Woodside

RESTAURANTS

Buck's / ★★

3062 WOODSIDE RD, WOODSIDE; 650/851-8010

For nearly two decades, Jamis MacNiven's cheery and eccentric restaurant has been one of the most unlikely spots for power breakfasts in all of Silicon Valley and the Peninsula. Where else can you find high-profile execs, entrepreneurs, and venture capitalists cutting deals as they chow down on huevos rancheros and silver-dollar pancakes under brightly painted cowboy hat lamps, while life-size marlin figurines, a 6-foot plaster Statue of Liberty, and a flying horse look on? Most of the design touches play into a tongue-in-cheek Western motif, a good fit in this wealthy, horsey community. The food, however, is a cut above chuck-wagon fare. Breakfast includes tasty and well-prepared renditions of the usual muffins, waffles, egg dishes, and the like; lunch ranges from chili to hot Dungeness crab sandwiches; and dinner features a freewheeling menu that has everything from Yankee pot roast to chicken piccata "so tender it will sing you to sleep" (it says so right on the mock-newspaper-style menu). *$$; AE, DIS, MC, V; no checks; breakfast, lunch, dinner every day; full bar; reservations recommended; www.buckswoodside.com; near Canada Rd.*

John Bentley's Restaurant / ★★★

2991 WOODSIDE RD, WOODSIDE; 650/851-4988

Housed in Woodside's first firehouse, John Bentley's resembles a snug cabin inside and out. But this is a classy kind of rustic, with wood paneling on the ceiling and walls, a potbellied stove, dangling light fixtures with ribbed-glass shades, chair backs fashioned out of verdigris wrought-iron leaves, and a brown and green color scheme that heightens the mountain-retreat mood. In keeping with the atmosphere of backwoods elegance, chef-owner Bentley serves fare that's bold yet refined and generously laced with rarefied ingredients: lobster-ginger wontons in a delicate broth, ravioli stuffed with artichokes and caramelized onions, medallions of venison with shiitakes and braised red cabbage. With options like apple tart with sun-dried-cherry ice cream and a milk chocolate crème brûlée so smooth it seemingly lacks molecules, desserts are a must here. *$$$; AE, MC, V; local checks only; lunch Tues–Sat, dinner Tues–Sun; beer and wine; reservations recommended; www.johnbentleys.com/home.html; between Hwy 280 and Canada Rd.* ♿

The Village Pub / ★★★

2967 WOODSIDE RD, WOODSIDE; 650/851-9888

Don't let the name mislead you: this pub in the hills of Woodside is hardly typical of the genre—unless you're used to encountering a parking lot full of Mercedeses, Jaguars, and BMWs in front of your favorite watering hole. You won't exactly find bangers and mash on the menu either—think refined American cuisine served in a modern, elegant setting. Chef Mark Sullivan has created an inspired menu with starters that include a selection of house-cured charcuterie, decadent sweetbreads inventively prepared with poached eggs and a brown-butter vinaigrette, and a smooth-as-silk gazpacho. Only a handful of entrées are offered nightly; some intriguing choices include seared rare ahi with provençal vegetables and toasted almonds, or roasted duck breast with a rich demi-glace sauce and zucchini blossom beignets. Or you can share sorrel roasted chicken served over a fragrant saffron risotto and field greens prepared for two. A number of good California and European wines are offered by the glass, and the expert sommelier is ready to assist. Living up to its name, the Village offers a pub menu with a burger, duck confit, and other not-so-standard pub fare. *$$$; AE, DC, DIS, MC, V; no checks; lunch Mon–Fri, dinner every day; full bar; reservations recommended; www.thevillagepub.net; 1 mile west of Hwy 280.*

Redwood City

LODGINGS

Hotel Sofitel San Francisco Bay / ★★★

223 TWIN DOLPHIN DR, REDWOOD CITY; 650/598-9000

This gray behemoth perched in a corporate park is distinguished by its pretty setting on a man-made lagoon and Gallic touches provided by the French management: filigreed ironwork above the entrance, old-fashioned Parisian street lamps scattered throughout the property, and a staff endowed with charming accents. The 319 spacious guest rooms are decorated in a French country motif and feature blond-wood furniture and amenities like desks, TVs, voice mail, imported toiletries, minibars, and turndown service. The lobby and restaurants boast a large sweep of windows that take full advantage of the Sofitel's waterfront location, and the hotel is equipped with a workout room, a par course, a health and beauty spa, and an outdoor pool. French regional food is served all day at the casual Gigi Brasserie, while the formal and well-regarded Baccarat restaurant specializes in classic French cuisine. *$$$$; AE, DC, MC, V; checks OK; www.hotelsofitelsfbay.com; turn on Shoreline Dr to reach the hotel's entrance.* ♿

San Carlos

RESTAURANTS

Creo La. / ★★★

344 EL CAMINO REAL, SAN CARLOS; 650/654-0882

It took a while for this restaurant serving terrific New Orleans–style food to catch on in San Carlos, but now that the food-savvy know to ignore its inauspicious El Camino Real location and humble facade, Creo La. has come into its own. Chefs Edwin Caba and Robin Simmons know how to craft a menu that ably represents the new, lighter side of Creole and Cajun cooking. They go right to the source for many of their dishes, flying out andouille sausage, Gulf shrimp, and several other top-notch ingredients from Louisiana. For appetizers, try the Shrimp Bourbon Street (lightly battered, flash-fried prawns served with a tangy orange marmalade–horseradish sauce), Satchmo's Special (red beans and rice with andouille sausage rings), or the crawfish hush puppies with rémoulade. Interesting salads are served, too, including a Caesar topped with bacon-wrapped fried oysters. The list of entrées includes everything from alligator piccata and pan-blackened catfish to chicken with corn-bread stuffing and crawfish étouffée. Creo La.'s lineup of desserts includes a not-to-be-missed silky Cajun Velvet Pie with a light-as-air peanut butter mousse filling. *$$; AE, DC, DIS, MC, V; no checks; dinner every day; beer and wine; reservations recommended; www.creolabistro.com; just north of Holly St.* ♿

Kabul Afghan Cuisine / ★★

135 EL CAMINO REAL, SAN CARLOS; 650/594-2840

Afghanistan's national cuisine has roots ranging from the Mediterranean to Southeast Asia. This family-run establishment re-creates these tastes for Northern California with the highest-quality ingredients, including well-marbled meats along with spices the owners procure on trips to Asia and the Middle East. Set in a corner of a small shopping center, Kabul's spacious interior is unexpectedly atmospheric, with glimmering, candlelit, whitewashed stucco walls studded with bright Afghani tapestries and costumes; pink and white tablecloths; and the low whine of sitar music discreetly in the background. The management and servers are charming and attentive (even when you wander in with children—the true test of a place's friendliness quotient). A few dishes shouldn't be missed: the fragrant charbroiled lamb chops marinated in yogurt, olive oil, fresh garlic, and black and white pepper; the splendid sautéed pumpkin topped with yogurt and a tomato-based ground-beef sauce; and *aushak* (leek-and-onion-filled dumplings topped with yogurt and a meat sauce). First-timers might enjoy Kabul's combination platter for lunch—a generous sampler of three popular appetizers. Another Kabul restaurant run by the same family is located in Sunnyvale. *$$; AE, DC, MC, V; checks OK; lunch Mon–Fri, dinner every day; beer and wine; reservations recommended; www.kabulcuisine.com; in the San Carlos Plaza, between Holly St and Harbor Blvd.*

San Mateo

RESTAURANTS

Ristorante Capellini / ★★

310 BALDWIN AVE, SAN MATEO; 650/348-2296

Opened in 1990, this dapper trilevel restaurant designed by Pat Kuleto was one of the first to bring big-city sophistication to San Mateo's dining scene. The antipasto, fried calamari, and *insalata con pera* (a seasonal salad of pears, endive, radicchio, arugula, pine nuts, and Gorgonzola in a champagne-shallot vinaigrette) make excellent starters. You might move on to one of the imaginative thin-crust pizzas or to entrées such as sole piccata, veal Milanese, or steak with a merlot-mushroom sauce. The pasta is usually excellent here, light and cooked al dente; the long lineup includes linguine with assorted seafood; four-cheese ravioli in a lemon-pesto cream sauce; and penne with pancetta, tomatoes, garlic, mushrooms, and smoked mozzarella. The creamy tiramisu ranks as the most popular dessert, but the *torta di limone* and the warm bread pudding served with brandy hard sauce and a scoop of vanilla gelato are also winners. *$$$; AE, DC, MC, V; no checks; lunch Mon–Fri, dinner every day; full bar; reservations recommended; www.capellinis.com; at the corner of South B St.*

Spiedo Ristorante / ★★

233 4TH AVE, SAN MATEO; 650/375-0818

Good Italian regional fare is served in an attractive, modern setting at this family-friendly restaurant. The owners are justly proud of their mesquite-fired rotisserie, from which emerge herb-kissed and succulent chicken, game hen, rabbit, and duck. Savvy choices from the grill include the salmon, lamb chops, and pork cutlets. The kitchen also has a pleasant way with pasta, turning out delicate noodles flavored by interesting sauces; the fettuccine with prawns, green peas, and basil, and the *tortelloni di ànitra* (hat-shaped pasta filled with duck and zucchini in a sun-dried tomato and wild mushroom cream sauce) are two winners. Pizzas are quite good here, too. When it's time for dessert, forsake the unremarkable gelato and opt for the tiramisu—the raspberry sauce gives this old standard an unexpected twist. *$$; AE, DC, DIS, MC, V; no checks; lunch Mon–Sat, dinner every day; full bar; reservations recommended; www.spiedo.com; between Ellsworth and B sts.*

231 Ellsworth / ★★★

231 S ELLSWORTH ST, SAN MATEO; 650/347-7231

In 2000, this upscale restaurant that caters to the refined palates of old-money Peninsulites from Hillsborough and other tony suburbs endured a major overhaul—everything from new ownership to an entire remodel. Fortunately, the mostly American menu continues to feature fresh seasonal produce and inspired offerings like marinated baby beets with ricotta salata and house-made potato gnocchi. A duck breast served with foie gras and rhubarb, roasted halibut with English pea and leek stew and caviar, and pork tenderloin with Walla Walla onion purée and summer truffles are typical of the complex, compelling entrées. Primo desserts include light and airy sugar-and-spice brioche doughnuts with rhubarb marmalade and buttermilk panna cotta, and a delicate warm chocolate fondant bathed in an unusual caramel and fleur de sel sauce—heaven on a plate. The prodigious cellar offers more than 800 fine wines from Europe and California. Service is usually impeccable, although when the restaurant gets packed, the pace of the meal can sometimes be measured in geologic time. You'll also find three-, five-, or seven-course prix-fixe dinner menus that are not outrageously priced. *$$$; AE, DC, DIS, MC, V; checks OK; lunch Mon–Fri, dinner Mon–Sat; full bar; reservations recommended; www.231ellsworth.com; between 2nd and 3rd aves.*

Burlingame

While many of the surrounding communities are indistinguishable from the next, Burlingame has emerged as a delightful suburban town with a downtown row laden with retailers like Pottery Barn, Banana Republic, J. Crew, and an Apple Store. The central way, Burlingame Avenue, also affords multiple outdoor dining options, perfect for enjoying the city's sunny weather (even when San Francisco itself is heavily blanketed by fog, Burlingame usually remains clear and bright).

RESTAURANTS

The Crepevine / ★★☆

1310 BURLINGAME AVE, BURLINGAME (AND BRANCHES); 650/344-1310

You could visit Crepevine ten times and still not sample everything you want to try. While we recommend the casual, California-style eatery (high, airy ceilings, chalkboard-on-the-wall menu, order-at-the-counter type of service) for brunch—the sweet and savory crepes are delectable, as are the cheese blintzes and pumpkin waffles—it's also a popular lunch and dinner spot with a wide array of pasta dishes, sandwiches, and salads. Claim a spot on the large open-air patio before the place gets too crowded. Crepevine now boasts six other locations in the Bay Area as well. *$$; AE, DIS, MC, V; no checks; breakfast, lunch, dinner every day; beer and wine; no reservations; www.crepevine.com; between Park and Primose rds.* ♿

Kuleto's Trattoria / ★★

1095 ROLLINS RD, BURLINGAME; 650/342-4922

A spin-off of the popular San Francisco restaurant that bears the same name, this Burlingame branch has been one of the area's see-and-be-seen places since it opened in 1993. The sophisticated decor (which isn't, believe it or not, a product of the restaurant's namesake, designer Pat Kuleto) is bright and lively, with expanses of polished wood, a smattering of booths swathed in handsome fabrics, a large wood-burning oven, and a multilevel dining area. Alas, the northern Italian food is not always as winning as the environment—it's not uncommon to see a diner swooning with ecstasy over a meal while her companion complains about his disappointing dish. Reliable selections include baby spinach salad with crispy pancetta and goat cheese; penne with house-made lamb sausage; or roasted duck with soft polenta, braised cabbage, and grappa-soaked cherry sauce. However, the staff is often helpful about steering you through the menu's shoals, and the pizzas, salads, and many of the roast meats and pasta selections are noteworthy. *$$; AE, DC, DIS, MC, V; no checks; lunch Mon–Fri, dinner every day; full bar; reservations recommended; www.kuletostrattoria.com; just west of Hwy 101.*

Straits / ★★☆

1100 BURLINGAME AVE, BURLINGAME, 650/373-7883

Like many Singaporean joints, Straits blends the best bits of Malaysian, Indonesian, Chinese, Indian, and Nonya fare and creates dishes that will keep you coming back for more. Try the marinated sweet chile chicken lollipops, the garlic noodles, or the shrimp pad thai. The outdoor tables along Burlingame Avenue are nice on warm afternoons (which are most days in sunny Burlingame). Straits has another location in San Francisco and a third in San Jose. *$$; AE, DIS, MC, V; local checks OK; lunch, dinner every day; full bar; reservations recommended; www.straitsrestaurants.com; at California Dr.* ♿

LODGINGS

Embassy Suites San Francisco Airport–Burlingame / ★★★

150 ANZA BLVD, BURLINGAME; 650/342-4600

This hotel's a towering pink-and-aqua spectacle more typical of the sunny Southland than Northern California. In front, a cobblestone drive encircles a Spanish-style fountain; just inside, another fountain gurgles in front of the junglelike atrium. Each of the 340 suites has a private bedroom and a separate living room complete with a refrigerator, a wet bar, a coffeemaker, a microwave, two color televisions, two telephones, and a pullout sofa bed. Ask for a room overlooking San Francisco Bay. You can amuse yourself by lounging in the indoor swimming pool or by checking out the action at Rings Lounge, a popular singles bar and restaurant specializing in hearty fare like steaks, ribs, and chops. *$$$; AE, DC, DIS, MC, V; no checks; www.embassyburlingame.com; just off Hwy 101.* ♿

Millbrae

RESTAURANTS

Hong Kong Flower Lounge / ★★★

51 MILLBRAE AVE, MILLBRAE; 650/692-6666

Hong Kong, probably the world's most competitive culinary arena, has hundreds of excellent restaurants vying to produce the freshest, subtlest, and most exciting flavors. In 1987 Alice Wong, whose family owns four Flower Lounges in and around that city, expanded their empire to California with a small restaurant on Millbrae's main drag (which was sold a few years back). Its success prompted her to open another, fancier branch on Millbrae Avenue. Fortunately, the food at the Millbrae location has remained legendary, thanks largely to the Hong Kong chefs, who continue to produce cuisine according to the stringent standards of their home city. The red, gold, and jade decor is pure Kowloon glitz (although the patrons are comfortably informal), and the service is outstanding. Among the best dishes on the vast menu are the exquisite minced squab in lettuce cups, the delicate crystal scallops in shrimp sauce, the fried prawns with walnuts, and any fish fresh from the live tank. An excellent Peking duck is served at a moderate price. *$$; AE, DC, DIS, MC, V; no checks; lunch, dinner every day; full bar; reservations recommended; at El Camino Real.*

South San Francisco

Flanked by San Bruno Mountain to the north and the bay to the east, South San Francisco is often mistaken as merely the southern part of the City by the Bay, when in actuality it is its own municipality. Home to **SFO INTERNATIONAL AIRPORT**, South City (as the locals call it) is many visitors' first stop in the Bay Area, though they may not even know it. True, it's largely residential, and the Hollywood-like "South San Francisco: the Industrial City" hillside sign that greets you isn't the most appealing welcome, but if you need a quick bite en route to your flight out, a small handful of neighborhood gems do exist.

RESTAURANTS

Di Napoli Ristorante & Pizzeria / ★★★

202 GRANDE AVE, SOUTH SAN FRANCISCO; 650/873-5252

This popular Italian eatery doesn't have a lot of seating but is big on authenticity and has thrived in old downtown South San Francisco for 18 years. The delightful *quatrro formaggio* or thin-crust Margherita pizza could hail from any southern port in Italy. We recommend creating your own pie from the long list of fresh, plucked-from-the-garden veggies, including roasted red pepper, artichoke, and caramelized onion. Or you can peruse the extensive menu, with plenty of seafood and dessert options, and order online; delivery is free (11am–11pm every day). *$$; AE, MC, V; no checks; lunch, dinner every day; beer and wine; no reservations; www.dinapolipizza.com; at Cypress Ave.* ♿

JoAnn's Café / ★★

1131 EL CAMINO REAL, SOUTH SAN FRANCISCO; 650/872-2810
Long a favorite of locals and celebrities like Joe Montana, JoAnn's was sold to its staff a few years back. The result is a fusion of old-school country café and Latin diner that packs the seats on weekends. Outdoor coffee service in the chilly fog is a nice touch for those waiting for a seat. Huge platters of locally produced food, friendly service, and an eclectic menu are some of the highlights at this hidden café. JoAnn's is best for breakfast, serving up steaming platters of pancakes and eggs Benedict. *$$; AE, MC, V; local checks only; breakfast, lunch, dinner every day; no alcohol; no reservations; at Del Paso Dr.* ♿

White Elephant Restaurant / ★★

146 HAZELWOOD DR, SOUTH SAN FRANCISCO; 650/873-8341
Once a comic book store, this small but quite popular and clean Thai eatery can easily be overlooked as it's tucked in residential district just off El Camino Real. The food here is best summarized in one word: fresh. Elegant and simple curry or noodle dishes come piping hot to your table before you've had a chance to dig into the corn cake or fried tofu appetizer. The Thai iced tea is house-made and some of the best around. *$$; AE, MC, V; no checks; lunch, dinner every day; beer and wine; no reservations; at Mosswood Wy.* ♿

LODGINGS

Inn at Oyster Point / ★★

425 MARINA BLVD, SOUTH SAN FRANCISCO; 650/737-7633
This small, pleasant hotel accentuates the positive (attractive, well-appointed rooms, a spectacular bay setting) and diminishes the negative (you have to wade through an industrial park to get here). In keeping with its marina setting, the modern Cape Cod–style inn is decked out in a snappy blue-and-white color scheme, and the 30 guest rooms have bay views, feather beds, and tile fireplaces. A continental breakfast is included in the price of the room, and there's free shuttle service to nearby San Francisco International Airport (by prior arrangement). A branch of Dominic's Italian restaurant occupies part of the first floor; its deck overlooks the marina and is a great place for lunch on a warm day. *$$$; AE, DC, DIS, MC, V; no checks; www.innatoysterpoint.com; take the Oyster Pt Blvd exit off Hwy 101, head toward the bay, and turn right at Marina Blvd.*

Pacifica

Due west of San Francisco's airport lies the coastal community of Pacifica that has long thrived as a beginner surfing hot spot and gateway to the wilder environs of this rugged coast. Travel south past this three-beach enclave along Highway 1 and the scenery shifts into untouched nature protected by state park regulations. Whale sightings are common from the many tide pool nature preserves, and the entire coastline breathes with a vibrancy not found in more populated areas. This is a place to escape the tumble and roil of modern society and perhaps swim with a seal or two. Don't forget to bring along an extra layer of warmth, like a sweater and long pants.

RESTAURANTS

Nick's Restaurant / ★☆

100 ROCKAWAY BEACH AVE, PACIFICA; 650/359-3900

This wayside Motel Six doppelgänger of a restaurant and bar, smack-dab in the middle of Rockaway Beach, represents the last ocean-side restaurant—besides Taco Bell—until you reach Half Moon Bay. The late-night jazz and lounge singers at Nick's might be best suited for the graying demographic, but the brunch will chase the hangover of any hard-partying adventurer out for an early morning drive down gorgeous Highway 1. The standard American cuisine includes omelets, a fantastic eggs Benedict, and enormous waffles with strawberry or blueberry smotherings. For the true fish aficionado, there's the seafood omelet stuffed with shrimp and fresh Dungeness crab, sautéed tomatoes, and onions. Friday and Saturday nights host live music in the lounge and an extensive dinner menu filled with massive seafood platters. *$$; AE, MC, V; no checks; breakfast, lunch, dinner every day; full bar; reservations recommended; www.nicksrestaurant.net; off San Marlo Wy.* ♿

CENTRAL COAST

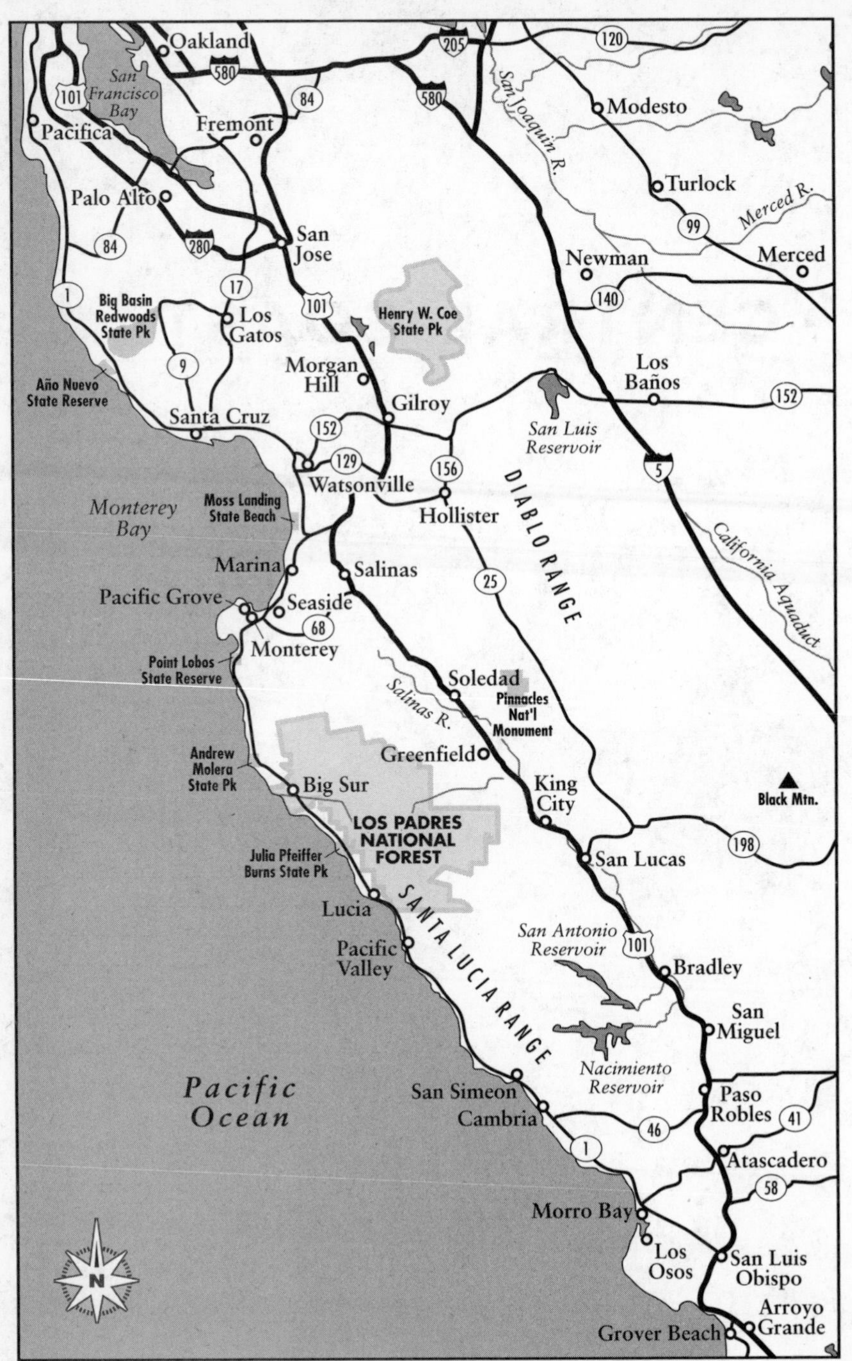
Oakland
San Francisco Bay
Pacifica
Fremont
Palo Alto
San Jose
Modesto
Turlock
Merced R.
San Joaquin R.
Newman
Merced
Big Basin Redwoods State Pk
Los Gatos
Henry W. Coe State Pk
Morgan Hill
Año Nuevo State Reserve
Santa Cruz
Gilroy
Los Baños
San Luis Reservoir
Watsonville
Hollister
DIABLO RANGE
Monterey Bay
Moss Landing State Beach
Marina
Salinas
Pacific Grove
Seaside
Monterey
California Aquaduct
Point Lobos State Reserve
Soledad
Salinas R.
Pinnacles Nat'l Monument
Greenfield
Andrew Molera State Pk
Big Sur
King City
Black Mtn.
LOS PADRES NATIONAL FOREST
Julia Pfeiffer Burns State Pk
San Lucas
Lucia
SANTA LUCIA RANGE
Pacific Valley
San Antonio Reservoir
Bradley
San Miguel
Nacimiento Reservoir
Pacific Ocean
San Simeon
Cambria
Paso Robles
Atascadero
Morro Bay
Los Osos
San Luis Obispo
Arroyo Grande
Grover Beach
N
1
9
17
25
41
46
58
68
84
99
101
120
129
140
152
156
198
205
280
580
5

CENTRAL COAST

With its dramatic coastlines, farmlands, forests, and unique small towns, Northern California's Central Coast offers up breathtaking beauty with laid-back style. Even though it's easily accessible from either San Francisco or Southern California, the Central Coast feels as though it's taken a time-out from the rush and noise of the rest of the world. It's the perfect place to spend hours collecting seashells or listening to the silence of the redwood trees, and you won't have to worry about bumping elbows with anyone. With 16 state and national parks, there's more than enough nature to go around.

The largest park on the Central Coast is one you might not see up close, unless you take a fishing or whale-watching excursion from Half Moon Bay, Santa Cruz, or Monterey, but its influence and importance is felt everywhere here. The Monterey Bay Marine Sanctuary, established in 1992, is a vast biologic conservatory that stretches from the mouth of the San Francisco Bay in the north to the tip of Big Sur in the south, encompassing one-fifth of California's coastline and covering 5,300 square miles. Monterey Canyon, the most dramatic submarine feature of the sanctuary, is more than 10,000 feet deep and rivals the Grand Canyon in size and topographic complexity. The nutrient-enriched seawater that upwells from its steep walls draws in more than 30 species of marine mammals, making it one of the Northern Hemisphere's most diversified underwater areas. On land, the Central Coast is dotted with beach towns, farm communities, and vacation destinations; underwater, it's an international hub.

ACCESS AND INFORMATION

Northern California's Central Coast includes nearly 400 miles of shoreline, from Pacifica in the north to Big Sur in the south. **HIGHWAY 1**, also named the Cabrillo Highway after the first Spanish explorer to lay claim to the land, is a scenic two-lane highway that meanders all along the coast, connecting with **HIGHWAY 92** at Half Moon Bay, **HIGHWAY 17** at Santa Cruz, and **HIGHWAY 101** near Monterey. The Central Coast's inland valleys are served by Highway 101, but anyone traveling the inland route from San Francisco will want to take **HIGHWAY 280** to avoid commuter traffic on the 101 San Francisco–San Jose stretch.

SAN FRANCISCO INTERNATIONAL AIRPORT (SFO) (650/821-8211; www.flysfo.com) offers passengers the largest international terminal in the nation, while visitors to points south—Santa Cruz to Big Sur—will appreciate the convenience of **SAN JOSE INTERNATIONAL AIRPORT** (408/501-7600; www.sjc.org). It's smaller than SFO and less congested but offers many of the same flights as its larger cousin to the north. Car rentals are available at both airports and in the larger cities, such as Santa Cruz and Monterey.

With a rainy season that lasts from November through March, and an average daily temperature of 60°F—that's year-round—no one's ever going to confuse the Central Coast with Malibu. During spring and summer, offshore breezes strip away the warm surface waters of the Pacific and bring frigid waters to the top. The result is a heavy marine layer (a.k.a. fog) that settles over the coast morning and evening. It's always wise to carry a sweater, as summer can be just as blustery as winter. This might not be everyone's idea of perfect beach weather, but when summer temps scorch the valleys there's a massive influx of cool-ocean-breeze worshippers. The best months are September and October, when the crowds disappear along with the fog.

Half Moon Bay Region

With the exception of Half Moon Bay, the picturesque stretch of shore between Moss Beach and Año Nuevo has been left undisturbed by development (thanks in part to the often blustery weather hereabouts). This lack of superluxe lodgings is a boon to nature lovers, as many of the beaches are open to the public. Check out the marine life at Moss Beach's Fitzgerald Reserve, or pay a visit to the elephant seals' breeding ground at Año Nuevo.

ACCESS AND INFORMATION

The fastest way to the Half Moon Bay region from San Francisco is to take the Highway 92 exit off Interstate 280, which leads straight into town. Far more scenic, however, is the drive along Highway 1, which, aside from the section known as Devils Slide, moves right along at a 50mph clip. The entrance to Half Moon Bay's Main Street is located about two blocks up (east) Highway 92 from the Highway 1 intersection. Head toward the Shell station, then turn right (south) onto Main Street until you cross a small bridge.

For more information, contact the **HALF MOON BAY VISITORS BUREAU** (235 Main St; 650/726-8380; www.halfmoonbaychamber.org or www.coastsidelive.com; open 9am–4pm Mon–Fri, 10am–3pm Sat).

Moss Beach

Don't take it personally if you've never heard of Moss Beach; this tiny town between Pacifica and Half Moon Bay has had a long history of being discreet. During the Prohibition years, bootleggers stored their illegal wares along the hollowed-out sea cliffs below and depleted them at the Moss Beach Distillery above. Today, despite the excellent selection of beaches and tide pools in the area, Moss Beach is anything but a tourist town—for shopping, dining, and such, a short drive down to Half Moon Bay is a requisite.

The highlight of Moss Beach is the **JAMES V. FITZGERALD MARINE RESERVE** (415/728-3584; www.fitzgeraldreserve.org). At high tide, one wonders what all the excitement is about, but come back at low tide and wow! Thirty-five acres of tidal reef house more than 200 species of marine animals—sea anemones, urchins, snails, hermit and rock crabs, starfish, sponges—making it one of the most diverse tidal basins on the West Coast (and one of the safest, thanks to a wave-buffering rock terrace 50 yards from the beach). It's OK to touch the marine life as long as you don't pick it up, but nothing—not even a rock—is available as a souvenir. Call the reserve before coming to find out about the tide and the docent-led tour schedules (tours are usually on Saturdays). No dogs are allowed, and rubber-soled shoes are recommended. It's located at the west end of California Avenue off Highway 1 in Moss Beach.

RESTAURANTS

Moss Beach Distillery / ★★

140 BEACH WY, MOSS BEACH; 650/728-5595

Used by bootleggers during Prohibition to store their illicit wares, this coastal grande dame was treated to a $2 million face-lift back in 1997. With its blue-painted walls, cozy dining alcoves, and massive patio and windows affording magnificent ocean views, the cliff-side landmark still has its beguiling 1920s beach-house atmosphere. The food has gotten considerably better, too. Gone is the pedestrian surf-and-turf fare; in its place are creative California–Mediterranean dishes such as grilled portobello mushrooms with cabernet sauce, shrimp tempura with a ginger vinaigrette, and a fork-tender pork chop enlivened by a mustard-shallot sauce and leek-buttermilk mashed potatoes. As if the views, historical setting, and good food weren't enough, the Distillery also lays claim to a couple of resident ghosts, including the famous Blue Lady, a flapper-era beauty who's said to haunt the place searching for her faithless lover. *$$; DC, DIS, MC, V; no checks; lunch Mon–Sat, dinner every day, brunch Sun (patio menu available all day); full bar; reservations recommended; www.mossbeachdistillery.com; from Hwy 1, take the Cypress Ave turnoff and turn right on Marine Blvd, which turns into Beach Wy.*

LODGINGS

Seal Cove Inn / ★★★

221 CYPRESS AVE, MOSS BEACH; 650/728-4114 OR 800/995-9987

Karen Brown Herbert (who published her own line of guidebooks) knows what makes a superior bed-and-breakfast, and she didn't miss a trick when she and her husband, Rick, set up their own. The result is a gracious, sophisticated B and B that somehow manages to harmoniously blend California, New England, and European influences in a spectacular seacoast setting. The large, vaguely English-style country manor has 10 bedrooms that overlook a colorful half-acre wildflower garden dotted with birdhouses. All rooms have fireplaces, fresh flowers, antique furnishings, original watercolors, grandfather clocks, hidden televisions with DVD players, and refrigerators stocked with free beverages. One thing's for sure: you won't starve here. Early in the morning, you'll find coffee and a newspaper outside your door, and a full breakfast is served wherever you prefer. In the afternoon, wine and hors d'oeuvres are offered in the dining room. The inn's extravagant backyard garden fronts open parkland with seaside meadows and a miniforest of cypress trees. On the other side of the park is the Fitzgerald Marine Reserve. *$$$$; AE, DIS, MC, V; checks OK; www.sealcoveinn.com; 6 miles north of Half Moon Bay on Hwy 1, then west on Cypress Ave.* ♿

Princeton-by-the-Sea

At the north end of Half Moon Bay is the small, quiet community of Princeton-by-the-Sea, anchored by the industrial-strength **PILLAR POINT HARBOR**, a major supplier to San Francisco's seafood market. Until recently it was a one-hotel town, but within the last couple of years Princeton has beefed up its tourism market by adding several new hotels and restaurants.

RESTAURANTS

Barbara's Fish Trap / ★

281 CAPISTRANO RD, PRINCETON-BY-THE-SEA; 650/728-7049

To get any closer to the ocean than Barbara's Fish Trap, you'd have to get your feet wet. Situated on stilts above the beach, Barbara's has indoor and outdoor dining with panoramic views of Half Moon Bay. The decor is classic fish-and-chips (complete with plastic checkered tablecloths, fishnets on the ceilings, and a wooden fisherman by the door), but the food is a cut above. Barbara's offers a large selection of deep-fried seafood as well as daily fresh fish specials such as tangy Cajun-spiced snapper. The garlic prawns, clam chowder, calamari tempura, and steamed mussels are all local favorites, as is the ever-important beer selection. Lunch is a far better deal than the inflated dinner prices; better yet, order some fried clams from the walkaway counter and go for a stroll down the wharf. *$$; no credit cards; local checks only; lunch, dinner every day; beer and wine; no reservations; 4 miles north of Half Moon Bay on Hwy 1, west on Capistrano Rd to Pillar Point Harbor.*

LODGINGS

Pillar Point Inn / ★★

380 CAPISTRANO RD, PRINCETON-BY-THE-SEA; 650/728-7377 OR 800/400-8281

Located on a bustling harbor with a commercial fishing fleet, sportfishing and whale-watching charters, a few popular restaurants, and a busy pier, this modern inn is surprisingly quiet. Cheery and reminiscent of Cape Cod, the inn's 11 sunny, smallish rooms have harbor views, private baths, gas fireplaces, feather beds, televisions with DVD players, VCRs, and video libraries. Breakfast, served in the common room, includes coffee, tea, juice, house-made granola, fresh fruit, and a daily hot entrée such as cheese-potato pie, quiche, or Belgian waffles. *$$$–$$$$; AE, MC, V; checks OK; www.pillarpointinn.com; 4 miles north of Half Moon Bay on Hwy 1, then west on Capistrano Rd.* ♿

Half Moon Bay

Victorian houses and boutiques line downtown Half Moon Bay, the oldest city in San Mateo County, while produce stands, U-pick farms, well-stocked nurseries, and flower farms ring its perimeter. Once a sleepy town whose main attraction was its annual Pumpkin Festival, Half Moon Bay has become a satellite city for neighboring Silicon Valley—and has seen its real estate prices rise right along with the sale of microchips. At once chichi and funky, it has an old-time Americana ambience that residents and visitors love; anyone witnessing its Fourth of July parade or annual Civil War Reenactment will get a kick out of the low-key, small-town hoopla. Half Moon Bay also has a history as a hippie haven: rocker Neil Young lives in the mountains off Highway 92, and tie-dyed establishments such as **MYSTIC GIFTS** (433 Main St; 650/712-1697; www.mysticgifts.us) and the **FLIGHT OF THE HAWK CENTER FOR CONTEMPORARY SHAMANISM** (650/562-1074; www.flightofthehawk.com) somehow fit right in with the flag-waving elders and cell-phoning commuters. Even though there's plenty to see and do, and enough good restaurants to keep you well fed from dawn to dusk, Half Moon Bay is the antithesis of bright lights, big city. From all indications it plans to stay that way—good news for those looking for a peaceful getaway.

Since 1970 the **HALF MOON BAY ART & PUMPKIN FESTIVAL** has featured all manner of squash cuisine and crafts, as well as the Giant Pumpkin weigh-in contest, won recently by a 974-pound monster. A Great Pumpkin Parade, pumpkin-carving competitions, pie-eating contests, and piles of great food pretty much assure a good time for all; for more information call the **PUMPKIN HOTLINE** (650/726-9652; www.miramarevents.com).

The best way to explore the small, flat town of Half Moon Bay and its beaches is on a beach cruiser–style bicycle, available for rent at the **BIKE WORKS** (520 Kelly St in downtown Half Moon Bay; 650/726-6708). Prices range from $10 an hour to $35 all day. Be sure to ask one of the staffers about the best biking trails in the area, particularly the wonderful beach trail from Kelly Avenue to Pillar Point Harbor.

Once you have explored the town, spend some time hiking through **PURISIMA CREEK REDWOODS** (650/691-1200), a little-known sanctuary frequented mostly by locals. Located on the western slopes of the Santa Cruz Mountains, the preserve is filled with fern-lined creek banks, lush redwood forests, and fields of wildflowers and berries that are accessible to hikers, mountain bikers, and equestrians along miles of trails. From the Highway 1/Highway 92 intersection in Half Moon Bay, drive 1 mile south on Highway 1 to Higgins Purisima Creek Road and turn left, then continue 4½ miles to a small gravel parking lot—that's the trailhead.

Another popular Half Moon Bay activity is deep-sea fishing. Even if you don't fish, it's worth a trip to **PILLAR POINT HARBOR** (4 miles north of Half Moon Bay off Hwy 1) to take in the pungent aroma of the sea; the rows of rusty trawlers and the salty men and women tending to endless chores evoke a sort of Hemingwayish sense of romance. Pillar Point Harbor is just that sort of big ol' fishing harbor. Visitors are encouraged to walk along the pier and even partake in a fishing trip. **HUCK FINN SPORTFISHING** (650/726-7133 or 800/572-2934) charges around $65, including rod and reel, for a day's outing—a small price to pay for 30 pounds of fresh snapper or salmon. Between December and March, whale-watching trips also depart on weekends from either Huck Finn (www.halfmoonbaywhalewatch.com; $45 for 3-hour trip) or **HALF MOON BAY SPORTFISHING** (650/726-2913; www.fishingboat.com; $40 for 3-hour trip) at Pillar Point Harbor.

Near the harbor is one of the most infamous surf beaches in California: **MAVERICK BEACH**. Maverick—which initially placed Northern California on the global surf scene—has some of the most volatile waves on the West Coast and, thus, is beloved by adrenaline junkies. An annual surf competition, one of the most celebrated events among hard-core surfers, takes place here if the weather's right (often it's not). On calmer days, though, secluded Maverick Beach is still a good place to escape the weekend crowds because, although everyone's heard about the beach, few know where it is (it's not on any map). Here's the dope: From Capistrano Road at Pillar Point Harbor, turn left on Prospect Way, left on Broadway, right on Princeton, then right on Westpoint to the West Shoreline Access parking lot (on your left). Park here then continue up Westpoint on foot toward the Pillar Point Satellite Tracking Station. Take about 77 steps, and on your right will be a trailhead leading to legendary Maverick Beach a short distance away.

If surfing isn't your thing, how about ocean kayaking? If you're one of those Type A people who can't just lie on the beach and relax, **CALIFORNIA CANOE & KAYAK** (Pillar Pt Harbor at the Half Moon Bay Yacht Club; 800/366-9804; www.calkayak.com) has the answer: for $49 they'll take you out on the bay for a half-day tour of Pillar Point Harbor, allowing you to get up close and personal with harbor seals, marine birds, and other wildlife; rentals are also available.

Back on land is the **ANDREOTTI FAMILY FARM** (329 Kelly Ave, halfway between Hwy 1 and the beach; 650/726-9461; open until 6pm year-round). If you like vegetables, you'll love this place. Every Friday, Saturday, and Sunday one of the family members slides open the old barn door at 10am sharp to reveal a cornucopia of just-picked artichokes, peas, brussels sprouts, beans, strawberries, and whatever else is growing in their adjacent fields. The Andreotti enterprise has been in operation since 1926, so it's a sure bet they know their veggies.

If you're a golfer, be sure to reserve a tee time at one of the two ocean-side 18-hole courses at **HALF MOON BAY GOLF LINKS** (2 Miramontes Pt Rd, next to the Ritz-Carlton; 650/726-1800; www.halfmoonbaygolf.com). The Old Course (still our favorite) was designed by Arnold Palmer and is rated among the top 100 courses in the country. The newer Ocean Course was designed by award-winning golf architect Arthur Hills in the tradition of Scotland's finest "links" courses, with challenges to rival those in Scotland. Reserve for both courses as far in advance as possible.

On your way out of town, be sure to stop at **OBESTER WINERY'S WINE-TASTING AND SALES ROOM** (12341 San Mateo Rd; 650/726-9463; www.obesterwinery.com; open 10am–5pm every day), which is only a few miles from Half Moon Bay up Highway 92. It's a pleasant drive—passing numerous fields of flowers, Christmas tree farms, and pumpkin patches—to this wood shack filled with award-winning wines. Behind the tasting room is a small picnic area that's perfect for an afternoon lunch break.

RESTAURANTS

Pasta Moon / ★★

315 MAIN ST, HALF MOON BAY; 650/726-5125

Like many California eateries these days, Pasta Moon features lots of locally grown organic produce and fresh fish. Start with an appetizer of Half Moon Bay artichokes à la grecque, served with Italian butter beans, arugula, and lemon vinaigrette, or house-smoked salmon with pickled pearl onions and parsley salad. *Secondi piatti* include Hawaiian butterfish baked in parchment paper with artichoke, capers, oven-dried tomatoes, white wine, lemon, and olive oil-poached potatoes; and baked eggplant parmesan with buffalo mozzarella, smoked provolone, tomatoes, garlic, and basil. The focaccia is heavenly, the house-made pasta seldom disappoints, and the thin-crust pizza creations delight pizza lovers. Pastas, breads, and pastries are all made on the premises. *$$; AE, DC, DIS, MC, V; local checks only; lunch, dinner every day, brunch Sun; full bar; reservations recommended; www.pastamoon.com; in the Tin Palace, at the north end of Main St, near Hwy 92.*

San Benito House / ★★

356 MAIN ST, HALF MOON BAY; 650/726-3425

A pastel blue Victorian on Half Moon Bay's Main Street, San Benito House has a candlelit dining room that's one of the prettiest on the Central Coast, decorated with country antiques, vases of fresh flowers, and paintings by local turn-of-the-century artists. At lunch, the deli café turns out top-notch sandwiches on fresh house-made bread, perfect for a repast in the garden or on one of the nearby beaches. At dinnertime the kitchen prepares such interesting European fare as homemade ravioli stuffed with fennel, fontina, and toasted almonds with creamy leek sauce or salmon topped with a lemon-caper vinaigrette on a bed of lentil ragout. Desserts are terrific and may include a strawberry-rhubarb crepe served with crème anglaise and strawberry sauce or a pear poached with ginger and port wine. Too stuffed to move? Consider spending the night upstairs in one of the dozen modest but cheerful guest rooms (the one above the garden is the best). Arrive a bit early for a predinner cocktail at the cozy old-fashioned saloon. *$$; AE, DC, MC, V; no checks (restaurant), advance checks OK (hotel); breakfast, lunch, dinner every day; full bar; reservations recommended; www.sanbenitohouse.com; at Mill St.* ♿

Sushi Main Street / ★★

696 MILL ST, HALF MOON BAY; 650/726-6336

The food is Japanese, the decor is Balinese, and the background music might be anything from up-tempo Latin to bebop American. Hard to envision, yes, but these elements come together beautifully at Sushi Main Street, a funky yet tranquil oasis in the heart of town. Grab a seat at the L-shaped sushi bar, pull up a chair at one of the rust-colored asymmetrical slate tables, or, if you're feeling limber, plunk yourself down at the large, low table designed for traditional cross-legged dining. You might want to tickle your tonsils with a drop of the special sake (served room temperature in a traditional wooden box) or nosh on a kelp salad (a crisp, sesame-laden mixture of Japanese seaweeds) before diving into your main course. You can choose from a wide range of sushi and sashimi, from arctic surf clams to marinated mackerel. For a Zen sense of wholeness, top off your meal with green-tea ice cream or a dessert roll with papaya, plum paste, sesame seeds, and teriyaki sauce. *$$; MC, V; checks OK; lunch, dinner every day; beer, wine, and sake; reservations recommended; www.sushimainstreet.com; just off Main St.*

LODGINGS

Beach House Inn at Half Moon Bay / ★★★

4100 N CABRILLO HWY/HWY 1, HALF MOON BAY; 650/712-0220 OR 800/315-9366

This three-story Cape Cod–style building overlooking Pillar Point Harbor offers 54 deluxe suites with enough amenities to make you feel right at home. Each guest room features a separate sleeping area, step-down living room with fireplace, private patio or balcony, wet bar, refrigerator, microwave, two TVs, and five-CD player. Oversize baths offer deep soaking tubs and separate showers. A small swimming pool and roomy Jacuzzi spa on the south-facing terrace afford views of Surfer's Beach and local surfers—a perfect place to warm up on a foggy morning. If the spa and the calming sound of surf aren't enough to work out those stress-related kinks, make an appointment with the Beach House Day Spa for a massage or aromatherapy wrap; for a small extra charge, the massage therapists will perform their healing ministrations in your room. A complimentary continental breakfast is served in the lobby. *$$$$; AE, DC, DIS, MC, V; checks OK; www.beach-house.com; 3 miles north of Half Moon Bay.*

Cypress Inn on Miramar Beach / ★★★

407 MIRADA RD, HALF MOON BAY; 650/726-6002 OR 800/832-3224

With Miramar Beach literally 10 steps away, this wonderful modern inn is the place to commune with the ocean along the Peninsula coast. From each of its 12 rooms you not only see the ocean but also hear it, smell it, even feel it when a fine mist drifts in with the morning fog. The cheerful wooden building, set at the end of a residential block, has beamed ceilings, skylights, terra-cotta tiles, colorful folk art, and warm, rustic furniture made of pine, heavy wicker, and leather: sort of a Santa-Fe-meets-California effect. All guest rooms in both the main Beach House building and the newer Lighthouse annex across the street are romantically outfitted with feather beds, gas fireplaces, private baths, and ocean views. Most have private balconies, and the enormous penthouse also boasts a two-person soaking tub. Breakfast is far above the standard B and B fare; expect fresh juices, croissants, a fruit parfait, and made-to-order entrées such as eggs Benedict and the inn's signature peaches-and-cream French toast. *$$$$; AE, MC, V; local checks only; www.cypressinn.com; 3 miles north of the junction of Hwys 92 and 1, turn west on Medio Rd, and follow it to the end.* ♿

Mill Rose Inn / ★★

615 MILL ST, HALF MOON BAY; 650/726-8750 OR 800/900-7673

One of the oldest bed-and-breakfasts on the Peninsula coast, the Mill Rose Inn fancies itself an old-fashioned English country house, with an extravagant garden and flower boxes as well as all the requisite lace curtains, antique beds, and nightstands. Romantics may love it here, but the inn's profusion of fabric flowers and slightly garish wallpapers (think William Morris on LSD) take it over the top for many folks; frankly, the overall effect is more Harlequin romance than authentic British country manor. But the rooms are spacious and chock-full of creature comforts, and the Jacuzzi, tucked inside a frosted-glass gazebo, is quite enjoyable on a chilly coastal evening. The six guest rooms have king- or queen-size feather beds, clawfoot tubs, fireplaces (with the exception of the Baroque Rose Room), and views of the garden. They also have telephones, televisions with cable and VCRs, well-stocked refrigerators, fresh flowers, chocolates, and liqueurs. *$$$–$$$$; AE, DIS, MC, V; checks OK; www.millroseinn.com; 1 block north of Main St.*

Old Thyme Inn / ★★

779 MAIN ST, HALF MOON BAY; 650/726-1616 OR 800/720-4277

Located on the quiet southern end of Main Street, this 1898 B and B is the epitome of Victorian style and grace. All of the seven guest rooms, painted in restful colors and decorated with well-chosen antiques, offer private baths, TVs and VCRs, and sumptuous queen-size feather beds topped with down comforters and imported linens. The Garden Room and the Thyme Room feature double whirlpool tubs and fireplaces. Every morning, innkeepers Rick and Kathy Ellis serve gourmet breakfasts with delectable entrées such as lemon-rosemary or banana-coconut crumb cake, quiche du jour, *chiles rellenos*, zucchini soufflé, or eggs Benedict. Wine and hors d'oeuvres are served daily in the parlor. *$$$–$$$$; AE, DC, DIS, MC, V; checks OK; www.oldthymeinn.com; near Filbert St.*

The Ritz-Carlton Half Moon Bay / ★★★★

ONE MIRAMONTES PT RD, HALF MOON BAY; 650/712-7000

From the moment you enter the Ritz-Carlton estate, perched high above the Pacific on the edge of a bluff, it's as if you've been transported to the craggy Scottish coast (the hotel's prime position between two golf courses only further enhances this image). You really need a map to navigate the grounds, as you could easily get lost exploring. Each room comes equipped with your typical five-star amenities: spa robes and slippers, an honor bar, a refrigerator, three telephones with voice mail, a safe, a TV and DVD player, and luxury bath products. The marble bathrooms are large with showers and soaking tubs. Ask for a room with an ocean view—spectacular. Guests also have access to the Colony Club tennis courts, racquets, and ball machine; basketball court; both golf courses; swimming pool, hot tub, sauna, and water aerobic equipment; fitness center; beauty salon; 16,000-square-foot spa; boutique; Roman mineral bath; and much, much more. Heck, there's even a "technology" butler on hand to solve all your computer dilemmas. As if all that weren't enough, the hotel organizes fun family activities like S'mores Night and an outdoor Hot Chocolate Bar (liquor optional) on weekends. Try a blind tasting test in the wine room, ENO (housed beside the Conservatory Room), before eating the best meal (including breakfast) on the coast at Navio. *$$$$; AE, DIS, MC, V; no checks; www.ritzcarlton.com; at the end of Miramontes Pt Rd.* ♿

The Zaballa House / ★★

324 MAIN ST, HALF MOON BAY; 650/726-9123

The oldest building in Half Moon Bay, this 1859 pastel blue Victorian offers a few amenities that go beyond the usual B and B offerings. Homey, pretty, and unpretentious, the nine guest rooms in the main house are decorated with understated wallpaper and country furniture. Some have fireplaces, vaulted ceilings, or garden views. None have telephones, but three rooms have TVs. An addition houses three attractive (and costlier) private-entrance suites that feature kitchenettes, double Jacuzzis, large bathrooms, fireplaces, VCRs, and private decks. Each is decorated differently: Casablanca-inspired number 10 is a charming, airy room with skylights, ceiling fans, and light wood-and-wicker furniture; number 11 has a French country look; and number 12—the most opulent—uses red velvet and plaster pillars, busts, and cornices to create an over-the-top classical look that will thrill some and be Greek to others. In the evening, guests partake of wine, hors d'oeuvres, and cookies by the fireplace in the main house's snug, antique-filled living room. Pets are welcome (for a $10 fee). *$$–$$$; AE, DIS, MC, V; checks OK; www.zaballahouse.net; at the north end of town.*

Pescadero

Were it not for the near-mythical status of **DUARTE'S TAVERN** (see review), Pescadero would probably enjoy the sane, simple small-town life in relative obscurity. Instead, you can pretty much count on the town's population tripling on weekends as everyone piles into the bar and restaurant to see what all of the hubbub is about. Whether it's worth the visit depends mostly on your interest in seeking out Duarte's holy recipe for cream-of-artichoke soup.

AÑO NUEVO STATE RESERVE

You're not the only one having fun in the sun. For a seaside sex show, pull off Highway 1 between the coastal towns of Pescadero and Davenport (22 miles north of Santa Cruz) at **AÑO NUEVO STATE RESERVE** (800/444-4445, tickets; 650/879-0227, information; www.parks.ca.gov), a unique and fascinating breeding ground for northern elephant seals. A close encounter with a 16-foot-long, 2-ton male elephant seal waving his humongous schnoz is an unforgettable event. The seals are named after the male's dangling proboscis, which can grow up to a couple of feet long. The reserve is open year-round, but you'll see hundreds of these marine mammals during their mating season, which starts in December and continues through March. To access the reserve during the mating season, you must have a reservation for one of the 2½-hour naturalist-led tours (offered Dec 15–Mar 31). The tours are terrific and tickets are cheap, but they sell out fast, so plan about two months ahead (and don't forget to bring a jacket).

A few miles east of Duarte's Tavern on Pescadero Road is **PHIPPS RANCH** (2700 Pescadero Rd; 415/879-0787; www.phippscountry.com), a sort of Knott's Berry Farm back when it was a farm. Kids can play with the animals in the barnyard while Mom and Dad load up on the huge assortment of fresh, organically grown fruits and vegetables (including an amazing selection of dried beans) or browse the nursery and gardens. In the early summer, pick your own strawberries, olallieberries, and boysenberries in the adjacent fields. It's open 10am to 6pm daily (10am–5pm in winter). About 7 miles north of Pescadero on Highway 1 is the turnoff to Highway 84 and the legendary **SAN GREGORIO GENERAL STORE** (Hwy 84 at Stage Rd; 650/726-0565; www.sangregoriostore.com). Since 1889 this funky old place has been providing the nearby ranching and farming community with a bewildering assortment of "shoat rings, hardware, tack, bullshit, lanterns," and just about everything else a country boy needs to survive. It's truly worth a gander, particularly on Saturday and Sunday afternoons when the Irish R & B or Bulgarian bluegrass bands are in full swing. It's located 1 mile up Highway 84 from the Highway 1 intersection and is open 9am to 6pm daily.

At the turnoff to Pescadero is one of the few remaining natural marshes left on the Central Coast, the **PESCADERO MARSH NATURAL PRESERVE**. The 600 acres of wetlands—part of the Pacific flyway—are a refuge for more than 160 bird species, including great blue herons that nest in the northern row of eucalyptus trees. Passing through the marsh is the mile-long **SEQUOIA AUDUBON TRAIL**, accessible from the parking lot at Pescadero State Beach on Highway 1 (the trail starts below the Pescadero Creek Bridge).

RESTAURANTS

Duarte's Tavern / ★

202 STAGE RD, PESCADERO; 415/879-0464

Duarte's (pronounced DOO-arts) is a rustic gem, still owned and operated by the family that built it in 1894. Back then it was the place to buy a 10-cent shot of whiskey on the stagecoach ride from San Francisco to Santa Cruz. Nowadays Duarte's is half bar, half restaurant (when Duarte's tavern caught fire in 1927, local firefighters examined their priorities and sacrificed the restaurant to save the bar), but it's still set in an Old West–style wood-and-stucco building near Pescadero's general store. The dimly lit bar is typically filled with locals. The unassuming wood-paneled restaurant next door serves steak, prime rib, and plenty of fresh coastal fare such as red snapper, halibut, sole, sand dabs, and salmon in season. Most of the fruits and vegetables come from the Duartes' own gardens behind the restaurant. It's sort of a county misdemeanor if you don't start dinner with a bowl of cream-of-artichoke soup and finish with a slice of Lynn Duarte's famous melt-in-your mouth olallieberry pie. *$–$$; AE, MC, V; local checks only; breakfast, lunch, dinner every day; full bar; reservations recommended; www.duartestavern.com; downtown.*

LODGINGS

Costanoa / ★★☆

2001 ROSSI RD, PESCADERO; 650/879-1100 OR 877/262-7848

Set in a pristine wilderness bordering four state parks and 30,000 acres of hiking trails, Costanoa is a perfect place to get away from it all in grand style. With a wide variety of accommodations, you can choose exactly how rough you want to rough it. If you're a tenderfoot, stay in the lodge, a striking cabin-like structure with 40 superlative guest rooms. In keeping with Costanoa's eco-sensibilities, the rooms are decorated with natural materials: polished wood, slate tile, and pale, earth-toned hues. Room amenities include private baths, Bose stereo systems, refrigerators, robes, private decks, and access to the lodge's spa facilities and outdoor hot tub. Many rooms have fireplaces and soaking tubs. One step lower on the luxury ladder are the six duplex cabins. Each of the 12 cabin rooms features a vaulted ceiling, fireplace, and deck with porch swing that overlooks wild, lush terrain. The cabins don't have private baths, but one of six "comfort stations" (sleek and upscale, with heated floors, large showers, and dry saunas) is only a short walk away. Reserve one of the deluxe tent bungalows for Costanoa's most unique lodging experience. Their queen-size beds, down comforters, heated mattress pads, and retro-style furnishings will make you feel like Meryl Streep in *Out of Africa*. Less luxurious tent bungalows are also available, as is a small area for pitching your own tent or parking your RV. The General Store on the premises offers a coffee bar and deli with all the makings for a gourmet picnic. The small spa offers Swedish, deep tissue, or shiatsu massage; aromatherapy; a sauna; and a steam room. Activities include hiking, on-site mountain bike rentals and horseback riding, and a children's play area. *$$–$$$$; AE, DC, DIS, MC, V; no checks; www.costanoa.com; Hwy 1 between Pigeon Pt Lighthouse and the Año Nuevo State Reserve, 9 miles south of Pescadero.*

Santa Cruz and the Monterey Bay Area

Although the Santa Cruz Boardwalk and Monterey Bay Aquarium get the lion's share of visitors, there's much more to do in this mountains-meets-the-sea region than ride the country's oldest roller coaster or gawk at fish. For adventures off the beaten track, explore the redwood-studded valley setting of Ben Lomond, the historic mission at San Juan Bautista, or the bucolic little farming towns of Tres Pinos, Castroville, and Moss Landing.

ACCESS AND INFORMATION

HIGHWAY 1 and scenic but highly trafficked **HIGHWAY 17** lead right into the center of Santa Cruz. Just "over the hill" is **SAN JOSE INTERNATIONAL AIRPORT**, with plenty of major airlines and car rental companies. **GREYHOUND** (800/231-2222; www.greyhound.com) provides service to Santa Cruz's downtown bus terminal (425 Front St, Santa Cruz; 831/423-1800). The excellent **VISITORS INFORMATION CENTER** (1211 Ocean St, Santa Cruz; 831/425-1234 or 800/833-3494; www.santacruzca.org) boasts a friendly staff and lots of info about area attractions and events.

Highway 1 continues on with direct access to Monterey. From Highway 101, take the Highway 156–Monterey exit, which merges with Highway 1. The **MONTEREY PENINSULA AIRPORT** (Hwy 68 off Holsted Rd, 4 miles from Monterey; 831/648-7000; www.montereyairport.com) has nearly 100 arrivals and departures daily, with connections to all domestic and foreign airlines. Car rental offices of **AVIS**, **BUDGET**, and **NATIONAL** are located here. **AMTRAK**'s (800/USA-RAIL; www.amtrak.com) Coast Starlight route stops in Salinas; free bus service is provided for the 30-minute ride into downtown Monterey. The **MONTEREY COUNTY CONVENTION AND VISITORS BUREAU** (877-MONTEREY; www.monterey.com) has two visitor centers: one located in the lobby of the Maritime Museum at Custom House Plaza near Fisherman's Wharf, and the other at Lake El Estero on Camino El Estero. Both locations are open daily and offer maps, free brochures, and visitors' guides.

Ben Lomond

RESTAURANTS

Ciao! Bella!! / ★★

9217 HWY 9, BEN LOMOND; 831/336-9221

Ciao! Bella!! is a restaurant with a sense of humor: mannequin legs wearing fishnet stockings and platform shoes stick out of the ground by the entrance,

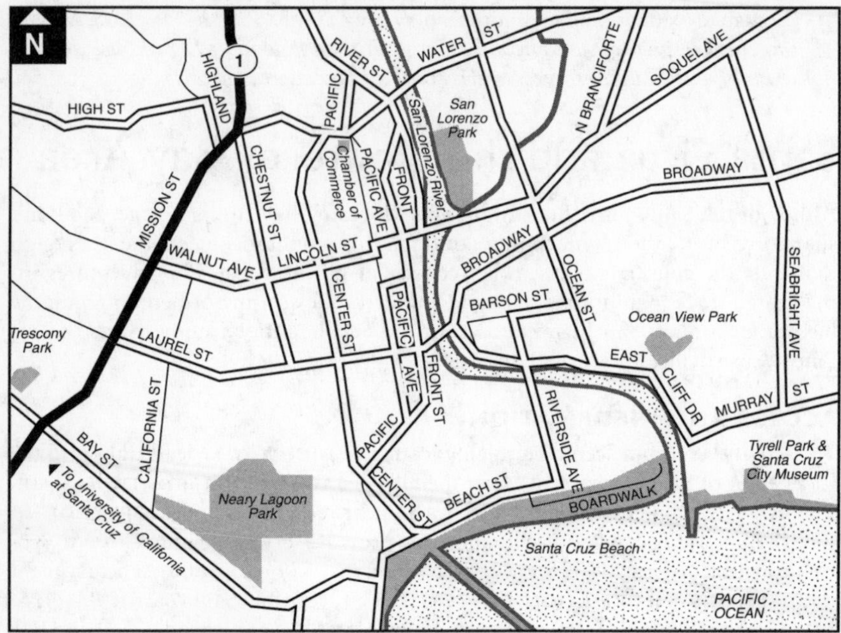

Santa Cruz

a parking slot is marked "Reserved for Elvis," and a Rapunzel-like sister mannequin leans out of a dormer above, letting down her hair, a perfect metaphor. Nestled in a mountain redwood grove in the San Lorenzo Valley, the roadhouse restaurant serves what owner Tad Morgan describes as "new California-Italian" cuisine. In addition to nightly specials, Ciao! Bella!! serves up hefty portions of pasta, ranging from Tutto Mare (prawns, clams, calamari, and fresh fish sautéed in cream and white wine) to Penne alla Napoletana (penne with tomatoes, basil, garlic, and mozzarella tossed in a marinara sauce). *Secondi piatti* include scampi as well as chicken with prosciutto, mozzarella, and spinach, topped with a sauce of basil, tomatoes, and garlic. Be sure to start with the Tuscan steamed clams and save room for the housemade desserts: zabaglione, tiramisu, and bread pudding. *$$; AE, DIS, MC, V; no checks; dinner every day; beer and wine; reservations recommended; www.ciaobellabenlomond.com; just south of town.*

Santa Cruz

Long regarded as a seaside nirvana for hippies and anyone else eschewing the conventional lifestyle, the Santa Cruz coast simply ain't what it used to be—spend a day on the boardwalk and you'll see more bike locks than dreadlocks. It all comes down to money, of course. Tourism is the big draw here: some 3 million annual visitors are the major source of income for the city, which in turn is doing everything possible to make Santa Cruz a respectable and safe place to bring the family. The result? A little of everything. Walk down gilded Pacific Avenue and you're bound to see the homeless mix it up with the alternative lifestylers as they hang out in front of a sea of yuppie shops and shiny cafés. The cultural dichotomy is glaringly manifest, but nobody seems to mind; rather, most locals are pleased with the turnout. As one resident put it, "Anything but Carmel."

The half-mile-long, 100-year-old **SANTA CRUZ BEACH BOARDWALK** (400 Beach St; 831/423-5590; www.beachboardwalk.com) is the last remaining beachfront amusement park on the West Coast. Take a spin on the famous Giant Dipper, one of the best and oldest wooden roller coasters in the country (with a great view at the top), then grab a seat on one of the intricately hand-carved horses on the 1911 Looff Carousel, the last bona fide brass ring merry-go-round in North America (both rides are listed on the National Register of Historic Places). Of course, the boardwalk (now a cement walk) also caters to hard-core thrill seekers who yearn for those whirl-and-twirl rides. Newer rides and attractions include a 3D Fun House, where you wear 3D glasses and walk through a space filled with optical illusions, and Ghost Busters, an interactive ride where you can zap ghosts with phasers as they zip by. Also part of the boardwalk is Neptune's Kingdom, an enormous indoor family recreation center whose main feature is a two-story miniature golf course. If you're among the crowds here on a Friday night in the summer, don't miss the boardwalk's free concerts, which feature retro rock 'n' roll from groups such as the Shirelles, the Drifters, and the Coasters.

Beaches are Santa Cruz's other crowning glory. On the north end of West Cliff Drive is **NATURAL BRIDGES STATE BEACH** (831/423-4609; www.thatsmypark.org), named after archways carved into the rock formations here by the ocean waves (only one of the three original arches still stands). The beach is popular with surfers, windsurfers, tide-pool trekkers, and sunbathers, as well as fans of the migrating monarch butterflies that roost in the nearby eucalyptus grove from late October through February. On the south end of West Cliff Drive is **LIGHTHOUSE FIELD STATE BEACH** (831/429-2850), the reputed birthplace of American surfing. This beach has several benches for sitting and gazing, a jogging and bicycling path, and a park with picnic tables, showers, and even plastic-bag dispensers for cleaning up after your dog (it's one of the few public places in town where canines are allowed). The nearby brick lighthouse is now home to the tiny **SANTA CRUZ SURFING MUSEUM** (West Cliff Dr at Lighthouse Pt; 831/420-6289; www.santacruzparksandrec.com; open 10am–5pm Wed–Mon in summer, noon–4pm Wed–Sun in winter; admission is free), the first of its kind in the world.

Between the lighthouse and the boardwalk is that famous strip of the sea known as **STEAMERS LANE**, the summa cum laude of California surfing spots (savvy surfers say this—not Southern California—is the place to catch the best breaks in the state). Watch some of the nation's best surfers ride the breaks, then head over to the marvelous (but often crowded) white-sand **SANTA CRUZ BEACH** fronting the boardwalk. The breakers are tamer

LEARN TO SURF, SANTA CRUZ STYLE

If you've always wanted to ride the waves hanging ten (toes), it's not too late to learn. **CLUB ED SURF SCHOOL** (831/464-0177 or 800/287-7873; www.club-ed.com), located on Cowell Beach in front of the West Coast Santa Cruz Hotel, is one of the most respected surfing schools in the world. Most days owner Ed Guzman and his staff teach a two-hour small group lesson for $80 that includes rental of a wet suit, surfboard, and water booties. The class starts on shore with yoga stretches on the surfboard, and goes on to include how to read waves, how to position yourself on the board, how to paddle, and, of course, how to stand up and actually surf. Guzman has designed special extrawide and thick surfboards so they catch waves well and are easy to stand up on, and he has taught wishful surfers from 4 years old up to 71 how to do it. Ed can also take paraplegics and quadriplegics out on his tandem board to experience the sensation of surfing. Classes are offered spring through fall. Contact Club Ed for information or reservations.

here, and free volleyball courts and barbecue pits make this a favorite spot for sunbathing, swimming, picnicking, and playing volleyball on the sand courts. In the center of the action is the 85-year-old **MUNICIPAL WHARF** (831/420-6025), where you can drive your car out to the shops, fish markets, and seafood restaurants.

VENTURE QUEST KAYAKING (831/427-2267; www.kayaksantacruz.com), located on the northeast end of the wharf, rents single-, double-, and triple-seater kayaks for exploring the nearby cliffs and kelp beds, where a multitude of sea otters, seals, sea lions, and other marine animals congregate. No experience is necessary, and all ages are welcome. Guided tours and moonlight paddles are also available.

Even if you can't paddle, the view of the Santa Cruz coast from the water shouldn't be missed. **STAGNARO FISHING TRIPS AND BAY TOURS** (831/427-2334; www.stagnaros.com) has a one-hour tour of the bay that cruises the harbor, swoops around the wharf, and passes by Seal Rock and back. They also offer sport-fishing and whale-watching trips in season. For a more elegant tour, sign up for the **CHARDONNAY** (831/423-1213; www.chardonnay.com), a 70-foot luxury yacht that sails year-round on sunset, ecology, wine-tasting, and whale-watching tours. Better yet, sign up for some surfing lessons. Both **COWELL'S BEACH SURF SHOP** (30 Front St; 831/427-2355) and **CLUB ED SURF SCHOOL** (831/464-0177 or 800/287-SURF; www.club-ed.com) offer surf lessons on Cowell Beach. Whether you take the two-hour group session, a private lesson, or a seven-day surf camp, they guarantee you'll get up.

The **PACIFIC GARDEN MALL** (a.k.a. Pacific Avenue), Santa Cruz's main shopping district, was hit hard by the Loma Prieta earthquake in 1989, but the entire area has been rebuilt, and it's shinier and spiffier than before. Major retailers such as the Gap and Starbucks have settled in alongside book, antique, and vintage clothing stores, movie theaters, and sidewalk cafés. As you make your way down the mall, look for the **OCTAGON BUILDING**, an ornate, eight-sided Victorian brick edifice built in 1882. The building once served as the city's Hall of Records and is now part of the **MUSEUM OF ART AND HISTORY** (705 Front St at Cooper St; 831/429-1964; www.santacruzmah.org).

The nearby **BOOKSHOP SANTA CRUZ** (1520 Pacific Ave; 831/423-0900) has an inventory worthy of any university town, with a particularly good children's section, an adjacent coffeehouse, and plenty of places to sit, sip, and read a bit of your prospective purchase. For great organically grown produce and other picnic-basket goodies, shop at the downtown **FARMERS MARKET** (Lincoln St, between Pacific Ave and Cedar St; www.santacruzfarmersmarket.org; open 2:30–6:30pm Wed year-round) and at the Westside location (2801 Mission St; open 9am–1pm Sat year-round).

Secrets of the sea are revealed at the **SEYMOUR MARINE DISCOVERY CENTER** (100 Shaffer Rd, at the end of Delaware Ave; 831/459-3800; www2.ucsc.edu/seymourcenter). The center's exhibit galleries, aquariums, and teaching laboratories provide an inside look at UC Santa Cruz's Institute of Marine Sciences. Children love the tide-pool touch tanks that allow them to handle—and learn about—sea stars, anemones, sea cucumbers, and other slimy marine life. Behind the gift shop are the skeletal remains of an 85-foot blue whale.

For some serious hiking and mountain biking, drive about 23 miles north to the 18,000-acre **BIG BASIN REDWOODS STATE PARK** (21600 Big Basin Wy, off Hwy 236, 9 miles north of Boulder Creek; 831/338-8860; www.bigbasin.org), California's first state park and its second-largest redwood preserve. Big Basin is home to black-tailed deer and mountain lions, and 80 miles of trails wind past 300-foot-high redwoods and many waterfalls.

Locomotive lovers, kids, and fans of Mother Nature should hop aboard one of the trains at **ROARING CAMP RAILROADS** (5355 Graham Hill Rd, Felton; 831/335-4484; www.roaringcamp.com). The Roaring Camp Train is a narrow-gauge steam-powered train that was originally used to haul redwood logs out of the mountains. It now takes passengers for a s-l-o-w 6-mile round-trip excursion up one of the steepest narrow-gauge grades in North America, passing through stately redwood groves as it winds its way to the summit of Bear Mountain. A second Beach Train route offers an 8-mile ride through mountain tunnels and along the scenic San Lorenzo River before stopping at the Santa Cruz Beach Boardwalk. Both trains are located on Graham Hill Road off Highway 17 in Felton (follow the signs); the Beach Train Railroad can also be boarded at the east end of the Santa Cruz boardwalk.

RESTAURANTS

El Palomar / ★★

1336 PACIFIC AVE, SANTA CRUZ; 831/425-7575

El Palomar, Mexican restaurant extraordinaire, is a Santa Cruz institution. You have two choices: sit inside in the shadowy, dramatic dining room with a vaulted ceiling that was the lobby of a '30s hotel, featuring beams painted in the Spanish manner and a huge mural depicting a Mexican waterfront village scene, or sit out in the happy, glassed-roof conservatory-patio, where the sun always seems to shine—you might squint and think you are in Mexico itself. If you need further convincing, have an Ultimate Margarita and munch on tortilla chips still warm from the oven. El Palomar is known for its seafood dishes, which are topped with exotic sauces, but traditional Mexican favorites such as burritos and tacos are also outstanding. *$$; AE, DIS, MC, V; local checks only; lunch, dinner every day, brunch Sun; full bar; no reservations; www. elpalomarcilantros.com; in the Pacific Garden Mall, near Soquel Ave.* ♿

Gabriella Café / ★★★

910 CEDAR ST, SANTA CRUZ; 831/457-1677

Downtown on Cedar Street is a small mission-style cottage with a tiny garden courtyard entry graced with cupid statues and ivy. Inside, the whitewashed walls are hung with art from local artists, and tables are draped with white linens. The rooms are small, and the tables are small too, so you can't stretch out, but the ambience and food are worth it. The homemade focaccia is perfect, served with roasted garlic, caponata, or basil pesto. The menu offers a crab and squash cakes appetizer with red pepper, red onion, and Meyer lemon aioli; a *caprese* salad with heirloom tomatoes, fresh mozzarella, fresh basil, and extra-virgin olive oil; and a daily changing gnocchi special that might include a truffle version. Main courses include pan-roasted pork loin with peach compote and summer vegetable slaw, and chicken Gabriella, a sautéed chicken breast with a marinade of prunes, apricots, olives, capers, oregano, and olive oil. *$$; AE, MC, V; local checks only; lunch, dinner every day, brunch Sun; beer and wine; reservations recommended; www.gabriellacafe.com; on Cedar St between Locust and Church sts.* ♿

Ristorante Avanti / ★★★

1711 MISSION ST, SANTA CRUZ; 831/427-0135

Most tourists who take one look at this unpretentious restaurant set in a humble strip mall keep on driving. The locals, however, are hip to Ristorante Avanti's fantastic food and considerate, professional service. In keeping with the Santa Cruz lifestyle, Avanti prides itself on serving "the healthiest meal possible" (think fresh, organic produce and free-range chicken, veal, and lamb). The modern, casual decor, with a long wooden counter dominating one of the small rooms and Italian ceramics scattered throughout, provides a welcome setting for aromatic, seasonal dishes such as sweet squash ravioli with sage butter, lasagne al forno, spaghetti with wild-mushroom and shallot duxelles, and orecchiette with salmon, Italian greens, mushrooms, and sun-dried tomatoes. The grilled lemon chicken and balsamic vinegar–marinated lamb chops also demonstrate the kitchen's skillful and delicate touch, and you simply can't go wrong with the daily specials. The menu changes with the seasons, and anything with wild mushrooms is prepared with locally gathered varieties. The ample and reasonably priced wine list contains selections from California, France, Spain, and Italy. *$$; AE, MC, V; local checks only; lunch Mon–Fri, dinner every day; beer and wine; reservations recommended; www.ristoranteavanti.com; near Bay St.* ♿

Walnut Avenue Café / ★★

106 WALNUT AVE, SANTA CRUZ; 831/457-2307

When the urge to brunch strikes, locals head to this downtown staple. The café serves breakfast and lunch only, featuring classic dishes with a creative flair: for example, eggs Benedict are served with shrimp and tomato or blackened ahi tuna. Tofu can be substituted for eggs in any breakfast scramble (in true Santa Cruz hippie fashion). *Sunset* magazine has even bestowed the eatery with the honor of "city's best breakfast." The daily pasta special is usually a safe bet for lunch, and salad, soup, sandwich, and burger offerings are many. If you request to dine alfresco on a sunny day, be prepared for a lengthy wait. So head there before the lunchtime rush or settle for indoor seating. *$$; AE, MC, V; no checks; breakfast, lunch every day; beer and wine; no reservations; www.walnutavenuecafe.com; at Commerce Ln.*

LODGINGS

The Babbling Brook Inn / ★★

1025 LAUREL ST, SANTA CRUZ; 831/427-2437 OR 800/866-1131

Ensconced in a fantastical garden with waterfalls, gazebos, and, of course, the babbling brook, Santa Cruz's oldest B and B offers 13 rooms, most named after famous artists. The original building was a gristmill, and the 200-year-old working mill wheel still churns water from a creek that flows through the property from high above town. The mauve-and-blue Van Gogh Room has a private deck, fireplace, beamed ceiling, and whirlpool tub for two. Peach and ivory predominate in the Cézanne Room, with its generous bath and canopy bed. The blue-and-white Monet Room has a corner fireplace, private deck, and view of the waterfall and footbridge. Breakfast is served in the comfortable lobby, and wine and snacks are also served there from 5:30 to 7:30pm. *$$$; AE, DC, DIS, MC, V; checks OK; www.babblingbrookinn.com; near California St.*

Casablanca Inn / ★

101 MAIN ST, SANTA CRUZ; 831/423-1570 OR 800/644-1570

Right across the street from the beach and wharf, the Casablanca Inn has a close-up view of the ongoing street carnival that is the Santa Cruz Beach Boardwalk. The 39 rooms are divided between the four buildings of the Cerf Mansion, a multilevel Spanish-style structure with a red-tile roof. Because the Cerf Mansion is a historic building, each room has a slightly different configuration, and rooms on the upper end of the rate scale have decidedly more personality. All guest rooms come with telephones, cable TVs, microwaves, and refrigerators; a good number feature fireplaces, kitchens, or private terraces; and 33 have ocean views. If you're in the mood for a party, reserve a room facing Beach Street; if you'd rather stay in a less boisterous environment, opt for a room in the Guest House or Carriage House. There's nothing very Moroccan about the hotel's Casablanca Restaurant (831/426-9063), a boardwalk bastion of California-continental cuisine, except, perhaps, the palpable air of romance. *$$$; AE, DC, DIS, MC, V; checks OK; www.casablanca-santacruz.com; at Beach St, on the waterfront.*

Cliff Crest Bed and Breakfast Inn / ★★

407 CLIFF ST, SANTA CRUZ; 831/427-2609

From its perch on Beach Hill high above the boardwalk, this antique-laden Victorian B and B offers five highly decorated rooms and a carriage house with an upstairs suite for those wanting more solitude. The more casual lobby and solarium features a fireplace, antique furniture, and the original owner's family photos. The entire house has carved woodwork, bright square panes of stained glass, intriguing nooks, claw-foot tubs, and converted gas-light fixtures. The Empire Room downstairs has a four-poster king bed and a fireplace, and the Rose Room upstairs boasts bay views, a sitting area, and an Eastlake bed, with a private bath across the hall containing a claw-foot bathtub and a profusion of lace. Two other guest rooms have fireplaces, all the rooms are equipped with telephones, and TVs are available upon request. The complimentary full breakfast is served downstairs in the solarium, or you can take it to your room. There is off-street parking, and you can walk to the wharf or boardwalk or to town. *$$$–$$$$; AE, DIS, MC, V; checks OK; www.cliffcrestinn.com; near 3rd St.*

The Darling House—A Bed-and-Breakfast Inn by the Sea / ★★

314 W CLIFF DR, SANTA CRUZ; 831/458-1958

Location, location, location. There are probably no better views in all of Santa Cruz than those you'll find at the Darling House, a Spanish Revival mansion built as a summer home for a Colorado cattle baron in 1910. From its vantage point a few yards from the water, you can see endless miles of gray-blue sea, boats, seagulls, and the lights of faraway towns. On chilly days a fire crackles in the living room's glorious art deco fireplace. The downstairs has not been gentrified, and the beautiful Craftsman-style living room has carved oak pillars and beveled glass windows. Upstairs, the large Pacific Ocean Room is decorated like a sea captain's quarters, with a crown Victorian bed, a fireplace, and a telescope to spy ships at sea. Across the hall, the Chinese Room features an exotic canopied, carved, and gilded Chinese rosewood wedding bed. The cottage out back has a kitchenette, a wood-burning stove, and two bedrooms—each with a double bed and a claw-foot tub. Owners Darrell and Karen Darling have preserved the beautiful woodwork and have outfitted all eight guest rooms with mostly American Victorian antiques; there are also fluffy robes in every closet. Karen's breakfasts include fresh fruit, homemade granola with walnuts, and oven-fresh breads and pastries. *$$$; AE, DIS, MC, V; checks OK; www.darlinghouse.com; on W Cliff Dr between the pier and the lighthouse.*

Capitola

Just east of Santa Cruz sits Capitola, a tiny, very popular resort town nestled around a small bay. The Mediterranean-style buildings, curved streets, white-sand beaches, outdoor cafés, and perpetually festive atmosphere seem more akin to the French or Italian Riviera than Monterey Bay. If you're staying on the coast for more than a day, and especially if you're around during the week, a visit to this ultraquaint hamlet is highly recommended. Park the car anywhere you can, feed the meter (bring quarters), spend an hour browsing the dozens of boutiques along the esplanade, then rest your bones at **ZELDA'S ON THE BEACH** sunny beachside patio (203 Esplanade; 831/475-4900) with a pitcher of margaritas. As in any upscale beach town, the ambience is breezy and informal, and you can go anywhere in a bathing suit with a cover-up.

At the west end of town is the bustling 867-foot-long **CAPITOLA PIER**—a great place to hang out, admire the view of the town, and, on weekends, listen to live music. Many anglers come here to try their luck at reeling in the big one (and you don't need a license to fish from a pier in California). If you'd rather try your luck out at sea, visit **CAPITOLA BOAT & BAIT** (1400 Wharf Rd; 831/462-2208; www.santacruzboatrentals.net; closed Jan–mid-Feb) at the end of the pier. Rates are reasonable and include fuel, safety equipment, and a map of the hot fishing spots. You can also rent fishing gear and purchase one-day licenses, so there's no excuse not to brave the open ocean—if only just for the halibut.

RESTAURANTS

Gayle's Bakery & Rosticceria / ★★

504 BAY AVE, CAPITOLA; 831/462-1200

Take a number and stand in line; it's worth the wait. A self-service bakery and deli, Gayle's offers numerous imaginative sandwiches, pastas, casseroles, roasted and barbecued meats, salads, cheeses, appetizers, breads, and treats. The variety is staggering and the quality top-notch. There's a good selection of wine, beer, bottled water, and espresso drinks, too. Once you've fought your way to the counter, you'll have the makings of a first-class picnic to take to one of the nearby parks or beaches. Daily specials range from carrot ginger soup to braised meatballs with red wine gravy. You can also eat your feast in the café's small dining area or on the heated patio. Gayle's Web site lists hot items and the next day's specials. *$; MC, V; checks OK; breakfast, lunch, dinner every day; beer and wine; no reservations; www.gaylesbakery.com; by Capitola Ave.*

Shadowbrook Restaurant / ★★

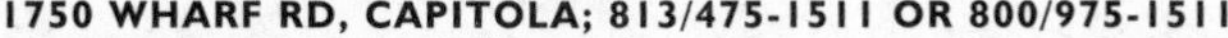

1750 WHARF RD, CAPITOLA; 813/475-1511 OR 800/975-1511

Known for years as the most romantic restaurant in the county, Shadowbrook is everyone's favorite place for proposals, birthdays, and anniversaries: the fun starts with the ride aboard the restaurant's funicular, a small cable railway that runs down through the ferny woods, past a waterfall, to the multistoried, woodsy restaurant bedecked in white lights. Now people are also beginning to come for the seasonal California–Mediterranean cuisine. Starters might include the signature crab cakes, artichoke hearts with lime-cilantro sauce, or tender calamari strips served with a Creole rémoulade. Some popular entrées include blackened lamb with roasted root vegetables, tender braised lamb shank, bacon-wrapped prawns with creamy polenta, and swordfish. Jack Daniels mud pie and New York–style cheesecake remain the most requested desserts. The best seats in the house are at the alfresco tables on the brickwork terraces, nestled romantically among rock gardens and rhododendrons; otherwise, opt for dining at the informal bar area with a view of the waterfalls and gardens. *$$$; AE, DC, DIS, MC, V; local checks only; dinner every day, brunch Sun; full bar; reservations recommended; www.shadowbrook-capitola.com; near the end of Capitola Rd.*

LODGINGS

The Inn at Depot Hill / ★★★

250 MONTEREY AVE, CAPITOLA; 831/462-3376 OR 800/572-2632

When Martha Stewart stayed here, she enthused about the Delft Room, with its antique Dutch tile fireplace, feather bed decked out in white Belgian lace, and collectible Dutch blue and white porcelains. Located in a 1910-era former Southern Pacific train depot, the Inn at Depot Hill sits on a bluff overlooking Capitola. Decorated with passionate attention to detail, the 12 guest rooms, lavishly designed to evoke international ports of call, seem to have sprung directly from the pages of *Architectural Digest*. The terra-cotta-walled Portofino Room, patterned after a coastal Italian villa, sports a stone cherub, ivy, frescoes, and a brick patio. No less charming is the Stratford-upon-Avon, a faux English cottage with a cozy window seat. The Railroad Baron Room has sumptuous red fabric walls, heavy gold silk drapes, and formal gilt mirrors. Every room has a TV and a VCR, a built-in stereo system, a gas fireplace, and a marble-appointed bathroom complete with a mini-TV and a coffeemaker. In the morning, there's a buffet of pastries, cereal, quiche, and a hot dish; in the evening, sweets and wine are set out in the downstairs parlor. *$$$$; AE, DIS, MC, V; checks OK; www.innatdepothill.com; near Park Ave, next to railroad tracks.*

Aptos

Most of Aptos's appeal is of the outdoor variety: beyond its handful of B and Bs, people come for the good hiking trails, state beaches, and state parks. Aptos has little in the way of tourist entertainment, leaving that up to neighboring Capitola and Santa Cruz. The focus here is on quality lodgings in quiet surroundings. The only drawback is that the beaches are too far to walk to from town, but if you don't mind the short drive, Aptos is the ideal place for a peaceful vacation on the coast. **SEACLIFF STATE PARK BEACH** has picnic tables with shade covers as well as the infamous Concrete Ship, built by the Navy to sail the coast but now permanently moored (it later became a dance hall) and looking very much like a concrete wharf. In the spring the local park in Aptos Village is home to a fun and funky blues festival.

RESTAURANTS

Cafe Sparrow / ★★

8042 SOQUEL DR, APTOS; 831/688-6238

Chef-owner Bob Montague and his wife, Julie, opened this quaint French country restaurant in June 1989. Then along came the October 17 Loma Prieta earthquake, reducing the café to little more than a pile of rubble. Fortunately, the couple didn't throw in the towel, and their remodeled restaurant is now a gem of a dining spot and a magnet for local gourmets. Two dining rooms, decorated with country furniture and a tentlike expanse of French printed fabric, provide a romantic backdrop for Montague's spirited culinary creations. Lunch may include a croissant layered with shrimp in lemon, fresh dill, and crème fraîche, or a bowl of creamed spinach with a vinaigrette salad and bread. Dinner, however, is when Montague puts on the Ritz. Start with a pâté of fresh chicken livers seasoned with herbs and Cognac. Then progress to such entrées as an Yvette salad—grilled chicken breast with pears topped with Brie, or lamb chops in a rich red-wine and mint sauce. Favorite desserts are profiteroles—puff pastries filled with custard or vanilla ice cream and smothered in Ghirardelli chocolate sauce. Nightly dinner specials include the entrée du jour, and a choice of soup or salad, plus bread pudding to top it all off. *$$; MC, V; checks OK; breakfast Sat, lunch Mon–Sat, dinner every day, brunch Sun; beer and wine; reservations recommended; www.cafesparrow.com; near Trout Gulch Rd.*

LODGINGS

Historic Sand Rock Farm / ★★½

6901 FREEDOM BLVD, APTOS; 831/688-8005

The word "nestled" was made for this inn, positioned on a woodsy knoll under a grove of redwoods. It originally was a 1,000-acre ranch and winery built in the 1880s by a doctor's family, who also built the Craftsman-style shingled mansion in 1910 from virgin redwood growing on the site. Lynn Sheehan, formerly chef at several of San Francisco's finest restaurants, and her mother, Kris Sheehan, who previously was innkeeper at the Wild Rose Inn in Sonoma, have restored the home back to its original glory, with European antiques and an obvious love for light, airy rooms. The living room features redwood box beams, leaded glass, and a mantel made of rare curly redwood. The Sun Porch Suite, a large, open room, has a private enclosed sunporch sitting area and access to a large outdoor hot tub. The Hidden Garden Suite opens onto a rose garden framed by a stone wall. The Morning Glory Room faces east; as the sun rises, the Eastlake-style brass queen bed glows with reflected light. Breakfast is a gourmet experience, usually served outdoors on the redwood deck under the trees. There are many nooks, crannies, hidden gardens, and old winery buildings to explore at this historic country retreat. *$$; MC, V; local checks only; www.sandrockfarm.com; on Freedom Blvd, ½ mile from Hwy 1.*

Seascape Resort / ★★

1 SEASCAPE RESORT DR, APTOS; 408/688-6800 OR 800/929-7727

This attractive condo-resort complex on 64 cliff-side acres offers spacious accommodations and plenty of creature comforts. The 285 guest suites and villas are arranged in a cluster of three-story stucco buildings and are available in studio or one- or two-bedroom configurations. Each suite and villa is outfitted with beach house–style furnishings in light colors of sand and blue and comes with a fireplace, a private balcony or patio, a TV, and a kitchenette. The studios are quite large, with mini kitchens, and the one- and two-bedroom villas are larger still, with complete kitchens, sitting areas, and, in the two-bedroom units, washer-dryers. All rooms and villas have balconies or patios. Largely given over to corporate functions during the week, the complex turns into a haven for couples and families on the weekend. For a fee the staff will provide wood and build a private bonfire on the beach, or you can just buy a bundle of wood from the resort and do it yourself. A paved path leads down through a small canyon to the beautiful beach, and guests enjoy member privileges at a nearby PGA-rated golf course and the Seascape Sports Club, which offers tennis, swimming, and a fully equipped gym. The resort also provides 24-hour room service, a summer children's program, and a spa offering massage and salon services. Fresh seafood is the specialty at Sanderlings, one of the on-site airy restaurants, with curvy light wood dividers and a mega-aquarium; Palapas serves upscale Mexican fare. *$$$$; AE, DC, MC, V; checks OK; www.seascaperesort.com; at Sumner Blvd, 9 miles south of Santa Cruz.* ♿

Rio Del Mar

Located on the ocean side of Highway 1 near Aptos, Rio Del Mar is a wide strip of welcoming sand, a jetty, and an upscale residential neighborhood, but the palisades of Rio Del Mar were once the site of the first crop of sugar beets in California, planted by sugar magnate Claus Spreckels.

RESTAURANTS

Bittersweet Bistro / ★★

787 RIO DEL MAR BLVD, RIO DEL MAR; 831/662-9799

Local gourmets love the Bittersweet, a sleek American bistro-style restaurant and wine bar featuring a patio for dining alfresco and a stylish mahogany, lacquer, and black-granite bar area. Pasta offerings include seafood puttanesca and five-cheese ravioli. For a main course, order the oak-roasted pork tenderloin with apple Calvados jus or the Bittersweet paella. The seasonal menu also features a range of pizzas from the wood-fired oven. The pretty-as-a-picture desserts range from lemon napoleon to ricotta cheesecake and chocolate mousse in a florentine cookie cup. The wine list is extensive and varied, with some interesting if pricey older vintages among its treasures. *$$$; AE, MC, V; local checks only; lunch and dinner every day, brunch Sun; full bar; reservations recommended; www.bittersweetbistro.com; take Hwy 1 south of Santa Cruz to the Rio Del Mar exit.* ♿

Gilroy

Will Rogers called Gilroy the only town in America where you can marinate a steak just by hanging it out on the line—and, yes, when the wind's blowing in the right direction, the aroma from the area's garlic fields is just about that strong. So it only made sense that the people of Gilroy decided in 1979 to celebrate their odoriferous claim to fame with the now-famous **GARLIC FESTIVAL** (408/842-1625; www.gilroygarlicfestival.com), held the last weekend in July. The three-day-long festivities attract throngs of people eager to try such oddities as garlic ice cream and garlic chocolate, and to enter their own stinking-rose recipes in the Great Garlic Cook-off. You can also buy any number of garlic-based foodstuffs and doodads. To find out about Gilroy before the age of garlic, visit the **GILROY HISTORICAL MUSEUM** (5th and Church sts; 408/848-0470). If bargain hunting, not garlic, happens to set your heart aflutter, be sure to stop at the **GILROY PREMIUM OUTLETS** center (Leavesley Rd, just east of Hwy 101; 408/842-3729), with 145 outlets for big-name retailers.

San Juan Bautista

This sunny little town is home to one of the most beautifully restored missions in California. Built just 2 feet away from the main trace of the San Andreas Fault, **MISSION SAN JUAN BAUTISTA** (831/623-2127; www.oldmissionsjb.org) was nearly destroyed by the 1906 quake, but locals raised the money to rebuild it. With its pretty chapel and gardens, the mission sits on a broad plaza surrounded by other well-preserved Spanish colonial buildings. Several rooms in the mission are preserved as well, such as the library for the priests, full of old leather-bound books and maps. Fans of Alfred Hitchcock's *Vertigo* will want to explore the bell tower from which Kim Novak's character fell to her death. San Juan Bautista is also home to the world-famous theater troupe **EL TEATRO CAMPESINO** (705 4th St; 831/623-2444; www.elteatrocampesino.com). Director Luis Valdez left the San Francisco Mime Troupe in the '60s to form this political theater group composed of migrant farmworkers. The group puts on plays throughout the year and is most famous for its Christmas plays, *La Virgen del Tepeyac* and *La Pastorela*, presented at the mission. Hikers, rock climbers, bird-watchers, and other nature lovers will want to explore the cliffs and caves of nearby **PINNACLES NATIONAL MONUMENT** (831/389-4485; www.nps.gov/pinn), a glorious 16,000-acre volcanic park located high in the hills above the Salinas Valley off Highway 101. The dark red contorted rock shapes and crumbling terraces sit on top of a still-active earthquake fault. If you can stay only a short while, visit the park's east side, which has the most dramatic rock formations and caves. Of the four self-guided trails, the favorite (and the easiest) is Moses Spring Trail.

Tres Pinos

If you blink, you'll miss Tres Pinos, located on Highway 25 south of Hollister. There's not much of a town, just an intersection; most people blast through here on the way to Pinnacles National Monument. It once was home to an agricultural community, but now migrant workers are being replaced by high-tech commuters and well-off retirees who live in the new housing developments that have spread outward from Hollister.

RESTAURANTS

Inn at Tres Pinos / ★★

6991 AIRLINE HWY, TRES PINOS; 831/628-3320

This dark, romantic restaurant in a former bordello built in 1880 makes for a surprising find in the tiny town of Tres Pinos outside Hollister. "Keep it fresh and keep it simple" is the credo here. Popular dishes include filet mignon with green peppercorn sauce, Fettuccine Fantasia (chicken, artichoke hearts, sun-dried tomatoes, olives, herbs, and garlic with a white-wine and cream sauce), and calamari sautéed in chardonnay and butter. Rustic but surprisingly elegant, the inn wins high praise for its desserts, from New York–style cheesecake with fresh raspberries and mango to a Granny Smith apple crisp. *$$$; AE, MC, V; local checks only; dinner Tues–Sun; full bar; reservations recommended; www.trespinosinn.com; 5 miles south of Hollister.* ♿

Moss Landing

Nature lovers have long revered Moss Landing's Elkhorn Slough as a prime spot to study egrets, pelicans, cormorants, terns, great blue herons, and many other types of aquatic birds, not to mention packs of frolicking harbor seals and otters. Besides hiking or kayaking, one of the best ways to explore this scenic coastal wetland is to embark on an **ELKHORN SLOUGH SAFARI** (831/633-5555; www.elkhornslough.com). Naturalist guides provide expert and enthusiastic commentary aboard a 27-foot-long pontoon boat, and special activities (such as Bird Bingo) are provided for children. Binoculars are available for rent, and coffee, soda, and cookies are served on the way back. The two-hour tours operate every day, year-round.

RESTAURANTS

Phil's Fish Market / ★★

7600 SANDHOLDT RD, MOSS LANDING; 831/633-2152

Turn at the Whole Enchilada (see review), keep driving inland on Sandholdt Road, over the short one-lane bridge and past fishing boats, and you'll come to Phil's Fish Market, a local institution owned by the eternally cheerful Phil DiGirolamo. It's much more than a fish market—it's a kind of community center, joke central, and indoor picnic spot as well as a restaurant and take-out place. And of course there are the fresh fish, lying in state on ice like sculptures in a museum. Beautiful fish, most of it caught that morning. If you like your fish still moving, there are banks of tanks full of undulating catfish, clunky lobsters, and mussels. Phil's most famous dish is cioppino-to-go, but he also offers lunch items including albacore salad and pizzas with shrimp and sun-dried tomatoes. For dinner there's fettuccine with lobster meat, bay scallops in saffron cream sauce, or blackened scallops Alfredo. Should you get addicted to Phil's grub, you can have his chowder base with clams and red potatoes (just add milk or cream) or his Lazy Man's Cioppino shipped overnight in a frozen vacuum gel pack to any place in the country. Phil even provides a kids' menu and live bluegrass music on Monday and Thursday nights. *$; AE, DC, DIS, MC, V; local checks only; lunch, dinner every day; beer and wine; no reservations; www.philsfishmarket.com; off Hwy 1 at the end of Sandholdt Rd.* ♿

The Whole Enchilada / ★

7902 HWY 1, MOSS LANDING; 831/633-3038

Fresh seafood is the focus of this upbeat Mexican restaurant on Highway 1. Gaily painted walls, folk-art decorations, and leather basket chairs lend an engaging south-of-the-border ambience. Voted "Best Mexican Restaurant" in a local readers' poll, the Whole Enchilada offers the usual lineup of burritos, tacos, chiles rellenos, and enchiladas on the comprehensive menu. But hold out for one of the more exotic regional specialties, such as Oaxacan tamales filled with fresh albacore or chicken, wrapped in a banana leaf and drenched in a rich, dark mole salsa. The catch of the day is right off the local fishing boats and prepared in the authentic Mexican coastal style. Wash it all down with a muy bueno Cadillac margarita. Service is warm and efficient, and little touches like crayons and plastic mermaids clinging to the drink cups make this a place your kids will like, too. *$$; AE, DC, DIS, MC, V; no checks; lunch, dinner every day; full bar; reservations recommended; www.wenchilada.com; at Moss Landing Rd.*

Castroville

Gilroy made history with garlic; Castroville chose the artichoke. The undisputed Artichoke Capital of the World, tiny Castroville celebrates its chokehold on the artichoke market during the annual **ARTICHOKE FESTIVAL**, held every third weekend in September. It's mostly small-town stuff: the crowning of the Artichoke Queen, a 10K run, artichoke cook-offs, and the Firefighters' Pancake Breakfast. The town's most famous queen of the thistle was Marilyn Monroe. The best souvenir in town is the postcard with an (apparently) nude model lying in a sea of artichokes. If that's too racy for you, you can still get deep-fried artichokes at almost every quick-food place.

Marina

LODGINGS

Sanctuary Beach Resort / ★★★

3295 DUNES DR, MARINA; 831/883-9478 OR 877/944-3863

Just north of Monterey, this sprawling resort is hidden back off the highway among the dunes. Set against the Monterey Bay National Marine Sanctuary, the resort occupies 19 acres of oceanfront land. Two- or four-unit plexes house the guest rooms. Wake up to the reddish glow of the Pacific sunrise just outside your window; the undulating dunes only further complete the peaceful scene. All rooms have a fireplace, flat-screen TV, snuggly robes, free wireless Internet, iPod dock, and mini-bar. And what could be more fun than having your own personal golf cart (sans driver) to use for the duration of your stay? Other resort amenities include an outdoor heated pool and spa, and a lavish Serenity Spa. It's the ultimate in romantic retreats, so book your honey—and a room—and head to this seaside haunt. Weekday rates are significantly lower than weekends (almost half in some cases). *$$$–$$$$; AE, DC, MC, V; checks OK; www.thesanctuarybeachresort.com; Reservation Rd exit off Hwy 1, 9 miles north of Monterey.* ♿

Monterey

Monterey is really two towns: Old Monterey (the historic part, including colonial buildings and Fisherman's Wharf) and New Monterey, home to Monterey Bay Aquarium and Cannery Row. If you're looking for the romantically gritty, working-class fishing village of John Steinbeck's novel *Cannery Row*, you won't find it here. Even though Monterey was the sardine capital of the Western Hemisphere during World War II, overfishing (among other factors) forced most of the canneries to close in the early '50s. Resigned to trawling for tourist dollars instead, the city converted its low-slung sardine factories along **CANNERY ROW** (www.canneryrow.com) into a rather tacky

RIDE THE WAVE: MONTEREY'S FREE SHUTTLE SERVICE

Eliminate the hassle and high price of parking on Monterey's crowded streets by catching a ride on the **WAVE** (Waterfront Area Visitor Express) shuttle, which operates from the end of May to September 1 and takes passengers to and from all the major waterfront attractions, including **FISHERMAN'S WHARF**, **CANNERY ROW**, and the **MONTEREY BAY AQUARIUM**. The free shuttle departs from the downtown parking garages at Tyler Street and Del Monte Avenue every 10 to 12 minutes and operates 10am–7pm every day. Other WAVE stops include many hotels and motels in Monterey and Pacific Grove. For more information call Monterey–Salinas Transit (831/899-2555).

array of boutiques, knickknack stores, yogurt shops, and—the Row's only saving grace—the world-famous Monterey Bay Aquarium. As you distance yourself from Cannery Row, however, you'll soon see that Monterey also has its share of pluses that help even the score: dazzling seacoast vistas, stately Victorian houses, wonderfully preserved historic architecture, and a number of quality lodgings and restaurants. More importantly, Monterey is only minutes away from Pacific Grove, Carmel, Pebble Beach, and Big Sur, which makes it a great place to set up base while exploring the innumerable attractions lining the Monterey coast.

Attracting nearly 2 million visitors each year, the **MONTEREY BAY AQUARIUM** (866 Cannery Row; 831/648-4888 or 800/756-3737; www.montereybay aquarium.org) is Monterey's jewel in the crown and a must-see experience. It's the largest aquarium in the United States, with more than 350,000 marine animals, birds, and plants on display in over 200 galleries and exhibits. One of the aquarium's main exhibits is a three-story, 335,000-gallon tank with clear acrylic walls that offers a stunning view of leopard sharks, sardines, anchovies, and other sea creatures swimming through a towering kelp forest. Even more impressive, however, is the Outer Bay, a million-gallon exhibit that showcases aquatic life in the outer reaches of Monterey Bay. Schools of sharks, barracuda, yellowfin tuna, sea turtles, ocean sunfish, and bonito can be seen through one of the largest windows on earth: a 78,000-pound acrylic panel that measures 15 feet high, 13 inches thick, and 54 feet long. The Deep Sea exhibit is the largest collection of live deep-sea species in the world, many of which have never been part of an exhibit before. Another popular exhibit is the sea otter "playground": be sure to stop by for the daily feedings. The Splash Zone caters to the little ones, with hands-on interactive tours through two shoreline habitats. Tip: You can avoid lines at the gate by ordering tickets in advance. Also, go in the early afternoon—by 2pm the crowds have thinned out and you'll have a much easier time getting an unobstructed view of the exhibits.

To get the flavor of Monterey's heritage, follow the 2-mile **PATH OF HISTORY**, a walking tour of the former state capital's most important historic sites and splendidly preserved old buildings—remember, this city was thriving under Spanish and Mexican flags when San Francisco was still a crude village. Free tour maps are available at various locations, including the **CUSTOM HOUSE** (at the foot of Alvarado St, near Fisherman's Wharf), California's oldest public building, and **COLTON HALL** (on Pacific St, between Madison and Jefferson sts), where the California State Constitution was written and signed in 1849. Call **MONTEREY STATE HISTORIC PARK** (831/649-7118) for more information.

Nautical history buffs should visit the **MARITIME MUSEUM OF MONTEREY** (5 Custom House Plaza, near Fisherman's Wharf; 831/372-2608; www.montereyhistory.org), which houses ship models, whaling relics, and the two-story-high, 10,000-pound Fresnel lens used for nearly 80 years at the Point Sur lighthouse to warn mariners away from the treacherous Big Sur coast.

One of the most enjoyable ways to spend a sunny day on the Monterey coast is paddling a sea kayak among the thousands of seals, sea lions, sea otters, and shorebirds that live within the **MONTEREY BAY NATIONAL MARINE SANCTUARY**. Another thrill is seeing the Monterey Bay Aquarium from the water. No kayaking experience is necessary—just follow behind the instructor for an interpretive tour of the bay. For reservations contact **MONTEREY BAY KAYAKS** (831/373-5357 or 800/649-5357; www.montereybaykayaks.com). Prices start at about $60 per person for a three-hour tour.

The landmark **FISHERMAN'S WHARF** (www.montereywharf.com), the former center of Monterey's cargo and whaling industry, is awash in mediocre restaurants and souvenir shops—although, with its seaside-carnival ambience, it's a place the kids might like. The best time to visit is in the winter or spring, when whale-watching trips sail regularly from the wharf. You'll have a number of tour companies to choose from; a popular choice is **CHRIS' FISHING TRIPS & WHALE WATCHING** (48 Fisherman's Wharf, 831/375-5951; www.chrissfishing.com), which offers whale-watching tours in season, as well as fishing excursions for cod, salmon, and whatever else is running. Serious shoppers will be better off strolling **ALVARADO STREET**, a pleasantly low-key, attractive downtown area with a much less touristy mix of art galleries, bookstores, and restaurants. Alvarado Street is also the site of the popular **OLD MONTEREY FARMERS MARKET AND MARKETPLACE**. Held every Tuesday year-round (open 4–8pm summer, 4–7pm winter), it's a real hoot, with more than 100 vegetable, fruit, and crafts vendors plus musicians and performers.

Children will love the **DENNIS THE MENACE PLAYGROUND** (Camino El Estero and Del Monte Ave, near Lake El Estero). Designed by cartoonist Hank Ketcham, it has enough climbing apparatuses to please a monkey. For fun on the water, take your Curious Georges on a paddleboat and pedal around **LAKE EL ESTERO** (831/375-1484). You can rent bicycles and inline skates at the **MONTEREY BAY RECREATION TRAIL**, which runs along the Monterey shore for 18 miles to Lovers Point in Pacific Grove. For a self-guided tour of the area's wineries, stop in at the **MONTEREY COUNTY VINTNERS ASSOCIATION** (831/375-9400; www.montereywines.org), where you can get a wine-tasting and touring map of Monterey County's excellent vineyards and wineries, many of which have public tasting rooms and picnic grounds.

On the third weekend in September top jazz talents such as Wynton Marsalis, Etta James, and Ornette Coleman perform at the **MONTEREY JAZZ FESTIVAL** (925/275-9255 for tickets, 831/373-3366 for information; www.montereyjazzfestival.org), one of the country's best jazz jubilees and the oldest continuous jazz celebration in the world. Tickets and hotel rooms sell out fast, so plan early—die-hard jazz fans make reservations at least six months before show time. Monterey also hosts a **BLUES FESTIVAL** (831/394-2652; www.montereyblues.com) in late June, which attracts a respectable but smaller crowd.

RESTAURANTS

Cafe Fina / ★★

47 FISHERMAN'S WHARF, MONTEREY;
831/372-5200 OR 800/THE-FINA

It's a surprise to find a fine restaurant in the carnival atmosphere of Fisherman's Wharf, but Cafe Fina certainly fits the bill. Owner Dominic Mercurio cooks with a wood broiler and wood-fired brick oven and offers fresh fish, mesquite-grilled chicken and beef, salads, house-made pasta with inventive herb sauces, salmon burgers, and pizzettes—little pizzas hot from the brick oven. Specialties are the seafood and pasta dishes, including clams with garlic butter, prawns and Pernod, and the flavorful Pasta Fina (linguine with baby shrimp, white wine, olives, clam juice, olive oil, tomatoes, and green onions). The food is delicious and carefully prepared, the atmosphere is casual and fun, and the vista is a maritime dream when the sea otters and sea lions are playing within view. Be sure to pick up a business card, which has a recipe for roasted garlic printed on the back. You can sit inside—request a window-side table—or walk up to the window and get a pizza or deep-fried artichoke hearts to go. *$$; AE, DC, DIS, MC, V; no checks; lunch, dinner every day; full bar; reservations recommended; www.cafefina.com; on Fisherman's Wharf.*

Duck Club / ★★★

400 CANNERY ROW (MONTEREY PLAZA HOTEL & SPA),
MONTEREY; 831/646-1707

The Monterey Plaza Hotel & Spa juts out into the bay and slings this restaurant over the starboard side so that the dining room frames the camera-worthy Monterey Bay National Marine Sanctuary. Executive chef James Waller has been running the exhibition kitchen and serving up sustainable seafood since 1997. Starts include wild shrimp in a mandarin orange syrup with almond sauce or grilled Dungeness crab cakes. The menu includes a tasty selection of grilled meats like California pork chops, Kobe short ribs, and roasted Steinbeck's Duck. *$$$$; AE, DC, DIS, MC, V; no checks; breakfast every day, dinner Wed–Sun; full bar; reservations recommended; www.montereyplazahotel.com; at Drake Ave.* ♿

East Village Coffee Lounge / ★★

498 WASHINGTON ST, MONTEREY; 831/373-5601

When you're traveling, sometimes it's nice to unwind at a neighborhood hangout. This large yet cozy coffee shop is our Monterey pick, with exposed brick walls, cushy seating, lofted ceilings, and multiple lounging rooms. Fresh baked goods, prepared on-site every day, include bagels, croissants, Danish pastries, brownies, and strudels. For lunch, you can order salads, panini, minisandwiches, or wraps. The beverage menu features organic coffee drinks, juices, ginger beer, and Italian sodas, as well as alcoholic options like sparkling sake, European beer, and wine by the glass or bottle. The shop also offers free wireless Internet for the computer-toting crowd, and live entertainment takes the stage a couple nights a week. *$; AE, DIS, MC, V; local checks only; breakfast, lunch every day; beer, wine, and sake; no reservations; www.eastvillagecoffeelounge.com; at Pearl St.* ♿

Fresh Cream / ★★★

99 PACIFIC ST, MONTEREY; 831/375-9798

At this upstairs aerie perched on a knoll, you can dine and have a bird's-eye view of Monterey Bay and Fisherman's Wharf. Specializing in French cuisine with hints of California influence, Fresh Cream thrills the eye and the palate all the way through dessert. Appetizers range from lobster ravioli with gold caviar to a smooth-as-silk goose liver pâté with capers and onions. Executive chef Gregory Lizza's luscious entrées include roasted duck with black currant sauce, the definitive rack of lamb dijonnaise, and a delicate poached salmon in saffron-thyme sauce. Vegetarians needn't feel left out; the tasty grilled seasonal vegetable plate is a cut above most veggie entrées. For dessert try the Grand Marnier soufflé or the amazing *sac au chocolat*. Service tends to be a bit on the formal side; the wine list is extensive and expensive. *$$$; AE, DC, DIS, MC, V; checks OK; dinner every day; full bar; reservations recommended; www.freshcream.com; Ste 100C in the Heritage Harbor complex, across from Fisherman's Wharf.* ♿

Montrio / ★★★

414 CALLE PRINCIPAL, MONTEREY; 831/648-8880

Curved lines, stools of woven branches, and soft-sculpture clouds overhead punch up the decor of this converted 1910 firehouse, and the waitstaff are cordial and insightful. The only edgy element here is the food, which has the lusty, rough-yet-refined flavors characteristic of Rio Grill and Tarpy's, two other local favorites founded by Montrio co-owners Tony Tollner and Bill Cox. An oak-fired rotisserie grill in the open kitchen lets you watch the action. Try such dishes as grilled salmon over beans and black rice in a citrus-cumin broth, or duck with wild rice and a dried plum–juniper reduction. The wine list, which received *Wine Spectator* magazine's Award of Excellence, includes many fine vintages by the glass. Or you can opt to sample a wee dram of single-malt Scotch or small-batch bourbon—and if it's a thrill you seek, try a Tombstone Martini, described on the menu as "soooo smooth it's scary."

STEINBECK COUNTRY

John Steinbeck's novel *Cannery Row*, set amid the sardine canneries of Monterey in the 1940s, begins with the line "Cannery Row is a stink, a poem, a grating noise." This doesn't exactly hold true anymore; the smell left when the canneries closed down in the 1950s. However, a few of Cannery Row's monuments remain, most notably the **WING CHONG GROCERY**, which now houses **KRISTONIO'S SHELL SHOP** (835 Cannery Row, Monterey; 831/375-4421). Stand across the street to see its vintage facade and imagine the Chinese immigrants who lived upstairs in its 22 hotel rooms; inside, be sure to check out the Steinbeck memorabilia room and the collection of authentic Chinese lanterns.

One of the best places to get a feel for Steinbeck's life and work is at the fascinating **NATIONAL STEINBECK CENTER** (1 Main St, Salinas; 831/775-4721; www.steinbeck.org). Opened in 1998, the center contains a theater that shows a short biographical film, multimedia exhibits, and a gallery with Steinbeck-themed art. This fun, family-oriented museum is no dusty shrine: kids (especially those who can read) will have a blast exploring the colorful interactive exhibits, which allow them to touch clothing and tools in a replica of the bunkhouse from *Of Mice and Men*, smell the sardines at a Monterey cannery, and try washing laundry as the Joads did in *The Grapes of Wrath*. If they get too rowdy, have them chill out in the refrigerated boxcar à la *East of Eden*. The on-site gift shop has a comprehensive collection of Steinbeck's works, and the museum's **ONE MAIN STREET CAFE** offers breakfast and lunch with regionally inspired dishes such as Gilroy Garlic Fries, Chicken Castroville, and Tortilla Flat Black Bean Soup.

Desserts are worth the calories, particularly the white nectarine pecan crisp with vanilla-bean ice cream. Surprisingly for such a stylish place, a kids' menu and crayons are available, which should keep junior diners as contented as their parents. *$$$; AE, DIS, MC, V; no checks; dinner every day; full bar; reservations recommended; www.montrio.com; near Franklin St.* ♿

Paradiso Trattoria / ★★

654 CANNERY ROW, MONTEREY; 831/375-4155

In 2008 this former Asian-inspired restaurant was renovated and transformed back to an Italian eatery—its original focus. The menu offers an amalgamation of Mediterranean cuisine, including lobster, crab risotto, eggplant Parmesan, linguine clams, and chicken scaloppine. Be warned: Many of the dishes come doused in butter or cream sauce; for dieters, it's not the healthiest place to dine. While the food is pretty tasty and likewise eclectic, Paradiso's greatest offering is the view, with waterfront seating overlooking the bay. If you're here for dinner, request a table by the window—and prepare to witness a spectacular sunset. Note: Restaurants along this stretch are particularly pricey, so if you're looking for a cheaper meal, venture farther away from the waterfront. *$$–$$$; AE, MC, V; checks OK; lunch, dinner every day; full bar; reservations recommended; between Prescott and Hoffman sts.*

Stokes Restaurant and Bar / ★★★

500 HARTNELL ST, MONTEREY; 831/373-1110

Formerly Stokes Adobe, the name was changed because too many people assumed the restaurant served basic Mexican food. Not likely in this sophisticated place. Dorothea and Kirk Probasco didn't miss a trick when they opened Stokes in 1996, snagging Brandon Miller as head chef and assembling a well-trained and friendly staff. The large interior space has been divided into several airy dining rooms with terra-cotta floors, bleached-wood plank ceilings, and Mediterranean-inspired wooden chairs and tables. It's a soothing showcase for Miller's terrific food, which he describes as "contemporary rustic." That means, for example, when he takes a pizza out of the oven, it won't always be perfectly round. Come for a full meal or just for tapas, like the fava bean crostini or crispy potatoes with aioli. Popular entrées include grilled lavender pork chop with leek–lemon bread pudding and pear chutney, and a roasted half chicken on a currant, candied pecan, and crouton salad. Don't let the "rustic" label fool you: this is extremely refined cooking that respects the individual flavors of the high-quality ingredients. Desserts are wonderful here, especially the chocolate lava cake. *$$; AE, MC, V; no checks; dinner every day; full bar; reservations recommended; www.stokesrestaurant.com; at Madison St.* ♿

Tarpy's Roadhouse / ★★★

2999 MONTEREY–SALINAS HWY, MONTEREY; 831/647-1444

Tarpy's may single-handedly give the word roadhouse a good name. Worth a hop in the car for a spin on Highway 68, this exuberant 1917 roadhouse restaurant set on 5 landscaped acres features a broad, sunny patio shaded by market umbrellas and a handsome Southwestern decor inside with rustic, bleached-wood furniture, golden stone walls, and whimsical art. Lunch emphasizes well-prepared sandwiches and salads, but dinner is when Tarpy's really shines. Appetizers might include grilled polenta with mushrooms and Madeira, fire-roasted artichokes with lemon-herb vinaigrette, and Pacific oysters with red wine–jalapeño mignonette. Entrées, cooked on a wood-burning grill, run the gamut from a bourbon-molasses pork chop or a Dijon-crusted lamb loin to sea scallops with saffron penne or a grilled vegetable plate with succotash. Desserts include lemon and fresh ginger crème brûlée, a triple-layer chocolate cake, and olallieberry pie. The wine list is thoughtfully selected, though skewed toward the expensive side. Tarpy's offers a kids' menu as well, with everything under $6. *$$$; AE, DIS, MC, V; no checks; lunch, dinner every day, brunch Sun; full bar; reservations recommended; www.tarpys.com; at Hwy 68 and Canyon Del Rey.*

LODGINGS

Tip: If you're having trouble finding a vacancy, try calling **RESORT 2 ME** (800/757-5646; www.resort2me.com), a local reservation service that offers free recommendations on Monterey Bay Peninsula hotels in all price ranges.

Casa Munras / ★★★

700 MUNRAS AVE, MONTEREY; 800/222-2446 OR 831/375-2411

Resplendent in wood and stone, Casa Munras decidedly sprawls across this compact area of downtown Monterey. With smaller accommodations upstairs in the main building and huge suites scattered about the grounds, this hotel is deceptively simple on the outside, but truly decadent inside. The spa features nine different massages, spiritual medicine like Reiki and craniosacral therapy, and a rather large assortment of skin treatments. A fitness center and heated pool are available to all customers, while the enchanting Jacuzzi set amidst palms and cushy lounge chairs is reserved for the Sano Spa. Blazing fires, exceptional service, a full bar and restaurant, and the centrality of this hotel make it worthy of a closer look. *$$–$$$; AE, DIS, MC, V; checks OK; www.hotelcasamunras.com; between Fremont and Abrego sts.*

Hotel Pacific / ★★★

300 PACIFIC ST, MONTEREY; 831/373-5700 OR 800/554-5542

The Hotel Pacific is a modern neo-hacienda hotel that blends in well with the authentic Old Monterey adobes it stands amid. A sparkling fountain burbles beside the entrance; inside you'll find handwoven rugs, terra-cotta tiles, and beamed ceilings soaring above rounded walls. Connected by tiled courtyards with hand-carved fountains, arches, and flowered pathways, a scattering of low-rise buildings holds 105 spacious suites. All rooms have private patios or terraces, fireplaces, hardwood floors, goose-down feather beds and two telephones. Ask for a room on the fourth level with a sneak peek of the bay, or a room facing the inner courtyard with its large fountain. A deluxe continental breakfast is provided in the morning, and guests may indulge in afternoon tea. Covered parking is available, too. *$$$$; AE, DC, DIS, MC, V; checks OK; www.hotelpacific.com; between Scott St and Del Monte Blvd.* ♿

Monterey Bay Inn / ★★★

242 CANNERY ROW, MONTEREY;
831/373-6242 OR 800/424-6242

Inside this attractive, 49-unit boutique hotel, you'll completely forget that the hustle and bustle of the town's tourist activity is at your doorstep (although it's located on the "quiet end" of the Cannery). Book an oceanfront room so you'll awake to the Pacific Ocean crashing below your window, and be sure to leave your breakfast card on your door at night, so in the morning you can enjoy a tray of fruit and baked goods from the comfort of your balcony. The rooms all have plush king-size beds, massive bathrooms, TVs, DVD and CD players, irons, safes, complimentary wireless Internet, coffeemakers, and binoculars for seal watching out your window. At night, dip into the rooftop

Jacuzzi and watch the lights of Monterey glimmer below you. If more R & R is in order, treat yourself to a massage or body scrub at the Serenity Salon & Spa. *$$$–$$$$; AE, DIS, MC, V; checks OK; www.montereybayinn.com; between Reeside and Drake aves.*

Monterey Plaza Hotel & Spa / ★★★½

400 CANNERY ROW, MONTEREY; 831/646-1700 OR 800/368-2468

Situated at the edge of Monterey Bay, the Monterey Plaza Hotel brings big-city style and services to Cannery Row. In contrast to the California beach-house decor often found in waterfront hotels, this place strikes a note of classic, sleek traditionalism, with a spacious lobby that gleams with Brazilian teakwood walls, Italian marble, and red Oriental-style carpeting. Beidermeier-style armoires and writing desks, cozy duvet bedspreads, and sumptuous marble baths carry the classic look into the hotel's 290 guest rooms and suites. And 24-hour in-room dining, a well-stocked honor bar, pay-per-view movies, and nightly turndown on request make guest rooms especially nice to cocoon in. Many of the rooms face the bay and feature private balconies that place you right above the lapping surf. The Plaza's 11,000-square-foot European-style spa has transformed it from simply a nice place to stay into something of a destination. Although the spa services are extra, use of the well-equipped fitness room is complimentary with any spa treatment. The hotel's Duck Club restaurant (see review) enjoys an enviable location right on the water and offers wood-roasted specialties; the adjacent Schooner's Bistro serves lighter fare. *$$$$; AE, DIS, MC, V; checks OK; www.montereyplazahotel.com; at Drake St.*

Old Monterey Inn / ★★★

500 MARTIN ST, MONTEREY; 831/375-8284 OR 800/350-2344

When was the last time you paid $300 for a room and felt you had underpaid? You may feel that way after a night at this elegantly appointed inn. Nestled among giant oak trees and gardens filled with rhododendrons, begonias, fuchsias, and ferns, this 1929 Tudor-style country inn positively gleams with natural wood, skylights, and stained-glass windows. The 10 beautifully decorated guest rooms, each with a private bath, are filled with charming antiques and comfortable beds with plump down comforters and huge, fluffy pillows. Nine rooms have fireplaces, and all rooms have telephones and TVs with VCRs. For the utmost privacy, request the lacy Garden Cottage, with a private patio, skylights, and a fireplace sitting room, but book it many months ahead because it is a favorite with honeymooners. The deluxe Ashford Suite is the largest, in a wing all its own. It has a sitting area with a fireplace, a separate dressing room, a king-size bed, an antique daybed, a very large "gentleman's tub," and a panoramic garden view. Breakfast, taken in the formal dining room or en suite, might include orange blossom French toast, crepes, artichoke strata, or waffles. You'll also find a delightful afternoon tea and evening hors d'oeuvres. *$$$$; MC, V; checks OK; www.oldmontereyinn.com; near Pacific St.*

FATHER OF CALIFORNIA MISSIONS

Junípero Serra, born on Mallorca in 1713, was a Franciscan friar who was sent to the New World to administer the church's missions in Baja ("lower") California (in present-day Mexico). He was later sent north to found missions in the ports of San Diego and Monterey in the little-explored Alta ("upper") California, a Spanish territory populated with "heathen" natives and threatened by Russian imperialism. On reaching Monterey Bay, Father Serra conducted, with great pageantry, the services that finally symbolized the definitive presence of the Spanish in Alta California.

Though small of stature and quiet of nature, Serra ultimately went on to found a total of 9 thriving missions before his death in 1784. The mission chain eventually totaled 21, situated a day's travel apart (on horseback) along **EL CAMINO REAL** ("the royal road"), which stretched up through present-day California from Mexico. Highway 101 runs along this historic route.

Spindrift Inn / ★★★

652 CANNERY ROW, MONTEREY; 831/646-8900 OR 800/841-1879

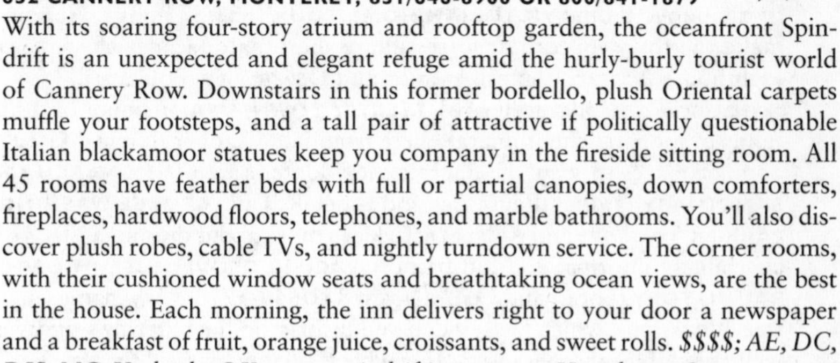

With its soaring four-story atrium and rooftop garden, the oceanfront Spindrift is an unexpected and elegant refuge amid the hurly-burly tourist world of Cannery Row. Downstairs in this former bordello, plush Oriental carpets muffle your footsteps, and a tall pair of attractive if politically questionable Italian blackamoor statues keep you company in the fireside sitting room. All 45 rooms have feather beds with full or partial canopies, down comforters, fireplaces, hardwood floors, telephones, and marble bathrooms. You'll also discover plush robes, cable TVs, and nightly turndown service. The corner rooms, with their cushioned window seats and breathtaking ocean views, are the best in the house. Each morning, the inn delivers right to your door a newspaper and a breakfast of fruit, orange juice, croissants, and sweet rolls. *$$$$; AE, DC, DIS, MC, V; checks OK; www.spindriftinn.com; at Hawthorne St.*

Pacific Grove

In 1875, Methodists set up a summer retreat, pitching tents near what is now Lovers Point. Before long, board-and-batten cottages were built right over the tents, and in some of those former cottages current residents still find scraps of the original tent material in the eaves. As one might suppose, things were pretty buttoned up for a while, and Pacific Grove once even had an ordinance that residents' curtains must be open during the day so no hanky-panky could transpire. The town was incorporated in 1889, just about the time Robert Louis Stevenson visited and said, "I have never been in a place that seemed so dreamlike." This beautiful Victorian seacoast village is still a bit dreamlike and retains its decorous old-town character, though it's loosened its collar a bit since the early days, when dancing, alcohol, and even the Sunday newspaper were banned. Less tourist-oriented than Carmel, less commercial than Monterey, P.G. (as locals call it) exudes peace and tranquility.

Geographically, Pacific Grove begins at the Monterey Bay Aquarium and ends at the 17-Mile Drive gate. Introduce yourself to the town by strolling the 4 miles of trails that meander between the white-sand beaches and rocky tide-pool-dotted coves at **LOVERS POINT BEACH** (off Ocean View Blvd on the east side of Point Piños) and **ASILOMAR STATE BEACH** (off Sunset Dr on the west side of Point Piños). Be sure to sit and enjoy the view from the landmark **LOVERS POINT** (named for lovers of Jesus Christ, not the more carnal kind) and keep an eye out for sea otters sleeping atop the kelp beds—there are tons of them here.

At the tip of **POINT PIÑOS** (Spanish for "Point of the Pines") stands the Cape Cod–style **POINT PIÑOS LIGHTHOUSE** (Asilomar Blvd at Lighthouse Ave; 831/648-5716), the oldest continuously operating lighthouse on the West Coast, built in 1855. This National Historic Landmark is open to the public from 1 to 4pm Thursday through Monday, and admission is free.

P.G. is famous for its Victorian houses, inns, and churches, and hundreds of them have been declared historically significant by the Pacific Grove Heritage Society. Every October, some of the most artfully restored are opened to the public on the **VICTORIAN HOME TOUR** (831/373-3304). If you can't make the tour, you can at least admire the ornate facades clustered along Lighthouse Avenue, Central Avenue, and Ocean View Boulevard.

Pacific Grove bills itself as **BUTTERFLY TOWN, USA**, in honor of the thousands of monarchs that migrate here from late October to mid-March. Two popular places to view the alighting lepidoptera are the **MONARCH GROVE SANCTUARY** (at Lighthouse Ave and Ridge Rd) and **GEORGE WASHINGTON PARK** (at Sinex Ave and Alder St). To learn more about the monarchs, visit the charmingly informal and kid-friendly **PACIFIC GROVE MUSEUM OF NATURAL HISTORY** (Forest and Central aves; 831/648-5716; www.pgmuseum.org; free admission), which has a video and display on the butterfly's life cycle, as well as exhibits of other insects, local birds, mammals, and reptiles. For good books and international gifts, amble over to **BOOKWORKS** (667 Lighthouse Ave; 831/372-2242), where yellow crime tape festoons the mystery section and there's an easy chair for reading, along with an extensive array of magazines and newspapers.

Around the corner from the Monterey Bay Aquarium is the **AMERICAN TIN CANNERY PREMIUM OUTLETS** center (125 Ocean View Blvd; 831/372-1442), where more than 40 clothing, shoes, and accessories stores—including Anne Klein, Bass, London Fog, Reebok, Big Dog, OshKosh B'Gosh, Samsonite, and Izod—sell their wares for up to half of what you'd normally pay. Particularly worth a look are the amazing deals at the Woolrich outlet, where many items are 50 percent off.

For more information about P.G., call or visit the **PACIFIC GROVE CHAMBER OF COMMERCE** (831/373-3304 or 800/656-6650; www.pacificgrove.org), located at the corner of Forest and Central avenues.

RESTAURANTS

Fandango / ★★★

223 17TH ST, PACIFIC GROVE; 831/372-3456

Fandango, the name of a lively Spanish dance, is the perfect moniker for this kick-up-your-heels restaurant specializing in Mediterranean country cuisine. It's a big, sprawling, colorful place with textured adobe walls and a spirited crowd filling six separate dining rooms; the glass-domed terrace in back, with its stone fireplace and open mesquite grill, is especially pleasant. Start with a few tapas—perhaps spicy sausage, roasted red peppers, or a potato-and-onion frittata. If you're feeling adventurous, order the Velouté Bongo Bongo, an exotic creamy soup with oysters, spinach, and Cognac. For the main course, choose from the flavorful Paella Fandango (served at your table in a huge skillet), pasta puttanesca (tomatoes, basil, garlic, capers, and olives), bouillabaisse Marseillaise, osso buco, or the 26-ounce porterhouse steak, with tarragon and Cognac herbed butter. For dessert, try the profiteroles filled with chocolate ice cream and topped with hot fudge sauce. *$$$; AE, DC, DIS, MC, V; no checks; lunch Mon–Sat, dinner every day, brunch Sun; full bar; reservations recommended; www.fandangorestaurant.com; near Lighthouse Ave.*

Red House Cafe / ★★

662 LIGHTHOUSE AVE, PACIFIC GROVE; 831/643-1060

A trim, 103-year-old, red brick house in downtown Pacific Grove is the deceptively modest setting for some of the most adroit cooking on the Monterey Peninsula. It offers a handful of humble-sounding dishes at breakfast and lunch—items such as Irish oatmeal, Belgian waffles, pastries, a mixed green salad, roast beef on sourdough, a BLT, and eggs any way you like them as long as they're scrambled. Sit in one of the snug, country cottage–style dining rooms or enjoy the ocean breezes on the porch with its smattering of wicker chairs and tables for two. Often local salmon or other Monterey Bay seafood is on the menu, and the crab cakes are to die for, full of succulent crab and not much else. Locals love it here and often have a favorite menu item they always order. Perfectly cooked, every dish demonstrates the kitchen's insistence on first-rate ingredients—heck, even the toast and jam tastes like a gourmet treat. On the sidewalk outside there is a large, round embedded stone engraved with the word JOY. When you take your first bite you will see why. *$; cash only; breakfast Sat–Sun, lunch, dinner Tues–Sun; beer and wine; reservations recommended; www.redhousecafe.com; at 19th St.*

Taste Cafe & Bistro / ★★★

1199 FOREST AVE, PACIFIC GROVE; 831/655-0324

Although this restaurant is a bit hard to see on Forest Avenue, in a small mini-mall with only one entry, food lovers seek out Taste Cafe. You'll be hard-pressed to find higher-quality food for the same price anywhere else on the coast. The menu combines rustic French, Italian, and California cuisines made from the best and freshest local produce, seafood, and meats. Lunch could be a grilled eggplant sandwich with smoked Gouda cheese and caramelized onion on toasted focaccia, or chicken-apple sausages with au gratin potatoes. At dinner, start your meal with house-cured salmon carpaccio with a mustard-dill dressing or butternut squash agnolotti. Move on to entrées such as marinated rabbit with braised red cabbage or lean pork medallions with sautéed napa cabbage, onions, celery, and apples. Be sure to save room for one of the wonderful desserts: warm brioche pudding with apricot coulis and crème fraîche, or a bittersweet chocolate torte. The interior is simple—airy, high-ceilinged, and graced with beautiful flower arrangements. The word is out on this terrific restaurant, so call well ahead for reservations, especially for weekend dinners. *$$; AE, MC, V; checks OK; dinner every day; beer and wine; reservations recommended; www.tastecafebistro.com; at Prescott Ave.* ♿

LODGINGS

Gatehouse Inn / ★★

225 CENTRAL AVE, PACIFIC GROVE; 831/649-8436 OR 800/753-1881

This big yellow Victorian looks a bit like the haunted house at Disneyland, but much cheerier. When State Senator Benjamin Langford built the ocean-view mansion in 1884, Pacific Grove was less a town than a pious Methodist meeting ground, separated from wicked, worldly Monterey by a white picket fence. Langford's domain is now an enticingly eccentric B and B, where the nine individually decorated guest rooms range in style from Victoriana to Persia to beach house. All guest rooms have private baths and queen-size beds, with the exception of the Cannery Row Room, which has a king-size bed. The Langford Room ranks as the inn's most luxurious, with an ocean-view sitting room, a potbellied stove, and a claw-foot bathtub that commands a stunning view of the coast. Looking for something more exotic? You might try the Turkish Room. You'll find hors d'oeuvres, tea, and wine in the lobby every evening and a full breakfast buffet with house-baked breads every morning, and you can even help yourself to cookies and beverages from the kitchen any time. *$$$; AE, DIS, MC, V; checks OK; www.gatehouse-inn.com; at 2nd St.*

Lighthouse Lodge and Suites / ★★

1150 AND 1249 LIGHTHOUSE AVE, PACIFIC GROVE; 800/858-1249

Less than a block from the ocean, the Lighthouse Lodge and Suites is really two entities with rather distinct personalities. The lodge consists of 64 motel-like rooms and suites—complete with large TVs, minibars, refrigerators, and microwaves—that are ideally suited for families, particularly when booked as part of the hotel's discount vacation package. Those seeking more luxurious accommodations should spring for one of the 31 newer suites down the hill and across the road. The Cape Cod–style suites—all with beamed ceilings, plush carpeting, fireplaces, wing chairs, vast bathrooms with marble whirlpool tubs, large-screen TVs, mini-kitchens, and king-size beds—glow in peacock hues of purple, green, and fuchsia. The overall effect is a bit nouveau riche, but riche all the same. A full breakfast and afternoon poolside barbecue are included in the room rate. After breakfast take a morning stroll around the grounds, cleverly landscaped with fountains and native plants, or go for a swim in the outdoor heated pool. Pets are welcome for $25 a night. *$$ (lodge), $$$–$$$$ (suites); AE, DC, DIS, MC, V; no checks; www.lhls.com; at Asilomar Blvd.*

The Martine Inn / ★★☆

255 OCEAN VIEW BLVD, PACIFIC GROVE; 831/373-3388 OR 800/852-5588

Perched like a vast pink wedding cake on a cliff above Monterey Bay, this villa with a Mediterranean exterior and a Victorian interior is one of Pacific Grove's most elegant bed-and-breakfasts. Built in 1899 for James and Laura Parke (of Parke-Davis Pharmaceuticals), the inn has two dozen spacious guest rooms, all with private baths and high-quality antiques. Owner Dan Martine has accumulated the best collection of ornately carved armoires on the planet. Most rooms have wood-burning fireplaces; all have views of the water or the garden courtyard with its delightful dragon fountain. If you feel like splurging, the Parke Room on the top floor is outstanding. Originally the master bedroom, it has three walls of windows with views of the waves crashing against the rocks, an 1860s Chippendale Revival bedroom set complete with four-poster canopy bed, a sitting area, a claw-foot tub, and a massive corner fireplace. No matter which room you choose, you'll find a silver basket of fruit and a rose waiting for you upon arrival, and a newspaper at your door in the morning. Several intimate sitting rooms offset three large common areas: the library, the main dining room (with a dazzling view of the bay), and the breakfast parlor. Martine serves an elaborate and well-prepared breakfast, and offers wine and hors d'oeuvres in the late afternoon in the formal parlor with its baby grand piano. *$$$–$$$$; AE, DIS, MC, V; checks OK; www.martineinn.com; 4 blocks from Cannery Row.*

Seven Gables Inn / ★★★☆

555 OCEAN VIEW BLVD, PACIFIC GROVE; 831/372-4341

Set in an immaculate yellow Victorian mansion built in 1886 and surrounded by gardens, this family-run inn commands a magnificent view of Monterey Bay. Chock-full of formal European antiques, Seven Gables will seem like paradise to those who revel in things Victorian. Once you're ensconced in one of the 25 guest rooms, which are divided among the main house, a guest house, and a smattering of cottages, the warm and welcoming staff will see to your every comfort. The uniquely appointed rooms feature gorgeous ocean views, private baths with luxurious bath amenities, and queen-size beds with down comforters. A pull-out-all-the-stops breakfast is served by the house chef in the ocean-view dining room, and tea service is set out every afternoon. *$$$$; MC, V; checks OK; www.pginns.com; at Fountain Ave.*

CENTRAL COAST THREE-DAY TOUR

DAY ONE: *Marine magic*. Get up early, grab a latte and a bagel to go, and start the day by exploring the teeming tide pools of the **JAMES V. FITZGERALD MARINE RESERVE** at Moss Beach. Enjoy lunch at **MOSS BEACH DISTILLERY**, then browse the shops along Half Moon Bay's quaint Main Street or rent a beach cruiser and take a leisurely bike ride along the shoreline. Drive south on Highway 1 to check in to your deluxe tent bungalow at **COSTANOA** in Pescadero. For an ocean view of the setting sun, take a hike on the **PAMPAS HEAVEN LOOP TRAIL**. Start at the main trailhead at Costanoa, cross Whitehouse Creek Bridge, and follow Whitehouse Creek Trail to the loop. Try **DUARTE'S TAVERN** in Pescadero for dinner or bring your own fixin's and fire up one of the barbecues in the camp.

DAY TWO: *Sweet nature and spas*. Rise early and walk the **REDWOOD NATURE TRAIL** to commune with the flora and fauna in **BIG BASIN REDWOODS STATE PARK**. Return to Costanoa for continental breakfast, a shower, and a sauna; don't forget to stock up on gourmet goodies for the road at **COSTANOA'S GENERAL STORE**. Take Highway 1 south and follow the signs to Pacific Grove and **17-MILE DRIVE** for a tour of some of the world's most expensive real estate. Exiting

Pebble Beach and the 17-Mile Drive

How much are a room and a round of golf at Pebble Beach these days? Let's put it this way: If you have to ask, you can't afford it. If the 6,000-or-so residents of this exclusive gated community had their way, Pebble Beach would probably be off-limits to mere commoners. Perhaps more of an indignity, though, is the $9.25-per-car levy required to trespass on their gilded avenues and wallow in envy at how the ruling class recreates (though if you grab a drink at the Lodge or Spanish Bay, they'll refund your entrance fee). If you have no strong desire to tour corporate-owned hideaways and redundant—albeit gorgeous—seascapes along the famous 17-Mile Drive, save your lunch money; you're not really missing anything that can't be seen elsewhere along the Monterey coast (just drive along the coast on Ocean View Boulevard in Pacific Grove and you'll see pretty much the same views). Then again, some folks swear that cruising past Pebble Beach's mansions and manicured golf courses is worth the admission just to contemplate the lifestyles of the very rich.

If you decide to pay the toll, you'll see everything from a spectacular Byzantine castle with a private beach—the **CROCKER MANSION** near the Carmel gate—to several tastefully bland California Nouvelle country-club establishments in perfectly maintained forest settings. Other highlights include the

17-Mile Drive at Ocean Avenue will put you right in the center of Carmel's many boutiques and restaurants. After lunch at **CASANOVA RESTAURANT**, you can opt for a little shopping or a walk along glorious **CARMEL BEACH**. Head to Carmel Valley to spend the night at **BERNARDUS LODGE**. Before dinner at the lodge's **MARINUS** restaurant, freshen up with a dip in the pool, or indulge in a massage or facial at the luxurious on-site spa.

DAY THREE: *Big Sur-prises*. After breakfasting on your private terrace, enjoy a game of tennis, bocce ball, or croquet at Bernardus, or a round of golf at one of Carmel Valley's championship courses. Travel south on Highway 1 for a look at literary memorabilia in the **HENRY MILLER LIBRARY** and lunch at Big Sur's **NEPENTHE RESTUARANT**. Browse the **PHOENIX GIFT SHOP** at Nepenthe for imported treasures and locally made jewelry, soaps, and aromatic oils before driving a few miles north to the **POST RANCH INN**. After checking in to your mountain- or ocean-view cabin, take the walking trail down to the inn's Olympic-size pool for a late afternoon swim, or drink in an amazing view of the Pacific (and predinner cocktails, if you like) while relaxing in the giant hot tub known as the Basking Pool. End the day with dinner at Post Ranch's romantic **SIERRA MAR** restaurant and some stargazing from the restaurant patio.

often-photographed gnarled **LONE CYPRESS** clinging to its rocky precipice above the sea; miles of hiking and equestrian trails winding through groves of native pines and wildflowers, with glorious views of Monterey Bay; and **BIRD ROCK**, a small offshore isle covered with hundreds of seals and sea lions (bring binoculars). Self-guided nature tours are outlined in a variety of brochures, available for free at the gate entrances and at **THE INN AT SPANISH BAY** and **THE LODGE AT PEBBLE BEACH** (see reviews).

There are five entrances to the **17-MILE DRIVE**, each manned by spiffy security guards, and the entire drive takes about one to two hours (though you can whiz by the highlights in 30 minutes). Your best bet is to avoid the busy summer weekends and come midweek. Visitors may enter the 17-Mile Drive for free on foot or bike, although cyclists are required to use the Pacific Grove gate on weekends and holidays. For more information, contact the **PEBBLE BEACH RESORT** (831/624-3811; www.pebblebeach.com).

LODGINGS

The Inn at Spanish Bay / ★★★★

2700 17-MILE DR, PEBBLE BEACH; 831/647-7500 OR 800/654-9300

Set on the privately owned 17-Mile Drive, this sprawling modern inn—consistently ranked among the top resorts in the world—defines deluxe. Its 270 luxuriously appointed rooms and suites perched on a cypress-dotted bluff have gas fireplaces, quilted down comforters, and elegant sitting areas. Most have private patios or balconies with gorgeous views of the rocky coast or the Del Monte Forest. Three of the most deluxe suites even come with grand pianos. The bathrooms, equipped with all the modern conveniences you could want, are appropriately regal. Hotel guests have access to eight tennis courts, an outdoor swimming pool, a 22,000-square-foot full-service spa and salon, and miles of hiking and equestrian trails. Along with the well-respected Roy's at Pebble Beach (831/647-7423), the resort also has an Italian restaurant, Peppoli (831/647-7433), which serves rich Tuscan fare. *$$$$; AE, DC, MC, V; checks OK; www.pebblebeach.com; near the Pacific Grove entrance.* ♿

The Lodge at Pebble Beach / ★★★½

1700 17-MILE DR, PEBBLE BEACH; 831/647-7500 OR 800/654-9300
Despite greens fees of $495 (hey, it includes a cart), Pebble Beach remains the mecca of American golf courses, and avid golfers feel they have to play it at least once before retiring to that Big Clubhouse in the Sky. The guest rooms are tastefully decorated, swathed in soothing earth tones and outfitted with a sophisticated, modern decor. There are 161 suites and rooms, most with private balconies or patios, brick fireplaces, sitting areas, and gorgeous views. All the usual upscale amenities are provided, from phones by the commode to honor-bar refrigerators to robes. The whole effect is very East Coast country club. Four restaurants cater to visitors, most notably Club XIX, featuring a mix of French and Californian cuisine, and the Stillwater Bar and Grill (831/625-8524), with a menu that offers seafood, steak, and even hamburgers. Jackets for men are required at Club XIX. Hotel guests have preferred tee times at the world-famous Pebble Beach, Spanish Bay, and Spyglass Hill golf courses, as well as access to the ocean-side Beach & Tennis Club, an outdoor swimming pool, a 22,000-square-foot full-service spa and salon, and miles of hiking and equestrian trails. *$$$$; AE, DC, DIS, MC, V; checks OK; www.pebblebeach.com; near the Carmel Gate.* ♿

Carmel

In the not-so-distant past, Carmel was regarded as a reclusive little seaside town with the sort of relaxed Mediterranean atmosphere conducive to such pursuits as photography, painting, and writing. Robert Louis Stevenson, Upton Sinclair, and Ansel Adams all found Carmel peaceful and intellectually inspiring enough to settle down here. They wanted to be left alone, and fought street improvements and numbered house addresses to ensure their seclusion. The charmingly ragtag bohemian village of yesteryear has long since given way to a major tourist hot spot brimming with chichi inns, art galleries, and house-and-garden shops offering $300 ceramic geese and other essentials. Traffic—both vehicular and pedestrian—can be maddeningly congested during the summer and on weekends, and prices in the shops, hotels,

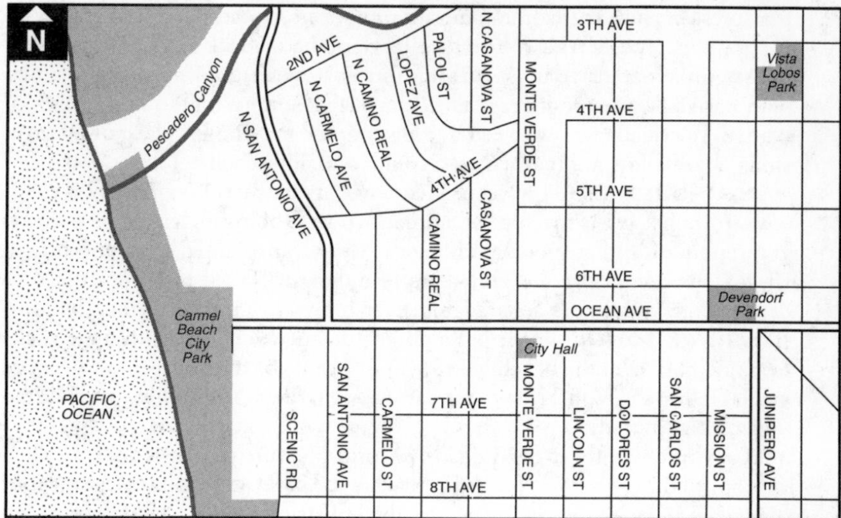

Carmel

and restaurants tend to be high. The funny thing is, no matter how crowded or expensive Carmel gets, nobody seems to mind. Enamored of the village's eclectic dwellings, expensive boutiques, quaint cafés, and silky white beaches, tourists arrive in droves during the summer to lighten their wallets and darken their complexions. Just be sure to make your reservations far in advance, and leave plenty of room on the credit cards—you'll need it. And bring your dog if you have one; many inns welcome them with doggy biscuits at the desk and pet beds in the rooms, and in many shops it's perfectly OK to bring Fido in to browse.

Without doubt, the best way to see Carmel is on foot. **CARMEL WALKS** (831/642-2700; www.carmelwalks.com) offers a two-hour guided walk through the town's most interesting paths and courtyards, including Hugh Comstock's storybook cottages and the homes of famous former denizens such as feminist Mary Austin, photographer Edward Weston, and poet Robinson Jeffers. Tours cost $25 and are offered at 10am Tuesday through Friday, and at 10am and 2pm on Saturday; meet in the courtyard of the **PINE INN** (Lincoln St at Ocean Ave).

The restored **MISSION SAN CARLOS BORROMEO DEL RÍO CARMELO**, better known as the **CARMEL MISSION** (3080 Rio Rd, at Lasuén Dr, several blocks west of Hwy 1; 831/624-3600; www.carmelmission.org), is located next to **MISSION TRAILS PARK**, with 5 miles of winding paths dotted by wildflowers, willows, deer, and redwoods. Established in 1770, the Carmel Mission was the headquarters of Father Junípero Serra's famous chain of California missions—and his favorite (Serra is buried in front of the altar in the sanctuary, which is marked with a plaque). The vine-covered baroque church with its 11-bell Moorish tower, completed in 1797, is one of California's architectural treasures. Be sure to see the main altar, with its Gothic arch and elaborate decorations, and Serra's restored cell, where he died in 1784. The mission houses three extensive museums, and its surrounding 14 acres are planted with native flowers and trees. The cemetery has more than 3,000 graves of Native Americans who worked and lived in the mission; in place of a gravestone, many plots are marked by a solitary abalone shell.

TOR HOUSE (26304 Ocean View Ave at Stewart Wy; 831/624-1813; www.torhouse.org), the former home of poet Robinson Jeffers, is a rustic granite building that looks as though it were transplanted from the British Isles. Constructed over several years beginning in 1914, today it's the residence of one of Jeffers's descendants. Even more intriguing is the nearby four-story **HAWK TOWER**, which Jeffers built for his wife, Una, with huge rocks he hauled up from the beach below. Guided tours of the house and tower are available for a fee on Friday and Saturday by reservation only (no children under 12 admitted).

Are you ready for a good dose of Mother Nature's great wonders? Then visit one of the town's two beautiful beaches. **CARMEL CITY BEACH**, at the foot of Ocean Avenue and the town's shopping district, tends to be overcrowded in the summer (though its chilly aquamarine water is unsafe for swimming), but the gorgeous white sand and towering cypresses are worth the price of sunbathing among the hordes. Or head a mile south on **SCENIC DRIVE** to spectacular **CARMEL RIVER STATE BEACH**, where the locals go to hide from the tourists (though swimming is unsafe here, too). The Carmel River enters the Pacific at this point, and you'll see a bird sanctuary frequented by pelicans, hawks, sandpipers, kingfishers, willets, and the occasional goose. **MIDDLE BEACH** and **MONASTERY BEACH** lie beyond. These areas are remarkably scenic, but Mother Nature saved her best efforts for the 1,276-acre **POINT LOBOS STATE RESERVE** (on Hwy 1 approximately 3 miles south of Carmel; 831/624-4909 for park information, 831/624-8413 for scuba-diving reservations; http://pt-lobos.parks.state.ca.us). More than a dozen Point Lobos trails lead to ocean coves, where you might spy sea otters, harbor seals, California sea lions, large colonies of seabirds and, between December and May, migrating California gray whales. Some trails will even take you to one of the two naturally growing stands of Monterey cypress remaining on earth (the other stand is in Pebble Beach on the 17-Mile Drive). For more nearby hiking recommendations, see the Big Sur section in the following pages.

Shopping is a popular pastime in Carmel—at least for those who don't blanch at astronomical price tags. Not only is its downtown packed with interesting little boutiques, but also just outside of town lie two luxe suburban malls: **THE BARNYARD** (on Hwy 1 at Carmel Valley Rd; 831/624-8886) and **THE CROSSROADS** (on Hwy 1 at Rio Rd; 831/625-4106). **OCEAN AVENUE** between Junipero and San Antonio avenues has its share of tourist-schlock shops, it's true, but hit the side streets for some fine adventures in consumerland. Numerous quality art galleries are located between Lincoln and San Carlos streets and Fifth and Sixth avenues. Particularly noteworthy is the **WESTON GALLERY** (6th Ave at Dolores St; 831/624-4453), which showcases

19th- and 20th-century photographers' works, including a permanent display featuring such famous Carmelites as Edward Weston, Ansel Adams, and Imogen Cunningham. If you want to tour the galleries, pick up a copy of the Carmel Gallery Guide from the Carmel Visitor Information Center.

Carmel has an active theater scene, perhaps best represented by the **PACIFIC REPERTORY THEATRE COMPANY** (831/622-0100; www.pacrep.org), which puts on an outdoor musical and a Shakespeare festival each summer and performs other classics such as *The Madness of George III* and *Death of a Salesman* in its indoor theater year-round.

The annual month-long **CARMEL BACH FESTIVAL** (831/624-2046; www.bachfestival.com) offers numerous concerts, recitals, lectures, and discussion groups—some are even free. In addition to Bach masterpieces, you'll hear scores by Vivaldi, Scarlatti, Beethoven, and Chopin. The most sought-after ticket of the event is the formal concert in the mission (book far ahead for that one). The classical music celebration begins in mid-July; series tickets are sold starting in January, and single-event tickets (ranging from $10 to $50) go on sale in April.

For more information about Carmel, call or visit the **CARMEL VISITOR INFORMATION CENTER** (800/550-4333 or 831/624-2522; www.carmelcalifornia.org; open 9am–5pm Mon–Fri), located on San Carlos Street between 5th and 6th avenues. The information center is amply stocked with maps, brochures, and publications on area attractions and lodgings. There's also a visitor information kiosk at Carmel Plaza, on Ocean Avenue between Junipero and San Carlos streets. It's open from 11am to 5pm on Saturday year-round, and Wednesday through Sunday Memorial Day through Labor Day.

RESTAURANTS

Anton & Michel / ★★

MISSION ST, CARMEL; 831/624-2406 OR 866/244-0645

This longtime Carmel favorite overlooks the Court of the Fountains with its Louis XV lions and verdigris garden pavilions. Anton & Michel's elegant dining room has pink walls, white wainscoting, and tall, slender pillars adorned with curlicue cornices. Despite the interesting decor, the continental cuisine isn't exactly daring, but it's extremely well prepared. Standouts include the rack of lamb with an herb-Dijon mustard au jus, grilled veal with a spinach-Madeira sauce, and medallions of ahi tuna with a black-pepper-and-sesame-seed crust and a wasabi-cilantro sauce. Anton & Michel also offers traditional French desserts such as crepes suzette, cherries jubilee, and chocolate mousse cake with sauce anglaise. Service is courtly, and the extensive wine list has garnered many *Wine Spectator* magazine awards. *$$$; AE, DC, DIS, MC, V; no checks; lunch, dinner every day; full bar; reservations recommended; www.carmelsbest.com; between Ocean and 7th aves.*

Casanova Restaurant / ★★

5TH ST, CARMEL; 831/625-0501

The former home of Charlie Chaplin's cook, this sunny cottage with a Mediterranean feel attracts happy throngs of locals and tourists alike. Casanova specializes in Italian and French country–style dishes; the pasta creations, such as linguine with seafood served in a big copper pot, are particularly fetching. At dinner, there is a required three-course prix-fixe menu, so don't come just to graze on appetizers. Lunch on the big patio out back is informal and fun, with heaters keeping patrons warm on chilly afternoons. Inside, the cottage is a jumble of nooks and crannies decked out in rustic European decor. Casanova prides itself on its extensive and reasonably priced wine list, including the well-received Georis merlot and cabernet, produced by one of the restaurant's owners. Cap off your meal with one of Casanova's superb desserts; the many choices include a Basque-style pear tart and a chocolate custard pie with whipped cream, nuts, and shaved dark and white Belgian chocolates. *$$; MC, V; no checks; lunch, dinner every day, brunch Sun; full bar; reservations recommended; www.casanovarestaurant.com; between San Carlos and Mission sts.* ♿

The Cottage / ★★

LINCOLN ST, CARMEL; 831/625-6260

The Cottage seems like the place rich Carmel housewives might convene for a weekly cup of tea and rousing book club discussion. Its brick-walled interior and fireplaces give it a cozy edge, while floral touches add a Laura Ashley flair. But the breakfast is surely why you come to this downtown establishment (and it's served all day, every day). Try the panettone French toast, one of the six types of eggs Benedict (like the Crab 'n' Spinach or Lox 'n' Onion), or a stack of fruit cakes (strawberry, raspberry, or blueberry) in powdered sugar and cinnamon. Egg dishes are accompanied by fresh fruit, hash browns or Cottage Potatoes, and a choice of bread. Dinner may begin with the artichoke soup (a secret recipe!), followed by fresh Monterey Bay salmon topped with a lemon caper sauce, served with hollandaise vegetables and garlic mashed potatoes, and finished off with the house specialty, gingerbread in lemon sauce. *$$; MC, V; no checks; breakfast, lunch every day, dinner Thurs–Sat; wine; reservations recommended (dinner); www.cottagerestaurant.com; between Ocean and Seventh sts.*

Flying Fish Grill / ★★

MISSION ST, CARMEL; 831/625-1962

Hidden on the ground level of the Carmel Plaza shopping center, this ebullient newcomer is worth seeking out for its fun, stylish atmosphere and superb seafood. The interior is a maze of booths and tables flanked by an expanse of warm, polished wood and crisp blue-and-white banners. Chef-owner Kenny Fukumoto offers creative East-West fusion dishes such as Yin-Yan Salmon (roast salmon on angel hair pasta sprinkled with sesame seeds and served with a soy-lime cream sauce); panfried Chilean sea bass with almonds, whipped potatoes, and a Chinese cabbage and rock shrimp stir-fry; and, his specialty, a rare peppered ahi tuna on angel hair pasta. New York steak and a couple of flavorful Japanese clay pot dishes (seafood or beef) that you cook at your own table round out the menu. There's also a tempting lineup of desserts, including Chocolate Decadence, a warm banana sundae, and an assortment of delicate sorbets. *$$; AE, DIS, MC, V; no checks; dinner Wed–Mon; beer and wine; reservations recommended; between Ocean and 7th aves, in Carmel Plaza.*

Grasing's Coastal Cuisine / ★★★

6TH AVE, CARMEL; 831/624-6562

Noted chefs Kurt Grasing and Narsai David teamed up to open this eponymous restaurant (formerly the Sixth Avenue Grill), which serves a more casual version of the contemporary California-Mediterranean cuisine Grasing previously turned out at tony eateries like San Mateo's 231 Ellsworth. At lunch, you'll find superb pastas, salads, sandwiches, and entrées such as bronzed salmon with grilled portobellos, roasted potatoes, and garlic. Dinner starters might include potato, wild rice, and zucchini pancakes with house-cured salmon and crème fraîche, or a savory three-onion tart with a fennel sauce and balsamic syrup. Main courses range from wild-mushroom stew with creamy polenta, to roast duck with an orange-port glaze, or local swordfish over orzo pasta with snow peas, bok choy, and ponzu sauce. The dining room is a cheerful stage for Grasing's inspired cooking, with Milano-modern furnishings, textured ocher walls, cathedral ceilings, and witty sculptures and art. The wine list is ample and thoughtfully selected, desserts are diet-busting delights. *$$; AE, DC, MC, V; local checks only; lunch, dinner every day; beer and wine; reservations recommended; www.grasings.com; at Mission St.* ♿

Katy's Place / ★

MISSION ST, CARMEL; 831/624-0199

A few steps from the city library is Katy's Place, the locals' favorite spot in Carmel for breakfast. The country kitchen–style restaurant specializes in comfort food: big helpings and endless variations of pancakes, waffles, and eggs, including a dynamite eggs Benedict. Eat in the pretty dining room or on the patio under the redwood trees. This is a great place to bring the kids. *$; no credit cards; local checks only; breakfast, lunch every day; beer and wine; no reservations; www.katysplacecarmel.com; between 5th and 6th aves.* ♿

La Dolce Vita / ★★

SAN CARLOS ST, CARMEL; 831/624-3667

Those in the mood for authentic Italian food in a casual atmosphere will enjoy this restaurant, a local favorite. The terrace, which overlooks the street, is popular for both sunny lunches and moonlit dinners (heaters take the chill off when necessary). The main dining room is more gussied up, resembling a cozy trattoria with slate floors, light wood furniture, and peach-toned walls. Specialties include the transporting Ravioli alla Rachele (homemade spinach ravioli stuffed with crab and cheese in a champagne cream sauce, topped with scallops and sun-dried tomatoes) and Gnocchi della Nonna (fresh potato dumplings with a choice of tomato or Gorgonzola-sage cream sauce—ask for a little of both). A range of individual-size pizzas is also available, along with *secondi piatti* ranging from traditional osso buco to calamari steak drizzled with sun-dried tomato pesto, lemon juice, and crisp orvieto wine. The waitstaff can be a bit cheeky at times, but hey, with food this *bellissima*, you're not likely to get your feathers ruffled. *$$; MC, V; local checks only; lunch, dinner every day; beer and wine; reservations recommended; between 7th and 8th aves.* ♿

Pacific's Edge / ★★★★

120 HIGHLANDS DR (HIGHLANDS INN), CARMEL; 831/622-5445

Perched on an eyebrow cliff over Highway 1 in the Highlands area is Pacific's Edge, the Highlands Inn Park Hyatt Hotel's flagship restaurant. If you are going to break the bank for one special evening, this is the place. Named one of America's best restaurants by *Wine Spectator* magazine, it serves inspired California cuisine in a gorgeous setting with panoramic 180-degree views of the coastline (reserve well in advance for a table at sunset). Starters might include farm-fresh artichokes with basil mayonnaise, potato-wrapped ahi tuna, or grilled quail with creamy rosemary polenta. Entrées on the three- to five-course menu range from grilled Monterey Bay salmon in an onion-rosemary sauce to roasted rack of lamb with white truffle potatoes. Choosing the appropriate wine shouldn't be a problem—the inn's wine cellar has consistently won *Wine Spectator*'s Grand Award. Valet parking is free. *$$$; AE, DC, DIS, MC, V; checks OK; dinner every day, brunch Sun; full bar; reservations recommended; www.pacificsedge.com; 4 miles south of Carmel.*

Rio Grill / ★★

101 CROSSROADS BLVD, CARMEL; 831/625-5436

This noisy Southwestern-style grill is packed with a lively crowd from opening till closing. The salads—such as organic mixed greens with aged goat cheese, seasoned walnuts, and curry vinaigrette—are wonderfully fresh, and appetizers—like the ever-popular onion rings and fried Monterey Bay squid with orange-sesame dipping sauce—draw raves. The tasty barbecued baby back ribs and the herb-crusted chicken with crispy broccoli-corn risotto cakes are good bets for the main course, as is the pumpkin seed–crusted salmon with chipotle-lime vinaigrette and roasted red pepper–potato cakes. Don't miss the French fries with rosemary aioli. Desserts include a killer olallieberry pie and caramel-apple bread pudding. While the atmosphere may be chaotic, the service isn't, and the grill boasts a large wine list, with many selections available by the glass. They also have a kids' menu that's easy on the wallet. *$$; AE, DIS, MC, V; no checks; lunch, dinner every day, brunch Sun; full bar; reservations recommended; www.riogrill.com; in the Crossroads Shopping Village, at Hwy 1 and Rio Rd.* ♿

LODGINGS

Cypress Inn / ★★

LINCOLN ST, CARMEL; 831/624-3871 OR 800/443-7443

One of the more elegant hotels in Carmel, this Spanish Colonial–style inn in the center of town is owned by movie star and animal-rights activist Doris Day. Pets, naturally, are more than welcome. In fact, the immaculate hotel even provides dog beds for its four-footed guests. The 34 guest rooms come in a wide variety of sizes, shapes, and locations. Try to book a tower suite, with the bedroom reached by a winding stair, plus whirlpool tub, arched windows, and bookshelves complete with books. All rooms contain some thoughtful touches: fresh fruit, bottles of spring water, chocolates left on the pillow at night, and a decanter of sherry. Some have sitting rooms, wet bars, private verandas, and ocean views; all have marble bathrooms, fruit baskets, nightly turndown service, and special blankets for pets. Light sleepers should ask for a room on the second floor. Downstairs there's a spacious Spanish-style open-beam living room with a comforting fire and a friendly bar that dishes out coffee and a continental breakfast in the morning, and libations of a more spirited kind at night. Posters of Doris Day movies add a touch of glamour and fun to the decor. *$$$–$$$$; AE, DIS, MC, V; checks OK; www.cypress-inn.com; at 7th Ave.*

Highlands Inn / ★★★

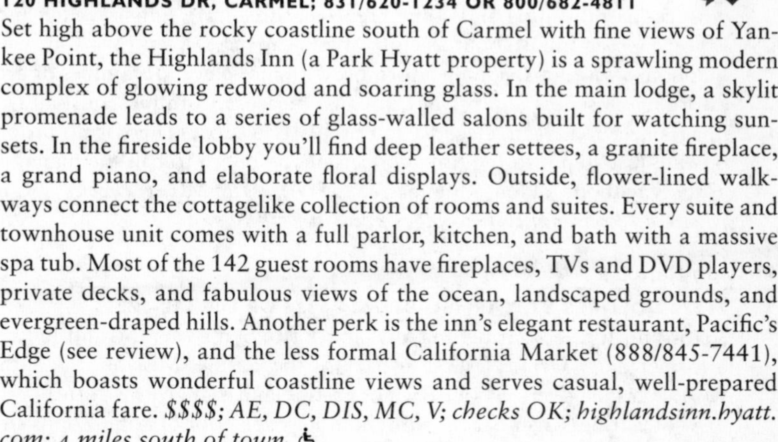

120 HIGHLANDS DR, CARMEL; 831/620-1234 OR 800/682-4811

Set high above the rocky coastline south of Carmel with fine views of Yankee Point, the Highlands Inn (a Park Hyatt property) is a sprawling modern complex of glowing redwood and soaring glass. In the main lodge, a skylit promenade leads to a series of glass-walled salons built for watching sunsets. In the fireside lobby you'll find deep leather settees, a granite fireplace, a grand piano, and elaborate floral displays. Outside, flower-lined walkways connect the cottagelike collection of rooms and suites. Every suite and townhouse unit comes with a full parlor, kitchen, and bath with a massive spa tub. Most of the 142 guest rooms have fireplaces, TVs and DVD players, private decks, and fabulous views of the ocean, landscaped grounds, and evergreen-draped hills. Another perk is the inn's elegant restaurant, Pacific's Edge (see review), and the less formal California Market (888/845-7441), which boasts wonderful coastline views and serves casual, well-prepared California fare. *$$$$; AE, DC, DIS, MC, V; checks OK; highlandsinn.hyatt.com; 4 miles south of town.* ♿

La Playa Hotel / ★★★

CAMINO REAL, CARMEL; 831/624-6476 OR 800/582-8900

Originally built in 1904 as a wedding gift for a member of the Ghirardelli chocolate family, this Mediterranean villa–style luxury hotel spills down a terraced, bougainvillea-and-jasmine-strewn hillside toward the sea. The classic and subdued lobby sets the tone, with Greek caryatid priestess figures holding up the fireplace mantel. Paths lit by gas street lamps wind among lush gardens with cast-iron gazebos and past a heated swimming pool festooned with mermaids, La Playa's mythical mascots. The 75 guest rooms and suites are comfortable, with hand-carved furniture, TVs, and nightly turndown service. Many overlook the gorgeous courtyard. To do La Playa right, invest in one of the five cottages, some of which are nestled in the gardens. These have varying numbers of rooms, and four of them offer full kitchens, fireplaces, and private patios. The hotel's restaurant, the Terrace Grill (831/624-4010), has a fine view of the gardens and serves such seasonal fare as artichoke ravioli, grilled shrimp risotto, and chicken breast stuffed with dried cherries, cranberries, and walnuts. Reserve a massage, a facial, or other services at the hotel's Garden Spa (831/227-3279). *$$$–$$$$; AE, DC, MC, V; checks OK; www.laplayahotel.com; at 8th Ave.* ♿

Lincoln Green Inn / ★★

26200 CARMELO ST, CARMEL; 831/626-4006

If you're looking for a place to pop the question and promise a rose garden in a cottage built for two, you could do worse than make your pitch in one of Lincoln Green Inn's four cottages. Located at Carmel Point just across the road from picturesque River Beach, the white, green-shuttered cottages (named Robin Hood, Maid Marian, Friar Tuck, and Little John) occupy a bucolic English garden setting. Each storybook cottage features a living room with cathedral ceiling and stone fireplace; three have full-size kitchens. The Lincoln Green Inn is about as close as you can get to your own Carmel summer house without spending a fortune; it's a nice place for families or groups, affording closeness and privacy in equal measure. Antiques and sailing ship images accent a clean, elegant Hamptons-style decor. There is no proprietor on-site; just step into the tiny wooden phone booth to call the management at the Vagabond's House Inn. *$$$–$$$$; AE, DIS, MC, V; checks OK; www.vagabondshouseinn.com/cottages.html; at 15th Ave.*

Mission Ranch / ★★★

26270 DOLORES ST, CARMEL; 831/624-6436 OR 800/538-8221

Actor and former Carmel mayor Clint Eastwood owns this inn located on a former dairy farm. Nestled in back of the Carmel Mission, the authentic working ranch overlooks a carpet of pastureland that gives way to a dramatic view of Carmel River Beach, with the craggy splendor of Point Lobos stretching just beyond. When Eastwood bought the property in the late 1980s, he poured a ton of money and a lot of love into restoring the Victorian farmhouse, cottages, bunkhouse, and other buildings. The result is simply wonderful. The peaceful, Western-style spread offers everything a guest needs to feel comfortable—without a single silly frill. Most of the 31 rooms are housed in Western ranchlike buildings with slight porch overhangs. They are sparsely but tastefully appointed, with props from Eastwood's films, such as the clock from *Unforgiven*, nonchalantly scattered among the furnishings. Handmade quilts grace the custom-made country-style wooden beds that are so large you literally have to climb into them, and each guest room has a phone, TV, and bathroom. Rates include a continental breakfast served in the tennis clubhouse. The informal Restaurant at Mission Ranch (831/625-9040), under separate management, serves hearty American-style fare. The place's only flaw is that the piano bar can get a little rowdy, and guests in the structures closest to the restaurant may find themselves reaching for earplugs in the middle of the night. *$$–$$$$; AE, MC, V; checks OK; www.missionranchcarmel.com; at 15th Ave.* ♿

Carmel Valley

Carmel Valley is a relaxed, ranchlike enclave where horses and wine are the main draws for those who need wide-open spaces. There's no coastal fog here, so prepare for sunny skies for your outing. Some of California's most luxurious golf resorts lie in this valley, and it's also studded with interesting specialty nurseries and wine-tasting rooms. Some believe the valley's growing conditions are similar to those of the Bordeaux wine area of France.

From Carmel, take Highway 1 to Carmel Valley Road. About 5½ miles into the valley you'll see a French-style château. It's the **CHATEAU JULIEN WINE ESTATES** (8940 Carmel Valley Rd; 831/624-2600; www.chateaujulien.com; 8am–5pm Mon–Fri, 11am–5pm Sat–Sun), open for tastings and picnics. Each of its wines is produced from 100 percent Monterey County grapes. Taste estate wines such as the 1999 chardonnay, the 1998 cabernet sauvignon, and the 1998 merlot. In the cool, high-ceilinged tasting room, pick up copies of recipes such as Pears in Port with Juniper and Ginger.

Roughly 9 miles into the valley, pull in to the parking lot for the **GARLAND RANCH**, a park with acres of open space. Follow the trail sign down the steps into the woods, across a wooden bridge over the murmuring Carmel River, and on into an open valley with the Santa Lucia Mountains rising ahead. Many people walk their dogs here or hike the scenic trails, or do birdwatching—pick up a *Checklist of Birds* brochure at the usually unstaffed visitor center to mark those you've seen. The center also provides hiking maps: try the 1¼-mile Lupine Loop or the 1½-mile Rancho Loop. The park has an area set aside for mountain biking, too, plus picnic tables in the lower area just beyond the Carmel River.

LODGINGS

Bernardus Lodge / ★★★★

415 CARMEL VALLEY RD, CARMEL VALLEY; 831/659-3131 OR 888/648-9463

You'll sigh with satisfaction the moment you enter Bernardus Lodge, Carmel Valley's swankiest boutique resort, where check-in is seamless from the time you drive up; upon entering the lobby, you're offered a glass of chilled white wine and an escort to your room. The simple, elegant colonial-flavor lodge is the vision of Bernardus Vineyard and Winery owner Ben Pon, who spared no expense getting everything just right. Situated on a terraced hillside dotted with ancient oaks and pines and affording grand vistas of the surrounding Santa Lucia Mountains, the lodge offers terra-cotta- and lemon-colored buildings that hold 57 guest rooms and suites, two restaurants, two tennis courts, bocce and croquet courts, a swimming pool, and a full-service spa and salon. Each generously sized guest room features a stone fireplace, an antique armoire, a sitting area with sofa and chairs, vaulted ceilings, French doors, a private patio, and a king-size feather bed with soft-as-silk Frette linens. The spa is a restorative haven; be sure to reserve spa treatments when you make your room reservation—weekend appointments fill up far in advance. The delectable Marinus restaurant (831/658-3595) offers French-inspired Wine Country cuisine. Wickets Bistro, a less formal environment, also draws upon an extensive wine list and penchant for local, fresh ingredients. Although jacket and tie are optional in both establishments, a slightly snooty waitstaff may make you wish you'd worn your Sunday best. *$$$$; AE, DC, DIS, MC, V; no checks; www.bernardus.com; at Los Laureles Grade.* ♿

Carmel Valley Ranch / ★★★

1 OLD RANCH RD, CARMEL VALLEY; 866/282-4745

This haven for golf and tennis enthusiasts (and corporate retreaters) on a 400-acre spread is about as plush a ranch as you're ever likely to encounter. The 144 guest suites are arranged in low-lying condolike clusters on the rolling hills; each suite features cathedral ceilings, a wood-burning fireplace, a well-stocked refreshment center, two TVs, three phones, a private deck, and a richly appointed bathroom. Some of the pricier suites come with a dining area and a kitchenette. Guests use the whirlpools located throughout the resort. You might need that whirlpool after a full day of activities at the ranch: golf at the Pete Dye 18-hole course (renovated in 2007), tennis on one of a dozen clay and hard-surface courts, guided nature hikes, biking, nearby horseback riding, workouts with a personal trainer at the fitness club, or a dip in one of two swimming pools. When you're ready to relax, you can also indulge in a facial or a manicure offered in-suite, or perhaps a couple's massage followed by champagne and chocolate-covered strawberries. The ranch has three restaurants, including the signature restaurant by Michel Richard, Citronella, a masterful blend of French and California cuisines. In 2008, Carmel Valley Ranch debuted a completely transformed main lodge. *$$$$; AE, MC, V; checks OK; www.carmelvalleyranch.com; off Carmel Valley Rd.* ♿

Stonepine / ★★★★

150 E CARMEL VALLEY RD, CARMEL VALLEY; 831/659-2245

This exquisite Mediterranean villa (the former country home of the Crocker banking family) rises in terraced splendor among 330 acres of Carmel Valley's oak-covered hills. Surrounded by cypress, imported stone pines, and wisteria trailing from hand-carved Italian stone pillars, the inn has eight guest suites throughout Château Noel (named after owner Noel Hentschel), three houses, and the idyllic (and astronomically expensive) Briar Rose Cottage, a two-bedroom affair with a private rose garden, living room, dining room, kitchen, and bar. The suites in the main house are studies in formal splendor; all have French antique furnishings, spa tubs, down comforters, and fluffy robes, and five of them feature fireplaces. The cost of your room includes a big breakfast; for an additional charge you may partake of a wine reception followed by an elegant five-course estate dinner in the dining room. During the day, float in the jewel-like swimming pool, play tennis, explore the ranch's trails, or horse around at the Stonepine Equestrian Center. Beware: The equestrian staff takes horseback riding mighty seriously, and more than one city slicker has suffered a bruised ego as well as a sore derriere after a turn on the trails. *$$$$; AE, MC, V; checks OK; www.stonepinecalifornia.com; 13 miles east of Hwy 1.* ♿

Big Sur

Originally El Pais Grande del Sur (the Big Country to the South) Big Sur encompasses 90 miles of rugged, spectacular coastline that stretches south from Carmel to San Simeon. A narrow, twisting segment of Highway 1 (built with convict labor in the 1930s) snakes through this coastal area, and the mist-shrouded forests, plunging cliffs, and cobalt sea bordering the road make the drive one of the most beautiful in the country, if not the world. The region is so scenic that some folks favor giving it national park status; others, however, recoil in horror at the thought of involving the federal government in the preservation of this untamed land and have coined the expression "Don't Yosemitecate Big Sur."

Keeping your Big Sur visit low-stress is challenging since driving Big Sur can be a bit confusing. Some of the park names sound so similar (too many Pfeiffers!), and it's hard to watch the road, take in the scenery, and still be ready to stop in time when you come to a park or gallery of interest. It will help if you can come either off-season or midweek, when traffic along Highway 1 is fairly light. Another tip: Come in the spring, April through early June, when the golden California poppies, yellow mustard, and purple lupines brighten the windswept landscape.

Whether you're cruising through for the day or you've booked a few nights at a resort, be sure to spend some time hiking in the gorgeous **POINT LOBOS STATE RESERVE** (for more details on the reserve, see the Carmel section). Farther south, Highway 1 crosses Bixby Creek via the 268-foot-high, 739-foot-long **BIXBY BRIDGE** (also known as the **RAINBOW BRIDGE**), a solitary, majestic arch built in 1932 that attracts lots of snap-happy photographers. Nearby is the automated **POINT SUR LIGHTHOUSE** (off Hwy 1, 19 miles south of Carmel; 831/625-4419; www.pointsur.org), situated 360 feet above the surf on Point Sur, a giant volcanic-rock island. The lighthouse was built in 1889 and is the only complete turn-of-the-century light station open to the public in California. Inexpensive (though physically taxing) three-hour guided lighthouse tours are offered on Saturday and Sunday year-round, with additional tours on Wednesday and Thursday during the summer and full-moon tours every month (be sure to take a jacket, even in the summer months).

Hikers and bicyclists often head farther south to navigate the many trails zigzagging through the sycamores and maples in 4,800-acre **ANDREW MOLERA STATE PARK** (831/667-2315; www.parks.ca.gov), the largest state park on the Big Sur coast. A mile-long walk through a meadow laced with wildflowers leads to the park's 2-mile-long beach harboring the area's best tide pools. A few miles down Highway 1 on the inland side is one of California's most popular parks, **PFEIFFER–BIG SUR STATE PARK** (831/667-2315; www.parks.ca.gov). Here, 810 acres of madrona and oak woodlands and misty redwood canyons are crisscrossed with hiking trails, and many paths provide panoramic views of the sea. The Big Sur River meanders through the park, too, attracting anglers and swimmers who brave the chilly waters. Nearby, the unmarked Sycamore Canyon Road (the only paved, ungated road west of Hwy 1 between the Big Sur Post Office and Pfeiffer–Big Sur State Park) leads to beautiful but blustery **PFEIFFER BEACH** (follow the road until it ends at a parking lot, about 2 miles from Hwy 1) with its white-and-mauve sands and enormous sea caves.

If your idea of communing with nature is a comfy chair in the shade, grab a seat on the upper deck of the fabled **NEPENTHE RESTAURANT** (see review), perched 800 feet above the roiling Pacific. Four miles south of Nepenthe is the **COAST GALLERY** (831/667-2301; www.coastgalleries.com), a showplace for local artists and craftspeople featuring pottery, jewelry, and paintings, including watercolors by author Henry Miller, who lived nearby for more than 15 years. The author's fans will also want to seek out the **HENRY MILLER LIBRARY** (just beyond Nepenthe Restaurant on the east side of Hwy 1; 831/667-2574; www.henrymiller.org). In addition to a great collection of Miller's books and art, the library serves as one of Big Sur's cultural centers and features the art, poetry, prose, and music of locals; it's open Thursday

ESALEN: A BIG SUR RETREAT FOR MIND, BODY, AND SPIRIT

To Esalen we can give thanks—or blame—for bringing terms like self-actualization, peak experience, encounter group, and Gestalt therapy into the popular lexicon, and for that essential contribution to instant enlightenment, the hot tub. Originally located at the ocean's edge, the baths were a source of controversy during Esalen's first two decades, generating rumors of drug use and public sex. In the early '60s, founders Michael Murphy and Richard Price tried to keep the lid on, so to speak, by declaring the baths chastely separate-sex, but the demand for co-ed nudity eventually overrode them. In 1998, El Niño storms caused extensive damage to the baths and the towering slope that rises above them. The baths were moved to the top of the bluff, where they'll remain until the original bath site is repaired. They're still co-ed and clothing-optional and continue to be popular with Esalen guests, but the wild antics are long gone. Hey, it's not the '60s anymore.

More than 40 years have passed since the heady days when Alan Watts and Joseph Campbell debated the mysteries of the universe, Joan Baez gave impromptu concerts, and George and Ringo flew in with the Maharishi in tow, but Esalen continues to be a countercultural enclave for spiritual seekers. A smorgasbord of more than 500 annual workshops dealing with trauma, art and creativity, massage, yoga, martial arts, and relationships offer enough options to keep anyone's body, mind, and spirit in proper working order. Shared lodgings and all meals are included. For more information, call 831/667-3000 or visit www.esalen.org.

through Sunday in the summer, Friday through Sunday in the winter. Seekers of other sorts flock to **ESALEN INSTITUTE** (831/667-3000; www.esalen.org), the world-famous New Age retreat and home of heavenly massages and hot springs that overlook the ocean.

At the southern end of Big Sur is beautiful **JULIA PFEIFFER BURNS STATE PARK** (800/444-7275; www.bigsurcalifornia.org), with 4,000 acres to roam. You'll find some excellent day hikes here, but if you just want to get out of the car and stretch your legs, take the quarter-mile Waterfall Trail to 80-foot-high **MCWAY WATERFALL**, one of the few falls in California that plunges directly into the sea. Keep an eye open for the sea otters that play in McWay Cove. But wherever you trek through Big Sur, beware of the poison oak—it's as ubiquitous as the seagulls hovering over the coast.

RESTAURANTS

Big Sur River Inn / ★

HWY 1, BIG SUR; 831/667-2700 OR 800/548-3610

The Big Sur River Inn is exactly the kind of restaurant you would expect to find in a mountain community—a large, rustic cabin (circa 1934), built and furnished entirely with rough-hewn woods, warmed by a large fireplace surrounded by comfy chairs, and occupied by jeans-clad locals sharing the day's news over beers at the corner bar. In the summer most everyone requests a table on the shaded back deck, which overlooks a picturesque stretch of the Big Sur River. Since the restaurant caters to the inn's guests, it's open morning till nightfall. Breakfast is all-American (eggs, pancakes, bacon, omelets, and such), as are lunch and dinner. The menu offers pasta, burgers, chicken sandwiches, salads, fish-and-chips, and a whole lot more. Recommended plates are the Black Angus Burger with a side of beer-battered onion rings, or a big platter of the Roadhouse Ribs served with cowboy beans. Wash either down with a cool glass of Carmel Brewing Co. Amber Ale, and you're ready to roll. *$; AE, DC, DIS, MC, V; no checks; breakfast, lunch, dinner every day; beer and wine; no reservations; www.bigsurriverinn.com; on Hwy 1 at Pheneger Creek, 2 miles north of Pfeiffer–Big Sur State Park.*

Nepenthe Restaurant / ★

48510 HWY 1, BIG SUR; 831/667-2345

This venerable Big Sur institution has been operating for more than half a century and still draws in the crowds. Located 800 feet above the ocean, Nepenthe commands views of the Big Sur coastline that will make you gasp. It is a friendly, family-owned and managed place, and therein lies part of its appeal. Originally a log cabin that housed Lolly and Bill Fassett and their five children, it became Nepenthe when they realized that the only way to keep their family amply fed was to open a restaurant. The log cabin remains, but over the years Nepenthe has grown to encompass the entire bluff it rests upon. The restaurant boasts a full bar, and two outdoor areas offer lots of room for alfresco dining. Even after warnings about overpriced meals, locals insist visitors to Big Sur should try Nepenthe at least once. The fare tends toward standard American with a twist. Starters include Cajun poached shrimp and Castroville artichoke; entrées include a choice of fresh fish, steaks, and broiled or roast chicken. Burgers and salads should keep kids and vegetarians happy. Be sure to check out Nepenthe's Phoenix Gift Shop on your way out. Located one flight of stairs below Nepenthe Restaurant is the far less expensive Cafe Kevah (831/667-2344), an order-at-the-counter café where breakfast is served all day and lunch offers a spicy chicken brochette, a grilled salmon with salsa verde, quesadillas, and a Caesar salad. *$$; AE, MC, V; no checks; lunch, dinner every day; full bar; reservations required for parties of 5 or more; www.nepenthebigsur.com; 27 miles south of Carmel.*

Sierra Mar / ★★★

HWY 1 (POST RANCH INN), BIG SUR; 831/667-2800

Situated high on the ridge, the Sierra Mar Restaurant at Post Ranch Inn is a gorgeous, cliff-hugging restaurant that has been hailed as one of the best on the Central Coast. It serves a sophisticated brand of California cuisine in a serene expanse of wood, brushed metal, and glass that lets you drink in the incredible views along with the costly wine. When you can wrest your eyes from the ocean and focus on the four-course prix-fixe dinner menu, which changes daily, you might see such sumptuous starters as pine-smoked squab with ginger and cilantro; mussel soup with saffron and potatoes; and perhaps a salad of lettuces (organic, of course) mixed with shaved fennel, oranges, Parmesan, and a Campari vinaigrette. Main courses include such bounty as roast rack of venison with glazed chestnuts and huckleberries, truffled fettuccine with asparagus and English peas, and roasted guinea fowl with potato gnocchi and pearl onions. Finish off your feast with a plate of assorted house-made sweets. *$$$; AE, MC, V; local checks only; breakfast, lunch, dinner every day; full bar; reservations recommended; www.postranchinn.com; 30 miles south of Carmel.* ♿

LODGINGS

Deetjen's Big Sur Inn / ★

48865 HWY 1, BIG SUR; 831/667-2377

Don't blink or you'll miss this charming cluster of ramshackle cabins as you head around the curve on Highway 1 just south of Ventana. Located in a redwood canyon, most of the cabins are divided into two units, each with dark wood interiors, hand-hewn doors without locks or keys (they can be secured with the hook and eye from within, though), and nonexistent insulation. Some have shared baths, and many are cozy in a rustic sort of way, but they're definitely not for everyone. If you stay in one of the two-story units (some with fireplaces or wood-burning stoves), be sure to request the quieter upstairs rooms. The cabins near the river offer the most privacy. Grandpa's Room, 13, has a bed built just under a large window overlooking the creek, and also has a pedal organ. Deetjen's Big Sur Inn Restaurant, which has garnered a loyal following, serves good Euro-California cuisine that takes advantage of local produce and seafood. The setting is rustic-romantic, with white walls, dimly lit old-fashioned lamps, and antiques in every nook. A wood-burning stove provides heat on chilly winter nights. *$–$$$; MC, V; checks OK; www.deetjens.com; on Hwy 1, 4 miles south of Pfeiffer–Big Sur State Park.*

Post Ranch Inn / ★★★★

HWY 1, BIG SUR; 831/667-2200 OR 800/527-2200

The inn's deceptively simple exteriors harmonize with the forested slopes, while windows, windows everywhere showcase the breathtaking vistas of sky and sea that define Big Sur. Architect Mickey Muennig propped up six of the inn's units (known as the Tree Houses) on stilts to avoid disturbing the surrounding redwoods' root systems and sank others into the earth, roofing them with sod. Inside, the lodgepole construction and wealth of warm woods lend a rough-hewn luxury. The Post Ranch Inn is one of the original eco-hotels, where the affluent can indulge in sumptuous luxury and still feel politically correct. The water is filtered; visitors are encouraged to sort their paper, glass, and plastic garbage; and the paper upon which guests' rather staggering bills are printed is recycled. Despite this ecologically correct attitude, the folks behind the Post Ranch Inn haven't forgotten about the niceties of life. The 40 rooms have spare—but by no means spartan—decor, including fireplaces, massage tables, king-size beds, and sideboards made of African hardwoods (non-endangered, naturally). Designer robes hang in the closets; the well-equipped bathrooms come with whirlpool tubs. A continental breakfast and guided nature hikes are included in the room rates; the massages, facials, herbal wraps, and yoga classes are not. The inn's restaurant, Sierra Mar (see review), serves a sophisticated brand of California cuisine in a stunning setting. *$$$$; AE, MC, V; checks OK; www.postranchinn.com; 30 miles south of Carmel.*

Ventana Inn & Spa / ★★★★

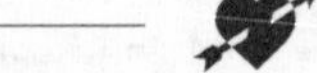

48123 HWY 1, BIG SUR; 831/667-2331 OR 800/628-6500

Set 1,200 feet above the Pacific Ocean on the brow of a chaparral-covered hill in the Santa Lucia Mountains, this modern, weathered cedar inn is serene, contemplative, and very discreet, which explains why celebrities such as Goldie Hawn, Barbra Streisand, and Francis Ford Coppola have been vacationing here since 1975. Its 60 spacious rooms, decorated in an upscale country style and divided among 12 low-rise buildings, look out over the plunging forested hillsides, wildflower-laced meadows, or roiling waters of the Big Sur coast. Since you're already splurging, go ahead and book a cedar-lined Vista Suite, which comes with an ocean-view deck with a private outdoor spa, a fireplace, and an oversize bathroom with an open slate shower. The inn's other big draw is Cielo Restaurant (*cielo* is Spanish for "heaven"), which delivers panoramic patio views of 50 miles of coastline at prices that can be equally breathtaking. Although critics have been unanimous in praising the restaurant's aesthetics, a revolving-door parade of chefs has kept them uncertain about the quality of the food since Jeremiah Tower's star turn here many years ago. *$$$$; AE, DC, DIS, MC, V; checks OK; www.ventanainn.com; 28 miles south of Carmel, 2 miles south of Pfeiffer–Big Sur State Park.*

The San Simeon Coast

Along the San Simeon coast, it looks a little like Wyoming with a coastline. The dramatic open ranch scenery reveals more surprises the farther south you drive. There are cow-studded pastures, pristine beaches, windswept cliffs, and tree-shaded country roads. The area's diversity is part of its appeal: you can bask in sunshine at ocean's edge, bicycle through lush vineyards, ride horses along rural back roads, and shop a boulevard of chic boutiques—all in one day. Glorious vacation destinations are sprinkled throughout the sometimes funky beachfront towns. The coastline itself has a distinct personality: sunny white-sand beaches segue into rocky, cliff-lined shores, then give way to calm, picturesque bays. No matter how many visitors it gets, the San Simeon coastal region always retains something of the frontier flair of pioneer ranchers. Although the area is best known for Hearst Castle, other destinations are tucked into the inland mountains and valleys, where citrus orchards and vineyards beckon to the discerning traveler.

Before you get to Hearst Castle, cross Highway 1 to the sheltering bay where William Randolph Hearst's father in the 1880s built a wharf, pier, and mission-style warehouses for the operation of what was then a massive cattle ranch. His son would later use the port to bring in the voluminous building materials and furnishings for the castle, including crates of exotic animals for his private zoo (the zebras you see grazing with cattle alongside the highway are remnants of that short-lived endeavor).

If you have time to see only one museum or monument on your trip to the Central Coast, make it **HEARST CASTLE** (750 Hearst Castle Rd, San Simeon; 800/444-4445; www.hearstcastle.com; day tours $20 adults, $10 kids; evening tours $30 adults, $15 kids), named this country's best monument by readers of *Condé Nast Traveler* magazine. The lavish palace that publishing magnate William Randolph Hearst never called a castle, but always referred to as "the ranch" or "the Enchanted Hill," sits high above the coastline, and at a distance it does look like a fairy-tale castle. It's opulently and almost haphazardly furnished with museum-quality treasures purchased by Hearst, a man of indiscriminate taste and inexhaustible funds who spent years traveling to Europe, buying up complete interiors and art from ancestral collections. Touring the house you'll see carved ceilings from Italian monasteries, fragments of Roman temples, lavish doors from royal castles, and a breathtaking collection of Greek pottery carelessly displayed among equally priceless volumes in the library. The estate boasts two swimming pools—one indoor, one outdoor—whose grandiose opulence must be seen to be believed.

Now operated as a State Historic Monument by the Department of Parks and Recreation, the landmark Hearst Castle can be seen only by guided tour; four separate itineraries cover different areas of the estate. It's sometimes possible to buy tour tickets after you arrive at Hearst Castle, but it is smart to make reservations in advance, particularly if you are coming in summer. There is plenty of free parking; nearby at the visitor center you board a tour bus that takes you the 5 miles up to the castle, where your tour guide awaits. Consult the Web site or call for information on tour schedules and advance ticket purchases.

ACCESS AND INFORMATION

The San Simeon coast is almost smack in between San Francisco and Los Angeles—a little under a five-hour drive from each hub. Because it's located along windy Highway 1, there is no quick way to get there—though taking Highway 101 (whether coming from the south or the north) and cutting west at Highway 46 near Paso Robles will be your best bet, shaving off valuable time on your journey.

The **SAN SIMEON CHAMBER OF COMMERCE** (250 San Simeon Ave, Ste 3A, San Simeon; 805/927-3500; www.sansimeonchamber.org), staffed by friendly local volunteers and stocked with free maps and visitor info, is located inside the Cavalier Plaza Shopping Center and open Monday through Friday from 9am to 1pm. Down the road, the **CAMBRIA CHAMBER OF COMMERCE** (767 Main St, Cambria; 805/927-3624; www.cambriachamber.org) has extended office hours—9am to 5pm Monday through Friday, and noon to 4pm on Saturday and Sunday.

Due to its location on the Pacific Ocean, the San Simeon coast never gets all that hot. Then again, it doesn't get all that cold either: winters are mild and rainy. Most days, no matter the season, start off blanketed by a layer of fog, which usually burns off by midday. For the best weather, visit the region during spring or fall.

LODGINGS

Ragged Point Inn & Resort / ★★☆

19019 HWY 1, RAGGED POINT; 805/927-4502

Perched on a grassy cliff high above the ocean, this modern woodsy complex offers views as spectacular as any farther north in pricey Big Sur. Part of an upscale rest-stop complex that includes a gas station, mini-mart, gift shop, snack bar, and the Ragged Point Inn restaurant, the motel itself has been upgraded. Each of the spacious 22 rooms features an oceanfront balcony or patio, along with separate heating controls for getting cozy on blustery nights. The furnishings are both contemporary and comfortable, and the motel is set back a ways from the other roadside facilities, so you can count on silence and seclusion. Foxes and raccoons are often spotted scurrying around the grounds. Take the walking trail out to the bluff, where you can look down on the ocean and sometimes see sea otters bobbing among the kelp. San Simeon and Cambria are a 25-minute drive south, but the restaurant is good enough to eat all your meals here if you want. Ask for an upstairs room to get the best view and the most privacy; the first-floor rooms, however, are a good value and also have views other hotels would brag about. *$$; AE, DIS, MC, V; checks OK; www.raggedpointinn.com; 15 miles north of Hearst Castle.* ♿

Cambria

Cambria is almost terminally cute. What saves it is genuine small-town friendliness, several fine restaurants, and shops offering high-quality goods, including art, crafts, housewares, and boutique clothing. The town's bread and butter are visitors to Hearst Castle, but it would stack up well against any romantic escape destination in California. Both chic and countrified, this sophisticated little village combines the best elements of both Northern and Southern California. The town's name reportedly compares the natural beauty of the area to the lush, rolling countryside of Wales, whose ancient name was Cambria.

The town has two sections: the East Village and the West Village, both full of restored Victorians, art galleries, antique stores, boutiques, and exceptional restaurants, nestled among pine-blanketed hills. Across the highway, however, **MOONSTONE BEACH** (named for the translucent milky stones that wash ashore) is lined with inns of wildly varying designs, from Tudor to modern, offering an opportunity to sleep alongside the breaking surf and stroll windswept beaches populated by seals and sea lions. For an introduction to the area, stop by the **CAMBRIA CHAMBER OF COMMERCE** (767 Main St; 805/927-3624; www.cambriachamber.org).

RESTAURANTS

Linn's Main Binn / ★★

2277 MAIN ST, CAMBRIA; 805/927-0371

This is just the kind of place you want to find on a family trip: unassuming, welcoming, and offering a specialty worth traveling to find. The steaming chicken potpies and the Yankee pot roast are delicious. Other winners are homemade daily soups, hearty sandwiches, and fresh-from-the-farm salads; at breakfast, sweet treats like berry-covered waffles and pancakes prevail. But don't miss the legendary berry pies, especially the olallieberry. The olallieberry bread pudding is also transcendent. The in-town outlet for the popular Linn's Fruit Binn, this casual all-day restaurant also carries straw hats, decorative housewares, gifts, and a selection of Linn's food products such as fancy fruit butters and berries in port wine. Every town should have a spot like this, where a reliably good meal doesn't have to be an event and where you'll feel equally welcome stopping in for just a slice of warm pie and a glass of ice-cold milk. *$; AE, DIS, MC, V; checks OK; breakfast, lunch, dinner every day; beer and wine; no reservations; www.linnsfruitbin.com; 1 block east of Burton Dr.* ♿

The Sow's Ear Cafe / ★★★★

2248 MAIN ST, CAMBRIA; 805/927-4865

Gourmets in the know head for this humble-sounding place, considered the very best in town. One of Cambria's tiny old cottages, now sandwiched in a row of shops, has been transformed into a warm, romantic hideaway right on Main Street, where the best tables are in the fireside front room, lit just enough to highlight its rustic wood-and-brick decor. You'll find contemporary California cuisine, but the number-one dish is the chicken-fried steak with Grandma-style gravy plus chicken and dumplings. Other standouts are salmon prepared in parchment, local swordfish with lemon-sesame glaze, and grilled pork loin glazed with chunky olallieberry chutney. Although dinners come complete with soup or salad, do share one of the outstanding appetizers—the calamari melts in your mouth, and the marinated goat cheese perfectly accompanies the restaurant's signature marbled bread baked in terra-cotta flowerpots. The wine list is among the area's best, featuring outstanding Central Coast vintages, with a large number available by the glass. If you have only one nice dinner in town, make this the place. *$$; DIS, MC, V; no checks; dinner every day; beer and wine; reservations recommended; www.thesowsear.com; ½ block east of Burton Dr.* ♿

LODGINGS

Cambria Pines Lodge / ★★★

2905 BURTON DR, CAMBRIA; 805/927-4200 OR 800/445-6868

As you drive up the steep hill from town, the road curves into thick woods dense with Monterey pines, and it's hard to believe an important lodging could be so far away from the action below. But that's part of the charm of Cambria Pines Lodge. Equal parts vacation lodge and summer camp, the lodge is composed of 31 buildings, from simple, old-fashioned cabins to larger rooms in two-level buildings (pack light if you stay in these units, since you'll have to drag your luggage up or down stairs). At the heart of the resort is the main lodge, built in the early 1990s around the great stone hearth of the original 1927 building (destroyed by fire). It all has a welcoming, communal feel. Nearly all of the rooms have fireplaces, contemporary furniture, coffeemakers, and cable TVs. The only swimming pool on the village side of town is on these grounds—an indoor pool heated for year-round use, plus a sauna and whirlpool. The massage facility in a nearby building is run by a separate business. Inside the main lodge, there's a moderately priced restaurant and large fireside lounge with occasional live music. *$–$$; AE, DIS, MC, V; checks OK; www.cambriapineslodge.com; take Burton Dr uphill from the center of town.* ♿

Olallieberry Inn / ★★★

2476 MAIN ST, CAMBRIA; 805/927-3222 OR 888/927-3222

A beautiful 1873 Greek Revival house sits like a prim dowager on Main Street at the edge of the East Village in Cambria, within strolling distance of the best shops and restaurants, but in a calmer zone a bit away from the bustle. Guest quarters are teeming with antiques, floral wallpaper, and Victorian lace. Six rooms are in the main house; though all have private baths, three of the baths are across the hall rather than en suite. The nicely renovated carriage house has two spacious rooms overlooking a creek; another has a view of trees and hills. Six rooms have fireplaces. The most charming of them all is Room at the Top, a sunny nook where you can relax fireside in a white wicker chaise or soak in the antique claw-foot tub. A complete breakfast is included, such as Alaskan sourdough pancakes with hash-brown eggs. The staff sets out cookies or cakes in the early afternoon. Later in the day, wine from the local Paso Robles winery Arciero is served with crackers, the inn's famous curry pâté, and a popular olive spread. A warm artichoke dip baked in a sourdough bread ball is also served, plus fresh vegetables with dip and tropical salsas. Ask about off-season packages with local restaurants. *$$; AE, MC, V; checks OK in advance; www.olallieberry.com; from Hwy 1, turn east on Main St.*

Paso Robles

Early on, Paso Robles was known for its hot mineral springs. The mission padres often brought their sick here to be healed by bathing in the thermal waters. More recently, the tawny rolling hills around Paso Robles (Spanish for "pass of oak trees") were dotted with cattle and framed with orderly almond orchards. But today every hill is stitched with grapevines, and wineries with tasting rooms appear around almost every curve.

In 2003, a 6.6 earthquake damaged much of the heralded renaissance of the town (and even killed two people), but you'd never know it visiting today. Following the quake, the people of Paso (as locals call it) regrouped and took stock of what was left. This spurred a major renovation, and shortly after, Paso saw a boom of top-notch restaurants, hotels, shops, and art galleries enter the downtown scene.

Part of the up-and-coming Central Coast wine country, Paso Robles currently boasts more than 40 wineries (see "Touring Paso Robles Wineries"). The town is also proud of its faintly checkered past: it was established in 1870 by Drury James, uncle of outlaw Jesse James (who reportedly hid out in these parts). In 1913, pianist Ignace Jan Paderewski came to live in Paso Robles, where he planted zinfandel vines on his ranch and often tickled the ivories in the Paso Robles Inn.

The well-preserved turn-of-the-century sleepy downtown could have inspired the script of *The Music Man.* At the center of town is **CITY PARK** (Spring and 12th sts), a green gathering place—complete with festival bandstand. Several downtown side streets are lined with splendid historic Victorian, Craftsman, and Queen Anne homes, all shaded by grand trees. Drive along Vine Street between 10th and 19th streets for a superb peek into the past, including the **CALL-BOOTH HOUSE** (1315 Vine St; 805/423-9174; www.callboothhouse.com), a carefully restored Victorian listed on the National Register of Historic Places, which is now a small inn with three rooms for rent.

The **PASO ROBLES PIONEER MUSEUM** (2010 Riverside Ave, near 21st St across the railroad tracks; 805/239-4556; www.pasoroblespioneermuseum.org) is worth a visit for insight into the heritage of a working frontier town.

The small museum is filled with artifacts presented as a series of life-size dioramas illustrating the town's history, ranging from Native American settlements and vintage ranching equipment to a primitive turn-of-the-century medical office.

Antique hounds have been flocking to Paso Robles since long before the wine country explosion, and downtown still proves fertile hunting ground for treasure seekers. The best are the giant mall-style stores, each representing dozens of dealers; you can easily spend hours in just one building. Two reliable choices are **ANTIQUE EMPORIUM MALL** (1307 Park St; 805/238-1078), with 55 vendors, and **GREAT AMERICAN ANTIQUES MALL** (1305 Spring St; 805/239-1203), which has 40 vendors. For more information, contact the **PASO ROBLES CHAMBER OF COMMERCE** (1225 Park St; 805/238-0506 or 800/406-4040; www.pasorobleschamber.com) and ask for the *Guide to Antique Shops* or log onto the city's Web site (www.prcity.com).

RESTAURANTS

Artisan / ★★★

1401 PARK ST, PASO ROBLES; 805/237-8084

The latest "big city"–like eatery to occupy downtown Paso real estate, Artisan is a contemporary bistro with a focus on wild-caught or sustainably farmed foods. Many ingredients are procured from local farmers markets. It's not surprising, really, that once you step inside, both the crisp decor and the culinary delights will remind you more of an urban center like San Francisco than tiny Paso. Executive chef Chris Kobayashi (Chef Koby) does hail from the north, having graduated from the Culinary Institute of America in Napa Valley and worked at restaurants like Asia de Cuba in San Francisco's Clift Hotel before migrating south. Start with the intense smoked Gouda and porter fondue or the bloodred gazpacho; order the smoked salmon with Finnish potatoes, bacon, and brown-butter béarnaise sauce for a main; and finish with the peach crumble or Scharffen Berger chocolate brownies. The wine list is heavy with selections from local vineyards. *$$–$$$; AE, DIS, MC, V; lunch, dinner every day, brunch Sun; full bar; reservations recommended; www.artisanpasorobles.com; at 14th St.*

Berry Hill Bistro / ★★

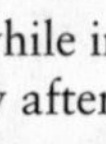

1114 PINE ST, PASO ROBLES; 805/238-3929

This is *the* lunch spot in town, and if you happen to befriend a local while in Paso, chances are you'll stumble upon him again here during the early afternoon hours. With a French countryside ambience—flowers and fruit decorate the tablecloths; skylights and floor-to-ceiling windows allow ample sunshine into the room—the first thing you'll probably wonder is, what exactly is up with all of those roosters? The theme is comfort food, and Berry Hill does warm sandwiches particularly well. Pad your stomach with the turkey, brie, apple, and cranberry sandwich or the chicken, pesto, and artichoke panino before you head out to the wineries and get your vino on, and don't pass on the garlic fries—they're top-notch. *$$; AE, DIS, MC, V; local checks only; lunch, dinner every day; full bar; no reservations; on the town square between 11th and 12th sts.* ♿

Bistro Laurent / ★★★

1202 PINE ST, PASO ROBLES; 805/226-8191

Although it was inevitable that fine dining would follow here on the heels of fine wine, chef-owner Laurent Grangien nevertheless created quite a stir when he opened this cozy yet chic bistro. With his extensive French cooking background and his Los Angeles restaurant experience (at the well-respected Fennel), Grangien offers a California-tinged style of French cuisine while maintaining an unpretentious atmosphere that locals love. Banquette-lined walls make virtually every table in the historic brick building a cozy private booth, and there's alfresco dining on a romantic patio. While you peruse Bistro Laurent's impressive list of Central Coast and French wines, you'll enjoy a complimentary hors d'oeuvre that changes daily (goat cheese toasts, perhaps, or a croustade of mushrooms with red wine vinaigrette). Menu highlights include traditional bistro fare such as roasted rosemary garlic chicken, pork loin bathed in peppercorn sauce, or ahi tuna in red wine reduction, depending on the season. Adventurous diners will choose the four-course tasting menu, which changes nightly, with a glass of wine paired to each course. During lunchtime, the shady patio magically becomes its own separate restaurant, dubbed Petite Marcel, and serves a simple, weekly changing provençal menu that may include two or three salads, pizzas, and a meat and a fish item. *$$; MC, V; no checks; lunch, dinner every day; beer and wine; reservations recommended; www.bistrolaurent.com; at the corner of 12th St.* ♿

Deborah's Room / ★★★★

11680 CHIMNEY ROCK RD (JUSTIN WINERY), PASO ROBLES; 805/238-6932 OR 800/726-0049

Ridiculously delicious and classy farm fare with superb pairings in an exclusive, plush dining room are the necessary ingredients found at Deborah's, the glitzy restaurant housed inside Justin Winery. The intimacy of eating at this 25-seat establishment—set deep in the vineyard—just cannot be compared to larger restaurants. The chef pays special attention to seasonal, locally produced meats and vegetables, so the menu is an ever-evolving creation sure to please a discerning palate. The nightly four-course prix-fixe dinner (plus a mini cheese course) may look something like this: pumpkin soup and risotto for starters, braised short ribs with truffle potato purée for a main, and baked chocolate mousse for the finale. If you plan on indulging your inner oenophile—and we highly recommend you do—the winery will arrange complimentary transportation to and from dinner. On weekends, brunch is served on the gorgeous patio surrounded by greenery, with misters or heat lamps, depending on the weather. *$$$$; AE, MC, V; no checks; breakfast every day for winery guests, dinner every day (one seating), lunch Sat–Sun; wine only; reservations required; www.justinwine.com; about 15 miles west of downtown Paso Robles.*

TOURING PASO ROBLES WINERIES

Wine touring in Paso Robles is reminiscent of another, unhurried time; here it's all about enjoying a relaxed rural atmosphere and driving leisurely along country roads from winery to winery. Three major wine events are held here every year: the **ZINFANDEL FESTIVAL** in March, the **WINE FESTIVAL** in May, and the **HARVEST WINE AFFAIR** in October. For a wine-touring brochure and information on events and area wineries, contact the **PASO ROBLES VINTNERS & GROWERS** (800/549-WINE; www.pasowine.com). Meanwhile, any time of year is fine for dropping by the following wineries:

EBERLE WINERY: Winemaker Gary Eberle is sometimes called the "grandfather of Paso Robles's wine country" by the local vintners who honed their craft under his tutelage. A visit to Eberle includes a look at its underground caves, where hundreds of aging barrels share space with the Wild Boar Room, site of Eberle's monthly winemaker dinners. *3810 Hwy 46E, 3½ miles east of Hwy 101; 805/238-9607; www.eberlewinery.com.*

EOS ESTATE WINERY AT ARCIERO VINEYARDS: Follow the checkered flag to the 650 acres of wine grapes owned by former race-car driver Frank Arciero, who specializes in Italian varietals like nebbiolo and sangiovese. The facility includes a self-guided tour, race car collection, spectacular rose garden, and picnic area. *5625 Hwy 46E, 6 miles east of Hwy 101; 805/239-2562 or 800/249-WINE; www.eosvintage.com.*

JUSTIN VINEYARDS & WINERY: At the end of a scenic country road lies the

LODGINGS

Adelaide Inn / ★☆

1215 YSABEL AVE, PASO ROBLES; 805/238-2770 OR 800/549-PASO

Though clearly not in an elegant neighborhood—it's tucked in among gas stations and coffee shops—this immaculate hotel is nicely isolated from its bustling surroundings. Lush, manicured gardens are screened from the street by foliage, a relaxing outdoor hot tub is secluded inside a redwood gazebo, and a miniature golf course/putting green gives you a chance to practice your stroke. The result is a surprisingly quiet, comfortable property tended with a loving care that's rare among lower-priced inns—and this place is truly a bargain: rooms start under $100 per night in summer. The accommodations are clean and comfortable, with an extra warmth that's a cut above standard motels; unexpected amenities include refrigerators, coffeemakers, hair dryers, and complimentary newspaper, plus work desks in some rooms and data ports in all rooms. No wonder it's popular with business travelers as well as families. The property is constantly being upgraded with new carpeting, boutique winery of ex-Angelenos Justin and Deborah Baldwin, whose best wine is Isosceles, a sophisticated Bordeaux-style blend with splendid aging potential. Since 1987 the Baldwins have commissioned a different artist each year to interpret their gorgeous Tuscan-style property for the label, and the results are on display throughout the complex. *11680 Chimney Rock Rd, 15 miles west of Hwy 101; 805/238-6932; www.justinwine.com.*

MERIDIAN VINEYARDS: Meridian is the largest local producer, the Central Coast's best-known label, and where you'll get the most polished, Napa-like tasting experience. The grounds are beautiful, featuring a man-made lake surrounded by rolling hills. *7000 Hwy 46E, 7 miles east of Hwy 101; 805/237-6000; www.meridianvineyards.com.*

TOBIN JAMES CELLARS: With a Wild West theme based on the unpredictable personality of colorful winemaker Tobin James (who claims with a wink that he must be a descendant of the James Gang), this winery is fun and unpretentious. Don't think he's not serious about his craft, though—Tobin James's zinfandel and late-harvest zinfandel are both award winners. *8950 Union Rd, at Hwy 46E, 8 miles east of Hwy 101; 805/239-2204; www.tobinjames.com.*

YORK MOUNTAIN WINERY: The first winery to be established in Paso Robles, York Mountain stands on land originally deeded by Ulysses S. Grant. Inside the 100-year-old stone tasting room, look for a dry chardonnay with complex spice overtones and reserve cabernets made from hand-selected grapes. *7505 York Mountain Rd, off Hwy 46W, 7 miles west of Hwy 101 in Templeton; 805/238-3925.*

curtains, and other niceties, so everything always looks fresh. The center of the complex is an outdoor heated pool. Morning fruit and muffins are provided in the lobby. *$–$$; AE, DC, DIS, MC, V; no checks; www.adelaideinn.com; at 24th St just west of Hwy 101.* ♿

Hotel Cheval / ★★★★

1021 PINE ST, PASO ROBLES; 805/226-9995 OR 866/522-6999

This absolutely delightful boutique hotel is surely Paso's finest; everything about it—location, service, design, amenities—is flawless. But if an equestrian motif doesn't suit you, you might consider heading elsewhere: Each of the 16 well-appointed rooms—Trumpator, Hanover, Darley, Rosebud—is named for a famous racehorse and features appropriate memorabilia. While no two rooms are alike, general amenities include flat-screen TVs (DVD players available upon request), fireplaces, complimentary wireless Internet, and spa robes and slippers. Some have sundecks, patios, lounges, window seats, and bathtubs. The rooms—all beautifully appointed with travertine showers and headboards made of leather, sea grass, and carved wood—are centered on a courtyard, with ample comfortable seating and fire pits for lounging. In-room spa treatments are also available. The Pony Club downstairs is, of course, horseshoe shaped; grab a cocktail there before heading down the street for some quality cuisine—in a horsedrawn carriage pulled by the hotel's resident Clydesdale, Chester (Fri and Sat evenings). There's also live music (Thurs–Sat nights), and a generous breakfast spread is delivered to your room each morning. *$$$–$$$$; AE, DIS, MC, V; checks OK; www.hotelcheval.com; at 10th St.* ♿

JUST Inn Bed & Breakfast / ★★★½

11680 CHIMNEY ROCK RD (JUSTIN WINERY), PASO ROBLES; 805/238-6932 OR 800/726-0049

More wineries really should follow Justin's cue by offering fine food, lodging, wine tastings, and a complimentary bottle all in a single breathtaking setting. In fact, you could stay at 160-acre Justin Winery for a week and never have to leave (and many guests do just that). The winery doesn't advertise its four rooms (other than on its Web site), but then again, it doesn't really need to, as loyal clients (and fans of the most popular cult favorite wine, Isosceles) keep them filled to capacity. Each room offers wireless Internet, a flat-screen TV, robes, the option of in-room massage, a complimentary bottle of Justin wine, and concierge service. With its marble bath, Hydro Spa, and wood-burning fireplace, the 1,200-square-foot Sussex Suite is popular with honeymooners (though the winery hosts only four weddings a year). But the two-story Bordeaux Suite, located in the wine tank building, is surely the inn's gem: decorated in maroon and gold, boasting a private kitchen and dining room, and occupying 1,400 square feet, it's truly fit for royalty. All guests are treated to a country breakfast at Deborah's Room (see review) and complimentary tastings throughout their stay. Justin Wine Society members receive a 20 percent lodging discount. *$$$–$$$$; AE, MC, V; www.justinwine.com; about 15 miles west of downtown Paso Robles.*

La Bellasera / ★★★

206 ALEXA CT, PASO ROBLES; 805/238-2834

Don't let the location of La Bellasera—literally in the parking lot of a Hampton Inn, alongside Highway 101—deter you from trying out this large hotel with a boutique-y feel. The interior is sophisticated, new (the whole place is just two years old), and carefully decorated to resemble a chateau in Southern Italy (it just might achieve this illusion, too, if it weren't situated next to a freeway). Each of the 60 rooms is oversize and immaculate, with a whirlpool spa, a deluxe bathroom with stone shower, a full-size sofa or chaise lounge, robes, a plasma TV, an iPod dock, and a computer with Internet access. Most rooms have fireplaces. The staff is exceptionally friendly and will give you a tour of the premises even if you aren't staying there. Also on-site: Enoteca restaurant, a spa, a swimming pool, a wine cellar, a fitness center, a laundry room, a gift shop, and a concierge. *$$–$$$; AE, DIS, MC, V; no checks; www.labellasera.com; at Hwy 101.* ♿

Paso Robles Inn / ★★

1103 SPRING ST, PASO ROBLES; 805/238-2660

The Paso Robles Inn has some rich history. People once came by stagecoach to dip in the hot springs here. Designed by famed architect Stanford White and built in 1891, the "absolutely fireproof" structure burned to the ground in 1940, except for the separate ballroom, which in 2001 was rebuilt to house meeting rooms and 12 oversize guest rooms with whirlpool tubs, private patios, microwave ovens, and refrigerators. The rest of the inn was reconstructed in the 1940s, and its Spanish architecture and tile reflect the passion for the Mission Revival style that was in full swing at that time. A stroll through lushly landscaped grounds leads guests to a footbridge over the creek meandering through this oak-shaded property and to 68 bungalow-style motel rooms with convenient carports. Well shielded from street noise, these units are simple and plain, but many guests consider them charming and nostalgic (although they are not cheap). Don't bother to stay here if the only rooms available start with 1 or 2—they're small, decorated in a bleak motel style with free-form swipes of brown paint on the walls, and close enough to the street to be noisy. A large heated pool near the creek makes for great afternoon dips, and the dining room (with cocktail lounge) serves three diner-style meals daily. *$–$$$; AE, DC, DIS, MC, V; no checks; www.pasoroblesinn.com; between 10th and 12th sts.* ♿

Summerwood Inn and Winery / ★★★

2130 ARBOR RD, PASO ROBLES; 805/227-1111

Across from its own Summerwood Winery, about a five-minute drive from the center of town, this AAA four-diamond bed-and-breakfast is a fine place to base yourself for a wine-tasting tour of nearby wineries. Though the main building—a white clapboard cross between Queen Anne and Southern plantation style—looks old, it was actually built in 1994. This means guest rooms are extraspacious and bathrooms ultramodern, though the entire inn is furnished with formal English-country antique reproductions. The winery's vine-planted acres are just steps from the inn's back patio and visible from every room's private balcony. Each of the nine rooms is named for a wine (Syrah, Bordeaux, Chardonnay) and has a gas fireplace, a balcony, a color satellite TV, a telephone, terry cloth bathrobes, and bedside bottled water. Luxury is achieved through small, thoughtful touches; you'll find fresh flowers accompanying everything from the Godiva chocolate on your pillow with turndown service to the early-morning coffee-and-scones spread on the sideboard downstairs. The room rate includes full breakfast, afternoon wine and hors d'oeuvres, and late-night cookies. For a romantic splurge, the Moscato Allegro Room features an in-room whirlpool for two, and the top-floor Cabernet Suite is as rich and decadent as an aged wine, with sumptuous furnishings, a seven-headed shower, and an ultraprivate patio with a view. *$$–$$$$; AE, MC, V; checks OK (at time of reservation); www.summerwoodwine.com; at Hwy 46W, 1 mile west of Hwy 101.* ♿

Morro Bay

Morro Rock is a 23-million-year-old volcanic-plug dome outcropping that is a registered California Historical Landmark. Vast and filled with birds and sea mammals, scenic Morro Bay is named for the peculiarly shaped Morro Rock anchoring the mouth of the waterway, one of nine remaining extinct volcanic rocks, called the Nine Sisters, along the coast. This ancient towering landmark, whose name comes from the Spanish word for a Moorish turban, is inhabited by the endangered peregrine falcon and other migratory birds. Across from the rock, a monstrous oceanfront electrical plant mars the visual appeal of the otherwise pristine bay. In the summer the town is overrun with sunburned tourists, and no one would call it an elegant seaside village. But it's unpretentious, and outside the town proper are some wonderful hiking trails.

If you're only going to be in Morro Bay for a day or for a few hours, there are a number of parks in which to enjoy quick picnics, a swim in the bay, or even some fishing. **COLEMAN PARK**, at the Embarcadero and Coleman Drive, has barbecues, fishing, and swimming in Morro Bay. **KEISER PARK** at Atascadero Road and Highway 1 offers barbecues and cool places to relax. At **MORRO ROCK CITY BEACH**, at the foot of Coleman Drive, you'll find barbecues, fishing, swimming, and surfing in the bay. **BAYSHORE BLUFFS PARK**, at the west end of Bayshore Drive, offers a bluff-top picnic area with a path to the beach. And finally, **TIDELANDS PARK**, at the Embarcadero between Olive and Fig, has good fishing plus swimming in the bay.

Morro Bay touts itself as a place "where the sun spends the winter," but no matter the season, the views of the Pacific, the great seafood, and the sunset make it a must-stop for any traveler in the area. Call the **MORRO BAY HARBOR DEPARTMENT** (805/772-6254) for information.

Los Osos

Located just south of Morro Bay and around the bird estuary, this quiet community is prime territory for bird-watching, hiking, and tide pooling. Most people seek it out as the gateway to **MONTANA DE ORO STATE PARK** (805/528-0513), which encompasses sand dunes, jagged cliffs, coves, caves, and reefs. Named "mountain of gold" by the Spanish for the golden poppies that carpet the hillsides each spring, the park contains trails for hiking, biking, and horseback riding, as well as restrooms and picnic facilities. Easily reached tide pools offer glimpses of starfish, anemones, crabs, and other residents. Stop first at the **VISITOR CENTER AND RANGER HEADQUARTERS** in the historic **SPOONER RANCH HOUSE** for hiking maps and directions to trails, to learn the history of this former ranch, and to see videos of local and natural history, including displays on hawks, bobcats, and coyotes. The **BLUFFS TRAIL** is an easy but breathtaking 4-mile round-trip hike atop the

Montana de Oro State Park bluffs—the trail dips down to tide pools, making it a true peak-hiking experience.

Tucked into the landscape on the south side of the bay near the corner of Pine and Ramona avenues and adjacent to the tidal flats, this secluded preserve has spring-fed ponds, a stream, and a marsh and upland area that is home to turtles, monarch butterflies, wetland birds, and many endangered species. Walk its decks and bridges and simply stand, look, and listen in this magical place. The **MORRO COAST AUDUBON SOCIETY** (805/772-1991; www.morrocoastaudubon.org) owns and maintains the 24-acre preserve; call to hear which rare birds have recently been spotted.

The San Luis Obispo Coast

The San Luis Obispo Coast area includes a wide range of coastal and inland agricultural lands, with towns as varied as the charming creek-side university town of San Luis Obispo to the old working fishing port of San Luis Pier to the raffish beach towns of Avila Beach and Pismo Beach and the former ranching towns of Arroyo Grande and Santa Maria. In the past 20 years the area has become an important wine region, including the Edna Valley and Arroyo Grande Valley areas. One of the largest ranges of sand dunes in the world stretches for miles at Pismo Dunes and Oceano Dunes.

ACCESS AND INFORMATION

Compared to the San Simeon coast, San Luis Obispo is a cinch to reach. One of the state's main highways, US 101, runs right through the center of town. Rugged Highway 1 is also an option if you're in the mood for scenery, but it is a longer, more lagging journey. If you're entering the city from the east, take Highway 46 or 41 to US 101, and then head south. **AMTRAK** (800/USA-RAIL; www.amtrak.com) offers daily service into San Luis Obispo from the Bay Area (Oakland) and Los Angeles.

You can find all you need to know at the downtown **SAN LUIS OBISPO VISITORS CENTER** (1039 Chorro St; 805/781-2777; www.visitslo.com), which is open Sunday to Wednesday from 10am to 5pm, Thursday to Saturday from 10am to 7pm. Pick up the comprehensive *Visitors Guide* and self-guided *Points of Interest Walking Tour* to navigate your visit.

Because San Luis Obispo is situated about 10 degrees inland, you'll get some hot and sticky summer days (well, for Central California, at least), much warmer than those along San Simeon. Prepare accordingly, bringing lightweight clothing for the daytime and a jacket for when the inevitable nighttime breeze picks up.

San Luis Obispo

San Luis Obispo is one of the prettiest towns on the coast. With two rivers running through it, a vibrant mission, and an art-filled downtown alive with music and events along the river walk, it's easy to spend several hours just wandering this enchanting place. While it appears quiet, many big-city transplants have settled down here. With its beautiful surrounding countryside, relaxed yet vital college-town atmosphere, charming neighborhoods of historic cottages, and developing wine region nearby, SLO—as the locals call it—has been growing by leaps and bounds. But even with the influx of new residents and commerce, SLO's downtown is wonderfully compact and perfect for exploring on foot, while the sparkling coastline is only minutes away.

Start at the **MISSION SAN LUIS OBISPO DE TOLOSA** (751 Palm St; 805/781-8220; www.missionsanluisobispo.org) or the **CHILDREN'S MUSEUM** and wander along **SAN LUIS CREEK**, where you'll come upon sculptures, musicians playing, and several informal restaurants with great views of the creek. You can stop along the way and listen to the water, or sip a glass of wine on a deck overlooking the creek bank. There is also a small amphitheater where bands often perform.

Like several other charming Central Coast towns, this one began life as a Spanish mission outpost. Founding friar Junípero Serra chose this valley in 1772, drawn by reports of friendly natives and bountiful food, and established the Mission. The mission has the dubious honor of being the first to use the now-traditional red tile roof after its original thatched roofs repeatedly fell to the burning arrows of local Chumash Indians. The church sanctuary is simple, its high white walls adorned with hand-painted garlands, with heavy beams overhead. The altar is surrounded by green marble; behind it there's gold-painted detail, and high above, a large Eye of God beams down. The mission gardens are shady with orange and lemon trees and a huge olive tree. Daisies, foxgloves, and roses provide color, and mission bell lighting fixtures light the paths at night. The well-restored mission church, padres' quarters, and colonnade are in the heart of town, fronted by the pedestrian-friendly **MISSION PLAZA**, a pretty park that serves as SLO's town square for festivals and other events.

ACCESS AND INFORMATION

A tiny **SLO COUNTY AIRPORT** (903-5 Airport Dr; 805/541-1038) is just 3 miles south of downtown and served by small carriers like America West, American Eagle, and United Express. A bit bigger and offering a wider range of flights, **SANTA BARBARA AIRPORT** (601 Firestone Rd; 805/967-7111; www.flysba.com) is located 100 miles south.

GREYHOUND (150 South St; 805/543-2121 or 800/231-2222; www.greyhound.com) runs daily buses to Los Angeles, Santa Barbara, and San Francisco.

AMTRAK (1011 Railroad Ave; 805/541-0505 or 800/USA-RAIL; www.amtrak.com) has north- and southbound trains passing through daily as part of the Coast Starlight route, which travels from Seattle to Los Angeles, and Pacific Surfliner route, from San Luis Obispo to San Diego.

San Luis Obispo's **REGIONAL TRANSIT AUTHORITY** (1150 Osos St; 805/781-4472; www.slorta.org) operates buses daily except Sunday across the region, including the neighboring cities of Paso Robles, San Simeon, Cambria, Morro Bay, and Pismo Beach.

The **SAN LUIS OBISPO CHAMBER OF COMMERCE** (1039 Chorro St; 805/781-2777; www.visitslo.com) offers a helpful *Points of Interest* brochure. The brochure outlines three walking tours: a Downtown District walk, which includes the **AH LOUIS STORE** (800 Palm St), where Chinese laborers working on the railroad shopped; a Historic Core Walk, which stops by the **HAYES–LATIMER ADOBE** (642 Monterey St); and a San Luis Creek Walk. At the chamber of commerce, pick up the colorful *Visitors Guide*, which is packed with useful information.

On Thursday nights everyone comes out, rain or shine, for the **FARMERS MARKET** (Higuera St, between Osos and Nipomo sts; open 6–9pm Thurs), a beloved local tradition. Emptied of auto traffic, Higuera Street fills with a colorful and festive assemblage of vendors and entertainers. Shoppers stroll through, clutching bags of luscious fruits and vegetables, fresh flowers, locally made arts and crafts, and warm baked goods. The sounds of Peruvian street musicians, old-fashioned brass bands, or lively dance troupes fill the air as the tantalizing aroma of oak barbecue wafts from sidewalk grills. Come hungry and graze your way through a classic SLO evening.

RESTAURANTS

Buona Tavola / ★★★

1037 MONTEREY ST, SAN LUIS OBISPO; 805/545-8000

Situated next to the art deco Fremont Theater, this upscale dining room and its charming outdoor patio offer well-prepared northern Italian cuisine in a setting that's fancy enough for special occasions but welcoming enough for the casually dressed. Checkerboard floors and original artwork adorn the warm, intimate interior, while lush magnolias, ficuses, and grapevines lend a garden atmosphere to alfresco seating out back. Begin by choosing one of the traditional cold salads on the antipasti list, then proceed to a main course menu that highlights delicious homemade pastas. Chef-owner Antonio Varia offers entrées such as *agnolotti di scampi allo zafferano*—half-moon purses pinched around a scampi filling, then smothered in saffron cream sauce; fish such as fresh Norwegian salmon; and meat entrées such as *costelette d'agnello*, rack of lamb marinated with rosemary, sage, thyme, and garlic, and served with a rosemary-Dijon reduction. For dessert try the deceptively simple *crema di vaniglia*—vanilla cream custard with caramel or chocolate sauce. The wine list is a winner, with traditional Italian offerings accented by stellar choices from the surrounding wine region. There's now a second location up the road in Paso Robles. *$$; AE, DIS, MC, V; local checks only; lunch Mon–Fri, dinner every day; beer and wine; reservations recommended; www.btslo.com; between Osos and Santa Rosa sts.* ♿

Corner View / ★★☆

1141 CHORRO ST, SAN LUIS OBISPO; 805/546-8444

After a simple lunch of tomato bisque and tuna salad that will make you say *aah*, you'll be taking note of Corner View with plans to come back. Located along a shaded downtown shopping way, Corner View attracts a professional clientele and a wide range of ages, not just the university students who populate the other nearby establishments. Its rather roomy interior ensures that you'll never wait too long for a table, although during peak lunch hours the place is absolutely hopping. Corner View is one of only two places on the coast that serves sand dabs, a flatfish delicacy, but the burger is one of the most popular items on the menu The wine list is extensive, and 25 varieties are offered by the glass. On the weekends, the restaurant turns into a bar and stays open as late as 1:30am. *$$; AE, MC, V; no checks; lunch, dinner every day; full bar; reservations recommended; www.cornerviewrestaurant.com; at Marsh St.* ♿

Downtown Brewing Company / ★☆

1119 GARDEN ST, SAN LUIS OBISPO; 805/543-1843

Hang out with the area's collegiate population at this local-brew-pub-makes-good success story. Its many homemade beers—the most famous are Pale Ale, Amber Ale, and Porter—have created such a buzz that they're now nationally distributed. Located downtown in a historic 100-year-old brick commercial building, the Company offers a bar downstairs and a cavernous dining room upstairs. Illuminated by industrial skylights and filled with hardy wooden tables and chairs, the restaurant is comfortable, although it can get loud. The menu—burgers, deep-fried appetizers, and other pub basics—is far from gourmet, but quite satisfying with a tall cold one. This is a great place to meet friends, celebrate a sports victory, or grab a premovie bargain bite. *$; AE, DIS, MC, V; local checks only; lunch, dinner every day; full bar; no reservations; www.dtbrew.com; between Higuera and Marsh sts.* ♿

NoVo / ★★★

726 HIGUERA ST, SAN LUIS OBISPO; 805/543-3986

Minimalist design and quirky art frame the interior of this Asian-Brazilian-Mediterranean tapas restaurant. When the weather is pleasant, the creekside outdoor seating makes an idyllic setting for an adventurous meal. The food ranges from satés and meat- or tofu-filled lettuce wraps to curries and out-of-this-world shrimp-and-avocado spring rolls. Many different sake selections, a huge wine list, and fresh, organic tea round out the meal. *$$–$$$; AE, MC, V; no checks; lunch, dinner every day, brunch Sun; beer and wine; reservations recommended; www.novorestaurant.com; between Garden and Broad sts.*

LODGINGS

Apple Farm Inn / ★★½

2015 MONTEREY ST, SAN LUIS OBISPO; 805/544-2040 OR 800/255-2040

The rooms are quieter and more elegant than you'd expect at this ultra-popular getaway near Highway 101. The entire complex—which includes a restaurant, gift shop, and working cider mill—exhibits an over-the-top Victorian-style cuteness, with floral wallpaper, fresh flowers, and sugar-sweet touches. No two guest rooms are alike, although each has a gas fireplace, large bathroom with plush terry cloth robes, canopy or brass bed, and lavish country decor. Some bedrooms open onto cozy turreted sitting areas with romantic window seats, while others have wide bay windows overlooking the creek that rambles through the property. Morning coffee and tea are delivered to your room, or you can opt for breakfast in bed at an additional cost. Rooms in the motel-style Trellis Court cost less, have virtually the same amenities as those in the main inn (including fireplaces and cozy decor), and include a discount voucher for breakfast at the restaurant, a great value without sacrificing a bit of luxury. The complex has a heated outdoor swimming pool and whirlpool, and there's unlimited hot apple cider on hand in the lobby. While you're here, be sure to try the restaurant's famous hot apple dumplings. *$$$ (main inn), $$ (Trellis Court); AE, DIS, MC, V; checks OK; www.applefarm.com; just south of Hwy 101.* ♿

Garden Street Inn / ★★★

1212 GARDEN ST, SAN LUIS OBISPO; 805/545-9802

When you first step inside this beautifully furnished and maintained inn, the whole effect is so grand you might expect to be greeted by a butler. The gracious Italianate Queen Anne bed-and-breakfast near downtown was built in 1887 and fully restored in 1990, a monument to Victorian gentility. Each bedroom and suite is decorated with well-chosen antique oak armoires, opulent fabric or paper wall coverings, and vintage memorabilia. Choose one with a claw-foot tub, fireplace, whirlpool bath, or private deck—whatever suits your fancy. The Field of Dreams room has a baseball theme, and the classic car–themed Concours d'Elegance suite has a tan damask spread, wing chairs, a sitting room, and a black fireplace. Guests enjoy breakfast in the morning room, where the sun filters through original stained-glass windows, and evening wine and cheese. But beware: Guests have frequently complained about the late-night excess street noise from both traffic and bar hoppers (which is the drawback to staying in such a prime downtown location). *$$; AE, MC, V; checks OK; www.gardenstreetinn.com; between Marsh and Pacific sts.* ♿

Madonna Inn / ★★

100 MADONNA RD, SAN LUIS OBISPO; 805/543-3000 OR 800/543-9666

Know before you go: This place is universally embraced for its over-the-top kitsch factor. But take a break from good taste and step into this eccentric hotel of fantasy rooms where faux-rock waterfalls, velvet-flocked wallpaper, marbled mirrors, and deep shag carpeting are just the beginning. The 110 rooms are individually decorated in themes so unusual that the Madonna Inn sells 110 different postcards—just in case your friends can't believe you slept in digs reminiscent of *The Flintstones*. Before you call for reservations, check the Web site for photos of every unique room. Favorites include the all-rock Caveman rooms, featuring waterfall showers and giant animal-print rugs. Other over-the-top options are the Austrian Suite and English Manor, which look pretty much like they sound. Many guests of this Disneyland for adults come back every year and request their favorite rooms, and the Madonna hosts hundreds of honeymooners each year. The rooms are spacious and very comfortable; if the loud decor doesn't keep you up, there's a very good night's sleep to be had. A surprisingly good coffee shop adjoins a delectable European bakery. Don't miss the Gold Rush dining room, an eyeful beyond description that's flaming with fuchsia carpet, pink leather booths, and gold cherub chandeliers. The inn now boasts a spa with a pool and six treatment rooms. *$$–$$$$; AE, DIS, MC, V; checks OK; www.madonnainn.com; Madonna Rd exit off Hwy 101.* ♿

Avila Beach

Avila Beach is a bit like Rip Van Winkle, just waking up from a period when it was effectively asleep for three years. Because of an environmental tragedy from seepage of underground crude oil, the town had to be destroyed to be saved and was essentially leveled, especially along the waterfront. The cleanup is now complete, and the still-bare town is just starting to flourish with attractive seating, benches complete with bas-relief starfish so lifelike they look as if they might slither off. Plans for restaurants and bars are in the works, and soon Avila Beach should spring back to the sunny and popular resort it once was, just a bit less funky.

LODGINGS

Avila la Fonda / ★★★☆

101 SAN MIGUEL ST, AVILA BEACH; 805/595-1700

It seems a bit off-kilter to have a hotel this nice, modeled after a 19th-century Mexican village, in such a laid-back, oddball town—especially one of this caliber and with such impeccably designed rooms. Each of the 30 suites, with a red and orange color scheme and terra-cotta tiled floors, has a Jacuzzi for two, a fireplace, a plasma TV, a CD player, an iPod dock alarm clock, wireless Internet (loaner laptops available upon request), robes, a hairdryer, an iron and board, and a complimentary basket of snacks. Everything in the kitchen honor bar is available for the taking; just make sure you keep tally of what you owe and pay at the end of your stay. A DVD, CD, and book library offers a wide selection of entertainment options, and an outdoor lanai with a barbecue kitchen, fireplace, and wet bar is the perfect place to throw a fete. A cozy 24-hour hospitality room stocks complimentary drinks and fresh-baked cookies. The organic spa, Nekkidd, provides a range of services and sells organic clothing. One drawback: Avila la Fonda lacks air-conditioning (the rooms only have fans), which can be a problem during sweltering summer days (though the nights cool off significantly in this coastal town). *$$$–$$$$; AE, MC, V; no checks; www.avilalafonda.com; at 1st St.* ♿

Sycamore Mineral Springs Resort / ★★★

1215 AVILA BEACH DR, AVILA BEACH; 805/595-7302 OR 800/234-5831

This sprawling historic resort drew guests for decades thanks to its mineral springs, and it still does now, with upgraded decor and new accommodations called the West Meadow Suites. Discovered in 1886 by prospectors drilling for oil, the bubbling mineral springs provide relaxation and rejuvenation in an idyllic natural setting. Sycamore Springs feeds close to 75 private mineral baths on the property—many rooms have their own spa tubs on attached decks or balconies, and two dozen more freestanding hot tubs are tucked away on the wooded hillside above the spa. Hot tub rentals for nonguests are available 24 hours a day, and a half-hour soak is included with any massage or facial. The spacious guest rooms, many of which have fireplaces, are in contemporary condo-style two-story buildings, reached via a long walking bridge arching over Avila Beach Drive and San Luis Creek. The resort's Gardens of Avila restaurant isn't much to look at, but its outdoor setting shines and its fare is casually elegant, if slightly expensive. *$$–$$$$; AE, DIS, MC, V; local checks only; www.sycamoresprings.com; 1 mile from Hwy 101.* ♿

Pismo Beach/Shell Beach

Pismo is about the beach. Forget about chic. Shorts, a T-shirt, sandals, a beach hat, and lots of sunscreen are all you need to pack. The native Chumash, who lived here as far back as 9,000 years ago, named Pismo Beach for the *pismu*, or tar, found in the sand. In the 1900s, with saloons, brothels, and a dance hall established, the town had become a tourist getaway for wild times, and that reputation was furthered during the Depression when Pismo Beach became a well-known source for illicit booze. Currently, it's merely a time-warp shrine to days when California beach towns were unpretentious places meant for just goofing off. Couples and families wander around town with no agenda except to soak up the sun. There is an upscale side to all this, but it's a bit north at Shell Beach, where the newer beachfront resorts can be quite elegant.

Near Pismo Beach—and claimed by Oceano, Grover Beach, and even inland Nipomo—lies a stretch of extraordinary sand dunes. Walk along the shifting sands at **PISMO STATE BEACH** (enter at Grand Ave) or, alternatively, visit the **PACIFIC DUNES RANCH RIDING STABLES** (1207 Silver Spur Pl; 805/489-8100; www.pacificdunesridingstables.com) in Oceano; they'll outfit you with a horse to match your riding ability and send you (alone or with a guide) along their private trail to the dunes, where you can gallop along the surf's edge or just mosey around. The Pismo dunes are also the only place in California where it's legal to drive on the beach—in the specially designated **OCEANO DUNES STATE VEHICULAR RECREATION AREA** (805/473-7230), accessed via a ramp from Pier Avenue in Oceano. A 5½-mile sand highway at the ocean's edge parallels the mountainous dunes; you can take the family car onto the sand highway, but the dunes themselves are off-limits to all but four-wheel-drive and all-terrain vehicles. For information on guided hikes to the dunes, contact the **DUNES CENTER** (805/343-2455; www.dunescenter.org; open 10am–4pm Thurs–Sun) in Guadalupe.

If you don't have your own off-road vehicle for running the dunes, you might want to sign up for a wild Hummer ride with **PACIFIC ADVENTURE TOURS OF OCEANO** (805/481-9330; www.pacificadventuretours.com). The one-hour tour explores the dunes and beach in their luxury four-by-four.

RESTAURANTS

Giuseppe's Cucina Italiana / ★★★

891 PRICE ST, PISMO BEACH; 805/773-2870

The enticing aroma wafting from this always-crowded standout on Pismo Beach's Italian restaurant row is enough to lure you inside. Known county-wide for consistently good home-style food, generous portions, and a friendly, casual ambience, Giuseppe's can get a little boisterous, but it retains a classy touch just a notch above the usual family-style pizza joint. White linen rather than red-checked tablecloths set the stage for a menu that offers both traditional Southern Italian–style fare (pizza, lasagne, veal parmigiana), and trattoria-influenced California cuisine such as peppercorn-seared ahi tuna and individual gourmet pizzas. Dinners come with soup or salad; try the "alternate" salad, butter lettuce with creamy Gorgonzola. Appropriately, given its seaside location, Giuseppe's menu includes plenty of ocean fare—favorites include an appetizer of clams stuffed with shrimp, scallops, and lox, baked in the wood-fired oven and served with aioli. *$$; AE, DIS, MC, V; local checks only; lunch Mon–Fri, dinner every day; full bar; no reservations; www.giuseppesrestaurant.com; at Pismo Ave.* ♿

Splash Cafe / ★★☆

197 POMEROY AVE, PISMO BEACH; 805/773-4653

Splash Cafe is the kind of place people can wander into with sandy feet, wearing a damp bathing suit. They come looking for a great bowl of clam chowder, and this informal place does not disappoint. While Pismo Beach is famous for clams, they aren't sold commercially, so any chowder is made with imported bivalves. Although Splash is basically a burger stand with a short menu and just a few tables, locals agree its creamy New England–style chowder is the best in town, which explains why the place makes 10,000 gallons annually. If you like, you can order it in a sourdough bread bowl. If that's not enough of a meal, the menu also includes fish-and-chips, hamburgers, corn dogs, hot dogs, and other sandwiches. *$; MC, V; local checks only; breakfast, lunch, dinner every day; beer and wine; no reservations; www.splashcafe.com; between Pomeroy St and the pier.* ♿

LODGINGS

Cottage Inn by the Sea / ★★☆

2351 PRICE ST, PISMO BEACH; 805/773-4617 OR 888/440-8400

You might think you have wandered into a British seaside resort in Cornwall when you see this cottage-style enclave with brown half-timber construction and a rounded thatch-style roof. There's even a vine-covered wishing well. Paths wind around the buildings on their way to the beach. This is one of the newest inns on Shell Beach, although it looks completely established. The rooms are romantic but more dignified than cloying, with reproductions of antiques, curtains with Roman shades, wallpaper with little roses, armoires, and wrought-iron beds. Each room has a fireplace, a microwave oven, a coffeemaker, an iron and ironing board, and a small refrigerator. Room rates are based entirely on the view, with nonview rooms beginning under $100 on weekdays. There are an inviting sundeck and a small glassed-in pool, and a spa right on the bluffs overlooking a dramatic stretch of the Pacific. The complimentary continental breakfast is served in the breakfast room or on the patio. *$–$$$; AE, DC, DIS, MC, V; no checks; www.cottage-inn.com; on Price St just off Hwy 101.* ♿

Dolphin Bay Resort & Spa / ★★★

2727 SHELL BEACH RD, PISMO BEACH; 805/773-4300

Whereas beachside condo complexes are standard in Florida and along the eastern seaboard, it's unique to find such resorts along the Central California coast. This makes Dolphin Bay a standout, but that's not the only reason. Built in 2006, all of the suites are between 900 and 2,000 square feet and feature private terraces, fully equipped gourmet kitchens with stainless steel appliances, separate dining and living rooms with queen-size sofa sleepers and large plasma TVs, and laundry facilities. Some have fireplaces and air-jet Jacuzzi tubs. Everything is very green, with an in-house recycling program and L'Occitane products dispensed from wall mounts. Complimentary valet parking and wireless Internet are additional perks. Although the resort welcomes families, one of the three buildings is for adults only, as are the private hot tubs. The Lido Restaurant with indoor and outdoor dining serves two meals a day and changes its menu three times a year. While most guests choose to lounge by the pool, the resort does have direct beach access. (Fun fact: part of *Pirates of the Caribbean 2* was filmed along this exact stretch of coast). Near the beach, there are lawn cabanas, a bocce court, and a fire pit, as well as the option to have a private dinner on the edge of the cliff. The Fireside Grill, located by the pool and lit with tiki torches, holds a barbecue on Friday and Saturday from May to November. The resort can also arrange golf excursions and winery tours. *$$$$; AE, DIS, MC, V; www.thedolphinbay.com; off Hwy 101.* ♿

SeaVenture Resort / ★★★

100 OCEAN VIEW AVE, PISMO BEACH; 800/662-5545

This heavenly beachfront find is the only local upscale resort that's not on Shell Beach. Located right on Pismo Beach, it offers exceptional pampering without a trace of pretentiousness. Each room is decorated in a soothing blend of deep greens, with thick carpeting, white plantation-style furnishings, and a gas-burning fireplace. With the beach directly below, private balconies or decks are welcoming enough, but in addition almost all rooms have irresistible private hot tubs with soft leatherette rims. Whether the night is foggy or clear, slide into the spa tub, and the invigorating yet ethereal experience is worth the entire cost of the room—or slip into mindlessness with a movie rental from the hotel's video library. In the morning, a continental breakfast basket is delivered to your door. Another nice amenity: the free use of beach cruiser bicycles or beach surreys. Free beach chairs and towels are also a plus. If you're still not relaxed, SeaVenture has an on-site therapeutic massage center, and the restaurant offers dinner room service and a lovely brunch. *$$–$$$$; AE, DC, DIS, MC, V; checks OK; www.seaventure.com; from Price or Dolliver sts follow Ocean View Ave to the beach.* ♿

WINE COUNTRY

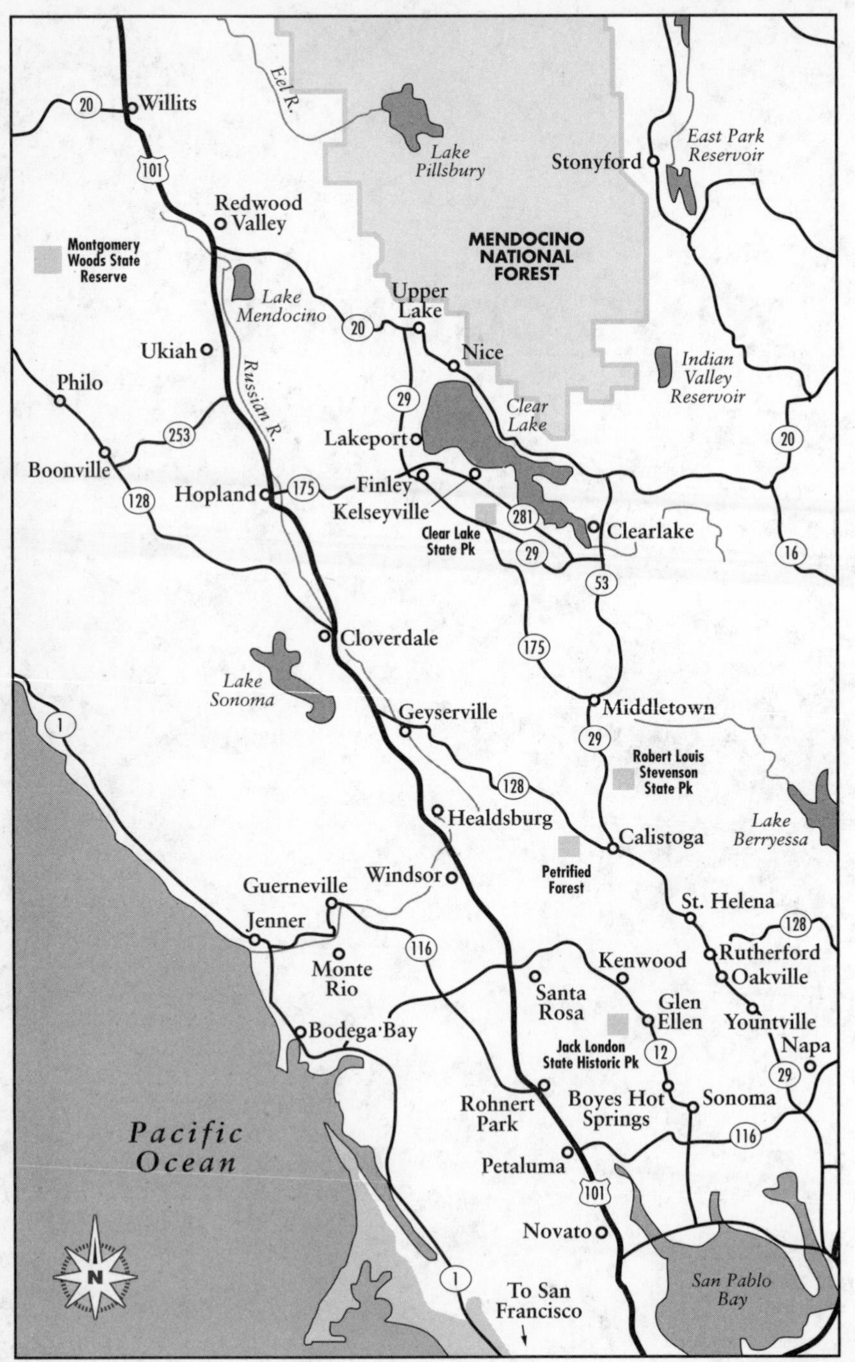
Willits
Eel R.
Lake Pillsbury
Stonyford
East Park Reservoir
Redwood Valley
Montgomery Woods State Reserve
MENDOCINO NATIONAL FOREST
Lake Mendocino
Upper Lake
Ukiah
Nice
Indian Valley Reservoir
Philo
Russian R.
Clear Lake
Lakeport
Boonville
Finley
Hopland
Kelseyville
Clear Lake State Pk
Clearlake
Cloverdale
Lake Sonoma
Geyserville
Middletown
Robert Louis Stevenson State Pk
Healdsburg
Calistoga
Lake Berryessa
Windsor
Petrified Forest
Guerneville
St. Helena
Jenner
Rutherford
Oakville
Kenwood
Monte Rio
Santa Rosa
Glen Ellen
Yountville
Bodega Bay
Jack London State Historic Pk
Napa
Rohnert Park
Boyes Hot Springs
Sonoma
Pacific Ocean
Petaluma
Novato
To San Francisco
San Pablo Bay
N
20
101
175
29
253
128
281
53
16
1
116
12

WINE COUNTRY

Napa and Sonoma are two of the top tourist attractions in the United States, with little wonder. When you combine supernatural scenic beauty with nearly year-round excellent weather, top-notch restaurants, and world-class wines, what's not to like? These qualities have made the region, which includes pastoral Anderson Valley and its fringe of Mendocino County towns, a popular destination for oenophiles and gourmets alike. And for the nature lover who comes along for the ride, Wine Country delivers some of America's most stunning vistas. Like competitive siblings of the same robust family, these areas contain many similarities, but each also retains its individual personality.

ACCESS AND INFORMATION

There are two main options for those arriving in the Wine Country by air. Fly into **SAN FRANCISCO INTERNATIONAL AIRPORT (SFO)** (located off Hwy 101, just south of San Francisco; 650/821-8211; www.flysfo.com) or **OAKLAND INTERNATIONAL AIRPORT (OAK)** (1 Airport Dr; 510/563-3300; www.flyoakland.com), and then rent a car, since that is by far the best way to tour this largely rural area.

Driving from San Francisco, you will likely hit more traffic, and the route can be tricky: from the airport, head north on Highway 101 toward San Francisco. Take the 101 North/Duboce/Mission Street exit, stay right, then turn right onto Mission Street/US 101 North. Turn left onto South Van Ness, which will take you north across the city. Turn left onto Lombard and follow signs to the Golden Gate Bridge. Cross the bridge and continue on Highway 101 north.

In Novato, exit onto Highway 37. For the town of **SONOMA**, head east on 37 for about 8 miles. Take a left onto Highway 121 north (Infineon Raceway will be on your left). You are now in the Sonoma Valley. Stay on 121 and take Highway 12 north.

For **NAPA**, follow the directions above but stay on 121, following signs for Napa until you reach Highway 29, which will then take you the length of the valley to your destination. Travel time to Napa from SFO is approximately 2 hours (1½ hours to Sonoma); add an extra hour or more during rush hour. For other Sonoma County destinations, stay on 101 and continue north.

Napa is easily accessible from the East Bay side of the Bay Area, and that makes the Oakland Airport a good choice (Oakland flights can also be cheaper and less inclined to be delayed by fog than flights to and from SFO). From Oakland, take Highway 80 north to Vallejo, then take the Highway 37 exit going west. This will take you to Highway 29, where you will go right (north) to Napa. As you approach Napa, the road will split; for downtown Napa, stay to the right and follow the signs that say Lake Berryessa/Downtown Napa. (You can also take one of four downtown Napa exits off of Highway 29.) For the rest of the Napa Valley, stay to the left and follow signs for 29 north.

If you want to rent a car but would rather skip the Bay Area traffic, you can take a shuttle bus to Napa, Sonoma, or Santa Rosa and rent a car there. Evans Airport Shuttle (707/255-1559) has scheduled shuttles to and from both airports to Napa. You'll need to take a short taxi ride to downtown Napa's rental car companies. **SONOMA AIRPORTER** (800/611-4246; www.sonomaairporter.com) connects all of Sonoma Valley's towns with SFO. **SONOMA COUNTY AIRPORT EXPRESS** (707/837-8700; www.airportexpressinc.com) has scheduled rides to and from Santa Rosa and both airports. Car rentals available in Napa and Santa Rosa include **AVIS**, **BUDGET**, **ENTERPRISE**, and **HERTZ**.

If driving is simply not an option, your choices are limited. The Wine Country doesn't have the best public transportation, so you'll need to either set up camp in a walkable city, such as downtown Napa or downtown Sonoma, or hire someone to drive you to the attractions. The **NAPA VALLEY CONFERENCE AND VISITORS BUREAU** (1310 Napa Town Center, off 1st St, Napa; 707/226-7459; www.napavalley.com) can arrange bicycle, van, and limousine tours of the wineries.

The **SONOMA VALLEY VISITORS BUREAU** (453 1st St E, Sonoma; 707/996-1090; www.sonomavalley.com) has winery tour information. Both the Napa and the Sonoma Valley visitors bureaus can connect you with group and private tour services.

Napa Valley

Given that Napa Valley is the country's most extensive adult playground for food, wine, and luxury lovers, it's almost fitting that the 35-mile-long stretch of grape-strewn real estate surrounding rural Highway 29 is right up there with kid-oriented Disneyland as one of the most visited destinations in California. Around 5 million visitors annually make the grape escape to the valley's towns and world-renowned wineries, resorts, and restaurants, which means roads and attractions can be more tightly packed than a cluster of heavy-hanging chardonnay fruit—especially in high season (March through November). During this time the traffic on Highway 29 that gets you to your next winery can be as loathsome as big-city gridlock. But no matter. Spring displays vibrant green hills and bright yellow mustard blossoms, summer brings everyday sunshine and hillsides fat with fruit; fall explodes with brilliant autumnal colors and the excitement of harvest, and winter makes for even more excuses to indulge in some of the world's best food and wine. You'll be quick to realize road congestion is a small price to pay for paradise.

There are other costs to the visitor, too. Popularity has resulted in most wineries charging a tasting fee—which can range from $5 for sips of a few current releases to $30 for a single glass at Opus One—and most hotels jacking up rates, so break open the piggy bank before you come.

Lodging information, winery maps, and details about parks, hot-air balloon rides, and other recreational pastimes like the **NAPA VALLEY WINE TRAIN**

(707/253-2111), a dining train that traverses the valley floor, are available at the **NAPA VALLEY CONFERENCE AND VISITORS BUREAU** (1310 Napa Town Center, off 1st St, Napa; 707/226-7459; www.napavalley.com).

Napa Valley Wineries

Staff at most wineries assume that the folks who walk through their doors are not wine connoisseurs, and they welcome questions. During the congenial process of touring their facilities and sampling various vintages, they try to show visitors what makes their product unique. So if you've ever dreamed of entering a fine restaurant and confidently describing the exact style of wine you like and want, this is the place to learn how to do it—and what fun the learning is!

Although most vintners now charge you to taste their wines, tours are usually free. Some require reservations, but don't let that deter you: many establishments, especially those in residential areas, are required to limit the number of guests at any one time.

Since Napa has more than 280 wineries, it's safe to say you won't see them all in a weekend. A good plan of attack is to choose the ones you most want to visit and then tour three or four a day—with a leisurely lunch break somewhere in between. Leave room in your schedule for the serendipitous detour, because this is the best way to make new discoveries. Napa's wineries are mainly clustered along **HIGHWAY 29** and the **SILVERADO TRAIL**, two parallel roads running the length of the valley. On summer weekends, the traffic on 29 slows to a standstill, so the wise traveler will look for alternatives. But even when the coast is clear for putting the pedal to the metal, *don't speed along these roads*! Local law enforcement officers have little to do other than making sure tourists aren't cruising the area after one too many sips of chardonnay.

When planning your winery visits, keep in mind that most open around 10am and close by 5pm. Some summer hours are extended, but it's a good idea to confirm open hours before you hit the road. Here's a roster of some of the Napa Valley's most popular wineries, many of which offer free tours of their facilities:

BEAULIEU VINEYARDS (1960 St. Helena Hwy, Rutherford; 800/373-5896; www.bvwines.com). Nicknamed "BV," this winery housed in a historic estate is the third-oldest continuously operating winery in Napa Valley and is famous for its cabernet sauvignon. Tastings cost $15.

BERINGER VINEYARDS (2000 Main St, St. Helena; 707/967-4412; www.beringer.com). The Napa Valley's oldest continuously operating winery features a stately old Rhineland-style mansion and good tours of the vineyards and caves. It's well known for its chardonnay, cabernet sauvignon, and white zinfandel. You can taste current vintages for $10 or arrange private tastings starting at $35.

CHÂTEAU MONTELENA WINERY (1429 Tubbs Ln, Calistoga; 707/942-5105; www.montelena.com). This stunning French château–style winery

NAPA VALLEY'S WINE HISTORY

Napa's famous wine region began with a bang. Mount St. Helena was once an active volcano, and its eruptions left the valley with the loamy soil in which grapes thrive. The first person to take advantage of this development was also Napa's first American settler; George Yount planted vineyards in 1838 and shared the fruits of his labor with other thirsty pioneers.

By the latter half of the 19th century, European immigrants began making their mark, establishing a wine industry in the valley. Many of their names can still be seen on today's vintages: Charles Krug (**CHARLES KRUG WINERY**); Jacob Schram (**SCHRAMSBERG VINEYARDS**); Gustave Niebaum (**NIEBAUM-COPPOLA ESTATE WINERY**); and Frederick and Jacob Beringer (**BERINGER VINEYARDS**).

By the 1890s the industry was thriving, with more than 140 wineries in operation, when disaster struck in the form of phylloxera, a louse that destroys the grapes' roots. (A hundred years later, phylloxera would strike again—forcing grape growers to replant the majority of their vineyards.) In 1919, a plague more deadly than any parasite finished off Napa's wine industry: Prohibition. Only a handful of wineries survived—by making blessed sacramental altar wine.

is built of stone and is celebrated for its chardonnay. The beautiful setting includes a lake with two islands and wonderful gazebos. Tastings will set you back $15.

CLIFF LEDE VINEYARDS (1473 Yountville Cross Rd, Yountville; 800/428-2259; www.cliffledevineyards.com). Previously S. Anderson, the new owners changed the name on the marquee, but they still produce both sparkling and still wines. They charge $20 for a flight of three wines.

CLOS PEGASE (1060 Dunaweal Ln, Calistoga; 707/942-4981; www.clospegase.com). Designed by architect Michael Graves, this stunning, modern facility offers grand outdoor sculpture, a "Wine in Art" slide show, and good guided tours of the winery, caves, and art collection. You can taste four wines for $15 here.

DOMAINE CHANDON (1 California Dr, Yountville; 707/944-2280; www.chandon.com). Excellent sparkling wines as well as chardonnay, pinot noir, and its rustic cousin pinot meunier (pronounced muh-NYAY) come from this winery's handsome building and its stunning landscaped grounds. There's a four-star dining room (Étoile Restaurant), fantastic guided tours, and a "salon" where you can sip bubbly ($16 per glass) and order snacks inside or on the terrace.

THE HESS COLLECTION WINERY (4411 Redwood Rd, Napa; 707/255-1144; www.hesscollection.com). A stone winery in a remote and scenic mountainside location, the Hess Collection is well known for its cabernet sauvignon and chardonnay. But art lovers are equally smitten with the

By 1960, only 25 wineries remained in Napa Valley. Instead of grapes, the sleepy farming community raised cattle, walnuts, and prunes. But the next three decades would witness an amazing resurrection of Napa's wine industry.

Through a dedication to quality, a handful of winemakers gradually began to elevate the stature of Napa's wines, attracting international attention. Still, California vintages were always considered second-rate to France until a landmark event occurred in 1976, known as the Paris Tasting. Organized to coincide with the American Bicentennial, the blind tasting was held in Paris, with French judges. And to every Napa Valleyite's joy and amazement, Napa Valley wines won—in both the white and red categories. The French judges cried foul and demanded to see their tasting notes again. But when they dried their eyes, the facts remained: a Château Montelana chardonnay and a Stag's Leap cabernet sauvignon had beaten all the grand crus from France. *Time* magazine immediately dispatched a team of journalists to Napa to cover the story, and winemakers and oenophiles alike headed to the valley to find out what all the fuss was about. Today the region boasts more than 280 wineries, and no one is surprised anymore when Napa vintages garner international awards.

Contemporary American and European art gallery showcased in a dramatic building, part of an informative self-guided tour. Tastings are $10.

MERRYVALE VINEYARDS (1000 Main St, St. Helena; 707/963-2225; www.merryvale.com). Merryvale's romantic, historic stone winery offers daily tastings for a small fee and (by appointment only) informative, thorough tasting classes on Saturday and Sunday mornings. The winery is best known for its cabernet, but it's got loads of other tasty varietals to sample, too.

OPUS ONE (7900 St. Helena Hwy, Oakville; 707/944-9442; www.opusonewinery.com). Robert Mondavi started this extraordinary venture in collaboration with France's Baron Rothschild. In a dramatic bermed (earth-sheltered) neoclassical building, tours and expensive wine tastings ($30 for a 4-ounce glass) are offered by appointment.

ROBERT MONDAVI WINERY (7801 St. Helena Hwy, Oakville; 888/766-6328; www.robertmondaviwinery.com). This huge, world-famous winery, housed in a mission-style building, offers $25 tastings, excellent tours of the facilities and specialty tours, a famous cooking school, and numerous special events.

RUBICON ESTATE WINERY (1991 St. Helena Hwy, Rutherford; 800/782-4266; www.rubiconestate.com). Filmmaker Francis Ford Coppola now owns the former Inglenook grand château, built in the 1880s. The stunning estate and winery features displays on Coppola's film career and Inglenook's history, plus an enormous gift shop stocked with wine, books, gourmet foods, and even Coppola's favorite cigars. Daily wine tastings are $25; tours of the extensive grounds are included in the fee and are first come, first served.

SCHRAMSBERG VINEYARDS (1400 Schramsberg Rd, Calistoga; 707/942-6668; www.schramsberg.com). Schramsberg's first-rate sparkling wines are showcased in attractive, historic facilities and extensive caves. Enchanting $35 guided tours are available by appointment.

STERLING VINEYARDS (1111 Dunaweal Ln, Calistoga; 707/942-3300; www.sterlingvineyards.com). Sterling offers an excellent self-guided tour through its sleek, white Mediterranean-style complex perched on a hill. Access is via an agonizingly short aerial tramway ($20, including a tasting of five wines) offering splendid views, and there's a vast room with panoramic vistas of the surrounding countryside.

Napa

At the southernmost end of Napa Valley is the sprawling part-pretty, part-industrial city of Napa, where about half of the county's 130,000-plus residents live. Although its name is synonymous with wine, most of the valley's wineries are actually several miles north of town. Though most tourists previously zoomed past the city for the more pastoral Wine Country towns to the north, Napa—founded in 1848 and boasting stunning Victorian structures—is coming into its own. Thanks to ridiculous housing prices to the south, ongoing restorations, and new restaurants and attractions, downtown Napa is getting hot, hot, hot and offers plenty of reasons to pull off the highway before heading north.

After a glorious restoration, the **NAPA VALLEY OPERA HOUSE** (1030 Main St; 707/226-7372; www.nvoh.org), where Jack London once gave readings, reopened in 2003 with its first performance since 1914. The principal theater in the 116-year-old structure is known as the Margrit Biever Mondavi Theater because of the winemaking family's restoration leadership. Nearby, the riverfront historic **HATT BUILDING** (500 Main St; 877/251-8500) features a boutique hotel, shops, restaurants, and an adorable bakery.

For the traffic-weary traveler, downtown Napa provides a base from which a plethora of Victorian bed-and-breakfasts, restaurants, and attractions can all be accessed on foot. Lodging reservations and walking tour maps are available through the **NAPA VALLEY CONFERENCE AND VISITORS BUREAU** (1310 Napa Town Ctr, Napa; 707/226-7459; www.napavalley.com). For a break from seeing the sights, stop at **ABC BAKING COMPANY** (1517 3rd St; 707/258-1827) and enjoy goodies like espresso, killer breakfasts, sandwiches, and chocolate-caramel cake. Or browse the large selection of books on the Wine Country at **COPPERFIELD'S** (3900A Bel Aire Plaza; 707/252-8002), then walk down to **NAPA VALLEY ROASTING COMPANY** (948 Main St; 707/224-2233) to read your selections over a latte. Around the corner drop into **BOUNTY HUNTER RARE WINE AND PROVISIONS** (975 1st St; 707/255-0622; www.bountyhunterwine.com), a sleek and sexy place to saddle up to the sophisticated Western-inspired bar, sip or buy wines, and snack on gourmet appetizers any time of day or late into the evening.

RESTAURANTS

Angèle / ★★½

540 MAIN ST, NAPA; 707/252-8115

Pronounced AHN-zhel, this family effort by Claude Rouas (Auberge du Soleil and Piatti founder) and daughters Bettina and Claudia is a wonderful combination of truly captivating surroundings and cozy and classic French country cuisine. It's the wood beam ceiling, candlelight, sleek bar, and heated riverfront patio seating that set the stage. Then the ovation-worthy performance begins with attentive service, decadent oxtail and lentil salad with tangy ravigote dressing, steamed mussels in braised fennel broth, and the town's best gourmet hamburger, and ends with finales of sorbet and coffee pot de crème. Despite the chic environs, kids are welcomed and accommodated here, which—along with yummy French fries—is one reason wine industry heavyweights make this the spot for family night out. *$$; AE, MC, V; local checks only; lunch, dinner every day; full bar; reservations recommended; www.angelerestaurant.com; at the Napa River.*

Bistro Don Giovanni / ★★★

4110 ST. HELENA HWY, NAPA; 707/224-3300

An absolute favorite for locals, Bistro Don Giovanni manages to be all things to all people. The bar is a preferred perch for gathering and chatting over a glass of wine or a complete dinner. The bright dining room is comfortable and bustling, and the heated patio overlooking a fountain and vineyards is perfect year-round. Donna and Giovanni Scala are the masterminds behind the perfectly al dente pasta (try it with rich duck ragout); superb thin-crust pizzas with exotic toppings like fig, prosciutto, and balsamic; and the beet and haricot vert salad, which is as vibrant as it is flavorful. Meat dishes are also fantastic. The wine list, although skewed toward expensive California vintages, is extensive and imaginative, and dessert beckons with such offerings as watermelon granita and textbook tiramisu. *$$; AE, DC, DIS, MC, V; local checks only; lunch, dinner every day; full bar; reservations recommended; www.bistrodongiovanni.com; on Hwy 29, just north of Salvador Ave.*

Cole's Chop House / ★★

1122 MAIN ST, NAPA; 707/224-6328

Some may have considered opening an expensive American steak house in predominantly blue-collar Napa a raw idea, but from the beginning owner Greg Cole has welcomed brisk business to this bright, airy restored historic building, built in 1886. Apparently meat lovers don't hesitate to pay around $30 for aged steak without accompaniments served in downtown's most upscale environment. Whether you mosey up to the bar, dine alfresco on the charming courtyard patio, or soak in the old-meets-new ambience of stone walls, hardwood floors, cushy booths, and beamed ceilings, you need not stick with steak: additional menu classics include a tangy Caesar salad, rich oysters Rockefeller, veal, lamb, and a few vegetarian dishes thrown in for modern measure. Old-school side dishes, such as creamed spinach, are ordered à la carte, the wine list emphasizes expensive reds, and a city-smart cocktail menu rounds out the retro drinking and dining options. *$$$; AE, DC, MC, V; local checks only; dinner Tues–Sun; full bar; reservations recommended; www.coleschophouse.com; behind the big pink movie theater on Soscol Ave, just north of 1st St.* ♿

Foothill Café / ★★★

2766 OLD SONOMA RD, NAPA; 707/257-2270

This hidden gem is favored by locals who know to turn off the main streets and into the eastern Napa neighborhood for great food at amazingly low prices. Despite the ongoing attention to chef-owner Jerry Shaffer's (of San Francisco's Masa's and St. Helena's original Miramonte) American restaurant, the space maintains its sense of whimsy; even decorative items, such as wrought-iron artwork by a local artist, are fanciful. Virtually anything from the big oak oven is a sure thing. Dessert favorites include classic vanilla-bean and Cognac crème brûlée. Like the rest of the menu items, wines are affordably priced. *$$; AE, MC, V; local checks only; dinner Wed–Sun; beer and wine; reservations recommended; from Hwy 29 go west on Imola Ave, right at Foster Rd, left on Old Sonoma Rd; in J&P Center.* ♿

Pearl / ★★

1339 PEARL ST, STE 104, NAPA; 707/224-9161

This homey establishment is a favorite with locals, mainly because it's been one of the few places in town where you can count on friendly—albeit woefully slow—service and consistently good fare. Owners Nickie and Pete Zeller divide duties; Nickie presides over the kitchen, and Pete runs the front of the house. The menu offers something for all tastes and budgets, running the gamut from an array of raw and prepared oyster appetizers to goat cheese pizzas to an Asian-inspired ahi tuna sandwich with red cabbage coleslaw to a hearty triple pork chop with mashed potatoes. Pearl is located in a terra-cotta-colored stucco building, with a cute patio on the street and live music on the patio on summer weekends. *$$; MC, V; local checks only; lunch, dinner Tues–Sat; beer and wine; reservations recommended; www.therestaurantpearl.com; at Franklin.*

Villa Corona / ★

3614 BEL AIRE PLAZA, NAPA; 707/257-8685

This low-key Mexican restaurant in a mall serves such clean, delicious, authentic cuisine that local chefs come here on days off. Stand in line, order from the counter, grab a number, and settle down at one of the tables amid brightly colored walls or at one of the few patio tables outside. After a short wait, huge plates will come your way. Classic burritos—especially pork *carnitas*—are outstanding; the homemade corn tortillas and delicious red sauce make the tacos and enchiladas other favorites. Prawns are flavor-packed with

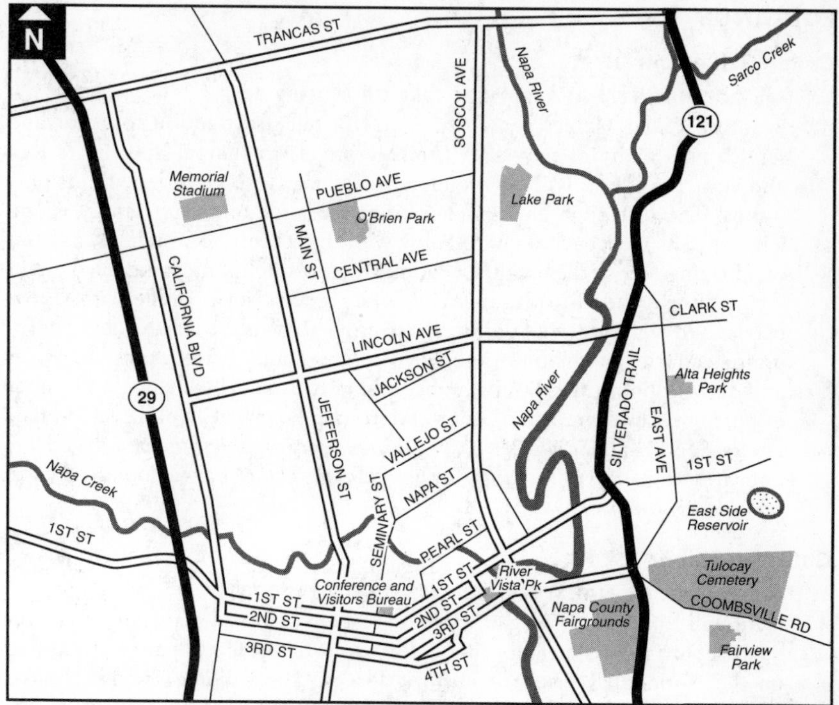

Napa

garlic butter or spicy hot sauce, and all the usual suspects—chimichangas, chiles rellenos, tamales, tostadas—are just as good. Breakfast includes *chilaquiles* (scrambled eggs with tortilla strips and salsa), huevos rancheros, and *machaca* (eggs and roasted pork scramble). *$; MC, V; no checks; breakfast, lunch, dinner Tues–Sun; beer and wine; no reservations; off Trancas St hidden in the southeast corner of the mall.*

Zuzu / ★★★

829 MAIN ST, NAPA; 707/224-8555

Downtown Napa's favorite neighborhood restaurant is this comfy, rustic-chic, come-as-you-are joint serving tapas and tasty wines at great prices. A no-reservation policy means you might have to wait for a table in the small downstairs dining room, along the compact wine bar, or upstairs in the quieter loft. But chef Angela Tamura's Moroccan barbecued lamb chops with a sweet-spicy sauce; tangy paella topped with braised meats, shellfish, and a dollop of aioli; and apple empanadas are worth it—especially when practically every dish is less than $10 and comes with convivial atmosphere, an eclectic wine list, and a good time that often costs three times the price in these parts. *$; AE, MC, V; no checks; lunch Mon–Fri, dinner every day; beer and wine; no reservations; www.zuzunapa.com; at Third St.*

LODGINGS

Cedar Gables Inn / ★★

486 COOMBS ST, NAPA; 707/224-7969 OR 800/309-7969

Beautiful Cedar Gables may be a B and B, but its attention to decor and service puts many of the valley's upscale hotels to shame. Innkeepers Ken and Susie Pope have worked wonders with their 1892 Victorian and its nine rooms. The historic theme extends from the large and cozy family room, where guests meet each night to enjoy wine and cheese or watch TV in front of a blazing fire, to the breakfast room, where a full hot morning meal might include homemade breads, in-season fruit, French toast soufflé with strawberries and walnuts, or a Southwest casserole. Rooms are lavishly and appropriately adorned with tapestries, gilded antiques, and in five rooms, fireplaces and/or whirlpool tubs. Bonuses uncommon to B and Bs include a decanter of port in each room, robes, irons and ironing boards, CD players, and hair dryers. *$$$; AE, DIS, MC, V; checks OK; www.cedargablesinn.com; from Hwy 29 exit onto 1st St, follow signs to downtown, turn right on Coombs St, and proceed to corner of Oak St.*

Churchill Manor / ★★

485 BROWN ST, NAPA; 707/253-7733 OR 800/799-7733

Churchill Manor is an elegant, meticulously maintained mansion, incongruously set in a modest neighborhood. Built in 1889 by a local banker, it is listed on the National Register of Historic Places. The Colonial Revival house, which rises three stories above an expanse of beautiful gardens, is graced by stately pillars and a large, inviting veranda. Each of the 10 immaculate guest rooms features antique furnishings, ultraplush carpeting, a fireplace, and an elegant private bath; the king rooms have two-person soaking tubs and separate showers. Rates include a full breakfast served in the marble-floored sunroom, fresh-baked cookies and coffee or tea in the afternoon, and a wine-and-cheese reception in the evening. When you're not out touring the local wineries, you may tickle the ivories of the grand piano in the parlor, play croquet on the lovely side lawn, or tour Old Town Napa on the inn's tandem bicycles. *$$; AE, DIS, MC, V; checks OK; www.churchillmanor.com; at Oak St.*

La Résidence Country Inn / ★★

4066 ST. HELENA HWY, NAPA; 707/253-0337

Set back in the trees along busy Highway 29, this multimillion-dollar inn has 25 guest rooms scattered throughout three buildings separated by a heated swimming pool and an elaborate gazebo. The main house, a Gothic Revival mansion built in 1870 by a former New Orleans riverboat captain, contains nine comfortable guest rooms beautifully decorated with designer fabrics and American antiques. Most have sitting rooms and fireplaces; all have CD players and private baths. Airier accommodations can be found in the modern French-style barn across the plaza. Filled with simple pine antiques, these spacious rooms have fireplaces, private baths, and French doors that open onto small patios or balconies. The most recent addition is the Cellar House, where three suite-type rooms have king-size beds, cable TVs, fireplaces, and wet bars. A delicious gourmet breakfast is served downstairs in the barn in a cheery, sunny dining room. Although La Résidence is undeniably one of the region's loveliest small inns, its location next to the highway detracts from the away-from-it-all feel that B and Bs usually try to cultivate. *$$$$; AE, DC, DIS, MC, V; no checks; www.laresidence.com; on Hwy 29, next to Bistro Don Giovanni.*

Silverado Resort / ★★

1600 ATLAS PEAK RD, NAPA; 707/257-0200

Golfers and tennis players flock to this 1,200-acre estate, and it's easy to see why. The Silverado boasts two perfectly maintained 18-hole golf courses designed by Robert Trent Jones Jr. and the largest tennis complex in North America, with 17 championship courts. If you're not into golf or tennis, however, there's little reason to stay here; the 280 unprepossessing rooms seem to have been designed for people who don't plan to spend much time indoors. The standard rooms are individually decorated in a condolike warren. One- and two-bedroom suites overlooking the golf course are prettier but tend to be equally soulless. A few minutes' drive from the main complex are the more secluded Oak Creek East accommodations, street after street of mind-numbingly similar houses and condominiums owned by country-club members and rented out to guests. Numerous swimming pools dot the extensive grounds—popular spots to cool off on the valley's sweltering summer days. The resort's clubhouse and restaurants are located in the magnificent colonnaded Southern Gothic mansion at the heart of the main complex. Vintners Court, a formal dining room dominated by a glittering chandelier and a white grand piano, is open only on Friday nights for a seafood buffet. The fancy Royal Oak serves steak and seafood nightly. For a more casual meal, order a club sandwich or a hamburger at the Silverado Bar & Grill. Though the restaurants are unmemorable, the property's full-service spa is definitely worth visiting. *$$$$; AE, DC, DIS, MC, V; checks OK; www.silveradoresort.com; from Hwy 29, turn right onto Trancas St (Trancas St will become Hwy 121), then turn left onto Atlas Peak Rd.*

Yountville

Given that the commercial hub is about three blocks long, sleepy little Yountville, located 9 miles north of Napa off Highway 29 and founded in the mid-19th century by pioneer George Clavert Yount (reportedly the first American to settle in Napa Valley), has developed quite a reputation as a top-notch destination. The hullabaloo began with **THE FRENCH LAUNDRY** (see review), which has been touted as the best restaurant in the United States—and the most impossible to get into. But on the heels of its success came two glorious

French bistros, **BOUCHON** and **BISTRO JEANTY** (see reviews); a handful of expensive inns; more foot traffic to the small collection of boutiques; and the destination eatery **BOUCHON BAKERY** (6528 Washington St; 707/944-BAKE), famed chef Thomas Keller's takeout spot selling stunning fresh-from-the-oven French breads, sandwiches, and pastries.

RESTAURANTS

Bistro Jeanty / ★★★

6510 WASHINGTON ST, YOUNTVILLE; 707/944-0103

Philippe Jeanty was a culinary pioneer in Napa. He came from France to head Domaine Chandon's now-legendary kitchen back when the region was known more for cattle and prunes than for four-star wines. After 20 years at Chandon, he left to open his own place in Yountville, and it's been a success ever since, with the James Beard Foundation nominating Jeanty for his ingenuity more than once. Bistro Jeanty represents the rare perfect marriage of setting and cuisine, perhaps because Jeanty designed the whole thing himself, modeled on the small French bistros from his childhood. The details are flawless—from the window boxes with geraniums outside to the antiques and specials chalkboard inside. A large "community table" by the front door seats the diners without partners or reservations and is a favorite of locals who drop by. The food remains true to Jeanty's heritage: lamb tongue salad, haricots verts, sole meunière, steak tartare, and a dreamy coq au vin—all well followed by a sinfully luxurious crème brûlée, which includes a surprise layer of chocolate mousse. *$$$; MC, V; no checks; lunch, dinner every day; full bar; reservations recommended; www.bistrojeanty.com; at Mulberry St.*

Bouchon / ★★☆

6534 WASHINGTON ST, YOUNTVILLE; 707/944-8037

Thomas Keller opened this small bistro to handle the overflow business from the French Laundry and as a late-night gathering place for the valley. Bouchon looks like a miniature Paris bistro—one with such a sophisticated, elegant atmosphere that you immediately feel stylish simply by walking through the door. A zinc bar is put to good use serving raw seafood specialties such as oysters, mussels, and langoustines. The fare is traditional bistro français: foie gras, quiche du jour, charcuterie, onion soup gratin, steak *frites*, mussels marinières, and for dessert, tarte Tatin and profiteroles with ice cream and chocolate sauce. Don't miss the French fries—they're the best in the valley—or the pristine and oh-so-pretty butter lettuce salad. The short menu of appetizers, entrées, and desserts served until 12:45am daily lures the post-work restaurant crowd. *$$$; AE, MC, V; local checks only; lunch, dinner every day; full bar; reservations recommended; www.bouchonbistro.com; across from the Vintage 1870 shopping center.*

The French Laundry / ★★★★

6640 WASHINGTON ST, YOUNTVILLE; 707/944-2380

A serious dining affair awaits those who are fortunate (or persistent) enough to snare a reservation at the French Laundry, the top-ranked restaurant in the country. Draped in ivy, surrounded by herb gardens, and bearing the most incognito sign announcing its purpose, the discreet restaurant is occupied by brilliant chef Thomas Keller, who designs unbelievably intricate meals accompanied by stellar wines, and faultless (and, yes, formal) service. Here it's all about edible artistry and everything is coddled, sculpted, ornamented, and coaxed to beyond perfection. The prix-fixe tasting menu—always lavish, extraordinary, and very precious—offers a choice of five or nine courses that change daily and invariably are accompanied by more than one amuse-bouche. Think rich scrambled duck eggs with truffle sauce; a velvety sabayon of pearl tapioca with Bagaduce oysters and osetra caviar; fresh fava bean agnolotti with roasted abalone mushrooms and Madras curry emulsion; perfectly grilled prime beef with shiitake mushrooms; and to-die-for butterscotch pot de crème. There's also a multicourse lunch, which is best enjoyed on the patio. Reservations are accepted up to two months in advance. Good luck getting through to a receptionist, though. *$$$$; AE, MC, V; local checks only; lunch Fri–Sun, dinner every day; beer and wine; reservations required; www.frenchlaundry.com; at Creek St.*

Mustards Grill / ★★☆

7399 ST. HELENA HWY, YOUNTVILLE; 707/944-2424

Some critics call Mustards' feisty American regional cuisine comfort food, but that's too complacent a description for the vigorous, spicy, vaguely Asian-influenced bistro fare served here. Chef Cindy Pawlcyn's popular restaurant keeps it casual with a big open kitchen, white walls, dark wood wainscoting, and a black-and-white checkerboard floor. Appetizers range from seared ahi with wasabi cream and sesame crackers to Caesar salad with Parmesan croutons. The menu changes frequently but might include tea-smoked Peking duck with almond-onion sauce, lemon and garlic chicken with garlic mashed potatoes, and chipotle-rubbed quail with wild mushroom tamale and jicama-radish slaw. *$$; AE, DC, MC, V; no checks; lunch, dinner every day; full bar; reservations recommended; www.mustardsgrill.com; south of the Vintage 1870 shopping center.* ♿

LODGINGS

Maison Fleurie / ★★

6529 YOUNT ST, YOUNTVILLE; 707/944-2056 OR 800/788-0369

Built in 1873, this beautiful, ivy-covered brick-and-fieldstone hotel was a bordello and later a 4-H clubhouse before it opened in 1971 as the Napa Valley's first bed-and-breakfast inn. Purchased by the owners of the Four Sisters Inns company (who also run the charming Petite Auberge in San Francisco and Pacific Grove's Gosbey House), the old Magnolia Hotel was reborn as Maison

Fleurie in 1994 and endowed with a French country feel. Seven of the guest rooms are located in the main house, with its thick brick walls, terra-cotta tiles, and vineyard views; the remaining six are divided between the old bakery building and the carriage house. All have private baths, and some feature fireplaces, private balconies, sitting areas, and patios. After a long day of wine tasting, unwind at the pool or soak your tired dogs in the outdoor spa tub. The inn also provides bicycles for tooling around town. *$$$; AE, MC, V; no checks; www.maisonfleurienapa.com; at Washington St.*

Villagio Inn & Spa / ★★★★

6481 WASHINGTON ST, YOUNTVILLE; 800/351-1133

The Villagio is the place to treat yourself to the full five-star experience (and have the dough to afford it). With a Tuscan-style ambience, Villagio runs like one sophisticated, well-oiled machine—from the check-in to the service to the food preparation. The 112 rooms are divided into four types: perimeter courtyard, interior courtyard, one-bedroom minisuites, and suites with connecting rooms. Each guest room is quite spacious with perks like a refrigerator (complete with free bottle of wine), Molton Brown bath products, a fireplace, an oversize sunken tub, a flat-screen TV, and a set of spa robes. The complimentary breakfast spread and afternoon champagne buffet are a real treat, and should you need a more substantial meal, the inn is within short walking distance of more Michelin Star restaurants than you can count on one hand. And the whole experience just got a little bit sweeter thanks to the 2008 addition of a 13,000-square-foot terra-cotta-tiled spa, with 16 treatment rooms in separate men's and women's wings. Any of the additional five luxury spa suites will make you want to call Villagio home, with their fireplaces, daybeds, steam showers, and private outdoor terraces and jet tubs. Midweek room prices can be as much as 50 percent of the weekend cost, so if money's an issue, try for non-peak times and you might just get lucky. *$$$$; AE, DIS, MC, V; no checks; www.villagio.com; downtown.*

Vintage Inn / ★★

6541 WASHINGTON ST, YOUNTVILLE; 707/944-1112 OR 800/351-1133

Spread throughout a 23-acre estate, the Vintage Inn provides the Napa Valley traveler with a host of creature comforts in a modern setting. The 80 large, cheery rooms, bathed in soothing earth tones and wood accents, are all equipped with fireplaces, Jacuzzi tubs, refrigerators, patios or verandas, ceiling fans, and plush private baths. Guests may take a dip in the heated pool or outdoor spa, play a game of tennis, order room service, sip a spirit at the bar, or rent the inn's bikes or private limo for a tour of the Wine Country. You'll also be treated to complimentary wine on arrival, a buffet breakfast served with glasses of bubbly, afternoon tea, and access to the heated outdoor pool and hot tub, and spa services at their sister property Villagio Inn & Spa (see review), located down the block. *$$$$; AE, DC, DIS, MC, V; no checks; www.vintageinn.com; just east of Hwy 29.*

Oakville

Other than several world-class wineries, Oakville's main claim to fame is the **OAKVILLE GROCERY CO.** (7856 St. Helena Hwy, at Oakville Cross Rd; 707/944-8802; www.oakvillegrocery.com), a local icon and old-fashioned country market complete with a fading Drink Coca-Cola sign outside. It's not a scene for the claustrophobic; any given noontime will find this homey establishment clogged with tourists lined up to buy gourmet deli treats. But those who brave the scene will find a fine variety of local wines, a small espresso bar tucked in the corner, and pricey but delicious picnic supplies ranging from pâté and caviar to sliced-turkey sandwiches and freshly made sweets.

Rutherford

RESTAURANTS

Rutherford Grille / ★★★

1180 RUTHERFORD RD, RUTHERFORD; 707/963-1792

This Southwestern-style restaurant has long been a favorite for everyone from bikers to billionaires, boasting both indoor and outdoor seating (with heat lamps for cool evenings). The menu is a strange amalgamation of dishes—deviled eggs for appetizers, bangers and mash or fajitas and lamb for entrées—but oddly enough, it works. The chef uses mostly locally grown or made products, and the restaurant even has a garden where it extracts mint for mojitos, and arugula and tomatoes for other fare. The colcannon potatoes—which incorporate sautéed cabbage and green onions and are topped with parsley and extra-virgin olive oil—are spectacular, and other specialties include rotisserie chicken, grilled ostrich medallions, and a steak and enchilada platter. Strawberry shortcake, Oreo cookie ice cream sandwich, and raspberry apple crisp à la mode round out the dessert menu. Pet friendly, Rutherford Grill allows guests to bring their dogs while dining alfresco. Although wine is clearly the drink of choice (and cheap by Napa Valley standards, especially since you can bring your own for no cork fee), the grill is particularly good at cocktail mixology. There is often a long line for seating, so be prepared to either wait or arrive early. *$$–$$$; AE, MC, V; no checks; lunch, dinner every day; full bar; reservations recommended; www.hillstone.com; at Hwy 29.* ♿

LODGINGS

Auberge du Soleil / ★★★★

180 RUTHERFORD HILL RD, RUTHERFORD; 707/963-1211 OR 800/348-5406

The exclusive 33-acre, 50-unit resort, inspired by the sunny architecture of southern France, is nestled in an olive grove on a wooded hillside above the

Napa Valley. Here it's all about exclusivity in the form of cottages and suites you could get lost in, complete with rough-textured adobe-style walls, white French doors and windows, and shocking pink textiles that are whimsical upon first encounter and old hat by the second or third visit. Each cottage has four guest rooms. Suites have very private entrances and patios or balconies. Upstairs rooms, which boast vaulted, exposed-beam ceilings, are particularly posh, but even the humblest accommodations are sinfully hedonistic, with fireplaces, CD players, original artwork, comfortable furnishings, candles, sitting areas, tiled floors, and to-die-for bathrooms. Two rooms lack fireplaces but have king-size beds and French doors that open onto private terraces. Tack on the pool, the valley's best spa, a gym, and the restaurant serving excellent Wine Country cuisine (go for terrace seating!), and there's little reason to leave. *$$$$; AE, DIS, MC, V; checks OK; www.aubergedusoleil.com; north of Yountville—from the Silverado Trail, turn right on Rutherford Hill Rd.*

Rancho Caymus Inn / ★★★

1140 RUTHERFORD RD, RUTHERFORD; 707/963-1777 OR 800/845-1777

With adobe walls, wood-burning fireplaces, wood floors, and Native American–style fabrics, Rancho Caymus Inn looks like it was transported from a Southwestern ranch to Northern California's Wine Country. An attractive dual-level inn with 26 rooms, it was named for the Kaimus tribe that once inhabited the land. Rooms have shaded terraces, wet bars, telephones, TVs, hair dryers, and coffeemakers. The sleeping area is set apart from the sitting room by two stairs and railing, giving the feeling that you're staying in a house and not a mere hotel room. Most everything in the bathroom—floor, shower walls, sink—is lined with pretty glazed terra-cotta tiles. A basic complimentary continental breakfast is served at the on-site restaurant, La Toque. One downside: there is no Internet access, but if you're on vacation, maybe it's a good idea to step away from the computer in the first place. *$$–$$$; AE, MC, V; no checks; www.ranchocaymus.com; just off Hwy 29.* ♿

St. Helena

For many years St. Helena has been entrenched in a never-ending battle to preserve its exclusive, small-town way of life—instead of becoming one more tourist haven for Wine Country visitors. Citizens have filed injunctions against everything from the Napa Valley Wine Train (forbidding it to stop in town) to Safeway (the grocery giant wanted to build a supermarket larger than the one that already exists). Needless to say, Wal-Mart was out of the question. As a result, **MAIN STREET** has retained its Victorian Old West feel and historic structures like **STEVE'S HARDWARE** (1370 Main St; 707/963-3423).

Just off the main drag you can find more down-home pleasures at the **NAPA VALLEY OLIVE OIL MANUFACTURING COMPANY** (835 Charter Oak Ave; 707/963-4173), an authentic and ramshackle Italian deli and general store stuffed to the rafters with goodies like dried fava beans, biscotti, salami, and fresh mozzarella. For great gifts, be sure to pick up a bottle or two of the top-notch extra-virgin olive oil or the olive oil soap. Just south of town, the New York gourmet superstore **DEAN & DELUCA** (607 S St. Helena Hwy; 707/967-9980; www.deandeluca.com) sells a mind-boggling array of cheeses, wines, deli items, specialty foods, and cookware.

An excellent way to rub elbows with locals and find great edibles is to attend the **ST. HELENA FARMERS MARKET** (Crane Park, off Hwy 29, east on Sulphur Springs Ave, right on Crane Ave; 707/486-2662), held 7:30am to noon every Friday from May through October. For a picnic, take your treats to **LYMAN PARK** (on Main St between Adams and Pine) and sit on the grass or in the beautiful little white gazebo where bands sometimes perform summer concerts. A more bucolic picnic spot is **BALE GRIST MILL STATE HISTORIC PARK** (Hwy 29, 3 miles north of St. Helena).

RESTAURANTS

Martini House / ★★★★

1245 SPRING ST, ST. HELENA; 707/963-2233

Well, Pat Kuleto has done it again: he's created a restaurant in the far reaches of Wine Country that entices people to drive for miles just to see what all the fuss is about. And it's well worth the trip. The restaurant captures the best bits of the area, from antique pieces to Native American artifacts, such as the woven baskets on display throughout the establishment. Kuleto recruits some of the Bay Area's best chefs to man his kitchens, as he managed to do in this case, bringing in executive chef and co-owner Todd Humphries from San Francisco's popular Campton Place. Start with one of his creamy soups, like the asparagus or carrot and ginger, followed by a butter-poached lobster tail with artichokes, pearl onions, and crispy potatoes. Top it off with chocolate custard cake with espresso mascarpone and salted caramel ganache. Three different prix-fixe choices are available, including the chef's market, the mushroom menu, and the chef's tasting menu, with wine pairings optional (though the cocktails are quite delightful, too). *$$$; AE, DC, MC, V; no checks; lunch Fri–Sun, dinner every day; full bar; reservations recommended; www.martinihouse.com; at Oak St.* ♿

Taylor's Automatic Refresher / ★★

933 MAIN ST, ST. HELENA; 707/963-3486

Anyone who knows how tiresome fancy food can get might understand why Taylor's Refresher, a classic burger stand straight out of the 1950s, is a favorite among even the region's top chefs and the nation's best-regarded food editors. Sure, the 1949-built outdoor diner is a looker, with its yesteryear fast-food-shack design and outdoor seating. But more important, it doles out some darned good burgers—juicy, thick, and served with all the toppings. Wine Country living doesn't get much better than a patty smothered with cheese, accompanied by fries and a creamy shake or fizzy root beer float—or

ROBERT LOUIS STEVENSON'S TIME IN NAPA

The Scottish author Robert Louis Stevenson came to California in search of Fanny, a married woman 10 years his senior whom he'd met and fallen in love with in France. By the time he arrived by ship in San Francisco, he was half dead from bronchitis, his condition worsening as he waited for Fanny to obtain a divorce. By then he was penniless and critically ill.

The couple married in May 1880 and, in an attempt to restore the groom's health, spent their last $10 on a honeymoon cabin at a hot springs resort in Calistoga—a region even then famed for its restorative powers. With their money gone, they spent the summer in the old bunkhouse of an abandoned silver mine on Mount St. Helena. Their neighbors were grizzly bears, mountain lions, and rattlesnakes.

Dry weather and sunshine did, in fact, restore Stevenson's health. He describes his adopted home in a memoir, *Silverado Squatters:*

The house, after we had repaired the worst of the damages, and filled in some of the doors and windows with white cotton cloth, became a healthy and a pleasant dwelling-place, always airy and dry, and haunted by the outdoor perfumes of the glen. Within, it had the look of habitation, the human look . . . . And yet our house was everywhere so wrecked and shattered, the air came and went so freely, the

a nice glass of wine. Those who beg to differ can always belly up for a good old-fashioned corn dog; steak, fish, or chicken taco; or veggie burger. *$; AE, MC, V; local checks only; lunch, dinner every day; beer and wine; no reservations; www.taylorsrefresher.com; right on the highway, you can't miss it.* ♿

Terra / ★★★★

1345 RAILROAD AVE, ST. HELENA; 707/963-8931

If you can have only one dinner out while visiting Napa Valley, have it at Terra. Housed in a historic stone building with high ceilings and arched windows, Terra's subdued dining rooms have an ineffable sense of intimacy about them. Fervid tête-à-têtes, however, are more likely to revolve around Terra's fine southern French–northern Italian food than around amore. Yet this isn't the sort of food that screams to be noticed; chef Hiro Sone, who won the James Beard Foundation's Best California Chef award in 2003, creates incredible food that never grandstands. Though the menu changes with the seasons, tried-and-true standbys include fried rock shrimp with organic greens and chive mustard sauce; broiled sake-marinated rock cod with shrimp dumplings; spaghettini with tripe, tomato, and butter beans; and grilled, dry-aged New York strip steak with sautéed vegetables and anchovy garlic sauce. Sone's wife and business partner, Lissa Doumani, is behind the outstanding desserts, which *sun found so many portholes, the golden outdoor glow shone in so many open chinks, that we enjoyed, at the same time, some of the comforts of a roof and much of the gaiety and brightness of alfresco life. A single shower of rain, to be sure, and we should have been drowned out like mice. But ours was a California summer, and an earthquake was a far likelier accident than a shower of rain.*

The writer admits more than the weather was a draw to Napa: "I was interested in California wine. Indeed, I am interested in all wines, and have been all my life. . . . " To this end, he spent time with Jacob Schram, who founded **SCHRAMSBERG VINEYARDS**.

While Stevenson idled on the mountain with Fanny, his family accepted the news of his marriage. The couple returned to Scotland, where Stevenson wrote *Treasure Island*. Mount St. Helena is said to be the inspiration for Spyglass Hill.

Today, at **ROBERT LOUIS STEVENSON STATE PARK**, you can hike up rugged, solitary Mount St. Helena to the site where the newlyweds squatted; a stone monument of a book marks the spot. In St. Helena, the **SILVERADO MUSEUM** (1490 Library Ln; 707/963-3757; www.silveradomuseum.org) houses one of the world's largest collections of Stevenson memorabilia. Documentary filmmakers from Scotland have, ironically, made the pilgrimage to Napa to research one of their most distinguished native sons.

might include strawberries drenched in a cabernet-and-black-peppercorn sauce served with vanilla ice cream, or a sculptural tiramisu. Service is formal yet friendly, and the wine list highlights local producers. *$$$$; DC, MC, V; local checks only; dinner Wed–Mon; beer and wine; reservations recommended; www.terrarestaurant.com; between Adams and Hunt sts, 1 block east of Main St.*

Tra Vigne & Cantinetta / ★★½

1050 CHARTER OAK AVE, ST. HELENA; 707/963-4444 (RESTAURANT) OR 707/963-8888 (CANTINETTA)

The Italian-style courtyard dining is pure heaven, the Tuscan-inspired food is exceptionally fresh, and almost everything is made on the premises. The menu is seasonal, but you can usually find excellent fritti of fried prawns and vegetables in Arborio rice flour served with mustard vinegar, or expert wood-fired pizza specials such as a classic Margherita. Pastas run the gamut from traditional to outrageous—such as rigatoni with tomatoes, pecorino, and basil; or ravioli with eggplant, ricotta, mozzarella, tomato conserva, and warm oregano crumbs. Entrées might include grilled wild king salmon with fresh chickpeas, Blue Lake beans, and Meyer lemon sauce; roasted organic chicken breast with roasted carrots, potatoes, escarole, and garlic-lemon jus; and a savory grilled lamb sirloin with rapini and olive jus. Servers are knowledgeable, witty, and efficient. The wine list includes a carefully chosen array of Italian and Napa Valley bottles. For a lighter lunch, food to go, or wine tastings, amble over to the less-expensive Cantinetta Tra Vigne. *$$$; CB, DC, DIS, MC, V; no checks; lunch, dinner every day (restaurant); lunch every day (cantinetta); full bar; reservations recommended; www.travignerestaurant.com; off Hwy 29.*

Wine Spectator Greystone Restaurant / ★★

2555 MAIN ST, ST. HELENA; 707/967-1010

When you first spot Greystone perched high atop a hill, you'll catch your breath, as it's the closest thing to a castle you'll find in the United States. The building, which formerly housed the Christian Brothers winery, was constructed in 1889 out of local tufa stone. The restaurant is on the first floor of the Culinary Institute of America (it's named for *Wine Spectator* magazine, which donated $1 million to the school's scholarship fund), and is in a large, noisy room with a fireplace and a display kitchen surrounded by a bar. The CIA's students play an integral role in restaurant preparations that tend to trot the globe in their inspiration. Appetizers nod to the East with curried cauliflower soup with turmeric oil and bow to Spain with steamed mussels with chorizo, romesco sauce, and grilled bread. Entrées say *olé!* with fire-roasted poblano peppers stuffed with fresh corn polenta, ricotta cheese, and black bean sauce, and accentuate the local bounty with fillet of beef with original Point Reyes blue cheese, heirloom tomatoes, shoestring potatoes, and red wine sauce. The extensive wine list offers something for every taste and price range. The basement houses a decent cookware emporium, complete with great gadgets and cookbooks. *$$$$; AE, DC, MC, V; local checks only; lunch, dinner every day; full bar; reservations recommended; www.ciachef.edu; at Deer Park Rd.*

LODGINGS

El Bonita Motel / ★

195 MAIN ST, ST. HELENA; 707/963-3216 OR 800/541-3284

Thanks to an extensive remodeling, El Bonita is indeed bonita. Hand-painted grapevines grace many of the room entrances, and inside the walls are colored a faint pink, with floor-length baby blue drapes and pink-and-baby-blue floral bedspreads. Each of the 41 rooms has a private bath, cable TV, refrigerator, microwave, coffeemaker, phone, and—for a little more money—whirlpool bath. Huge oak trees surround the motel, a heated kidney-shaped swimming pool sits in front, and a sauna and an outdoor whirlpool are on the premises; massages are available by appointment. The rates vary from month to month (depending on business), but in general you (and your pet) can get a reasonably priced room. El Bonita fronts Highway 29, so try to reserve a room as far from the street as possible. *$$; AE, DC, DIS, MC, V; no checks; www.elbonita.com; just south of downtown St. Helena on Hwy 29.*

Harvest Inn / ★★☆

1 MAIN ST, ST HELENA; 707/963-9463 OR 800/950-8466

Set on 8 acres of impeccably manicured gardens, the country estate–style Harvest Inn is easily one of the classiest hotels in all of Napa Valley. You'll need the map provided at check-in just to navigate the sprawling grounds. Of the 74 suites, the Vineyard rooms are the best in the house, and all have back porches with hot tubs. All rooms are massive, with large stone fireplaces, flat-screen TVs and DVD players, luxurious beds, and spacious bathrooms that feature a spread of L'Occitane bath products. While the accommodation is top-notch, the service doesn't always follow suit: After a recent change in management, employees seem a bit disinterested in actually doing their jobs and uneducated in the amenities of the hotel—they've been known to lose reservations from time to time and misdirect guests. Still, if it's comfort you seek and couldn't care less about an attentive staff, Harvest Inn is the place for you. Included with your stay is a superb breakfast at the hotel's Wine Country Kitchen; follow it up with a dip in one of the two pools (open 24 hours). *$$$; AE, DIS, MC, V; no checks; www.harvestinn.com; on Hwy 29 at the south entrance to St. Helena.* ♿

The Ink House Bed and Breakfast / ★

1575 ST. HELENA HWY, ST. HELENA; 707/963-3890

This gorgeous Italianate Victorian inn, built in the shape of an ink bottle by Napa settler Theron Ink in 1884, would merit three stars if it weren't for its no-star location along a busy, noisy stretch of Highway 29. The three-story yellow-and-white home has seven sumptuously decorated guest rooms, plus a lavish living room and three parlors, one with an old-fashioned pump organ. The B and B's most interesting architectural feature is the glass-walled cupola observatory that sits atop the house like the stopper of an inkwell and offers a sweeping 360-degree view of the Napa Valley hills and vineyards. The best (and quietest) room is the spacious, high-ceilinged French Room, with its richly carved French oak bed graced by an elegant quarter canopy. The rooms at the front of the house are for sound sleepers only. The innkeeper is incredibly friendly and helpful, and she'll keep you nourished with a full country breakfast, plus wine and appetizers in the afternoon. *$$$; MC, V; checks OK; www.inkhouse.com; at Whitehall Ln.*

Inn at Southbridge / ★★☆

1020 MAIN ST, ST. HELENA; 707/967-9400 OR 800/520-6800

This sister to the swanky Meadowood Napa Valley resort (see review) fills the gap between Napa's ultraluxe digs and its ubiquitous bed-and-breakfast inns. Designed by the late William Turnbull Jr., the 21-room inn is part of a terracotta-hued complex that dominates a long block on St. Helena's main drag. Inside, there's not much in the way of common areas, but the guest rooms are almost Shaker in their elegant simplicity, with white piqué cotton comforters, candles, fireplaces, vaulted ceilings, and French doors opening onto private balconies. Guest privileges are available at the exclusive Meadowood Napa

Valley resort, though the on-site Health Spa Napa Valley offers a plethora of spa services, a swimming pool, and exercise equipment. In the courtyard, a sign boasting a big red tomato sets the mood at Pizzeria Tra Vigne, the stylish pizzeria neighboring the inn. Sit on one of the bar stools facing the open kitchen and order the clam pie, a winning pizza combo. *$$$$; DC, MC, V; checks OK; www.innatsouthbridge.com; between Charter Oak Ave and Pope St.*

Meadowood Napa Valley / ★★★★

900 MEADOWOOD LN, ST. HELENA; 707/963-3646 OR 800/458-8080

Rising out of a surreal green sea of fairways and croquet lawns, Meadowood's pearl-gray New England–style mansions are resolutely East Coast. Winding landscaped paths and roads connect the central buildings with smaller lodges scattered over 256 acres; the lodges are strategically situated near an immaculately maintained nine-hole golf course, two croquet lawns (with a full-time croquet pro on hand), seven championship tennis courts, and a 25-yard lap pool. The 85 exorbitantly priced accommodations range from one-room studios to four-room suites, each with a private porch and wet bar. The suites tucked back in the woods are the most private, but the Lawnview Terrace rooms are the best, with their vaulted ceilings, massive stone fireplaces, and French doors opening onto balconies that overlook the croquet green. All guests have access to the swimming pool, outdoor whirlpool, and well-equipped health spa that offers a weight room, aerobics classes, massages, and numerous other ways to pamper your body. The octagonal Restaurant at Meadowood, which serves California Wine Country cuisine, has a high ceiling and a beautiful balcony overlooking the golf course. The more informal Grill at Meadowood offers breakfast, lunch, and dinner daily. *$$$$; AE, DC, DIS, MC, V; checks OK; www.meadowood.com; off the Silverado Trail.*

Calistoga

Mud baths, mineral pools, and massages are still the main attractions of this charming little spa town, founded in the mid-19th century by California's first millionaire, Sam Brannan. Savvy Brannan made a bundle of cash supplying miners in the gold rush and quickly recognized the value of Calistoga's mineral-rich hot springs. In 1859 he purchased 2,000 acres of the Wappo Indians' hot springs land, built a first-class hotel and spa, and named the region Calistoga (a combination of the words California and Saratoga). He then watched his fortunes grow as affluent San Franciscans paraded into town for a relaxing respite from city life.

Generations later, city slickers are still making the pilgrimage to this strip of spas. These days, however, more than a dozen enterprises touting the magical restorative powers of **MINERAL BATHS** line the town's Old West–style streets. You'll see an odd combo of stressed-out CEOs and earthier types shelling out dough for a chance to soak away their worries and get the kinks rubbed out of their necks. While Calistoga's spas and resorts are less glamorous than the Fairmont Sonoma Mission Inn & Spa (see review in Lodgings section of Sonoma), many offer body treatments and mud baths you won't find anywhere else in this part of the state. Among the most popular spas are **DR. WILKINSON'S HOT SPRINGS** (1507 Lincoln Ave; 707/942-4102; www.drwilkinson.com), where you'll get a great massage and numerous other body treatments in a rather drab setting; **CALISTOGA SPA HOT SPRINGS** (1006 Washington St; 707/942-6269; www.calistogaspa.com), a favorite for families with young children that boasts four mineral pools in addition to several body-pampering services; **INDIAN SPRINGS** (1712 Lincoln Ave; 707/942-4913; www.indianspringscalistoga.com) for pricey spa treatments in a historic setting and the best (and largest) mineral pool in the area (you can even see—and hear—the steam from one of the geysers feeding hot mineral water into the pool); and **LAVENDER HILL SPA** (1015 Foothill Blvd/Hwy 29; 707/942-4495; www.lavenderhillspa.com), which provides aromatherapy facials, seaweed wraps, mud baths, and other sybaritic delights in one of the most attractive settings in town.

After you've steamed or soaked away all your tensions, head over to the pretty outdoor patio at **CALISTOGA INN** (1250 Lincoln Ave; 707/942-4101; www.calistogainn.com) for a tall, cool drink. Try one of the house-brewed beers or ales, but save your appetite for one of the better restaurants in town. Once you're rejuvenated, stroll down the main street, **LINCOLN AVENUE**, and browse through the many quaint shops marketing everything from French soaps and antique armoires to silk-screened T-shirts and saltwater taffy. For a trip back in time to Calistoga's pioneer past, stop by the **SHARPSTEEN MUSEUM AND BRANNAN COTTAGE** (1311 Washington St; 707/942-5911; www.sharpensteen-museum.org). Just outside of town you can marvel at **OLD FAITHFUL GEYSER** (1299 Tubbs Ln, 2 miles north of Calistoga; 707/942-6463; www.oldfaithfulgeyser.com), which faithfully shoots a plume of 350°F mineral water 60 feet into the air at regular intervals.

Other natural wonders abound at the **PETRIFIED FOREST** (4100 Petrified Forest Rd, off Hwy 128, 6 miles north of town; 707/942-6667; www.petrifiedforest.org), though if you aren't a trained geologist, it might be hard to appreciate those towering redwoods turned to stone when **MOUNT ST. HELENA** erupted 3 million years ago. For a splendid view of the entire valley, hike through the beautiful redwood canyons and oak-madrona woodlands in **ROBERT LOUIS STEVENSON STATE PARK** (off Hwy 29, 8 miles north of Calistoga; 707/942-4575) to the top of Mount St. Helena.

RESTAURANTS

All Seasons / ★★½

1400 LINCOLN AVE, CALISTOGA; 707/942-9111

Many restaurants in the Napa Valley have elaborate wine lists, but none compare to this café's award-winning roster. The rear of the restaurant—a retail wine store with a tasting bar—stocks hundreds of first-rate foreign and domestic selections at remarkably reasonable prices. If nothing catches your fancy on the restaurant's regular wine list, ask to see the shop's enormous computerized catalog. The All Seasons menu is structured around wine as well as the seasons: the appetizers, such as salmon tartare with crispy taro-root chips and wasabi emulsion, are recommended to accompany sparklers, chardonnay, and sauvignon blanc; entrées such as braised short ribs with polenta cake, wild mushrooms, and red wine sauce are paired with zinfandel and Rhône wines; and oven-roasted Colorado lamb sirloin with port-roasted figs or gratin of potato and turnip are matched with merlot or cabernet. The enthusiastic and opinionated servers can usually steer you safely to the better choices on the changing menu. *$$; DIS, MC, V; local checks only; lunch Fri–Sun, dinner every day; beer and wine; reservations recommended; www.allseasonsnapavalley.com; at Washington St.*

Wappo Bar & Bistro / ★★

1226-B WASHINGTON ST, CALISTOGA; 707/942-4712

Husband-and-wife chefs Aaron Bauman and Michelle Matrux opened this zesty bistro in 1993 and immediately began collecting accolades for what Bauman describes as "regional global cuisine." Confused? Well, even Bauman admits the cuisine is hard to pinpoint, merrily skipping as it does from the Middle East to Europe to Asia to South America to the good old USA. The small menu changes often, but this culinary United Nations has embraced such diverse dishes as Thai noodle and green papaya salad with shredded vegetables, herbs, peanuts, marinated chicken, and ginger-lime dressing; and yogurt-lemon marinated chicken skewers with orzo pasta and Greek salad. One dish that turns up often due to popular demand: chiles rellenos stuffed with basmati rice, crème fraîche, currants, and fresh herbs, dipped in a blue cornmeal batter, deep-fried, and served on a bed of walnut-pomegranate sauce. This is ambitious, imaginative cooking, and the talented chefs usually pull it off with aplomb. *$$; AE, MC, V; local checks only; lunch, dinner Wed–Mon; beer and wine; reservations recommended; www.wappobar.com; off Lincoln Ave.*

LODGINGS

The Chanric Inn / ★★★★

1805 FOOTHILL BLVD, CALISTOGA;
707/942-4535 OR 877/281-3671

With Wine Country B and Bs springing up all over the place, it takes some really stellar hospitality to get noticed. But Channing McBride and Ric Pielstick, life partners and co-owners of Chanric Inn—a play on their names, in case you're late to the party—have already created a reputation for themselves that goes far beyond Calistoga's confines in just their three years in service. It's not just the six immaculately decorated guest rooms, the stunning living room and show-kitchen areas, or the added accoutrements like biscotti, bottled water, and Aveda bath products en suite. It's the welcoming attitude that permeates the inn, right down to the resident golden retriever Dinnegan, who's always on hand for a snuggle. It's as if you were already a part of their big, loving family before you arrived. As if you needed another reason to stay, Ric is a culinary school–trained chef and whips up the best three-course brunch you'll find in these parts, starting with a basket of pastries, followed by a starter of red Anjou pear with sabayon mousseline, and topped off with a main course of chived eggs on fontina toast with sauteed spinach, mushroom duxelles, and white truffle oil. (Those who want to take home some of Ric's panache in the kitchen should check the inn's Web site for a schedule of his culinary classes.) Massage rooms plus a swimming pool and hot tub in back are the icing on the cake. If you have a craving for a midnight snack, the kitchen wet bar—fully stocked with snacks and wine—is open 24/7. *$$$–$$$$; AE, MC, V; no checks; www.thechanric.com; ½ mile west of Lincoln Ave on Hwy 128.*

Cottage Grove Inn / ★★

1711 LINCOLN AVE, CALISTOGA; 707/942-8400 OR 800/799-2284

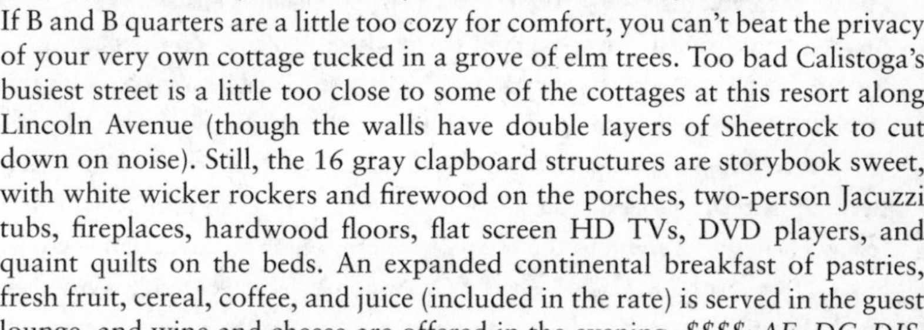

If B and B quarters are a little too cozy for comfort, you can't beat the privacy of your very own cottage tucked in a grove of elm trees. Too bad Calistoga's busiest street is a little too close to some of the cottages at this resort along Lincoln Avenue (though the walls have double layers of Sheetrock to cut down on noise). Still, the 16 gray clapboard structures are storybook sweet, with white wicker rockers and firewood on the porches, two-person Jacuzzi tubs, fireplaces, hardwood floors, flat screen HD TVs, DVD players, and quaint quilts on the beds. An expanded continental breakfast of pastries, fresh fruit, cereal, coffee, and juice (included in the rate) is served in the guest lounge, and wine and cheese are offered in the evening. *$$$$; AE, DC, DIS, MC, V; checks OK; www.cottagegrove.com; at Wappo Ave.*

Indian Springs / ★

1712 LINCOLN AVE, CALISTOGA; 707/942-4913

This historic inn was built in 1860 by Sam Brannan, the founder of Calistoga, on a site where Native Americans used to erect sweat lodges to harness the region's thermal waters. A procession of palm trees leads to the accommodations—17 rustic and casually furnished wooden cottages with partial kitchens, which appeal to families eager to cavort in the resort's huge hot-springs-fed swimming pool. Indian Springs also offers a playground and the full gamut of spa services (massages, facials, mud baths, and more). The spa is open to the public, but the wonderful pool is restricted to spa and hotel guests. *$$$; DIS, MC, V; checks OK; www.indianspringscalistoga.com; between Wappo Ave and Brannan St.*

Clear Lake Area

California's largest freshwater lake, Clear Lake once had more than 30 wineries ringing its shore. Prohibition put an end to all that in 1919. The land was converted to walnut and Bartlett pear orchards, and only in the past few decades have

WINE COUNTRY THREE-DAY TOUR

DAY ONE: *Glamorous Napa.* The ultimate Napa experience begins at **AUBERGE DU SOLEIL HOTEL** with a leisurely breakfast on the patio overlooking the valley (also available to nonguests). Drive your convertible south down the **SILVERADO TRAIL**—taking in the vineyard views—and make a right onto Yountville Cross Road to catch the morning tour at **CLIFF LEDE VINEYARDS**. Buy a bottle of Diva to take home. Cruise west along Yountville Cross Road to downtown Yountville for a 12:30pm lunch reservation at **BISTRO JEANTY**. Next, head north on Highway 29 to the **RUBICON ESTATE WINERY**. Try the claret, buy wine paraphernalia in the gift shop, and peruse Francis Ford Coppola's movie memorabilia collection upstairs. Continue north along 29 to **BERINGER VINEYARDS** and investigate the lovely Rhine House, then visit the tasting room. Stroll along St. Helena's **MAIN STREET** before heading on to have a Tuscan-inspired dinner down the road on the patio at **TRA VIGNE**. Then head back to your room at Auberge du Soleil for a good night's rest.

DAY TWO: *Scenic Sonoma.* From Napa, begin your day with a woodsy drive along the hairpin curves of **OAKVILLE GRADE** (which, closer to Sonoma, will become first Dry Creek Road, then Trinity Road). At Glen Ellen, turn left and follow Highway 12 south to the town of Sonoma. Grab a cappuccino and pastry at **CUCINA VIANSA** (25200 Arnold Dr, Sonoma; 800/995-4740; www.viansa.com) then begin shopping in the gourmet deli for the day's picnic lunch. Walk

the grapes (and the wineries) been making a comeback. This area may one day become as celebrated as Napa and Sonoma, but unlike these trendy stepsisters to the south, there ain't nothin' nouveau about Clear Lake. Country music wafts from pickup trucks, bored (and bared) youths wander the roads aimlessly (perhaps in search of their shirts), and there's generally not a whole lot going on until the weekend boaters and anglers arrive.

Middletown

If you're traveling north from the Napa Valley to Clear Lake, stop at the well-regarded **LANGTRY ESTATE AND VINEYARDS** (21000 Butts Canyon Rd, 6 miles east of Middletown; 707/987-2385; www.langtryestate.com), a 23,000-acre estate owned by British actress Lillie Langtry in the 1880s. Take a tour of the winery and taste the buttery chardonnays and the trendy blend of reds called Meritage. For the lowdown on what to expect up ahead in the Clear Lake region, contact the county-run **LAKE COUNTY VISITORS CENTER** (6110 E Hwy 20, Lucerne; 707/274-5652 or 800/525-3743; www.lakecounty.com; open 9am–5pm every day).

around the plaza and continue gathering goodies from the **SONOMA CHEESE FACTORY** and whatever else strikes your fancy. Drive north of town to **RAVENSWOOD WINERY** for some of the best zinfandels around. Take your picnic to **BARTHOLOMEW PARK WINERY**, and after tasting the wines and visiting the museum, lunch on the 400-acre grounds and walk the trails. Next stop is historic **BUENA VISTA WINERY** (try the cream sherry), followed by a visit to **GUNDLACH BUNDSCHU WINERY**, where you can hike up the hill to view the valley below. Drive back into Sonoma for dinner on the vine-covered patio at **DELLA SANTINA'S** before heading back to the hotel.

DAY THREE: *Calistoga mud baths.* Breakfast again at Auberge du Soleil, then begin the day with the breathtakingly beautiful tram ride up the mountain to **STERLING VINEYARDS**, where you can taste wines on the patio. Next head south to **WINE SPECTATOR GREYSTONE RESTAURANT** and while away a couple of hours eating lunch, touring the building, watching a cooking demo, and visiting the basement cookware marketplace. Head back to Calistoga for an afternoon of sybaritic pleasures at **INDIAN SPRINGS**, the region's historic Victorian spa. Have a mud bath or facial, then soak up the sun in the enormous mineral springs–fed swimming pool. Enjoy a relaxed dinner at **ALL SEASONS CAFÉ** before heading out of town. Drive south along the Silverado Trail, savoring the final vineyard views in the last dying rays of the sun.

Clear Lake

Clear Lake's informal annual blowout is on the **FOURTH OF JULY WEEKEND** (contact the Clear Lake Chamber of Commerce, 707/994-3600; www.clearlakechamber.com), when thousands of born-again patriots amass (and timorous locals split) for a three-day sunburnt orgy of flag waving, fireworks, waterskiing, and a parade. If you want to dive into the aquatic activities on boats of all shapes and sizes, contact **FUNTIME RV PARK & CAMPGROUND** (6035 Old Hwy 53, Clear Lake; 707/994-6267) or **ON THE WATERFRONT** (60 3rd St, Lakeport; 707/263-6789), which also rents Jet Skis and Sea-Doos.

Clear Lake also draws crowds eager to snag some of its largemouth bass, catfish, perch, and crappie. Although the lake has earned the title of bass capital of the West, there aren't any shops renting fishing equipment, so you'll have to tote your own. For more information on Clear Lake and its surrounding towns and wineries, call or drop by the **LAKE COUNTY VISITOR INFORMATION CENTER** (6110 E Hwy 20, Lucerne; 707/274-5652 or 800/525-3743; www.lakecounty.com; open 9am–5pm every day).

Lakeport

With its small, old-fashioned downtown, Lakeport is the prettiest town on Clear Lake. Formerly known as Forbestown (after early settler William Forbes), the area is usually very peaceful until summer, when people from outlying cities pack up their SUVs and caravan out here for fishing, camping, swimming, and wine tasting. **CLEAR LAKE STATE PARK** (off Soda Bay Rd, south of Lakeport; 707/279-4293; www.parks.ca.gov, search for "Clear Lake") is one of the area's main draws, with its campgrounds (no reservations available during off-season), miles of hiking trails, and a beach. Folks also flock to Lakeport every Labor Day weekend for the **LAKE COUNTY FAIR** (401 Martin St; 707/263-6181; www.lakecountyfair.com), featuring 4-H exhibits, livestock auctions, horse shows, and a carnival.

RESTAURANTS

Park Place / ★★

50 3RD ST, LAKEPORT; 707/263-0444

Ever since the Loon's Nest restaurant in nearby Kelseyville closed, there hasn't been much debate over Lake County's best restaurant. It's Park Place—a small lakeside café serving very good Italian and California-inspired food. Owners Barbara Morris and Nancy Zabel make fettuccine every day and serve it with simple, fresh sauces such as creamy Alfredo, zingy marinara, pesto, or *quattro formaggio*. Also highly recommended are Nancy's made-from-scratch soups (particularly the chunky Italian vegetable) and house-made focaccia sandwiches. Save room for the superb cheesecake. *$$; MC, V; checks OK; lunch, dinner every day; beer and wine; reservations recommended; off Main St, near the lake.*

Nice

LODGINGS

Featherbed Railroad Company / ★

2870 LAKESHORE BLVD, NICE; 707/274-8378 OR 800/966-6322

Nine cabooses that look as though they would be right at home in Disneyland are spread out underneath a grove of oak trees at this gimmicky but fun bed-and-breakfast. The freight-train cars are burdened with cutesy names, but they're equipped with feather beds, private baths (some with Jacuzzi tubs), and other amenities that make up for the silliness. Favorite train cars include two newer cabooses, the Orient Express (with a private deck) and the Casablanca (complete with a piano and bar), but it's the black and maroon La Loose Caboose (tackiest of them all, with a bordello decor, a deck, and a mirror over the bed) that's always booked. The Rosebud Caboose has a Jacuzzi tub for two. Breakfast is served at the Main Station, a century-old ranch house, in front of a cozy fire or on the porch overlooking the lake. A small pool and spa adjoin the house. *$$; AE, DIS, MC, V; no checks; www.featherbedrailroad.com; off Hwy 20, at the southwest end of town.*

Sonoma County

Many would argue that when it comes to comparing Sonoma Valley's Wine Country with Napa's, less is definitely more: Sonoma is less congested, less developed, less commercial, and less glitzy than its rival. Smitten with the bucolic charm of the region, oenophiles delight in wandering the area's back roads, leisurely hopping from winery to winery and exploring the quaint towns along the way. There are moments when—sitting in the sunshine at some of the beautifully landscaped wineries, inhaling the hot camphor smell of the eucalyptus trees, listening to a gurgling brook and the serenade of songbirds as you sip a glass of chilled sauvignon blanc—you think that even Eden would be a disappointment after Sonoma.

Sonoma Wine Country is informally divided into two regions: **SONOMA VALLEY** and **NORTHERN SONOMA COUNTY**. The valley is relatively condensed: about 40 wineries and a modest countrified social life revolve around downtown Sonoma and its historic plaza. Santa Rosa is the gateway to northern Sonoma County, where wineries are discovered along winding one-lane country roads, and famous growing areas such as Dry Creek promise killer zinfandel and intimate winery experiences.

Before setting out for this verdant vineyard-laced region, stop at the **SONOMA VALLEY VISITORS BUREAU** (453 1st St E; 707/996-1090; www.sonomavalley.com) for lots of free, helpful information about the area's wineries, farmers markets, historic sites, walking tours, recreational facilities, and seasonal events. If you're exploring northern Sonoma County, contact the **SONOMA COUNTY TOURIST PROGRAM** (800/576-6662) to order a free brochure, or visit their Web site (www.sonomacounty.com) for every possible thing you might want to know about the area.

Sonoma Wineries

California's world-renowned wine industry was born in the Sonoma Valley. Franciscan fathers planted the state's first vineyards at the Mission San Francisco Solano de Sonoma in 1823 and harvested the grapes to make their sacramental wines. Thirty-four years later, California's first major vineyard was planted with European grape varietals by Hungarian count Agoston Haraszthy at Sonoma's revered Buena Vista Winery. Little did the count know that one day he would become widely hailed as the father of California wine. Today many wineries dot the Sonoma Valley, most offering pretty picnic areas and free tours of their winemaking facilities. Alas, free tastings used to be the norm, but like Napa wineries, most Sonoma wineries also charge fees (usually around $10) to sample. Here's a roundup of some of Sonoma's best:

BARTHOLOMEW PARK WINERY (1000 Vineyard Ln, Sonoma; 707/935-9511; www.bartparkwinery.com). The winery sits in the midst of 400-acre

Bartholomew Memorial Park, making it one of the most beautiful settings in the valley and an exceptional picnic spot, complete with hiking trails. A museum displays photos by Victorian photographer Eadweard Muybridge, who documented viticulture practices from the 19th century. Tastings are $5.

BENZIGER FAMILY WINERY (1883 London Ranch Rd, Glen Ellen; 888/490-2739; www.benziger.com). Tram ride tours ($15) take visitors through the vineyards, and $10 tastings of their extensive portfolio are held in the wine shop.

BUENA VISTA CARNEROS (18000 Old Winery Rd, Sonoma; 800/678-8504). California's oldest premium winery (founded in 1857) is a large estate set in a forest with picnic grounds. Tours of the stone winery and the hillside tunnels are available, and a gallery features locals' artwork. Tastings start at $10.

CHÂTEAU ST. JEAN (8555 Sonoma Hwy/Hwy 12, Kenwood; 707/833-4134; www.chateaustjean.com). Beringer purchased Château St. Jean in 1996; since that time the mansion and 250-acre estate have undergone a dramatic renovation. So did the tasting room, which is now reminiscent of a Napa corporate winery, as opposed to its previous intimate atmosphere. Still, the place is beautiful with great picnic grounds. You can enjoy a few samples for $10–$15.

FERRARI-CARANO VINEYARDS AND WINERY (8761 Dry Creek Rd, Healdsburg; 707/433-6700; www.ferrari-carano.com). This cutting-edge facility features 5 acres of spectacular gardens. Ferrari-Carano made its reputation with its chardonnay but also offers top-notch fumé blanc and cabernet sauvignon, which you can sample for $5.

GLORIA FERRER CHAMPAGNE CAVES (23555 Hwy 121, Sonoma; 707/996-7256; www.gloriaferrer.com). This champagne house's subterranean cellars make for an excellent guided tour ($10). Since there's no actual tasting room, you can order your bubbly by the glass ($2–$10) and take it out on the balcony, which offers stunning views of the valley below.

GUNDLACH BUNDSCHU WINERY (2000 Denmark St, Sonoma; 707/938-5277; www.gunbun.com). Located in a grand historic building set on impressive grounds, Gundlach Bundschu is known primarily for its zinfandel but also makes several interesting German-style whites. Picnic facilities are available and tastings are $5.

KENWOOD VINEYARDS (9592 Sonoma Hwy/Hwy 12, Kenwood; 707/833-5891; www.kenwoodvineyards.com). Kenwood is renowned for its quaint wooden barns and red wines. The best of its zinfandel and cabernet grapes come from Jack London's old vineyard on Sonoma Mountain. Tastings start at $5.

KORBEL CHAMPAGNE CELLARS (13250 River Rd, Guerneville; 707/824-7000; www.korbel.com). In an ivy-covered brick building set in a redwood forest with a view of the Russian River, Korbel hosts informative tours and free tastings. The extensive and beautiful flower gardens are open for tours May through mid-October, and a deli offers great picnic items.

KUNDE ESTATE WINERY (9825 Sonoma Hwy/Hwy 12, Kenwood; 707/833-5501; www.kunde.com). The Kunde family has been growing grapes for

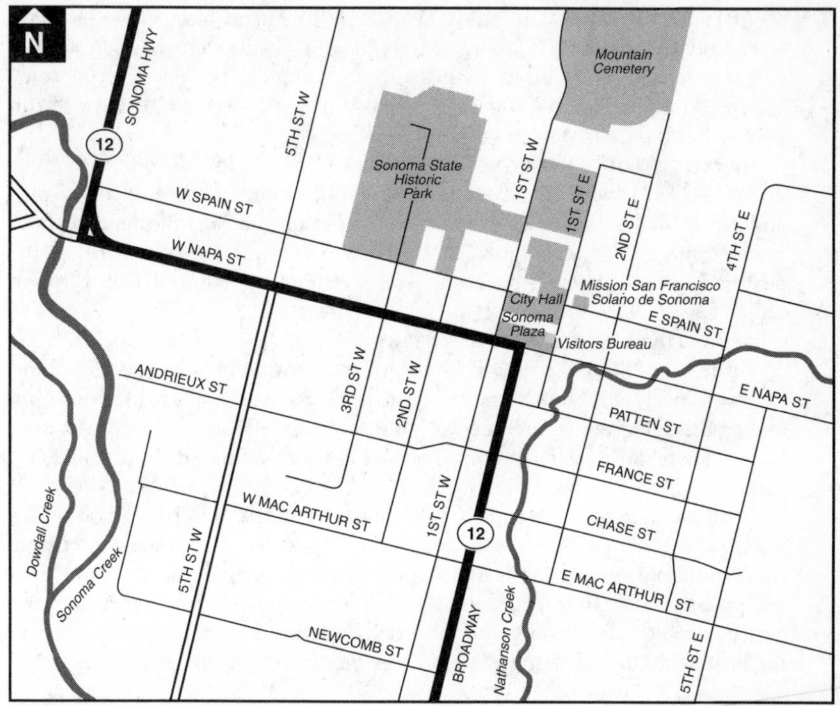

Sonoma

more than five generations, and today they're one of Sonoma County's largest suppliers. Their century-old winery sits in the middle of this lovely 2,000-acre setting. Tastings are $10 a flight.

LANDMARK VINEYARDS (101 Adobe Canyon Rd, Kenwood; 707/833-0053; www.landmarkwine.com). Home to the John Deere family descendants, this lovely intimate vineyard now sells rows of vines to any oenophile who wishes to purchase one (they're then invited to partake in the annual fall harvest). Catered lunches from an airy second-story room with vineyard views make for a great special occasion. Tastings are $5. You can take your wine out into the gardens, where there's a bocce court and horsedrawn wagon rides in the summer.

LEDSON WINERY & VINEYARDS (7335 Sonoma Hwy, Kenwood; 707/537-3810; www.ledson.com). Located in a modern-day castle complete with formal gardens and fountains, the winery offers a large array of wines for tasting ($10–$20) and a well-stocked deli.

MATANZAS CREEK WINERY (6097 Bennett Valley Rd, Santa Rosa; 707/528-6464; www.matanzascreek.com). A beautiful drive leads to this winery's attractive facilities surrounded by lavender. Matanzas offers outstanding chardonnay and merlot as well as guided tours and picnic tables. Tastings are $5.

QUIVIRA VINEYARDS (4900 W Dry Creek Rd, Healdsburg; 707/431-8333; www.quivirawine.com). Quivira is housed in a postmodern barn in a quiet vineyard setting. The winery is known for its zinfandel, but the superbly spicy Sauvignon Blanc Fig Tree Vineyard is worth trying as well. A tasting will run you $5 but the fee is waived with purchase.

RAVENSWOOD WINERY (18701 Gehricke Rd, Sonoma; 888/669-4679 or 707/933-2332; www. ravenswood-wine.com). Home of some of the tastiest zinfandels made, Ravenswood offers vintages that run the full range of styles from jammy to peppery. Along with $10–$15 tastings, the winery offers the perfect accompaniment—barbecue—on weekends, Memorial Day through Labor Day.

SEBASTIANI VINEYARDS & WINERY (389 E 4th St, Sonoma; 707/933-3230 or 800/888-5532; www.sebastiani.com). Sonoma's largest premium-variety winery, Sebastiani Vineyards provides tours of its fermentation room and aging cellar, which includes an interesting collection of carved-oak cask heads. There's also a slick, enormous tasting room–cum–gift shop where you can taste seven 1-ounce pours for $10.

VIANSA WINERY AND ITALIAN MARKETPLACE (25200 Arnold Dr, Sonoma; 800/995-4740; www.viansa.com). Modeled after a Tuscan village, these buildings and grounds are owned by the Sebastiani family. They produce several fine Italian-style wines, like dolcetto and nebbiolo. Grilled meats, gourmet Italian picnic fare, and local delicacies are available for enjoying on the beautiful hillside picnic grounds. Tastings start at $10.

Sonoma

Sonoma, one of the most historic towns in Northern California, is a good place to experience the region's Mexican heritage. Designed by General Mariano Vallejo in 1835, Sonoma is set up like a Mexican town, with an 8-acre parklike plaza in the center—complete with a meandering flock of chickens and crowing roosters. Several authentic adobe buildings hug the perimeter; most now house an assortment of boutiques, restaurants, and also the vintage **SEBASTIANI THEATRE** (476 1st St E; 707/996-2020; www.sebastianitheatre.com). **MISSION SAN FRANCISCO SOLANO DE SONOMA** (on the corner of E 1st St and E Spain St; 707/938-1519; www.californiamissions.com), a.k.a. the Sonoma Mission, is the northernmost and last of the 21 missions built by the Spanish fathers.

A stroll around the plaza area offers interesting shopping and an excellent bookstore, **READER'S BOOKS** (130 E Napa St; 707/939-1779; www.readersbooks.com). Or find everything for a Wine Country feast: cheeses and deli fare galore from the **SONOMA CHEESE FACTORY** (2 W Spain St; 707/996-1931; www.sonomacheesefactory.com). If you didn't have time to hit all the wineries you wanted, or if you're ready for a beer instead, stop by the **WINE EXCHANGE** (452 1st St E; 800/938-1794; www.wineexsonoma.com). You can taste wine and beer here, and choose from an enormous selection of each to complete your picnic. Listen to acoustic music on Thursday through Sunday nights at **MURPHY'S IRISH PUB** (464 1st St E; 707/935-0660), hidden in the courtyard behind the Sebastiani Theatre. Late-night wine tasting, live jazz, and tasty "small plates" are available at the extremely elegant **LEDSON HOTEL AND HARMONY CLUB** (480 1st St E; 707/996-9779; www.ledsonhotel.com), which serves breakfast, lunch, and dinner daily.

RESTAURANTS

Cafe La Haye / ★★★

140 E NAPA ST, SONOMA; 707/935-5994

Located just off the main plaza, this light-filled café blends two sensual pleasures: art and food. Paintings in the bold California Colorist–style cover the walls, and larger-than-life fantasy nudes float across the bathroom walls. Not to be outdone, the food is also a unique work of art. Brunch dishes offer surprising twists, like a poached egg with ham bobbing in a sea of white cheddar grits. Or try the ubiquitous eggs Benedict, updated here with roasted red peppers and shiitake mushrooms, served on an herb biscuit. Dinner offers a short menu of rustic European dishes, like seared black pepper–lavender fillet of beef with Gorgonzola potato gratin, or risotto and fish specials that change daily. The wine list is three times as long as the menu and, in keeping with the theme, offers some unusual Sonoma specialties. *$$; MC, V; local checks only; dinner Tues–Sat, brunch Sun; beer and wine; no reservations for brunch, reservations recommended for dinner; www.cafelahaye.com; just east of the plaza.*

Della Santina's / ★★

133 E NAPA ST, SONOMA; 707/935-0576

A fixture on the plaza for years, this popular and traditionally Italian dining room has a homey interior and a wonderful vine-laced brick patio tucked in back that's the place to dine when the weather is warm. The menu includes a good selection of light to heavy house-made pastas (the Gnocchi della Nonna with a tomato, basil, and garlic sauce would impress any Italian grandmother) and wonderful meats from the *rosticceria* (the chicken with fresh herbs is tender and perfectly spiced). Be sure to inquire about the *pasticceria*—and if panna cotta is among the offerings, nab it. Paired with an espresso, it's the perfect finale to a fine meal. *$$; AE, DIS, MC, V; local checks only; lunch, dinner every day; beer and wine; reservations recommended; www.dellasantinas.com; off 2nd St.*

the girl & the fig / ★★

110 W SPAIN ST (SONOMA HOTEL), SONOMA; 707/938-3634

"Country food with French passion" doesn't get more inviting than at the girl & the fig. Owner Sondra Bernstein's restaurant, which celebrates among other things the decadent fig, is a cozy spot where tables in the cheery yellow dining room with wood paneling are a wee bit tight, but all the better to get a sneak preview from your neighbor's plate. Patio seating is prime country dining when the weather's right. The chef prepares dishes such as fig salad with arugula, dried figs, pecans, chèvre, pancetta, and a fig-port vinaigrette; aromatic steamed mussels with Pernod, garlic, leeks, fresh herbs, and croutons; or savory pan-seared striped bass with roasted shallot and chive vinaigrette and mashed potatoes. Cheese lovers should splurge on the cheese menu featuring local productions. If nothing else, forks should stand at attention for the sensuous lavender crème brûlée or delicate chilled Meyer lemon soufflé with whipped cream and fruit compote. Just as exciting as the food is the trendsetting wine list, which goes against the Sonoma grain with Rhône-style California wines. *$$; AE, MC, V; checks OK; lunch, dinner every day; full bar; reservations recommended; www.thegirlandthefig.com; on Sonoma Plaza, on the ground floor of the Sonoma Hotel.* ♿

Juanita Juanita / ★½

19114 ARNOLD DR, SONOMA; 707/935-3981

For the occasions when heaven is a roadside shack, cold beer, and a heaping plate of nachos, Juanita Juanita is your savior. Locals are loyal to this spray-painted mural box of a restaurant, and no wonder. It's not every day that you can play Trivial Pursuit while digging into a plastic bucket of thick, crisp tortilla chips and zesty salsa, waiting for your grilled chicken quesadilla, beef enchilada, or fish taco. Hint: Come at off-hours to avoid the wait. *$; no credit cards; local checks only; lunch, dinner every day; beer and wine; no reservations; www.juanitajuanita.com; from Sonoma Plaza head west on W Napa St, turn right on Arnold Dr, and continue until you see the shack on the left side of the street.*

LODGINGS

El Dorado Hotel / ★★

405 1ST ST W, SONOMA; 707/996-3220 OR 800/289-3031

If you've had it with cutesy B and Bs, El Dorado Hotel is a welcome respite, offering 27 moderately priced rooms modestly decorated with terra-cotta tile floors, handcrafted furniture, and down comforters. Renovated by the team that created the exclusive Auberge du Soleil, each room has French doors leading to a small balcony overlooking the town square or the hotel's private courtyard—a pleasant, sunny spot where you can enjoy the complimentary continental breakfast. There's also a heated outdoor lap pool and concierge service to help you arrange your next Wine Country excursion. *$$$; AE, MC, V; checks OK; www.eldoradosonoma.com; at W Spain St, on the plaza's west side.*

Lodge at Sonoma / ★★½

1325 BROADWAY, SONOMA; 707/935-6600

This Marriott-owned resort allows for the intimacy of a high-end Sonoma County getaway without the exorbitant price. Ten acres of lush foliage house a hodgepodge of cottage rooms, suites, and lodge rooms, all of which are centered on a courtyard, where the pool and hot tub are located. The recently remodeled roomy accommodations all have soaking tubs, balconies, iPod alarm clocks, fridges, and flat-screen TVs with premier cable channels; most have fireplaces. Carneros Bistro & Wine in the main building serves a delicious breakfast, brunch, lunch, and dinner, and the adjoining Raindance Spa prides itself on pampering *au naturel*, with essences like mustard, lavender, grape seed, and olive oil all procured locally. The staff is extremely affable and accommodating. *$$–$$$; AE, MC, V; no checks; www.thelodgeatsonoma.com; at Napa Rd.*

Sonoma Chalet / ★★

18935 5TH ST W, SONOMA; 707/938-3129 OR 800/938-3129

So close, and yet so far: every room in this secluded Swiss-style farmhouse overlooks the grassy hills of a 200-acre ranch, giving you the impression that you're way out in the country. Fact is, you're at the edge of a suburban neighborhood—three-quarters of a mile from Sonoma's town square. There are four rooms in the two-story 1940s chalet (two of them share a bath) and three adorable private cottages, each with its own little sitting area, feather bed, fireplace or wood-burning stove, and kitchen. All of the rooms have decks or balconies with views, and each boasts an assortment of antiques, quilts, and collectibles that complement the rustic surroundings. In the morning, proprietor Joe Leese serves pastries, juices, yogurt, and granola in the country kitchen or, if you prefer, in the privacy of your cottage. *$$; AE, MC, V; checks OK; www.sonomachalet.com; follow 5th St W to the end, then continue west on the gravel road.*

Victorian Garden Inn / ★

316 NAPA ST E, SONOMA; 707/996-5339 OR 800/543-5339

This 1870s Greek Revival farmhouse with a wraparound veranda has one of the most inviting small gardens you'll ever see: lush bowers of roses, azaleas, and camellias encircle wonderful little tables and chairs, while flowering fruit trees bend low over Victorian benches. The inn's four guest rooms, decorated in white wicker and florals, are pretty, if a bit cloying. The most requested room is the Woodcutter's Cottage, favored for its comfy sofa and armchairs facing the fireplace and its private entrance and bath. In the evening, owner Donna Lewis pours glasses of wine and sherry for guests to enjoy in front of the parlor fireplace. Breakfast, served at the dining table, in the garden, or in your room, consists of granola, croissants, gourmet coffee, and fruit picked right from the garden. A big bonus is the large swimming pool in the backyard—a blessing during Sonoma's typically hot summer days—and a therapeutic hot tub located in the gardens. *$$$; AE, DC, MC, V; checks OK; www.victoriangardeninn.com; between 3rd St E and 4th St E, 2 blocks from the plaza.*

Boyes Hot Springs

LODGINGS

Fairmont Sonoma Mission Inn & Spa / ★★★

100 BOYES BLVD, BOYES HOT SPRINGS; 707/938-9000 OR 866/540-4499

With its ethereal, serene grounds and elegant pink stucco buildings, the Sonoma Mission Inn feels a bit like a convent—except that novitiates wear white terry-cloth bathrobes or colorful running suits instead of nuns' habits. And that indulgence, in body and spirit, is the order of the day. The recently renovated European-style spa offers everything from aerobics classes and Swedish massages to aromatherapy facials, seaweed wraps, and tarot card readings in perfectly groomed surroundings. You'll also find exercise rooms, saunas, Jacuzzis, a salon, yoga and meditation classes, and two swimming pools, one of which is filled with artesian mineral water. While the luxurious spa is the main draw, the inn has also reacquired its historic golf course, which had been sold during the Depression. Bathed in shades of light peach and pink, each of the more than 230 rooms features plantation-style shutters, ceiling fans, and down comforters. Some units have wood-burning fireplaces and luxe granite or marble bathrooms big enough for an impromptu tango. The inn's two restaurants, Sante and the Big 3 Diner, both serve Californian cuisine. Sante is one of the most expensive restaurants in Sonoma; the less-expensive Big 3 Diner offers such fare as light pastas, pizzas, and grilled items, as well as hearty breakfasts. *$$$$; AE, DC, DIS, MC, V; checks OK; www.fairmont.com/sonoma; just west of Hwy 12.*

Glen Ellen

There are more places and things named after Jack London in Sonoma County than there are women named María in Mexico. This cult reaches its apex in Glen Ellen, where the writer built his aptly named Beauty Ranch, an 800-acre spread now known as **JACK LONDON STATE HISTORIC PARK** (2400 London Ranch Rd, off Hwy 12; 707/938-5216; www.jacklondonpark.com). London's vineyards, piggery, and other ranch buildings are here, as well as a house-turned-museum containing his art collection and mementos (including a series of rejection letters London received from several publishers, who must have fallen over backward in their cushy chairs the day they learned London had become the highest-paid author of his time). Ten miles of trails lead through oaks, madrones, and redwoods, including a grove of oaks shading London's grave. If you'd rather ride than walk through London's land, let the friendly folks at the **TRIPLE CREEK HORSE OUTFIT** (located in Jack London State Historic Park; 707/887-8700; www.triplecreekhorseoutfit.com) saddle up a horse for you. Call for the lowdown on their guided horseback trips (reservations are required).

The tiny town of Glen Ellen was also the longtime home of the late celebrated food writer **M. F. K. FISHER**. It offers a couple of good restaurants, plus wine-tasting and antiquing excursions. The **WINE COUNTRY FILM FESTIVAL** (707/935-FILM or www.winecountryfilmfest.com), a three-week summer splurge of screenings and parties throughout Napa and Sonoma, is headquartered here.

RESTAURANTS

Glen Ellen Inn Oyster Grill & Martini Bar / ★★☆

13670 ARNOLD DR, GLEN ELLEN; 707/996-6409

If you're staying in Glen Ellen, it's nice to know you don't have to go far to find a good meal. In fact, Christian and Karen Bertrand's tiny, romantic restaurant is worth a drive from farther afield. The menu changes frequently but always features local cuisine at its freshest and in beautiful preparations. Dinner might include spinach, mission figs, walnuts, and chèvre in a chilled crepe, with port dressing; expertly seared ahi tuna in a wasabi cream sauce and port reduction; or grilled pork tenderloin with pineapple-mango chutney and smoked Sonoma Jack cheese polenta. The new martini bar adds 20 varieties of crafted concoctions to wash down the raw oysters. With just 15 white-clothed tables in the dining room and 15 more outside in the herb garden, service is personal and attentive, almost as if you've been invited into the Bertrands' home. *$$; AE, MC, V; local checks only; lunch Fri–Tues, dinner every day; beer, wine, and martinis; reservations recommended; www.glenelleninn.com; at O'Donnell Ln.*

LODGINGS

Beltane Ranch / ★★☆

11775 SONOMA HWY, GLEN ELLEN; 707/996-6501

Surrounded by vineyards at the foot of the Mayacamas Mountains, this century-old buttercup yellow and white clapboard farmhouse was a bunkhouse long before it was a bed-and-breakfast—but certainly the cowhands of old never had it so good. Each of the inn's five rooms is uniquely decorated; all have sitting areas, private baths, separate entrances, and a family antique or two. Ask for one of the upstairs rooms that opens onto the huge wraparound double-decker porch equipped with hammocks and a swing. Or if a little extra privacy is on your itinerary, go for the two-room Garden Cottage, which lies a few yards from the main house and has French doors that open onto a private garden and patio. All guests are welcome to the full country breakfast served in the garden or on the porch, which overlooks Sonoma's hillsides. Blissfully calm and beautiful, the whole place makes you feel as though you should be wearing a wide-brimmed hat and sipping a mint julep. Should you tire of lolling like a Southern belle, knock a few balls around the tennis court near the house, pitch horseshoes in the garden, or hike trails through the estate's 1,600 acres of vineyards and hills. *$$; no credit cards; checks OK; www.beltaneranch.com; on Hwy 12, 2.2 miles past the Glen Ellen turnoff.*

Gaige House Inn / ★★★½

13540 ARNOLD DR, GLEN ELLEN; 707/935-0237 OR 800/935-0237

From the outside, the Gaige House looks like yet another spiffed-up Victorian mansion, inevitably filled with the ubiquitous dusty antiques and family heirlooms. Inside, however, the Victorian theme comes to a screeching halt. All 15 rooms are spectacular, and each is individually decorated in an Indonesian plantation–style with an eclectic mix of modern art. Owners Ken Burnet Jr. and Greg Nemrow have a discerning sense of style that's evident from the in-room atriums in the Zen Suites with their private Japanese garden and waterfall to the Gaige Suite, which features a king-size four-poster canopy bed and an unbelievably large and luxe bathroom with a whirlpool tub that could easily fit a party of six (and probably has), as well as a huge wraparound balcony. The Studio Suites open onto a shaded deck and are within steps of a beautiful brick-lined 40-foot swimming pool surrounded by a large, perfectly manicured lawn. Included in the room rate—which is surprisingly affordable considering the caliber of the accommodations—is a two-course gourmet breakfast served at individual tables in the dining room and superb evening appetizers and wine. *$$$; AE, DIS, MC, V; checks OK; www.gaige.com; from Hwy 12, take the Glen Ellen exit.*

Kenwood

LODGINGS

Kenwood Inn & Spa / ★★★

10400 SONOMA HWY, KENWOOD; 707/833-1293 OR 800/353-6966

This posh inn resembles a centuries-old Italian pensione with freestanding accommodations around a garden court and pool. The 28 guest rooms are beautifully decorated, each with a fluffy feather bed, a fireplace, and a sitting area. Room 3, bathed in shades of gold, has a pleasant private balcony, and room 6 is a suite sporting a sitting room with a stereo, Jacuzzi, and balcony overlooking the vineyards and the swimming pool. The six-room, full-service spa pampers guests with Caudalie Vinotherapie treatments, which employ vine and grapeseed extracts. Breakfast, served in the new dining room, is an impressive spread that may include fresh fruit, polenta with poached eggs, and buttery house-made croissants. *$$$$; AE, MC, V; checks OK; www.kenwoodinn.com; on Hwy 12, 3 miles past Glen Ellen.*

Santa Rosa

Santa Rosa is the closest thing Sonoma County has to a big city, but it's more like a countrified suburb. Oddly enough, it's got more than its share of offbeat museums. Botanists, gardeners, and other plant lovers will want to make a beeline for the popular gardens and greenhouse at the **LUTHER**

BURBANK HOME & GARDENS (corner of Santa Rosa and Sonoma Ave; 707/524-5445; www.lutherburbank.org). Burbank was a world-renowned horticulturist who created 800 new strains of plants, fruits, and vegetables at the turn of the century. Pop culture fans will get a kick out of **SNOOPY'S GALLERY & GIFT SHOP** (1665 W Steel Ln; 707/546-3385; www.snoopygift.com), a "Peanuts" cartoon museum with the world's largest collection of Snoopy memorabilia, thanks to donations by the beagle's creator, the late Charles Schulz, who lived in Santa Rosa.

For music, magicians, and a plethora of fresh-from-the-farm food, head over to the wildly successful **SANTA ROSA DOWNTOWN MARKET** (707/542-2123; www.srdowntownmarket.com; 5–8:30pm Wed May–Aug) on downtown Santa Rosa's Fourth Street from B Street to D Street, which is closed to traffic for this festive event that draws folks from far and near. Another local crowd-pleaser is the annual **SONOMA COUNTY HARVEST FAIR** (1350 Bennett Valley Rd; 707/545-4200; www.sonomacountyfair.org), a wine-tasting, food-gobbling orgy held at the fairgrounds from late July to early August.

RESTAURANTS

Hana Japanese Restaurant / ★★★

101 GOLF COURSE DR, ROHNERT PARK; 707/586-0270

Unbeknownst to most visitors, this Japanese restaurant, located in a strip mall in Santa Rosa suburb Rohnert Park, is *the* place for sushi in Northern California. What it lacks in its almost motel-style decor it more than makes up for with mind-blowing raw and cooked fish dishes and astoundingly beautiful presentations created by chef-owner Ken Tominaga. Try tuna, salmon, albacore, and yellowtail; choose rolls that range from California or spicy salmon to tuna-belly-and-green-onion or soft-shell crab. But it's Ken's specials that really shine—such as foie gras with unagi (eel), sea-urchin egg custard, ahi poke, and octopus salad. For the sushi experience of your life, ask him to lead the way, but be sure to tell him up front how much you want to spend. Folks who aren't raw fish fans can choose from the huge lunch and dinner menu. Wash it down with one of the great premium sakes or a Japanese beer. At lunch, the bento boxes, domburi, and udon meals (complete with miso soup, Japanese pickles, salad, and rice) are great deals. *$$$; AE, DC, DIS, MC, V; no checks; lunch Mon–Sat, dinner every day; beer, wine, and sake; reservations recommended; www.hanajapanese.com; call for directions.* ♿

John Ash & Co. / ★★★

4330 BARNES RD (VINTNERS INN), SANTA ROSA; 707/527-7687

This casually elegant restaurant, founded by Wine Country cuisine guru John Ash, has topped the list of Santa Rosa's best restaurants for many years. It's pricey, but the service is expert, the food is fabulous, and the serene dining room with cream-colored walls, tall French windows, and a crackling fire will entice you to settle in for a good long time. The menu, under the direction of executive chef Jeffrey Madura, is a classic California hybrid of French,

Italian, Asian, and Southwestern cuisines. A meal might begin with such glorious dishes as iced Hog Island oysters on the half shell with a trio of sauces, followed by a sweet-and-sour molasses and ginger pork chop with goat cheese mashers. For dessert, diners swoon over the Vanilla-Mint Melt Down, a warm, flourless chocolate cake with a gooey chocolate truffle center, vibrant Tahitian vanilla syrup, mint oil, and crème anglaise. The large, reasonably priced wine list, showcasing Napa and Sonoma wines, also includes a good selection of ports, sherries, and dessert wines. For a taste of Wine Country cuisine at a fraction of the regular price, sit at the bar or on the patio and order from the Vineyard Cafe menu. *$$$; AE, DC, DIS, MC, V; local checks only; dinner every day; full bar; reservations recommended; www.vintnersinn.com/johnash.asp; next to Vintners Inn, off River Rd, at Hwy 101.*

Syrah / ★★☆

205 5TH ST, SANTA ROSA; 707/568-4002

Owners Josh and Regina Silvers preside over a local favorite, serving French-inspired American cuisine within a casual-chic historic building. Choose your table on the patio or near the open kitchen, where chef Josh (previously of Mustards in Napa Valley) prepares baked brioche and poached foie gras, which might be accompanied by marinated dried cherries in a terra-cotta pot, or sautéed crab cakes tenderly placed on an arugula salad with roasted beets and horseradish vinaigrette. Other starters include a moist duck confit with beluga lentil salad and succulent pork tenderloin. *$$$; DIS, MC, V; no checks; lunch Tues–Sat, dinner every day; beer and wine; reservations recommended; www.syrahbistro.com; at Davis St.*

Willi's Wine Bar / ★★☆

4104 OLD REDWOOD HWY, SANTA ROSA; 707/526-3096

Locals slink into this dark, low-slung, and laid-back spot for wine and a whimsical global dining adventure. Each dish bucks the expected—from artfully presented brandade spring rolls with herb salad and romesco to wonton-paper-wrapped scallop dumplings seasoned with lemongrass butter and pancetta. Pairing's not a problem thanks to 40 wines by the 2-ounce pour, glass, or half bottle. *$$; AE, MC, V; no checks; lunch Tues–Sat, dinner every day; beer and wine; reservations recommended; www.williswinebar.net; near River Rd.*

Zazu / ★★☆

3535 GUERNEVILLE RD, SANTA ROSA; 707/523-4814

Hiding out in a funky roadhouse a few miles from downtown Santa Rosa, rustic-chic Zazu has railroad-apartment-meets-clapboard-shack ambience—the perfect match for chef/co-owners Duskie Estes and John Stewart's Americana/Italian/farmers market–influenced comfort food. It's not uncommon to spot winemakers huddling around one of the copper-topped tables and devouring a crisp poppy seed–crusted soft-shell crab with ruby grapefruit, avocado, and poppy seed dressing; a robust star-anise rubbed duck with apricot sambal, crispy rice cake, and bok choy; a juicy, naturally raised

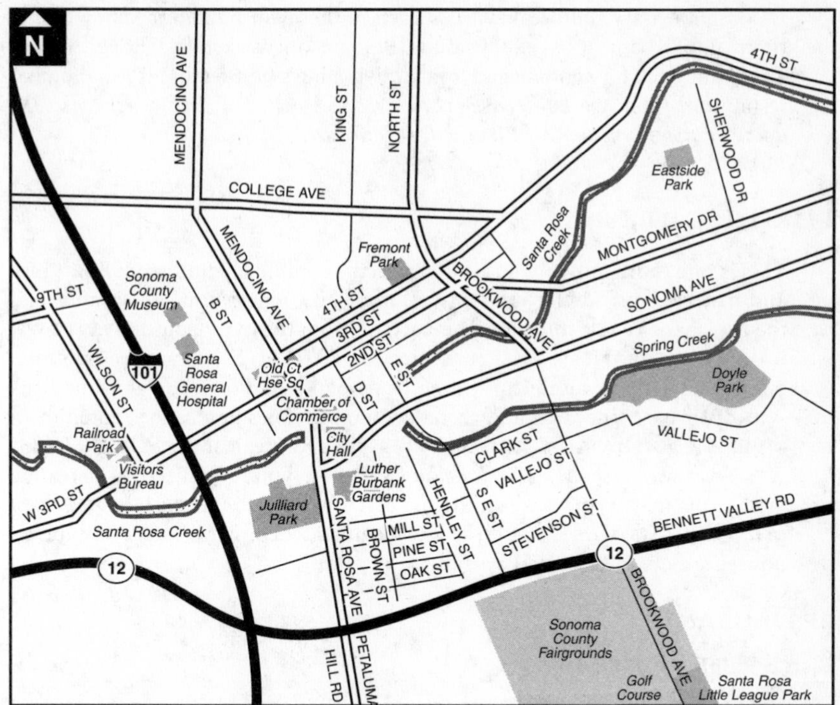

Santa Rosa

flatiron steak with Point Reyes blue cheese ravioli and roasted garlic; or the legendary slow-roasted balsamic pork shoulder with caramelized onions and mashed potatoes. No one can resist the retro-inspired dessert of homemade nutter-butter cookies with Scharffen Berger chocolate fondue. Wines focus on varietals made within a 50-mile radius and include lots of affordable options. *$$$; MC, V; local checks only; dinner Wed–Sun; beer and wine; reservations recommended; www.zazurestaurant.com; at Willowside Rd.*

LODGINGS

Vintners Inn / ★★

4350 BARNES RD, SANTA ROSA; 800/421-2584

The Vintners Inn combines the charm of a country inn with the conveniences of a modern hotel. Its four Provençal-style buildings are clustered around a central courtyard set amid vineyards. The inn's 44 rooms were renovated in 2002 to reflect a European sensibility with king-size beds, plush carpets, armoires and desks, and separate sitting areas; many have wood-burning fireplaces, too. The old-world antics don't extend to smoking, which is not allowed. French doors open onto a balcony or patio with a view of the vineyards or the landscaped grounds (ask for a room with a vineyard view facing away from Highway 101).

A complimentary full breakfast is served in the main building's sunny dining room until 10am on weekdays and 10:30am on weekends. Though there's also a fine deck for sunning and a Jacuzzi, the inn's best feature is its adjoining restaurant, John Ash & Co. (see review). *$$$$; AE, DC, MC, V; checks OK; www.vintnersinn.com; off River Rd, at Hwy 101.*

Healdsburg

This is one tourist town whose charm seems completely unforced. Boutiques and bakeries surround a pretty, tree-lined plaza where you can sit and read the newspaper while munching on pastries from the marvelous **DOWNTOWN BAKERY & CREAMERY** (308-A Center St; 707/431-2719; www.downtownbakery.net). In the summer, nothing beats paddling down the glorious Russian River past vineyards and secret swimming holes in a canoe rented from **RIVER'S EDGE KAYAK & CANOE TRIPS** (13840 Healdsburg Ave; 707/433-7247; www.riversedgekayakandcanoe.com). If you're in need of a respite from your activity-packed day trips, catch a flick at the **RAVEN THEATER** (415 Center St, 707/433-5448; www.raventheater.com), the area's best movie house for new releases and art films.

RESTAURANTS

Bistro Ralph / ★★☆

109 PLAZA ST E, HEALDSBURG; 707/433-1380

In a town where restaurants have been afflicted with the revolving door syndrome, simple yet stylish Bistro Ralph continues to thrive. Housed in a slender storefront on the square, Ralph Tingle's intimate bistro serves consistently excellent food, with a focus on local ingredients. Choice starters include grilled portobello mushrooms with white truffle oil and crispy Sichuan pepper calamari. The lamb dishes are always good, particularly the hearty spring lamb stew à la provençal, and the lamb shanks with crème fraîche–horseradish mashed potatoes. The lunch menu sticks to upscale salads and sandwiches, such as the grilled ahi or salmon sandwich and the popular lamb burger on a fresh roll, all three served with a pile of irresistible shoestring fries. The decor has a cozy, slightly industrial feel, with a dozen or so linen-topped tables, white brick walls, and a long concrete counter where you can watch chef Tingle perform culinary magic in the small open kitchen. *$$; MC, V; local checks only; lunch, dinner Mon–Sat; beer, wine, and martinis; reservations recommended; www.bistroralph.com; on the plaza.*

Zin / ★★

344 CENTER ST, HEALDSBURG; 707/473-0946

Located just off Healdsburg's main plaza, Zin specializes in updated versions of American classics, and each day features a blue plate special, such as meat loaf or St. Louis–style barbecued ribs. The dishes are particularly well suited to pairing with zinfandels (quite fittingly considering Sonoma is prime zin country), and the wine list features a whole page of them. The hush puppies with red pepper make a great starter—a mountain of them served hot and fluffy and grease free. Entrées include a succulent sliced duck breast served on a bed of garlic mashed potatoes topped by sautéed spinach. Grilled lamb chops come with asparagus and a giant helping of roasted new potatoes. This is a great place for those with hearty appetites, because portions are huge. Zin's architecture is Postmodern California Bomb Shelter—a concrete bunker trimmed in redwood—which, thankfully, has little to do with the aesthetic of the food. *$$$; AE, MC, V; local checks only; lunch, dinner every day; beer and wine; reservations recommended; www.zinrestaurant.com; 1 block from the plaza.*

LODGINGS

Belle de Jour Inn / ★★★

16276 HEALDSBURG AVE, HEALDSBURG; 707/431-9777

In a region where rampant Victoriana is all the rage, Belle de Jour's four romantic hillside cottages and large carriage house have a refreshingly spare, uncluttered feel. From the bedroom of the cottage called the Terrace Room, you can savor a fine view of the valley from the comfort of a giant Jacuzzi. Also recommended is the Caretaker's Suite with its lace-canopied four-poster bed, private deck with a vine-covered trellis, and blue-tiled whirlpool tub. All of the accommodations have fireplaces, ceiling fans, and refrigerators and are air-conditioned—a big plus around here in the summer. Innkeepers Tom and Brenda Hearn whip up a bountiful country breakfast and serve it on the deck of the main house. Also available to guests for an hourly fee is a chauffeured back-roads winery tour in the Hearns' 1925 Star touring car—something to consider if wine tasting makes you tipsy. *$$$; AE, MC, V; no checks; belledejourinn.com; 1 mile north of Dry Creek Rd, across from Simi Winery.*

Haydon Street Inn / ★★

321 HAYDON ST, HEALDSBURG; 707/433-5228 OR 800/528-3703

This pretty blue 1912 Queen Anne Victorian inn with a large veranda set behind a white picket fence offers eight cheery guest rooms, all with private baths. But your best bet is to rent one of the two larger rooms in the Victorian Cottage tucked behind the main house. The first floor of the cottage is not for rent, but the upstairs has been turned into two spacious rooms with vaulted ceilings, queen-size beds, high dormer windows, big whirlpool tubs, and loads of charm. In the morning you'll find a full country breakfast featuring such treats as green chile frittatas with basil and cilantro, fresh fruit or baked apples, and plenty of house-made muffins and croissants. *$$$; AE, DIS, MC, V; checks OK; www.haydon.com; at Fitch St.*

Healdsburg Inn on the Plaza / ★★★

112 MATHESON ST, HEALDSBURG; 707/433-6991 OR 800/431-8663

Originally built as a Wells Fargo Express office in 1900, this surprisingly quiet inn on the plaza has high ceilings and a lovely old staircase leading from the ground-floor art gallery to the nine attractive guest rooms upstairs; there is also one downstairs and a carriage house. The four rooms facing the plaza have beautiful bay windows; particularly engaging is the spacious pale yellow and white Song of the Rose Room, which has a king-size white iron and brass bed, a whirlpool tub, and a fireplace. One of the largest rooms is the Garden Suite, with its Jacuzzi, king-size bed, and private patio bedecked with flowers. All rooms have private baths with showers, TVs with VCRs, and air-conditioning; all but one have gas-log fireplaces and five have claw-foot bathtubs. A full breakfast and afternoon wine and snacks are served at tables for two in the glass-enclosed solarium. *$$$; MC, V; no checks; www.healdsburginn.com; on the plaza's south side.*

Hotel Healdsburg / ★★★

317 HEALDSBURG AVE, HEALDSBURG; 800/889-7188

Healdsburg's only full-service luxury hotel offers plush rooms, spa services, and instant access to downtown's adorable old-fashioned square. Upscale perks abound within the 55 sunny rooms, elegantly ornamented with Tibetan rugs, dark wood furnishings, goose-down duvets, TVs and DVD players, CD players, Frette bathrobes, large glittering bathrooms that beckon with walk-in showers and two-person tubs, wireless Internet, and French doors opening to private balconies overlooking the plaza. Though plaza shopping and dining is outside the front door, there's plenty of reason to hang around, specifically a grappa bar, an enormous garden pool, a full-service spa, a fitness room, and famed chef Charlie Palmer's excellent and expensive Dry Creek Kitchen, which serves seasonal cuisine accentuating pure flavors and local ingredients. A daily Gourmet Harvest Breakfast, included in the rates, is served in the hotel lobby. *$$$$; AE, DC, MC, V; checks OK; www.hotelhealdsburg.com; on the plaza.* ♿

Les Mars Hotel / ★★★★

27 NORTH ST, HEALDSBURG; 707/433-4211

For such an unassuming exterior, which is posh and inviting but blends in perfectly with the rest of Healdsburg, Les Mars opens its doors to reveal the most polished inn in the whole region (which is saying a lot, given Wine Country's five-star factor). Opened by the Mars family in 2005, the inn brings the best bits of European luxury to Healdsburg. The 16 rooms spread out over two floors feature hand-carved walnut panels, four-poster canopy beds, sitting areas, and vaulted ceilings, as well as more modern luxuries like marble showers, gas fireplaces, hydrotherapy jet tubs, spa robes, and flat-screen televisions. Room 303 is particularly charming, with brilliant sunlight and views overlooking Healdsburg's quaint downtown below. Added touches in each room such as fresh white roses, complimentary Voss water, breakfast delivered on a silver platter, a fireplace, and even a bedside book light make this place the *crème de la crème*. Not to mention its lobby-level restaurant, Cyrus, has nearly overtaken the French Laundry as the best place to dine in all of Wine Country. If you're going to splurge on any one stay in California, make it this one. Single travelers be wary, though: If you're not there with a partner, you'll really be wishing you were. *$$$$; AE, DIS, MC, V; no checks; www.lesmarshotel.com; at Healdsburg Ave.*

Geyserville

RESTAURANTS

Taverna Santi / ★★★☆

21047 GEYSERVILLE AVE, GEYSERVILLE; 707/857-1790

Until Santi opened downtown, there was really no need to visit the barren boondocks of Geyserville. Rather, it would be much more likely for those passing through to head a bit farther south to Healdsburg or east to Calistoga. But since Santi has been under the management of restaurant industry vet Doug Swett, it's had no trouble packing the house and bringing in guests from far and wide. (It's also an excellent spot to refuel after a day spent among the vines.) The board of house-cured *salumi* is perhaps the most popular in the antipasti category, as is the *insalata di pesce*. Follow with a *primi* like the *spaghettini al sugo calabrese*, then move onto a *secondi* like *pesce con tartufo bianco* (Arctic char, Jerusalem artichokes, black trumpets, Bloomsdale spinach, and white truffle oil). Wash it all down with one of the many local wine selections on hand, and indulge your sweet tooth by ordering the almond panna cotta or pumpkin cake. If you're looking for a quicker bite to eat, try Diavola Pizzeria and Salumeria, Santi's more casual sister next door. *$$$; AE, MC, V; lunch Wed–Sat, dinner every day; full bar; reservations recommended; www.tavernasanti.com; downtown.* ♿

LODGINGS

Hope-Bosworth House / ★★

21238 GEYSERVILLE AVE, GEYSERVILLE; 707/857-3356 OR 800/825-4233

Across the street from its showier cousin, the Hope-Merrill House (see review), the 1904 Hope-Bosworth House provides a cheery, informal, and less expensive place to stay. This Queen Anne–style Victorian inn has four bedrooms, all of which have full baths, including one with a Jacuzzi tub. The downstairs Sun Porch Room has the dry, woody fragrance of a summer cottage, and it reverberates each morning with birdsong from the backyard. Everyone's favorite, however, is the sunny and spacious Wicker Room with its old-fashioned white and pink flowered wallpaper. Guests are treated to the same elaborate breakfast as their neighbors, and they have access to the pool and other facilities at the Hope-Merrill House. *$$$; AE, DIS, MC, V; checks OK; www.hope-inns.com; from Hwy 101, take the Geyserville exit.*

Hope-Merrill House / ★★★

21253 GEYSERVILLE AVE, GEYSERVILLE; 707/857-3356 OR 800/825-4233

Since nearly every mediocre shack built in the late 19th century gets dubbed "Victorian," it's easy to forget the dizzying architectural and design heights reached during that period. This beautifully restored two-story 1870 Eastlake Stick has expansive bay windows and a back veranda furnished with comfortable cane chairs. The landscaping is formal and strictly symmetrical, with box hedges and weeping mulberries. The inn offers eight individually decorated guest rooms with private baths and queen-size beds. The fairest is the Peacock Room: images of gold, rose, and gray-blue peacocks strut around a ceiling border, a gas fireplace dominates one wall, and French doors open into a bathroom with an immense marble-topped two-person whirlpool tub. For the best views, ask for the Vineyard View Room or the Bradbury Room, which have fireplaces, two-person showers, and views of the property's swimming pool (closed in winter) and the pretty gardens. A hearty breakfast is included in the rates. *$$$; AE, DIS, MC, V; checks OK; www.hope-inns.com; from Hwy 101, take the Geyserville exit.*

Cloverdale

LODGINGS

Vintage Towers Bed and Breakfast Inn / ★★

302 N MAIN ST, CLOVERDALE; 888/886-9377

Listed on the National Register of Historic Places, this beautiful mauve mansion located on a quiet residential street has seven air-conditioned guest rooms. The three corner suites have tower sitting rooms (one round, one square, and one octagonal), sleeping quarters, and private baths. Particularly unique is the Vintage Tower Suite, which has its own private porch complete with a telescope for stargazing and a spiral staircase that descends to the yard. Downstairs you'll find a large dining room with a fireplace, a parlor, and a library. In the morning, there's a full gourmet breakfast in the dining room; the veranda is the spot to relax and snack on ever-available cookies, sodas, and other treats. *$$$; AE, DIS, MC, V; checks OK; www.vintagetowers.com; at 3rd St, off Cloverdale Blvd.*

Anderson Valley and Mendocino County Wine Region

For a glimpse of what Napa Valley looked like 30 years ago, visit the quiet, bucolic Anderson Valley. Once noted only for sheep, apples, and timber, the Anderson Valley has become the premier producer of cool-climate California wines such as chardonnay, gewürztraminer, and riesling. The enological future of this valley, whose climate is almost identical to that of the Champagne region of France, may also reside in the production of sparkling wine, now that some of France's best champagne makers have successfully set up shop here.

Anderson Wineries

Most of the Anderson Valley's wineries line the narrow stretch of Highway 128 that winds through this gorgeous, verdant 25-mile-long valley before it reaches the Pacific coast. Here are some of Anderson's premier wineries:

GREENWOOD RIDGE (5501 Hwy 128, Philo; 707/895-2002; www.greenwoodridge.com). Known for its white riesling (and cabernet and zinfandel produced in another region), Greenwood is the site of the annual California Wine Tasting Championships (for novices and pros) held on the last weekend of July; it also has a picnic area by a pond and a tasting room.

HANDLEY CELLARS (3151 Hwy 128, Philo; 707/895-3876; www.handleycellars.com). Popular for its chardonnay, which is free to taste, Handley has a tasting room full of exotic artifacts from around the world, and a picnic area in a garden courtyard.

HUSCH VINEYARDS (4400 Hwy 128, Philo; 800/554-8724; www.huschvineyards.com). The oldest winery in the Anderson Valley (founded in 1971), Husch produces chardonnay, pinot noir, and gewürztraminer, along with wines from its Ukiah vineyards. It offers free samples in a small, rustic redwood tasting room and also has picnic tables.

NAVARRO VINEYARDS (5601 Hwy 128, Philo; 707/895-3686; www.navarrowine.com). This small, family-owned winery pioneered the region's trademark wine (dry, fruity, spicy Alsatian-style gewürztraminer) and produces outstanding chardonnay, pinot noir, white riesling, and sexy straight-up grape juice. Navarro wines are sold only by mail order, at the winery, and in restaurants; the winery has a surprisingly large—and free—tasting menu.

PACIFIC ECHO CELLARS (8501 Hwy 128, Philo; 707/895-2065). In 1991 Scharffenberger Cellars was sold to Moët Hennessey, which has since begun bottling its traditional French sparkling wine under the generic-sounding label "Pacific Echo Cellars." The company still produces excellent brut, blanc de blancs, brut rosé, and *crèmant*. The tasting room is in a remodeled farmhouse. Tours are available.

ROEDERER ESTATE (4501 Hwy 128, Philo; 707/895-2288; www.roedererestate.com). This winery was established by one of France's most prestigious champagne producers. Inside the quietly elegant hillside facility, visitors can take tours by appointment to learn about the sparkling wine–making process. Inside the tasting room you can sample high-quality sparkling wines for a nominal fee.

Boonville

This speck of a town in the heart of the Anderson Valley is best known for a regional dialect called Boontling, developed by townsfolk at the beginning of the century. No one really speaks Boontling anymore, though a few old-timers remember the lingo. As in most private languages, a large percentage of the words refer to sex, a fact glossed over in most touristy brochures on the topic. Most people don't know what the Boontling word for beer is, but the folks at the **ANDERSON VALLEY BREWING COMPANY** (17700 Boonville Rd; 707/895-BEER; www.avbc.com; tours 11:30am, 3pm Thurs–Mon) definitely do and will tell you during brewery tours. While you're in town, grab a copy of the **ANDERSON VALLEY ADVERTISER** (www.theava.com), a rollicking, crusading (some say muckraking) small-town paper with avid readers from as far away as San Francisco and the Oregon border. **BOONT BERRY FARM** (13981 Hwy 128; 707/895-3576), an organic-produce market and deli in a small, weathered-wood building, turns out terrific treats.

LODGINGS

The Boonville Hotel and Restaurant / ★★★

14050 HWY 128, BOONVILLE; 707/895-2210

The decor of the Old West–style hotel is pleasantly austere, but feels more modern Shaker these days. Half of the rooms have private balconies, although two of them overlook the busy highway. Two newer suites and two cottages offer spacious separate sitting areas, making them well suited to those with kids in tow. (The staff hasn't seemed to figure out that the bare hardwood floors of the old hotel are not suited to the clomping of small children, a fact that can make sleeping near-impossible for the other guests.) The smaller rooms at the back of the hotel are quieter and less expensive. Medium-sized room 3, with its unique iron bed, is a good compromise between affordability, spaciousness, and peacefulness. Guests are treated to breakfast beverages in the sunny dining room. The restaurant, a gathering spot for local winemakers, is still one of the best north of the Napa Valley. Chef Schmitt (who for years cooked with his mother when she owned the French Laundry restaurant in Yountville) offers a fresh mix of California, Southwestern, and backwoods regional cuisine, such as sliced pork tenderloin with cumin, cilantro, and oranges, and chicken breast with roasted tomato–mint salsa. Reservations are recommended for the restaurant, especially in summer. From May through October, the hotel parking lot becomes the site of the festive Boonville Farmers Market (9:45am–noon Sat). *$$$; MC, V; checks OK; usually closed Jan; www.boonvillehotel.com; at Lambert Ln, in the center of town.*

Philo

There's not much to see in this hamlet, but about 2 miles west you'll find **GOWAN'S OAK TREE** (6600 Hwy 128; 707/895-3353), a great family-run roadside fruit-and-vegetable stand with a few picnic tables in back and a swing for road-weary tots.

Hopland

This small town's name originated from hops, an herb used to flavor beer. Hop vines once covered the region from the 1860s until mildew wiped out the crop in the 1940s. The only legacy left of that era today is the hops growing in the beer garden of **MENDOCINO BREWING COMPANY** (13351 S Hwy 101, Hopland; 707/744-1361; www.mendobrew.com), a location that's also home to several award-winning microbrews. Today, Hopland's rich alluvial soil is dedicated to the production of wine grapes and Bartlett pears.

While it may not look like much, a handful of fine lodging and dining options could put this up-and-coming spot on the map, primarily as a jump-off point to Anderson Valley's many vineyards. Before doing anything else after you arrive, drop by the central **SIP!** tasting room (13420 S Hwy 101; 707/744-8375; www.sipmendocino.com; open 11am–6pm every day), the only of its kind in the vicinity, to visit owner Bernadette Byrne, a 20-year veteran of the area's wine industry, and get an overview (and taste) of the best varieties around. Sip! will give you a chance to mingle with locals and tourists alike on its comfy, shaded patio.

RESTAURANTS

Bluebird Café / ★★

13340 S HWY 101, HOPLAND; 707/744-1633

It takes but a step through the door at this shabby diner to realize that this is a locals' spot. Although Hopland is the gateway to Anderson Valley's Wine Country, no one else in the establishment appears to be a tourist. Thus, don't be surprised when you're given the once over by all patrons not polite enough to keep their eyes on their own food. Still, the staff is pretty friendly (if a bit unattentive), and they certainly know how to cook up a mean scramble, eggs Benedict, or stack of steaming pancakes with fruit topping. The lunch menu, though, is this café's selling point: it serves just about any kind of burger meat you could want—ostrich, boar, elk, salmon, and regular ol' cow—as well as its signature dish, O&M (beer-battered onions and mushrooms). *$–$$; AE, MC, V; local checks only; breakfast, lunch every day, dinner Thurs–Mon; beer and wine; no reservations; downtown.*

The Crushed Grape Grille / ★★★

13500 S HWY 101, HOPLAND; 707/744-2020

Even if this restaurant weren't the only dinner spot in town (except for the Bluebird Café, which is only open at night on weekends), it would still be our pick based on its mix of casual atmosphere, inventive dishes, and inexpensive prices. Not to mention, nothing beats patio dining while watching a rousing game of bocce ball. (There are six on-site courts that both Crushed Grape patrons and local bocce ball–league members share.) Try the house-specialty red roasted pepper soup to start, followed by an entrée from the comfort cuisine menu (like the mini meatloaf with garlic mashed potatoes, gravy, and veggies) or one of the gourmet pizzas (the pear, Gorgonzola, arugula, red onion, and balsamic vinaigrette is a favorite). Top it all off with a warm piece of Kentucky Derby pie—à la mode, of course. *$$; MC, V; checks OK; lunch, dinner Tues–Sat; full bar; reservations recommended; www.thecrushedgrape.com; at Schoolhouse Plaza.* ♿

LODGINGS

The Hopland Inn / ★

13401 HWY 101, HOPLAND; 707/744-1890 OR 800/266-1891

Built as a stage stop in 1890, this haughty cream-colored combination of Gothic spires and gabled windows still looks like a luxurious frontier saloon-hotel, thanks to an $800,000 restoration in 1990. The lobby is dominated by a long, mirrored, polished-wood bar; and the gorgeous dark wood–paneled library is filled with interesting old books, velvet settees, shiny brass reading lamps, and a fireplace. A wide, curving wood stairway leads from the lobby to 21 charmingly decorated guest rooms on the second and third stories—all with private baths. The quietest rooms with the best views are on the south side of the hotel overlooking the backyard patio with a fountain, wrought-iron lampposts, and a giant oak tree. A continental breakfast is included in the rate. The hotel's restaurant, the Bar & Bistro at the Hopland Inn, serves acceptable but uninspired California cuisine. *$$$; AE, MC, V; checks OK; www.hoplandinn.com; downtown.*

Ukiah

Located in the upper reaches of the California Wine Country, Ukiah is still what Napa, Sonoma, and Healdsburg used to be—a sleepy little agricultural town surrounded by vineyards and apple and pear orchards. Peopled by an odd mix of farmers, loggers, and back-to-the-landers, Ukiah is a down-to-earth little burg with few traces of Wine Country gentrification. That doesn't mean there isn't any wine, however. **JEPSON VINEYARDS** (10400 Hwy 101; 800/516-7342; www.jepsonwine.com) produces a wide variety of wines, including chardonnay, sauvignon blanc, sparkling wine, and brandy, which is distilled in a copper alembic. Mendocino County's oldest winery, founded in 1932, is

PARDUCCI WINE ESTATES (501 Parducci Rd; 707/462-5350; www.parducci.com), an enterprise that produces a variety of reds and whites. And if you continue up the road a bit to the Redwood Valley, you'll find **FREY VINEYARDS** (14000 Tomki Rd, off Hwy 101, Redwood Valley; 707/485-5177 or 800/760-3739; www.freywine.com), one of the few wineries in the state that doesn't add sulfites to its wines and uses certified organically grown grapes. Sample the Frey family's petite syrah, cabernet, sauvignon blanc, and more.

Soak away the aches and pains of your long drive (Ukiah is a long drive from almost anywhere) at the clothing-optional **ORR HOT SPRINGS** (13201 Orr Springs Rd; 707/462-6277), or in North America's only warm and naturally carbonated mineral baths at **VICHY SPRINGS RESORT** (see review). Hikers will want to stretch their legs at **MONTGOMERY WOODS STATE RESERVE** (on Orr Springs Rd, off Hwy 101, 15 miles northwest of Ukiah; www.parks.ca.gov, search "Montgomery Woods"); it features 1,142 acres of coastal redwoods with a self-guided nature trail along Montgomery Creek. In town, the main attraction is the **GRACE HUDSON MUSEUM AND SUN HOUSE** (431 S Main St; 707/467-2836; www.gracehudsonmuseum.org), housing Hudson's paintings of Pomo Indians and a collection of beautiful Pomo baskets.

RESTAURANTS

Patrona / ★★★

130 W STANDLEY AVE, UKIAH; 707/462-9181

After patrolling the streets for something other than a fast-food joint, which upon initial encounter seems to be all that Ukiah has to offer, you'll be thrilled to stumble upon this out-of-place, midrange eatery. Big and open, with an interesting display of Native American ponchos, Patrona appears to attract large groups of locals celebrating birthdays, bachelorette parties, and other occasions. Start the night off with the crispy calamari in an orange-pepper glaze or the Gorgonzola, poached fig, and walnut pizza. Entrées are a wide selection of standard meat, seafood, and pasta dishes, while desserts are pretty basic fare, such as chocolate torte or apple crumble. The restaurant supports the local food market and only uses organic and seasonal ingredients, meaning the menu changes daily based on what's available. Owner Craig Strattman can be spotted mingling with his diners and ensuring that all have as fine an experience as possible. The wine list, comprising only Mendocino varietals, was carefully selected by the staff. *$$$; AE, MC, V; local checks only; dinner Tues–Sat; full bar; reservations recommended; www.patronarestaurant.com; at School St.* ♿

Schat's Courthouse Bakery and Cafe / ★

113 W PERKINS ST, UKIAH; 707/462-1670

Schat's Courthouse Bakery has been open in Ukiah since 1990, but its history dates back to Holland in the early 1800s—which is as far back as the fifth-generation baker brothers Zach and Brian Schat can trace the roots of a very long line of Schat bakers. In 1948, the Schat clan emigrated to California, bringing with them the hallowed family recipe for their signature Sheepherder's Bread, a semisour, dairy- and sugar-free round loaf that's so popular it's been featured in *Sunset* magazine's "Best of the West" column. What really separates Schat's Courthouse Bakery from the rest are the huge more-than-you-can-possibly-eat lunch items: made-to-order sandwiches, build-your-own baked potatoes, house-made soups, tangy Caesar salad, and huge slices of vegetarian quiche (served with bread and a salad), each for around five bucks. Located just off Highway 101, this is a great spot to load up on munchies while exploring the local Wine Country. *$$; MC, V; local checks only; breakfast, lunch Mon–Sat; beer and wine; reservations recommended; www.schats.com; from Hwy 101 take the Perkins St exit west; ½ block west of State St, across from the courthouse.*

LODGINGS

Sanford House Bed and Breakfast / ★★

306 S PINE ST, UKIAH; 707/462-1653

There's something indisputably small-town about this tall, yellow Victorian inn on a tree-lined street just west of Ukiah's Mayberry-like downtown. Peaceful, unhurried, and bucolic, Sanford House boasts only one Gothic turret, but it does have a big front porch dotted with white wicker chairs and an old-fashioned baby buggy, plus an English garden complete with a koi pond. Inside, antiques grace every room and everything is freshly painted, but it's far too comfortable and unpretentious to be called a showplace. The five guest rooms are named after turn-of-the-century presidents; the Taft Room, with its dark four-poster bed, floral fabrics, and a sort of spooky Princess Di doll in a wedding dress, is the most elegant, but equally pleasant is the spacious cream and green Wilson Room with its floral wallpaper, beautiful armoire, and sunny turret sitting area. *$$; MC, V; checks OK; www.sanfordhouse.com; from Hwy 101, take the Perkins St exit, head west, and turn left on Pine.*

Vichy Springs Resort / ★

2605 VICHY SPRINGS RD, UKIAH; 707/462-9515

Although the rejuvenating effect of the naturally carbonated mineral pools at Vichy Springs had been known by the Pomo Indians for hundreds of years, it wasn't until the mid-1800s that others caught on to the idea. Since then, this California Historic Landmark has attracted the likes of Ulysses S. Grant, Teddy Roosevelt, Mark Twain, and Jack London to the famed baths that have a mineral content identical to the famed pools in Vichy, France. With such a remarkable distinction and luminous history, one would expect a four-star resort with fancy bathhouses. Ironically, the estate was practically a disaster area for years until proprietors Gilbert and Marjorie Ashoff refurbished the 700-acre property and reopened it in 1989. Even with its face-lift, the resort is far from posh, though five creek-side rooms, all with private baths, and the two-bedroom Jack London Cottage bring the accommodations up a notch. Twelve more small, simply decorated guest rooms—all with private baths and most with queen-size beds—line a long ranch house–style building. If you're visiting with children, consider staying at one of the eight private cottages, each fully equipped with a kitchen, a wood-burning stove, and a shaded porch. Built more than 130 years ago, the eight indoor and outdoor baths remain basically unchanged (bathing suits required). Also on the grounds are a nonchlorinated Olympic-size pool filled with the therapeutic bubbly, a modern whirlpool bath, a small cabin where Swedish massages are administered, and 6 miles of ranch roads available to hikers and mountain bikers. Room rates include an expanded continental breakfast and unlimited use of the pools, which are rarely crowded. The baths are available for day use, too, and the resort has basic services for business travelers. *$$$; AE, DC, DIS, MC, V; checks OK; www.vichysprings.com; from Hwy 101, take the Vichy Springs Rd exit and head west.*

NORTH COAST

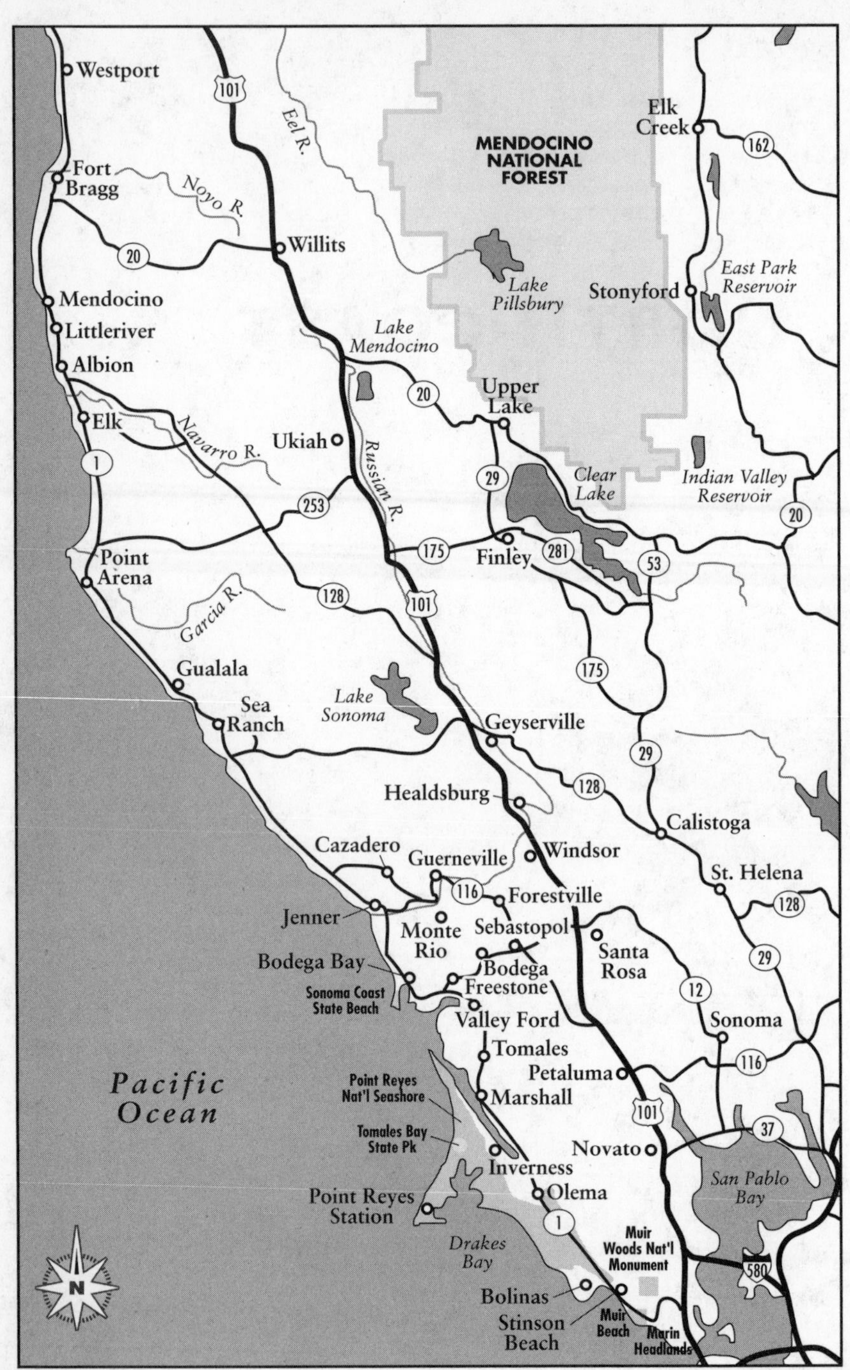
Westport
101
Eel R.
Elk Creek
162
MENDOCINO NATIONAL FOREST
Fort Bragg
Noyo R.
Willits
20
East Park Reservoir
Stonyford
Lake Pillsbury
Mendocino
Littleriver
Lake Mendocino
Albion
20
Upper Lake
Elk
Navarro R.
Ukiah
Russian R.
1
29
Clear Lake
Indian Valley Reservoir
253
20
175
Finley
281
53
Point Arena
Garcia R.
128
101
175
Gualala
Sea Ranch
Lake Sonoma
Geyserville
29
128
Healdsburg
Calistoga
Cazadero
Guerneville
Windsor
St. Helena
116
Forestville
128
Jenner
Monte Rio
Sebastopol
Santa Rosa
Bodega Bay
Bodega
29
Freestone
12
Sonoma Coast State Beach
Valley Ford
Sonoma
Tomales
116
Petaluma
Pacific Ocean
Point Reyes Nat'l Seashore
Marshall
101
Tomales Bay State Pk
37
Novato
Inverness
San Pablo Bay
Point Reyes Station
Olema
1
Drakes Bay
Muir Woods Nat'l Monument
580
N
Bolinas
Stinson Beach
Muir Beach
Marin Headlands

NORTH COAST

From the point where the Golden Gate Bridge touches the sunny shores of Marin County to the ruggedly beautiful timber- and trawler-dotted land and seascapes of Fort Bragg, the North Coast offers some of the most beautiful scenery on California's coastline. You can leave your ties and high heels at home, because informality reigns supreme in these parts. It's all about walks on the beach, farm-fresh cuisine, spectacular vistas, and forgetting your worries—if just for a while.

ACCESS AND INFORMATION

Two major highways provide access to the North Coast: **HIGHWAY 1**, the only route that runs along the coast, and **HIGHWAY 101**, the central artery that connects to Highway 1 via three main scenic roads. To enjoy the full-blown coast experience, take the Stinson Beach/Highway 1 exit from Highway 101 north and head west. Driving is always slow along the coast; on a good day it'll take you five hours to reach Mendocino. Here are four alternative Highway 1/Highway 101 combo routes to consider, depending on time constraints and how far north you want to travel. *First*: From Highway 101 take the Highway 1/Stinson Beach exit about 7 miles north of the Golden Gate Bridge. This is the quickest route to Muir Woods and Stinson Beach. *Second*: Exit from Highway 101 at Sir Francis Drake Boulevard, which will take you through West Marin to Olema, where Highway 1 and Sir Francis Drake Boulevard intersect (the quickest route to Point Reyes and Tomales Bay). *Third*: Traveling north on Highway 101, exit at Petaluma/Highway 116 west. Follow Bodega Avenue to Petaluma Valley Ford Road and continue on to Bodega Highway (the easiest route to Bodega Bay and Jenner). *Fourth*: Traveling north on Highway 101, exit at Highway 128 west (don't take the first "east" exit) just past Cloverdale, which will take you to Highway 1 just below Mendocino. This is by far the fastest route to Mendocino and Fort Bragg.

Once you exit Highway 101—avoid commute hours like the plague—you will be rewarded with scenic drives through idyllic pastoral settings and little traffic aside from the occasional moving house (a.k.a. motor home).

Expect more fog, wind, and cold weather as you travel north along the coast. Call **CALTRANS** (800/427-7623) or log on to www.dot.ca.gov for highway conditions. Stock up on provisions for the drive, bring Dramamine if you're prone to carsickness (which you will be on these roads), and pack layers of clothing. Oh yes, and don't forget the binoculars and wide-angle camera lens.

The **MARIN COUNTY CONVENTION & VISITORS BUREAU** (1 Mitchell Blvd, Ste B, San Rafael; 415/925-2060 or 866/925-2060; www.visitmarin.org) is an excellent Marin County information resource. Contact the **FORT BRAGG–MENDOCINO COAST CHAMBER OF COMMERCE** (332 N Main St, Fort Bragg; 707/961-6300; www.mendocinocoast.com) for information about the Mendocino area.

The Marin Coast

Although Marin County has one of the highest per-capita incomes in the nation, you won't find even a Motel 6 along the entire Marin coast, due partly to very restrictive zoning laws but mostly to the inaccessibly rugged, heavily forested terrain (it may look like a 15-minute drive from San Francisco on the map, but 90 minutes later you'll probably still be negotiating hairpin curves down the side of Mount Tamalpais). The only downside to the Marin coast's underdevelopment is the scarcity of affordable lodgings; expensive B and Bs reign supreme, which is fine if you don't mind spending $200 a night or more (with a two-night minimum, of course) for a bed and a bagel. Otherwise, the Marin coast is just short of Eden, a veritable organic playground for weary commuters and adventure-bound tourists.

Marin Headlands

On a sunny San Francisco day, there's no better place to spend time outdoors than in the Marin Headlands. For more than a century following the Civil War, this vast expanse of grass-covered hills and rocky shore was off-limits to the public, appropriated by the U.S. Army as a strategic base for defending the bay against invaders. Remnants of obsolete and untested defense facilities—dozens of thick concrete bunkers and batteries recessed into the bluffs—now serve as viewing and picnic sites for the millions of tourists who visit each year.

There's a wealth of scheduled activities offered daily within the 15-square-mile **GOLDEN GATE NATIONAL RECREATION AREA** (GGNRA), including birding clinics, bunker tours, wildflower hunts, and geology hikes. The **MARIN HEADLANDS VISITOR CENTER** (take the Alexander Ave exit, the second exit after crossing the Golden Gate Bridge, off Hwy 101 and follow signs; 415/331-1540; www.nps.gov/goga/marin-headlands.htm; open 9:30am–4:30pm every day), located within the headlands, houses plenty of information, including maps and pertinent facts about all the locations listed here.

The **MARINE MAMMAL CENTER** (415/289-SEAL; www.tmmc.org; open 10am–4pm every day; free), a popular Marin Headlands attraction, is a volunteer-run hospital for injured and abandoned mammals of the sea. Signs list each animal's adopted name, species, stranding site, and injury—the latter of which is usually human caused. The center is located at the east end of Fort Cronkhite near Rodeo Lagoon.

Closed to the public for several years due to storm damage, the precariously perched 1877 **POINT BONITA LIGHTHOUSE** (415/331-1540; open 12:30–3:30pm Sat–Mon) is once again thrilling those tourists brave enough to traverse the long, dark tunnel and seven small footbridges leading to the beacon. The reward for such courage is, among other things, a rare and sensational view of the entrance to the bay. The story goes that one 19th-century lighthouse keeper rigged ropes around his children to prevent them from slipping into the raging sea below.

Also within the Marin Headlands is **HAWK HILL** (located above Battery 129, where Conzelman Rd becomes one-way), one of the most remarkable avian sites in the western United States and the biggest hawk lookout in western North America. Record count in 1992 was more than 20,000 birds, including 21 species of hawk. The best time to visit is during September and October, when thousands of birds of prey soar over the hill each day.

Muir Woods

When you stand in the middle of Muir Woods (from Hwy 101 in Sausalito, take the Stinson Beach/Hwy 1 exit heading west and follow the signs; 415/388-2595; www.nps.gov/muwo; open 8am–sunset; $5 per person 16 years and older) surrounded by a canopy of ancient redwoods towering hundreds of feet skyward, it's hard to fathom that San Francisco is less than 6 miles away. It's a den of wooden giants; tourists speak in hushed tones as they crane their necks in disbelief, snapping photographs that don't begin to capture the immensity of these living titans.

Muir Woods can get absurdly crowded on summer weekends. Picnicking is not allowed, but there is a snack bar and gift shop at the entrance. It's typically cool and damp, so dress appropriately. And for an even more memorable experience, grab a brew and a bratwurst in the well-kept secret **TOURIST CLUB** (20 Ridge Ave, Muir Woods; 415/388-9987; www.touristclubsf.org), a German beer garden. You can join the club, or simply visit the first, third, or fourth weekend of any month between 1 and 6pm. Just remember to bring cash, as the bar doesn't accept credit cards.

Three miles west of Muir Woods, along Highway 1, is a small crescent-shaped cove called **MUIR BEACH**. Strewn with bits of driftwood and numerous tide pools, Muir Beach is a more sedate alternative to the beer 'n' bikini crowds at the ever-popular **STINSON BEACH** up north. If all you're looking for is a sandy, quiet place for some R & R, park your car right here and skip the trip to Stinson.

RESTAURANTS

The Pelican Inn / ★★

10 PACIFIC WY, MUIR BEACH; 415/383-6000

One of the better ways to spend a Sunday afternoon is to take a leisurely drive to this homey little English pub, grab a table at the glassed-in patio or by the fireplace, and gorge yourself proper on a steaming shepherd's pie. Rack of lamb, prime rib, and a few fish dishes are also on the menu, and in the bar you'll find a goodly number of British, Irish, and Scottish beers on tap. After lunch, burn a few calories with a stroll down Muir Beach. A high tea is available with 48-hour notice; Sundays feature a special pub roast carvery. *$$; MC, V; no checks; lunch, dinner every day; beer and wine; reservations recommended; www.pelicaninn.com; at the entrance to Muir Beach.* ♿

NORTH COAST THREE-DAY TOUR

DAY ONE: *Meet the giants.* Fuel up at the **DIPSEA CAFE** (200 Shoreline Hwy, Mill Valley; 415/381-0298). Follow the curves on Highway 1 to **MUIR WOODS**, home of the giant redwoods. Grab your jacket, pick up a trail guide at the entrance, and look up in awe. Take the 1-mile main trail loop to **CATHEDRAL GROVE**, where you might be inspired to grow a tree of your own. Live redwood burls are sold at the gift shop. Back on Highway 1, expect winding roads aplenty and gorgeous views as you wind down to **STINSON BEACH**. Get your toes wet in the sand or search for an elusive sand dollar. Refuel at the **PARKSIDE CAFE**, then move on to the **POINT REYES NATIONAL SEASHORE**. Check in at the **OLEMA INN** and enjoy a refreshing respite. Round 'em up and head for Main Street at **POINT REYES STATION**. Dinner's served at the **STATION HOUSE CAFE**. Be sure to mosey across the street to the **OLD WESTERN SALOON** (11201 Hwy 1, Point Reyes Station; 415/663-1661) for a nightcap before you hit the hay.

DAY TWO: *Earth-shaking events.* Time to see what's shaking at the **BEAR VALLEY VISITOR CENTER**: Stop at the seismograph station and check out the status of "the big one." Walk through the large picnic area in back of the visitor center and follow the signs to the half-mile-long **EARTHQUAKE TRAIL**. Walk along the San Andreas fault and examine the epicenter of the 1906 San Francisco earthquake. Then check out the **MORGAN HORSE FARM** and drop in to the sweat house at **KULE LOKO**, a re-created coast Miwok Indian village. For a great

Stinson Beach

On those treasured weekend days when the fog has lifted and the sun is scorching the Northern California coast, blurry-eyed Bay Area residents grab their morning paper and beach chairs, pile into their SUVs, and scramble to the sandy shores of popular Stinson Beach—the North Coast's nice-try answer to the fabled beaches of Southern California.

A 3½-mile stretch of beige sand provides elbow room for everyone to spread out beach blankets, picnic baskets, and toys. Swimming is allowed, and lifeguards are on duty from May through mid-September, though notices about riptides (plus the sea's toe-numbing temperatures and the threat of sharks) tend to discourage folks from venturing too far into the water. Call 415/868-1922 for recorded weather and surf conditions.

Joined at the hip with la playa is a village filled with art galleries, specialty shops, and informal cafés. There are plenty of adventurous things to do in the area. For example, **OFF THE BEACH BOATS** (15 Calle del Mar, next to the Stinson Beach Post Office; 415/868-9445) offers three-hour lessons on picnic, buy your provisions at **TOMALES BAY FOODS** and set out on Highway 1, bound for Tomales and **DILLON BEACH**. Spread out your blanket and soak up the fresh air and sweet sound of the surf. You'll be camping tonight, Tuscan-style, at the **SONOMA COAST VILLA**. Hang up your gear and prepare to be pampered. If you're still raring to go after watching the sunset, have dinner at the **DUCK CLUB**, or call it a day with a 90-minute massage.

DAY THREE: *Damme it all!* Let the fog burn off while you linger over a full breakfast at the villa. Set your compass north; take it easy on the curves. Cruise through Bodega Bay and pick up a quart of crab cioppino and some sodas at the **LUCAS WHARF DELI** (595 Hwy 1, Bodega Bay; 707/875-3522). The second pit stop is Jenner, home of **GOAT ROCK BEACH**. You can stand on the cliffs by the road and, with the aid of binoculars, get close-up views of the harbor seals congregated on the sandbar below. Dig into that cioppino while you're at it. Back in the car, hug the curves to Point Arena. Find out about those ships of the night and mysterious lights when you tour the **POINT ARENA LIGHTHOUSE AND MUSEUM**. On to Mendocino. Fortified with a sugar rush from the **TOTE FÊTE BAKERY**, stroll through the galleries and shops before making your way to **VAN DAMME STATE PARK** to hike the **FERN CANYON TRAIL**. Check in to the **MENDOCINO FARMHOUSE**, play with Molly the dog for a while on the front lawn, then head back to Mendocino for dinner at the **MOOSE CAFE** followed by a nightcap at **DICK'S PLACE** before settling in for the night with one of the cats at the farmhouse.

the basics of sea and surf kayaking. They also rent sea and surf kayaks, surfboards, bodyboards, and wetsuits.

Skinny-dipping is the trend at **RED ROCK** (www.redrockbeach.com), one of the few nude beaches on the Marin coast. Located about 1 mile south of Stinson Beach on Highway 1, it's easy to miss since you can't see it from the road. Park at the first dirt pull-off on your right after leaving Stinson and look for a steep path leading down to the water.

RESTAURANTS

The Parkside Cafe / ★★

43 ARENAL AVE, STINSON BEACH; 415/868-1272

During the day this popular neighborhood café bustles with locals and Bay Area beachgoers who stop for an inexpensive breakfast or lunch before shoving off to Stinson Beach around the corner. Morning favorites are the omelets, blueberry pancakes, and the not-to-be-missed raisin-walnut bread. For lunch there are basics like burgers, grilled sandwiches, and soups, as well as daily specials. Once the beach crowd departs, the kitchen starts preparing the seasonal evening menu, which might include oven-roasted Sonoma squab, pan-seared Alaskan halibut, or grilled filet mignon. On sunny days dine alfresco on the brick patio; otherwise, cozy up to the fire. For a quick bite to go, the café's snack bar sells great burgers, fries, and shakes daily from March through September, and on weekends from October through February. *$–$$; AE, MC, V; local checks only; breakfast, lunch, dinner every day; beer and wine; reservations recommended for dinner; www.parksidecafe.com; off Calle del Mar.* ♿

Bolinas

The beach town of Bolinas, a tight-knit community of free-spirited individuals, is one of the most reclusive towns in Northern California. Residents regularly take down highway signs pointing the way to their rural enclave, an act of rebellion that ironically has created more publicity for Bolinas than any road sign ever did. As a tourist, you don't have to worry about being chased out of town by a band of machete-wielding Bolinistas, but don't expect anyone to roll out the welcome mat, either. The trick is not to look like a tourist, but more like a Bay Area resident who's only here to buy some peaches at the **PEOPLE'S STORE** (14 Wharf Rd; 415/868-1433; open 8:30am–6:30pm every day).

What's the People's Store, you ask? It's a town landmark that's well known for its locally grown organic produce and exceptional service—the antithesis of the corporate supermarket. It's a little hard to find, hidden at the end of a gravel driveway (don't confuse it with the much larger general store down the street), but it's worth searching out just to see—and taste—the difference between Safeway and the Bolinas way.

Three side trips offer plenty of entertainment. Just before entering downtown Bolinas, turn right (west) on Mesa Road, left on Overlook Road, and right on Elm Road, and you'll dead-end at the **DUXBURY REEF NATURE RESERVE** (415/499-6387), the largest intertidal reef in North America. Rich tide pools harbor an array of starfish, lacy purple plants, sea anemones, and kelp. Check the tide conditions and wear appropriate shoes; the rocks are slippery. If you continue west on Mesa Road you'll reach the **POINT REYES BIRD OBSERVATORY** (415/868-1221; www.prbo.org; open dawn to dusk every day), where ornithologists keep an eye on more than 400 feathered species. Admission to the visitor center and nature trail is free, and visitors are welcome to observe the tricky process of catching and banding the birds. Banding hours vary seasonally; call 415/868-0655 for exact times. At the very end of Mesa Road is the **PALOMARIN TRAILHEAD**, which accesses beautiful coast and inland trails that stretch for more than 12 miles. The 6-mile round-trip trek passes several small lakes and meadows before it reaches **ALAMERE FALLS**, a freshwater stream that cascades down a 40-foot bluff onto **WILDCAT BEACH**.

BOLINAS LAGOON, a placid saltwater expanse that serves as refuge for numerous shorebirds and harbor seals, is just south of the town of Bolinas on Highway 1. Across from the lagoon is the **AUDUBON CANYON RANCH'S BOLINAS LAGOON PRESERVE** (415/868-9244; www.egret.org;

open 10am–4pm Sat–Sun and holidays mid-Mar–mid-July, by appt for groups; free), a 1,014-acre wildlife sanctuary that supports a major population of great blue herons and white great egrets. This is the premier spot along the Pacific coast to watch these immense, graceful seabirds as they court, mate, and build huge nests at the top of towering redwoods. Baby birds are usually in the nests by late April. The trails leading to the overlook are steep and often slippery. Wear sturdy shoes or boots.

Point Reyes National Seashore

Hiking, biking, swimming, sailing, windsurfing, sunbathing, camping, fishing, horseback riding, bird-watching, kayaking—all are fair game at this 71,000-acre sanctuary of forested hills, deep green pastures, and undisturbed beaches. Point Reyes is hardly a secret anymore—more than 2 million visitors arrive each year—but the land is so vast and varied that crowds are a rarity.

There are four towns in and around the Point Reyes National Seashore boundary: Olema, Point Reyes Station, Inverness Park, and Inverness. Choose one and you'll be within a stone's throw of the park. While the selection of lodging in Point Reyes is excellent, it's also expensive, with most rooms well over $150 per night. Be sure to make your reservation far in advance for the summer and holidays, and bring layers of clothing: Point Reyes gets chilly at night regardless of the season. If you're having trouble finding a vacancy, call the **INNS OF MARIN** (415/663-2000 or 800/887-2880; www.innsofmarin.com) or **WEST MARIN NETWORK** (415/663-9543) for information on available accommodations. The **WEST MARIN CHAMBER OF COMMERCE** (415/663-9232; www.pointreyes.org) is also a good source for lodging and visitor information.

Your first stop is the **BEAR VALLEY VISITOR CENTER** (Bear Valley Rd; 415/464-5100; www.nps.gov/pore; open 9am–5pm Mon–Fri, 8am–5pm Sat–Sun), located at the entrance to the Point Reyes National Seashore; follow the signs from Highway 1 in Olema. Pick up a free map and trail guide and chat with a friendly ranger about overnight campsites, weather forecasts, tide conditions, and special programs. Drive out to the **POINT REYES LIGHTHOUSE** (415/669-1534; open 10am–4:30pm Thurs–Mon, weather permitting) at the westernmost tip of the Point Reyes Peninsula. It's a 45-minute scenic excursion through windswept meadows and working dairy ranches—watch out for cows on the road. When the fog burns off, the lighthouse and the headlands provide a fantastic lookout point for spying gray whales and thousands of common murres that inundate the rocks below. Visitors have free access to the lighthouse via a windy 0.4-mile walk with a thigh-burning 308-step staircase.

If bivalves are your thing, stop off at **DRAKES BAY FAMILY OYSTER FARM** (off Sir Francis Drake Blvd, about 6 miles west of Inverness; 415/669-1149; www.drakesbayfamilyfarms.com). Eat 'em on the spot, or buy a bag for the road—either way, you're not likely to find California oysters as fresh or as cheap anywhere else. The oyster farm resides within **DRAKES ESTERO**, a

POINT REYES NATIONAL SEASHORE RULES AND REGULATIONS

You will find no gates or tollbooths on the roads leading in and out of Point Reyes; access is free and relatively unlimited, but you won't be allowed to park your car overnight here since car camping is prohibited (although the rangers won't stop you from taking an innocent midnight stroll on a clear night, they may stop by to check to see if you're all right). Most of the rules here are aimed at one of two goals: protecting park visitors from injuring themselves, and protecting rare and endangered wildlife from being trampled or otherwise disturbed by their admirers. Here are the basics: Dogs are allowed only on **KEHOE BEACH**, **PALOMARIN BEACH**, **NORTH BEACH**, **SOUTH BEACH**, and southern **LIMANTOUR BEACH**, but must be kept on leashes at all times. Don't take your dog on any hiking trails within the seashore boundaries. Camping is limited and very closely regulated. If you don't have a reservation and a permit for one of the four small backpacking camps in the park, you will not be allowed to spend the night. Permits are required for all fires, including beach fires. Bicycles are allowed on just 35 miles of the park's more than 140 miles of trails, and cyclists are required to yield right-of-way to every other class of trail user (especially equestrians). The 15mph bicycle speed limit is strictly enforced. Finally, disturbing or harassing any wildlife in the park is prohibited. Observe seasonal beach closures and trail restrictions that may become necessary to protect nesting, breeding, or molting animals. To plan your visits, contact one of three visitor centers: **BEAR VALLEY VISITOR CENTER** (Bear Valley Rd; 415/464-5100), the **KENNETH PATRICK VISITOR CENTER** (mile 14, Sir Francis Drake Blvd; 415/669-1250), or the **LIGHTHOUSE VISITOR CENTER** (end of Sir Francis Drake Blvd; 415/669-1534).

large saltwater lagoon on the Point Reyes peninsula that produces nearly 20 percent of California's commercial oyster yield. It's open 8am to 4:30pm every day.

A popular Point Reyes pastime is ocean kayaking. Don't worry, the kayaks are very stable and there are no waves to contend with because you'll be paddling through placid **TOMALES BAY**, a haven for migrating birds and marine mammals. Rental prices at **BLUE WATERS KAYAKING** (415/669-2600 or 888/546-2252; www.bwkayak.com) start at about $50 for a half day. You can sign up for a guided day trip, a naturalist tour, bird-watching and oyster-tasting excursions, and more.

As most ardent Bay Area mountain bikers know, **POINT REYES NATIONAL SEASHORE** boasts some of the finest mountain bike trails in the state. Narrow dirt paths wind through densely forested knolls and end with spectacular ocean views. A map is a must (available for free at the Bear Valley Visitor Center) since many of the park trails are off-limits to bikes. To rent a bike, call **CYCLE ANALYSIS** (415/663-9164 or 415/663-1645; www.cyclepointreyes.com).

Olema

RESTAURANTS

Olema Inn Restaurant / ★★★

10000 SIR FRANCIS DRAKE BLVD, OLEMA; 415/663-9559

A favorite destination restaurant of Marinites, the whitewashed, airy restaurant inn (see also Lodgings review) retains the elegance of a stage stop for upscale Victorian travelers and prides itself on its beautifully prepared fresh food. The dining rooms are bright, courtesy of big mullioned windows; the original woodwork has been refinished in pastels; and the floor is pine, refashioned from a 19th-century tobacco warehouse. The menu is small but consistent in quality; seafood lovers will want to sample the oysters, which come in myriad options, prepared in bacon, garlic, barbecue sauce, or heirloom tomatoes. Menus are planned around seasonal local produce and meats. In fact, much of the restaurant's produce is grown in an organic garden and an orchard on the premises. In balmy weather, guests may dine outdoors on the back patio. *$$$; AE, MC, V; checks OK; lunch Sat–Sun, dinner every day; beer and wine; reservations recommended; www.theolemainn.com; corner of Sir Francis Drake Blvd and Hwy 1.* ♿

LODGINGS

Olema Inn / ★★★

10000 SIR FRANCIS DRAKE BLVD, OLEMA; 415/663-9559

This 1876 building, a former stagecoach stop, is loaded with modern luxuries yet still manages to retain its period charm. It features six rooms with European Sleepworks mattresses, down comforters, and antique furniture. Four of the rooms have showers and baths, two have showers only. The decor is simple and elegant, in keeping with the style and era of the building: high ceilings, antique light fixtures, baths in Victorian-style white porcelain and chrome, and roomy armoires. Try to reserve room 3, which overlooks the garden and is the quietest of the six. Guests are encouraged to stroll behind the inn to the orchard, and on the stone pathways of the vegetable gardens. A complimentary breakfast of croissants, local cheeses, seasonal fruit, coffee, and juice is served in the dining room. *$$$; AE, MC, V; checks OK; www.theolemainn.com; corner of Sir Francis Drake Blvd and Hwy 1.*

Point Reyes Station

It feels like time stood still in this West Marin community (population well under 1,000) that was a rail town in the 1890s and is steeped in dairy-farming tradition. Maybe that's why so many weary Bay Area commuters flock to Point Reyes Station on weekends. The three blocks everyone calls Main Street are actually on Highway 1. It's worth waiting in line to sample the breads and pastries at the renowned **BOVINE BAKERY** (415/663-9420); if gourmet picnic goodies are on your list, head for **TOMALES BAY FOODS** (415/663-9335)—also home of the **COWGIRL CREAMERY**. Those Western gals sure know how to make ice cream and cheeses. **TOBY'S FEED BARN** (415/663-1223) is the place to buy farm-fresh fruits and vegetables, seeds, sunbonnets, local arts and crafts, and souvenir postcards. The **PINE CONE DINER** (415/663-1536) rustles up made-from-scratch biscuits and gravy every morning.

RESTAURANTS

The Station House Cafe / ★★

11180 HWY 1, POINT REYES STATION; 415/663-1515

For more than two decades the Station House has been a favorite stop for West Marin residents and San Francisco day-trippers. The menu changes weekly, but you can count on the kitchen creating daily wonders with local produce, seafood, and organic beef from Niman Ranch. Breakfast items range from French toast made with Il Fornaio bakery's sweet challah to buckwheat pancakes and roasted vegetable frittatas. For dinner, start with a platter of local oysters and mussels, followed by a braised lamb shank (made with Guinness Stout), salmon with roasted yellow pepper sauce, or one of the Station House's old standbys such as fish-and-chips with country fries and coleslaw. There's a good selection of wines, too. When the weather's warm, sit outside in the shaded garden area—particularly if you're eating breakfast here on a sunny day. In the summer, barbecued oysters are often served on the patio. *$$; DIS, MC, V; local checks only; breakfast, lunch, dinner every day (closed Wed in winter); full bar; reservations recommended; www.stationhousecafe.com; on Main St.* ♿

Inverness Park

LODGINGS

Blackthorne Inn / ★★★

266 VALLEJO AVE, INVERNESS PARK; 415/663-8621

With its four levels, five rooms, multiple decks, spiral staircase, sky bridge, and fire pole, the Blackthorne Inn is more like a tree house for grown-ups than a B and B. The octagonal Eagle's Nest, perched on the top level, has its own sundeck and a 360-degree view of the forest (the bath, however, is located across the sky bridge—a bit of an adventure on blustery nights); the

RIDING THE RIDGE

North and just east of Point Reyes National Seashore is **BOLINAS RIDGE TRAIL**, a moderate 22-mile round-trip mountain bike ride through beautiful vistas overlooking Kent Lake and Olema Valley. With no switchbacks or difficult climbs, and sparse use on weekdays, this is a good bike ride for beginners who have the strength for the climb but lack the technical skills necessary to keep from wiping out on steep downhill grades and tricky corners. Access is from the town of Fairfax or from Shoreline Highway/Highway 1. From Broadway in Fairfax, turn left at the stop sign onto Bolinas–Fairfax Road and follow it past Alpine Dam to the intersection with West Ridgecrest Boulevard. Backtrack on Bolinas–Fairfax Road for a tenth of a mile and look for the Bolinas Ridge trailhead on the north side of the road. Or from Shoreline Highway/Highway 1, look for Bolinas–Fairfax Road on the right approximately a tenth of a mile north of Audubon Canyon Ranch. Drive up a tenth of a mile past the intersection with West Ridgecrest Boulevard and look for the trailhead. Before setting out on this adventure, however, check with the **OLEMA VALLEY RANGER STATION** (415/464-5100) for updated trail condition information; both the road and trail are particularly vulnerable to inclement weather and are sometimes closed. To rent a mountain bike, call **CYCLE ANALYSIS** (415/663-9164 or 415/663-1645; www.cyclepointreyes.com).

spacious Forest View and Hideaway rooms, which share a bath, have sitting areas facing the woods; the outdoor treetop-level hot tub offers a great view of the stars. The main sitting room in the house features a large stone fireplace, a skylight, and beautiful stained-glass windows, and is surrounded by a huge deck. A country buffet breakfast, included in the room rate, is served on the upper deck when the sun is shining. *$$$$; MC, V; checks OK; www.blackthorneinn.com; from Inverness Park, go 1¼ miles up Vallejo Ave.*

Holly Tree Inn / ★★★

3 SILVERHILLS RD, INVERNESS PARK; 415/663-1554 OR 800/286-4655

Hidden within a 19-acre valley with a meandering creek and wooded hillsides is the blissfully quiet Holly Tree Inn. This family-owned B and B has four cozy guest rooms, each with a private bath (one with a fireplace) and decorated with Laura Ashley prints and country antiques. The large, airy living room has a fireplace and comfortable chairs where guests converse over afternoon tea. If privacy is what you're after, tucked in a far corner of the estate is the Cottage in the Woods, a two-room hideaway with a small fireplace, a king-size bed, and an old-fashioned bathtub from which you can gaze at the garden. Families or honeymooners should inquire about the separate Sea Star

Cottage—built on stilts over Tomales Bay—the two-bedroom Vision Cottage; they, along with the aforementioned Cottage in the Woods, also three have hot tubs. In the morning, enjoy a bountiful country breakfast, included in the room rate. *$$–$$$; AE, MC, V; checks OK; www.hollytreeinn.com; off Bear Valley Rd.*

Tomales

Most people don't even know the town of Tomales exists. Consisting of not much more than a general store, two churches, and a superb little bakery, the tiny ranching community looks pretty much as it did a hundred years ago. It's in a prime location, though—only 30 minutes' drive from Point Reyes National Seashore, yet far enough away to avoid the traffic and commotion. The 4-mile drive from Tomales to **DILLON BEACH** (via Dillon Beach Rd) is one of the most scenic routes on the Marin coast. There is a $7 day-use fee at the beach. The fishing pier and dune campgrounds at **LAWSON'S LANDING** (707/878-2443) also attract visitors.

Tomales is a popular stop for fresh raw and barbecued oysters. The **TOMALES BAY OYSTER COMPANY** (15479 Hwy 1, Marshall; 415/663-1242; www.tomalesbayoysters.com; open 8am–6pm every day) has been in business since 1909. They sell them by the dozen or in a sack of 100. Those in the know bring their own knives, lemons, cocktail sauce, and even bags of charcoal for the nearby barbecue pits.

Marshall

RESTAURANTS

Nick's Cove Restaurant / ★★★☆

23240 HWY 1, MARSHALL; 415/663-1033 AND 866/63-NICKS

Restaurant pioneer Pat Kuleto's most recent addition to Northern California, Nick's Cove is a little slice of rustic heaven overhanging Tomales Bay. Kuleto is known for his adult theme parks, and Nick's Cove is no exception: The restaurant's lodgelike ambience is authentic with Adirondack chairs on the deck, a fireplace in the living room, and stuffed animal heads mounted on the walls (vegetarians might consider dining elsewhere). The enclosed patio is the perfect dining venue on a pleasant evening. Nick's is the place to go for an oyster overload, with a changing menu of daily oyster specials by the dozen, an oyster potpie with oyster mushrooms and puff pastry crust, and a menu of other raw offerings. The chef seems to take offense if you don't at least sample an oyster. On the other hand, those who prefer their meals cooked can order the dry-aged, hand-cut steak with balsamic demi glace, Point Reyes blue cheese mashed potatoes, and haricots verts.

$$$–$$$$; AE, DC, DIS, MC, V; breakfast, lunch, dinner every day; full bar; reservations recommended; www.nickscove.com; on Tomales Bay. ♿

LODGINGS

Nick's Cove / ★★★☆

23240 HWY 1, MARSHALL; 415/663-1033 AND 866/63-NICKS

If you ate too many oysters at the adjoining restaurant (see review), you needn't stumble farther than a hundred feet to one of the 12 on-site cabins to take a load off your feet. All accommodations give the feeling you're staying in a secluded hunting cabin somewhere deep in the woods—only with five-star amenities. Five are located on the water, another four simply have bay views, and the remaining three are located creek side. Our favorite digs are Al's, where heated marble bathroom floors keep your tootsies nice and toasty before you soak a long while in the luscious clawfoot tub, and the roomy Bandits' Bungalow, a two-bedroom suite comprising nearly 800 square feet. All cabins offer kitchenettes, wood-burning stoves, wet bars, high-definition TVs, wireless Internet, safes, organic bath products by EO, robes, and slippers. *$$$–$$$$; AE, DC, DIS, MC, V; reservations recommended; www.nickscove.com; on Tomales Bay.* ♿

The Sonoma Coast

Mention Sonoma and everyone's immediate association is Wine Country. What few Californians seem to know, however, is that Sonoma County gerrymanders a hefty chunk of the coast as well—more than 50 miles of mostly undeveloped shoreline from Bodega Bay to Gualala. And judging from the mostly vacant state parks and beaches, even fewer Californians seem to know what a good thing they're missing as they migrate lemming-like to Mendocino or Carmel. The Sonoma coast isn't for everyone, though; there's little in the way of shopping, sightseeing, and such. It's more of a place where inlanders return annually to bury themselves in a book, wiggle their toes in the sand, and forget about work for a while.

Valley Ford

This sleepy little community is just a charming bend in the road for most coastal travelers. The Northern Pacific Railroad steamed through here in 1876, potato farming flourished in the 1920s, and today most of the just over one hundred residents are ranchers of cows or sheep. There were traffic jams in 1976 when the artist Christo installed his *Running Fence*, 18 feet high and 24½ miles long, through Valley Ford. Created from pure white silk, the undulating fence snaked over green rolling hills straight into the Pacific.

LODGINGS

Valley Ford Hotel / ★

14415 HWY 1, VALLEY FORD; 707/876-1983

The pleasant, old-fashioned Valley Ford Hotel, built in 1864 and well-maintained ever since, is a good choice for travelers who prefer the privacy of a hotel to the more social aspect of a B and B. Recently reopened under new owners, the hotel has six clean, spacious, and simply furnished rooms; each has a private bath and queen bed. For those who crave sports and company, there is a full bar with satellite TV in the cocktail lounge. After the game, many move on to the porch's old-timey rocking chairs or into the adjoining restaurant, Rocker Oysterfeller's, choosing dinner entrées like chicken saltimbocca or fillet Madagascar, served Wednesday through Sunday. The restaurant also serves weekend brunches on the patio, making it a good place to take a break on your way to the coast. *$$$; AE, MC, V; checks OK; www.vfordhotel.com; downtown.* ♿

Bodega Bay

When it comes to fancy restaurants, accommodations, and boutiques, Bodega Bay has a long way to go. There is only one three-star lodge and restaurant, and the town's most venerable store sells taffy and kites. This is odd, considering that Bodega Bay is only a few hours' drive from the Bay Area, a good two to three hours closer than Mendocino, and has all the beautiful scenery and golden beaches you could possibly hope for. Spend a few hours meandering through town and it becomes apparent that Bodega Bay is, for the most part, still a working-class fishing village. Most people start their day before dawn—mending nets, rigging fishing poles, and talking shop. But if all you want to do is breathe in some salty air and you couldn't care less about designer boutiques and dancing till dawn, come to Bodega Bay—ain't much here, which is precisely the point.

The **SONOMA COAST VISITORS CENTER** (850 Hwy 1, Bodega Bay; 707/875-3866; www.bodegabay.com or www.visitsonomacoast.com) is a good place to load up on free maps, guides, and brochures, including the *Bodega Bay Area Map & Guide*. This guide gives the exact locations of all the town's attractions, including nearby **BODEGA HEAD** (from downtown Bodega Bay, turn west on Eastshore Rd, go right at the stop sign onto Bay Flat Rd, and follow it to the end), the small peninsula that shelters Bodega Bay. You'll discover two superb walking trails that follow the ocean at the head. The first, a 4-mile round-trip trail, starts from the west parking lot, leads past the **BODEGA BAY MARINE LABORATORY** (707/875-2211; www.bml.ucdavis.edu), which conducts guided tours of its lab projects from 2 to 4pm on Fridays, and ends at the sand dunes of Salmon Creek Beach. An easier 1½-mile round-trip walk begins in the east parking lot and encircles the edge of Bodega Head. From December through April, Bodega Head also doubles as one of the premier whale-watching points along the California coast.

A great way to spend a lazy afternoon in Bodega Bay is at the docks, watching the rusty fishing boats unload their catches. **TIDES WHARF RESTAURANT** (835 Hwy 1, Bodega Bay; 707/875-3652) has the most active dock scene, including a viewing room near the processing plant that allows you to witness a fish's ultimate fate—a swift and merciless gutting by deft hands, followed by a quick burial in ice (kids are mesmerized by this). Just outside, sea lions linger by the dock, hoping for a handout.

Linking Bodega Bay and the nearby town of Jenner are the Sonoma coast state and county beaches, 16 miles of pristine sand and gravel beaches, tide pools, rocky bluffs, hiking trails, and one heck of a gorgeous drive along Highway 1. Although all the beaches are pretty much the same, the safest for kids is **DORAN PARK BEACH**, located just south of Bodega Bay. When the water's rough everywhere else, Doran is still calm enough for swimming, clamming, and crabbing (an added bonus: the adjacent Doran mud flats are a favorite haunt of egrets, pelicans, and other seabirds). The best tide pools are at the north end of **SALMON CREEK BEACH** (off Bean Ave, 2 miles north of town) or **SHELL BEACH**, a small low-tide treasure trove 10 miles north of Bodega Bay. If all you want to do is get horizontal in the sand, deciding which of the 14 beaches along Highway 1 looks the best will drive you nuts; just pick one and park.

RESTAURANTS

The Duck Club / ★★★

103 HWY 1 (BODEGA BAY LODGE & SPA), BODEGA BAY; 707/875-3525 OR 888/875-2250

Bodega Bay sure took its sweet time coaxing a premier chef to the coast, but now that Jeff Reilly (formerly the executive chef at Lafayette Park in Walnut Creek) is in town, gastronomes up and down the coast are coming to the Bodega Bay Lodge & Spa (see review) to sample his wares. "Sonoma County cuisine" best describes Reilly's penchant for local yields, with creations such as roasted Petaluma duck with Valencia orange sauce or a Sonoma farm-fresh asparagus strudel bathed in a mild curry sauce. *Le poisson du jour* comes straight from the docks down the street. Large windows overlook the bay, so be sure to beg for a table with a view when making the required reservation. The Duck Club offers a lengthy wine list with an extensive selection of Sonoma County labels. Picnic lunches are available upon request. *$$$; AE, DC, DIS, MC, V; no checks; breakfast, dinner every day; beer and wine; reservations required; www.bodegabaylodge.com; south end of town.* ♿

LODGINGS

Bodega Bay Lodge & Spa / ★★★

103 HWY 1, BODEGA BAY; 707/875-3252 OR 888/875-2250

Granted, the competition isn't very fierce, but it's safe to say that the Bodega Bay Lodge & Spa provides some of the Sonoma coast's finest accommodations. It's the view that clinches it: all 84 rooms—swathed in handsome hues of cardinal red and forest green, with fireplaces and stocked minibars—have private balconies with a wonderful panorama of Bodega Bay and its bird-filled wetlands. The lodge also offers six deluxe Ocean Club suites featuring Jacuzzi tubs for two, black granite fireplaces, and romantic ocean views. Should you ever leave your balcony, a short walk through elaborate flower gardens leads to an outdoor fieldstone spa and heated swimming pool overlooking the bay. A fitness center, sauna, and complimentary morning newspaper are part of the package, as is a complimentary wine hour from 5 to 6pm. Ask about the on-site facials, massages, and body treatments. More proof of Bodega Bay Lodge & Spa's top standing is its Duck Club restaurant (see review), easily the Sonoma coast's best. *$$$$; AE, DC, DIS, MC, V; checks OK; www.bodegabaylodge.com; south end of town.* ♿

The Inn at the Tides / ★★

800 HWY 1, BODEGA BAY; 707/875-2751 OR 800/541-7788

In Bodega Bay the architectural style of most structures is nouveau Californian—wood-shingled boxes with lots of glass—and the Inn at the Tides is no exception. Perched on a hillside overlooking Bodega Bay, it offers 86 units with bay views, spacious interiors, contemporary (albeit dated contemporary) decor, and all the usual amenities of an expensive resort: terry-cloth robes, coffeemakers, hair dryers, TVs, refrigerators, minibars, fresh flowers, continental breakfasts, and access to the indoor-outdoor pool, sauna, and whirlpool tubs. A few of the rooms have king-size beds, and most have fireplaces. The Inn at the Tides's restaurant, the Bay View, is open for dinner Wednesday through Saturday. It offers ocean views and has a romantic, somewhat formal ambience. *$$$; AE, DIS, MC, V; checks OK; www.innatthetides.com; across from the Tides Wharf.* ♿

Bodega

A quick trip to the town of Bodega, a few miles southeast of Bodega Bay off Highway 1, is a must for any Hitchcock fan. The attraction is a bird's-eye view of the hauntingly familiar **POTTER SCHOOL HOUSE** and **ST. TERESA'S CHURCH**, both immortalized in Hitchcock's *The Birds*, filmed here in 1961. The two or three boutiques in downtown Bodega manage to entice a few visitors to park and browse, but most people seem content with a little rubbernecking and finger pointing as they flip U-turns through the tiny town.

LODGINGS

Sonoma Coast Villa / ★★★☆

16702 HWY 1, BODEGA; 707/876-9818 OR 888/404-2255

If your idea of a vacation is a Mediterranean footbath, rejuvenating body massage, and soothing facial in a beautiful Tuscan setting, you're in luck. Along with a spa, an outdoor swimming pool, and an indoor whirlpool spa, the estate houses 12 spacious guest rooms featuring exposed wooden beams, wood-burning fireplaces, Italian slate floors, large marble walk-in showers or jetted tubs, well-stocked mini-refrigerators, TVs with VCRs, and private patios. Phones are not featured in this quiet refuge, but there are board games aplenty and a nine-hole putting green. Ask owners Susan and Cyrus Griffin if you can peek in the all-glass Tower Library Room perched at the top of the winding wrought-iron staircase. Cyrus will have been busy in the kitchen long before you rise, rustling up a hot country breakfast accompanied by fresh baked goods, served in the dining room with windows overlooking the lush gardens. *$$$$; AE, MC, V; checks OK; www.scvilla.com; 2 miles past Valley Ford.* ♿

Occidental

LODGINGS

The Inn at Occidental / ★★★

3657 CHURCH ST, OCCIDENTAL; 707/874-1047 OR 800/522-6324

Covered porches, wainscoted hallways, antique wicker furniture, walled-in English gardens, and a comfortable sitting parlor are all elegant reminders of the days when Occidental was a stopping point on the railroad between San Francisco and the Northwest. The 16 individually decorated rooms have private baths, beds topped with plump down comforters, comfortable sitting areas, and fireplaces, and are furnished with the innkeeper's vast collection of heirlooms, antiques, and original artwork. Most rooms also offer spa tubs for two and private decks. For the ultimate Sonoma escape pad, inquire about the separate Sonoma Cottage. Guests are treated to a full gourmet breakfast of fresh fruit, juices, homemade granola, freshly baked pastries, and hot entrées such as orange-thyme pancakes or French toast with jam—all served in the dining room or outdoors. *$$$$; AE, DIS, MC, V; checks OK; www.innatoccidental.com; off the Bohemian Hwy.* ♿

Sebastopol

Situated at the crossroads of Highway 116 and Highway 12, Sebastopol is the gateway between western Sonoma County and the North Coast. Gravenstein apples, the area's greatest claim to fame, were introduced in the late 1800s. The **APPLE BLOSSOM FESTIVAL** is held every April, and Christmas tree farms bustle during the holidays. Antique shopping is a popular pastime year-round. Gardeners will enjoy a walking tour of **GOLD RIDGE FARM** (7781 Bodega Ave; 707/829-6711; www.lutherburbank.org). This is where Luther Burbank, the world-renowned horticulturist, conducted plant-breeding experiments at the turn of the century. For more information, contact the **SEBASTOPOL VISITOR CENTER** (265 S Main St; 707/823-3032 or 877/828-4748; www.sebastopol.org).

RESTAURANTS

Stella's at Russian River Vineyards / ★★★

5700 GRAVENSTEIN HWY N, SEBASTOPOL; 707/887-2300

Foodies will think they have died and gone to heaven when they discover this little gem. Gregory Hallihan, the gregarious owner and California Culinary Academy graduate, brings years of experience, including a stint with the Ritz-Carlton in Hawaii, to Stella's. There is something for everyone on the ever-changing menu, from vegan, vegetarian, and seafood selections to old-fashioned rib-eye steak and pan-roasted chicken with Dijon and truffled mashed potatoes. Try the likes of coconut lentil soup or spicy grilled prawns with red jalapeño mango purée and pineapple couscous salad. You'll soon know why locals fill the place night after night; scoring a reservation can be difficult. Wine connoisseurs will also be pleased with the excellent choices, many from nearby vineyards. *$$; MC, V; checks OK; dinner Wed–Mon; beer and wine; reservations recommended; www.stellascafe.net; just before Forestville.* ♿

LODGINGS

Avalon / ★★★

11910 GRATON RD, SEBASTOPOL; 707/824-0880 OR 877/3AVALON

The secluded entrance to Avalon, a luxury bed-and-breakfast, conjures up images of a magical forest reminiscent of the knights of the Round Table. Hilary and Gary McCalla, the engaging owners and hosts, opened this charming Tudor-style B and B in early 2000. Avalon, a family name, coupled with the McCallas' love of old English legends, inspired the three beautifully decorated (and very spacious) suites. Each features a separate entrance, a gas fireplace with thermostat, a king-size bed, fine linens, a large private bath, a CD player, and local handmade soaps. Indoor exercise facilities are available for those who miss the gym, while the brave of heart might enjoy an invigorating plunge in the nearby swimming hole (or a soak in the outdoor hot tub). Tea is an afternoon ritual, and Hilary whips up a bountiful breakfast every morning. French Babies—scalloped puff pastries filled with Brie and fresh strawberries—are a specialty, along with baked pears or apples and homemade scones. *$$$$; AE, DC, MC, V; checks OK; 3-night minimum stay on holiday weekends; www.avalonluxuryinn.com; 3.3 miles off Graton Rd.*

The Sebastopol Inn / ★★

6751 SEBASTOPOL AVE, SEBASTOPOL; 800/653-1082

Guests at the Sebastopol Inn enjoy comfortable accommodations in a historic setting. Located behind the restored vintage Gravenstein Railroad Station in downtown Sebastopol, the inn exudes country charm. Constructed with vertical board-and-batten siding and topped with a verdigris copper roof, it has 31 rooms and suites. You can expect all the amenities of a boutique hotel, including queen- or king-size beds, coffeemakers, TVs, and full concierge service. Some rooms have fireplaces, whirlpool tubs, microwaves, and refrigerators.

Ask about the balcony rooms looking out on pristine wetland preserves, and bring a bathing suit for the heated pool and Jacuzzi in the garden courtyard. Right next door is the New Dawn Day Spa, offering a variety of treatments, including massage, body, facial skin care, and waxing. *$$–$$$; AE, DC, MC, V; checks OK; www.thesebastopolinn.com; downtown—look for the old train barn.* ♿

Vine Hill Inn / ★★

3949 VINE HILL RD, SEBASTOPOL; 707/823-8832

The rolling vineyards will remind you of Tuscany, but this beautifully restored 1897 Victorian farmhouse and its rambling country gardens belong in western Sonoma. You'll feel right at home, too, when you snuggle up in one of the four upstairs bedrooms. Furnished with charming antiques, each has a private bath; choose from a whirlpool tub or claw-foot bath with shower. An inviting porch or deck, with comfortable seating and glorious views, is never far away. How about a cool dip in the pool, a nap in the hammock, or an amusing game of table tennis? Wake up to the clucking of hens and the aroma of a hearty country breakfast. *$$$; AE, DIS, MC, V; checks OK; www.vine-hill-inn.com; follow Hwy 116 west to Vine Hill Rd.*

Forestville

From this tiny hamlet surrounded by redwoods you can launch an all-day canoe trip down the gentle Russian River. Set forth from **BURKE'S CANOE TRIPS** (707/887-1222; www.burkescanoetrips.com) from May through September, and someone there will pick you up 10 miles down the scenic river—a haven for turtles, river otters, egrets, and great blue herons—and take you back to your car. Also worth a detour is **KOZLOWSKI FARMS** (5566 Gravenstein Hwy; 707/887-1587; www.kozlowskifarms.com), a family farm that has turned into a gourmet-food business. The Kozlowskis' apple butter, jams, and vinegars are sold in specialty shops throughout Sonoma County and beyond.

RESTAURANTS

Topolos Russian River Vineyards Restaurant & Winery / ★

5700 GRAVENSTEIN HWY, FORESTVILLE; 707/887-2300

Greek food on the Russian River may be an oxymoron, but that hasn't stopped folks from lining up for Bob Engel and Christine Topolos's Mediterranean cuisine made from generations of Topolos recipes. Every meal at this family-owned restaurant—spartanly decorated, as most cafés are along the Aegean—comes with *tzatziki*, a garlic-laden cucumber-yogurt dip for bread, and a tomato stuffed with aromatic ratatouille. Follow that with an order of *mezes*: a plate of *dolmas*, *tiropita* (cheese-and-egg pies wrapped in flaky phyllo pastry), marinated eggplant, and feta. Then choose from such main courses as roast Petaluma duckling with a black currant–Madeira wine sauce, roast rack of baby lamb, or prawns Santorini, prepared with tomato, feta, and dill. Both Topolos wines (made here) and other local wines are served with dinner. Dessert, naturally, is a hunk of honey-drenched baklava. *$$$; AE, DC, MC, V; checks OK; lunch, dinner every day, brunch Sun (closed Mon and Tues in winter); wine only; reservations recommended; www.topolos.net; on Hwy 116, ¼ mile south of town.*

LODGINGS

Farmhouse Inn / ★★★

7871 RIVER RD, FORESTVILLE; 707/887-3300 OR 800/464-6642

Don't let the outside of the Farmhouse Inn's eight guest cottages fool you. At first glance these buildings tucked within a grove of trees look like roadside motel cabins. But step inside and you'll see that these little lodges are actually quite luxurious, with plush carpets, wood-burning fireplaces, CD players, saunas, thick robes, feather beds with down comforters and fine linens, European "rain" showerheads, and jumbo two-person Jacuzzis—all the toys you need for a romantic weekend in the Wine Country. The grounds, 6 acres of hills and redwoods, include a large swimming pool, a croquet course, and formal English gardens. Spa services—massages and facials—are also available. Guests gather for a hearty breakfast in the conservatory-style dining room or outdoors on the terrace. Expect to be treated to fruit, cereal, and hot dishes such as huevos rancheros or eggs Florentine. The inn's restaurant is also open to the public for dinner Thursday through Monday. *$$$–$$$$; AE, MC, V; checks OK; www.farmhouseinn.com; River Rd (at Wohler Rd).* ♿

Guerneville

The longtime residents of Guerneville—one of the busiest logging centers in the West during the 1880s—have seen their town undergo a significant change of face in every recent decade. Once it was a haven for bikers—the leather, not the Lycra, sort—then it became a hangout for hippies. Now it's a summer mecca for the Bay Area gay community and for naturalists attracted by the beauty of the redwoods and the Russian River. The town is a good launching spot for nature expeditions and winery touring. **KORBEL CHAMPAGNE CELLARS** (13250 River Rd; 707/824-7000; www.korbel.com), overlooking the vineyards and the Russian River, is one of the region's most popular wineries and offers free tastings. **ARMSTRONG WOODS STATE RESERVE** (17000 Armstrong Woods Rd; 707/869-2015) is a peaceful grove of spectacular ancient redwoods with hiking trails. Equestrians should saddle up at **ARMSTRONG WOODS PACK STATION** (707/887-2939; www.redwoodhorses.com), which offers 1½-hour and half- and full-day horseback rides with gourmet lunches, as well as overnight camping rides. From May through October, you can rent canoes, kayaks, and paddleboats at **JOHNSON'S BEACH & RESORT** (16241 1st St; 707/869-2022; www.johnsonsbeach.com) just under the main bridge.

Johnson's Beach is also home to the wildly popular **RUSSIAN RIVER JAZZ FESTIVAL** (707/869-2022; www.jazzontheriver.com), held every September. For more information, check out the **RUSSIAN RIVER CHAMBER OF COMMERCE & VISITORS CENTER** (16209 1st St, Guerneville; 707/869-9000 or 800/823-8800; www.russianriver.com).

RESTAURANTS

Applewood Restaurant / ★★★

13555 HWY 116 (APPLEWOOD INN), GUERNEVILLE; 707/869-9093 OR 800/555-8509

Folks at the nearby inn are apt to describe the Applewood Restaurant's design as rustic-barn architecture, but don't be fooled. When was the last time you saw a barn with lofty beam ceilings, two river-rock fireplaces, and spacious windows looking out to towering redwoods? Guests are invited to arrive in casual attire and linger over a romantic candlelit dinner impeccably prepared by executive chef Bruce Frieseke. In keeping with Applewood's culinary history, he focuses on the organic bounty from the inn's 2-acre garden and fruit orchard. Entrées range from a lavender roasted duck breast with huckleberries and baby carrots, to American red snapper with golden raisins, hazelnuts, and carrot sauce. Save room for the banana ice cream profiteroles with chocolate and caramel sauce. Wine lovers will be in heaven: there are more than 250 selections—many from local vineyards. *$$$; AE, MC, V; no checks; dinner Tues–Sat; beer and wine; reservations recommended; www.applewoodinn.com; 1 mile south of Guerneville.* ♿

Garden Grill / ★★

17132 HWY 116, GUERNEVILLE; 707/869-3922

With a menu of salads, sandwiches, and burgers, Garden Grill is the place you drop in on for a quick bite en route to a day full of outdoor fun. We're big fans of the Garden Grill Delight: a sandwich consisting of portobello mushrooms, Swiss cheese, roasted red peppers, spinach, tomatoes, red onion, and garlic aioli. The outdoor dining is an added bonus. *$–$$; MC, V; checks OK; breakfast, lunch, dinner Thurs–Mon; beer and wine; no reservations; www.gardengrill.net; just west of downtown Guerneville.*

Nit's Thai Creations / ★★

15025 RIVER RD, GUERNEVILLE; 707/869-3576

This traditional Asian joint has been written up in *Sunset* magazine for its inexpensive meals that taste delicious and use fresh veggies and organic products. The menu is pretty standard Thai fare, but the location (right on the river) and space (very roomy) make this a great casual dining spot for larger groups. Portions are big, so we recommend ordering a couple dishes family-style. *$$; AE, MC, V; no checks; lunch, dinner Thurs–Sun; beer and wine; reservations recommended; just east of downtown Guerneville.*

LODGINGS

Applewood Inn / ★★★½

13555 HWY 116, GUERNEVILLE; 707/869-9093 OR 800/555-8509

A grand old 1922 California Mission Revival mansion, formerly the country home of a wealthy banker, is the centerpiece of this tranquil inn and restaurant (see review). The 19 secluded rooms and suites, each individually decorated with attractive antiques and artwork, are located in three Mediterranean-style villas that surround a terraced garden courtyard and look out onto the surrounding redwoods, apple trees, and vineyards. All rooms have TVs, fresh flowers, and private baths, and many come with either a spa tub or a shower for two. Everyone feels pampered with lush Turkish cotton towels, European down comforters, and hand-pressed linens. The Gate House offers three contemporary suites featuring bedside fireplaces, whirlpool baths, couples' showers, and private decks. You'll discover cozy sitting areas, some with fireplaces, throughout the inn. There's a large outdoor swimming pool and spa beyond the stone courtyard and bubbling lion's-head fountain. Guests start the day with breakfast in the airy Applewood Restaurant (see review). *$$$–$$$$; AE, MC, V; no checks; www.applewoodinn.com; 1 mile south of Guerneville.* ♿

Boon Hotel + Spa / ★★★

14711 ARMSTRONG WOODS RD, GUERNEVILLE; 707/869-2721

New to the Russian River community in May 2008, Boon has already garnered a following of Bay Area residents who want a complete escape from city life—without traveling too far. Nestled among the serene redwoods, but situated in an odd sun-soaked clearing, the resort features 14 rooms that flank the saline swimming pool and hot tub (complete with cushy outdoor furniture imported from Thailand). The casual outdoor setting gives the whole place a more communal feel, and it's not unusual for a group of complete strangers lounging poolside to wind up hitting the town together for dinner and drinks. The owners, world travelers themselves, fashioned their first venture after Bali's eco-resorts. Accommodations have a soothing feng shui vibe to them, with minimal yet modern furniture done up in grays, purples, and the signature color, orange. We challenge you to find more comfortable beds than those on hand here (the owners made a point to invest in the coziest bedding they could find). Other amenities include eco-friendly EO bath products, fluffy cotton robes, TVs, DVD players, fireplaces, refrigerators, an outdoor bar, and massage treatment rooms. Pets are also welcome, and bikes are available for rent for just $5 a half day or $10 for the full. *$$–$$$; AE, MC, V; checks OK; www.boonhotels.com; ½ mile north of River Rd/Main St.* ♿

Jenner

About 16 miles north of Bodega Bay on Highway 1 is what seems to be every Northern Californian's "secret" getaway spot: Jenner. Built on a bluff rising from the mouth of the Russian River, the tiny seaside town consists of little

TICK TALK

After a walk through coastal forests or meadows, it's always a good idea to check for hitchhikers on your pant legs and socks. The western black-legged tick, bearer of the dreaded Lyme disease, awaits its prey at the tips of knee-high vegetation, then burrows its head into the victim's skin.

While there are dozens of old wives' tales on how to remove a tick (from dousing it in peanut butter to "unscrewing" it counterclockwise), the only real solution is to pull it straight out—without twisting or jerking—with tweezers. Grab the tick as close to the skin as possible and gently pull. If you have to use your fingers, be sure to use a tissue; afterward, wash your hands and the bite with warm, soapy water and apply an antiseptic.

Symptoms of Lyme disease include a bull's-eye marking or other rash around the bite, often accompanied by a fever or flulike feeling anywhere from a week to months after the encounter. Since Lyme disease can be fatal, it's a good idea to call your doctor or the Infectious Diseases branch of the **CALIFORNIA DEPARTMENT OF HEALTH SERVICES IN BERKELEY** (510/ 981-5100) if symptoms start to occur.

more than a gas station, three restaurants, two inns, and a deli, which means the only thing to do in town is eat, sleep, and lie on the beach—not a bad vacation plan. It is also two hours closer to the Bay Area than Mendocino, yet offers the same spectacular coastal scenery and a far better selection of beaches.

The sandbar at beautiful **GOAT ROCK BEACH** (707/875-3483), a breeding ground for harbor seals, becomes a major seasonal attraction during pupping season—March through May. Seals give birth on land, and orange-vested volunteers are usually around to protect the playful mammals, answer questions, and even lend binoculars for a closer look.

A serpentine 12-mile drive north of Jenner on Highway 1 takes you to the **FORT ROSS STATE HISTORIC PARK** (707/847-3286; www.parks.ca.gov), a fortress built by Russian fur traders in 1812. The fort's distinctive structures, including a stockade, a Russian Orthodox chapel, and the commandant's house, have been replicated and restored. Short history lessons are offered in the **FORT COMPOUND** (call ahead for times).

A great day trip from Jenner is the scenic drive along Highway 101 to **SALT POINT STATE PARK** (707/847-3221). There are 3,500 acres to explore and all kinds of things to do, including free diving off rocky beaches, tide pooling, and hiking through coastal woodlands. Simply pull the car over anywhere along Highway 1 and start walking. At the north end of the park on Kruse Ranch Road is the 317-acre **KRUSE RHODODENDRON PRESERVE** (707/847-3221), a forested grove of plants that grow up to 18 feet tall under a vast canopy of redwoods. Masses of vivid pink and purple flowers appear in early spring. Peak blooming time varies, but April is usually the month to see the world's tallest *Rhododendron californicum.*

RESTAURANTS

River's End / ★★

11048 HWY 1, JENNER; 707/865-2484

This popular restaurant, formerly run by chef-owner Wolfgang Gramatzki, is just as bustling as ever. The menu, which changes monthly, is decidedly eclectic, with entrées ranging from Indian curries to racklets of elk, coconut shrimp, pheasant breast, and locally harvested seafood. Lunch is more down to earth, with reasonably priced burgers and sandwiches. Local Sonoma meats, poultry, and organic vegetables are used whenever possible, including Sonoma microbrews and wines. Most tables have wonderful views of the ocean, as does the small outside deck—the perfect spot for a glass of Sonoma County wine. The hours tend to vary as much as the menu, so be sure to call ahead. *$$; MC, V; no checks; lunch, dinner Thurs–Mon (Fri–Mon Nov–Apr); full bar; reservations recommended; www.ilovesunsets.com; just north of town.* ♿

Sizzling Tandoor / ★

9960 HWY 1, JENNER; 707/865-0625

When the weather is warm and sunny, Sizzling Tandoor is the best place on the Sonoma coast to have lunch. This Indian restaurant is perched high above the placid Russian River, and the view, particularly from the outside patio, is fantastic. Equally great are the inexpensive lunch specials: huge portions of curries and kebabs served with vegetables, soup, pilau rice, and superb naan (Indian bread). Even if you don't have time for a meal, drop by and order some warm naan to go. *$; AE, DIS, MC, V; no checks; lunch, dinner every day; beer and wine; reservations recommended; at south end of the Russian River Bridge, south of Jenner.* ♿

Sea Ranch

Sea Ranch is undoubtedly one of the most beautiful seaside communities in the nation, due mostly to rigid adherence to environmentally harmonious architectural standards. Approximately 300 homes, some quite grand, are available as vacation rentals. There are eight or nine rental companies, charging as low as $200 to as high as $700 for two nights—rates are generally lower on the east side of Highway 1. The **SEA RANCH LODGE AND RESTAURANT** (707/785-2371 or 800/732-7262; www.searanchlodge.com) offers the only hotel accommodations. Return visitors often sample different locations—woods, meadows, ocean bluffs. For rentals contact **SEA RANCH RENTALS** (888/732-7262; www.searanchvillage.com) or **RAMS HEAD REALTY** (800/785-3455; www.ramshead-realty.com). Rentals also include use of the community's three outdoor heated swimming pools, tennis courts, and recreation center. The award-winning **SEA RANCH GOLF LINKS** (located along Sea Ranch's northern boundary at the entrance to Gualala Point Regional Park; 707/785-2468), a challenging Scottish-style 18-hole course, was designed by Robert Muir Graves and is open daily to the public.

The Mendocino Coast

There are four things first-time visitors should know before heading to the Mendocino coast. First, be prepared for a long, beautiful drive; there are no quick and easy routes to this part of California, and there's no public transportation, so traveling by car is your only option. Second, make your hotel and restaurant reservations as far in advance as possible because everything involving tourism books up solid during summers and holidays. Third, bring warm clothing. A windless, sunny, 80-degree day on the Mendocino coast is about as rare as affordable real estate. Fourth and finally, bring a lot of money and your checkbook. Cheap sleeps, eats, and even banks are few and far between along this stretch of shoreline, and many places don't take credit cards (though personal checks are widely accepted).

So where exactly is the Mendocino coast? Well, it starts at the county line in the town of Gualala and ends a hundred or so miles north at the sparsely populated stretch known as the Lost Coast. The focal point is the town of Mendocino, but the center of commerce—and the region's only McDonald's (if you can believe it)—is in Fort Bragg, 15 miles up the shore. Compared with these two towns, every other part of the Mendocino coast is relatively deserted—something to consider if you're looking to escape the masses. Spring is the best time to visit, when the wildflowers are in full bloom and the crowds are still sparse. Then again, nothing on this planet is more romantic than cuddling next to the fireplace on a winter night, listening to the rain and thunder pound against your little cottage. For more information, contact the **FORT BRAGG–MENDOCINO COAST CHAMBER OF COMMERCE** (217 S Main St, Fort Bragg; 707/961-6300; www.mendocinocoast.com).

Gualala

The southernmost town in Mendocino County, Gualala also happens to have the most mispronounced name in Mendocino County. Keep the G soft and you end up with "wah-LAL-ah," the Spanish version of *walali*, which is Pomo Indian patois for "water coming down place." The water in question is the nearby Gualala River, a placid year-round playground for kayakers, canoers, and swimmers.

Once a lively logging town, Gualala has tamed considerably since the days loggers literally climbed the saloon walls with their spiked boots. Though a few real-life lumberjacks still end their day at the Gualala Hotel's saloon, the coastal town's main function these days is providing gas, groceries, and hardware for area residents. On the outskirts, however, are several excellent parks, beaches, and hiking trails; combine this with the region's glorious seascapes, and suddenly little mispronounced Gualala emerges as a serious contender among the better vacation spots on the North Coast.

One of the most enjoyable activities on the California coast is river and sea kayaking, and the Gualala River is ideal for beginner kayakers. **ADVENTURE RENTS** (downtown Gualala in the Cantamare Center; 707/884-4386 or 888/881-4386; www.adventurerents.com) provides the necessary gear, instruction, and transportation of the kayaks and canoes to and from the river.

Of the six public beach access points along Highway 1 between Sea Ranch and Gualala, the one that offers the most bang for the $5 parking fee is the 195-acre **GUALALA POINT REGIONAL PARK** (707/785-2377). The park has 10 miles of trails through coastal grasslands, redwood forests, and river canyons, as well as picnic sites, camping areas, and excellent bird- and whale-watching along the mostly deserted beaches.

RESTAURANTS

St. Orres Restaurant / ★★★

36601 HWY 1 (ST. ORRES INN), GUALALA; 707/884-3335

St. Orres Restaurant is one of Gualala's star attractions and one of the main reasons people keep coming back to this region. The restaurant's constantly changing prix-fixe dinner menu focuses on North Coast cuisine, including a fair amount of wild game. Self-taught chef Rosemary Campiformio's dark and fruity sauces and sublime soups are perfectly suited to the flavorful game, resulting in a distinctly Northern California rendition of French country cuisine. It's an adventuresome menu she's put together: fresh wild salmon with zucchini cakes; grilled veal chop with garlic mashed potaotes, foie gras, and truffle Madeira sauce; rack of wild boar with Rosemary's spicy applesauce and apple pancakes. St. Orres's wine cellar stores a sizable selection of rich California reds that are well-suited for such hearty entrées. *$$$; MC, V; checks OK; breakfast (inn guests only), dinner every day (call ahead in winter); beer and wine; reservations recommended; www.saintorres.com; 2 miles north of Gualala on the east side of Hwy 1* . ♿

LODGINGS

St. Orres / ★★★

36601 HWY 1, GUALALA; 707/884-3303

In the early '70s, a group of young architects and builders, inspired by the Russian architecture of the early Northern California settlers, took their back-to-the-land dreams to Gualala and created this dazzling copper-domed inn from redwood timbers scrounged from old logging mills and dilapidated bridges. Located just off Highway 1 and within walking distance of a sheltered, sandy cove, St. Orres consists of 8 small, less expensive rooms with 3 shared baths in the main lodge (the 2 front rooms with ocean views are the best) and 13 private cottages scattered throughout the 50 acres of wooded grounds. The best cottage is the ultrarustic Wild Flower Cabin, a former logging-crew shelter furnished with a cozy sleeping loft, a wood-burning stove, an adorable outside shower overlooking the woods, and even a gaggle of wild turkeys waiting for handouts at your doorstep. Another top choice is the gorgeous Sequoia Cottage, a solid-timbered charmer tucked into the edge of the forest. Then again, all the cottages are pretty darn romantic. All guests start the day with a complimentary full breakfast (delivered to the cottages in baskets); spend the rest of the day lolling around the nearby beaches, then have dinner at St. Orres's superb restaurant (see review). Reserve a table for dinner (cost not included in room rate) when you make your room reservation; the restaurant is almost always booked. *$–$$; MC, V; checks OK; www.saintorres.com; 2 miles north of Gualala on the east side of Hwy 1.* ♿

Point Arena

Fifteen miles north of Gualala is one of the smallest incorporated cities in California, Point Arena. This former bustling shipping port currently has a population of just a few hundred; many residents are transplants from larger cities, and some have set up shop along the three-block Main Street.

The **POINT ARENA LIGHTHOUSE** (707/882-2777; www.pointarenalighthouse.com; open 10am–3:30pm every day) is the biggest attraction in the area. Built in 1870 after 10 ships ran aground here on a single stormy night, the fully operational lighthouse had to be rebuilt after the 1906 earthquake. But now it's solid enough for visitors to trudge up the six-story tower's 145 steps for a standout view of the coast—if the fog has lifted. A look through the dazzling 6-foot-wide lead-crystal lens is worth the hike alone. You'll find it at the end of scenic Lighthouse Road, about 5 miles northwest of downtown Point Arena off Highway 1. The fee for the tour, museum, and parking is $7.50.

Virtually isolated is the 5-mile sweep of shore, dunes, and meadows of **MANCHESTER STATE BEACH** (707/882-2463). Though several access roads off Highway 1 lead to the shore, the closest one to Point Arena also happens to be the best—the 15-minute walk across the dunes from the parking lot is a leg burner, but it's a small price to pay for your own private beach. Take the Stoneboro Road exit west off Highway 1; the beach is 2 miles north of the turnoff to Point Arena Lighthouse.

Elk

Once known as Greenwood, this tiny former logging town was renamed Elk by the postal service when someone realized there was another town in California called Greenwood. For such a small community of a couple hundred, it sure has a booming tourist trade: six inns, four restaurants, and one authentic Irish pub. Its close proximity to the big tourist town of Mendocino, a mere

30-minute drive up the coast, is one reason for its popularity. Elk's paramount appeal, however, is its dramatic shoreline; the series of immense sea stacks here creates one of the most awesome seascapes on the California coast.

LODGINGS

Greenwood Pier Inn / ★★★

5928 HWY 1, ELK; 707/877-9997

What separates this cliff-top wonder from the dozens of other precariously perched inns along Highway 1 are its rooms' fantastic interiors and the brilliant flower gardens gracing the property. The inn offers 14 guest rooms, including 3 detached cliff-hanging suites (Cliffhouse and the two Sea Castles) and the separate Garden Cottage. The whimsical avant-garde decor and tile and marble detailing in most rooms are the work of artist Kendrick Petty, who owns and operates this quartet of café, country store, garden shop, and seaside inn. Some units also feature Petty's colorful airbrush collages, and all the rooms have private baths, fireplaces or wood-burning stoves, ocean views, private decks, and CD players. The elegantly rustic Cliffhouse is a favorite, with its expansive deck, marble fireplace, whirlpool tub, and Oriental rugs. While the suites and Sea Castles are rather expensive, the rooms in the main house are moderately priced. Room rates include a continental breakfast delivered to your doorstep, and you can even have a café dinner brought to your room. In-room therapeutic massage and herbal facial massage are available as well. All guests have access to a hot tub on the cliff's edge. *$$$–$$$$; AE, MC, V; local checks only; www.greenwoodpierinn.com; center of town.* ♿

The Harbor House Inn / ★★★

5600 S HWY 1, ELK; 707/877-3203 OR 800/720-7474

Constructed in 1916 in the classic Craftsman style, the majestic redwood-sided, two-story Harbor House was originally an executive lodge for Goodyear Redwood Lumber Co. executives. There are six regally appointed rooms in the main house, all with classic and antique furnishings, fireplaces, decks, and private baths. And should you want a cottage nestled among the 3 acres of redwoods, there are four to choose from, intimate and tastefully appointed. Down comforters, feather beds, luxurious robes, and CD players come with all main-house and cottage rooms. A full breakfast and four-course dinner for two are included in the rates. *$$$$; MC, V; checks OK; www.theharborhouseinn.com; north end of Elk.*

Albion

A renowned haven for pot growers until an increase in police surveillance and property taxes drove most of them away, Albion is more a free-spirited ideal community than an actual town. A white wooden bridge, the last of its kind on Highway 1, marks the entrance to town.

RESTAURANTS

Albion River Inn Restaurant / ★★

3790 HWY 1, ALBION; 707/937-1919 OR 800/479-7944

Chef Stephen Smith has presided over the Albion Inn's ocean-view dining room for more than a decade, and contented diners keep coming back for more of his consistently good coastal cuisine. Fresh local produce complements such dishes as braised Sonoma rabbit, grilled sea bass, fennel-crusted ahi tuna, oven-roasted quail, and rock shrimp pasta. The extensive, award-winning wine list—more than 500 choices—includes hard-to-find North Coast labels. Arrive before nightfall to ooh and aah over the view. *$$$; AE, DIS, MC, V; checks OK; dinner every day; beer and wine; reservations recommended; www.albionriverinn.com; on the northwest side of the Albion bridge.* ♿

The Ledford House Restaurant / ★★½

3000 HWY 1, ALBION; 707/937-0282

It's rare when an ocean-view restaurant's food is as good as the view, but owners Lisa and Tony Geer manage to pull it off, serving provençal-style cuisine in a wonderfully romantic cliff-top setting. One part of chef Lisa's menu is reserved primarily for hearty bistro dishes such as Antoine's Cassoulet (lamb, pork, garlic sausage, and duck confit slowly cooked with white beans), potato gnocchi with a rosemary Gorgonzola cream sauce, and fresh fish stew in a white wine, tomato, fennel, and saffron broth. The other half is dedicated to the classics: rack of lamb, Pacific salmon, roast duckling, and New York steak. Vegetarian entrées and soups are always featured as well. With a view like this, a window table at sunset is a must. After dinner, sidle up to the bar and listen to the live music, featured nightly. *$$$; AE, MC, V; checks OK; dinner Wed–Sun (closed 3 weeks in Feb); full bar; reservations recommended; www.ledfordhouse.com; exit west off Hwy 1 at Spring Grove Rd.* ♿

LODGINGS

Albion River Inn / ★★★

3790 HWY 1, ALBION; 707/937-1919 OR 800/479-7944

This seaside inn, poised 90 feet above Albion Cove where the Albion River meets the sea, is one of the finest on the California coast—the kind of place where guests return again and again. Each of the 23 individually decorated New England–style cottages—situated right along the bluff—features distinctive furnishings, a king- or queen-size bed, and a fireplace. Additional perks for each room include binoculars for wildlife viewing, robes, a bottle of wine, fresh ground coffee, a refrigerator, the daily newspaper, and a private deck with Adirondack-style lounging chairs. If you really want to impress your partner, reserve one of the rooms with a spa tub for two set right next to a large picture window with postcard views of the coast. A full country breakfast, served in the restaurant (see review), is included in the rates. *$$$–$$$$;*

AE, DIS, MC, V; checks OK; www.albionriverinn.com; on the northwest side of the Albion bridge. ♿

Little River

Once a bustling logging and shipbuilding community, Little River is now more like a suburb of Mendocino. The town does a brisk business handling the tourist overflow from its neighbor 2 miles up the coast; vacationers in the know reserve a room in serene Little River and make forays into Mendocino only for dining and shopping.

The town is near **VAN DAMME STATE PARK** (707/937-5804), a 2,337-acre preserve blanketed with ferns and second-growth redwoods. One of the finest state parks on the Mendocino coast, it has a small beach, visitor center, and campground, but its main attraction is the 15 miles of spectacularly lush trails—ideal for a stroll or a jog—that start at the beach and wind through the redwood-covered hills. **FERN CANYON TRAIL** is the park's most popular, an easy and incredibly scenic 2½-mile hiking and bicycling path that crosses over the Little River. You can also hike or drive (most of the way) to Van Damme's peculiar **PYGMY FOREST**, an eerie scrub forest of waist-high stunted trees. To reach the Pygmy Forest by car, follow Highway 1 south of the park and turn up Little River Airport Road, then head uphill 2¾ miles.

LODGINGS

Glendeven Inn / ★★★

8221 HWY 1, LITTLE RIVER; 707/937-0083 OR 800/822-4536

This stately 1867 farmhouse resides among 2½ acres of well-tended gardens and heather-covered headlands that extend all the way to the blue Pacific. The 10 spacious rooms and suites feature an uncluttered mix of country antiques and contemporary art. Most have ocean views, fireplaces, and porches, and all have wireless Internet access. For the ultimate in luxury, stay in the Pinewood or Bayloft suites in the Stevenscroft Annex—each has a sitting parlor, fireplace, and partial ocean view. The cozy East Farmington Room, with its private garden deck and fireplace, is another good choice. Above the Glendeven Gallery, the inn's fine-arts boutique, sits the fabulous Carriage House Suite, a two-story redwood-paneled house ideal for families or two couples. After a hot country breakfast in bed—brought to your room in a basket—walk to the beautiful fern-rimmed canyon trails in nearby Van Damme State Park. *$$$–$$$$; AE, DIS, MC, V; checks OK; www.glendeven.com; 2 miles south of Mendocino.*

The Inn at Schoolhouse Creek / ★★

7051 HWY 1, LITTLE RIVER; 707/937-5525 OR 800/731-5525

Whereas most small inns located along the Mendocino coast have to make do with an acre or less, the Inn at Schoolhouse Creek has the luxury of spreading its 12 adorable cottages and 8 guestrooms amid 8 acres of beautiful flower gardens, lush meadows, and cypress groves. Most of the cottages are designed for couples, though a few can comfortably fit kids as well; our favorite is the secluded Cypress Cottage, with its private yard graced by an inviting pair of Adirondack chairs. All are luxuriously loaded with fireplaces, TVs with VCRs (DVD players available for borrow), CD players, phones, private baths, private entrances, and decks or adjoining garden seating areas. Rates include a bountiful buffet breakfast and evening wine and hors d'oeuvres, served on the front porch of the inn's 1862 Ledford farmhouse. Perhaps the best indulgence, however, is the inn's hot tub, perched at the top of a meadow overlooking the ocean. *$$$; MC, V; checks OK; www.innatschoolhousecreek.com; just south of Little River.* ♿

Little River Inn & Restaurant / ★★

7901 HWY 1, LITTLE RIVER; 707/937-5942 OR 888/466-5683

Set on a 225-acre parcel of oceanfront land, the Little River Inn is an ideal retreat for those North Coast travelers who simply can't leave their golf clubs or tennis rackets at home. The resort is often jokingly referred to as the poor man's Pebble Beach, complete with a nine-hole golf course, driving range, putting green, full-service salon and day spa, restaurant, and two lighted tennis courts. All the estate's 65 rooms and cottages offer ocean views, many feature fireplaces, and some also have whirlpool tubs (if you prefer to relax indoors, check out the inn's extensive video and DVD library). The antique-filled rooms in the main Victorian house are preferable to the north wing's motel-style units, which suffer from uninspired decor. The Little River Inn Restaurant is a casual place for breakfast, dinner, and weekend brunch. Dishes are made from mostly local products: fresh fish from nearby Noyo Harbor; lamb, beef, and potatoes from the town of Comptche; and greens and vegetables from local gardens. For breakfast try the popular Ole's Swedish Hotcakes. *$$–$$$$; AE, MC, V; checks OK; www.littleriverinn.com; across from the Little River Market and Post Office.* ♿

Stevenswood Lodge / ★★★

8211 HWY 1, LITTLE RIVER; 707/937-2810 OR 800/421-2810

Stevenswood Lodge is for people who want the comforts of a modern hotel—cable television, telephone, refrigerator, honor bar—without feeling like they're staying at a Holiday Inn. As it works out, not many Holiday Inns are surrounded on three sides by a verdant 2,400-acre forest, or located just a quarter of a mile from the Mendocino shoreline, or embellished with sculpture gardens and contemporary art displays throughout the grounds. The rooms and suites are outfitted with handcrafted burl-maple furniture, large windows with striking vistas (some with partial ocean views), private bathrooms, wood-burning fireplaces, TVs and DVD players, free long-distance calling, complimentary bottles of wine, and access to several shared decks. The lodge, built in 1988, also has two spas set within the forest canyon, as well as a restaurant offering upscale coastal cuisine. Rates include a full breakfast. *$$$–$$$$; AE, DC, DIS, MC, V; checks OK; www.stevenswood.com; 2 miles south of Mendocino.* ♿

Mendocino

The grande dame of Northern California's coastal tourist towns, this refurbished replica of a New England–style fishing village—complete with a white-spired church—has managed to retain more of its charm and allure than most North Coast vacation spots. Motels, fast-food chains, and anything hinting of development are strictly forbidden here (even the town's only automated teller is subtly recessed into the historic Masonic Building), resulting in the almost-passable illusion that Mendocino is just another quaint little coastal community. Try to find a parking space on a summer weekend, however, and the illusion quickly fades; even the four-hour drive fails to deter hordes of Bay Area residents.

Founded in 1852, Mendocino is still home to a few anglers and loggers, although writers, artists, actors, and other urban transplants now far outnumber the natives. Spring is the best time to visit, when parking spaces are plentiful and the climbing tea roses and wisteria are in full bloom. Start with a casual tour of the town, and end with a stroll around Mendocino's celebrated headlands. Suddenly the long drive and inflated room rates seem a trivial price to pay for visiting one of the most beautiful places on earth.

To tour Mendocino proper, lose the car and head out on foot to the **TOTE FÊTE BAKERY** (10450 Lansing St; 707/937-3383). Fuel up with a double cappuccino and cinnamon bun, then throw away your map of the town and start walking—the shopping district of Mendocino is so small it can be covered in less than an hour, so why bother planning your attack? One must-see shop is the **GALLERY BOOKSHOP & BOOKWINKLE'S CHILDREN'S BOOKS** (45098 Main St; 707/937-BOOK; www.gallerybooks.com), one of the best independent bookstores in Northern California, with a wonderful selection of books for kids, cooks, and local-history buffs (the original building burnt down in January 2008, but was fully restored a year later). Another is **MENDOCINO JAMS & PRESERVES** (440 Main St; 707/937-1037 or 800/708-1196; www.mendojams.com), a town landmark that offers free tastings—à la bread chips—of its luscious marmalades, dessert toppings, mustards, chutneys, and other spreads.

As with many towns that hug the Northern California coast, Mendocino's premier attractions are provided by Mother Nature and the Department of Parks and Recreation, which means they're free (or nearly free). **MENDOCINO HEADLANDS STATE PARK**, the grassy stretch of land between the village of Mendocino and the ocean, is one of the town's most popular sites. The park's flat, 3-mile trail winds along the edge of a heather-covered bluff, providing spectacular sunset views and good lookout points for spotting seabirds and

California gray whales. The headlands' main access point is at the west end of Main Street—or skip the footwork altogether and take the scenic motorist's route along Heeser Drive off Lansing Street. **MENDOCINO STATE PARK VISITOR CENTER** is located at Ford House (735 Main St; 707/937-5397).

About 2 miles north of Mendocino, off Highway 1, is the worst-kept secret on the coast: **RUSSIAN GULCH STATE PARK** (707/937-5804), a veritable paradise for campers, hikers, and abalone divers. After paying a small entry fee, pick up a trail map at the park entrance and find the path to **DEVIL'S PUNCH BOWL**—a 200-foot-long sea-carved tunnel that has partially collapsed in the center, creating an immense blowhole that's particularly spectacular during a storm. Even better is the 5½-mile round-trip hike along **FALLS LOOP TRAIL** to the **RUSSIAN GULCH FALLS**, a misty 35-foot waterfall secluded in the deep old-growth forest.

If you have a passion for plants and flowers, spend a few bucks on the admission fee to the **MENDOCINO COAST BOTANICAL GARDENS** (18220 Hwy 1; 707/964-4352; www.gardenbythesea.org), located 2 miles south of Fort Bragg. The nonprofit gardens feature 47 acres of plants—ranging from azaleas and rhododendrons to dwarf conifers and ferns—as well as a picnic area, retail nursery, and gift store.

The black sheep of Mendocino's hiking trails is **JUG HANDLE STATE RESERVE'S ECOLOGICAL STAIRCASE TRAIL** (707/937-5804). This 5-mile round-trip trail is a wonderful hike and gets surprisingly little traffic. The attraction is a series of naturally formed staircaselike bluffs—each about 100 feet higher and 100,000 years older than the one below it—that differ dramatically in ecological formation: from beaches to headlands to an amazing pygmy forest filled with waist-high, century-old trees. The trail entrance is located on Highway 1, 1½ miles north of the town of Caspar, between Mendocino and Fort Bragg.

After a full day of adventuring, why not top off the evening with a little nightcap and music? If you appreciate classical tunes and warm snifters of brandy, take a stroll down Mendocino's Main Street to the elegant bar and lounge at the **MENDOCINO HOTEL AND RESTAURANT** (see review). If blue jeans and baseball caps are more your style, hang out with the guys at **DICK'S PLACE** (45080 Main St; 707/937-5643), which has the cheapest drinks in town and the sort of jukebox 'n' jiggers atmosphere you'd expect from this former logging town's oldest bar. For a rowdy night of dancing and drinking, head a few miles up Highway 1 to **CASPAR INN** (Caspar Rd exit off Hwy 1, ¼ mile north of Mendocino and 4 miles south of Fort Bragg; 707/964-5565; www.casparinn.com), the last true roadhouse in California, where everything from rock and jazz to reggae and blues is played live Thursday through Saturday nights starting at 9:30pm (check the inn's Web site calendar for upcoming shows).

RESTAURANTS

Cafe Beaujolais / ★★★

961 UKIAH ST, MENDOCINO; 707/937-5614

Cafe Beaujolais started out as the finest little breakfast and lunch place in Mendocino. Then, over the years, the modest 1893 Victorian farmhouse morphed into one of the most celebrated restaurants in Northern California. The café has since lost much of its illustrious status, but the tradition of featuring locally grown organic produce, meat from humanely raised animals, and fresh, locally caught seafood continues. Carnival-glass chandeliers, oak floors, and heavy oak tables adorned with flowers add to the intimate country atmosphere. The menu changes weekly and usually lists about five main courses. A typical dinner may start with cider-braised Niman Ranch pork belly, followed by pan-roasted California sturgeon fillet, house-made tagliatelle, truffle emulsion sauce, wild mushrooms, beets, and snap peas. Try to avoid sitting in the bustling bench section, which has itsy-bitsy tables; rather, opt for the enclosed atrium overlooking the garden. For a take-home treat, you can buy Cafe Beaujolais's renowned "brickery breads" on their Web site or at the bakery in the restaurant foyer from 11am to around 3pm every day. *$$$$; AE, DIS, MC, V; checks OK; dinner every day; beer and wine; reservations recommended; www.cafebeaujolais.com; at Evergreen St.* ♿

MacCallum House Restaurant / ★★★

45020 ALBION ST, MENDOCINO; 707/937-0289 OR 800/609-0492

Using the freshest ingredients—seafood straight from the coast and organic meats and produce from neighboring farms and ranches—chef Alan Kantor, a graduate of the Culinary Institute of America, whips up some wonderful North Coast cuisine. Situated within an 1882 Victorian mansion and warmed by a crackling fire in the stone fireplace, this intimate restaurant is the ideal setting for Kantor's sophisticated, seasonally changing menu. Entrées may range from roasted Pacific salmon with saffron-pistachio risotto and arugula pesto to pan-seared Sonoma duck breast with huckleberry-honey vinegar sauce, and grilled Niman Ranch pork chops with walnut bread pudding and pear chutney. After dinner, stroll over to the Grey Whale bar for a martini. *$$$; MC, V; no checks; breakfast, dinner every day; full bar; reservations recommended; www.maccallumhousedining.com; between Kasten and Lansing sts.* ♿

The Moosse Cafe / ★★☆

390 KASTEN ST, MENDOCINO; 707/937-4323

One of the most popular restaurants in Mendocino is this petite café set in a New England–style home. The rather unorthodox modern interior is due partly to a 1995 fire—after burning to the ground, the entire place had to be rebuilt and redecorated. The menu changes seasonally and often includes locally grown herbs and vegetables. A popular combo is the superb Caesar salad and Rocky Range roast chicken with garlic mashed potatoes. Seafood specials range from crab cakes served over basmati rice with a roasted red pepper

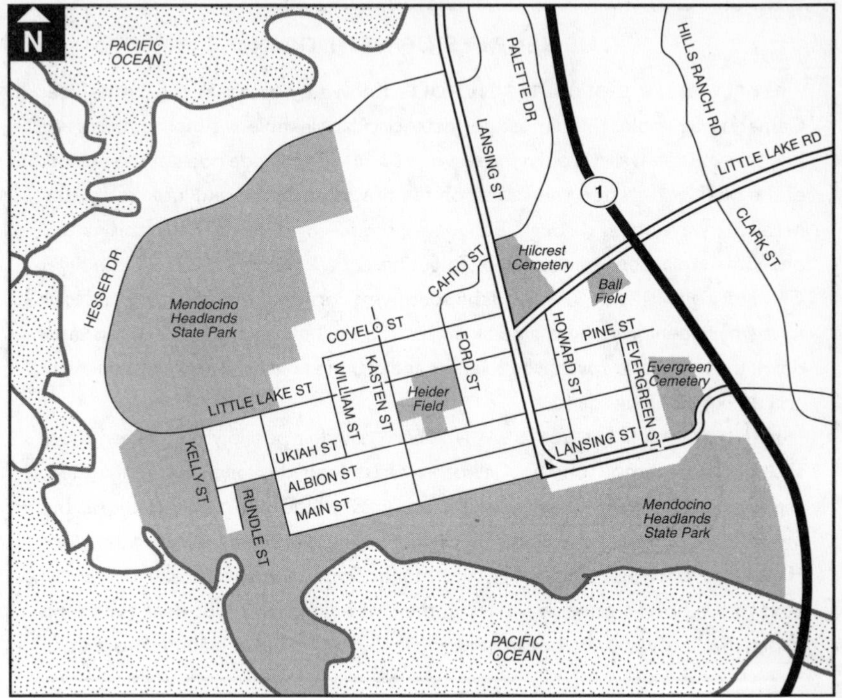

Mendocino

rémoulade to fresh grilled swordfish. The lavender-smoked double-thick pork chop served with roasted yam and apple purée is also quite good. Save room for the decadent house-made desserts. *$$$; MC, V; checks OK; lunch, dinner every day; beer and wine; reservations recommended; www.theblueheron.com; at the corner of Kasten and Albion sts.* ♿

955 Ukiah Street Restaurant / ★★★

955 UKIAH ST, MENDOCINO; 707/937-1955

This under-the-radar Mendocino restaurant is described by local epicureans as "the sleeper restaurant on the coast." Shortly after this building's construction in the 1960s, the region's most famous painter, Emmy Lou Packard, commandeered its premises as an art studio for the creation of a series of giant murals. Guests enter the establishment by way of a winding path flanked by much foliage, a labyrinth of greenery of sorts. The dramatic interior, with its split-level dining room, massive wood beams, 20-foot ceilings, and elegant table settings create the proper mood for the North Coast cuisine, which might include seared pork loin stuffed with prosciutto, crispy duck served with ginger-apple brandy sauce, and a thick swordfish steak resting in a red chile–tomatillo sauce. The upstairs section can get cramped and a little noisy, so try to sit downstairs—preferably at the corner window table—where the vaulted

THE SECRETS OF MENDOCINO

LITTLE RIVER'S SECRET SINKHOLE: Known by locals as the Little River Cemetery Sinkhole, this almost perfectly circular sinkhole is simply amazing. At low tide you can walk through the wave-cut tunnel to the tide pools at the bottom of the bluff; at high tide you can sit on the tiny sandy beach and look at the tunnel as the waves blast through. Either way, the feeling of being within this natural phenomenon is borderline sacred. To get here, park across from the Little River Cemetery on Highway 1, walk to the southwest corner of the cemetery, and look for a small opening in the chain-link fence. The sinkhole is only a few dozen yards down the trail, but be prepared to enter and exit the hole on all fours or you might end up buried alongside it.

MENDOCINO'S SECRET BEACH: There couldn't possibly be a cuter, more secluded little beach on the California coast than this one. Naturally, there are no signs pointing the way and it requires a little effort to get there, but my-oh-my is it worth the walk. First you need to find the Pine Beach Inn along Highway 1 between Fort Bragg and Mendocino. Take the Ocean Drive exit next to the hotel's giant sign, park in the small dirt parking lot near the tennis courts, walk toward the ocean, and you'll see the trailhead leading into a small

ceiling imparts a comfortable sense of space. *$$$; MC, V; checks OK; dinner Wed–Sun; beer and wine; reservations recommended; www.955restaurant.com; Ukiah and Evergreen sts, east end of town.* ♿

The Raven's Restaurant / ★★

HWY 1 AND COMPTCHE–UKIAH RD (THE STANFORD INN BY THE SEA), MENDOCINO; 707/937-5615 OR 800/331-8884

To complement their environmentally friendly lodge (see review), Joan and Jeff Stanford have taken a huge gamble and opened the region's only fine-dining vegetarian-vegan restaurant. The menu varies monthly to take advantage of seasonal organic produce, some of which derives from the lodge's own gardens. Dishes range from lighter fare—herbed Asiago polenta cakes sautéed in a roasted garlic–chardonnay sauce with local organic shiitake mushrooms (fantastic)—to hearty entrées such as tarragon roasted acorn squash filled with wild rice, shiitake mushrooms, roasted garlic, and caramelized apples. These are masterfully crafted dishes that explode the myth that it takes meat to make a meal. Though the dining room exudes a rustic elegance, dining attire is anything but formal. *$$; AE, DC, DIS, MC, V; checks OK; breakfast, dinner every day, brunch Sun; full bar; reservations recommended; www.ravensrestaurant.com; 1 mile south of Mendocino.*

forest. A five-minute walk through scrub pines and meadows rewards you with a billion-dollar view of the coast. At the bluff's edge, head south toward the green-roofed house, and you'll come to a small creek that provides easy access to the beach.

THE SECRET GORDON: Here's a little-known walk for people who love to sit alone for hours and watch the waves pound against stone. About a mile south of Mendocino along Highway 1, look for the Gordon Lane turnoff heading inland. Park on the raised dirt shoulder across from the Gordon Lane turnoff and look for a small opening in the barbed-wire fence. The unmarked half-mile trail through Chapman Point's meadows ends at an enormous rocky outcropping with a letter-box view of Mendocino far across the bay.

THE SECRET SUNSHINE: When the fog refuses to lift for days—even weeks—at a time during Mendocino summers, locals are sure to be found a few miles inland at the perpetually sunny "3.66 Beach" on the Navarro River. The small golden-sand beach fronts a placid pool of cool green river water that's ideal for swimming. To get here from Mendocino, head south on Highway 1, turn inland at the Highway 128 junction, and look for the 3.66 mile marker. Park along the road and take the short, well-worn path down to the beach.

LODGINGS

Agate Cove Inn / ★★★

11201 N LANSING ST, MENDOCINO; 707/937-0551 OR 800/527-3111

If there's a more beautiful coastal setting than the one at Agate Cove Inn, we've yet to discover it. The view from the inn's front lawn is so stunningly pretty—a sweeping vista of the sea and its surging waves crashing onto the rocky bluffs—you can't help but stare in silence as you sit on the inn's weathered wooden bench under the cypress tree. This well-run inn consists of a main house trimmed in blue and white surrounded by several single and duplex cottages; it offers seclusion, privacy, and views that in-town B and Bs just can't match. All cottages have light pine furnishings, casual country decor, king- or queen-size feather beds with Scandia Down comforters, CD players, TVs with VCRs (and a free video and CD library), and private decks, and all but one room have ocean views and fireplaces. Some have DVD players, Jacuzzis, and/or refrigerators. In the morning on your doorstep you'll find the *San Francisco Chronicle*, which you can peruse over a bountiful country breakfast in the main house's enclosed porch. *$$$$; AE, MC, V; checks OK; www.agatecove.com; ½ mile north of downtown.*

John Dougherty House / ★★★

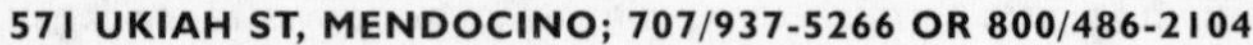

571 UKIAH ST, MENDOCINO; 707/937-5266 OR 800/486-2104

This classic saltbox is a wonderful example of why so many movies supposedly set in New England (*The Russians Are Coming*, *Summer of '42*) are actually filmed in Mendocino. The John Dougherty House features authentic Early Americana throughout: stenciled walls, Early American furniture, and all-cotton linens on the beds. Each of the eight rooms has a touch of individual charm, but your first choice should be either the Osprey Room or the Raven Room, which feature beautiful ocean views, decks, jet tubs for two, fire stoves, flat-screen TVs with DVD players, and king-size four-poster beds. Another favorite is Kit's Cabin—a cozy two-room cottage hidden in the flower garden that comes with a wood-burning stove and four-poster bed. All the other rooms have private baths, wood-burning fireplaces, and queen beds; the Starboard and Port cottages have jet tubs for two as well. An expansive breakfast including homemade bread and scones is served next to a crackling fire. *$$$–$$$$; DIS, MC, V; checks OK; www.jdhouse.com; Ukiah St just west of Kasten St.*

Joshua Grindle Inn / ★★★

44800 LITTLE LAKE RD, MENDOCINO; 707/937-4143 OR 800/GRINDLE

The most authentic of Mendocino's many New England–style B and Bs, this masterpiece was built in 1879 by the town's banker, Joshua Grindle. Startlingly white against a backdrop of wind-whipped cypress trees, the two-story beauty has lovely bay windows and a wraparound front porch trimmed with gingerbread arches. There are five Early American rooms in the clapboard house (including one with a whirlpool tub and fireplace), two in the saltbox cottage, three in an old-fashioned water tower set back in the trees, and two suites in the Lupe Gordon House. Top picks are any of the cute water-tower rooms or the Library Room with its four-poster bed, deep soaking tub, and 19th-century hand-decorated tiles encircling the wood-burning fireplace. All of the rooms have sitting areas and private baths. Sherry, snacks, and tea are offered in the afternoon, while a complimentary full breakfast is served in the dining room. In addition to the inn, the proprietors also offer a two-bedroom, two-bathroom ocean-view rental home with floor-to-ceiling windows, a large kitchen, and a wood-burning fireplace. *$$$$; MC, V; no checks; www.joshgrin.com; east end of Little Lake Rd.*

Mendocino Farmhouse / ★★½

43410 COMPTCHE RD, MENDOCINO; 707/937-0241 OR 800/475-1536

Once you emerge from deep within the redwood forest surrounding Marge Kamb's secluded estate, you know you're going to be very happy here. All six rooms—four in the farmhouse and two in the adjacent Barn Cottage—are filled with antique furnishings and fresh flowers from the surrounding English gardens and come with private baths, queen- or king-size beds, and, if you listen carefully, echoes of the nearby ocean; all but two have fireplaces as well. Each morning in the sitting room, Marge serves up a real country breakfast. *$$–$$$; MC, V; checks OK; www.mendocinofarmhouse.com; off Olson Ln.*

Mendocino Hotel & Garden Suites / ★★☆

45080 MAIN ST, MENDOCINO; 707/937-0511 OR 800/548-0513

The Mendocino Hotel, built in 1878, combines modern amenities—telephones, full bathrooms, room service—with turn-of-the-century Victorian furnishings to create a romantic yesteryear setting with today's creature comforts. The hotel's 51 rooms—all decorated with quality antiques, patterned wallpapers, and old prints and photos—range from inexpensive European-style rooms with shared baths to elaborate garden suites with fireplaces, king-size beds, balconies, and parlors. The Ocean View suites on the hotel's third floor have wonderful views of Mendocino Bay from their private balconies. Other favorites are the deluxe rooms with private baths, particularly rooms facing the sea. Breakfast and lunch are served downstairs in the verdant Garden Cafe. The hotel's intimate Victorian Dining Room serves California-style cuisine such as pan-seared ahi tuna, double-baked pork chops, and prime rib au jus. Budding sommeliers should inquire about the hotel's popular winemaker dinners. *$$–$$$$; AE, MC, V; checks OK; www.mendocinohotel.com; between Lansing and Kasten sts.* ♿

The Stanford Inn by the Sea / ★★★★

HWY 1 AND COMPTCHE–UKIAH RD, MENDOCINO; 707/937-5615 OR 800/331-8884

Hats off to Joan and Jeff Stanford, the environmentally conscious couple who turned this parcel of prime coastal property and the former Big River Lodge into something more than a magnificent resort. It's a true ecosystem, a place where plants, animals, and people coexist in one of the most unforgettable lodging experiences in California. Upon entering the estate you'll see several tiers of raised garden beds, where a wide variety of vegetables, herbs, spices, and edible flowers are organically grown for local grocers and restaurants. Watching your every move as you proceed up the driveway are the Stanfords' extended family of curious llamas. Guests may also bring along their own menagerie of critters, be they pet dogs, cats, parrots, or iguanas. Also on the grounds is a beautiful plant-filled greenhouse that encloses a grand swimming pool, sauna, and spa. There's also a mountain bike and canoe shop on the property. The inn's 23 rooms and 10 suites feature decks with ocean views, fireplaces or Waterford stoves, TVs with VCRs and DVD players, coffeemakers, telephones, wireless Internet, and sitting areas. The isolated, utterly romantic River Cottage sits right on the water's edge—an ideal honeymooners' hideaway. A cooked-to-order full breakfast, served in the Raven's Restaurant (see review), afternoon snacks, and evening wine and hors d'oeuvres are included in the price. *$$$$; AE, DC, DIS, MC, V; checks OK; www.stanfordinn.com; ½ mile south of Mendocino.* ♿

Whitegate Inn / ★★★

499 HOWARD ST, MENDOCINO; 707/937-4892 OR 800/531-7282

During movie shoots Julia Roberts, Mel Gibson, Bette Davis, and Angela Lansbury preferred to stay at the Whitegate Inn, one of the finest B and Bs in Mendocino. This beautifully restored 1883 Victorian mansion offers six rooms individually decorated with classic antiques, fireplaces, immaculate private baths, European feather beds with soft down comforters, European toiletries, TVs, and garden or ocean views. Our favorite is the Enchanted Cottage; secluded in the Victorian garden, it has a private entrance and deck, king-size bed, therapeutic jet tub, refrigerator, and TV and DVD player. In the morning a full breakfast is served in the dining room. *$$$–$$$$; MC, V; checks OK; www.whitegateinn.com; corner of Howard and Ukiah sts.*

Fort Bragg

Originally built in 1855 as a military outpost to supervise the Pomo Indian Reservation, Fort Bragg is still primarily a logging and fishing town proud of its century-old timber-and-trawler heritage.

Two popular festivals are celebrated annually: **PAUL BUNYAN DAYS** on Labor Day weekend features a big parade and log-cutting races, and the annual **WHALE FESTIVAL**, held the third Saturday of March, includes ranger-led talks about the cetaceans, a Whale Run, and a beer and chowder tasting.

If you've visited all of Mendocino's boutiques and still haven't shrugged the shopping bug, head over to historic downtown Fort Bragg. The building facades have been restored to their early 1900s look; inside you'll find shops, galleries, and restaurants—all within walking distance of each other. Two dangerous places for a credit card are the **UNION LUMBER COMPANY STORE** (corner of Main and Redwood sts) and **ANTIQUE ROW** (Franklin St between Laurel and Redwood).

One of the prettiest—and largest—public beaches on the Mendocino coast is **MACKERRICHER STATE PARK** (707/964-9112), located 3 miles north of Fort Bragg off Highway 1. The 8-mile shoreline is the perfect place to while away an afternoon, and it's free admission to boot. The highlight of the park is the **LAGUNA POINT SEAL WATCHING STATION**, a fancy name for a small wooden deck that overlooks the harbor seals sunning themselves on the rocks below.

One of the most popular attractions in Fort Bragg is the **SKUNK TRAIN** (100 Laurel St; 866/457-5865; www.skunktrain.com). The unusual name is derived from the odoriferous mix of diesel fuel and gasoline once used to power the train—you could smell it coming. Depending on which day you depart, a steam-, diesel-, or electric-engine train will take you on a scenic six- to seven-hour round-trip journey through the magnificent redwoods to the city of Willits and back again, crossing 31 bridges and trestles and cutting through two deep tunnels (half-day trips are offered daily from March 1 through the end of November). Reservations are recommended, especially in summer.

If you're passing through between December and April, be sure to watch the migrating California gray whales and humpback whales make their annual appearances along the North Coast. Although they're visible from the bluffs, you can practically meet the 40-ton cetaceans face to face by boarding one of the whale-watching boats in Fort Bragg. Just south of town, **NOYO FISHING CENTER** (32440 N Harbor, Noyo; 707/964-3000; www.fortbraggfishing.com) is the best source of information on whale-watching tours and sportfishing excursions.

RESTAURANTS

Egghead's / ★★★

326 N MAIN ST, FORT BRAGG; 707/964-5005 OR 707/964-8543

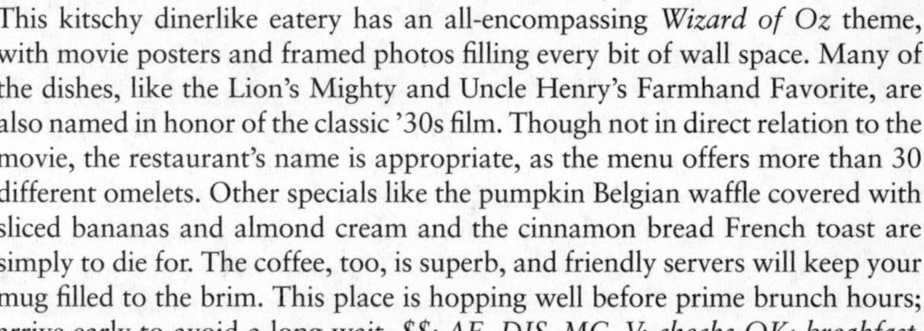

This kitschy dinerlike eatery has an all-encompassing *Wizard of Oz* theme, with movie posters and framed photos filling every bit of wall space. Many of the dishes, like the Lion's Mighty and Uncle Henry's Farmhand Favorite, are also named in honor of the classic '30s film. Though not in direct relation to the movie, the restaurant's name is appropriate, as the menu offers more than 30 different omelets. Other specials like the pumpkin Belgian waffle covered with sliced bananas and almond cream and the cinnamon bread French toast are simply to die for. The coffee, too, is superb, and friendly servers will keep your mug filled to the brim. This place is hopping well before prime brunch hours; arrive early to avoid a long wait. *$$; AE, DIS, MC, V; checks OK; breakfast, lunch Thurs–Tues; no alcohol; no reservations; www.eggheadsrestaurant.com; between Laurel St and E Redwood Ave.* ♿

North Coast Brewing Company / ★★

455 N MAIN ST, FORT BRAGG; 707/964-2739

This homey brewpub is the most happening place in town, especially at happy hour, when the bar and dark wood tables are occupied by boisterous locals. The pub is housed in a dignified, century-old redwood structure, and the beer is brewed on the premises in large copper vats displayed behind plate glass. A pale ale, wheat beer, stout, pilsner, and seasonal brew are always available, though first timers should opt for the inexpensive four-beer sampler—or, heck, why not indulge in the eight-beer sampler?—to learn the ropes. After your meal, browse the retail shop or take a free tour of the brewery. *$$; DIS, MC, V; checks OK; lunch, dinner every day; beer and wine; no reservations; www.northcoastbrewing.com; between E Pine and Laurel sts.* ♿

LODGINGS

Grey Whale Inn / ★★

615 N MAIN ST, FORT BRAGG; 707/964-0640 OR 800/382-7244

Wide doorways and sloped halls are the only vestiges of this popular inn's previous life as the town hospital, built in 1915. In 1978 this stately four-story redwood building was converted into one of the more comfortable and

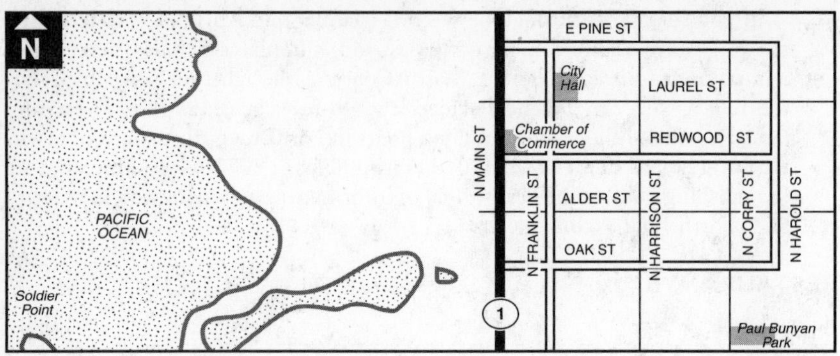

Fort Bragg

distinctive inns on the coast. Decorated with handmade quilts, heirlooms, and antiques, the 13 large guest rooms have private baths, TVs, and views of town or sea. The best guest rooms are the two penthouse rooms: Sunrise offers a view of the town, pretty wicker furniture, and a double whirlpool bath, while Sunset opens onto a private deck overlooking the ocean. Another good choice for romantically bent couples is the spacious and elegant Campbell Suite, which comes with a king bed, TV with VCR, and marble gas-log fireplace. The full buffet breakfast is served in the Craftsman-style breakfast room (with trays for carrying your food back to bed, if you prefer) and is included in the rates. There's even a game room with a pool table and foosball table. *$$–$$$; AE, DIS, MC, V; checks OK; www.greywhaleinn.com; corner of Main and 1st sts.* ♿

Historic Old Coast Hotel / ★★★

101 N FRANKLIN ST, FORT BRAGG; 707/961-4488 OR 888/468-3550

This charming downtown bed-and-breakfast seems to be off most travelers' radar, and for no apparent reason. With beyond reasonable prices, delightful rooms, and friendly service, it's one of our favorites in all of Mendocino County. The three wings of the building are centered on a well-groomed courtyard, and while the hotel itself has been welcoming guests since 1892, both the interior and exterior are still in excellent condition. Have the innkeeper, Michele, give you a guided tour, complete with the eccentricities (read: hauntings!) for which the hotel is known. The 15 rooms all come in different sizes, shapes, and themes. We like the Marilyn Monroe suite with vaulted ceilings and framed paraphernalia of the vixen. Other themes include Godfather, Elvis, and Lucille Ball. A central family room, complete with pool table, is where Michele serves up a scrumptious breakfast each morning. There's a sports bar and grill on site as well, but it's only open in spring and summer months. *$$–$$$; AE, DIS, MC, V; checks OK; www.oldcoasthotel.com; at E Oak St.* ♿

North Cliff Hotel / ★★

1005 S MAIN ST, FORT BRAGG; 707/962-2500

At the southern entrance to Fort Bragg, North Cliff occupies prime Mendocino real estate, perched on a particularly remarkable stretch of the coast (floor-to-ceiling windows and balconies maximize the view). A sprawling oceanfront lodge, it's also one of the few places in town that is neither a modest B and B nor a chain hotel. The furniture is a bit outdated with Laura Ashley–style touches, but rooms are massive, and all have fireplaces to keep the Pacific chill at bay. Some have Jacuzzis by windows overlooking the ocean. Other room amenities include a TV and VCR, an iPod dock, wireless Internet, robes, an iron, a hairdryer, a fridge, a safe, a microwave, and Bath and Body Works products. Complimentary continental breakfast, bottled water, and juice are included. *$$$; AE, DIS, MC, V; checks OK; at N Harbor Dr.* ♿

Willits

Ever since the widespread success of Laura Hillenbrand's 2001 novel *Seabiscuit* and the subsequent 2003 blockbuster film, the sensational racehorse has put this pinprick of a town on the map. Those who want to see the former home of Charles and Marcela Howard and the hotshot thoroughbred himself, where he's immortalized in bronze, can pay a visit to **RIDGEWOOD RANCH** (16200 Hwy 101; 707/459-5992; www.seabiscuitheritage.com).

A three-hour tour takes place at 9am one Saturday a month from May through October, including a video and visit to the "museum" (a dining hall where Seabiscuit's photos and press clippings hang), the old Howard home, the stables, and the paddock where his descendants still reside. The cost is $25 per person. A shorter, more kid-friendly tour is available at 9:30am on Monday, Wednesday, and Friday, June through September, for $15. No reservations are required, but because the ranch is small, it's best to call ahead and let them know you're coming.

RESTAURANTS

Purple Thistle / ★½

50 S MAIN ST, WILLITS; 707/459-4750

If you're looking for a good restaurant in the Willits area, head to the Purple Thistle, where you'll find the freshest fish around. It's a homey spot with a loyal following, good food, and friendly faces. Red snapper, prawns, chicken breast, or tofu can be served up grilled, Cajun-style, or in a tempura batter. In deference to unrepentant carnivores, however, Harris Ranch steaks have been added to the bill of fare. There are also plenty of vegetarian options made from almost entirely organic produce. *$; AE, DIS, MC, V; local checks only; lunch Tues–Fri, dinner Tues–Sat; beer and wine; reservations recommended; on Hwy 101, near Commercial St.* ♿

LODGINGS

Emandal Farm / ★

16500 HEARST POST OFFICE RD, WILLITS; 707/459-5439

Since 1908 this thousand-acre working farm situated along the Eel River has been a popular summer getaway for Bay Area families who long for a stint on the farm. The second and third generations of the Adams family own and run Emandal Farm, and they happily let children and their parents assist with the daily chores, such as feeding the pigs, milking the goats, tending the garden, and gathering eggs in the chicken coop. Guest may also enjoy the Adamses' private sandy beach on the river or explore trails meandering through the valley. At night a campfire circle inevitably forms. The 19 rustic redwood cabins, nestled under a grove of oak and fir trees, are not equipped with much—just single and queen-size beds, cold spring water, and electricity. The bathrooms and showers are housed in a separate, communal facility. The Adamses prepare a healthy, hearty breakfast, lunch, and dinner (two meals on Sunday), all included in the room price. Expect fare like omelets stuffed with garden-fresh vegetables, garden lasagne with homemade noodles, barbecued chicken, and homemade bread that's baked fresh daily. Although no alcohol is permitted at tables, guests may bring beer and wine in to the cabins. *$$; MC, V; checks OK; open late July–late Sept; www.emandal.com; 16 miles east of town (call for directions).*

Westport

If you've made it this far north, you're either lost or determined to drive the full length of Highway 1. If it's the latter, then you'd best stock up on a sandwich or two at the **WESTPORT COMMUNITY STORE & DELI** (24980 Abalone St on N Hwy 1; 707/964-2872) because this is the northernmost town on the Mendocino coast, and you still have a looooong way to go.

LODGINGS

DeHaven Valley Farm & Country Inn / ★★★

39247 HWY 1, WESTPORT; 707/961-1660

This remote 1875 Victorian farmhouse, with its sublime rural setting and access to a secluded beach, comes complete with a barnyard menagerie of horses, sheep, goats, and donkeys. If the animals aren't enough to keep you amused, try a game of croquet or horseshoes, do a little bird-watching or horseback riding, or take a meditative soak in the hot tub set high on a hill overlooking the ocean. The inviting parlor has deep, comfortable couches, while the six guest rooms in the house and the three nearby cottages are decorated with colorful comforters and rustic antiques; some even have fireplaces. In the morning, you'll wake to such complimentary treats as apple pancakes or potato-artichoke frittata. The small DeHaven Valley Farm Restaurant offers a commendable prix-fixe multicourse dinner menu Friday and Saturday (and some Thursdays in summer) that might go like this: cucumber salad, asparagus soup, freshly baked sweet French bread, entrées such as roasted pork tenderloin with apple horseradish or freshly caught salmon, and a killer apple strudel for dessert. Reservations are required. *$$–$$$; AE, MC, V; checks OK; 1.7 miles north of Westport.*

Howard Creek Ranch / ★★★

40501 N HWY 1, WESTPORT; 707/964-6725

Located off a remote stretch of Highway 1 near the tiny town of Westport, this isolated 40-acre ranch, which Mendocino County has designated a historic site, appeals to travelers who want to really get away from it all. For more than two decades, proprietors Sally and Charles (a.k.a. Sunny) Grigg have been renting out three cabins, four guest rooms in the 1871 Farmhouse, and six rooms in the renovated 1880s Carriage Barn. The rooms in the farmhouse feature separate sitting areas, antiques, and homemade quilts, while the barn units—each one handcrafted by Charles, a master builder with a penchant for skylights—have curly grain redwood walls and Early American collectibles. The separate Beach House, with its freestanding fireplace, skylights, king-size bed, large deck, and whirlpool tub, is a great romantic getaway. A hot tub and sauna are perched on the side of a hill, as are Sally's guardian cows, sheep, llamas, and horses. In the morning, Sally rings the breakfast bell to alert her guests that it's eatin' time—and the hearty country fare is definitely worth getting out of bed for. Note: Pet dogs are welcome with prior approval. *$$–$$$; AE, MC, V; checks OK; www.howardcreekranch.com; 3 miles north of Westport.*

REDWOOD EMPIRE

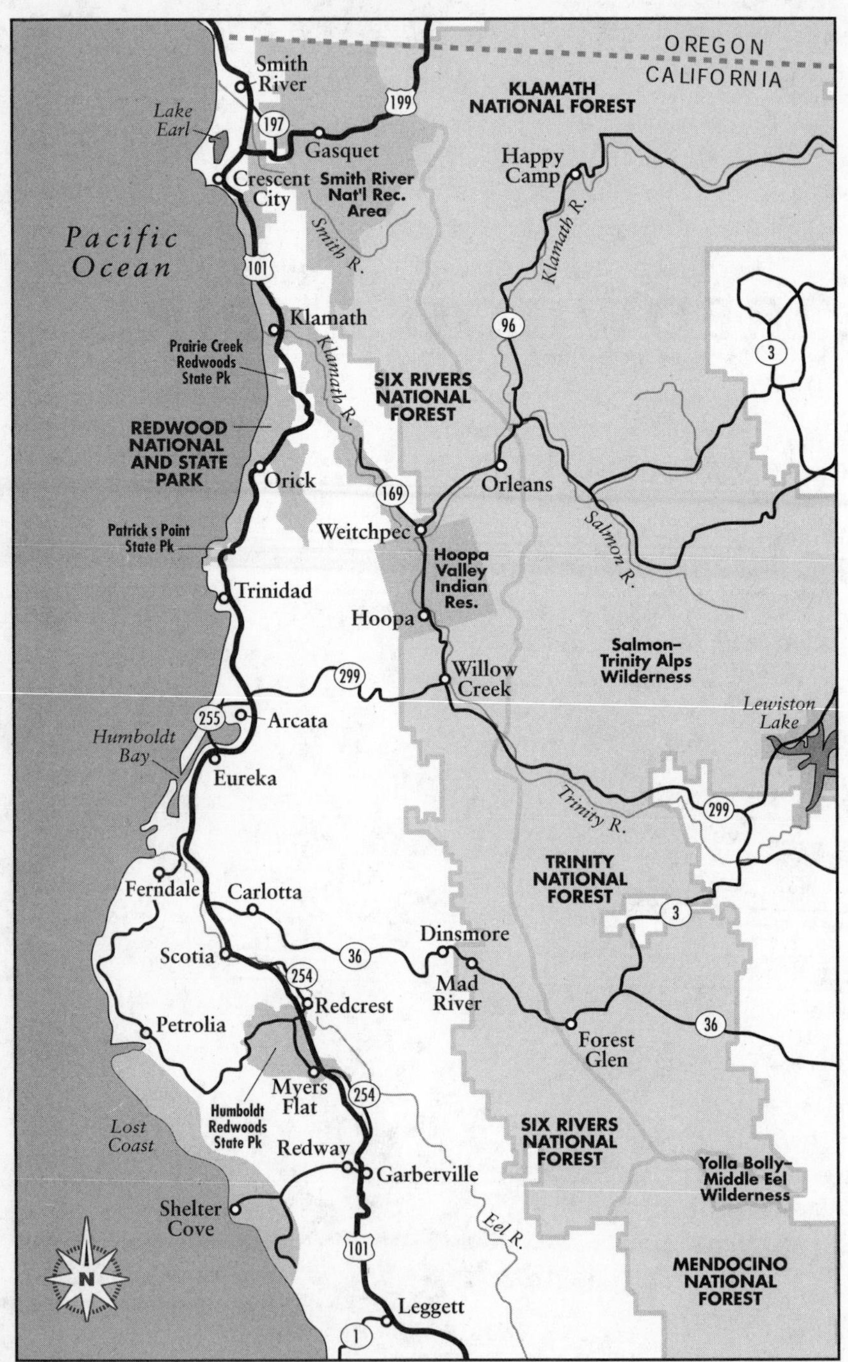
OREGON
CALIFORNIA
KLAMATH NATIONAL FOREST
Smith River
199
Lake Earl
197
Gasquet
Happy Camp
Crescent City
Smith River Nat'l Rec. Area
Smith R.
Klamath R.
Pacific Ocean
101
Klamath
96
3
Prairie Creek Redwoods State Pk
Klamath R.
SIX RIVERS NATIONAL FOREST
REDWOOD NATIONAL AND STATE PARK
Orick
Orleans
169
Weitchpec
Salmon R.
Patrick s Point State Pk
Hoopa Valley Indian Res.
Trinidad
Hoopa
Salmon–Trinity Alps Wilderness
299
Willow Creek
255
Arcata
Lewiston Lake
Humboldt Bay
Eureka
Trinity R.
299
TRINITY NATIONAL FOREST
Ferndale
Carlotta
3
Dinsmore
Scotia
36
254
Mad River
Redcrest
Petrolia
36
Forest Glen
Myers Flat
254
Humboldt Redwoods State Pk
Lost Coast
SIX RIVERS NATIONAL FOREST
Redway
Garberville
Yolla Bolly-Middle Eel Wilderness
Shelter Cove
Eel R.
101
MENDOCINO NATIONAL FOREST
N
Leggett
1

REDWOOD EMPIRE

Considering that California's Redwood Coast contains the most spectacular coastal forests in the world—including the world's tallest tree—it's surprising how few tourists care to venture north of Mendocino to get there. Perhaps it's the myth that the upper coast is permanently socked in with rain and fog, and that the only places to stay or eat are cheap motels and greasy diners. Or it could be the seemingly infinite road that snakes its way up the coast, heading nowhere in particular (or so it might appear); many intrepid drivers realize this halfway and often turn back.

Like most myths, of course, this isn't true (at least it's no longer true). Granted, the coastal weather can be miserable, but the fog usually burns off by the afternoon, and the rain—well, bring an umbrella; it's the price you pay for vacationing among the thirsty redwood giants. And while there are no Hyatts or Hiltons this far north, the Redwood Coast offers something even better: a wealth of small, personable inns and bed-and-breakfasts run by proprietors who bend over backward to make your stay as enjoyable as possible. The food? Combine the northern region's penchant for organic gardening with a year-round supply of just-off-the-boat seafood, and you have the ingredients for remarkably fresh and healthy gourmet cuisine.

The reason for the Redwood Coast's recent upswing in fine dining and accommodations is that an increasing number of Bay Area baby boomers are migrating northward for a little more elbow room. Among the pilgrims are a number of noted chefs and innkeepers who have pulled up their big-city stakes and relocated in small towns such as Eureka and Arcata to open their own restaurants or inns. This, combined with the region's beautiful scenery and absence of crowds, has made the Redwood Coast one of the premier—and relatively unknown—tourist destinations in California. You can camp, hike, fish, cycle, kayak, beachcomb, whale watch, and bird-watch, or just enjoy having a magnificent forest practically to yourself.

For those who can't survive without good restaurants, interesting boutiques, and a few bookstores to browse, Eureka, the largest town in northwestern California (population 25,000), has all those hallmarks of civilization in and around its picturesque Old Town. Located on historic Humboldt Bay, it also has a number of bed-and-breakfast inns that are as fine as any in far more expensive locales. Just 16 miles away, the entire village of Ferndale has been designated both a National and State Historical Landmark for its well-preserved Victorian architecture. If your perfect bliss is the total absence of civilization, however, the romantically named Lost Coast is as remote and empty as the most confirmed misanthrope could desire. This 850-square-mile area south of Ferndale and north of Westport, with more than 75 miles of coastline, has few roads, and though several towns are shown on maps, it is almost uninhabited. Backpackers love the beaches with their pristine tide pools, abundant wildlife, remnants of legendary shipwrecks, and miles and miles of solitude.

REDWOOD EMPIRE THREE-DAY TOUR

DAY ONE: *Bagels to beaches.* Start things off with a bagel and coffee at **LOS BAGELS** in Arcata, followed by a stroll around **ARCATA PLAZA**. Then hop in your car and head 20 miles north of Eureka to Trinidad, a tiny fishing village of white clapboard houses overlooking Trinidad Bay. Admire the view then purchase a few pounds of smoked salmon at **KATY'S SMOKEHOUSE**. Continue north on Highway 101 along the coast through Orick, the burl capital of the world. Keep an eye peeled for burl artists deftly wielding small chain saws. About 5 miles farther, take the **NEWTON B. DRURY SCENIC PARKWAY**—a 10-mile trip through the unspoiled scenery of **PRAIRIE CREEK REDWOODS STATE PARK**, with herds of Roosevelt elk, giant trees, fern canyons, and beaches along the way. As beautiful as it is, you can't dawdle too long, because you have to go back the way you came, following the signs to **PATRICK'S POINT STATE PARK**, 5 miles north of Trinidad. Here you can look for whales, hunt for semiprecious stones on **AGATE BEACH**, and wander through **SUMEG**, a Yurok Indian village with redwood houses and a sweat lodge still used for traditional ceremonies. Another option—and hugely recommended in the fall—is a short hike into **TALL TREES GROVE** to see the tallest tree in the world, followed by a drive along Howland Hill Road through **JEDEDIAH SMITH REDWOODS STATE PARK**. Head back to Trinidad, check in to the **LOST WHALE BED AND BREAKFAST INN**, and enjoy a soak in the ocean-view hot tub at sunset before you finish the day with dinner at the nearby **LARRUPIN' CAFE**.

DAY TWO: *All about town.* After breakfast at the inn, head to Eureka, stroll the **OLD TOWN** with its restored Victorian shops, and take a few photos of the **CARSON HOUSE** mansion, possibly the finest Victorian anywhere (but you can't

ACCESS AND INFORMATION

US HIGHWAY 101 stretches north from Willits in northern Mendocino County to Humboldt County and Eureka on the coast, then farther north to Crescent City and into Oregon. The seldom-visited Lost Coast can be reached by the **MATTOLE ROAD**, which starts just north of Weott at the southern boundary of the Avenue of the Giants, runs north and west to the hamlets of Honeydew and Petrolia, and reaches the coast just south of Cape Mendocino. From there it continues north to Ferndale.

Three other roads for the adventuresome lead east over the mountains: **CALIFORNIA 36** runs from Fortuna along the Van Duzen River to Dinsmore and Mad River, ending at Interstate 5 in Red Bluff (past Mad River the going gets really rough, and the road is sometimes closed in winter); **CALIFORNIA 299** follows the Klamath and Trinity rivers to Weaverville and Lewiston, then continues on to Interstate 5 in Redding; and **CALIFORNIA 199** parallels the go in, as it's privately owned). After having a sandwich and truffle at **RAMONE'S BAKERY & CAFE**, hop aboard the **MADAKET**, the oldest passenger vessel on the Pacific Coast, for a tour of Humboldt Bay. For dinner you can choose between gobs of basic, rib-stickin' food at the historic **SAMOA COOKHOUSE** or an elegant dinner at **RESTAURANT 301**, the best restaurant on the North Coast. Then it's off to the Victorian village of Ferndale, just a hop away, for a performance at the **FERNDALE REPERTORY THEATRE**. Spend the night in the village's most elegant B and B, the fabled **GINGERBREAD MANSION**, where you can wind down with a soak in matching claw-foot tubs.

DAY THREE: *Lumbering among the giants*. After a lavish B and B breakfast, you're on the road to Scotia for a glimpse of a real company town, built entirely of redwood, and owned by the Pacific Lumber Company. It's so clean and tidy it's almost surreal. Take the self-guided tour through one of the last sawmills in the area (and the world's biggest sawmill). It will give you a perspective on your next destination, the **AVENUE OF THE GIANTS**. The Avenue was originally a stagecoach road, and it winds some 32 miles along the Eel River through stunning groves of coast redwoods. Be sure to take a walk through **FOUNDERS GROVE**. For lunch, grab a bite in the down-home **ETERNAL TREEHOUSE CAFE** in tiny Redcrest, complete with country or gospel music coming from the kitchen. Don't dally, though, because you're going to want to check in to the historic **BENBOW INN** as early as possible so you can catch a few rays on its private beach before dinner in the restaurant. Afterward, see what's happening across the road at Lake Benbow's outdoor stage—jazz, pop, reggae, or Shakespeare—under the stars and the redwoods, with the lake as a backdrop.

Smith River (nationally designated a wild and scenic river, and California's only undammed river system) north and east to Oregon and Interstate 5 at Grants Pass. Travel tip: A popular option among families and groups is to rent a small motor home for transportation and book a series of inns and motels for sleeping; look in the phone directory under "Motor Home—Renting and Leasing" for the nearest motor home rental outfit or contact **CRUISE AMERICA** (480/464-7300 or 800/671-8042; www.cruiseamerica.com), the largest RV rental company in the nation.

The **ARCATA/EUREKA AIRPORT** in McKinleyville (11 miles north of Eureka) is served by Alaska Airlines/Horizon Air (800/252-7522; horizonair.alaskaair.com) and United Express (800/241-6522; www.united.com). Rental cars are available there. **GREYHOUND BUS** (800/231-2222; www.greyhound.com) offers service along Highway 101; there are two buses each way daily for travelers from San Francisco and Oregon.

Tourism is the area's number-two revenue generator, gaining fast on timber, and information about tourist destinations is plentiful. Contact the **HUMBOLDT COUNTY CONVENTION AND VISITORS BUREAU** (1034 2nd St, Eureka; 800/346-3482; www.redwoodvisitor.org) or the **CRESCENT CITY–DEL NORTE COUNTY CHAMBER OF COMMERCE** (1001 Front St, Crescent City; 707/464-3174 or 800/343-8300; www.northerncalifornia.net) for information.

The Lost Coast and Shelter Cove

The Lost Coast is proof that if you don't build it, they won't come. What wasn't built between Ferndale and Rockport was a coastal road: the geography of the 90-mile stretch—steep mountain ranges abutting rocky shore—wouldn't allow it. The result is the last untamed and undeveloped region of the California coast, a place where two cars following each other are considered a convoy and where more cows than people lie on the beach (seriously). Popular with campers, backpackers, and fishers, the Lost Coast is beginning to see a hint of gentrification at its only seaside town, Shelter Cove. Otherwise, the land is inhabited mainly by ranchers, retirees, and alternative lifestylers (a.k.a. hippies), the latter of which have made the Lost Coast one of the most productive pot-growing regions in the world.

The Lost Coast also makes for a fantastic day trip by car. Of the three entrance points into the region—Garberville, Humboldt Redwoods State Park, and Ferndale—the most scenic route is through the state park. From Highway 101 take the State Park turnoff and follow the Mattole Road all the way to Ferndale and back onto Highway 101. The three- to four-hour, 75-mile drive transports you through lush redwood forests, across golden meadows, and along miles of deserted beaches (well, if you don't count the cows). Be sure to fill up your gas tank, and bring a jacket if you plan to venture anywhere on foot.

RESTAURANTS

Cove Restaurant / ★

10 SEAL CT, SHELTER COVE; 707/986-1197

At the north end of a small runway for private planes, this rather remote restaurant is situated in an A-frame beach house with two-story-high picture windows, an outdoor dining area, and a spectacular view of the untamed Lost Coast. The menu's offerings are wide ranging and well prepared: charbroiled steak cut to order, Cajun-style fish (we're talking right out of the water), grilled chicken, juicy hamburgers, and piles of fresh shellfish. All meals are served with a choice of a creamy clam chowder, shrimp salad or green salad, and house-made bread. Desserts range from fresh fruit pies (snatch a slice of the wonderfully tart wild blackberry if it's available) to chocolate mousse and cheesecake.

$$; MC, V; checks OK; lunch Sun, dinner Thurs–Sun; full bar; reservations recommended; www.sheltercoverestaurant.com; off Lower Pacific Dr.

LODGINGS

Shelter Cove Oceanfront Inn / ★★

26 SEAL CT, SHELTER COVE; 707/986-7002

Snoozing seals, grazing deer, and migrating whales are just some of the sights you'll see in Shelter Cove, the Lost Coast's only oceanside community. Once you leave Highway 101 in Garberville, prepare to navigate along 24 miles of steep, twisting tarmac that passes through rocky grasslands and patches of forest before reaching the cove (good brakes are a must). At the end of the journey you'll reach the Shelter Cove Oceanfront Inn, a handsome beachhouse-style building built smack-dab on the shoreline. All rooms have an oceanview balcony, wireless Internet, satellite TV with HBO, a fridge, and a microwave. The next step up is booking one of the two Jacuzzi rooms, which are larger and outfitted with a telescope, leather chairs, king-sized bed, and in-room Jacuzzi tub. It's definitely worth upgrading to a suite, which not only has a sprawling private deck overlooking the Pacific—complete with your own gas barbecue—but a fully equipped kitchen, living room, and king-size bedroom, as well. Serious R & R is the theme here: soak up sun on the deck, play a round of golf across the street, or walk to the nearby black sand beach via a direct-access staircase from the inn, 'cause there ain't nothin' to do around here except relax. *$$; AE, MC, V; checks OK; www.sheltercoveoceanfrontinn.com; off of Surf Point.*

Garberville

RESTAURANTS

Woodrose Cafe / ★

911 REDWOOD DR, GARBERVILLE; 707/923-3191

This homey small-town coffee shop is the social center of Garberville and a good place to break your fast with their renowned green chile omelet before heading deep into the Lost Coast. Black-and-white prints by local artists hang on the textured peach walls, and in back there's a small outdoor patio perfect for basking in the sun and wolfing down healthy fare such as tofu scramble, granola, vegetarian garden burgers, organic-fruit shakes, and chunky vegetable-based soups served with sourdough garlic bread. Organic produce is used whenever possible. Everything is skillfully and tastefully prepared, and you'll certainly leave feeling well nourished. *$; no credit cards; checks OK; breakfast, lunch every day (open Sat–Sun until 1pm); beer and wine; no reservations; www.woodrosecafe.com; from Hwy 101, take the Garberville exit.*

LODGINGS

Benbow Inn / ★★

445 LAKE BENBOW DR, GARBERVILLE; 707/923-2124 OR 800/355-3301

From its sophisticated afternoon tea to its beautifully cultivated gardens of primroses, narcissus, tulips, and roses, this elegant Tudor-style inn built in 1926 is a little slice of England nestled in the redwoods. A National Historic Landmark, the inn (named after the family who built it) has hosted such luminaries as Herbert Hoover, Eleanor Roosevelt, and Charles Laughton. The 55 guest rooms vary in size and amenities; the priciest accommodations, such as the Honeymoon Cottage, include private patios overlooking the river, Jacuzzis, and fireplaces readied with kindling. All rooms have complimentary wireless Internet, telephones, decanters of sherry, coffee, robes, hairdryers, and irons. The aristocratic (and expensive) dining room is lined with carved-wood and marble sideboards, and the large-paned windows provide a great view of the river and gardens. The menu changes frequently but always features seafood, beef, pasta, and poultry dishes. Of course, as British etiquette dictates, complimentary afternoon tea and scones are served in the lobby at 3pm, hors d'oeuvres in the lounge at 5pm, and port wine in the lounge at 9pm. Beautiful Benbow Lake State Park is right out the front door, and a golf course is across the highway. Tennis courts are nearby. *$$–$$$$; AE, DIS, MC, V; checks OK; www.benbowinn.com; from Hwy 101, take the Benbow Dr exit.*

Redway

RESTAURANTS

The Mateel Cafe / ★★

3344 REDWOOD DR, REDWAY; 707/923-2030

With its fresh, healthful food and lively atmosphere, the Mateel has become a social and cultural magnet for the southern Humboldt region (SoHum to the natives). Lunch and dinner are served in three areas: the main dining room, which has high-backed wooden booths and a modest collection of watercolors by local artists; the African-style Jazzbo Room, decked out in giraffe decor; and the covered patio, the preferred spot on warm days and nights. A worldly selection of food is served here, ranging from roast rack of lamb to seafood linguine, Louisiana tiger prawns, Thai tofu, and fresh seafood specials of the day. All entrées are served with appetizers, soup or salad, and house-made pita bread. If you're not up for one of the full meals, try a stone-baked pizza (there are more than 20 toppings to choose from) or an organic salad such as the napa cabbage, spinach, and chicken salad topped with tomatoes and almonds and a curry dressing. *$$–$$$; MC, V; checks OK; lunch, dinner Mon–Fri; beer and wine; no reservations; www.mateelcafe.com; from Hwy 101, take the Redway exit to downtown.* ♿

Myers Flat

LODGINGS

Myers Country Inn / ★

12913 OLD REDWOOD HWY/AVE OF THE GIANTS, MYERS FLAT; 707/943-3259 OR 800/500-6464

The two-story, wood-framed Myers Inn, constructed in 1860 and restored in 1906, sits just outside Humboldt Redwoods State Park in Myers Flat, a hamlet reminiscent of a cardboard-cutout saloon town. Ten comfortable, sparkling clean guest rooms—all individually decorated and with private baths—have been renovated with an eye toward upscale country charm. Verandas encircle the building on both floors, providing every room with a balcony that has a view of the town, mountains, and forest. A large wood-burning fireplace in the common room keeps guests warm at night. Although the inn is close to the highway—it was once a stage stop—the nearby Eel River and redwoods seem to absorb most of the noise. The forest also provides plenty of superb hiking and biking trails. *$$; AE, MC, V; no checks; www.myersinn.com; in the center of town.*

Redcrest

RESTAURANTS

Eternal Treehouse Cafe / ★

26510 AVE OF THE GIANTS, REDCREST; 707/722-4247 OR 707/722-4262

Located on the scenic Avenue of the Giants, the Eternal Treehouse is an all-American cafe right down to the house-made pies and country-and-western music flowing out of the kitchen. This family-run café serves the best biscuits and gravy in the county, as well as wholesome daily specials such as corned beef and cabbage served with potatoes, carrots, and a choice of soup or salad—all for less than the price of a movie. *$; MC, V; checks OK; breakfast, lunch, dinner every day; no alcohol; no reservations; from Hwy 101, take the Redcrest exit.*

Scotia

LODGINGS

Scotia Inn / ★★☆

100 MAIN ST, SCOTIA; 707/764-5338

This grand three-story hotel, constructed entirely of redwood, is the pride of Scotia, one of the last company-owned towns in America. In fact, the whole town is built of redwood—no surprise once you discover the town's owner is the Pacific Lumber Company. Built in 1923, the Scotia Inn has 2 guest rooms downstairs and 20 spacious rooms on the second floor, each gussied up with Arts and Crafts furnishings, period antiques, and an abundance of flowery patterns. The inn's private bathrooms are equipped with showers and clawfoot tubs. The elaborate Redwood Room restaurant, handsomely decorated in rust, green, and burgundy and lit by gas transition chandeliers, serves American fare such as steak, prime rib, elk, and seafood featuring locally grown vegetables and berries. The wine list is excellent and the service always friendly. For classic, hearty steak-house grub in a less formal setting, you can also dine nightly at the inn's Steak and Potato Pub. *$$–$$$; AE, DIS, MC, V; checks OK; www.townofscotia.com/scotia-inn.html; at Mill St, directly across from the mill; from Hwy 101, take the Scotia exit.*

Mad River

LODGINGS

Journey's End Resort / ★

200 MAD RIVER RD, MAD RIVER; 707/574-6441

This remote resort is settled on the edge of little-known Ruth Lake, a well-hidden man-made lake that's a 1½-hour winding drive from the coast. Created in 1962, the lake is frequented by serious anglers in search of its sizable trout and black bass, which explains why a good number of guests at Journey's End are fisher folk (and the rest are typically water-skiers and jet-skiers). The motel's no-frills guest rooms are clean and warm, equipped with two firm double beds and a bathroom with a shower. A cabin on the premises sleeps up to five people and is supplied with a dishwasher, stove, microwave, refrigerator, and a barbecue on the porch—all you need to bring is food. Evening entertainment is left to the imagination rather than the networks, and if that doesn't suffice, there's a game-filled saloon with a satellite TV. The resort also has a grocery store, a laundry, basic fishing and boating supplies, and a small restaurant that specializes in made-from-scratch pizzas and range-fed, hand-cut rib eyes and New York steaks served with house-made fries, sautéed mushrooms, and grilled onions. *$$; AE, DIS, MC, V; no checks; www.thejourneysend.com; at the northeast end of Ruth Lake, 9 miles south of Hwy 36.*

Ferndale

Even if Ferndale isn't on your itinerary, it's worth taking a detour off Highway 101 to stroll for an hour or two down the colorful **MAIN STREET**, browsing through the art galleries, gift shops, and cafés strangely reminiscent of Disneyland's "old town." Ferndale, however, is for real and hasn't changed much since it was the agricultural center of Northern California in the late 1800s. In fact, the entire town is a National Historic Landmark because of its abundance of well-preserved Victorian storefronts, farmhouses, and homes. What really distinguishes Ferndale from the likes of Eureka and Crescent

City, however, is the fact that Highway 101 doesn't pass through it—which means no cheesy motels, liquor stores, or fast-food chains.

For a trip back in time, view the village's interesting memorabilia—working crank phones, logging equipment, and a blacksmith shop—at the **FERNDALE MUSEUM** (515 Shaw St at 3rd St; 707/786-4466; www.ferndale-museum.org). Not officially a museum, but close enough, is the **GOLDEN GATE MERCANTILE** (421 Main St.; 707-786-4891). Part of this general store hasn't been remodeled (or restocked) in more than 50 years, giving you the feeling that you're walking through some sort of time capsule or movie set. Far less historic but equally engrossing are the pedal-powered, amphibious entries in the wacky three-day World Championship Great Arcata to Ferndale Cross-Country Kinetic Sculpture Race on display at the **KINETIC SCULPTURE MUSEUM** (580 Main St at Shaw St; no phone). The dusty, funky museum is unlike anything you've ever seen, but it seems a fitting tribute to a race that gives eccentricity new meaning.

Another worthy Ferndale attraction is the leisurely drive along scenic **CENTERVILLE ROAD**. The 5-mile excursion starts at the west end of Main Street downtown and passes by several ranches and dairy farms on the way to the **CENTERVILLE BEACH COUNTY PARK**. If you continue beyond the park and past the retired naval facility, you'll be rewarded with an incredible view of the Lost Coast to the south. On the way back, just outside of town on the north side of the road, keep an eye out for **FERN COTTAGE**, a restored 1865 Victorian farmhouse built by the late state senator Joseph Russ, one of the first Ferndale settlers. Tours of the farmhouse are by appointment only; call 707/786-4835 to make a reservation.

In keeping with its National Historic Landmark status, Ferndale has no movie theaters. It has something better: the **FERNDALE REPERTORY THEATRE** (447 Main St; 707/786-5484; www.ferndale-rep.org). Converted in 1972 from a movie theater, the 267-seat house hosts live performances by actors from all over Humboldt County. The revolving performances run pretty much year-round and range from musicals to comedies, dramas, and mysteries. Tickets are reasonably priced and, due to the popularity of the shows, reservations are advised. For more information on Ferndale's upcoming events and activities, visit the town's Web site (www.victorianferndale.org/chamber).

RESTAURANTS

Curley's Grill / ★★½

400 OCEAN AVE (A VICTORIAN INN), FERNDALE; 707/786-9696

Longtime restaurateur and Ferndale resident Curley Tait decided it was finally time to open his own business. In 1995 he opened Curley's Grill in a little hole-in-the-wall on Main Street, and it was a big hit—so much so that Curley eventually relocated to fancy, spacious digs in the Victorian Inn several blocks down the street. The reason Curley's place is considered the best in town? He doesn't fool around: the prices are fair, the servings are generous, the food is good, and the atmosphere is bright and cheerful. Recommended starters are the grilled polenta with Italian sausage, fresh mushrooms, and sage-laden tomato sauce, and the moist tortilla-and-onion cake served with a tangy onion salsa. For the main course the meat loaf with garlic mashed potatoes or the fall-off-the-bone barbecued baby back ribs will leave you happily stuffed. Indulge in the house-made breads and desserts, and take a look at Curley's collection of Marilyn Monroe memorabilia, including Marilyn Merlot wine and martinis. On sunny afternoons, request a seat on the shaded back patio. *$$; DIS, MC, V; checks OK; breakfast Sat–Sun, lunch, dinner every day; beer and wine; reservations recommended; www.victorianvillageinn.com/curleys.htm; corner of Ocean Ave and Main St.*

LODGINGS

The Gingerbread Mansion / ★★★

400 BERDING ST, FERNDALE; 707/786-4000 OR 800/952-4136

The awe-inspiring grande dame of Ferndale, this peach-and-yellow Queen Anne inn is a lavish blowout for Victoriana buffs. Gables, turrets, English gardens, and architectural gingerbread galore have made it one of the most-photographed buildings in Northern California. The mansion has been through several reincarnations since 1899, including stints as a private residence, a hospital, a rest home, an apartment building, and even an American Legion hall before it was converted into a B and B in 1983. All 11 guest rooms have queen- or king-size beds and private baths. For the ultimate in luxury, though, reserve the Empire Suite, an orgy of marble and columns with twin fireplaces and a lavish bathing area. In the morning all guests awaken to a sumptuous breakfast in the formal dining room that overlooks the garden. An extravagant afternoon tea is served in one of five parlors, each handsomely furnished with Queen Anne, Eastlake, and Renaissance Revival antiques. Even if you're not staying in Ferndale, it's worth stopping by for a tour, scheduled from noon to 4pm daily. *$$$–$$$$; AE, MC, V; checks OK; www.gingerbread-mansion.com; at Brown St, 1 block south of Main St.*

Shaw House Inn Bed and Breakfast / ★★★

703 MAIN ST, FERNDALE; 707/786-9958 OR 800/557-SHAW

This Carpenter Gothic beauty, the oldest structure in Ferndale and the oldest B and B in California, is modeled after the titular manse of Nathaniel Hawthorne's *House of the Seven Gables*, complete with numerous balconies, bay windows, and jutting gables. It was built in 1854 by Ferndale founder Seth Louis Shaw and is listed on the National Register of Historic Places. A gazebo and fish pond highlight the inn's well-tended 1-acre yard, verdantly graced with 25 varieties of mature trees. The B and B has been meticulously restored and filled with books, photographs, and all manner of memorabilia. Each of the eight individually decorated guest rooms—replete with antiques, luxurious fabrics, and period fixtures—has a private bath, and four have private entrances. Three rooms have balconies overlooking the tranquil cottage garden, and the Fountain Suite has its own fireplace (a romantic must on those chilly nights). Pets are welcome for a fee of $30 a night. Each morning guests feast on homemade breakfast fare such as mushroom-leek frittatas, quiches, crepes, and house-baked breads. *$$$; DIS, MC, V; checks OK; www.shawhouse.com; on Main St, just east of downtown Ferndale.*

A Victorian Inn / ★★☆

400 OCEAN AVE, FERNDALE; 707/786-4949 OR 888/589-1808

If you can get your honey past the jewelry store on the first floor, you'll love the romantic rooms at this conveniently located bed-and-breakfast and country inn in the heart of Ferndale. Built in 1890 entirely of North Coast redwood, the inn is one of the most photographed buildings in the region. This ornately constructed and spacious inn has 12 guest rooms, all with private baths and some with fireplaces and sitting areas. The high-ceilinged rooms are individually decorated with charming wallpaper, antiques, formal draperies, and period fixtures, as well as TVs, CD players, telephones, and wireless Internet access. If you're traveling with the family, request a room with an additional trundle bed. Included in the room rate is a full breakfast served at Curley's Grill (see review), located in the inn. *$$–$$$; AE, DIS, MC, V; checks OK; www.victorianvillageinn.com; corner of Ocean Ave and Main St.*

Eureka

Named after the popular gold-mining expression "Eureka!" (Greek for "I have found it"), the heart of Eureka is **OLD TOWN**, a 13-block stretch of shops, restaurants, and hotels, most of them housed in painstakingly preserved Victorian structures. It's bordered by First and Third streets, between C and M streets. One of the finest Victorian architectural masterpieces is the multigabled-and-turreted **CARSON MANSION** (on the corner of 2nd and M sts), built of redwood in 1886 for lumber baron William Carson, who initiated the construction to keep mill workers occupied during a lull in the lumber business. Although the three-story, money-green mansion is closed to the public (it's now a snooty men's club), you can stand on the sidewalk and click your Kodak at one of the state's most-photographed houses. For more Old Town history, stroll through the **CLARKE MEMORIAL MUSEUM** (240 E St at 3rd St; 707/443-1947), which has one of the top Native American art displays in the state, showcasing more than 1,200 examples of Hupa, Yurok, and Karok basketry, dance regalia, and stonework. A block away, there's more Native American artwork, including quality silver jewelry, at the **INDIAN ART & GIFT SHOP** (241 F St at 3rd St; 707/445-8451 or 800/566-2381), which sells many of its treasures at reasonable prices.

If you need a good book at a great price, stop by the **BOOKLEGGER** (402 2nd St at E St; 707/445-1344), a marvelous bookstore in Old Town with thousands of used paperbacks (especially mysteries, Westerns, and science fiction) as well as children's books and cookbooks. If purple potatoes, cylindra beets, and other fancy foods are on your shopping list, you're in luck, because you'll find them at the **FARMERS MARKETS** held weekly in Eureka and Arcata. Most of the produce is grown along the local Eel and Trinity rivers and is sold at bargain prices. For more information call the North Coast Growers Association (707/441-9999).

Before you leave Eureka, be sure to take a bay cruise on skipper Leroy Zerlang's **MADAKET**, the oldest passenger vessel on the Pacific Coast. The 75-minute narrated tour—a surprisingly interesting and amusing perspective on the history of Humboldt Bay—departs daily from the foot of C Street in Eureka and gets progressively better after your second or third cocktail. For more information, call **HUMBOLDT BAY HARBOR CRUISE** (707/445-1910). Afterward, stroll over to the **LOST COAST BREWERY** (617 4th St, between G and H sts; 707/445-4480; www.lostcoast.com) for a fresh pint of Alleycat Amber Ale and an order of buffalo wings.

RESTAURANTS

Los Bagels / ★

403 2ND ST, EUREKA; 707/442-8525

Simply put, this is Eureka's best bagel shop. For a full review of the original Los Bagels, see the Restaurants section of Arcata. *$; no credit cards; local checks only; breakfast, lunch Wed–Mon; no alcohol; no reservations; www.losbagels.com; at E St in Old Town.* ♿

Ramone's Bakery & Cafe / ★

209 E ST, EUREKA; 707/445-2923

Before you start exploring Old Town, start your day with an espresso and a cinnamon roll at Ramone's, Eureka's best bakery since 1986. Everything on the menu—pastries, breads, chocolate truffles, soups, salads, sandwiches—is made from scratch every morning without preservatives or dough conditioners. Along with huge sandwiches made with freshly baked breads, the café offers daily lunch specials such as lasagne and quiche. You can either order your goods to go—there's plenty of bench seating in Old Town—or dine in the café's small self-service dining room. At any time of the day it's a great place to stop in for a light, inexpensive meal. *$; no credit cards; local checks only; breakfast, lunch every day; no alcohol; no reservations; www.ramonesbakery.com; in Old Town.*

Restaurant 301 / ★★★

301 L ST (HOTEL CARTER), EUREKA; 707/444-8062 OR 800/404-1390

Seafood direct from local fisheries, one of the finest wine lists in the nation, and herbs, vegetables, and edible flowers from the hotel's extensive gardens are just a few of the highlights at Restaurant 301, Eureka's finest restaurant. Diners, seated at window-side tables overlooking the waterfront, may either order à la carte or splurge on the Discovery Menu, a prix-fixe five-course affair that pairs each course with suggested wines by the glass. A typical dinner may begin with an artichoke, green lentil, and fennel salad, followed

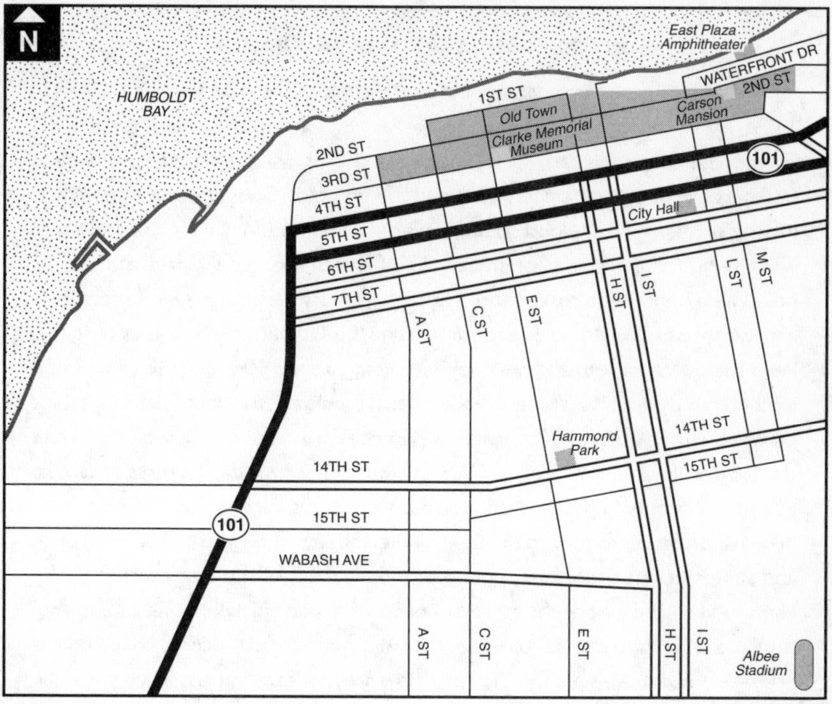

Eureka

by a warm chèvre cake appetizer or a savory saté of grilled marinated quail, then on to main entrées such as a grilled duck breast served with a seasonal fruit and zinfandel sauce, or tender grilled medallions of filet mignon served with smoked oyster dressing and a green peppercorn glaze. For dessert, the fresh rhubarb tart drizzled with lemon-curd sauce is superb. Restaurant 301's astounding wine list—courtesy of the 301 Wine Shop and Wine Bar within the hotel—is a recipient of the Grand Award from *Wine Spectator* magazine. *$$–$$$; AE, DC, DIS, MC, V; checks OK; breakfast, dinner every day; full bar; reservations recommended; www.carterhouse.com; at 3rd St in Old Town.* ♿

LODGINGS

Abigail's Elegant Victorian Mansion Bed & Breakfast / ★★

1406 C ST, EUREKA; 707/444-3144

This inn is a jewel—a National Historic Landmark built in 1888 and lovingly maintained by owners Doug "Jeeves" Vieyra and Lily Vieyra. If you're a fan of Victoriana, be prepared for a mind-blowing experience. Each of the four guest rooms upstairs has furnishings reflecting a different period, place, or personage. The light-filled Lillie Langtry Room, named for the famed 19th-century chanteuse who once sang at the local Ingomar Theatre, has an

PLEASE, SIR, MAY I HAVE SAMOA?

Visiting the Eureka area without a stop at the **SAMOA COOKHOUSE** (707/442-1659; www.samoacookhouse.net) is like visiting Paris without seeing the Eiffel Tower. This enormous barnlike building is the last surviving cookhouse in the West (it's been in operation since 1893) and a Humboldt County institution. When logging was king in redwood country, every mill operation had a cookhouse that was the hub of life in the community. Lumbermen worked six days a week, 12 hours a day, and were served three hot meals a day. Appetites were enormous, and waitresses rushed back and forth from the kitchen to the tables trying to keep the platters filled. Today's cookhouse patrons are served in the exact same lumber-camp style, where everyone is seated elbow to elbow at long tables covered with checkered oilcloths. Few decisions are required—just sit down and the food will come until you say "Uncle!" Breakfast typically features sausages, biscuits, scrambled eggs, and potatoes as well as a choice of French toast, hash browns, or pancakes (not to mention all the coffee and OJ you can drink). Lunch and dinner include soup, salad, potatoes, and the meat-of-the-day, which might be ham, fried chicken, pork chops, roast beef, barbecued chicken, or fish. Mind you, the food isn't haute cuisine (except for the delicious bread, which is baked on the premises), but there's plenty of it, and prices are modest. And just when you think you're about to burst, along comes the fresh-baked pie. After your meal, spend a few minutes waddling through the adjoining logging museum to see a wonderful collection of logging tools and photographs of early lumber and shipping activities in Eureka. The cookhouse name, by the way, comes from the old company town of Samoa, so-called because Humboldt Bay resembles the harbor at Pago Pago. From Eureka on Highway 101, take the Samoa Bridge to the end, turn left on Samoa Road, then left on Cookhouse Road.

impressive four-poster oak bed and a private bath down the hall. The French country–style Governor's Room sleeps up to three, has a private bath, and offers a distant view of the bay. The Vieyras have a great array of old (1905–40) movies and a collection of popular music from the same era, which guests often enjoy in the common room. Then there's Doug's obsession with antique autos—he's frequently seen motoring around (with guests on board) in his 1928 Model A Ford. The Vieyras are incredibly attentive hosts: they'll lend you bicycles, serve ice-cream sodas and lemonade while you play croquet on the manicured lawn, show you the way to their Finnish sauna and Victorian flower garden, pore over road maps with you, and make your dinner reservations. Lily, trained as a French chef (and Swedish masseuse), prepares a morning feast. *$$–$$$; MC, V; no checks; www.eureka-california.com; at 14th St.*

Carter House, Hotel Carter, Bell Cottage, Carter Cottage / ★★★★

301 L ST, EUREKA; 707/444-8062 OR 800/404-1390
What is now one of the finest accommodation-and-restaurant complexes on the upper North Coast started serendipitously in 1982, the year Eureka resident Mark Carter converted his newly built dream home—a four-story, five-bedroom Victorian reproduction—into an inn. In 1986, Mark, a former builder, added the 23-room Hotel Carter across the street, and four years later he refurbished the Bell Cottage, an adjacent three-bedroom Victorian home built in 1890. In 1991, next door to the other two, he added Carter Cottage, an entire house that's been lavishly furnished as a honeymoon getaway: a chef's kitchen, two fireplaces, a grand bathroom with a whirlpool tub for two, a private deck, and even a wine cellar. The foursome of inn, hotel, and two cottages offers a contrasting array of luxury accommodations, ranging from rooms with classic Victorian dark-wood antique furnishings in the house and cottages to a softer, brighter, more contemporary look in the hotel. Amenities include baskets filled with wine and specialty foods, concierge services, a videotape and CD library, tea-and-cookie bedtime service, and wine and hors d'oeuvres in the evening. Included in the room rate is a full breakfast featuring fresh-baked tarts, muffins, cinnamon buns, breads, fresh fruit, and an ever-changing array of entrées, juices, and strong coffee. The highly acclaimed Restaurant 301 (see review), is located on the first floor of Hotel Carter and is widely regarded as one of the North Coast's top spots for dining. *$$$–$$$$; AE, DC, DIS, MC, V; checks OK; www.carterhouse.com; at 3rd St in Old Town.* ♿

Arcata

Home to **CALIFORNIA STATE UNIVERSITY AT HUMBOLDT**, a liberal arts school, Arcata is like most college towns in that everyone tends to lean toward the left. Environmentalism, artistry, good breads, and good bagels are indispensable elements of the Arcatian philosophy, as is a cordial disposition toward tourists, making it one of the most interesting and visitor-friendly towns along the North Coast.

The heart of this seaside community is **ARCATA PLAZA**, where a statue of President McKinley stands guard over numerous shops and cafés housed in historic buildings. A walk around the plaza—with its perfectly manicured lawns, hot dog vendor, and well-dressed retirees sitting on spotless benches—is enough to restore anyone's faith in small-town America. At the plaza's southwest end is its flagship structure, **JACOBY'S STOREHOUSE** (791 8th St at H St; 707/822-4500; www.jacobystorehouse.com), a handsomely restored 1857 brick pack-train station that now holds shops, offices, and restaurants. If you need a new book, the **TIN CAN MAILMAN** (1000 H St at 10th St; 707/822-1307) is a terrific used-book store with 130,000 hard- and softcover titles, including a few collector's items.

You can see (and touch!) 3-billion-year-old fossils and view various California flora and fauna exhibits at Humboldt State University's **NATURAL HISTORY MUSEUM** (13th and G sts, downtown; 707/826-4479). Queue up at the **MINOR THEATRE** (1101 H St at 10th St; 707/822-3456), which offers a wide range of first-run and classic college films at starving-student prices (the daily matinees are particularly cheap). After the flick, savor a pitcher of Red Nectar Ale at the **HUMBOLDT BREWING COMPANY** (856 10th St at G St, next to the Minor Theatre; 707/826-2739); brewery tours are offered, too.

Once you've toured the downtown area, it's time to explore Arcata's numerous parks and preserves. A two-minute drive east of downtown on 11th Street will take you to Arcata's beloved **REDWOOD PARK**, a beautiful grassy expanse—ideal for a picnic—complemented by a fantastic playground that's guaranteed to entertain the tots. Surrounding the park is the **ARCATA COMMUNITY FOREST**, 600 acres of lush second-growth redwoods favored by hikers, mountain bikers, and equestrians; before you go, pick up a free guide to the forest's mountain-biking or hiking trails at the **ARCATA CHAMBER OF COMMERCE** (1635 Heindon Rd at Janes Rd; 707/822-3619; www.arcatachamber.com).

The best way to spend a summer Sunday afternoon in Arcata is at the **ARCATA BALLPARK** (707/822-3619), where only a few bucks buys you nine innings of America's favorite pastime hosted by the Humboldt Crabs semipro baseball team. With the brass band blasting and the devoted fans cheering, you'd swear you were back in high school. Most games are played Wednesday, Friday, and Saturday (doubleheader) evenings and Sunday afternoons in June and July. The ballpark is located at the corner of Ninth and F streets in downtown Arcata, but don't park your car anywhere near foul-ball territory.

RESTAURANTS

Abruzzi / ★★

780 8TH ST, ARCATA; 707/826-2345

Named after a region on the Italian Adriatic, Abruzzi is located on the bottom floor of the historic Jacoby's Storehouse, a mid-19th-century brick complex that's been converted into the Arcata Plaza shopping and dining complex. If you have trouble finding the place, just follow your nose: the smell of garlic and fresh bread will soon steer you to this popular restaurant, where you'll be served an ample amount of artfully arranged food in a romantic setting of dark wood and dim lighting. Meals begin with a basket of warm breads from a local bakery, followed by such highly recommended dishes as sea scallops with langoustines tossed with cheese tortellini, *linguine pescara* (prawns, calamari, and clams tossed in a light Sicilian tomato sauce), range-fed veal piccata, or any of the fresh seafood specials. The standout dessert is the Chocolate Paradiso—a dense chocolate cake set in a pool of champagne mousseline. The restaurant's owners also run the Plaza Grill on the third floor of the same building—a great place to sip a glass of wine in front of the

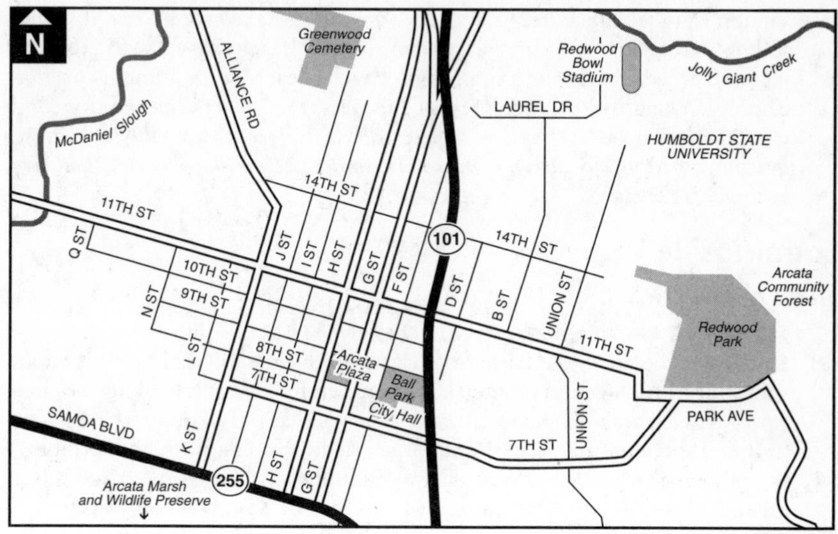

Arcata

fireplace at the end of the evening. *$$; AE, DIS, MC, V; checks OK; dinner every day; full bar; reservations recommended; www.abruzziarcata.com; at H St in the Arcata Plaza.* ♿

Folie Douce / ★★

1551 G ST, ARCATA; 707/822-1042

To say Folie Douce just serves pizza is like saying Tiffany just sells jewelry. "Designer pizza" is a more apt description: mole chicken with tomatoes, roasted peppers, jalapeño, and queso fresco; green coconut curried prawns with fresh mango, jalapeño, and cilantro; salami and Brie with mozzarella and apricot jam—all made with fresh ingredients from local farmers and baked to perfection in a wood-fired oven. If the unorthodox pizzas don't set your heart aflutter, the appetizers and entrées will. Start with the artichoke-heart cheesecake appetizer, perhaps followed by a brandy-flambéed filet mignon topped with Roquefort cheese and green peppercorns, or the rosemary and mustard grilled lamb chops topped with a roasted garlic and red wine demi-glace. You'll appreciate the award-winning yet reasonably priced wine list as well. Locals love this festive, brightly painted bistro, so reservations, even for early birds, are strongly recommended. *$$; DIS, MC, V; checks OK; dinner Tues–Sat; beer and wine; reservations recommended; www.holyfolie.com; between 15th and 16th sts.* ♿

Los Bagels / ★

1061 I ST, ARCATA; 707/822-3150

This emporium is a popular town hangout where you'll see lots of folks scanning the morning paper while munching on bagels layered with smoked salmon, smoked albacore, or lox. Try some fresh-baked challah or, if you're feeling particularly adventurous, a poppy seed bagel topped with jalapeño jam and cream cheese, or a multigrain bagel smeared with hummus or guacamole. Owing to Los Bagels' brisk business, the owners opened a second location in Eureka (see review). *$; no credit cards; local checks only; breakfast, lunch Wed–Mon; no alcohol; no reservations; www.losbagels.com; between 10th and 11th sts.* ♿

LODGINGS

Hotel Arcata / ★

708 9TH ST, ARCATA; 707/826-0217 OR 800/344-1221
Located at the northeast corner of Arcata's winsome town plaza, this handsome turn-of-the-century hotel has been carefully restored to its original state, evoking an ambience of Arcata's halcyon days. (It wouldn't take much to imagine Humphrey Bogart and Grace Kelly strolling through the lobby.) If you're not inclined to stay at the more sumptuous Lady Anne B and B (see review), this is definitely the next best choice. The 85 individually decorated rooms—many with claw-foot tubs—range from inexpensive small singles to quiet minisuites and a large Executive Suite that overlooks the plaza. A few modern amenities include cable TV, coffeemaker, data port, and shuttle service to the airport. Continental breakfast is complimentary, and on the premises—under different management—is a Japanese restaurant, Tomo. The hotel also offers guests free passes to the health club and indoor pool just a few blocks down the street. Pets are accepted with a per-day fee and a one-time deposit. *$$; AE, CB, DC, DIS, MC, V; no checks; www.hotelarcata.com; at the corner of 9th and G sts.*

The Lady Anne / ★★

902 14TH ST, ARCATA; 707/822-2797
Just a few blocks from Arcata Plaza in a quiet residential neighborhood, this exquisite example of Queen Anne architecture has been painstakingly restored. Five large and airy guest rooms are individually decorated with antiques, burnished woods, English stained glass, Oriental rugs, and lace curtains. The inn's two parlors are stocked with several games, as well as a grand piano and other musical instruments that you're welcome to play. Honeymooners should request the Lady Sarah Angela Room, with its cozy four-poster bed and pleasant bay view. When the weather is warm, relax on the Lady Anne's veranda or head out to the lawn for a game of croquet. Breakfast (beg for the Belgian waffles) is served in the grand dining room, which is warmed by a roaring fire in the winter. Several great restaurants are a short walk away at Arcata Plaza. *$$; MC, V; checks OK; www.arcataplaza.com/lodging; at I St.*

WASTE GOES IN, PRIDE COMES OUT

The small town of Arcata, just north of Eureka, has garnered international praise for turning an abandoned industrial and landfill site into the beautiful 154-acre **ARCATA MARSH AND WILDLIFE SANCTUARY**, with miles of trails, more than 100 varieties of plants, and more than 200 species of birds—including egrets, osprey, hummingbirds, and night herons. Not so unusual, you say? It wouldn't be, except that this natural splendor contains the 49 acres of oxidation ponds that treat Arcata's wastewater. Time, water, plants, bacteria, and fungi purify the wastewater that circulates through six marsh systems before it is finally released into Humboldt Bay. Natural processes in the marshes simultaneously purify the wastewater and feed marsh plants that attract birds, fish, and other wildlife. The community has received many awards and lots of press for the marsh, leading to its slogan, "Arcata residents flush with pride." Each Saturday at 8:30am and 2pm, local docents give free one-hour guided tours of the preserve—rain or shine—at the cul-de-sac at the foot of South I Street (reservations aren't required). Or just pick up a free self-guided walking-tour map of the preserve, available at the **ARCATA CHAMBER OF COMMERCE** (1062 G St at 11th St; 707/822-3619).

Trinidad

In the early 1850s Trinidad was a booming supply town with a population of 3,000; now it's one of the smallest incorporated cities in California, encompassing a little rocky bluff that a handful of anglers, artists, retirees, and shopkeepers call home. A sort of Mendocino-in-miniature, cute-as-a-button Trinidad is known mainly as a sportfishing town: trawlers and skiffs sit patiently in the bay, awaiting their owners or tourists eager to spend an afternoon salmon fishing. Scenery and silence, however, are the town's most desirable commodities; if all you're after is a little R & R on the coast, Trinidad is among the most peaceful and beautiful areas you'll find in California.

There's plenty to see and do in the Trinidad region. Five miles north of Trinidad, off Patrick's Point Drive, is **PATRICK'S POINT STATE PARK**, a 640-acre ocean-side peninsula with lush, fern-lined trails that wind through foggy forests of cedar, pine, and spruce. The park was once a seasonal fishing village of the Yurok Indians. Nowadays it's overrun with campers in the summer, but it's still worth a visit. Stroll down **AGATE BEACH** (keep an eye out for the semiprecious stones), climb the stone stairway up to the house-size **CEREMONIAL ROCK**, and admire the vistas from the **RIM TRAIL**, a 2-mile path along the cliffs where you can sometimes spot sea lions, harbor seals, and gray whales. In 1990 descendants of the original Native American settlers reconstructed **SUMEG**, an authentic Yurok village within the park, and visitors are welcome. A map and guide to all of the park's attractions are included in the vehicle day-use fee; call 707/677-3570 for more details.

The **HUMBOLDT STATE UNIVERSITY MARINE LABORATORY** (570 Ewing St at Edwards St; 707/826-3671; www.humboldt.edu/~marinelb) features various live marine life displays, including a touch tank and tide pools; it's open to the public from 9am to 4:30pm Monday through Friday and noon to 4pm Saturday and Sunday. Then again, why not catch your own sea critters? A day spent sportfishing off Trinidad's bounteous coast is more fun and much easier than you probably think. You simply drop your prerigged line into the water, reel it in when something's tugging on the other end, and throw your catch in the burlap sack at your feet. The crew does all the dirty work of cleaning and cutting your fish. Trinidad's two sportfishing charter boats—which operate seasonally—are the 36-foot **JUMPIN' JACK** (707/839-4743 or 800/839-4744 in CA; www.trinidadbaycharters.net) and the 45-foot **SHENANDOAH** (707/677-3625). Both charters offer morning and afternoon trips daily from **TRINIDAD PIER**, and walk-on customers are welcome. The five-hour salmon or rockfish hunt costs about $70 per person, which includes all fishing gear. One-day fishing licenses can be purchased on board the *Jumpin' Jack*. If you're lucky enough to reel in a lunker salmon, haul it to **KATY'S SMOKEHOUSE** (740 Edwards St; 707/677-0151; www.katyssmokehouse.com) just up the road from the pier; have them smoke it up and wrap it to go—or even send it via UPS to your home. Katy's salmon jerky isn't bad, either.

RESTAURANTS

Larrupin' Cafe / ★★★

1658 PATRICK'S PT DR, TRINIDAD; 707/677-0230

Situated on a quiet country road 2 miles north of Trinidad is the region's finest restaurant. You'll like this place from the moment you walk in the front door and admire the eclectic blend of Indonesian and African artifacts, colorful urns full of exotic flowers, and romantic candlelit tables. Dinner always starts with an appetizer board stocked with gravlax, pâté, dark pumpernickel, apple slices, and sauce, followed by a red- and green-leaf salad tossed with a Gorgonzola vinaigrette. The best menu items are the ones barbecued over mesquite fires, such as the pork ribs doused in a sweet-and-spicy barbecue sauce; the barbecued Cornish game hen served with an orange-and-brandy glaze; and a generous cut of fresh halibut, basted with lemon butter and served with mustard-flavored dill sauce. In winter the wood-burning fireplace gives off welcomed warmth; in warmer weather, request a table on the bamboo-fenced patio near the reflecting pool. Note: They don't take credit cards and the hours tend to vary seasonally, so be sure to call ahead and bring plenty of cash. *$$; no credit cards; checks OK; dinner Thurs–Sun; beer and wine; reservations recommended; www.larrupin.com; from Hwy 101, take the Trinidad exit and head north on Patrick's Pt Dr.* ♿

LODGINGS

The Lost Whale Bed and Breakfast Inn / ★★★

3452 PATRICK'S PT DR, TRINIDAD; 707/677-3425 OR 800/677-7859

The Lost Whale isn't just a place to stay overnight; it's a destination in itself—particularly for families with small children. The traditional Cape Cod–style building, constructed in 1989, stands alone on a 4-acre grassy cliff overlooking the sea, with a private stairway leading down to miles of deserted rocky beach. The innkeepers manage to give romancing couples lots of space and solitude, yet they also have created one of the most family-friendly inns on the California coast. Five of the inn's eight soundproof rooms have private balconies or sitting alcoves with views of the Pacific, two rooms have separate sleeping lofts, and all have private baths and queen-size beds. After a day on the inn's private beach or at neighboring Patrick's Point State Park, relax in the outdoor hot tub while listening to the distant bark of sea lions or looking out for whales. Kids can romp around on the playground, which has a small playhouse with its own loft. You'll also enjoy the huge breakfasts—casseroles, quiches, home-baked muffins, fresh fruit, locally smoked salmon—and the snacks provided throughout the day and evening. *$$–$$$; AE, DIS, MC, V; checks OK; www.lostwhaleinn.com; from Hwy 101, take the Seawood Dr exit and head north for 11 miles on Patrick's Pt Dr.*

Trinidad Bay Bed and Breakfast / ★★

560 EDWARDS ST, TRINIDAD; 707/677-0840

Perched 175 feet above the ocean on a bluff overlooking Trinidad's quaint fishing harbor and the rugged California coast, this postcard-perfect Cape Cod–style inn is the dream house of owner Mike Morgan, a San Francisco native who fell in love with the area while vacationing here. After buying the place in 2004, he redecorated and gave each room a theme: Tide Pool, Redwoods, Trinity Alps, and Crab Pot—all named for local attractions. The four guest rooms (two standard rooms and two suites) all come with private bathrooms. Both suites have private entrances, comfortable sitting rooms, spectacular views of Trinidad Bay, and breakfast-in-bed service. Despite the busy summer season and small size of the inn, Mike leaves one room unbooked so that fellow travelers have the opportunity to magically stumble upon the inn as he once did a few years back. Other amenities include complimentary wireless, late checkout, and free airport pickup. *$$$; MC, V; checks OK; www.trinidadbaybnb.com; from Hwy 101, take the Trinidad exit to Main St and turn left on Trinity St.*

Orick and Redwood National and State Parks

The burl art capital of the world, Orick looks more like a huge outdoor gift shop than a town. What's burl art, you ask? Well, take a sizable chunk of redwood, do a little carving here and there with a small chain saw, and when it resembles some sort of mammal or rodent, you have yourself a piece. There are thousands of burl pieces to choose from here, ranging from the Abominable Burlman to Sasquatch and the Seven Dwarfs. Several roadside stands have viewing booths where mesmerized tourists watch the redwood chips fly. Orick is also the southern entry to **REDWOOD NATIONAL AND STATE PARKS**; 1 mile south of town off Highway 101 is the **REDWOOD INFORMATION CENTER** (707/464-6101, ext. 5265; www.nps.gov/redw; open 9am–5pm every day), where visitors can pick up a free park map and browse through geologic, wildlife, and Native American exhibits.

Of course, the best way to experience the parks and their magnificent redwoods is on foot. The short **FERN CANYON TRAIL** leads through an incredibly lush fern grotto. The **LADY BIRD JOHNSON GROVE LOOP** is an easy one-hour self-guided tour that loops 1 mile around a gorgeous grove of redwoods. Closer to shore is the **YUROK LOOP NATURE TRAIL** at Lagoon Creek, located 6½ miles north of the Klamath River bridge on Highway 101; the 1-mile self-guided trail gradually climbs to the top of rugged sea bluffs—with wonderful panoramic views of the Pacific—and loops back to the parking lot. Perhaps the summa cum laude of trails is the **BOY SCOUT TREE TRAIL**, a 6-mile round-trip hike through a cool, damp forest brimming with giant ferns and majestic redwoods.

To see the world's tallest tree—we're talkin' 368 feet tall and 14 feet in diameter—you'll first have to go to the Redwood Information Center near Orick to obtain a free map and permit—only 50 issued per day—then drive to the trailhead of **TALL TREES GROVE**. You still have to walk a steep 1⅓ miles from the trailhead to the grove, but the reward is one of the most beautiful and awe-inspiring walks you'll ever take—particularly in the fall, when the brilliant yellow maple leaves blanket the ground.

RESTAURANTS

Rolf's Park Cafe / ★

123664 HWY 101, ORICK; 707/488-3841

After decades of working as a chef in Switzerland, Austria, San Francisco, and even aboard the presidential SS *Roosevelt*, the trilingual Rolf Rheinschmidt decided it was time to semi-retire. He wanted to move to a small town to cook, and towns don't get much smaller than Orick with a population around 500. So here, among the redwoods, Rheinschmidt serves up good bratwurst, wiener schnitzel, and crepes suzette. His specialty is marinated rack of spring lamb, and he has some unusual offerings such as wild boar, buffalo, and elk steak (the truly adventurous should get the combo platter featuring all three). Each dinner entrée includes lots of extras: hors d'oeuvres, salad, vegetables, farm-style potatoes, and bread. And ever since the debut of Rheinschmidt's German Farmer Omelet—an open-faced concoction of ham, bacon, sausage, mushrooms, cheese, potatoes, and pasta, topped with sour cream and salsa and garnished with a strawberry crepe—breakfast in Orick has never been the same. *$$; MC, V; local checks only; breakfast, lunch, dinner every day in summer (typically open Mar–Sept); beer and wine; no reservations; 2 miles north of Orick.* ♿

Klamath

From the looks of it, the town of Klamath hasn't recovered much since it was washed away in 1964, when 40 inches of rain fell within 24 hours. All that remains are a few cheap motels, trailer parks, tackle shops, and boat rental outlets, kept in business by the numerous anglers who line the mighty Klamath River, one of the finest salmon and steelhead streams in the world. The scenery around the river is extraordinary; Redwood National Park and Klamath National Forest have some incredible coastal drives and trails that even the timid and out-of-shape can handle with aplomb.

Stretch out your legs at the lofty **KLAMATH OVERLOOK**, which stands about 600 feet above an estuary at the mouth of the Klamath River. A short but steep trail leads down to a second overlook that's ideal for whale watching and taking photographs. To get there from Highway 101, take the Requa Road turnoff, north of the Klamath River bridge. For more hiking recommendations, read about Redwood National and State Parks in the Orick section.

One of the premier coastal drives on the Redwood Coast starts at the mouth of the Klamath River and runs 8 miles south toward **PRAIRIE CREEK REDWOODS STATE PARK**. If you're heading south on Highway 101, take the Alder Camp Road exit just south of the Klamath River bridge and follow the signs to the river mouth. Northbound travelers should take the Redwood National and State Parks Coastal Drive exit off the Newton B. Drury Scenic Parkway. Campers and cars with trailers are not advised. The narrow, partially paved road winds through stands of redwoods, with spectacular views of the sea and numerous turnouts for picture-taking (sea lions and pelicans abound) and short hikes. Keep an eye out for the World War II radar station disguised as a farmhouse and barn.

If you've never toured the mighty Klamath River aboard a giant jet boat, you're missing out on one heck of a thrill ride. These incredibly powerful and fast boats take visitors from the estuary upriver to view bear, deer, elk, osprey hawks, otters, and other wildlife along the riverbanks. They typically operate May through October. For more information and reservations, contact **KLAMATH RIVER JET BOAT TOURS** (707/482-5822 or 800/887-JETS; www.jetboattours.com).

LODGINGS

The Requa Inn / ★

451 REQUA RD, KLAMATH; 707/482-1425 OR 866/800-8777

The Requa Inn (pronounced RECK-wah) was established in 1885, and despite going through several owners, four name changes, one relocation, and a major fire that burned it to the ground in 1914 (it was rebuilt the same year), this venerable riverside inn is still going strong. The slow pace, beautiful surroundings, and rustic simplicity give this boxy ol' inn its charm, and the inexpensive rates only add to the appeal. The 10 spacious guest rooms are modestly decorated with antique furnishings and have private baths with showers or claw-foot tubs. Four rooms offer views of the lower Klamath River, and all are refreshingly TV- and phone-free. Most guests, however, spend their time in the spacious sitting room, reading or doing jigsaw puzzles beside the wood-burning fireplace, or just sipping wine while admiring the view from the large picture window. Both breakfast and dinner are served in the dining room, where guests feast on large portions of simple, straightforward dishes made with fresh ingredients. Excellent hiking trails through the Redwood National Park surround the lodge, and during salmon season you'll undoubtedly meet some ardent fishermen and dine on huge servings of the freshest possible salmon. *$–$$; DIS, MC, V; checks OK; www.requainn.com; from Hwy 101, take the Requa Rd exit and follow the signs.* ♿

Crescent City

Because it's the northern gateway to the popular **REDWOOD NATIONAL AND STATE PARKS** (for park highlights, see Orick section), one might assume Crescent City would be a major tourist mecca, rife with fine restaurants and hotels. Unfortunately, it's not. Cheap motels, fast-food chains, and mini-malls are the main attractions along this stretch of Highway 101, as if Crescent City exists only to serve travelers on their way someplace else. The city is trying, however, to enhance its image, and if you know where to go (which is anywhere off Highway 101), there are actually numerous sites worth visiting and several outdoor-recreation options that are refreshingly nontouristy. You won't want to make Crescent City your primary destination, mind you, but don't be reluctant to spend a day lolling around here, either; you'd be surprised what the town has to offer besides gas and groceries.

For starters, take a side trip to the **NORTH COAST MARINE MAMMAL CENTER** (424 Howe Dr in Beach Front Park, at the north end of Crescent City Harbor; 707/465-MAML; www.northcoastmmc.org). This nonprofit organization was established in 1989 to rescue and rehabilitate stranded or injured marine mammals. Staffed by volunteers and funded by donations, the center is the only facility of its kind between San Francisco and Seattle, providing emergency response during environmental disasters and assisting marine researchers by collecting data on marine mammals. The center is open to the public every

HEAVEN ON EARTH VIA THE HOWLAND HILL ROAD

For car-bound cruisers who want to take a journey through an unbelievably spectacular old-growth redwood forest, there's a hidden, well-maintained gravel road called **HOWLAND HILL ROAD** that winds for about 12 miles through the misty, silent groves of **JEDEDIAH SMITH REDWOODS STATE PARK**. Heading north on Highway 101, turn right on Elk Valley Road at the south end of Crescent City (at the 76 gas station) and follow it to Howland Hill Road, which will be on your right. After driving through the park, you'll end up near the town of Hiouchi, and from there it's a short jaunt northwest on Highway 199 to get back to Highway 101. Plan at least two to three hours for the 45-mile round-trip, or all day if you want to do some hiking among the world's tallest trees—in what many consider one of the most beautiful places in the world. Trailers and motor homes are not allowed.

day year-round, and visitors are welcome to watch the volunteers in action, make a donation, and buy a nature book or two at the gift shop.

Other interesting local sites include the operational **BATTERY POINT LIGHTHOUSE** (707/464-3089), built in 1856 on a small island off the foot of A Street. Guided tours of the lighthouse and the light keeper's living quarters are offered 10am to 4pm Wednesday through Sunday (April through September), tide permitting (you have to cross a tide pool to get there). Next, head to the **B STREET PIER** (at the south foot of B St) and do some fishing and crabbing off the city's 800-foot-long pier. Crabbing is simple: throw the prebaited net into the water (don't forget to tie the other end to the pier), wait about 10 minutes, then pull it up and see what's for supper. Because it's a public pier, you don't even need a fishing license.

If you're not one to get your hands dirty, take a shoreline tour along **PEBBLE BEACH DRIVE** from the west end of Sixth Street to Point St. George. You're bound to see a few seals and sea lions at the numerous pullouts. End the tour with a short walk though a sandy meadow to **POINT ST. GEORGE**, a relatively deserted bluff that's perfect for a picnic or beach stroll. On a clear day, look out on the ocean for the **ST. GEORGE REEF LIGHTHOUSE**, reportedly the tallest (146 feet above sea level), deadliest (several light keepers died in rough seas while trying to dock), and most expensive ($704,000) lighthouse ever built.

One of the prettiest picnic sites on the California coast is along **ENDERTS ROAD** at the south end of town. Drive 3 miles south on Highway 101 from downtown, turn right on Enderts Road (across from the Ocean Way Motel), and continue 2⅓ miles. Park at the **CRESCENT BEACH OVERLOOK**, lay your blanket on the grass, and admire the ocean view. Type A personalities can drive to the end of Enderts Road and take the 1.2-mile round-trip hiking trail to Enderts Beach. In the summer, free ranger-guided tide pool and seashore walks are offered when the tides are right, starting at the beach parking lot. For specific tour times, call 707/464-6101, ext. 5265.

Crescent City's best-kept secret, however, is the **LAKE EARL WILDLIFE AREA**, a gorgeous habitat replete with deer, rabbits, beavers, otters, red-tailed hawks, peregrine falcons, bald eagles, songbirds (some 80 species), shorebirds, and migratory waterfowl that share these 5,000 acres of pristine woodlands, grasslands, and ocean shore. Hiking and biking are permitted, but you'll want to make the trip on foot with binoculars in hand to get the full effect of this amazing patch of coastal land. To get there, take the Northcrest Drive exit off Highway 101 in downtown Crescent City and turn left on Old Mill Road. Proceed 1½ miles to the park headquarters at 2591 Old Mill Road (if it's open, ask for a map) and park in the gravel lot. Additional trails start at the end of Old Mill Road. For more information, call the **DEPARTMENT OF FISH AND GAME** (707/464-2523).

And if you're planning to explore the Redwood National and State Parks, be sure to pick up a free map and guide at the **REDWOOD NATIONAL PARK HEADQUARTERS AND INFORMATION CENTER** (1111 2nd St at K St; 707/464-6101, ext. 5064).

RESTAURANTS

Beachcomber Restaurant / ★

1400 HWY 101S, CRESCENT CITY; 707/464-2205

Although several trendy eateries have made a brave stand in Crescent City, they've all fallen by the wayside. Perched right on the beach a couple of miles south of Crescent City's center, the venerable Beachcomber Restaurant has been the locals' favorite for a reliably good meal since 1975. If you can live with the hokey nautical theme (scatterings of driftwood, fishnets, and buoys dangling above a dimly lit dining room), the restaurant does a commendable job of providing fresh seafood—halibut, red snapper, lingcod, shark, sturgeon, Pacific salmon—that is refreshingly free of heavy or complicated sauces. The Beachcomber also specializes in flame-broiled steaks, cooked to your specification on an open madrone-wood barbecue pit. Thick cuts of prime rib are the special every Saturday and Sunday. Ask for a booth by the window and start the evening with the steamer-clam appetizer: 1½ pounds of the North Coast's finest. *$$; MC, V; no checks; dinner every day (Thurs–Sat in winter); beer and wine; reservations recommended; 2 miles south of downtown.* ♿

LODGINGS

Crescent Beach Motel / ★

1455 HWY 101S, CRESCENT CITY; 707/464-5436

Crescent City has the dubious distinction of being the only city along the coast without a swanky hotel or B and B. There is, however, an armada of inexpensive accommodations, the best of which is the Crescent Beach Motel. A color scheme of brown, beige, and green complements the simply furnished interiors, and all but 4 of the 27 rooms are within steps of the beach. Most units have queen-size beds and color TVs. The small lawn area and large sundecks overlooking the ocean are great places to kick back and enjoy some true R & R. Another perk: You can get a pretty good seafood dinner right down the street at the Beachcomber Restaurant (see review). *$; AE, DIS, MC, V; no checks; www.crescentbeachmotel.com; 2 miles south of downtown.* ♿

Curly Redwood Lodge / ★

701 HWY 101S, CRESCENT CITY; 707/464-2137

Built in 1957 with lumber milled from a single ancient redwood, the Curly Redwood Lodge looks as if it's been preserved in a time capsule from the '60s, the kind of place where you might have stayed as a kid during one of those cross-country vacations in the family station wagon (with wood paneling, of course). Granted, it's not as fancy as the newer chain motels down the highway, but it's loaded with old-school charm (as well as the requisite TVs and telephones), lean on price, and generously spacious—particularly the two-room suites, which are perfect for families. As an added bonus, both the beach and the Beachcomber Restaurant (see review) are right across the highway. *$; AE, DC, MC, V; no checks; www.curlyredwoodlodge.com; 2 miles south of downtown on Hwy 101.*

NORTH MOUNTAINS

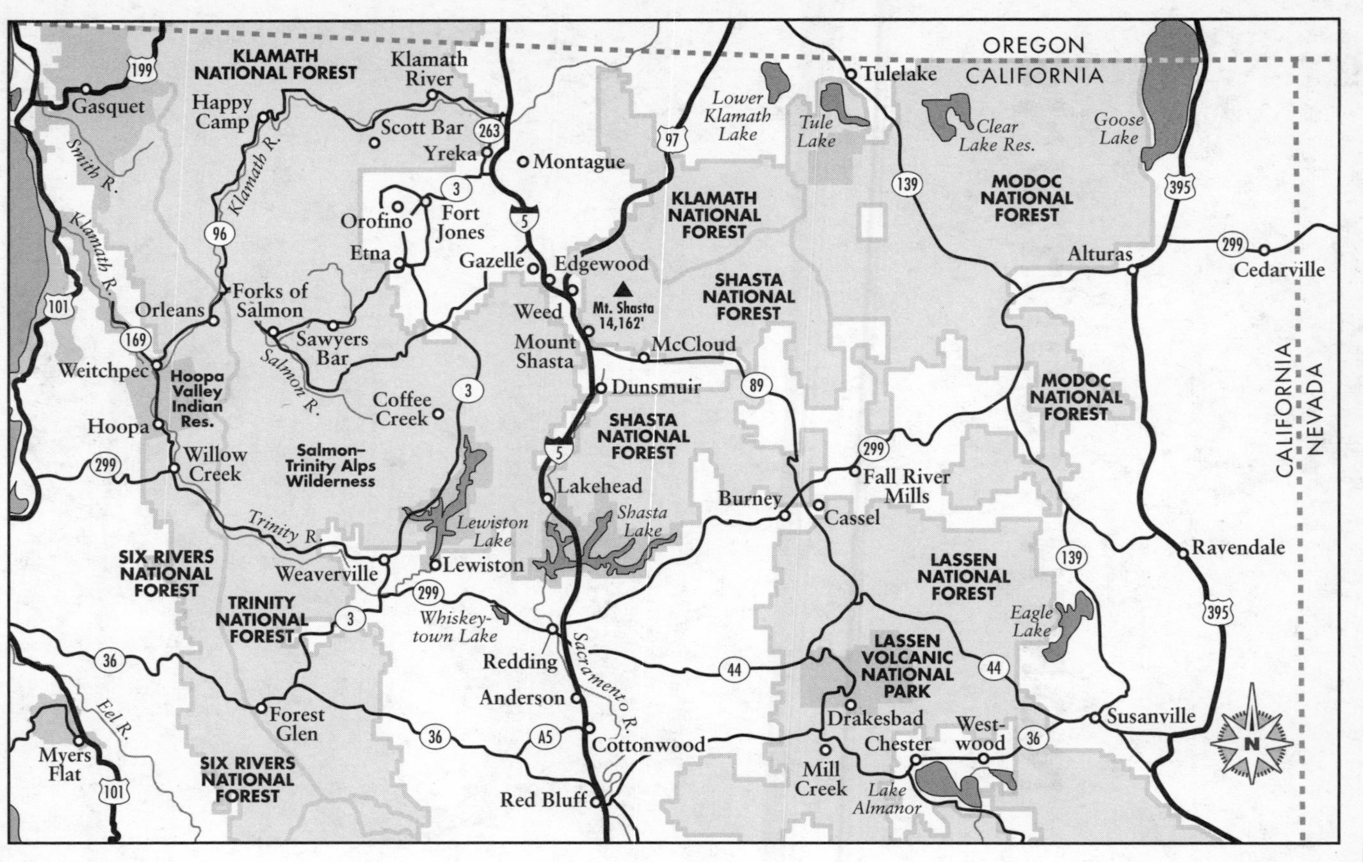
OREGON
CALIFORNIA
CALIFORNIA
NEVADA
KLAMATH NATIONAL FOREST
Klamath River
Gasquet
Happy Camp
Scott Bar
Yreka
Montague
Lower Klamath Lake
Tule Lake
Tulelake
Clear Lake Res.
Goose Lake
MODOC NATIONAL FOREST
Smith R.
Klamath R.
Klamath R.
Orofino
Fort Jones
KLAMATH NATIONAL FOREST
Etna
Gazelle
Edgewood
Mt. Shasta 14,162'
SHASTA NATIONAL FOREST
Alturas
Cedarville
Forks of Salmon
Orleans
Weed
Mount Shasta
McCloud
Sawyers Bar
Weitchpec
Hoopa Valley Indian Res.
Salmon R.
Coffee Creek
Dunsmuir
MODOC NATIONAL FOREST
Hoopa
SHASTA NATIONAL FOREST
Willow Creek
Salmon–Trinity Alps Wilderness
Lakehead
Fall River Mills
Burney
Cassel
Shasta Lake
Trinity R.
Lewiston Lake
Lewiston
SIX RIVERS NATIONAL FOREST
Weaverville
Ravendale
LASSEN NATIONAL FOREST
TRINITY NATIONAL FOREST
Whiskeytown Lake
Eagle Lake
Redding
Sacramento R.
LASSEN VOLCANIC NATIONAL PARK
Eel R.
Anderson
Forest Glen
Drakesbad
Susanville
Westwood
Chester
Cottonwood
Myers Flat
Mill Creek
Lake Almanor
SIX RIVERS NATIONAL FOREST
Red Bluff
N
199
263
97
139
395
3
5
96
299
101
169
89
3
5
299
139
299
395
3
44
44
36
36
A5
36
101

NORTH MOUNTAINS

As you drive north toward Redding up the flat, uninspiring Interstate 5 corridor, snow-topped Mount Shasta appears as a white smudge at the end of the highway. Venture a little closer and the imposing volcano soon dominates the horizon. This unforgettable sight heralds your approach to California's northern mountains. Step out of your car and you'll feel as though you've stepped back in time to a simpler (and, frequently, less expensive) way of life. This area offers everything a pleasure-seeking visitor could hope for: prime fishing, bird-watching, boating, waterskiing, mountain biking, rock climbing, camping, hiking, river rafting, kayaking, golfing, and, in winter, every kind of snow sport.

This little piece of California is nature's unspoiled, uncrowded playground. You can detoxify in one of the many gorgeous mineral springs; hang out on a houseboat on Shasta Lake; explore the tortured lava caves and steaming thermal vents in Lassen Volcanic National Park; take a scenic ride on the dinner train departing from the adorable little town of McCloud; bike or cross-country ski the 10-mile paved path at Lake Almanor; or, if you're in really good shape, climb the magic mountain itself.

Accommodations in this part of the state range from wonderful wood cabins lit by kerosene lanterns to luxurious bed-and-breakfasts. Some very good restaurants are tucked away in places you've probably never heard of—Weaverville, Dunsmuir, and Chester—which makes touring California's northern mountain towns a constant culinary adventure.

ACCESS AND INFORMATION

The region is predominantly medium-high mountain ranges (the Cascades, the Salmon, and Siskiyou mountains), with high desert and rangeland to the east. The three major highways run north-south. **INTERSTATE 5** from Los Angeles and Sacramento leaves the Central Valley at Redding (the largest town in the northern mountains region) and continues to Dunsmuir, Mount Shasta City, Weed, and Yreka, then on to Oregon. **US 395** heads north from Reno, Nevada, through high desert and not much else until it gets to Alturas, then leaves California via its lonely northeastern corner. **HIGHWAY 89**, the curviest of the three north-south routes, starts from US 395 north of Reno and heads northwest to Lake Almanor and Chester. It winds its way through Lassen Volcanic National Park past Burney and McCloud, skirting the great mountain, then joins Interstate 5 just south of Mount Shasta City.

East-west roads through this country are mostly mountainous. **HIGHWAY 299** from Arcata to Redding via Weaverville is officially described as going "from the Redwood Coast to the Valley Oaks," neglecting any mention of the roller-coaster curves. From Redding it continues east to Alturas. **HIGHWAY 44** is the best route to Lassen Volcanic National Park from Redding.

The only airport in the region is the **REDDING MUNICIPAL AIRPORT (RDD)**, served by two airlines, Alaska Airlines/Horizon Air (800/252-7522; horizon air.alaskaair.com) and United Express (800/241-6522; www.united.com).

NORTH MOUNTAINS THREE-DAY TOUR

DAY ONE: *Trail and rail.* Spend the first night in Chester at the **BIDWELL HOUSE BED AND BREAKFAST INN**. In the morning, grab breakfast at the B and B and then stop at one of the grocery stores downtown and get picnic fixings before you head out to **LASSEN VOLCANIC NATIONAL PARK**, where you can stretch your legs by walking the **BUMPASS HELL TRAIL** past wildflowers, hissing fumaroles, steam vents, and assorted mud pots. Back in the car, continue north on Highway 89 around Mount Lassen, briefly stopping at 129-foot-high **MCARTHUR-BURNEY FALLS** to watch some of the 200 million gallons of water that fall there daily. A short trip through the pines will get you to McCloud to board the **SHASTA SUNSET DINNER TRAIN** for a fine dinner with Mount Shasta as a backdrop. Repair to the **MCCLOUD BED AND BREAKFAST HOTEL** for the night.

DAY TWO: *Up a mystic mountain.* Fuel up at the B and B, then move on to Mount Shasta, stopping at **MOUNT SHASTA BOARD & SKI PARK** to rent a mountain bike and gear. Take the ski lift to the top (elevation: 6,600 feet) and bike back down to the lodge. Repeat this as many times as your nerves and muscles will allow. Then make the short drive to Mount Shasta City, stopping

Car rentals are available there. The closest major airport is **SACRAMENTO INTERNATIONAL AIRPORT (SMF)** (916/929-5411; www.sacairports.org; 150 miles south of Redding).

GREYHOUND BUS (800/231-2222; www.greyhound.com) serves the towns along Interstate 5, and Amtrak's **COAST STARLIGHT TRAIN** (800/USA-RAIL; www.amtrak.com) from Seattle to Los Angeles makes two stops a day (one each way) at Dunsmuir and Redding.

For more information, contact the **REDDING CONVENTION AND VISITORS BUREAU** (777 Auditorium Dr, Redding; 800/874-7562; www.visitredding.org) or the **SHASTA CASCADE WONDERLAND ASSOCIATION** (800/326-6944; www.shastacascade.org), which offers information on Lassen, Modoc, Plumas, Siskiyou, Shasta, and Trinity counties.

Redding and the Shasta Lake Area

About 20 minutes north of Redding, Shasta Lake, the largest reservoir in California and "Houseboat Capital of the World," is a perfect introduction to the pleasures of the region and the ideal place for fishing, waterskiing, or just lounging with a good book in the sun on a houseboat. Be sure to stop in Redding for homey pleasures and a bit of local history.

at **LILY'S** for lunch on the deck before you check in at the **MOUNT SHASTA RANCH BED AND BREAKFAST**. Do some serious lounging on the front lawn for late-afternoon views of America's most photogenic mountain before you get back in the car for a short jaunt to Dunsmuir for dinner at **CAFE MADDALENA**. Afterward, take a walk in the town's restored historic railroad section along Sacramento Avenue.

DAY THREE: *Nature's temple*. After a scrumptious breakfast at the inn, head for the beautiful upper Sacramento River (it's more of a stream here) down to Shasta Lake, stopping first for a ferry ride across the lake to visit the **LAKE SHASTA CAVERNS**, which boast towering limestone columns, followed by a stop at **SHASTA DAM**. Take the tour of the dam, descending 600 feet into its bowels to view its dynamos and turbines. Then it's on to Redding, with a stop at **BUZ'S CRAB** for a quick Louie and a cold drink before heading west into the Trinity Alps to Weaverville. Walk around this 1850s gold-mining town that reeks of history and peek in at the old **CHINESE MINERS' TAOIST TEMPLE** on Main Street. End your tour with one of **LA GRANGE CAFE**'s great dinners, two short blocks from the temple, before heading to the **BRIDGEHOUSE BED AND BREAKFAST** to unwind.

Redding

What was once just a stopover en route to Mount Shasta is now a destination itself thanks to a lively waterfront area and an ongoing renovation along the downtown's main street. A popular attraction here is the $15 million, 34,000-square-foot **TURTLE BAY EXPLORATION PARK** (530/243-8850 or 800/TURTLEBAY; www.turtlebay.org), which provides a hands-on exploration of the natural world. On the banks of the Sacramento River, the park houses a museum, a river aquarium, the Butterfly House (May–Sept), live animals, a forest camp, several history and science exhibits, an art gallery, a café, and activities for all ages. Walk along an elevated boardwalk through a riparian forest and seasonal wetland or come face to face with white sturgeon, bull trout, and perch at the largest freshwater native fish aquarium in California. The art gallery displays a selection of original Ansel Adams photographs, and the Exploration Hall traces the historical path of the Wintu Indians. The museum is part of an $84 million complex, which will eventually include a pedestrian bridge over the Sacramento River linking the museum to the north bank.

The 10-mile long **SACRAMENTO RIVER TRAIL** meanders along the town's riverbanks and over a stress-ribbon concrete bridge—the only bridge of its kind in the country. A recent addition to the riverfront is the architecturally stunning **SUNDIAL BRIDGE**, built by Spanish artist Santiago Calatrava. The 710-foot-long, 21-story-tall pylon bridge with a translucent glass surface spans the river without footings in the water and is the largest sundial structure in the world. Free live music is performed by the bridge on Friday nights throughout the summer from 7 to 10pm.

For a guided tour of the river—and by an interesting means of transportation at that—call Bruce and Robin Reynolds at **SHASTA GLIDE 'N RIDE** (530/242-1150 or 866/466-4111; www.shastaglidenride.com) and cruise the area by Segway. Choose a one-, two-, or three-hour tour and pass over the Sundial Bridge, throughout the arboretum, and by the turtle pond. Night Glides are offered on Friday and Saturday nights in summer. On Free 'fer Fridays daytime tours are buy-one-get-one-free (though these sell out quickly, so reserve well in advance).

This section of the river also offers good year-round fishing for steelhead, trout, and salmon; for information about where to cast your line, call Redding's world-class fly-fishing store, the **FLY SHOP** (800/669-3474 or 530/222-3555; www.flyshop.com). **WHISKEYTOWN LAKE**, west of Redding, offers great beaches, windsurfing, and sailings; for information, call the lake's visitor center (530/246-1225).

RESTAURANTS

Buz's Crab / ★

2159 EAST ST, REDDING; 530/243-2120

Every day the bounty of the North Coast is hauled over the hills into California's parched interior to Buz's seafood market. With Naugahyde booths and Formica tables, this ain't no pretty place for a romantic dinner for two, but Buz's earns its star for doing what it does perfectly. The seafood baskets offer much more than your standard fish-and-chips: you'll find everything here—from stuffed prawns, oysters, scallops, and clam strips to calamari, catfish, Cajun halibut, and crisp potato rounds. From December through May, order the fabulous crab (just plucked from the boiling crab pots on the patio), along with a slab of Buz's fresh-baked sourdough bread. Be sure to ask for a free copy of their excellent cioppino recipe. *$–$$; MC, V; local checks only; lunch, dinner every day; beer and wine; no reservations; www.buzscrab.com; north of W Cypress Ave and Pine St.*

Cheesecakes Unlimited & Cafe / ★★

1080 E CYPRESS AVE, REDDING; 530/244-1775

Cory Gabrielson and Nicholas Parker started Cheesecakes Unlimited as a wholesale cheesecake business, then opened a small café that offers light meals—so now you can have your cake and eat croissant sandwiches and freshly made salads, too. A couple of winners are the house-smoked salmon salad (with tomatoes, cucumbers, asparagus, and oregano vinaigrette) and the prawn and pasta salad with roasted garlic and herbed vinaigrette dressing. Of course, the New York–style cheesecakes (lemon, chocolate-chocolate, raspberry, almond amaretto, and mocha Baileys) are the kind you'd never want to pass up—or even share. *$; AE, DIS, MC, V; checks OK; lunch Mon–Fri; beer and wine; reservations recommended; at Churn Creek Rd.* ♿

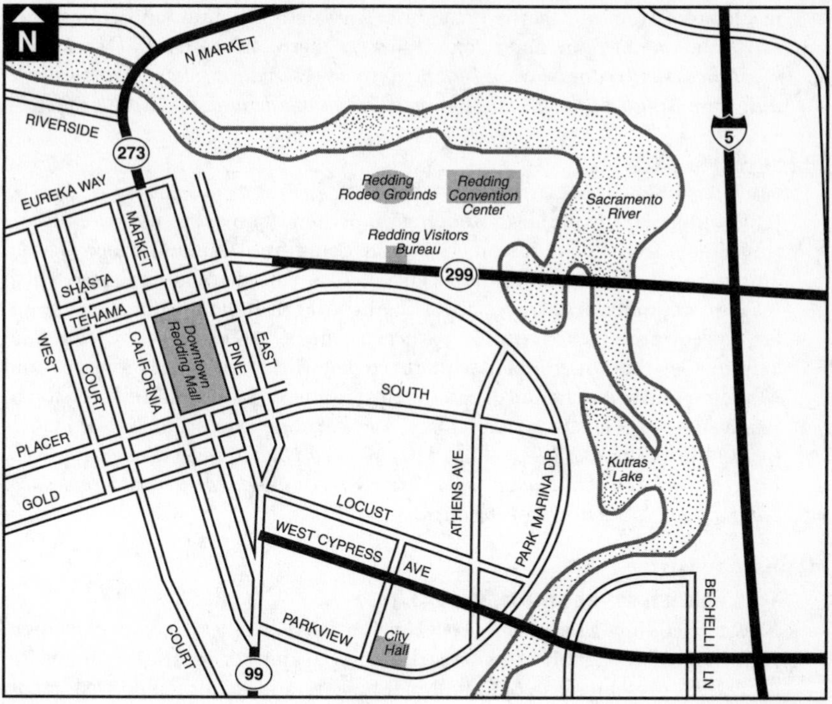

Redding

Gironda's / ★★★

1100 CENTER ST, REDDING; 530/244-7663

Hidden in a residential area, Gironda's is easy to miss—you wouldn't stumble upon it unless you were specifically looking for it. That's probably why it's packed to the brim with locals who frequent this place for its novel-size menu of all things pasta. We recommend trying one of the seven types of ravioli, like the sun-dried tomato and egg, or the Florentine and ricotta drenched in creamy basil pesto. The Chicago-style pizzas are also tasty, and seafood lovers can indulge in the fish, mussels, prawn, and clam cioppino or shrimp piccata. Don't pass up the fried artichoke starter dipped in beer batter and served with Gorgonzola sauce. Delivery is available, as is a kids' menu. *$$; AE, DIS, MC, V; local checks only; lunch Mon–Fri, dinner every day; full bar; reservations recommended; www.girondas.com; at Trinity St.*

Jack's Grill / ★★

1743 CALIFORNIA ST, REDDING; 530/241-9705

A 1930s tavern, Jack's Grill is a beloved institution in Redding—so beloved, in fact, that few even grumble over the typical two-hour wait for a table on weekends. But be forewarned: This is a carnivores-only club, specializing in huge, juicy 1-pound steaks, tender brochettes, and thick steak sandwiches. The meaty meals are served with garlic bread, a green salad, a potato, and coffee. Jack starts cooking at 5pm, and hungry folks get there early. *$$; AE, DIS, MC, V; local checks only; dinner Mon–Sat; full bar; no reservations; www.jacksgrillredding.com; south of the downtown mall, between Sacramento and Placer sts.*

La Gondola / ★★

630 N MARKET ST, REDDING; 530/244-6321

La Gondola is so popular in Redding that when it moved to its current location, loans from loyal customers kept it going until the new place was up and running. The restaurant specializes in northern Italian cuisine, which features creamier, less spicy sauces than southern Italian food. Some popular entrées are chicken stuffed with prosciutto cooked in white wine and cream; filet mignon topped with roasted garlic, caramelized onions, and Madeira; and spinach- and cheese-filled agnolotti. The restaurant's version of tiramisu—with layers of chocolate, mascarpone cheese, and Kahlua—is justifiably famous. *$$; AE, DIS, MC, V; local checks only; dinner Tues–Sat, brunch Sun; beer and wine; reservations recommended; www.lagondolaca.com; a few blocks north of the Sacramento River.* ♿

Moonstone Bistro / ★★

3425 PLACER ST, REDDING; 530/241-3663

New to Redding, Moonstone seems uncharacteristically trendy for this town. (But its poshness is offset by its strip-mall parking-lot location.) Dishes are as artfully presented as you'd find in a big city and might include fish tacos, prosciutto-wrapped seared scallops, tuna casserole, or duck cassoulet. The old-fashioned Moonstone burger is served on a scallion roll and rarely disappoints. Dessert is a must-order, with seasonal specials like seven-layer gingerbread cake. Sunday brunch is popular, with delightful concoctions like a Spicy Bloody Mary, Moonstone Sorbet Cocktail, or classic mimosa. *$$–$$$; AE, DIS, MC, V; lunch, dinner every day, brunch Sun; full bar; reservations recommended; www.moonstonebistro.com; east of Buenaventura Blvd.* ♿

LODGINGS

Bridgehouse Bed and Breakfast / ★★★½

1455 RIVERSIDE DR, REDDING; 530/247-7177

The newly opened Bridgehouse looks like a page out of a contemporary home-style design magazine. The four bedrooms feature flat-screen TVs, spa robes, hair dryers, 500-thread-count sheets, and Ghirardelli chocolates on the pillows; the two upstairs have views of the nearby river and train trestle. The second-story Sundial Bridge Room is the largest with a king-size bed, double pedestal sink, massage tub, and balcony. Breakfasts are phenomenal; the owner frequently serves up some family recipes, like delectable quiches, stuffed French toast strata, and a Belgian waffle bananas Foster that will surely turn you into a repeat visitor. *$$–$$$; AE, MC, V; checks OK; www.reddingbridgehouse.com; at Market St.* ♿

Tiffany House Bed and Breakfast Inn / ★★

1510 BARBARA RD, REDDING; 530/244-3225

Perched on a hill above town, Brady and Susan Stewart's beautifully refurbished Cape Cod–style home offers three guest rooms and a cottage, a swimming pool, and a fine view of Mount Lassen. The Victorian Rose Room features charming cupola windows and a claw-foot bathtub. If you're an early bird, you'll appreciate the Tierra Room and the larger Oak Room, which both offer great sunrise views. Each room has a queen-size bed and a private bath. Guests are welcome to lounge in the antique-filled music parlor, where old-time sheet music is stacked on the piano. Another parlor houses a game table and a fireplace, an ideal retreat on cool nights. If you prefer total privacy (and can fork over a few more bucks), rent the attractive guest cottage, where you can bask in the luxurious indoor spa. *$$–$$$; AE, DIS, MC, V; checks OK; www.tiffanyhousebb.com; off Benton Dr.*

Shasta Lake

To fully appreciate Shasta Lake's 370 miles of shoreline, view the lake by boat. And while you're at it, keep your eye on the sky for a glimpse of the mighty bald eagle, the largest bird of prey in North America. Shasta Lake is currently the home of quite a few pairs of the endangered bird—the largest nesting population of bald eagles in California. For information about other lake attractions and houseboat rentals, contact the **REDDING CONVENTION AND VISITORS BUREAU** (800/874-7562; www.visitredding.org) or the **SHASTA CASCADE WONDERLAND ASSOCIATION** (530/365-7500; www.shastacascade.org).

If you're heading up to Shasta Lake on I-5, the monolithic 3,640-foot-long **SHASTA DAM** (from I-5, take the Shasta Dam Blvd exit and follow the signs; 530/275-4463) is a great place to pull over for a lengthy pit stop. Shasta is the second-largest and second-tallest concrete dam in the United States (it contains enough concrete to build a 3-foot-wide sidewalk around the world) and one of the most impressive civil engineering feats in the nation. The visitor center and viewing area are rather ho-hum, but the free 45-minute dam tour is outstanding. It kicks off with a speedy elevator ride into the chilly bowels of the 15-million-ton, 602-foot-high structure—definitely not recommended for claustrophobes. Dam tours are scheduled from 9am to 4pm every day; call for information and winter and holiday hours.

About 10 miles north of the dam is another popular attraction: guided tours of the impressive, crystal-studded stalagmites and stalactites in the **LAKE SHASTA CAVERNS** (from I-5, take the Shasta Caverns Rd exit and follow the signs; 530/238-2341; www.lakeshastacaverns.com). Getting there is an adventure in itself; after you pull off the highway and check in at cavern headquarters, you'll have to hop aboard a ferry for a 15-minute trip across Shasta Lake, then climb onto a bus for a white-knuckle ride up to the caverns (open every day, year-round). And anglers take note: The stretch of the Sacramento River between Shasta Lake and Mount Shasta is one of the top spots in the country for trout fishing, so don't forget to pack the rod and reel. For tips on touring the area north of Shasta Lake, see the Mount Shasta section in this chapter.

The Trinity Alps Region

National forest blankets 70 percent of Trinity County, which includes the stunning Trinity Alps north of Highway 299. The area is chock-full of good fishing spots, especially on the **TRINITY RIVER**, **TRINITY LAKE**, and **LEWISTON LAKE**. Mountain bikers, hikers, and horseback riders flock to the scenic 50-mile **WEAVER BASIN TRAIL**, which circles Weaverville.

Lewiston

LODGINGS

Old Lewiston Inn / ★★

DEADWOOD RD, LEWISTON; 530/778-3385 OR 877/778-3385

This B and B on the banks of the Trinity River's fly-fishing-only section caters—surprise—to fly-fishers. It has seven guest rooms: three small rooms in the 1875 Baker House and four rooms in the adjoining inn. Most have private baths. A favorite is the Baker House's Herbert Hoover Room, where the 31st president once slept. The inn accommodations have less history but more elbow room, with private entrances and decks overlooking the Trinity River. The Old Lewiston Inn also has a hot tub for unwinding after a day of touring or trout fishing. While you're having your hearty country breakfast, you can keep an eye out the back door for fish rising in the river. *$$; DIS, MC, V; checks OK; www.theoldlewistoninn.com; ½ block from the bridge.* ♿

Weaverville

Founded nearly 150 years ago by gold miners, the little rural town of Weaverville, population 4,000, is the largest town in Trinity County (an area the size of Rhode Island and Delaware combined). While cruising through the historic downtown district, keep your peepers open for the peculiar outdoor spiral staircases that grace many of the homes—they're remnants of the days when a different person owned each floor. For a bit of gold rush and Weaverville history, stroll down Main Street and visit the small **JAKE JACKSON MUSEUM** (780 Main St; 530/623-5211). Adjacent to the museum is **JOSS HOUSE STATE HISTORIC PARK**, site of the oldest Chinese temple, the Temple of the Forest Beneath the Clouds (530/623-5284), in the United States. The well-preserved temple was built by immigrant Chinese miners in 1874 and is worth a peek (and the nominal entrance fee); call for information on temple tours.

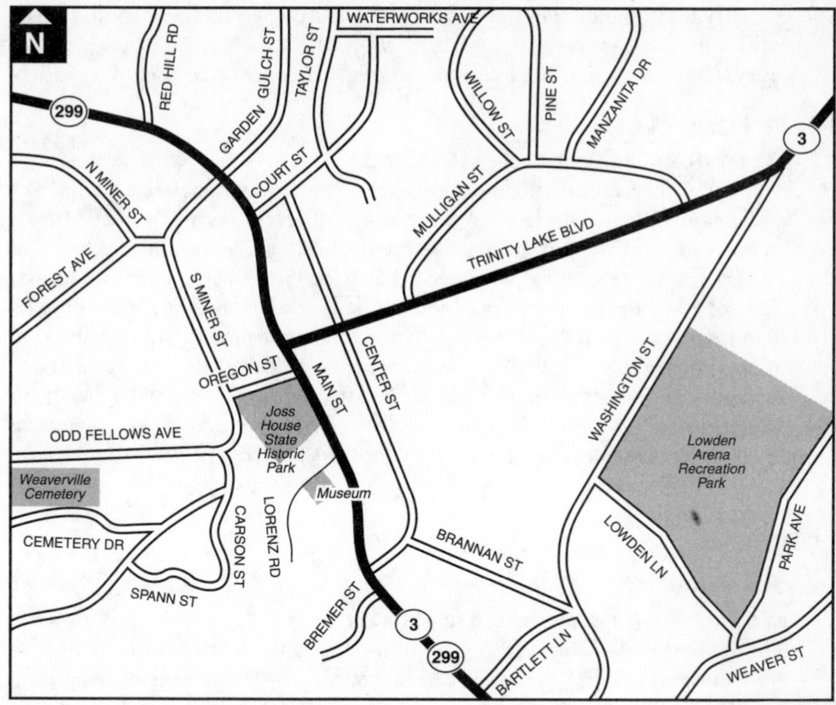

Weaverville

Another town highlight is the grueling **LA GRANGE CLASSIC MOUNTAIN BIKE RACE**, typically held the first weekend in June. To find out more about this mountain town's activities, call the **TRINITY COUNTY CHAMBER OF COMMERCE** (530/623-6101 or 800/487-4648). For information about fishing in the region, visit the helpful staff at **TRINITY FLY SHOP** (530/623-6757), located at the bottom of Ohio Hill in Lewiston.

RESTAURANTS

La Grange Cafe / ★★★

226 MAIN ST, WEAVERVILLE; 530/623-5325

Named after a nearby mine, La Grange Cafe serves the best food in the county. Start your dinner with chef-owner Sharon Heryford's exceptionally fresh salad tossed with an Italian dressing and chunks of blue cheese. Then sink your teeth into her charbroiled marinated steak served with black bean chili, or try one of the game dishes such as venison loin chops or buffalo burger steak. There are a lot of seafood, chicken, and pasta choices, too. An excellent and moderately priced wine list boasts more than 100 selections. And then there's the sweet stuff: berry cobbler, banana cream pie, and old-fashioned bread pudding are made on the premises. La Grange is located in a big, airy brick building in the town's historic area, with a lot of room for the folks who flock to the place. *$$; AE, DIS, MC, V; checks OK; lunch, dinner every day, brunch Sun; full bar; reservations recommended; on Hwy 299.* ♿

Noelle's Garden Cafe / ★★

252 MAIN ST, WEAVERVILLE; 530/623-2058

This snug, cheerful café in an old two-story house has a phalanx of windows and a sunny outside deck. Proprietor Noelle Roget's specialties include Austrian strudel (a flaky puff pastry filled with shrimp, veggies, and cheeses) and a hefty veggie melt served with her home fries spiced with garlic and onion. The seasonal dinner menu may include such dishes as a perfectly cooked lime-marinated halibut or a stir-fry prepared with jumbo shrimp, chicken, or fresh vegetables. She also offers an array of baked desserts, and if the espresso cake is up for grabs, grab it. *$; MC, V; local checks only; breakfast, lunch every day Memorial Day–Labor Day (Wed–Mon Labor Day–Memorial Day), dinner Fri–Sat (year-round); beer and wine; no reservations; 1 block west of Oregon St.*

LODGINGS

Red Hill Motel / ★

RED HILL RD, WEAVERVILLE; 530/623-4331

The Red Hill's 14 well-maintained auto-court units (cabins with small covered garages) would have made a great set for a '40s film noir starring Lauren Bacall and Humphrey Bogart. So put on your best Bogart fedora and step back in time by booking a night or two at these one- or two-bedroom cabins, decorated with authentic pre–World War II furnishings (except for the remote-control cable TVs and in-room phones, of course). Owners Patty Holder and her husband restored this jewel, surrounded by a rolling green lawn and ponderosa pines. Spend the day reeling in rainbow trout on the Trinity then prepare your catch for supper at the Red Hill's fish-cleaning station. Or kick back in a lawn chair under the pines and think about the good ol' days, when life was simpler, the fish were bigger, and folks were named Claudette, Clark, Ida, and Humphrey. The friendly Red Hill folks permit pets, too. *$; AE, DIS, MC, V; no checks; across from the U.S. Forest Service station on Main St, at the west end of town.*

Weaverville Hotel / ★

203 MAIN ST, WEAVERVILLE; 800/750-8920

This hotel has been in operation since 1861—a few fiery interruptions notwithstanding (it burned to the ground several times in the town's early days). Under Jeanne and Brian Muir it has been totally restored and refurbished. Though the rooms are posh, they have no phones or TVs, thus ensuring that guests slip into Weaverville's more relaxed tempo. Instead, there is a phone booth in the hall (restored, of course), and a flat-screen TV/VCR in a lounge behind the more formal lobby. Most of the seven rooms have gas log fireplaces, and all have private showers as well as claw-foot tubs and spas. In colder seasons, the four-poster queen beds are converted to feather beds. Coffee, tea, and cookies are always available, and guests can use the gym across the street. Because of the antique furnishings, the hotel is not suitable for children under 12. *$$–$$$; AE, MC, V; checks OK; www.weavervillehotel.com; in the center of town.*

Willow Creek

RESTAURANTS

Cinnabar Sam's / ★

19 WILLOW WY, WILLOW CREEK; 530/629-3437

If you travel between the Pacific coastline and Redding, be sure to stop for a bite at Cinnabar Sam's. A popular hangout for rafters and kayakers, this restaurant is decked out in Western memorabilia: antique gas pumps, old photographs, and movie posters from the golden days—the salad bar is even in a claw-foot tub. A favorite breakfast dish is the Claim Jumper: ham, scrambled eggs, hash browns, onions, bell peppers, sausage, and cheese. For lunch or dinner, try the popular do-it-yourself fajitas, the behemoth burger, the sirloin steak, or the barbecued ribs. *$; AE, DIS, MC, V; checks OK; breakfast, lunch, dinner every day; beer and wine; no reservations; at Hwy 299, at the east end of town.* ♿

Forks of Salmon

LODGINGS

Otter Bar Lodge / ★★★

14026 SALMON RIVER RD, FORKS OF SALMON; 530/462-4772

Surrounded by a pond and acres of mowed green grass, this seven-bedroom ranch-style lodge features oak floors, French doors, and lots of glass—all in an effort to bring the outdoors indoors. Two living rooms, two kitchens, a sauna, and a hot tub are also available to guests. The cedar-roofed, white-washed rooms have private decks and down comforters on the beds, and some are stocked with good books. Reserve the romantic Tower Room, an upstairs retreat lined with windows offering views of the fir trees, or try one of the three cabins. Otter Bar Lodge doubles as a world-class kayaking school and offers some of the most beautiful mountain-biking trails in the state. The food is terrific—no ranch-style meat and potatoes here. Instead, look for paella, snapper Veracruz, and other sophisticated delights on the ever-changing menu. Breakfast offerings include veggie omelets, homemade granola, and berry pancakes. Weeklong stays are required. All meals are included in the weekly rate. *$$$$; MC, V; checks OK; open mid-Apr–Sept 30; www.otterbar.com; 15 miles east of Somes Bar.*

Coffee Creek

South of Etna on Highway 3 is the postage-stamp-size town of Coffee Creek, which supposedly got its name from a miner's pack train that spilled coffee into the town's creek, although some claim the name came from the spring runoff, which colors the creek brown. Whatever the case, this town dates back to the gold rush days of the 1850s. There aren't many places to dine around here, but your best bet is the **FOREST CAFE** (Hwy 3 at Coffee Creek Rd; 530/266-3575). Venture a little farther south and you'll see **TRINITY LAKE** (also known as Clair Engle Lake in honor of an environmentally conscious local politician), a popular haunt of anglers and other lovers of the great outdoors.

LODGINGS

Ripple Creek Cabins / ★★

EAGLE CREEK LOOP, COFFEE CREEK; 530/266-3505 OR 510/531-5315

Set amid tall pines and cedars where Ripple Creek enters the Trinity River, all seven of Jim and Michele Coleman's well-furnished cabins have amply stocked kitchens (wow!—corkscrews and garlic presses!) and private baths. Most of the cabins accommodate two to six people. There's also a four-bedroom house for rent—ideal for a family reunion or group retreat. Diversions include table tennis, bicycles, a volleyball and badminton court, and a swimming hole. For a $10 fee, you can even bring your pooch along. *$–$$; no credit cards; checks OK; www.ripplecreekcabins.com; off Hwy 3.* ♿

Mount Shasta and the Yreka Area

Magnificent, snowcapped Mount Shasta, soaring 14,162 feet into the sky, is the largest volcano (by mass) in the contiguous 48 states. Shasta is a dormant volcano; it's not dead, just sleeping until it decides to blow its snowy stack—something it hasn't done since the late 1700s. Nestled about the peak are the railroad, mill, and lumber towns of Dunsmuir, McCloud, and Weed, along with Mount Shasta City. Traveling north toward the Oregon border, you'll discover the rustic treasures and rough-and-tumble pleasures of more small towns set in the great outdoors.

Dunsmuir

When a Southern Pacific train ran off the tracks in 1991 and spilled an herbicide in the Sacramento River, it killed all aquatic life for 45 miles along the river. And it darn near killed Dunsmuir. But this pretty, historic railroad town has a population of roughly 2,000 resilient residents who have brought the town back with a vengeance. Using a financial settlement from Southern

Pacific, the townsfolk have gussied up their community and hope to make Dunsmuir a major California tourist destination. They may just succeed. In addition to the beautiful natural surroundings, stylish gift shops and restaurants have sprung up on the city's streets (particularly on Dunsmuir and Sacramento avenues). Furthermore, trophy-size wild trout now abound in the Sacramento River, and the community slogan is "Home of the best water on earth." Fortunately, not all of the tourists are coming to Dunsmuir by car, thanks to the Amtrak train that stops here daily. Call the **DUNSMUIR CHAMBER OF COMMERCE AND VISITORS CENTER** (800/DUNSMUIR; www.dunsmuir.com) for the nitty-gritty.

RESTAURANTS

Cafe Maddalena / ★★★

5801 SACRAMENTO AVE, DUNSMUIR; 530/235-2725

The owners of Cafe Maddelena, chef Brett LaMott and his wife, Nancy, came here after establishing the wildly popular Trinity Cafe in Mount Shasta. They have expanded the previous menu, which was predominantly Sardinian, to include authentic dishes from southern France, Spain, and North Africa. Offerings may include zarzuela (a Spanish shellfish stew in a tomato-saffron broth); herb-roasted lamb rack with ratatouille; an exotic couscous with a tagine of yam, carrots, and prunes; or a pan-seared filet mignon with sauce *vin de minervois*. The menu changes seasonally, and everything is made fresh daily, including the bread and desserts. The wine list includes Italian, French, and Spanish labels to complement the entrées. During the summer months, request a table outside under the grape arbor. *$$; AE, DIS, MC, V; checks OK; dinner Thurs–Sun (closed Jan); beer and wine; reservations recommended; www.cafemaddalena.com; 1 block west of Dunsmuir Ave across from the Amtrak station and the Sacramento River.*

LODGINGS

Railroad Park Resort/The Caboose Motel

100 RAILROAD PARK RD, DUNSMUIR; 530/235-4440

A must for railroad buffs but a maybe for everyone else, the Railroad Park Resort's funky Caboose Motel offers quiet, comfortable lodgings in a boxcar and 23 refurbished cabooses (cabeese?) from the Southern Pacific, Santa Fe, and Great Northern railroads. Most have king- or queen-size beds with small bay windows or rooftop cupolas. The Boxcar (room 20) is decorated in country antiques and has a small private patio. Motel management also rents out four cabins. All guests have access to the pool and Jacuzzi—not to mention a great view of nearby Castle Crags. Guests may bring along their small pets for an extra $15. And if you're a big prime rib fan, you're in luck: that's the specialty of the Railroad Park Resort Restaurant. *$–$$; MC, V; checks OK; www.rrpark.com; 1 mile south of town.* ♿

McCloud

A company-built mill town, McCloud bills itself as "the quiet side of Mount Shasta." And true to its motto, this is a relatively sleepy place, but its many sumptuous B and Bs attract anglers, hikers, and other nature lovers who spend their waking hours outdoors, as well as those bleary-eyed city folk who long for little more than a warm bed and some solitude. Whatever your attraction to this neck of the woods, you can introduce yourself to the area by hopping aboard the **SHASTA SUNSET DINNER TRAIN** (530/964-2142; www.shastasunset.com), which follows a historic turn-of-the-century logging route. Now, as then, the steep grades, sharp curves, and a unique switchback at Signal Butte are still part of the route, though today's passengers ride in cars handsomely restored in wood and brass. As you nosh on a very good dinner in your railcar, you'll be treated to views of Mount Shasta, Castle Crags, and the Trinity Alps. The 40-mile, three-hour journey is run by the McCloud Railway Company year-round and costs $97.50 per person, including dinner.

In the summer, you can watch—or, better yet, join—the McCloud locals as they kick up their heels every night from May to September in the town's air-conditioned dance hall, **DANCE COUNTRY** (530/964-2992; www.mcclouddancecountry.com). Dancing—especially square dancing—is a favorite pastime here, so if you want to promenade your partner or swing to the beat, call for the latest schedule. This part of the northern mountains is also extraordinarily rich in outdoor-recreational opportunities; see the Mount Shasta section for details.

LODGINGS

The Guest House / ★★★

606 W COLOMBERO DR, MCCLOUD; 530/964-3160

Built in 1907 for McCloud timber baron J. H. Queal, this stately, two-story mansion became the McCloud River Lumber Company's guest house after Queal's death in 1921. Herbert Hoover, Jean Harlow, and various members of the Hearst family dallied here in the '20s and '30s, but soon afterward the house fell into disrepair. Restored as a country inn and restaurant, McCloud Guest House reopened its doors in 1984. In 2003, new ownership brought new life to this wonderful inn. Downstairs in the lobby and dining room are delicately wrought cabinetry, beveled glass, antique wallpaper, and a massive stone fireplace. The inn's five spacious guest rooms have four-poster beds and antique furnishings. A multicourse spa breakfast is served with offerings like fresh-fruit smoothies, Belgian waffles, potato pancakes, and, sometimes, freshly baked scones with Devonshire cream. *$$; MC, V; checks OK; www.historicalmccloudguesthouse.com; at the west end of town.*

McCloud Bed and Breakfast Hotel / ★★★★

408 MAIN ST, MCCLOUD; 530/964-2822 OR 800/964-2823

Built in 1916, the McCloud Bed and Breakfast Hotel has earned a highly coveted spot on the National Register of Historic Places. Its meticulous restoration was completed in 1995, and now the hotel offers 15 beautiful guest rooms gussied up with antiques, decorator fabrics, and, in many cases, tall four-poster beds. Each room also has a private bath. Telephones, TVs, and complimentary wireless Internet are available in the lobby. Gourmet breakfasts of fresh fruit, house-made bread, and a hot dish are served in the lobby area (though if you're staying in a suite, you can have the meal delivered to your room). Lunch and dinner are also available for guests. If you happen to tire of McCloud's numerous outdoor attractions, kick back in the hotel lobby's comfortable chairs and sofas and borrow one of the many books, games, and puzzles stashed here. *$$–$$$; AE, DIS, MC, V; checks OK; www.mccloudhotel.com; from exit off Hwy 89, follow signs to the historic district.* ♿

McCloud River Inn / ★★★

325 LAWNDALE CT, MCCLOUD; 530/964-2130 OR 800/261-7831

At this inn, yet another of the delightful bed-and-breakfasts in charming McCloud, the innkeepers knock themselves out to make sure their guests have a good time. Built at the turn of the century as headquarters for the McCloud River Lumber Company, the inn has been beautifully restored, and its five guest rooms are filled with period-style furnishings. All have private bathrooms (one with a spa tub and one with a claw-foot soaking tub). Breakfast is a big attraction, with fresh fruit, pastries, and frittata. The inn has massage therapists on call and a flower and gift shop. *$–$$$; AE, DIS, MC, V; checks OK; www.mccloudriverinn.com; at the north end of town.*

Mount Shasta

Mount Shasta is only the fifth-highest peak in the state, but unlike its taller cousins, which are clustered with other large mountains, this volcano stands alone, a position that seems to intensify its grandeur. "Lonely as God and white as a winter moon" is how author Joaquin Miller described this solitary peak in the 1870s. The mountain dominates the horizon from every angle, and on clear days it's visible from as far away as 150 miles.

Some Native Americans who lived in its shadow believed Mount Shasta was the home of the Great Spirit and vowed never to climb its sacred slopes, which they viewed as an act of disrespect. Today, men and women from around the world pay tribute to the volcano by making the spectacular trek to the top. This is not a mountain for novice hikers, but with some basic mountain climbing instruction and a good study of Shasta's various routes, physically fit adventurers can safely reach its stunning summit ("It's just like climbing stairs nonstop from 9 to 5," says one veteran climber). You can buy a good map of the mountain and rent crampons, an ice ax, and sturdy, insulated climbing boots at the **FIFTH SEASON** (300 N Mount Shasta Blvd at Lake St; 530/926-3606 store, 530/926-5555 mountain report; www.thefifthseason.com), staffed by experienced and helpful mountaineers. Beginners eager to climb Mount Shasta can take an all-day lesson in basic mountain-climbing skills from the folks at **SHASTA MOUNTAIN GUIDES** (530/926-3117; www.shastaguides.com), who also lead three- and four-day guided climbs. And whether you're a beginner or an expert climber, visit the **MOUNT SHASTA RANGER DISTRICT OFFICE** (204 W Alma St off N Mount Shasta Blvd; 530/926-4511), which provides up-to-date climbing literature as well as friendly advice. Get your free (and mandatory) hiking permit while you're there. If all this climbing sounds a wee bit intimidating, there is an easier way. In past years, many folks have made their way up Mount Shasta via a chairlift (though it doesn't reach the peak) and down on skis. **MOUNT SHASTA BOARD & SKI PARK** (at the end of Ski Park Hwy, off Hwy 89, 10 miles east of I-5; 530/926-8610 ski resort, 530/926-8686 snow report; www.skipark.com) offers mostly intermediate runs with nary a mogul in sight, and the cost of the lift ticket won't require taking out a second mortgage on your home. Ski Park also has a ski and snowboard rental and repair shop, restaurant, snack bar, and ski school. In the summer, the resort provides naturalist-led walks, mountain-biking trails accessible by chairlift (bike rentals are available, too), and an indoor recreational climbing wall for people of all ages and abilities. About a quarter-mile down the highway is the **NORDIC LODGE** (on Ski Park Hwy; 530/926-8610), a cross-country ski center with several miles of groomed tracks.

If you prefer to admire Mount Shasta from afar, visit **CASTLE CRAGS STATE PARK** (from I-5, take the Castle Crags State Park exit, about 13 miles south of Mount Shasta; 530/235-2684), one of California's geologic wonders. The park's enormous 6,500-foot spires of ancient granite are visible from the highway, but they deserve a much closer look. If you're anxious to really stretch your legs, hike up the park's moderately strenuous 2.7-mile **SUMMIT DOME TRAIL** to the base of the crags—the view of Mount Shasta alone is worth the trip. Less adventurous souls can stroll along the 1-mile **ROOT CREEK** or **INDIAN CREEK TRAILS** or picnic among the pines and wildflowers.

For another unforgettable experience, splurge on a guided white-water-rafting trip down the mighty **KLAMATH RIVER**. Daredevils can soar down the narrow, steep chutes appropriately called Hells Corner and Caldera, while saner souls (including children) can navigate the much less perilous forks. Trips are also available on the upper Sacramento, the Trinity, and other nearby rivers. One-day trips range from $80 to $145 (multiday trips are also available). Call the **TURTLE RIVER RAFTING COMPANY** (530/926-3223 or 800/726-3223; www.turtleriver.com) for more details.

The town of Mount Shasta offers two good (and safe) attractions that won't even make a dent in your wallet: the free **SISSON MUSEUM** (530/926-5508; www.mountshastasissonmuseum.org) showcases changing exhibits on local history, nature, geology, and Native American life, and its adjacent **MOUNT SHASTA FISH HATCHERY** (take Lake St across the freeway, turn left on Hatchery Rd, and head to 3 N Old Stage Rd; 530/926-2215; www.fishmtshasta.com), the oldest hatchery in the West, keeps thousands of rainbow and brown trout, including a few biggies, in the holding ponds. For a little pocket change you can purchase some fish food and incite a fish-feeding frenzy. For more information, contact the **MOUNT SHASTA VISITORS BUREAU** (300 Pine St at Lake St; 530/926-4865).

RESTAURANTS

Billy Goats Tavern / ★✯

107 CHESTNUT ST, MOUNT SHASTA; 530/926-0209

This gritty pub is where you go for a quick bite to eat or if you don't feel like donning your fancier duds and heading to Lily's (see review). The food is solid though basic—burgers and sandwiches are popular; most dishes come loaded with cheese, salt, and/or garlic—and service is speedy, though not particularly friendly. But the beer's the reason most people visit this watering hole. The 12 taps rotate 70 microbrew varietals, and the tavern also has an archive of 100 bottled beers. *$; AE, MC, V; no checks; lunch, dinner every day; beer only; no reservations; www.billygoatstavern.com; at Orem St.* ♿

Lily's / ★★

1013 S MOUNT SHASTA BLVD, MOUNT SHASTA; 530/926-3372

This popular place offers very good California cuisine with an ethnic flair. Start your dinner with spicy jalapeño pasta or baked Brie and follow that with an entrée of prime rib, Chicken Rosie (a chicken breast browned in butter and simmered with raspberries, hazelnut liqueur, and a hint of cream), or the terrific enchiladas *suizas*, stuffed with crab, shrimp, and fresh spinach. Lunch offerings are equally imaginative, and if you're looking for something a little different from the usual breakfast fare, try Lily's cheesy polenta fritters. Lily's is *the* place in town to get your Sunday brunch on, so snag a table early in the morning. *$$; AE, DIS, MC, V; local checks only; breakfast, lunch Mon–Fri, dinner every day, brunch Sat–Sun and holidays; beer and wine; reservations recommended; www.lilysrestaurant.com; from I-5, take the Central Mount Shasta exit.*

Michael's Restaurant / ★

313 MOUNT SHASTA BLVD, MOUNT SHASTA; 530/926-5288

Michael and Lynn Kobseff have been running this estimable little restaurant since 1980, which makes them old-timers on the ever-changing Mount Shasta restaurant scene. Some of their best lunchtime offerings are the crisp, greaseless fried zucchini appetizer, the French fries, and a terrific Cajun turkey melt. Their Italian dinners will satisfy those with lumberjack-size appetites, especially the combination ravioli and linguine plate. Lynn makes all the desserts in-house. The small but varied wine list features several bargains. *$; AE, DIS, MC, V; local checks only; lunch, dinner Wed–Sat; full bar; reservations recommended; from I-5, take the Central Mount Shasta exit.* ♿

MYSTIC MOUNTAIN

Native Americans have always considered Mount Shasta a holy mountain, the home of the Great Spirit. Over the years, spiritual seekers, New Age believers, and other metaphysical folk have also pronounced it one of the most powerful sacred sites in North America; organizations such as the Creative Harmonics Institute, the Ascended Master Teaching Foundation, the Temple of Cosmic Religion, I AM Activity, Planetary Citizens, and the Radiant School of Seekers and Servers have, at one time or another, made the base of the mountain their temporal home. And then there are the people inside the mountain. Lemurians, believed by some to be highly evolved beings descended from an ancient civilization called Lemuria, can supposedly materialize at will and may (it is said) occasionally show themselves to the faithful. Strange lights and noises on Mount Shasta are sometimes attributed to these folk. There is also an Indian legend that claims ancient lizard people once built a city beneath the mountain. And, indeed, one visitor allegedly spotted a "lizard person" in 1972.

The most famous metaphysical assembly in recent decades was the 1987 Harmonic Convergence, a gathering of 5,000 people who met at Mount Shasta to create a cosmic consciousness providing "attunement to the planet and to higher galactic intelligences." Four UFOs and an angel announcing the beginning of heaven on earth reportedly appeared. The UFOs could be attributed to the saucer-shaped clouds that form around the mountain, emanating beams of light—a perfectly feasible explanation, scientists say. The angel remains a mystery.

Today around Mount Shasta you can take workshops employing sweat lodges, ceremonial circles, and Peruvian whistling vessels to awaken your inner warrior or to retrieve your soul. Locals not of the New Age persuasion have occasionally been heard to refer to their spiritual neighbors as "cosmic muffins," but for the most part, all is peace and harmony here. At the very least, you can get really good vegetarian food in town.

If you're interested in learning about the mountain's alleged mystical powers, visit the delightfully funky **GOLDEN BOUGH BOOKSTORE** (219 N Mount Shasta Blvd at Lake St, Mount Shasta City; 530/926-3228), where the staff can give you the lowdown and direct you to multimedia, books, and all matter of spiritual info.

Trinity Cafe / ★★★

622 N MOUNT SHASTA BLVD, MOUNT SHASTA; 530/926-6200

When Bill and Crystal Truby moved here, they brought the best aspects of their Napa Valley roots to Mount Shasta. They may have traded vineyards for snowy peaks, but when you settle in for dinner at the Trinity Cafe, you could easily believe you are in Napa. The menu combines the flair and eclecticism of Wine Country cooking with the Mount Shasta penchant for healthy dishes, using fresh produce from the local farmers market and locally raised game. Try the cabernet braised lamb with mint pesto, grilled Pacific king salmon on panzanella salad, whole roasted tilapia with saffron risotto, or grilled vegetables stacked with polenta and fresh mozzarella. The wine list is predominantly California, with featured wines to complement the nightly specials. *$$; AE, MC, V; checks OK; dinner Tues–Sat; beer and wine; reservations recommended; between Jessie and Ivy sts.* ♿

LODGINGS

Mount Shasta Ranch Bed and Breakfast / ★★

1008 W. A. BARR RD, MOUNT SHASTA; 530/926-3870 OR 877/926-3870

This comfortable 70-year-old bed-and-breakfast inn with gabled windows and hip roofs offers large rooms, large baths, large views, and even large breakfasts. In addition to five guest rooms in the main building, the B and B has five rooms in a carriage house and a two-bedroom cottage. The main house, decorated with antiques and Oriental rugs, has the largest guest rooms (four of them sleep up to four people each), plus huge private bathrooms sporting original 1920s fixtures. The carriage house's five units are smaller and share two bathrooms but have great views of Mount Shasta and the rugged Siskiyous. Come morning, indulge in a hearty breakfast that might include cream-cheese-filled waffles with fresh fruit toppings, crepes bursting with local blackberries, plump sausages, a fresh fruit salad, and good strong coffee. Afterward, curl up with a book in front of the main lodge's gargantuan stone fireplace, or work off those waffles by hiking, swimming, playing a few rounds of table tennis or pool, or soaking in the inn's hot springs spa. *$–$$; AE, DIS, MC, V; checks OK; www.stayinshasta.com; south of the fish hatchery.* ♿

Mount Shasta Resort / ★★★

1000 SISKIYOU LAKE BLVD, MOUNT SHASTA; 530/926-3030 OR 800/958-3363

If you think people who live to hit little golf balls should get a life, you'll have second thoughts when you see the incredibly scenic Mount Shasta Resort. The prospect of spending all day on a rolling green lawn and breathing in clean air under the towering presence of Mount Shasta is alluring—even to those who can't tell a driver from a nine iron. The 50 one- and two-bedroom Craftsman-style chalets have all the creature comforts and they're located on the forested shore of Lake Siskiyou, where you can swim, fish, sailboard, kayak, canoe, or rent paddleboats. What? Left your putter at home? Don't despair. You can buy a new one here or consider such pastimes as fishing, hiking, mountain biking, or skiing—they're all within putting distance of the resort. Chalet rentals vary seasonally. Ask about the special golf packages offered in summer, the ski packages in winter, or the romantic getaway deals year-round. *$$–$$$; AE, DC, DIS, MC, V; local checks only; www.mountshastaresort.com; from I-5, take the Central Mount Shasta exit, go west, turn left on Old Stage Rd, veer onto W. A. Barr Rd, and turn left on Siskiyou Lake Blvd.* ♿

Strawberry Valley Inn / ★★

1142 S MOUNT SHASTA BLVD, MOUNT SHASTA; 530/926-2052

Strawberry Valley owners have combined the privacy of a motel and the personal touches of a B and B to create this terrific 14-room inn surrounded by a lush garden and towering oaks. Guest rooms are individually decorated with kitschy but fun color-coordinated fabrics; if you prefer lots of room to romp, ask for a two-room suite. Amenities include cable TV with HBO, iPod docks, and plush bedding that makes you want to jump on the bed in childish fashion. A buffet breakfast featuring fresh fruit, granola, oatmeal, waffles, and pastries is set up next to the inn's stone fireplace (those who want to dine in private may take a tray to their room). Complimentary wine is poured at the cocktail hour every evening in the beautifully decorated main house. *$; AE, DIS, MC, V; no checks; www.strawberryvalleysuites.com; from I-5, take the Central Mount Shasta exit.* ♿

Weed

Nestled on the north flank of Mount Shasta, this little lumber town doesn't offer much to the tourist, except, perhaps, the popular "I got high on Weed, California" T-shirt.

LODGINGS

Stewart Mineral Springs / ★

4617 STEWART SPRINGS RD, WEED; 530/938-2222

Hidden in a forested canyon at the end of a twisting country road, Stewart Mineral Springs is a great place to commune with nature and unwind from the rigors of daily life. To ensure that you get the R & R you deserve, start off with a visit to the bathhouse, located across the creek at the end of the footbridge, for a detoxifying mineral bath, a sauna, and maybe even a plunge in the creek or the large pond. You can sleep in one of the two inexpensive but spiritually enriching tepees (bring your own bedding) or in one of the five more comfortable (though spartan) little cabins with kitchens. If you plan to cook in your cabin, buy food before you get to this remote locale—convenience stores and burger emporiums are, thankfully, not a part of the scenery here, though the resort does have a restaurant serving breakfast, lunch, and dinner. The five-bedroom A-frame is perfect for large groups of up to 10 people, and there are 10 modest motel rooms. Camping and RV sites are available as well. *$; DIS, MC, V; checks OK; www.stewartmineralsprings.com; about 7 miles northwest of Weed; call for directions.*

Etna

RESTAURANTS

Etna Brewing Company / ★

131 CALLAHAN ST, ETNA; 530/467-5277

As Benjamin Franklin said, "Beer is proof that God loves us and wants us to be happy." Well, here's a little piece of happy. Originally established in 1872, the Etna Brewery was a thriving concern in the small town of Etna for 47 years before being shut down by Prohibition in 1919. In 1990, the brewery came back to life with the opening of the Etna Brewing Company, Siskiyou County's first microbrewery. The brewery changed hands again in 2001 and has been producing award-winning, all-natural beer ever since (including an outstanding root beer). To wash that beer down, you can choose from a full deli-style menu with sandwiches, wraps, salads, and standard pub fare—burgers, hot dogs, chili, and such. Tours of the brewery are also available. *$; AE, DIS, MC, V; checks OK; lunch, appetizers Wed–Sun (call ahead for seasonal hours); beer and wine; no reservations; www.etnabrew.co; at Lovers Ln.*

Lassen Volcanic National Park and the Northeast

Surprisingly, many Californians have never even heard of Lassen Volcanic National Park, much less been there. In fact, it's one of the least crowded national parks in the country, forever destined to play second fiddle to its towering neighbor, Mount Shasta. This is reason enough to go, since the park's 108,000 acres (including 50 beautiful wilderness lakes) are practically deserted, even on weekends. But don't stop here. From Drakesbad to Mill Creek, this area of panoramic vistas, aspen-lined creeks, and popular lakes is worth exploring.

Lassen Volcanic National Park

The heart of the park is 10,457-foot Lassen Peak, the largest plug-dome volcano in the world (its last fiery eruption was in 1915, when it shot debris 7 miles into the stratosphere). For decades Lassen held the title of the most recently active volcano in the continental United States; it lost that distinction in 1980, when Washington's Mount St. Helens blew her top. The volcano also marks the southernmost end of the Cascade Range, which extends to Canada. A visitors' map calls the park "a compact laboratory of volcanic phenomena"—an apt description of this pretty but peculiar place. In addition to wildflower-laced hiking trails and lush forests typical of many national parks, parts of Lassen are covered with steaming thermal vents, boiling mud pots, stinky sulfur springs, and towering lava pinnacles—constant reminders that Mount Lassen is still active.

Lassen Park's premier attractions in the summer and fall are sightseeing, hiking, backpacking, and camping (sorry, no mountain bikes allowed). The $10-per-car entrance fee, valid for a week, gets you a copy of the "Lassen Park Guide," a handy little newsletter listing activities, hikes, and points of interest. Free naturalist programs are offered daily in the summer, highlighting everything from flora and fauna to geologic history and volcanic processes. If you have only a day here, spend it huffing up the mountain on the Lassen Peak Hike, a spectacular 2½-mile zigzag to the top. Most hikers can make the steep trek in four to five hours—just don't forget to bring water, sunscreen, and a windbreaker. Another great—and much easier—trail is the 3-mile Bumpass Hell Hike, named after a mid-19th-century tour guide. Poor ol' Kendall Bumpass lost a leg on this one, but that was long before park rangers built wooden catwalks to safely guide visitors past the pyrite pools, steam vents, seething mud pots, and noisy fumaroles that line the trail.

Mount Lassen Park attracts a hardier breed of tourists in the winter, when the park's main thoroughfare is closed and the chief modes of transportation are snowshoes and cross-country skis. Smaller roads are plowed only from the north and south park entrances up to the ranger stations, and on sunny weekends parking lots are filled with families enjoying every kind of snow toy imaginable. On Saturday afternoons from January through March, a loquacious naturalist will take anyone who shows up at the **LASSEN CHALET** (at the park's south entrance, 5 miles north of the junction of Hwys 36 and 89) by 1:30pm on a free two-hour eco-adventure across the park's snowy dales. You must be at least eight years old, warmly dressed, and decked out in boots. Free snowshoes are provided (although a small donation for shoe upkeep is requested) on a first-come basis. Pack a picnic lunch. For more details, call **PARK HEADQUARTERS** (530/595-4480).

For the best lodgings and restaurants near the park, see the Drakesbad, Chester, Lake Almanor, and Mill Creek sections in this chapter.

Drakesbad

LODGINGS

Drakesbad Guest Ranch / ★★★★

WARNER VALLEY RD, DRAKESBAD; 530/529-1512

Hidden in a high mountain valley inside Lassen Volcanic National Park, the Drakesbad Guest Ranch is probably the worst-kept secret in California. Demand for this mountain retreat's 19 rooms is so high that it's often booked several months (and sometimes a year or two) in advance. Fortunately, plans made that far ahead often change, and February through June are good times to call to take advantage of cancellations. At night, kerosene lamps cast a warm yellow glow over the rustic accommodations; there's no electricity, except in the lodge. The tables, chairs, and bedsteads are made of smooth-sanded logs and branches. There are a half dozen pleasant rooms upstairs in the main lodge, but

BIGFOOT STEPPED HERE

Consider yourself forewarned: California's North Mountains are Sasquatch territory. Also known as Bigfoot, this huge, hairy, apelike mammal has been the subject of hundreds of reports in and around Trinity County, including three sightings within 10 miles of each other (by different people) in the Shasta-Trinity National Forest in 1999. There's a Bigfoot Wing in the **WILLOW CREEK/CHINA FLAT MUSEUM** (corner of Hwys 299 and 96 in Willow Creek; 530/629-2653) that commemorates the elusive creature. You'll know you're in the right place when you see the 23-foot redwood carving of Bigfoot out front. The museum contains dozens of plaster casts of large footprints discovered in the Northern California wilderness as well as a Bigfoot research center.

The legend of the man-beast has been around forever, known in many countries and by many names: as Yeti, the abominable snowman; as one of the Mound People; as Sasquatch, a name that comes from an ancient tribal language in British Columbia; and as Bigfoot. Information compiled from thousands of reputed sightings in North America has been organized into a composite description. Bigfoot is typically described as standing 7 to 12 feet tall and as weighing 250 to 400 pounds. Experts on the subject maintain that such creatures live in family groups in North America, and that an average family group consists of 8 members. Bigfoot is nocturnal, lives in caves, and has enhanced night vision, smell, and hearing. You will be relieved to know that the California Sasquatch is a vegetarian, while in the southern part of the United States, Bigfoot is a carnivore. This creature swims well, runs fast, is painfully shy—although curious—and apparently smells really, really bad.

The search for Sasquatch has gone high-tech in recent years, with investigators carrying tape recorders, motion detectors, infrared cameras, and night scopes into the wild. Sharing information on the Internet has enabled searchers to pursue patterns and similarities among the reported encounters. In spite of the footprints, sightings, blurry photographs, and tapes, however, no verifiable physical evidence of Sasquatch has been found. A California Department of Fish and Game spokesperson in Redding declared that while Bigfoot sightings do occur in Trinity County, the agency probably won't investigate the most recent ones. "We don't have a management plan for Bigfoot," he explained.

you might prefer one of the four quieter cabins at the edge of the woods, a good place to watch wildlife. The lodge's guest rooms and each of the cabins have their own sinks and toilets, but showers are in a shared facility. If you want a private bathroom, inquire about the two-room duplex (rented to a minimum of four people) or one of the six rooms in the bungalows at the edge of the meadow. One of the ranch's star attractions is the thermal swimming pool, fed by a natural hot spring and open 24 hours a day. Breakfast, lunch, and dinner (included in the price of lodging) are better than what you might expect in a national park. The breakfast buffet includes fresh fruit, hot and cold cereals, buttermilk pancakes, and excellent sausages. For lunch you can eat at the buffet or order a sack lunch. Dinner is a fancier affair. The popular Wednesday-night cookouts feature barbecued steak and chicken, plus pasta and an assortment of salads. *$$$$; DIS, MC, V; checks OK; closed mid-Oct–mid-June, depending on weather conditions; www.drakesbed.com; about 17 miles north of Chester, call for directions.* ♿

Burney/Fall River Mills

LODGINGS

Clearwater Lodge on the Pit River / ★★★★

24500 PIT ONE POWERHOUSE RD, FALL RIVER MILLS; 888/600-5451 OR 530/336-5005

Several years ago this unique fly-fishing getaway moved several miles east to expanded and spiffier quarters. The new digs are at a former Pacific Gas & Electric compound next to the Pit River. The lodge is in a magnificent 1921 Arts and Crafts building, built of lava rock, stained glass and old-growth fir. It has been lovingly restored and updated with modern amenities. Guests are pampered with the only gourmet cooking for miles around, and enjoy leisure activities centered on some of the West's most beautiful and legendary trout streams like Hat Creek, the Fall and McCloud Rivers, and the nearby Pit. Fly-fishing is paramount here, with lessons for beginners and excursions to prime spots for seasoned anglers. For those few who don't want to fish there is river rafting, golf, horseback riding, mountain biking, and bird-watching (bald eagles and ospreys abound). There are a variety of plans available, starting at single lodging including meals for $175 a day. *$$$$; AE, MC, V; checks OK; open late Apr–mid-Nov; www.clearwaterlodge.com; ¼ mile south of CA 299 between Burney and Fall River Mills at PG&E's Pit River Powerhouse One.* ♿

Alturas

RESTAURANTS

Nipa's California Cuisine / ★

1001 N MAIN ST, ALTURAS; 530/233-2520

You won't find seared tuna in loquat sauce here. Nipa's version of California cuisine is actually spicy Thai food—and it's the finest fare of any kind in Modoc County. Located in an old drive-in burger joint that's been transformed into a contemporary café decorated with Thai artifacts, Nipa's serves such classic favorites as tom yum kung, a fragrant soup packed with prawns and mushrooms; pad thai, the satisfying pan-fried-noodle dish with prawns, chicken, egg, bean sprouts, green onions, and a sprinkling of ground peanuts; and a spicy, succulent red curry made with prawns, chicken, or beef simmered in coconut milk. Wash it all down with a deliciously sweet Thai iced tea. *$; MC, V; local checks only; lunch, dinner every day; beer and wine; no reservations; 1 block south of Hwys 299 and 395.*

Cedarville

North of Alturas, Highway 299 turns east and crosses the narrow, little-known, and seldom-visited Warner Mountains, where antelope often graze. Then the highway descends into the aptly named Surprise Valley, a onetime oasis for Overland Trail emigrants after the rigors of the Nevada desert, and Cedarville, a little old-fashioned town of a bygone time. As one local poet put it, Cedarville is "where the pavement ends, and the West begins."

Isolated by the Warner Mountains on one side and the western edge of the Great Basin on the other, Cedarville attracts an interesting mix of travelers: in addition to the usual hunters, fly-fishers, history buffs, and bird- and wildlife watchers, you'll find paleontologists and paleobiologists drawn to the plentiful animal and plant fossils found in this part of the Great Basin. Whatever lured you here, there are a lot of hot springs to help rejuvenate those weary bones after a day of exploring.

RESTAURANTS

Country Hearth Restaurant & Bakery / ★☆

551 MAIN ST, CEDARVILLE; 530/279-2280

The Country Hearth should be called the Country Heart for all the love owner Janet Irene puts into the meals served in her homey, pine-paneled dining room with its wood-burning stove. Bite into her good hamburgers served on toasted, fresh-baked rolls, or try the nightly special "country-cooked meal," which might feature pork chops or chicken-fried steak. Irene makes all the breads, rolls, pastries, and desserts, which are included in the price of dinner. You can also purchase baked goods for the trip home. *$; MC, V; no checks; breakfast, lunch, dinner every day; beer and wine; reservations recommended; south of Hwy 299.*

Chester

LODGINGS

The Bidwell House Bed and Breakfast Inn / ★★★

1 MAIN ST, CHESTER; 530/258-3338

The beautifully restored Bidwell House, fronted by a yard of aspens and cottonwoods, looks out over mountain meadows and the broad expanse of Lake

Almanor. The former home of Chico pioneer John Bidwell, it opened as a B and B in 1991. The 14 guest rooms are furnished with antiques and a few have wood-burning stoves; most have private baths, and seven units are equipped with Jacuzzi tubs. A cottage that sleeps up to six makes an ideal family retreat. Be sure to show the kids the Bidwell House's pretty, enclosed downstairs porch fancied up with wicker furniture, a Gibson Girl sketchbook, and antique doll buggies and tricycles. The inn's manager is a creative pastry chef, so guests are treated to delicious breakfast dishes such as fresh-fruit crepes washed down with frothy frappés, served in the airy dining room. If you're around in September, don't miss the popular cowboy poetry reading—it's a hoot. *$$–$$$; MC, V; checks OK; www.bidwellhouse.com; east end of town.*

Lake Almanor

RESTAURANTS

Wilson's Camp Prattville & Carol's Cafe / ★

2932 ALMANOR DR W, LAKE ALMANOR; 530/259-2464

Certainly the oldest and funkiest place at Lake Almanor, Camp Prattville has been around since 1928, when it was founded by Frank and Nettie Wilson. Daughter-in-law Carol Wilson Franchetti, along with her partner, Ken Wilson (one of four generations of Wilsons who have worked here), now runs the restaurant, which offers breakfast, lunch, and dinner in a small dining room crowded with knickknacks. The menu is prodigious, and breakfasts are served until 1pm. Sandwiches and French fries are among the better offerings, but save room for dessert, especially the terrific bread pudding with applejack hard sauce and the house-made pies with delicate, flaky crusts. When the weather is warm, eat lunch at one of the picnic tables on the deck overlooking the lake. *$; MC, V; checks OK; breakfast, lunch, dinner every day (closed mid-Oct–Apr); beer and wine; reservations recommended; www.camp-prattville.com; on the lake's west shore.*

LODGINGS

Dorado Inn / ★★

4379 HWY 147, LAKE ALMANOR; 530/284-7790

What sets the Dorado apart from the other resorts along Lake Almanor's commercialized east shore are the spectacular Mount Lassen and lake views from the decks outside the cottages. All of the Dorado's seven cabins (a combination of two-bedroom cottages and one-room units) are near the water's edge, and they have fully equipped kitchens, private bathrooms, electric heat, and wood-burning stoves. In addition to soaking in the view, most visitors spend their time sunbathing and lounging lakeside, boating, fishing, swimming, or playing badminton or basketball. *$$; no credit cards; checks OK; open Apr–Dec; www.doradoinn.com; on the lake's east shore.* ♿

Mill Creek

RESTAURANTS

St. Bernard Lodge / ★★

44801 HWY 36E, MILL CREEK; 530/258-3382

The St. Bernard Lodge was constructed in 1912 to house workers building the dam at Big Meadows (now known as Lake Almanor), and in 1929 it was picked up and moved to its present location, where it started a new life as a public lodge. Although there are seven comfortable rooms upstairs, most Mill Creek residents come here for the famous St. Bernard Burgers: a three-quarter-pound patty of lean chuck served on a fresh-baked bun (all breads are baked on-site). You can also sink your teeth into prime rib, steak, fried chicken, and fried or sautéed fish. Before your meal, sip a cocktail in the antique bar with painted glass windows; afterward, head outside for a stroll along the deck and around the trout pond. *$$–$$$; AE, DIS, MC, V; checks OK; breakfast, lunch Sat–Sun, dinner Thurs–Mon; full bar; reservations required; www.stbernardlodge.com; on the south side of Hwy 36, 10 miles west of Chester.*

LODGINGS

Mill Creek Resort / ★★

1 HWY 172, MILL CREEK; 530/595-4449

If it's peace and solitude you're after, look no further. The Mill Creek Resort makes you feel as though you've stepped back in time to a quieter, gentler, and infinitely more affordable era (somewhere around 1925). A picture-postcard general store and coffee shop serve as the resort's center, and nine housekeeping cabins are rented on a daily or weekly basis. The units are clean and homey, with vintage '30s and '40s furniture. Seclusion is one of the main charms of the place, though it's not far from cross-country skiing trails and Lassen Volcanic National Park. Pets are welcome. *$; no credit cards; checks OK; www.millcreekresort.net; 3 miles south of Hwy 36.* ♿

SIERRA NEVADA

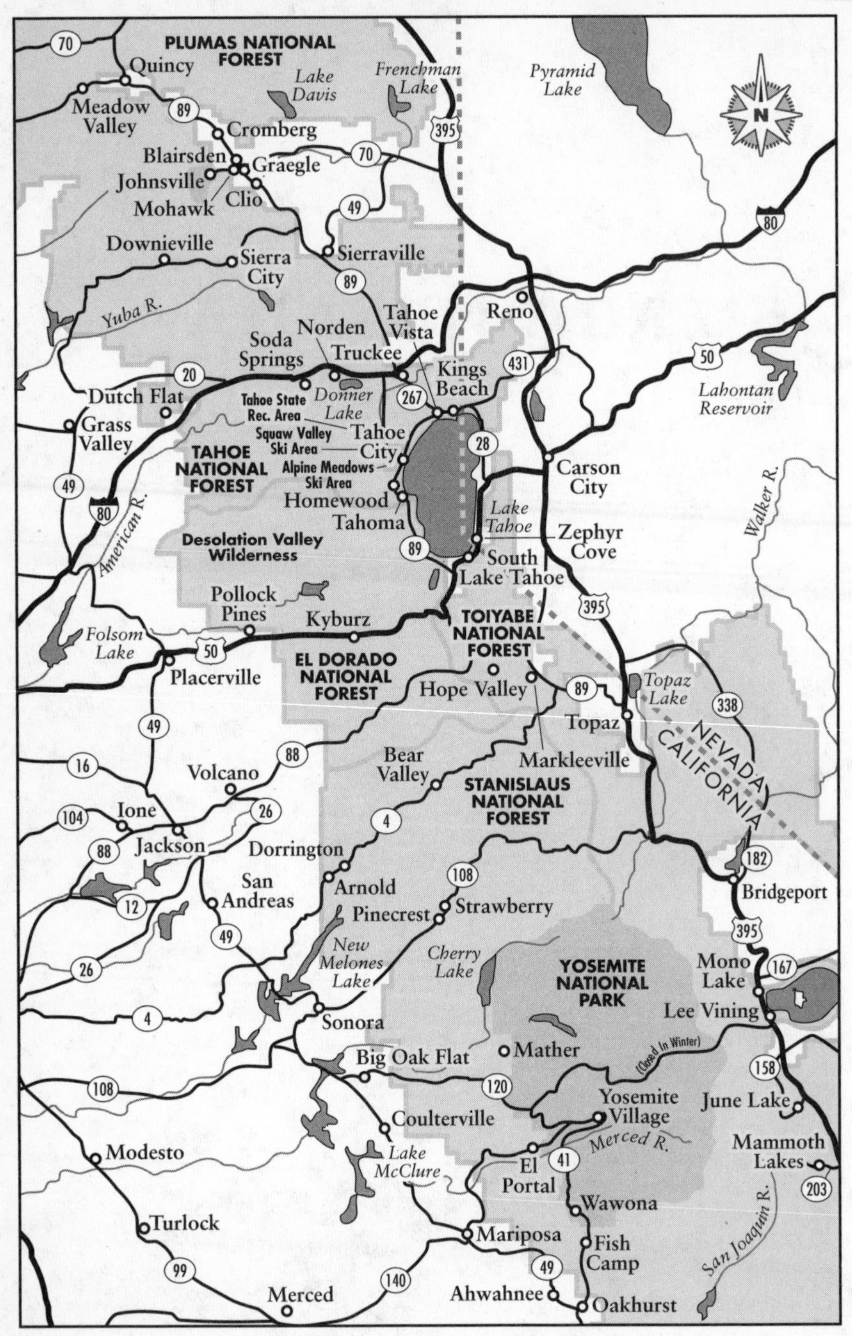
PLUMAS NATIONAL FOREST
Quincy
Meadow Valley
Lake Davis
Frenchman Lake
Pyramid Lake
Cromberg
Blairsden
Graeagle
Johnsville
Clio
Mohawk
Downieville
Sierra City
Sierraville
Yuba R.
Reno
Tahoe Vista
Norden
Soda Springs
Truckee
Kings Beach
Lahontan Reservoir
Dutch Flat
Tahoe State Rec. Area
Donner Lake
Grass Valley
Squaw Valley Ski Area
Tahoe City
TAHOE NATIONAL FOREST
Alpine Meadows Ski Area
Carson City
Homewood
Tahoma
Lake Tahoe
Zephyr Cove
Walker R.
American R.
Desolation Valley Wilderness
South Lake Tahoe
Pollock Pines
Kyburz
TOIYABE NATIONAL FOREST
Folsom Lake
Placerville
EL DORADO NATIONAL FOREST
Hope Valley
Topaz Lake
Topaz
NEVADA
CALIFORNIA
Volcano
Bear Valley
Markleeville
STANISLAUS NATIONAL FOREST
Ione
Jackson
Dorrington
San Andreas
Arnold
Pinecrest
Strawberry
Bridgeport
New Melones Lake
Cherry Lake
YOSEMITE NATIONAL PARK
Mono Lake
Lee Vining
Sonora
Mather
Big Oak Flat
(Closed In Winter)
Coulterville
Yosemite Village
June Lake
Merced R.
Modesto
Lake McClure
El Portal
Mammoth Lakes
Wawona
Turlock
Mariposa
Fish Camp
San Joaquin R.
Merced
Ahwahnee
Oakhurst
70
89
395
49
80
20
267
431
50
28
16
88
26
104
4
12
108
338
182
167
158
120
41
203
99
140

SIERRA NEVADA

The Sierra Nevada is home to two of the state's most popular destinations—Lake Tahoe and Yosemite. Keep in mind, however, that this mountain range is massive and offers dozens of other vacation destinations that are almost as gorgeous and far less crowded. If you have your heart set on the Lake or the Valley, remember, lots of other folks do, too.

In fact, Lake Tahoe and Yosemite are gradually being loved to death, although ambitious steps have long been discussed to slow the environmental damage to two of the most beautiful places on earth. Preservation of Lake Tahoe's cobalt-blue water and crisp mountain air has become a priority for both the community and the state. A plan to drastically cut back the number of cars allowed in Yosemite Valley (using low-polluting or zero-emission motor coaches from outlying parking lots) is still being argued over and is subject to change with each shift in prevailing political fortunes. In any case, try to plan your visit to either area for the spring or fall, when there are far fewer cars and people.

If you're after a more peaceful, but not primitive, communion with nature, take a peek at the Lakes Basin Area (about an hour's drive north of Truckee). This remote region has an assortment of lakeside lodges so sweetly simple and pleasant you'll remember them forever. On the eastern side of the Sierra Nevada, the haunting Mono Lake, a 60-square-mile desert salt lake with strangely beautiful limestone tufa spires, is like nothing you've ever seen before. Nearby Bodie is the most eerily authentic ghost town in California, kept in a state of "arrested decay" by park rangers. The Mammoth Lakes area, farther south, offers every kind of snow sport in winter, plus hiking, biking, and world-famous fishing in summer. It also has the Devils Postpile National Monument, 60-foot-tall rock columns formed 100,000 years ago from molten lava. And if you're feeling frisky, the 211-mile John Muir Trail, which connects Yosemite with Kings Canyon and Sequoia national parks, is accessible here.

ACCESS AND INFORMATION

The 400-mile-long Sierra Nevada mountain range begins northwest of Quincy with 6,500-foot peaks, eventually rising to 14,494 feet at Mount Whitney, the highest summit in the continental United States. From there, going south, they decrease in height, ending in the desert near the town of Mojave.

The **HIGHWAY SYSTEM** through the Sierra looks like a ladder with two north-south, all-weather highways forming the legs: US 99 in the Central Valley just west of the foothills, and in the high desert to the east of the Sierra escarpment, US 395, one of the West's most beautiful scenic drives. The rungs are a series of east-west roads—highways in the north and increasingly narrow and twisting (though gorgeous) lanes as you progress south: **HIGHWAY 70**, from Oroville to Quincy; **HIGHWAY 49**, from Grass Valley to Sierraville; **INTERSTATE 80**, from Sacramento to Truckee and Reno; **US 50**, from Sacramento to South Lake Tahoe and Carson City; **HIGHWAY 88**, from Jackson to Kirkwood and the Hope Valley; **HIGHWAY 4**, from Stockton to Angels Camp to Markleeville; **HIGHWAY 108**, from Modesto to Sonora to just north of Bridgeport; and **HIGHWAY 120**, from Manteca to Groveland. Some are closed in winter.

FRESNO–YOSEMITE INTERNATIONAL AIRPORT (FYI) (559/621-4500; www.flyfresno.org) is approximately 65 miles from Yosemite and the southern Sierra. **MAMMOTH AIRPORT (MMH)** is served by Mammoth Air Charter (888/934-4279). **RENO/TAHOE INTERNATIONAL AIRPORT (RNO)** (775/328-6400 www.renoairport.com) is approximately 45 miles from Lake Tahoe and 175 miles from Mammoth and the eastern Sierra. **SACRAMENTO INTERNATIONAL AIRPORT (SMF)** (www.sacairports.org/int) is approximately 100 miles from Lake Tahoe and the northern and central Sierra. The **AMTRAK** (800/USA-RAIL; www.amtrak.com) **CALIFORNIA ZEPHYR** from San Francisco to Chicago stops at Truckee, with Amtrak bus service to South Lake Tahoe; the **SAN JOAQUIN TRAIN** from Oakland to Bakersfield stops at Merced, with Amtrak bus service to Yosemite.

GREYHOUND (800/231-2222; www.greyhound.com) has daily service from Sacramento to Lake Tahoe and Reno, and from Sacramento to Truckee and Reno. **VIA ADVENTURES** (800/VIA-LINE; www.via-adventures.com) has four buses each day from Merced to Yosemite. The South Shore Chamber of Commerce's **TAHOE-CASINO EXPRESS** (866/89-TAHOE) makes 11 round-trips each day between Reno and South Lake Tahoe casinos. **EASTERN SIERRA TRANSIT AUTHORITY** (800/922-1930; www.easternsierratransitauthority.com) offers bus/van service along Highway 395 each day between Reno, Mammoth, Bishop, Lone Pine, and Ridgecrest.

YARTS (877/98-YARTS; www.yarts.com), the Yosemite Area Regional Transportation System, began running regional transit buses in 2000. YARTS offers an affordable, dependable alternative to travelers who would rather ride a bus from outlying communities into Yosemite Valley than drive their vehicles into Yosemite and park. It provides service to and from Mariposa, Merced, and Mono counties.

Visitor information is available from a variety of locations: **JUNE LAKE CHAMBER OF COMMERCE** (760/648-7584; www.junelakeloop.org), **LAKE TAHOE CENTRAL RESERVATIONS** (888/434-1262; www.gotahoenorth.com), **LAKE TAHOE VISITORS AUTHORITY** (800/AT-TAHOE or 775/588-5900; www.bluelaketahoe.com), **LEE VINING CHAMBER OF COMMERCE AND MONO LAKE VISITOR CENTER** (Hwy 395 and 3rd St, Lee Vining; 760/647-6629; www.leevining.com), **MARIPOSA COUNTY VISITORS BUREAU** (866/HALFDOME or 209/966-7081; www.homeofyosemite.com), **TUOLUMNE COUNTY VISITORS BUREAU** (800/446-1333 or 209/533-4420; www.thegreatunfenced.com), and **YOSEMITE AREA TRAVEL INFORMATION** (www.yosemite.com).

The Lake Tahoe region has dozens of other Web sites that are loaded with information, including www.skilaketahoe.com, www.laketahoeconcierge.com, www.virtualtahoe.com, www.tahoereservations.com, www.tahoesbest.com, and www.tahoevacationguide.com.

Lake Tahoe Area

Frontiersman Kit Carson was guiding General John Frémont's expedition across the Sierra Nevada in 1844 when he stumbled on an immense, deep blue body of water, a lake so vast the native Washoe Indians called it *tahoe* (big lake). Carson was the first white man to see Tahoe, North America's largest alpine lake and the eighth deepest in the world (its deepest point is at 1,685 feet). If completely drained, Tahoe would cover the entire state of California with 14 inches of water.

Despite all its great ski resorts, Tahoe is actually most crowded in the summer, when thousands flock here to cool off at the lake (although what constitutes public shoreline versus private waterfront is still a matter of heated debate between home owners and county supervisors). Warm-weather activities abound: boating, waterskiing, bicycling, hiking, rock climbing, hot-air ballooning, horseback riding . . . you name it. Unfortunately, the area pays dearly for its myriad attractions in the form of tremendous traffic jams, water and air pollution, and a plethora of fast-food joints and condos erected before tough building restrictions were imposed. Despite these glaring scars, Lake Tahoe remains one of the premier outdoor playgrounds of the West, dazzling visitors with its soaring Sierra peaks and twinkling azure waters.

For a grand introduction to the area, take a leisurely 72-mile drive around the lake itself. **HIGHWAYS 50**, **89**, and **28** hug the shore, providing gorgeous views from the car. Several sights merit pulling over for a closer look, so be prepared to stop and haul out your camera (or camcorder) along the way. Topping the not-to-be-missed list are **EMERALD BAY** (off Hwy 89), one of the most photographed sights in the world; **CAVE ROCK TUNNEL**, the 200-foot-long granite tunnel along Highway 50 on the East Shore; and **SAND HARBOR STATE PARK** (off Hwy 28, on the East Shore), one of the lake's prettiest—and least visited—beaches. Allow about three hours to loop around the lake, or longer if you're traveling on a summer weekend, on a holiday, or when the road is covered with snow.

Dutch Flat

RESTAURANTS

Monte Vista Inn / ★

OFF I-80, DUTCH FLAT; 530/389-2333

For about 60 years, the Monte Vista has been a roadhouse catering to locals—and to travelers lucky enough to find it. The comfortable inn is built of logs and indigenous stone; the kitchen prepares generous portions of California cuisine, ranging from mesquite-grilled steaks to scampi sautéed with fresh mushrooms and garlic, and the freshly baked pies taste as good as they look. Live music gets the bar hopping on the weekends. *$$; MC, V; local checks only; dinner every day; full bar; reservations recommended; www.montevistainn.com; at the Dutch Flat exit, 9 miles east of Colfax.* ♿

Soda Springs

RESTAURANTS

Engadine Cafe / ★★★

RAINBOW RD (ROYAL GORGE'S RAINBOW LODGE), SODA SPRINGS; 530/426-3661

Within Royal Gorge's Rainbow Lodge (see review) is the charming Engadine Cafe. Breakfasts are for folks with let's-scale-a-mountain appetites and feature a wide range of choices, from a belly-packing stack of whole wheat pancakes to three-egg omelets bursting with smoked ham, mushrooms, scallions, and Swiss cheese. Lunches are simple and satisfying and might include pasta with fresh eggplant, tomato, and mushroom sauce or a juicy burger with all the fixin's. In the evenings the kitchen turns out an eclectic mix of terrific fare, such as Swiss fondue for two and several daily seafood specials. The back deck looks out over the garden into the pines and is great for summer dining. *$$; MC, V; no checks; breakfast, lunch, dinner every day; full bar; reservations recommended; www.royalgorge.com; take Rainbow Rd exit off I-80S and drive west.* ♿

LODGINGS

Ice Lakes Lodge / ★★

1111 SODA SPRINGS ROAD, SODA SPRINGS; 530/426-3871

If you want to avoid the ubiquitous Tahoe traffic and droves of holiday tourists, consider a stay at the Ice Lakes Lodge. Few people know that this beautiful lakeside lodge even exists. The 26 guest rooms all have private baths, queen- or king-size beds, telephones, and TVs. The upper-level rooms offer private decks (book these rooms in the winter), while the ground-floor rooms have petite porches and instant access to the small, sandy beach (summer only). The lake is ideal for swimming, sailing, and canoeing, and safe for small kids to play in. The lodge's restaurant serves breakfast, lunch, and dinner daily and has a bar and lounge that overlook the lake. They'll even make box lunches for your outdoor adventures—the forest is right across the street, and the Sugar Bowl ski resort is only four minutes away via shuttle. *$$; AE, DIS, MC, V; local checks only; www.icelakeslodge.com; take Donner Pass Rd exit off I-80, then drive 4 miles south on Soda Springs Rd.* ♿

Royal Gorge's Rainbow Lodge and Wilderness Lodge / ★★

RAINBOW RD, SODA SPRINGS; 800/666-3871, 530/426-3661, OR 800/500-3871 (OUTSIDE NORTHERN CALIFORNIA ONLY)

In 1922, the Rainbow Lodge was built of hand-hewn timbers and local granite at a bend in the Yuba River. Each of the lodge's 32 rooms comes with a private bath, a shower and sink, or just a sink (with a bath down the hall). Rooms 12, 14, 23, and 24 overlook the river. Within the lodge is the very pleasant Engadine Cafe (see review). Breakfast is included with a night's stay. The Rainbow Lodge also offers cross-country skiers accommodations in its Wilderness Lodge, a handsome structure that's tucked away in a remote part of the cross-country course and accessed via an open sleigh pulled by a snowcat. The private guest rooms are equipped with bunks or double beds. *$$–$$$; MC, V; no checks; main lodge open year-round, Wilderness Lodge open during ski season only; www.royalgorge.com; take Rainbow Rd exit off I-80S and drive west.* ♿

Norden

LODGINGS

Clair Tappaan Lodge / ★

19940 DONNER PASS RD, NORDEN; 800/679-6775 OR 530/426-3632

Hardy souls who want to meet new people, limit expenses, and don't mind a few housekeeping tasks should hike on in to this massive structure near the Donner Summit; guests carry their own bedding and luggage 100 yards uphill from the road. Dorm-style rooms vary from two-person cubicles to family bunk rooms and a men's and women's dorm (the romantically inclined should note that most beds are single bunk beds). The living room is warmed by a fireplace, and a library, hot tub, and resident masseuse help you relax. Meals are included, and you're expected to help with basic chores. Guests get hot breakfasts and sack lunches to take skiing or hiking (slopes and trails are close by, and the area receives the highest average snowfall in the Sierra Nevada). The dinners here are casual, healthy, and filling affairs served family-style. *$; MC, V; checks OK; www.sierraclub.org/outings/lodges; from I-80, take the Soda Springs/Norden exit, then drive 2.4 miles east on Donner Pass Rd.*

Donner Summit

A whirl of white in the winter, the Donner region was named after the 89 members of the ill-fated Donner party, who journeyed by wagon train to the area in October 1846. They had come from the Midwest and were bound for the West Coast but were trapped here by an early winter storm. The **EMIGRANT TRAIL MUSEUM** in **DONNER MEMORIAL STATE PARK** (12593 Donner Pass Rd, south of I-80; 530/582-7892 for general park information, 800/444-7275 for camping reservations) tells the group's grim story of starvation, cannibalism, and—for some members—survival. Nowadays the snow-blanketed Donner region is a major downhill and cross-country ski destination in the winter, and in the summer the long fingers of its sparkling azure lake are dotted with sailboats, dwarfed by the imposing forested slopes and granite palisades. Donner Lake is a great fishing and boating retreat (a public boat ramp is on the west side), and a public beach rims the east end of the lake. The 350-acre state park, adjacent to the lake, also offers campsites, picnic tables, and hiking trails.

SIERRA NEVADA THREE-DAY TOUR

Note: This itinerary is possible only from early summer to fall, when the High Sierra mountain passes are snow-free and open to traffic. It begins in Oakhurst in the foothills just south of Yosemite.

DAY ONE: *Into the woods.* Arrive the night before and check in at **CHÂTEAU DU SUREAU** (see review in the lodging section of Oakhurst), one of the most elegant inns in the West. Have dinner and breakfast at the château's four-star restaurant to fuel up for the mountaineering ahead. On the way to Yosemite, take a short detour to see the **MARIPOSA GROVE** of sequoias, including one of the world's largest trees, the **GRIZZLY GIANT**. Entering **YOSEMITE NATIONAL PARK** by the southern entrance, you'll see **TUNNEL VIEW**, one of the best scenic views of the park and the subject of a famous Ansel Adams photograph. Once you're in the valley, stop at the visitor center and take the two-hour open-air tram tour, or grab a map, rent bikes, and conduct your own tour. And don't worry if you don't see everything, because once you've been here, you're hooked; you'll return again and again. Finish your tour early enough to check in to your room at the majestic **AHWAHNEE HOTEL** and have a drink in the Great Lounge before dinner in the hotel's legendary dining room.

DAY TWO: *Summits and spooks.* Enjoy a big breakfast at the Ahwahnee, then cross the High Sierra on Highway 120. The road is barely two lanes, but the scenery is as breathtaking as the altitude, so take your time and enjoy the ride. Before you reach the 9,945-foot summit at **TIOGA PASS** (the highest motor

LODGINGS

Loch Leven Lodge / ★

13855 DONNER PASS RD, DONNER LAKE; 530/587-3773 OR 877/663-6637

If you want to get away from the crowds but would like easy access to Tahoe's restaurants and shops, this quiet lodge has been satisfying guests for more than 50 years. Each of its eight small units faces beautiful Donner Lake, and all but one have kitchens. You can bask in the sun on the 5,000-square-foot deck or head over to the putting green (clubs and balls are provided). The lodge also has picnic tables, lawn and fishing chairs, a barbecue, a spa, and a rowboat. Lower-level rooms offer the best lake views, although passersby occasionally walk past the exposed windows. If you're traveling with the gang, reserve the two-level town house that sleeps eight and has a fully equipped kitchen. *$$; MC, V; checks OK; www.lochlevenlodge.com; 1½ miles from I-80 (take the Donner Lake exit and turn left on Donner Pass Rd).*

vehicle pass in California), stop and stretch your legs at beautiful **TUOLUMNE MEADOWS**, with the Tuolumne River on one side and soaring granite peaks on the other. Then drop down some 3,000 feet to Highway 395, and just north of the town of Lee Vining, stop at the **MONO BASIN SCENIC VISITORS CENTER** to get the scoop on the eerie lake and its otherworldly tufa towers of calcium. Next, take the lonely 12-mile detour to the magical mining town of **BODIE**. You'll swear this road doesn't go anywhere, but then you go over a rise and are transported back in time to 1920. From here it's north on Highway 395 to Highway 89, over the Monitor Pass, and on to Markleeville for dinner at the small Italian restaurant **VILLA GIGLI**. After dinner it's a short trip to Hope Valley and a night in one of the rustic cabins at **SORENSEN'S RESORT**. Quite a change from the luxury of the Ahwanee and du Sureau, but just right for this side of the Sierra.

DAY THREE: *By the big, blue water*. Enjoy your country breakfast at Sorensen's, because you're about to leave the simple, timeless charm of the remote High Sierra and head 15 miles north over the Luther Pass for the glitz, glamour, and gambling of **SOUTH LAKE TAHOE**. Drop your bags off at the **BLACK BEAR INN**, then take the two-hour lake cruise aboard the **TAHOE QUEEN**, an authentic Mississippi stern-wheeler. Pick up a picnic lunch at **SPROUTS**, then head across the state line to **ZEPHYR COVE** to indulge in some quality beach time on the beautiful golden sands. As the sun sets, enjoy a romantic Italian dinner at **CAFÉ FIORE** and after dinner head for the tables or slot machines at one of South Lake's many casinos (Harrah's, MontBleu, etc.) to try your luck.

Truckee

This popular little city packed with appealing shops, restaurants, and some terrific bed-and-breakfast inns started out in the mid-1800s as a railroad-lumber town with the construction of the first transcontinental railroad over Donner Summit. The settlement's transformation from a dirty, run-down, one-horse town to a bustling city began in the 1970s. Today visitors arrive by car, bus, and the eastbound or westbound Amtrak passenger trains that stop at the yellow depot. The notable **BOOKSHELF AT HOOLIGAN ROCKS** (11310 Donner Pass Rd, at the west end of the Safeway shopping center; 530/582-0515 or 800/959-5083) is one of the Sierra Nevada's best bookstores (it's named after a nearby outcropping of rocks where miscreants were once tarred and feathered). The Bookshelf also has branches in Quincy (373 W Main St; 530/283-2665) and Tahoe City (in the Boatworks Mall; 530/581-1900). In the summer, popular Truckee attractions include the **CANNIBAL CAR CRUISE** in July, the **FOURTH OF JULY PARADE**, and the **TRUCKEE CHAMPIONSHIP RODEO** in August. The **TRUCKEE RIVER REGIONAL PARK**

(½ mile south of town on Hwy 267) has softball diamonds, picnic tables, tennis courts, an 18-hole disk golf course, and an outdoor amphitheater offering music programs and wedding rentals throughout the summer.

In December, when snow blankets the town and bright little white lights twinkle in the windows of the century-old facades along **COMMERCIAL ROW**, Truckee truly looks like a picture from a fairy tale. All winter long the town swarms with skiers taking advantage of its proximity to many first-rate alpine and cross-country ski areas. Others brave the freezing temperatures to engage in the 10-day winter carnival called **SNOWFEST IN MARCH** or take a ride over the river and through the woods in a sleigh drawn by Clydesdales or Percherons. For more information, contact the **TRUCKEE CHAMBER OF COMMERCE** (530/587-2757; www.truckee.com).

RESTAURANTS

Cottonwood Restaurant & Bar / ★★

10142 RUE HILLTOP, TRUCKEE; 530/587-5711

The Cottonwood Restaurant stands high on a hill, affording a great view of Truckee's bright lights from the spacious dining room and deck (if it's warm, dining on the deck is a must). The eclectic seasonal menu ranges from Southwestern to Creole to Mediterranean fare. Begin the evening by sharing the garlic-slathered whole-leaf Caesar salad meant to be eaten with your fingers—it's one of the best dishes on the menu. Entrées might include a braised free-range rabbit cassoulet with andouille sausage and white beans or a seafood stew of shellfish, prawns, scallops, and boudin sausage in a saffron-tomato broth served over linguine. If available, the fresh berry-apple crisp à la mode makes a sweet finale. Local musicians often entertain guests Thursday through Saturday nights. *$$; DIS, MC, V; checks OK; dinner every day; full bar; reservations recommended; www.cottonwoodrestaurant.com; above town, right off Hwy 267 at Hilltop Lodge, just beyond the railroad tracks.*

Dragonfly / ★★★

10118 DONNER PASS RD, TRUCKEE; 530/587-0557

The talented Billy McCullough pleased the local epicureans by opening this small Old Town Truckee restaurant in 2001. His Asian-California cuisine is an eclectic blend of Thai, Japanese, Indian, and Malaysian influences—quite the dining adventure. A typical dinner may start with Thai-style seared sea scallops with rice, vermicelli noodle salad, and red curry saté sauce. The main entrée may be an Asian noodle bowl with Australian lobster tail, prawn, smoked chicken, andouille, mussels, udon noodles, snap peas, and yellow Thai curry broth. (Truckee, you've come a long way, my friend.) Even the wine list is refreshingly diverse. McCullough generously shares his recipes, so be sure to ask him if you're inclined. *$$; DIS, MC, V; local checks only; lunch, dinner every day; beer and wine; reservations recommended; www.dragonflycuisine.com; downtown.*

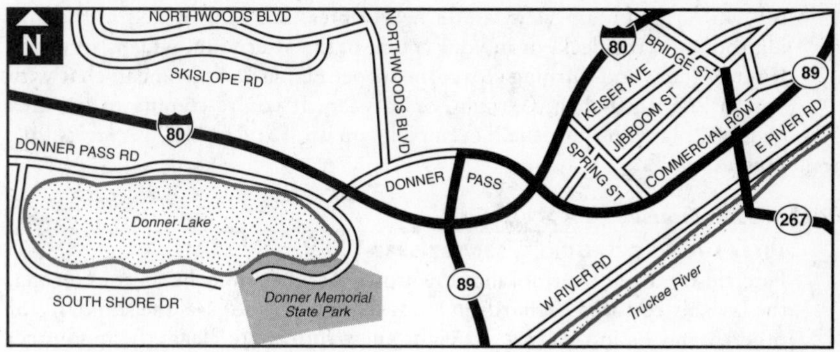

Truckee

Moody's Bistro & Lounge / ★★★

10007 BRIDGE ST (THE TRUCKEE HOTEL), TRUCKEE; 530/587-8688

The art deco–Ella Fitzgerald ambience of Moody's once inspired Paul McCartney to sit down at the piano and sing a few tunes for the stunned staff and patrons. It was an understandable urge considering the atmosphere: jazz combos in full swing and the bartenders pouring perfect Manhattans. The menu is equally hip, with choices ranging from effete (seared Sonoma foie gras with Bing cherry compote and port-balsamic syrup) to meat-and-potatoes ("Big Ass" all-natural Salmon Creek Farms pork chops served with peach sauce, potato purée, and a crispy salad). If there aren't any superstars on stage, request a seat at the open-air patio, and be sure to arrive a bit early for a predinner cocktail. *$$; AE, DC, DIS, MC, V; local checks only; lunch, dinner every day, brunch Sat–Sun; full bar; reservations recommended; www.moodysbistro.com; at Donner Pass Rd, in the Truckee Hotel.*

Truckee Trattoria / ★

11310-1 DONNER PASS RD, TRUCKEE; 530/582-1266

Conveniently located right off Interstate 80 within the Gateway Plaza, this popular and casual Italian café focuses primarily on pastas and roasted meats. Try the fettuccine with tender strips of chicken and broccoli in a garlic cream sauce, and polish the meal off with gelato, tiramisu, biscotti, or strawberry napoleon. Then hit the road again, well fed and ready for bed. *$–$$; DIS, MC, V; checks OK; dinner Wed–Mon; beer and wine; reservations recommended; at the west end of the Safeway shopping center.* ♿

LODGINGS

Hania's Bed & Breakfast Inn / ★★

10098 HIGH ST, TRUCKEE; 530/582-5775 OR 888/600-3735

Built in 1884, this pretty Victorian bed-and-breakfast has guest rooms decorated in Southwestern style. All the rooms have queen-size beds with down comforters, private baths, and TVs with VCRs. There's a year-round hot tub with a mountain view, and a hearty breakfast is provided in the dining room, on the deck, or in your room. In the afternoon, wine is served in front of the wood-burning stove. Innkeeper Hania Davidson can chat with you in English, Polish, German, or Russian. If you're coming to the area by train, plane, or bus, she'll even pick you up. *$$; AE, MC, V; checks OK; downtown.* ♿

Richardson House / ★★★

10154 HIGH ST, TRUCKEE; 530/587-5388

Perched on a hill overlooking downtown Truckee and the Sierra Nevada, the lavishly restored Richardson House (built in 1886) sets the standard for other B and Bs in the area. Its eight guest rooms are elegantly appointed; six have private bathrooms, and two adjoining suites share a bath. Some units have fireplaces, and Aunt Klara's Room offers every convenience for wheelchair-bound patrons. The vittles are first-rate, too. Soufflés, quiches, French toast, pancakes, hot cereal, and freshly baked scones are just some of the treats offered at the buffet breakfast. Guests are welcome to lounge in the parlor or spend time reclining on outdoor wicker furniture. Discount packages for skiers include lift tickets and bus transportation to nearby ski resorts. *$$–$$$; AE, DIS, MC, V; checks OK; www.richardsonhouse.com; at Spring St.* ♿

The Truckee Hotel / ★★

10007 BRIDGE ST, TRUCKEE; 800/659-6921

Built in 1873, this handsome establishment is one of the oldest operating hotels in the Sierra Nevada. There are 37 guest rooms with full-, queen-, or king-size beds, many with elaborately carved wooden headboards; 8 rooms have private baths and the other 29 have wash basins and share bathrooms. The various room configurations can accommodate one to five people, and the north-facing units at the back of the hotel are the quietest. Included in the rate is an expanded continental breakfast provided in the parlor, where late-afternoon tea is also served on weekends. Skiers will appreciate the ski racks and lockers. The hotel also houses Moody's Bistro & Lounge (see review). *$–$$; AE, MC, V; no checks; www.truckeehotel.com; at Donner Pass Rd.*

North Shore Lake Tahoe

Although the California–Nevada border basically bisects Lake Tahoe down the middle, leaving the west side in California and the east side in Nevada, the lake is more commonly referred to in terms of its north and south shores. The **SOUTH SHORE** area is the most populous and urban, where you'll hear all those slot machines ringing. If you'd rather steer clear of the one-armed bandits, head for the **NORTH SHORE**. There you'll find fewer casinos (and tourists) and more of everything else, including Tahoe's best alpine and cross-country ski resorts, first-rate restaurants, and luxurious lodgings. The best source for information about the

North Shore is the **NORTH LAKE TAHOE RESORT ASSOCIATION OR NORTH LAKE TAHOE VISITORS AND CONVENTION BUREAU** (530/583-3494 or 530/581-8703; www.tahoefun.org). This is also the place to call if you're having trouble finding a North Shore hotel room or campsite (a common problem during peak seasons) or need information on ski packages.

The hot summer weather brings a phenomenal array of lakeside activities, and many don't cost a dime. Day hikers should head for the trails next to the **TAYLOR CREEK VISITOR CENTER** (south shore of the lake, 5 miles south of Emerald Bay, just past Baldwin Beach; 530/543-2674). It's the starting point for several well-marked trails, ranging from an easy half-mile stroll to a 10-mile leg-burning trek. Serious mountain bikers shouldn't miss huffing up and down the famous 24-mile **FLUME TRAIL**, which provides fantastic views of the lake; the trailhead begins at **NEVADA STATE PARK AT SPOONER LAKE** on the lake's eastern shore. Casual and asphalt-only pedalers can vie with in-line skaters, joggers, and strollers for room on North Tahoe's 15-mile-long paved trail, which begins at **SUGAR PINE POINT STATE PARK** on the West Shore and stretches north along the lake to Dollar Point on the North Shore. There's also a 3½-mile paved trail that parallels the Truckee River and passes through Tahoe City; the trail starts at the turnoff to **ALPINE MEADOWS** ski resort on Highway 89. For the truly lazy (or crazy) rider, Northstar-at-Tahoe, Kirkwood, and Squaw Valley USA ski resorts offer miles of trails accessible by chairlift or cable car—simply let the lifts tote you and your bike up the mountains, then spend the day cruising (or careening, if you wish) down the slopes.

If you weren't able to pack all your recreational toys, **PORTER'S SKI & SPORT** (501 N Lake Blvd, Tahoe City; 530/583-2314; www.porterstahoe.com) has the best prices in town for outdoor rental equipment—everything from bikes to skates to rackets, as well as a full line of snow skis, water skis, and snowboards.

To try your luck at blackjack or craps, make the short drive to Nevada. Although the North Shore's casinos are more subdued and less glitzy than the South Shore's high-rolling high-rises, the dealers are still adept at taking your money. If you're a greenhorn, this is a good place to learn the ABCs of the games, especially during off-hours. North Shore casinos include the **TAHOE BILTMORE LODGE AND CASINO** (775/831-0660; www.tahoebiltmore.com); **CAL-NEVA RESORT, SPA, AND CASINO**, (800/225-6382; www.calnevaresort.com); **HYATT REGENCY LAKE TAHOE** (775/832-1234); and **CRYSTAL BAY CLUB CASINO** (775/833-6333; www.crystalbaycasino.com).

North Lake Tahoe also offers a few nocturnal alternatives to the dice and the slots, but nightlife definitely isn't the North Shore's best attribute. During ski season, the lounge of the **RIVER RANCH LODGE** (see review in the Lodging section of Alpine Meadows) has a raging après-ski scene, with ski bums from all over kicking back and chowing down on cheap hors d'oeuvres. There's usually live music nightly at **BULLWHACKER'S PUB**, a popular locals' hangout located at the Resort at Squaw Creek (see review in the Lodgings section of Squaw Valley).

Tahoe Vista

RESTAURANTS

Le Petit Pier / ★★★

7238 N LAKE BLVD, TAHOE VISTA; 530/546-4464

Le Petit Pier, with three intimate dining rooms and dazzling views of the lake, has been North Lake Tahoe's finest French restaurant for more than 30 years. The menu features such mouthwatering appetizers as escargots in Roquefort butter, and the exquisite entrées range from seafood to a superb rack of lamb. Also deservedly popular is the pheasant Souvaroff for two with foie gras and a rich demi-glace encrusted in puff pastry (but give the chef 24 hours notice). Le Petit Pier's wine list has won *Wine Spectator* magazine's Award of Excellence. When making a reservation, request a table by the window, and be sure to arrive before sunset—you don't want to miss this view. *$$$; AE, DC, DIS, MC, V; local checks only; dinner Wed–Mon; full bar; reservations recommended; on Hwy 28 at the west end of town.* ♿

LODGINGS

Franciscan Lakeside Lodge / ★

6944 N LAKE BLVD, TAHOE VISTA; 530/546-6300 OR 800/564-6754

The best of the North Lake's motels, the Franciscan offers access to a private beach and pier, mooring buoys, a heated swimming pool, volleyball nets, a croquet set, horseshoe pits, a children's play area, and nearby tennis courts, ski areas, and a golf course. Its 54 plain but adequate accommodations include studios, one- and two-bedroom units (and a four-bedroom house), full kitchens, private bathrooms, TVs, phones, and daily housekeeping service. The lakefront cottages have large porches overlooking the water (of course, they're the first to get booked, so make your reservations early). *$–$$; AE, MC, V; checks OK; www.franciscanlodge.com; on Hwy 28, 1 mile west of Hwy 267.*

Kings Beach

RESTAURANTS

Log Cabin Café & Ice Cream / ★

8692 N LAKE BLVD, KINGS BEACH; 530/546-7109

The funky Log Cabin Café is the locals' favorite for breakfast in Lake Tahoe. The owner's penchant for freshness is what makes the place such a hit: croissants and muffins are baked every morning, the orange juice is fresh squeezed, and the fluffy Belgian waffles are topped with fresh fruit and nuts. The large lunch menu features everything from tofu burgers to pizza. Near the lakeshore is a picnic area where you can cool off with ice cream sundaes and sodas, served from 11am to 11pm throughout the summer. *$; MC, V; checks OK; breakfast, lunch every day; beer and wine; no reservations; on Hwy 28, ⅓ mile east of Hwy 267.* ♿

Squaw Valley

LODGINGS

PlumpJack Squaw Valley Inn / ★★★

1920 SQUAW VALLEY RD, SQUAW VALLEY; 530/583-1576 OR 800/323-ROOM

Restaurateurs Bill Getty (yes, those Gettys) and San Francisco Mayor Gavin Newsom, the dashing duo who own the highly regarded PlumpJack Cafe in San Francisco, teamed up to create one of Tahoe's most stylish and sophisticated hotels and restaurants. The entire establishment, with its handsome industrial-deco theme, bears a strong resemblance to its San Franciscan counterpart. Guest rooms are loaded with comforts, from terry-cloth slippers to thick down comforters atop expensive mattresses. The hotel boasts mountain views from each of its 61 rooms, as well as a swimming pool, two spas, a retail sports shop, ski rentals and storage, complimentary parking, and room service from the terrific café from 7am to 10pm. The adjoining PlumpJack Cafe offers upscale cuisine and service regardless of your attire (this is, after all, a ski resort) and a tempting menu of modern American dishes, such as milk-brined double-cut pork chops with Yorkshire pudding and summer vegetables, and spicy Maine soft-shell crab with pickled ginger vinaigrette and chile tobiko. Those already familiar with PlumpJack Cafe in San Francisco know that the reasonably priced wine list is among the nation's best. *$$$; AE, DC, DIS, MC, V; checks OK; www.plumpjackcafe.com; off Hwy 89.* ♿

Resort at Squaw Creek / ★★★★

400 SQUAW CREEK RD, OLYMPIC VALLEY; 530/583-6300 OR 800/327-3353

Ranked among the top 50 resorts in North America by *Condé Nast Traveler,* the Resort at Squaw Creek is paradise for skiers, golfers, and tennis players. The resort offers a plethora of amenities—from parking valets, a concierge, and room service to children's programs, a shopping promenade, three swimming pools, a fitness center and spa (with a full-service salon, body wraps, and mud baths), 20 miles of groomed cross-country ski trails, an equestrian center, and even an ice-skating rink. Furthermore, it's only a stone's throw from the Squaw Creek chairlift, which accesses the entire Squaw Valley USA ski area. The 405 rooms, suites, and bilevel penthouses feature minibars, closed-circuit televisions, Nintendos, and Starbucks in-room service. In addition to a deli, a pub, a game lounge, and an outdoor café, the resort offers three restaurants: the Six Peaks Grille, which serves French-American cuisine; an outdoor ski lodge–style sit-down; and the Ristorante Montagna, where you can dine alfresco on wood-oven-baked pizzas and house specials. Be sure to ask about the midweek packages, which can knock a hefty amount off the normally exorbitant rates. *$$$$; AE, DC, DIS, MC, V; checks OK; www.squawcreek.com; off Hwy 89.* ♿

Alpine Meadows

LODGINGS

River Ranch Lodge / ★★

HWY 89, ALPINE MEADOWS; 530/583-4264 OR 866/991-9912

Established in 1888, the current rustic structure was built in 1950. The River Ranch's best rooms feature private balconies that overlook the Truckee River. All of the 19 rooms have private baths, antique or lodgepole pine furnishings, down comforters, TVs, and phones with data ports. Rooms 9 and 10, the farthest from the road, are the quietest and have the best river views from their private decks. In the winter, the lodge is a skier's paradise, a mere five-minute drive from both Squaw Valley USA and Alpine Meadows ski resorts (the Alpine Meadows stay-and-ski packages are outstanding); in the summer, guests relax on the huge patio overlooking the river. A continental breakfast is included in the surprisingly reasonable rates. The River Ranch's spectacular cocktail lounge has been a locals' haven for years and is an immensely popular après-ski spot. Also a big hit is the handsome River Ranch Lodge Restaurant, which serves fresh fish, steaks, and something you probably don't cook at home: wood-oven-roasted Montana elk loin with a dried Bing cherry–port sauce. *$–$$$; AE, MC, V; no checks; www.riverranchlodge.com; at Alpine Meadows Rd, 3½ miles from Lake Tahoe and Tahoe City.* ♿

Tahoe City

RESTAURANTS

Bridgetender Tavern and Grill / ★

65 W LAKE BLVD, TAHOE CITY; 530/583-3342

Any bar with Jägermeister on tap is worth a visit. The fact that the Bridgetender has 20 other beers on tap and great burgers is icing on the cake. Despite its location next to Tahoe City's most popular tourist attraction—Fanny Bridge—Tahoe's foremost tavern has always been a locals' hangout. The menu is basic—burgers, salads, sandwiches, and various appetizers—but the food is filling and cheap. Cholesterol-phobes will appreciate the healthful, low-fat chicken salad sandwich. In the summer, the patio is always packed with giddy tourists unfamiliar with the effects of alcohol at high altitudes. *$; DIS, MC, V; no checks; lunch, dinner every day; full bar; no reservations; on Hwy 89 at Fanny Bridge, downtown.* ♿

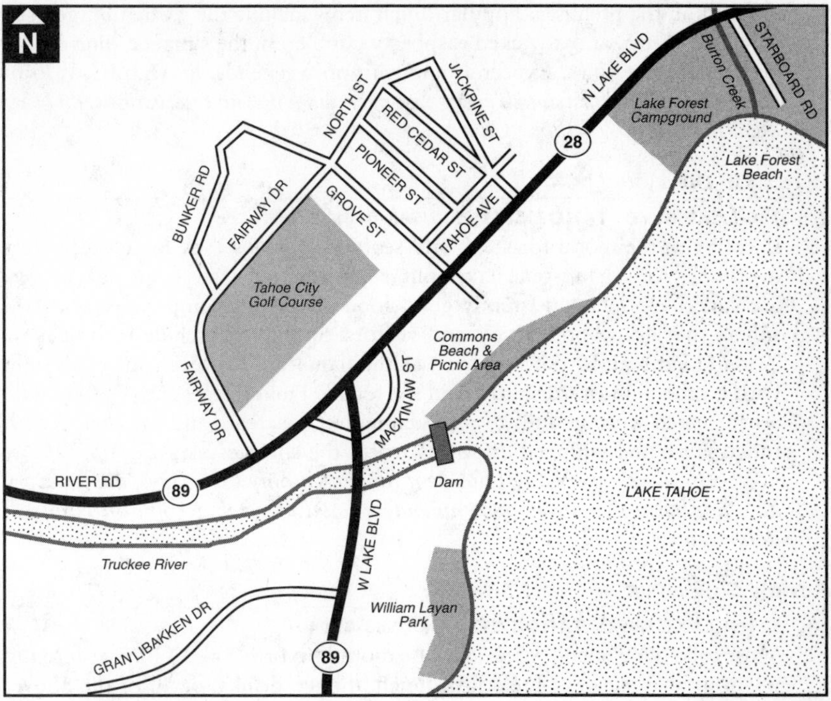

Tahoe City

Christy Hill / ★★★

115 GROVE ST, TAHOE CITY; 530/583-8551

Perched 100 feet above the lake, the venerable Christy Hill restaurant is one of the finest—and most expensive—restaurants in Tahoe City. The menu changes seasonally but always offers a wide selection of fresh seafood and choice-cut meats. Christy Hill's experienced servers (most have been here at least 10 years) know the menu and extensive wine list well, so don't hesitate to seek their advice. Dessert is a wonderful excuse to extend your evening here; try the warm summer fruit cobbler with house-made vanilla ice cream or the chocolate pot de crème with crème chantilly. Arrive before sunset to admire the spectacular view. *$$$; AE, MC, V; checks OK; dinner Tues–Sun; beer and wine; reservations recommended; www.christyhill.com; off Hwy 28/ N Lake Blvd, behind the Village Store.*

Fire Sign Café / ★★

1785 W LAKE BLVD, TAHOE CITY; 530/583-0871

This converted old Tahoe home has been a favorite breakfast stop for locals since the late 1970s. Just about everything here is made from scratch, including the coffee cake and muffins that accompany generous servings of bacon and eggs. Even the savory, thinly sliced salmon used in the eggs Benedict is smoked on the premises. Popular lunch items include the garden burger, the chicken burrito, and a wicked raspberry cobbler. In the summer, dine on the deck under the pines. Expect a long wait on weekends. *$; AE, MC, V; local checks only; breakfast, lunch every day; beer and wine; no reservations; on Hwy 89, 2 miles south of Tahoe City.* ♿

Jake's On the Lake / ★★

780 LAKE BLVD, TAHOE CITY; 530/583-0188

If you're in the mood for steak and seafood, Jake's serves some of the best in Tahoe. This handsome lakefront restaurant—the sweeping lake views are superb—offers consistently good food and service, and a casual atmosphere that draws both locals and visitors. Specialties include rack of New Zealand lamb and fresh fish, such as the flame-broiled seven-spice ahi tuna with a saffron mustard sauce. And the terrific Hula Pie dessert (Oreo cookie crust topped with mounds of macadamia nut ice cream and smothered with fudge sauce and whipped cream) is worth the splurge. *$$; AE, DIS, MC, V; no checks; lunch every day June–Sept (lunch Sat only Oct–May), dinner every day; full bar; reservations recommended; www.jakestahoe.com; on Hwy 28, downtown.* ♿

Rosie's Café / ★★

571 N LAKE BLVD, TAHOE CITY; 530/583-8504

Most folks who spend a few days or more in North Lake Tahoe eventually wind up at Rosie's for breakfast, lunch, dinner, drinks, or all of the above. This humble Tahoe institution serves large portions of traditional American fare, and the dish that tourists always return for is the hearty Yankee pot roast (the perfect dish for those cold winter nights), served with mashed potatoes and gravy and a side of sautéed vegetables. Bring the kids; they get their own special menus and free balloons. *$$; AE, DC, DIS, MC, V; no checks; breakfast, lunch, dinner every day; full bar; no reservations for breakfast and lunch, reservations recommended for dinner; www.rosiescafe.com; downtown.*

Wolfdale's / ★★★

640 N LAKE BLVD, TAHOE CITY; 530/583-5700

Chef-owner Douglas Dale is known for his innovative California cuisine that's often accented with Asian touches. His short, frequently changing menu offers an intriguing mix of one-of-a-kind, light, beautifully arranged dishes that range from very good to sublime. Everything served in this casually elegant restaurant is prepared on the premises; you might begin your meal with a soft-shell crab tempura, followed by roasted quail stuffed with fennel sausage and onions served on a bed of kale. Many of Wolfdale's regular patrons dine at the small bar, and in the summer you can sit outdoors and enjoy the view of Lake Tahoe through the trees. *$$$; MC, V; no checks; dinner Wed–Mon (dinner every day July–Aug); full bar; reservations recommended; www.wolfdales.com; on Hwy 28, downtown.* ♿

LODGINGS

The Cottage Inn / ★★

1690 W LAKE BLVD, TAHOE CITY; 530/581-4073 OR 800/581-4073

This is one of the more appealing places to stay in Tahoe City. Shaded by a thick grove of pine trees, each of the inn's unique country cottages has a stone fireplace, a private bath with a ceramic-tile shower, a thick and colorful quilt on the bed, and a TV with a VCR. A full country breakfast, included in the price, is served at the family-style tables in the main lodge's dining room or on the outside deck. After breakfast, read the morning paper in the comfortable sitting room, take a steam in the Scandinavian sauna, or work on your tan at the nearby private beach and dock. *$$; MC, V; checks OK; www.thecottageinn.com; on Hwy 89, 2 miles south of town.*

Sunnyside Restaurant & Lodge / ★★

1850 W LAKE BLVD, TAHOE CITY; 530/583-7200 OR 800/822-2754

Built as a private home in 1908, this handsome mountain lodge and restaurant is one of the few grand old lodges left on the lakeshore. It offers 23 guest rooms complete with small decks, all but four of which have unobstructed views of Lake Tahoe. The best of the bunch are the bright and airy lakefront units (suites 30 and 31 and rooms 32 to 39). A complimentary continental breakfast buffet is served every morning, and later on, locals and visitors assemble for lunch, dinner, or a drink on the huge deck overlooking the lake, beach, and marina. The Chris Craft Dining Room serves well-prepared California cuisine and specializes in fresh seafood. In the winter the lodge attracts a sizable après-ski crowd to watch ski flicks while munching on the inexpensive bar food. *$$$; AE, MC, V; no checks; www.sunnysideresort.com; on Hwy 89, 2 miles south of town.*

Homewood

LODGINGS

Chaney House / ★★★

4725 W LAKE BLVD, HOMEWOOD; 530/525-7333

The European-style Chaney House was built by Italian stone masons in the 1920s. Each of the four individually decorated rooms has a private bath and a queen- or king-size bed. The attractive Honeymoon Hideaway is a detached, very private unit with a fireplace and a granite Jacuzzi for two. Gary and Lori Chaney serve an elaborate breakfast on the patio (weather permitting), overlooking their private beach and pier. Lori likes to get creative in the kitchen—she often whips up such treats as French toast stuffed with cream cheese and topped with hot homemade blackberry sauce and crème fraîche, or a wonderful concoction of scrambled eggs mixed with artichokes, vermouth, and cheese. The Chaney House books up quickly, so make your reservation at least a month in advance. *$$; DIS, MC, V; checks OK; www.chaneyhouse.com; on Hwy 89, 1 mile north of Ski Homewood.*

Rockwood Lodge / ★★★

5295 W LAKE BLVD, HOMEWOOD; 530/525-5273 OR 800/LE-TAHOE

Situated on the west shore is one of the prettiest B and Bs in Lake Tahoe. Although you may be disconcerted by the requirement that you remove your shoes before entering (seasoned guests bring their own slippers), all is forgiven when your feet sink into the plush carpet. The lodge, located just across the street from the lake, has five rooms with lake or forest views. In the evenings guests often play backgammon and sip cordials by the fireplace in the sitting room. A generous breakfast is served at 9am in the dining room or on the outdoor patio (early rising skiers and golfers are also provided for). *$$–$$$; MC, V; checks OK; www.rockwoodlodge.com; on Hwy 89, next to Ski Homewood.*

Tahoma

LODGINGS

Tahoma Meadows Bed & Breakfast / ★★

6821 W LAKE BLVD, TAHOMA; 530/525-1553 OR 866/525-1553

Owners Ulli and Dick White are veterans of the hospitality industry and two of the nicest people you're likely to meet on the lake. This popular B and B consists of 14 cabins perched on a gentle slope among sugar pines and flowers. The units are individually decorated; each cozy little red cabin has a private bath, a discreetly placed TV, and a comfy king- or queen-size bed; four units have gas-log fireplaces. The largest cabins, Tree House and Sugar Pine, are ideal for families seeking privacy and plenty of elbow room. A full breakfast is served in the main lodge at the independently owned Stoneyridge Cafe, which also serves dinner Thursday through Saturday. Nearby activities include skiing at Ski Homewood, fly-fishing at a private trout-stocked lake (Dick, an avid fly-fisherman, can give you tips), sunbathing on the lakeshore just across the street, and hiking and biking at nearby trails. *$$; AE, DIS, MC, V; checks OK; www.tahomameadows.com; on Hwy 89, 8½ miles from Tahoe City.*

South Shore Lake Tahoe

Three premier attractions separate South Lake Tahoe from its more subdued northern counterpart: glitzy casinos with celebrity entertainers, long stretches of sandy beaches, and the massive **HEAVENLY SKI RESORT**, one of the largest ski resorts in North America. If skiing the slopes followed by gambling until 3am is your idea of paradise, then you're in for a treat.

Most of the weekend warriors who flock here on Friday afternoons book their favorite lodgings weeks—if not months—in advance. Follow their lead and plan early. For long-term stays, consider renting a condo with a group of friends. As soon as you roll into town, stop at the **LAKE TAHOE VISITOR AUTHORITY** (3066 Lake Tahoe Blvd; 530/544-5050; www.bluelaketahoe.com), where you'll find an entire room filled with free maps, brochures, and guidebooks to the South Lake region. And if you risked traveling to Tahoe without a hotel reservation, contact VirtualTahoe.com (800/210-3459; www.virtualtahoe.com) or www.tahoe reservations.com for help finding a vacancy.

In the summer, droves of tourists and locals arrive by bike, car, or boat at the **BEACON** (see review) to scope out the beach, babe, and bar scene—easily the best on the lake. In addition to **JAMISON BEACH**, the other popular public beaches are **NEVADA BEACH** (on Elk Point Rd, 1 mile east of Stateline, Nevada), which has spectacular views of Lake Tahoe and the Sierra Nevada, and **EL DORADO BEACH** (off Lakeview Ave in downtown S Lake Tahoe)—not as pretty but much closer to town.

Tahoe's brilliant-blue lake is so deep it never freezes, so it's navigable even in the dead of winter. One way to get on the water is to book a trip on the **TAHOE QUEEN** (775/589-4906 or 888/896-3830; www.zephyrcove.com; reservations required), an authentic Mississippi stern-wheeler that regularly offers Emerald Bay sightseeing tours and dinner-dance cruises.

The latest big tourist attraction in South Lake is **GONDOLA AT HEAVENLY** (775/586-7000; www.skiheavenly.com). The $20 million state-of-the-art gondola consists of "cars" that transport you from the South Shore's downtown area up the steep mountainside to Heavenly Ski Resort's 14,000-square-foot observation deck. The 2½-mile ride rises to an elevation of 9,123 feet, offering passengers incredible views of Lake Tahoe, Carson Valley, and Desolation Wilderness. The gondola is located a half-block west of Stateline, a short walk from the downtown hotels.

The South Lake's number-one nighttime entertainment is, of course, the casinos. The top guns on this side of the lake are **HARRAH'S**, **MONTBLEU**, **HARVEYS**, and the **HORIZON**, all of which are squeezed next to each other along Highway 50 and burn enough bulbs to light a small city. Even if you can't afford to gamble your paycheck, stroll through the ruckus to watch the high rollers or gawk at those just-one-more-try players mesmerized by the flashy money machines. If you want to try your luck, a mere $10 can keep you entertained for quite a while on the nickel slots. Or spend the night on the dance floor at **NERO'S 2000 NIGHTCLUB** (55 Hwy 50, Stateline, Nevada; 775/586-2000) in Caesars, or visit **TURTLE'S SPORTS BAR AND DANCE EMPORIUM** (4130 Lake Tahoe Blvd, S Lake Tahoe; 530/543-2135) in the Embassy Suites.

For more than a century, **DAVID WALLEY'S HOT SPRINGS & SPA**, (2001 Foothill Rd, 2 miles north of the east end of Kingsbury Grade, near Genoa, Nevada; 775/782-8155; www.davidwalleys.com) has been the place for South Lake residents to unwind after a hard day of skiing or mountain biking (even though it's about an hour-long drive from town). For $20 you can jump into six open-air pools (each is set at a different temperature) and watch ducks and geese at the nearby wildlife area. If a good soak doesn't get all the kinks out, indulge in a rubdown at the resort's massage center.

South Lake Tahoe

RESTAURANTS

The Beacon Bar & Grill / ★★

1900 JAMISON BEACH RD, S LAKE TAHOE; 530/541-0630

On a warm summer afternoon, there's no better place on the South Shore to sit outside, sip on a frosty Rum Runner (a blend of light and dark rums and seven juices), and say to yourself, "This is the life." Located right on Jamison Beach, the Beacon is where locals go to bask in the sun and gawk at the tourist scene. Lunch fare favorites include the Beacon Burger and Camp Richardson clam chowder, and dinner specialties range from fresh seafood to New York steak. In the summer the Beacon hosts jazz, reggae, country, and rock 'n' roll bands. Tip: Bring strong sunscreen—the alpine sun will cook you in minutes. *$$; AE, DIS, MC, V; no checks; lunch, dinner every day, brunch Sat–Sun; full bar; reservations recommended; www.camprich.com; off Hwy 89, 2½ miles north of the Hwy 50 junction, at Camp Richardson.* ♿

Café Fiore / ★★★

1169 SKI RUN BLVD #5, S LAKE TAHOE; 530/541-2908

In an area littered with chain restaurants and fast-food joints, Fiore is a gem. To begin, order a heaping basket of the melt-your-soul garlic bread, followed by an appetizer of the eggplant crepes. For a main, sample one of the pasta dishes like fettuccine alla calabrese, tossed with garlic, artichoke hearts, broccoli, olives, pine nuts, and fresh tomatoes in a light white wine sauce. In warm months, request to sit on the rustic outdoor patio. For a more intimate setting, ask for one of the candle-lit indoor tables. The service is stellar and the wine list goes on for days. Fiore even boasts multiple *Wine Spectator* awards for its selections. You pretty much always need a reservation to get in here, as it is, in one word, *magnifico. $$$; AE, MC, V; no checks; dinner every day; beer and wine; reservations recommended; www.cafefiore.com; at Tamarack Ave.* ♿

Evan's American Gourmet Café / ★★★

536 EMERALD BAY RD, S LAKE TAHOE; 530/542-1990

You can tell from the rather dated decor that this establishment's raison d'être is the food. The ever-changing menu features an eclectic and impressive blend of international cuisine styles (these folks were doing the chic fusion-cuisine thing before it had a name). The philosophy here is to use only the finest, freshest ingredients and to not overwhelm them with heavy sauces or overstylized culinary technique, which results in dishes like loin of lamb, crusted with ginger, orange, and bread crumbs and served with coconut jasmine rice. After dinner, try one of the lavish desserts. The wine list, with nearly 300 labels, is as engaging as the food. Seating is limited, so be sure to call ahead for reservations. *$$$; DIS, MC, V; no checks; dinner every day; beer and wine; reservations required; www.evanstahoe.com; on Hwy 89, 1 mile north of the Hwy 50 junction, at 15th St.*

The Naked Fish / ★★★

3940 LAKE TAHOE BLVD, S LAKE TAHOE; 530/541-3474

Yes, this sushi restaurant is a long way from the ocean, but the nigiri, maki, and sashimi served here are fresh, butter-soft, and oh-so-flavorful. This locally owned Japanese restaurant has a laid-back atmosphere, and in the spirit of a true sushi bar, the Japanese chefs are friendly and talkative, particularly if you buy them a beer. Pay close attention to the "specials" board—this is where the real action is. The live scallop sashimi special we ordered was so fresh, the deftly shelled medallions were still moving, and the presentation was edible art. Full dinners (such as the classic teriyaki standbys) are available, but it's the outstanding nigiri (the fresh salmon rocks) and flavorful, inventive rolls that draw the locals in droves. *$$; AE, DC, DIS, MC, V; no checks; lunch Sat–Sun, dinner every day; beer and wine; reservations recommended for parties of 6 or more; www.thenakedfish.com; at the junction of Hwy 50 and Pioneer Trail.* ♿

The Red Hut / ★

2723 LAKE TAHOE BLVD, S LAKE TAHOE; 530/541-9024

Satisfying South Lake locals and tourists since 1959, this all-American coffee shop, complete with an L-shaped Formica counter, red vinyl booths, and a bubble-gum machine, has become so popular the owners had to add a waiting room. The Red Hut's success is based primarily on its good coffee, hefty omelets with a variety of fillings, friendly servers, and, best of all, low prices. Lunch follows the same all-American formula with a menu of mostly burgers and sandwiches (try the grilled cheese with fresh avocado). While the food isn't anything to swoon over, it beats the buns off the fast-food chains down the street. *$; cash only; breakfast, lunch every day; no alcohol; no reservations; www.redhutcafe.com; ½ block south of Lake Tahoe Blvd, 4 miles east of Stateline, Nevada.*

Sprouts Natural Foods Café / ★★

3123 HARRISON AVE, S LAKE TAHOE; 530/541-6969

You don't have to be a granola-loving, long-haired, hippie type to realize that Sprouts is among the best places in town for a healthy, inexpensive meal. If the line out the door doesn't convince you, then perhaps a bite of the marvelous mayo-free tuna sandwich (made with yogurt and lots of fresh veggies) will. Almost everything is made on the premises. Order at the counter, scramble for a seat, and listen for one of the buffed and beautiful servers to call out your name and deliver your tray of earthly delights. This is also an excellent place to pick up a picnic lunch for a skiing, hiking, or mountain-biking expedition. *$; no credit cards; local checks only; breakfast, lunch, dinner every day; no reservations; on the corner of Hwy 50 and Alameda St.*

Wide Awake Conscious Café / ★★☆

3434 LAKE TAHOE BLVD, S LAKE TAHOE; 530/541-7400

This hippy-dippy spot, which supports all things fair trade and eco-friendly, is always bustling with those drawn to its organic offerings. And rightfully so—the breakfast is so good, it's not a matter of if you'll come back, it's *when*. Try a frittata with sun-dried tomato, garlic, sweet onion, and fresh basil, or order one of the belly-filling sweet crepes like the chocolate with caramelized bananas and powdered sugar. Coffee and tea come in mugs the size of bowls, so you won't leave without a caffeine jolt. Lunch items include dishes like chicken curry, wraps, and mac and cheese. The only problem is that the café tends to run out of its most popular items—like flavored bagels and other pastries—well before noon, so arrive early. *$$; DIS, MC, V; no checks; breakfast, lunch every day (dinner every day in winter); no reservations; www.wideawakecafe.com; between Fairway Ave and Johnson Blvd.* ♿

LODGINGS

Black Bear Inn Bed & Breakfast / ★★★

1202 SKI RUN BLVD, S LAKE TAHOE; 530/544-4451 OR 877/232-7466

The Black Bear Inn is a fine example of what a lot of money, excellent taste, and an incredible collection of early American antiques can produce. The inn consists of five rooms in the main lodge and three cabins of varying sizes set within a 1½-acre landscaped garden. Each of the spacious guest rooms has a king-size bed, a private bathroom, a TV/VCR/DVD player (with complimentary access to a DVD library), a gas fireplace, and towels and robes for the trip to the gazebo spa. The cabins are popular with honeymooners, who often prefer to have their breakfast—fresh-baked muffins, omelets, eggs Benedict, and other hearty dishes—delivered in bed. The cabins also have fully equipped kitchens or kitchenettes. One complaint: the location. Although this gorgeous B and B is just down the street from the Heavenly Ski Resort, it's also situated in one of the seediest parts of town. *$$$–$$$$; MC, V; checks OK; www.tahoeblackbear.com; off Hwy 50.* ♿

Historic Camp Richardson Resort & Marina / ★

JAMISON BEACH RD AND HWY 89, S LAKE TAHOE; 530/541-1801

This popular family retreat just a few miles outside town seems worlds away from the bustle of South Lake Tahoe. The lodge offers 28 sparsely furnished rooms with private baths and is only a five-minute walk from the lake. Even closer to the water are 39 homey cabins and the small, 7-room Beach Inn (the rooms are slightly larger than the main lodge's and have lake views, TVs, and telephones). The best cabins are near Jamison Beach and are usually reserved far in advance (only some of them are available in the winter). In the summer the resort provides guests with an ice cream parlor, a general store (which carries beer and wine), camping facilities, hiking and biking trails, volleyballs and nets, horseshoes and pits, and equipment rentals for almost anything that floats or rolls. Another perk: one of South Lake's best restaurants and bars, The Beacon Bar & Grill (see review) is just a short walk away. Staying at Richardson Resort is sort of like being at camp, and it's a great place to take the kids. *$$; AE, MC, V; no checks; www.camprich.com; 2½ miles west of the Hwy 50 junction.*

Lakeland Village Beach & Ski Resort / ★★

3535 LAKE TAHOE BLVD, S LAKE TAHOE; 530/544-1685 OR 800/822-5969

Although a few of Lakeland Village's buildings are located on busy Highway 50, the 19-acre resort has more than 1,000 feet of beachfront property, two tennis courts, and two swimming pools—all beyond the sight and sound of the traffic. The condominium resort's 260 units, ranging from studios to five-bedroom town houses, are individually owned and best suited for families. The most desirable town houses front the lake and get booked quickly during peak season; the studio rooms in the main lodge and the one-bedroom suites are the least expensive. All units come with fireplaces, fully equipped kitchens, private balconies, and daily housekeeping service. Perks include free shuttle service to Heavenly and the casinos, children's activities in the summer, beach barbecues, and an underground parking garage. *$$–$$$; AE, DIS, MC, V; checks OK; www.lakeland-village.com; between Ski Run Blvd and Fairway Ave.* ♿

Marriott's Timber Lodge & Grand Residence Club / ★

1001 HEAVENLY VILLAGE WY, S LAKE TAHOE; 877/45-GRAND

These colossal Marriott lodgings offer a whopping 464 units ranging from studios to three-bedroom condos. The "alpine village" consists of the two adjacent vacation ownership resorts (which also sell rooms on a per-night basis) and the Heavenly Village, a sort of alpine-style mall with shops, restaurants, bars, an ice skating rink, a movie theater, a ski gondola, an arcade, a . . . well, you get the picture. If you're into the corporate faux-village thing, you and your family will enjoy the easy access to all the usual resort amenities; just don't expect a lick of originality, personalized service, or bargains. And although most of the well-appointed guest rooms are quite spacious and come with fully equipped kitchens, quality is lacking—our toilet didn't work, nor did the shower drain; the mattress was painfully firm. *$$$–$$$$; AE, DIS, MC, V; no checks; www.marriottvillarentals.com; downtown.* ♿

Zephyr Cove

LODGINGS

Zephyr Cove / ★★

HIGHWAY 50 AT ZEPHYR COVE, NEVADA; 775/589-4906

Zephyr Cove is one of Lake Tahoe's best (and least crowded) family destinations. Set in a shady grove of pines, the resort's 28 cabins range from studios and cottages to four-bedroom cabins. Each has a front porch with patio furniture, cable TV with HBO, a telephone, Internet access, a bathroom, and a fully equipped kitchen. OK, so it's not the Ritz, but the cabins are clean, inexpensive, and reasonably comfortable. Besides, you'll spend most of your time at the resort's beautiful gold-sand beach, catching a comfy buzz on mai tais at the

Sunset Bar while the kids take turns on the rented jet ski. Pedal boats, kayaks, canoes, and ski boats are also available for rent, and the pier is the launching point for lake cruises. The Zephyr Cove Restaurant serves breakfast, lunch, and dinner daily, and it's a short drive to the restaurants and casinos in South Lake Tahoe (free shuttle service, even). Pets are allowed with a per-night fee. *$$; AE, DIS, MC, V; no checks; www.zephyrcove.com; 4 miles north of Stateline, Nevada, on Hwy 5.*

Hope Valley

LODGINGS

Sorensen's Resort / ★★★

14255 HWY 88, HOPE VALLEY; 530/694-2203 OR 800/423-9949

Since 1926, Sorensen's cluster of 30 cabins has offered access to first-rate cross-country skiing in the winter (the resort rents skis and snowshoes), prime hiking, horseback riding, rafting, mountain biking, and llama treks in late spring and summer, and a terrific display of colors in the fall. There's good trout fishing here, too. Accommodations range from inexpensive, rustic-but-comfy cabins to grand, modern chalets. Norway House features an open-loft bedroom, a kitchen, and a living/sleeping room, ideal for groups of up to eight people, while the cozy Waterfir Cabin is the best choice for couples. If you rent one of the three smaller, less expensive cabins (Piñon, Lupine, and Larkspur), which don't have kitchens, breakfast for two is included in the cost of your stay. There are also fully furnished homes available, ideal for families. Sorensen's Country Cafe is open only to guests for breakfast, lunch, and dinner, and the food is a cut above most mountain resort fare. Sorensen's also runs the nearby Hope Valley Store and Cafe, which offers a modest menu of hot dogs, hamburgers, and similar fare from Memorial Day through Labor Day—a good place for a quick, inexpensive meal. *$$; AE, MC, V; checks OK; www.sorensensresort.com; 5 miles northwest of Woodfords.* ♿

Markleeville

This tiny mountain town's claim to fame is the annual **DEATH RIDE TOUR OF THE CALIFORNIA ALPS**, a grueling 128-mile bike trek over five mountain passes (16,000 feet of climbing) that's renowned among bicyclists as one of the top 10 cycling challenges in the United States. The tour, limited to the first 2,500 prepaid applicants, is held the first Saturday after July 4; contact the **ALPINE CHAMBER OF COMMERCE** (530/694-2475; www.deathride.com) for more information.

The only place worth visiting in Markleeville, besides the exceptional Villa Gigli Trattoria (see review), is the **CUTTHROAT BAR** (530/694-2158), located within the Wolf Creek Restaurant. (Alas, gone is the collection of brassieres hanging from the bar's ceiling.) Just outside of town is the popular **GROVER**

HOT SPRINGS STATE PARK (4 miles west of Markleeville at the end of Hot Springs Rd; 530/694-2248; open 9am–9pm every day in summer, 2–9pm weekdays and 9am–9pm weekends in winter), where you may soak in the plain but soothing mineral pools year-round (bathing suits required).

RESTAURANTS

Villa Gigli Trattoria / ★★★

145 HOT SPRINGS RD, MARKLEEVILLE; 530/694-2253

Located on a remote hillside is Gina and Ruggero Gigli's Villa Gigli, a quintessential mom-and-pop café. Every Saturday and Sunday morning Ruggero, who was raised in a small town in Tuscany, rolls pasta dough, bakes breads, and stuffs cannelloni in preparation for his two dozen or so nightly guests, most of whom have traveled hours to get here and made reservations weeks in advance—it's that special. The menu usually consists of four pasta dishes, two vegetarian and two with meat, salad in the summer or soup in the winter, a dessert, and fresh-brewed coffee. Sparse, yes, but when you consider that Ruggero makes all the breads, pastas, sauces, and desserts by hand, without assistance in his tiny kitchen, it's amazing there are any choices. To find out what's on the menu, just give him a call. Prices are surprisingly low: an entrée with a bottle of the house red costs half as much as you'd pay in other three-star establishments in the Sierra Nevada. *$$; no credit cards; checks OK; dinner Sat–Sun (May–Oct); beer and wine; reservations required; www.ruggerogigli.com; 2 blocks west of downtown, then west on Hot Springs Rd.* ♿

The Lakes Basin Area

The scenic **GOLD LAKE ROAD**, which starts at Highway 49 just east of Sierra City and ends several miles south of Graeagle, is a spectacular 14-mile stretch of tarmac that zigzags through verdant valleys dotted with farms, historic buildings, deer, cows, and horses. It passes nearly a dozen sky blue lakes—there are 30 within the Lakes Basin Area—most of them either visible from the highway or within easy walking distance. The **LAKES BASIN CAMPGROUND**, located right off the road, offers 24 sites on a first-come, first-served basis; call the Beckwourth Ranger District station (530/836-2575) for details. Most of the lodges in the basin are quite rustic, and folks in the area like it that way. Whether you fancy horseback riding through meadows rife with wildflowers, fishing in roaring rivers, hiking through magnificent red fir forests, or mountain biking on rugged, hilly trails, you'll find it here. The lakeside lodges book up quickly, so make reservations well ahead of time or try your luck at catching a last-minute cancellation. Bear in mind that the seasonal resorts tend to have a high turnover of chefs, so menus and the quality of the fare may change considerably from one season to the next. In the winter, the basin closes and the unplowed road becomes a haven for snowmobilers.

RESTAURANTS

Sardine Lake Resort / ★★

END OF SARDINE LAKE RD AT LOWER SARDINE LAKE, LAKES BASIN AREA; 530/862-1196 (SUMMER ONLY)

When the stress of daily life begins to take its toll and you long for an escape to some peaceful, far-from-it-all retreat, Sardine Lake should spring to mind. The towering, craggy peaks of the Sierra Buttes are mirrored in this lake, where the tranquil forest is restorative for even the most frazzled city folk. The resort's proprietors, the Hunt family, take full advantage of the splendid setting, serving cocktails before dinner in a small gazebo that juts over the lake. The food is good, with a small but nicely rendered selection of meat, seafood, and poultry dishes. Restaurant reservations several weeks in advance are a must. Unfortunately, the resort's nine cabins are often filled by a long list of returning clients, so successfully reserving one can seem, as one frustrated lad put it, "downright impossible." *$$; no credit cards; checks OK; dinner Fri–Wed (open mid-May–mid-Oct); full bar; reservations required; off Gold Lake Rd, 2 miles north of Hwy 49.*

LODGINGS

Gold Lake Lodge / ★

GOLD LAKE RD, LAKES BASIN AREA; 530/836-2350

Gold Lake Lodge sits in the heart of the Lakes Basin Area (elevation 6,620 feet) within hiking distance of stunning High Sierra scenery and numerous lakes. Bear Lake is the closest (a one-third-mile hike), and Gold Lake is a five-minute drive by car. Nine tidy little cabins are available, most sleeping three to four people; each of the six standard cabins has a private bathroom, and the other three share a detached bathing facility just across the lawn. There is also one tent cabin for those who want to get closer to nature. Every cabin has electricity, a small front patio with a table and chairs, and housekeeping service. Breakfast and dinner are included in the rates, and meals are served in the lodge's dining room (open to nonguests, too). Sack lunches for hikers are available. Dinner specials range from lasagne to fried chicken, and the lodge's sun tea is the perfect antidote to a hot summer day. *$$$; MC, V; checks OK; open Father's Day–mid-Sept; www.goldlakelodge.com; 7 miles south of Hwy 89.*

Gray Eagle Lodge / ★★★

ON GOLD LAKE RD, LAKES BASIN AREA; 800/635-8778

Gray Eagle Lodge is set in the heart of spectacular scenery at the northern edge of the Lakes Basin Area. The resort's 18 refurbished cabins have small decks, private baths, wall-to-wall carpeting, mini-refrigerators, and queen- or king-size beds with electric blankets and comforters. Breakfast and dinner, included in the room rates, are served in the lodge's dining room. Dinner might include a carrot-curry soup with fresh ginger and an entrée of grilled salmon with a Mediterranean salsa accompanied by a garlic-polenta flan and baby green beans. The extensive wine list features primarily California labels and is the best in the Lakes Basin Area. If you're not staying at the lodge, dinner reservations are required. *$$–$$$; MC, V; checks OK; open May–Oct; www.grayeaglelodge.com; west of Gold Lake Rd.* ♿

Packer Lake Lodge / ★★

3901 PACKER LAKE RD, LAKES BASIN AREA; 530/862-1221

Built in 1926, Packer Lake Lodge steadfastly maintains its combination of good food and—at a 6,218-foot elevation—great scenery. The tall pines, gently rippling waters, and profusion of wildflowers provide an atmosphere of serene seclusion. Accommodations are in 14 simply furnished cabins, ranging from rustic lakeside log cabins with shared bathrooms to three-room buildings with kitchens and private baths. Each cabin has its own rowboat, too. The single-room main lodge has a tiny store that primarily sells candy bars and fishing supplies, a full bar, a reading and games nook, and a small dining room. Dinner fare includes meat dishes, pasta, and the "you-catch-it-and-clean-it-and-we'll-cook-it" trout special. Nonguests are welcome for dinner (reservations required). *$–$$$; MC, V; checks OK; open May–Oct; www.packerlakelodge.com; off Sardine Lake Rd, 4½ miles north of Hwy 49.*

Salmon Lake Lodge / ★

SALMON LAKE RD, LAKES BASIN AREA; 530/852-0874

You can't drive to this 1920s-era resort; instead, you have to drive to the north shore of Salmon Lake and telephone the lodge to send over a ferry (or you can hike a little less than a mile around the lake's splendid western rim). The 10 tent cabins offer canvas roofs, rough-wood walls, built-in double beds and single bunks, mini-refrigerators, and electric stoves; you need to bring a sleeping bag, towels, dishes, cooking gear, an ice chest, and groceries (showers and a washing machine—but no dryer—are available in a separate building). The three ridge-top cabins with their beautiful views are the favorites, and each has a fully equipped kitchen. Also highly sought after is the lakeshore cabin, which has its own dock. Salmon Lake is great for swimming and boating, and rowboats, sailboats, canoes, and kayaks are provided at no extra cost. You can also paddle a boat or take a barge to a lake island for a biweekly barbecue. *$$; no credit cards; checks OK; open June–mid-Oct (weather permitting); www.salmonlake.net; 1 mile west of Gold Lake Hwy.* ♿

Clio

RESTAURANTS

The Wigwam Room / ★★★★

349 BEAR RUN (NAKOMA GOLF RESORT), CLIO; 877/462-5662

Well, if that don't beat all . . . Frank Lloyd Wright's scions have bought themselves a major chunk of land in the area above Graeagle and built a gated community—the pièce de résistance of which is a sensational clubhouse, restaurant, and spa complex. The development is called, appropriately, Gold Mountain. The restaurant serves very good food that changes seasonally—Angus beef, fresh produce, and baked goods from scratch, with an impressive array of menu choices for breakfast, lunch, and dinner. If you'd like to check out the place without busting the budget, come at lunchtime for good salads and sandwiches at remarkably reasonable prices. The nearby little railroad town of Portola is sprucing itself up a bit in case its glitzy neighbors wander down the hill. It's worth a gander, too, as is the Portola Railroad Museum (530/832-4131), where you can fulfill your lifelong fantasy to drive a train. *$$$; AE, MC, V; checks OK; breakfast, lunch, dinner every day (Apr–Oct), Wed–Sun (Nov–Mar); full bar; reservations recommended; www.nakomaresort.com; County Rd A-15 between the towns of Clio and Portola.* ♿

Mohawk, Blairsden, and Graeagle

The tiny towns of Mohawk, Blairsden, and Graeagle sit cheek by jowl, so to speak—each is located less than a mile from the other. In Mohawk, there's not much left except an old, well-maintained little cemetery, a deteriorating but interesting log cabin that was once the town's stage stop, a pleasant deli-restaurant, and the funky **MOHAWK TAVERN** (530/836-1241), a friendly watering hole adorned with signs labeling it the Mohawk Convention Center and City Hall. Blairsden boasts a nursery, a hardware store, several restaurants—including a cute sandwich shop popular with the locals, the **TIN ROOF** (190 Bonta St, Blairsden; 530/836-1497)—and a truly great bakery (and coffee shop), the **VILLAGE BAKER** (340 Bonta St, Blairsden; 530/836-4064).

About a quarter mile south of Blairsden is the picturesque little city of Graeagle, a former company town of the California Fruit Growers Exchange. Fruit growers once had a lumber mill here that made wooden boxes for storing produce, but it's gone now and the millpond has been converted into a family swimming area with grassy banks, gravel beaches, brown trout, and paddleboat rentals; in the winter, the pond is often a resting place for gaggles of Canada geese. Graeagle modestly bills itself as the "Home of the World's Finest Golf Clubs" (there's a custom golf club store here), and there are six golf courses in the area; for **GOLFING INFORMATION**, call or stop by Williamson Realty (Hwy 89; 530/836-0112) in the Graeagle Village Center. Other outdoor activities include tennis, hiking, and horseback riding. The rest of the town consists of a little grocery store, a tearoom, an antique shop, and a handful of other small businesses—most are located in former company houses painted barn red with white trim. For more information and a brochure on the area, contact the **PLUMAS COUNTY VISITORS BUREAU** (800/326-2247; www.plumascounty.org).

RESTAURANTS

Grizzly Grill Restaurant and Bar / ★★★

250 BONTA ST, BLAIRSDEN; 530/836-1300

Owner Lynn Hagen is a true pioneer in this neck of the woods: she introduced baby greens, Muscovy duck, and Asiago cheese into this meat-and-potato belt. Next thing you know she'll be hosting martini and cigar nights. Her light, relaxed restaurant is a fine spot to have dinner or just a drink at the long bar staffed by a congenial crew. The Grizzly's menu will warm a yuppie's heart: main courses range from a perfectly grilled Norwegian salmon with tomatoes, capers, and toasted garlic chips, to hearty lamb shanks with French white beans, caramelized onions, mushrooms, rosemary, and a merlot sauce. The small, daily dessert menu often holds some gems, and there is an extensive wine list. Many items are available in two sizes, and there are early-bird specials for those dining between 5:30pm and 6:30pm. *$–$$; MC, V; checks OK; dinner every day; full bar; reservations recommended; www.grizzlygrill.com; near the junction of Hwys 70 and 89.*

LODGINGS

River Pines Resort / ★★

8296 HWY 89, GRAEAGLE; 530/836-2552 OR 800/696-2551

Set alongside the Feather River, the River Pines is a popular family retreat that folks return to year after year. It's fun and affordable, and it offers enough activities to keep any Type A vacationer entertained: a large pool and Jacuzzi with a poolside bar and snack bar, trout fishing, table tennis, shuffleboard, and horseshoes. It's also only a quarter mile from a stable with horseback riding excursions; nearby are several tennis courts and six golf courses. The resort has 63 units, including 18 cabins. Each cabin has a fully stocked kitchen and a private bathroom; the one-room cabins have a futon and either a queen-size bed or two twins, while the two-room cabins have a queen, two twins, and a futon. The resort's other rooms are reminiscent of a standard motel; some rooms have kitchens and sitting areas. Lunches of hamburgers, hot dogs, and pizza are served poolside or at the pool bar. Sharing the grounds is the popular Coyote Bar & Grill (530/836-2002), which serves good Southwestern food. And they make a margarita that'll knock your huaraches off. *$$; DIS, MC, V; checks OK; www.riverpines.com; at the north end of town, on the south side of the Feather River.* ♿

Johnsville

This tiny, charming town, established by the Sierra Buttes Mining Company in the 1870s, is a California treasure. It was built for the gold miners and their families, who didn't want to live next to the brothels and gambling centers in the nearby mining camps. Surrounded by the densely forested **PLUMAS-EUREKA STATE PARK**, Johnsville is a mix of abandoned miners' shacks and restored ones that serve as private residences. In between the historic buildings are some new homes, most built to meet the Johnsville Historical Society's strict design guidelines. As you drive down Main Street, note the striking old barn red **JOHNSVILLE HOTEL**, now a private home, and the toylike firehouse across the street with a bell in its steeple and a horse-drawn fire wagon inside. Among the many wonderful artifacts at the **PLUMAS-EUREKA STATE PARK MUSEUM** are a working blacksmith shop and a five-story, 60-stamp mill where gold was processed. A nearby campground straddles pretty Jamison Creek, and across the street from the museum is the diminutive **MORIARITY HOUSE**, a completely restored miner's home with furnishings and equipment used by the 10-member Moriarity family in 1901. For museum and campground information, call 916/638-5883. A mile up Johnsville's main road is a quaint, no-frills downhill ski resort for beginner to intermediate skiers. For environmental reasons, the state park opted to replace the historic Poma lift with a new chairlift in its footprint.

RESTAURANTS

The Iron Door / ★★

5417 MAIN ST, JOHNSVILLE; 530/836-2376

Johnsville supports one business, and this is it. The Iron Door restaurant has occupied the century-old general store and post office building since 1961, and it hasn't changed much since then. Behind the bar hangs a drawing of the last miner in Johnsville, who worked his claim on Jamison Creek until the 1950s. The soups are thick and hearty, and the main bill of fare is heavy with beef, lobster, and fowl. And since the restaurant's owner is from Bavaria, you can also bite into several excellent and authentic schnitzels. A good selection of beer and wine rounds out the offerings. *$$; MC, V; local checks only; dinner Wed–Mon (open Apr–Nov); full bar; reservations required; in Plumas-Eureka State Park, 5 miles west of Graeagle.* ♿

Cromberg

RESTAURANTS

Mount Tomba Inn / ★

60300 HWY 70, CROMBERG; 866/920-8725

Mount Tomba Inn has managed to survive and thrive in a sparsely populated area where businesses regularly go belly-up. The place is not only a restaurant, but also a shrine to John Wayne—every dish is named after one of the Duke's movies (well, except for the nameless vegetarian plate). Mount Tomba's specialty is prawns—big, meaty, tender prawns, the way the Duke would have liked 'em. You can get them deep fried, boiled with drawn butter, or sautéed in garlic butter, olive oil, lemon, and white wine. And of course, no John Wayne shrine would be complete without every cut of beef, from filet mignon to prime rib. Included in the price of every cowboy-size dinner is an excellent made-from-scratch soup (served in a large tureen), a nothing-special tossed green salad, a basket of warm bread, rice or a baked potato with all the trimmings, coffee, and a choice of sherbet, vanilla ice cream, or a chocolate sundae. *$–$$; DIS, MC, V; checks OK; dinner Tues–Sun (Apr–Oct), Fri–Sun (Nov–Mar); full bar; reservations recommended; www.mttombainn.com; ½ mile east of town, 17 miles from both Quincy and Portola.* ♿

LODGINGS

Twenty Mile House / ★★★

OLD CROMBERG RD, CROMBERG; 530/836-0375

Set on the middle fork of the Feather River, the Twenty Mile House has been a tranquil haven for travelers since 1854, when it served as a stagecoach stop. The two-story brick building is set amid 250 acres of wildflowers, evergreens, and wildlife, and four guest bedrooms are offered in the main house, all with private bathrooms. Tucked into the nearby forest next to Jackson Creek are three housekeeping cabins; each sleeps four and has a kitchen, a bedroom, and a deck. Breakfast for guests is served in the main house's country kitchen or on the front porch. Anglers are particularly partial to Twenty Mile House since 2 miles of the Feather River run through the inn's private property. Some years ago proprietor Barbara Gage stocked the river with wild and native trout, and their population is maintained by limiting the number of fly-fishers and enforcing a strict catch-and-release policy. *$$$; no credit cards; checks OK; www.twentymilehouse.us; 1 mile south of Hwy 70, 7 miles northwest of Graeagle, and 18 miles southeast of Quincy.* ♿

Quincy

Situated in a tranquil valley at the head of the beautiful Feather River Canyon, surrounded by national forest, Quincy is a pretty little mountain town struggling mightily to hang on to its small-town charm. The old town is centered on an imposing Victorian courthouse in a grassy plaza. The adjacent **PLUMAS COUNTY MUSEUM** (500 Jackson St; 530/283-6320) is a gem, with handsomely displayed early California artifacts. There's one 1930s art deco movie theater playing one movie—the essence of small-town life (**TOWN HALL THEATER**; 530/283-1140). That essential element of civilized living, a decent bookstore, is satisfactorily provided by the **BOOKSHELF** (373 Main St; 530/283-BOOK), and there's a variety of interesting downtown restaurants. The surrounding wilderness, punctuated by numerous lakes and streams, is perfect for every kind of outdoor recreation you can think of, particularly if you're looking for solitude. This is still a relatively remote area of California, and that is part of its appeal.

RESTAURANTS

Moon's / ★

497 LAWRENCE ST, QUINCY; 530/283-0765

A popular local hangout since the mid-'70s, Moon's is a roomy, ramshackle, rustic wooden building with four separate dining areas, including a formal dining room and an open-air patio. The strong scent of garlic and yeast is a dead giveaway to the house specialties: pizza, pasta, and other classic Italian dishes. The thick lasagne, heavily laden with sausage, is one of the kitchen's best efforts, as is the Mushrooms St. Thomas, a spinach, mushroom, and Italian-sausage casserole. Moon's is ideal for families, offering something to suit just about every taste. *$; AE, MC, V; checks OK; dinner Tues–Sun; beer and wine; reservations recommended; at Plymouth St.* ♿

Morning Thunder Café / ★

557 LAWRENCE ST, QUINCY; 530/283-1310

With its stained glass window, vine-laced trellis, and macramé plant holder, the Morning Thunder Café may look a bit like a hippie haven, but those details are just leftovers from its impetuous youth. Breakfast has always been the draw here, with dishes like huevos rancheros and three-egg spinach, cheese, and mushroom omelets. The portions are huge, and the biscuits are as large as a prizefighter's fist. The restaurant also serves lunches of enormous hamburgers and freshly made soups. In fact, the delicious Boston clam chowder has become such a hit that the café's regulars insist on having it every Friday. *$; MC, V; no checks; breakfast, lunch every day; beer and wine; no reservations on weekends; downtown.*

Sweet Lorraine's / ★

384 MAIN ST, QUINCY; 530/283-5300

On a sunny day, Sweet Lorraine's patio is the best spot in Quincy to kick back after touring the nearby Plumas County Museum or the shops along Main Street. The cook here sticks to simple dishes, nicely prepared—the pan-seared salmon with portobello mushroom ragù and roasted garlic mashed potatoes is a good choice. Soups, breads, and desserts are freshly prepared in-house, and there's beer on tap and a selection of wines. Relax and enjoy the small pleasures of a peaceful, picturesque little town. *$–$$; MC, V; local checks only; lunch Mon–Fri, dinner Mon–Sat; beer and wine; reservations recommended; downtown.*

LODGINGS

The Feather Bed / ★

542 JACKSON ST, QUINCY; 530/283-0102 OR 800/696-8624

This 1893 Victorian inn, proudly punctuated with colonnades on its teal and peach front porch, features five cozy, turn-of-the-century country-style guest rooms with private baths. There are also two quaint little cottages behind the house. Some rooms have terrific deep claw-foot soaking tubs; others have gas fireplaces. After refueling on the full breakfast served in the dining room, borrow a bike from proprietor Bob Janowski and take a spin around Quincy. You can also easily walk from the Feather Bed to the heart of the quaint town. *$$–$$$; AE, DC, DIS, MC, V; checks OK; www.featherbed-inn.com; at Court St, 1 block south of Hwy 70.* ♿

Greenville

LODGINGS

Yorkshire House Bed and Breakfast / ★

421 MAIN ST, GREENVILLE; 530/284-1794

If you really want to get off the beaten path, explore Indian Valley, a mountainous meadowland tucked between the Feather River and Lake Almanor. The Yorkshire, named by co-owner Angie Dalton for her birthplace in England, is located in the largest of the towns in the area, Greenville. With four suites to choose from, friendly hosts, and a full breakfast of yogurt, fruit, locally made sausages, and fresh muffins—all for a modest price—you may think about moving in permanently. This is fisher-folk heaven, with lots of lakes and reservoirs offering both native and planted trout as well as bass. Round Valley Reservoir, a warm-water fishery and Greenville's source of water, is just 4 miles away and shelters more than 100 resident species of birds. *$–$$; AE, MC, V; checks OK; www.yorkshirehousebb.com; 2 blocks east of Hwy 89.*

Bear Valley Area

Tucked away in the central Sierra Nevada some 7,000 feet above sea level is the small town of Bear Valley, home of the popular **BEAR VALLEY MOUNTAIN RESORT COMPANY** and the **BEAR VALLEY CROSS-COUNTRY AREA.** (See Skiing the Sierra Nevada at the end of this chapter for contact information.) In the summer, more than 100 miles of the cross-country ski trails become prime mountain-biking territory.

Bear Valley

LODGINGS

Bear Valley Lodge and Village Resort / ★★

3 BEAR VALLEY RD, BEAR VALLEY; 209/753-2327

Bear Valley Lodge, the center of this small mountain community, is a full-service year-round resort that appeals to families and sports enthusiasts. There are cross-country and downhill ski facilities nearby (ask about the skiing/lodging package deals here) and plenty of mountains, trails, lakes, and streams to explore. Another bonus is the resort's 7,000-foot elevation, which helps keep the scorching summer heat at bay. There are 51 guest rooms (including three suites), a restaurant and bar, and a heated swimming pool (open in summer only). Bear Valley Lodge Restaurant, catering to a mostly captive audience, offers California cuisine—steak, fish, chicken, pasta, vegetarian entrées, salads—and a children's menu. *$$; AE, MC, V; checks OK; www.bearvalleylodge.com; from Hwy 4E go left on Bear Valley Rd.* ♿

Lake Alpine Lodge / ★

4000 HWY 4, BEAR VALLEY; 209/753-6350

This quaint summer resort situated on Lake Alpine is an excellent choice for families. It features a fireplace so large you can walk into it, a spacious deck overlooking the lake, and a game room equipped with a pool table and video games. Eight of the nine rustic, fully equipped cabins have kitchens and outdoor barbecues, and all come with a shower, a deck, and a view of the lake. The lodge also offers several "upscale camping" cabins, each furnished with four twin beds, a barbecue ring, and access to public bathrooms (available mid-June–Labor Day only). The Lake Alpine Lodge Cafe serves breakfast, lunch, and dinner in the summer, and there's a small saloon as well as a convenience market that sells bait, tackle, and camping equipment. Laundry facilities and public showers are also available, as are boats and mountain bike rentals. *$$; MC, V; local checks only; open May 1–Oct 1; www.lakealpinelodge.com; at Ebbets Pass/Lake Alpine.* ♿

Dorrington

LODGINGS

The Dorrington Hotel and Restaurant / ★★

3431 HWY 4, DORRINGTON; 209/795-5800 OR 209/795-1140

A few miles from magnificent Calaveras Big Trees State Park sits the Dorrington Hotel, built in 1852 and used as a stagecoach stop, a depot for stockmen, and—because of its 5,000-foot elevation—a summer resort where people could beat the heat. Surrounded by some of the largest pines and sequoias in California, this country hotel has five antique-filled rooms, which share bathrooms. There's also a one-room cabin next door with a kitchenette, a large stone fireplace, and a spa tub. Complimentary sherry and fruit are left in the room, and a continental breakfast is served there in the morning. The hotel's casual dining room offers northern Italian–style dinners in the $15 to $30 range. *$$; DIS, MC, V; checks OK; www.dorringtonhotel.com; near Board's Crossing.*

Arnold

RESTAURANTS

Tallahan's Café / ★★★

1225 OAK CIRCLE, ARNOLD; 209/795-4005
Partners Kathleen Minahan and Bruce Tallakson serve up hearty yet sophisticated fare in their comfortable country café, a happy surprise in this rustic setting. Try the red chard and onion ravioli with mushrooms, dried cherries, white wine, and feta cheese or the risotto with tiger prawns and New Mexico sausage. Sandwiches are imaginative creations here too, such as the thinly sliced tri-dip with red onion, spinach, avocado, cheddar cheese, and red-chile aioli in a chipotle chile tortilla. The best spot to dine is on the deck, if weather permits. *$$; AE, DIS, MC, V; local checks only; lunch, dinner Fri–Tues (closed 2 weeks in mid-Nov and 3rd week in May); beer and wine; reservations recommended; off Hwy 4 at Cedar Center.* ♿

Pinecrest

RESTAURANTS

Steam Donkey Restaurant / ★

421 PINECREST LAKE RD, PINECREST; 209/965-3117
Named after a steam-powered logging machine used to drag timber to the railroad, this popular barbecue house is usually packed with Sonorans, who make the 32-mile trek up to Dodge Ridge for the Steam Donkey's highly rated ribs, steaks, and chicken. Many of the regular patrons are ex-loggers, who likely feel right at home among all the logging memorabilia scattered throughout the restaurant. *$–$$; MC, V; checks OK; lunch Sat–Sun (every day in summer), dinner every day; full bar; reservations recommended; www.pinecrestlakeresort.com/Donkey.htm; off Pinecrest Ave and Hwy 108.* ♿

Yosemite National Park and Beyond

What was once the beloved home of the Ahwahneechee, Miwok, and Paiute Indians is now a spectacular playground for 4 million annual visitors. Designated a national park in 1890, thanks in part to Sierra Club founder John Muir, 1,170-square-mile Yosemite is only slightly smaller than the state of Rhode Island. During the peak season, crowds typical of Disney World clog the 7-square-mile valley for a glimpse of some of nature's most incredible creations, including 4,500-foot-high **EL CAPITAN**, the largest piece of exposed granite on earth, and 2,425-foot-high **YOSEMITE FALLS**, the highest waterfall in North America and fifth highest in the world. The Yosemite area also offers access to the bird-watching shores of **MONO LAKE** and the outdoor haven of the **MAMMOTH LAKES** region.

Yosemite National Park

To avoid most of the crowds, visit Yosemite in the spring or early fall, when the wildflowers are plentiful and the weather is usually mild. You can virtually escape civilization by setting up a tent in Tuolumne Meadows (closed in winter), where numerous trails wind through the densely forested and sparsely populated high country. This grande dame of national parks is actually most dazzling—and least crowded—in the winter, the time of year Ansel Adams shot those world-renowned photographs of the snow-laced valley. Unfortunately, most of the hiking trails (and Tuolumne Meadows) will be inaccessible then, and the drive may be treacherous. Snow and ice limit access to the park, and many of the eastern passes may be closed; call for **HIGHWAY CONDITIONS** (800/427-ROAD). Those who do brave the elements, however, will be rewarded with a truly unforgettable winter vista.

No matter what the time of year, visitors to Yosemite National Park must pay its friendly rangers a $20-per-car entrance fee or $10 per person (17 years and older) per week for visitors on foot, horseback, motorcycle, or bus (annual Yosemite Passes are a bargain at only $40). In return, you receive a seven-day pass, a detailed park map, and the *Yosemite Guide*, a handy tabloid featuring the park's rules, rates, attractions, and current exhibits. One of the best ways to sightsee on the valley floor is by bike. **CURRY VILLAGE** (209/372-8333) and **YOSEMITE LODGE** (801/559-4884) have bike stands that rent one-speed cruisers (and helmets) daily. More than 8 miles of paved bicycle paths wind through the eastern end of the valley, but bicycles (including mountain bikes) are not allowed on the hiking trails.

Day hikers in the valley have a wide variety of trails to choose from, and all are well-charted on the visitors' map. The best easy hike is the **MIRROR LAKE/MEADOW TRAIL**, a 2-mile round-trip walk (5 miles if you circle the lake) that provides a magnificent view of Half Dome. More strenuous is the popular hike to **UPPER YOSEMITE FALLS**, a 7.2-mile round-trip trek with a spectacular overview of the 2,425-foot drop. (Don't wander off the trail, or you may join the unlucky souls who have tumbled off the cliffs to their deaths.) The granddaddy of Yosemite hikes is the very steep ascent to the top of 8,840-foot **HALF DOME**, a 17-mile, round-trip, 10- to 12-hour-long thigh-burner that requires Schwarzeneggerlike gusto and the nerve to hang on to climbing cables anchored in granite—clearly not a jaunt for everyone. When the snowstorm season hits, many people haul out their snowshoes or cross-country skis for valley excursions, or snap on their alpine skis and schuss down the groomed beginner/intermediate hills of **BADGER PASS SKI** (Glacier Point Rd; 209/372-8430; www.yosemitepark.com/BadgerPass.aspx).

If you'd rather keep your feet firmly planted on lower ground, tour the **YOSEMITE VALLEY VISITOR CENTER** (Village Mall, Yosemite Valley; 209/372-0200; www.nps.gov/yose), which houses some mildly interesting galleries and museums. The center's Indian Cultural Museum hosts live demonstrations of the native Miwok and Paiute methods of basket weaving, jewelry making, and other crafts. Nearby are a reconstructed Miwok-Paiute village, a self-guided

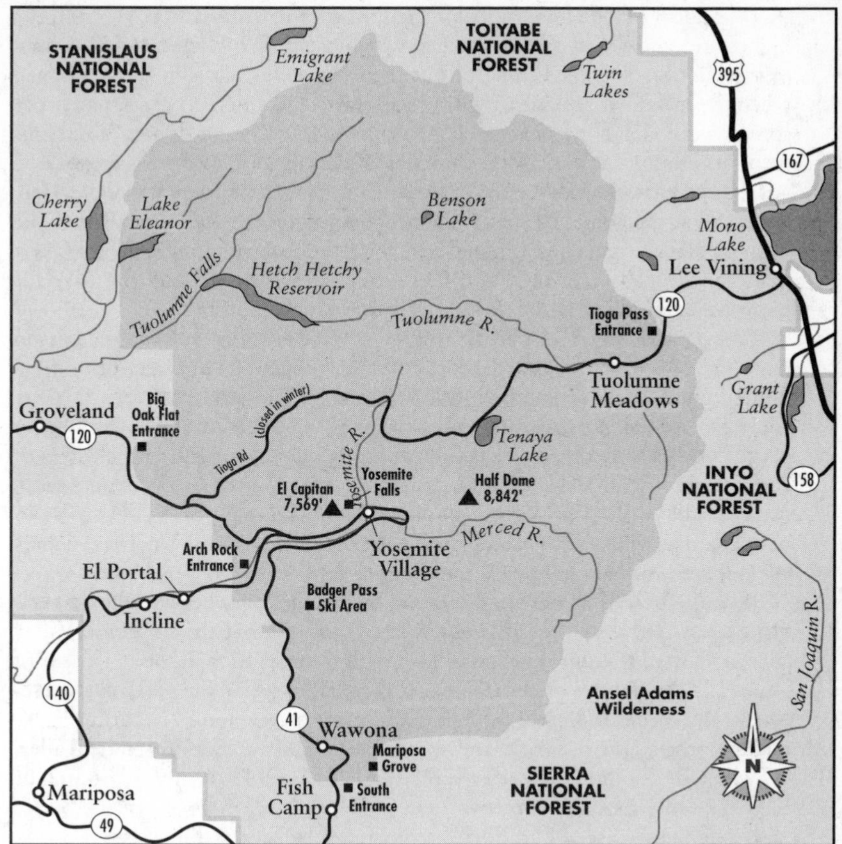

Yosemite National Park

nature trail, and an art gallery showcasing the master photographer whose name is almost synonymous with this place: Ansel Adams.

Unless bumper-to-bumper traffic is your idea of a vacation in the woods, skip Yosemite Valley during summer weekends. **GLACIER POINT** (at the end of Glacier Point Rd), a rocky ledge 3,215 feet above the valley floor, has what many consider one of the best vistas on the continent: a bird's-eye view of the entire valley and a panoramic expanse of the High Sierra. The view is particularly striking at sunset and under a full moon. The point is open only in the summer.

At the southern entrance to the park, 35 miles south of the valley, lies **MARIPOSA GROVE**, home to some of the planet's largest and most ancient living things. The most popular attraction is the 2,700-year-old **GRIZZLY GIANT**, the world's oldest sequoia. Pick up a self-guided trail map in the box at the grove trailhead, or attend one of the free ranger-led walks, offered regularly; check the *Yosemite Guide* for current schedules.

Due north of Yosemite Valley is the famous **TIOGA PASS** (Hwy 120), the highest automobile pass in California, which crests at 9,945 feet (and is closed in the winter). The ideal time to tour the 60-mile stretch is in early summer, when the meadows are dotted with wildflowers and you can occasionally spot some wildlife lingering near the lakes and exposed granite slopes. Numerous turnouts offer prime photo opportunities, and roadside picnic areas are located at **LEMBERT DOME** and **TENAYA LAKE.** This is also the route to **TUOLUMNE MEADOWS**, the gorgeous subalpine meadows along the Tuolumne River. The meadows are a popular camping area (half the campsites are available on a first-come, first-served basis and half require reservations) and the base for backpackers heading into Yosemite's beautiful high country.

Backpackers are required to obtain a **WILDERNESS PERMIT** in person (call 877/833-6777 for more information). The permits are free, but only a limited number are distributed. The 3½-mile hike to **MAY LAKE** is a favorite route for backpackers, as is the 6-mile hike to the **GLEN AULIN HIGH SIERRA BACKPACKER'S CAMP**, a spectacular spot for pitching a tent. Five clusters of canvas cabins (call 801/559-4909 for details), for four to six occupants each, are available to backpackers in the High Sierra region; prices average $145 per person per night and include breakfast, dinner, and a shower. These cabins are booked through an annual lottery each fall.

If you're partial to viewing Yosemite by car, pick up a copy of the **YOSEMITE ROAD GUIDE** or the *Yosemite Valley Tour* audio at the Yosemite Valley Visitor Center. It's almost as good as having Ranger Rick in the back seat of your car. City slickers might also want to consider seeing the park on **HORSEBACK**; the thrill (and ease) of riding a horse into Yosemite's beautiful backcountry just might be worth the splurge. Select a stable in Yosemite Valley, Wawona, or Tuolumne Meadows, then call 209/372-8348, 209/375-6502, or 209/372-8427 to make a reservation.

While the sightseeing in Yosemite is unparalleled, the dining is not. Bring as much of your own food as possible, because most of the park's restaurants offer mediocre (or worse) cafeteria-style food; the only exception is the lofty Ahwahnee Restaurant, but you'll have to fork over a bundle to eat there.

Park accommodations range from less than $25 per night for a campsite to more than $200 nightly for a room at the Ahwahnee Hotel. Reservations are required for most Yosemite **CAMPSITES**—only a few are available on a first-come, first-served basis. The valley campsites near the Merced River offer easy access to the park's most sought-after attractions, but not much in the way of privacy. Moderately priced **MOTEL ROOMS** are available at the valley's basic-but-adequate Yosemite Lodge (a quick walk from Lower Yosemite Falls). Spartan **CABINS** (some are nothing more than wood frames with canvas covers; others are heated in the winter) offer inexpensive alternatives to camping, and they're popular with families. Curry Village has 427 canvas tent cabins that sleep up to five people. Bathroom facilities are shared and, to avoid tempting the always-hungry bears, no food or cooking is allowed. These lodgings are actually just one step up from camping, but if you adopt the right "roughing it" attitude, they can be a lot of fun—sort of like summer camp. There are also tent cabins at Tuolumne Meadows Lodge and Yosemite Lodge. Campgrounds in Yosemite can be reserved up to five months in advance through the National Park Reservation Service (877/444-6777; www.reservations.gov). During the busy season, June through September, all valley campsites sell out within hours of becoming available. Online reservations may be booked through www.yosemitepark.com. Keep in mind that reservations held without deposit must be confirmed by 4pm on the scheduled day of arrival. Otherwise, you'll lose your reservation. Vacation-home rentals (with full kitchens) can also be reserved, but they cost a pretty penny; for more information call **YOSEMITE WEST COTTAGES AND VACATION HOME RENTALS** (559/642-2211; www.yosemitewest.com). Additional information on Yosemite National Park is available online at www.yosemitepark.com and www.nps.gov/yose. There's also a central 24-hour recorded information line for the park (209/372-0200).

LODGINGS

Ahwahnee Hotel / ★★★

YOSEMITE VALLEY, YOSEMITE NATIONAL PARK; 801/559-4884

The majestic Ahwahnee Hotel stands against the soaring cliffs of Yosemite and is among the most idyllic hotels in California. The 123 rooms are spacious, with double or king-size beds and large bathrooms; a few even boast a view of Half Dome (try to reserve one of the more spacious cottages, which cost the same as rooms in the main hotel). The Ahwahnee Restaurant is more noteworthy for its ambience than for its cuisine; arrive well before nightfall to admire the view. The food is certainly the best in the region and has improved of late, but don't expect a gourmet affair. Those in the know apply far in advance for lottery tickets to the Bracebridge Dinner, a three-hour feast held every Christmas that 60,000 people try to sign up for—though, alas, only 1,750 gain admission. *$$$–$$$$; DC, DIS, MC, V; checks OK; www.yosemitepark.com; take Hwy 120 east into Yosemite Valley and follow signs to hotel.* ♿

Wawona Hotel / ★

HWY 41, YOSEMITE NATIONAL PARK; 801/559-4884

Four miles from the park's entrance, the Wawona—the Ahwahnee Hotel's more rustic cousin—is the oldest resort hotel in the state. Most of the 104 rooms are small, and only about half have private bathrooms. This National Historic Landmark's biggest drawback is its distance from the park's most popular attractions. The giant sequoias in the nearby Mariposa Grove are inviting, but they don't compare to the cliffs and vistas elsewhere in Yosemite. Amenities include a nine-hole golf course, tennis court, riding stable, and 1917 "swimming tank." The dining room has usually offered little more than upscale institutional food, though lately the quality has improved considerably. However, the year-round Sunday brunch and the Saturday-evening summer lawn barbecues are a treat. *$$; AE, DC, DIS, MC, V; checks OK; www.yosemitepark.com; southwest corner of the park, 27 miles from Yosemite Valley.* ♿

Groveland

LODGINGS

Berkshire Inn / ★★

19950 HWY 120, GROVELAND; 209/962-6744 OR 888/225-2064

Most guests come to the Berkshire Inn for a weekend of white-water rafting on the Tuolumne River; for boating, golfing, or hiking at the nearby Pine Mountain Lake Recreation Area; or for an overnight stop on their way to Yosemite. Situated on 20 wooded acres, this sprawling lodge has six large guest rooms and four suites, all with private bathrooms and private entrances; some also have decks. Guests are encouraged to relax on the inn's wood decks overlooking the surrounding mountains, as well as in two large common areas with comfy couches, TVs, and VCRs. Guests share access to the large gazebo overlooking the countryside. Other perks include complimentary wine and a large continental breakfast. It's a warm, friendly place that's perfect for families, hikers, or groups of rafters. *$$; AE, DIS, MC, V; checks OK; www.berkshireinn.net; 2 miles east of town, look for the international flags.*

Evergreen Lodge / ★★

33160 EVERGREEN RD, GROVELAND; 209/379-2606 OR 800/93-LODGE

The key to truly enjoying Yosemite National Park is to stay clear of the brutal crowds. You accomplish this by booking a rustic little cabin at the Evergreen Lodge, which is located just a few miles from both the Groveland and Hetch Hetchy gateways to the park. The 70 recently renovated/built cabins are scattered throughout a grove of towering pines; each comes with a private bathroom, rocking chairs on the front porch, and TVs. Rates include a continental breakfast; dinner is served daily at the lodge's restaurant. There's also a small general store and deli, a beer garden, outdoor dining, a hot tub area, a campfire/amphitheater area, a recreation center, and guided trips in and around Yosemite. The lodge is surrounded by numerous hiking trails; access to tennis courts, a pool, and horseback riding are right down the road at neighboring Camp Mather. *$–$$; AE, DIS, MC, V; checks OK; www.evergreenlodge.com; off Hwy 120, turn left at Hetch Hetchy/Evergreen Rd.*

Groveland Hotel / ★★

18767 MAIN ST, GROVELAND; 209/962-4000 OR 800/273-3314

Constructed in 1849, the Groveland Hotel is one of the region's oldest buildings. Several years ago, the hotel underwent a million-dollar renovation, adding a modern conference center and a saloon. Despite the costly upgrades, the place still manages to retain some of the charm of yesteryear. Its 17 guest rooms aren't large, but they are attractive, and down comforters and private baths make them quite comfortable. The best rooms are the two-room suites equipped with spa tubs and fireplaces. Along with an authentic gold rush–era saloon, the hotel has an old-fashioned restaurant serving American classics, and the wine list has won the *Wine Spectator* Award of Excellence. Another plus: the hotel is pet-friendly. *$$$; AE, DC, DIS, MC, V; checks OK; www.groveland.com; downtown, east side of Main St.* ♿

Fish Camp

RESTAURANTS

Narrow Gauge Inn / ★★

48571 HWY 41, FISH CAMP; 559/683-7720

An attractive old inn and restaurant nestled in the thick of the Sierra National Forest, the Narrow Gauge is one of the Mariposa Grove area's best restaurants. You'll find down-home service here, as well as views of Mount Raymond and a cozy country ambience. The inn's specialty is thick cuts of well-prepared meats: everything from charbroiled rib eye to fillet of ostrich. Pasta, chicken, and seafood are available as well, and all dinners include a house-made soup or salad, fresh vegetables, and rice or potatoes (baked or garlic mashed). There's a well-edited wine list, too. The inn offers 26 rooms with balconies; ask for one of the four creek-side rooms, which have particularly splendid views. Narrow Gauge also offers a heated swimming pool and a spa. *$$; DIS, MC, V; no checks; dinner every day (open Apr 9–Oct 20); full bar; reservations recommended; www.narrowgaugeinn.com; 4 miles south of Yosemite National Park's south gate.*

LODGINGS

Tenaya Lodge at Yosemite / ★★★

1122 HWY 41, FISH CAMP; 559/683-6555 OR 888/514-2167

Tenaya Lodge is a full-service resort located just 2 miles from the entrance to Yosemite National Park. Built in 1990 and rebuilt in 1999, the lodge has 244 rooms, all with mountain and forest views and private baths. Amenities include outdoor and indoor pools and a small fitness center with a steam room, sauna, and whirlpool. Sierra Restaurant offers breakfast and Cal-Ital entrées like grilled sterling salmon and lobster with orecchiette pasta. The Parkside Deli specializes in picnic lunches to go, and Jackalope's Bar and Grill offers casual fare like pizza and burgers. The lodge's events desk offers mountain bike rentals, tours of Yosemite, white-water rafting, rock climbing, horseback riding, and other outdoor activities. Camp Tenaya has nature walks, arts and crafts, and music for kids, and lodge personnel can arrange daily baby-sitting services for infants. *$$$; AE, DC, DIS, MC, V; checks OK; www.tenayalodge.com; 2 miles south of Yosemite National Park's southwest gate.* ♿

MADAME MOUSTACHE AND THE ITALIAN GHOST

"Good-bye God, I'm going to Bodie," wrote a little girl whose family was moving to the most infamous gold rush boomtown in California.

Located in high desert country along the western slopes of the Sierra Nevada, Bodie had a population of about 8,000 brave souls in 1879 and a lurid history of stagecoach holdups, robberies, killings, saloons and dance halls, and loose women (Madame Moustache was a favorite). During one brief lull in the action, the local newspaper, tongue in cheek, commented, "Bodie is becoming a summer resort—no one killed here last week."

The town bustled with white-topped prairie schooners; horses and wagons filled with ore, wood, hay, and lumber; and daily stages carrying bars of gold bullion guarded by men with sawed-off shotguns. Some $32 million in gold was mined in Bodie's hills during the area's short but intense heyday. After the mines played out, the town went into decline, and by 1882 most of the townsfolk had moved on. Fires finished off many of the remaining buildings. Today Bodie is a ghost town, designated a National Historic Site and State Historic Park. It is maintained in a state of "arrested decay," which means the remaining buildings are preserved but not rebuilt or changed in any way.

What you see is so eerily authentic and strange—pants still hanging next to a steamer trunk, dusty schoolbooks tossed on desks, desert winds howling through

Bridgeport

LODGINGS

The Cain House: A Country Inn / ★★

340 MAIN ST, BRIDGEPORT; 760/932-7383 OR 800/433-2246

James Stuart Cain made his fortune in the rough-and-tumble boomtown of Bodie. However, later generations of Cains (perhaps weary of Bodie's sanitation problems and brothels) moved over the hill to the comparatively genteel cow town of Bridgeport. Set in one of the most picturesque valleys in the eastern Sierra, Bridgeport is backed by granite peaks in the west and sage- and piñon-covered desert hills in the east. This modest, turn-of-the-century inn, owned by the obliging Marachal Gohlich, is a tribute to Cain. Each of the seven individually decorated guest rooms has a private bath, a king- or queen-size bed with a quilt and down comforter, and a TV tucked inside an armoire. In the morning expect good, dark coffee (a rare treat on this side of the Sierra) and a hearty breakfast, including house-made muffins. *$$; AE, DIS, MC, V; checks OK; www.silvermapleinn.com; at the north end of town.*

a town jail known for vigilante justice—that ghost stories naturally abound. Some say a little girl, buried in the cemetery and known as "the Angel of Bodie," has been heard calling for her daddy and plays with the occasional unsuspecting visitor's child. Park aides tossing rocks down a mine shaft claim to have heard a calm voice saying "Hey, you," coming from within the blocked-up, caved-in mine. Another park employee opened a house that had been locked up for the winter and smelled fresh-cooked Italian food.

In addition to its ghostly inhabitants, Bodie is open to visitors all year—but winters can be fierce. At 9,000 feet, Bodie gets chilly even in summer. Mark Twain once said that the breaking up of one winter and the beginning of the next were the only seasons he could distinguish in Bodie. The *Carson Tribune* observed, "The weather is so cold in Bodie that four pairs of blankets and three in a bed is not sufficient to promote warmth." There are no food, drink, or tourist accommodations in the park—just the pure remains of the wild, wild West.

To get to Bodie, take US 395; 7 miles south of Bridgeport, take State Route 270. Go 10 miles to the end of the paved road and continue 3 more miles on the unfinished road. Call ahead (760/647-6445) for road and weather conditions. Admission is $5 per person 17 and older; free for 16 and under. For more information, visit www.bodie.com.

Mono Lake

Set at the eastern foot of the Sierra Nevada and ringed with fragile limestone tufa spires, this hauntingly beautiful 60-square-mile desert salt lake is a stopover for millions of migratory birds that arrive yearly to feed on the lake's trillions of brine shrimp and alkali flies (*mono* means "flies" in the language of the Yokuts, the Native Americans who live just south of this region). While numerous streams empty into Mono (pronounced MOE-no) Lake, there is no outlet. Instead, the lake water evaporates, leaving behind minerals washed down from the surrounding mountains. The result is an alkaline and saline content that is too high for fish (three times saltier than the sea) but ideal for shrimp, flies, and human swimmers. Right off Highway 395 is the **MONO BASIN SCENIC AREA VISITORS CENTER** (760/647-3044; www.monolake.org; open every day in summer, Thurs–Mon in winter), a modern, high-tech edifice that would make any taxpayer proud. The center offers scheduled walks and talks, and it has an outstanding environmental and historical display with hands-on exhibits that will entertain the kids. After touring the visitor center, head for the **SOUTH TUFA AREA** at the southern end of the lake and get a closer look at the tufa formations and briny water.

June Lake

RESTAURANTS

Carson Peak Inn / ★★

JUNE LAKE LOOP, JUNE LAKE; 760/648-7575

This red building, located a few miles past the town of June Lake, has led several former lives, most recently as an American Legion headquarters, a dance hall, and a pizza parlor. Now it's one of the better restaurants in the area, serving hearty dinners such as melt-in-your-mouth filet mignon smothered with sautéed mushrooms and Australian lobster tail (a rarity in these parts). Portions are large, so arrive hungry. They also offer a vegetarian plate and a special menu for kids. *$–$$$; AE, DIS, MC, V; checks OK; dinner every day; beer and wine; reservations recommended; off Hwy 395.* ♿

Mammoth Lakes

At the base of 11,053-foot Mammoth Mountain are nearly a dozen alpine lakes and the sprawling town of Mammoth Lakes—a mishmash of inns, motels, and restaurants primarily built to serve patrons of the popular Mammoth Mountain Ski Area. Ever since founder Dave McCoy mortgaged his motorcycle in 1938 to buy his first ski lift, folks have been coming here in droves to carve turns and navigate moguls at one of the best downhill ski areas in the United States. In addition to skiing, the region has been famous for decades for its fantastic fishing holes. The trout is king here, and several fishing derbies celebrate its royal status. This natural kingdom is no longer the exclusive domain of anglers and skiers, however. Word has gotten out about Mammoth's charms, attracting every kind of outdoor enthusiast and adventurer to this spectacular region in the heart of the High Sierra.

Whether you've migrated to the Mammoth area to ski, fish, golf, play, or simply rest your weary bones, stop by the **MAMMOTH LAKES VISITORS CENTER/RANGER STATION** (Hwy 203, just before the town of Mammoth Lakes; 760/924-5500), or contact the **MAMMOTH LAKES VISITORS BUREAU** (760/934-2712 or 888-GO-MAMMOTH; www.visitmammoth.com). You'll find wall-to-wall maps, brochures, and day planners, as well as copies of the Forest Service's excellent (and free) *Winter Recreation Map* and *Summer Recreation Map*, which show the area's best routes for hiking, biking, sledding, snowmobiling, and cross-country skiing. If you need to rent ski gear or practically any other athletic or outdoor equipment, visit the bustling **KITTREDGE SPORTS** shop (3218 Main St, next to the Chevron gas station, Mammoth Lakes; 760/934-7566; www.kittredgesports.com).

Once you've unpacked your bags, it's time to lace up your hiking boots and explore. A top attraction is **DEVILS POSTPILE NATIONAL MONUMENT** (760/934-2289), one of the world's premier examples of basalt columns. The 60-foot-tall, slender rock columns rise 7,560 feet above sea level and were formed nearly 100,000 years ago when molten lava erupted from Mammoth Mountain, cooled, and fractured into multisided forms; they've become such a popular attraction that between June 15 and September 15, rangers close the access road to daytime traffic and require visitors without special permits to travel by shuttle. Shuttles pick up riders every 15 minutes at the Mammoth Mountain Ski Area parking lot on Minaret Road, off Highway 203W, and drop them off at a riverside trail for the less-than-half-mile walk to the monument. (To reach the access road, take Hwy 203W from US 395, go through the town of Mammoth, and continue 17 miles west.)

After you've seen the Postpile, follow the trail for another 2 miles to the beautiful **RAINBOW FALLS**, where the **SAN JOAQUIN RIVER** plunges 101 feet over an ancient lava flow into a deep pool, often creating rainbows in the mist. If you follow the trail another 3 miles from the falls to **REDS MEADOW**, you'll be at one of the entrance points to the 228,500-acre **ANSEL ADAMS WILDERNESS**, a popular backpacking destination highlighted by the jagged **MINARETS**, a series of steep, narrow volcanic ridges just south of massive Mount Ritter.

True to its name, the Mammoth Lakes area boasts 10 lakes (none of which, oddly enough, are named Mammoth). The largest and one of the most striking is **LAKE MARY** (head west on Main St, which turns into Lake Mary Rd, drive past Twin Lakes, and continue on until you see it), and even though it's set high in the mountains, it's easy to get to. Numerous hiking trails at Lake Mary lead to nearby smaller, less-crowded lakes, including **HORSESHOE LAKE**, a great place for swimming (the water is slightly warmer than in neighboring lakes). Trout fishers frequently try their luck at Lake Mary, although most anglers prefer **CONVICT LAKE**, where you can rent a boat and stock up at the Convict Lake Resort's tackle shop (from Hwy 395 a few miles south of town, take the Convict Lake Rd exit, just south of Mammoth Lakes Airport; 760/934-3800). Another hot spot for snagging trout is **HOT CREEK** (on Hot Creek Hatchery Rd, just off Hwy 395 at the north end of Mammoth Lakes Airport), the most popular catch-and-release fishery in California (on average, each trout is caught and released five to six times a month). Only a few miles of the creek are accessible to the public—the rest is private property.

MOUNTAIN BIKING is another hugely popular sport here in the summer, when the entire Mammoth Mountain Ski Area is transformed into one of the top bike parks in the country. The national Norba mountain bike championship race (on Minaret Rd, off Hwy 203W) takes place here, too; call the Mammoth Lakes Visitors Bureau for details. You can buy an all-day pass to 60 miles of single-track trails and a gondola that will zip you and your bike up to the top of the mountain. It's all downhill from there (be sure to wear a helmet), with trails ranging in difficulty from the mellow "Paper Route" ride to the infamous "Kamikaze" wheel-spinner. If you don't want to pay to ride a bike, there are dozens of great trails in the area where mountain bikes are permitted. There's a variety of rent-and-ride packages available; for more information, call 800/MAMMOTH or log onto www.mammothmountain.com.

With winter comes an onslaught of downhill skiers, who journey here to schuss the slopes of **MAMMOTH MOUNTAIN SKI AREA** (see Skiing the Sierra Nevada). Unfortunately, it can be one of the country's most crowded ski areas, particularly on weekends, when more than 10,000 Los Angelenos make the lengthy commute. (Tip: About 90 percent of the skiers arrive on Friday night and leave Sunday afternoon, so come on a weekday.) If you've ever witnessed the traffic jams converging on the ski area's parking lot, you know why veteran Mammoth skiers always park their wheels in town and take the shuttle to the resort. These shuttles are not only convenient, but they're also free. And no matter where you're staying in Mammoth Lakes, a **MAMMOTH AREA SHUTTLE** (www.mammothweb.com/transportation/shuttleroute.cfm) stop is most likely nearby. The ubiquitous buses run from 7am to 5:30pm every day during the ski season, and they swing by their stops every 15 minutes to shuttle skiers to one of the resort's three entrances.

Mammoth Lakes also has mile upon mile of perfectly groomed cross-country ski trails winding through gorgeous stretches of national forest and immense meadows. Nordic skiers of all levels favor the **TAMARACK CROSS-COUNTRY SKI CENTER** (Lake Mary Rd, 2½ miles southwest of town; 760/934-2442; www.tamaracklodge.com) at Tamarack Lodge in Twin Lakes, which offers 25 miles of groomed trails, extensive backcountry trails, lessons, rentals, and tours.

Dozens of natural hot springs dot the Mammoth area, although most of the remote ones are kept secret by tourist-weary locals, who probably wouldn't make you feel very welcome even if you discovered one. Visitors are definitely welcome, however, at the more accessible springs, including the free **HOT CREEK GEOLOGIC SITE** (take the Hot Creek Hatchery Rd exit off Hwy 395, at the north end of Mammoth Lakes Airport, and follow the signs), where the narrow creek feeds into a series of artificial pools—some only big enough for two, others family-size. These pools are equipped with cold-water pipes that usually keep the water temperature toasty yet not unbearably hot. The Forest Service discourages soaking in the pools because of sporadic spurts of scalding water—yes, there is a small risk of getting your buns poached—but most people are more concerned about whether or not to show off their birthday suits (swimsuits are optional). Call the Mammoth Lakes Visitors Bureau for more details.

Granted, life is often one big outdoor party in Mammoth Lakes, but when the annual **MAMMOTH LAKES JAZZ JUBILEE** (www.mammothjazz.org) swings into gear, hold on to your Tevas—nearly everyone in this toe-tapping town starts kicking up their heels when a dozen world-class bands start tootin' their horns. This three-day jazz extravaganza usually happens the first weekend after the Fourth of July. A much more sedate but definitely worthwhile musical event is the annual **SIERRA SUMMER FESTIVAL** (www.sierrasummerfestival.org), a tribute to everything from chamber to classical music that begins in late July and winds down in early August.

RESTAURANTS

The Mogul / ★

1528 TAVERN RD, MAMMOTH LAKES; 760/934-3039

Your server skillfully charbroils fresh fish, shrimp, and steak under your watchful eye here at the Mogul, voted Mammoth's best steak house several years in a row by *Mammoth Times* readers. Although it's not cooked at the table, the Mammoth cut of prime rib is a local favorite. The restaurant's success is based in part on large portions and the use of old family recipes for such favorites as baked beans and sweet Cinnamon Charlotte, a cupcake topped with ice cream and cinnamon sauce. Kids get their own menus and Mogul balloons. *$$; AE, DIS, MC, V; no checks; dinner every day; full bar; reservations recommended; 1 block south of Main St, off Old Mammoth Rd.*

Nevados / ★★

6060 MINARET RD, MAMMOTH LAKES; 760/934-4466

One of Mammoth's finest restaurants is packed almost every night with locals and Los Angelenos on holiday. The entrées are so utterly satisfying—and reasonably priced—that nary a complaint is heard about the food or service. Though all menu items are available à la carte, for only a few dollars more you can enjoy a prix-fixe three-course meal with any dish on the three-part menu. A recommended trio is the strudel appetizer of wild mushrooms and rabbit with roasted shallots and grilled scallions, followed by an entrée of braised Provimi veal shank with roasted tomatoes and garlic mashed potatoes, and, for dessert, a fantastic warm pear and almond tart sweetened with caramel sauce and vanilla-bean ice cream. *$$–$$$; AE, MC, V; checks OK; dinner every day; full bar; reservations recommended; at Minaret Rd.*

Roberto's Mexican Café / ★★

271 OLD MAMMOTH RD, MAMMOTH LAKES; 760/934-3667

Before you hit the slopes, pad your stomach at Roberto's, where portion sizes could feed a whole family. (Note: Ordering both a burrito *and* a chile relleno for one is completely unnecessary.) Our recommendations include the chipotle chicken wings and vegetarian-friendly-yet-filling Juanitas Burrito. No matter what you choose, it will arrive loaded with cheese (the lactose intolerant may want to dine elsewhere). If the downstairs is packed, ask to eat upstairs at the bar. Margaritas aside, tequila cocktails are the house specialties and have saucy names like Pink Taco (Don Julio Silver, Patron, grapefruit juice), and Horny Bob (Hornitos Reposada tequila, triple sec, sweet and sour). *$$; MC, V; checks OK; breakfast, lunch, dinner every day; full bar; reservations recommended; at Meridian Blvd.*

Skadi / ★★

587 OLD MAMMOTH RD, MAMMOTH LAKES; 760/934-3902

Ian Algerøen, chef-owner of Skadi, was chef at the popular Nevados (see review) before realizing his own unique culinary vision. The food here is a mix of Scandinavian and Italian Alpine, with a bit of San Francisco thrown in. *Bon Appétit* magazine has called Skadi "the most inventive restaurant in Mammoth," and so it is. Entrées include roast maple-leaf duck with juniper, aquavit, and lingonberries and pan-roasted, crispy-skin salmon with horseradish and chives, served with mashed potatoes and roasted beets. The desserts are noteworthy, particularly the tasting of four of the house-made chocolate delights and the honey-roasted wild strawberries with passion fruit sorbet. *$$$; AE, MC, V; checks OK; dinner every day; beer and wine; reservations recommended; www.restaurantskadi.com; corner of Chateau and Old Mammoth rds.*

Whiskey Creek Mountain Bistro / ★

24 LAKE MARY RD, MAMMOTH LAKES; 760/934-2555

Both skiers and locals head to Whiskey Creek for two things: great steaks and a swinging bar scene. In the '70s this place was a raging singles hangout for the juiced-up L.A. crowd, and though it's calmed down a bit since then, it's still the most rockin' restaurant in Mammoth. The downstairs dining room's most popular entrées include the bacon-wrapped meat loaf and South Carolina pork chops, both served with a side of roasted garlic mashed potatoes. After dinner, head upstairs and enjoy live music every night from 9pm until at least 1am—and don't forget to dust off your cheesy come-on lines. *$$; AE, DC, DIS, MC, V; local checks only; dinner every day; full bar; reservations recommended at Minaret Rd.*

LODGINGS

Mammoth Mountain Inn / ★

1 MINARET RD, MAMMOTH LAKES; 760/934-2581 OR 800/228-4947

This mammoth-size inn is a popular haven for downhill skiers—you can't get any closer to the slopes—and in the summer the guests are primarily mountain bikers, fly-fishers, hikers, and horseback riders. The 173 guest rooms come with all the usual amenities—telephones, TVs and DVD players, and double or queen-size beds—but suffer from thin walls and a rather uninspired decor. Your best bet is to rent a junior suite in the refurbished section or, if you're bringing the family, one of the 40 condo units, which can house up to 13 guests. Other perks include a whirlpool spa, child-care facilities, a game room, a playground, and shuttle service. The only downside is the 10-minute drive into town. The hotel's Yodler Pub, Mountainside Grill, and Dry Creek Bar are open year-round. *$$–$$$; AE, MC, V; checks OK; www.mammothmountain.com; at Mammoth Mountain Ski Area, 4 miles from downtown.*

Sierra Lodge / ★★

3540 MAIN ST, MAMMOTH LAKES; 760/934-7231 OR 800/356-5711

Unlike most lodges in the area, Sierra Lodge, built in 1991, has no rustic elements in any of its 35 spacious rooms. The decor here is quite contemporary: amenities include cable TVs, telephones, kitchenettes, and partial mountain views from private balconies. The two-bedroom suite is ideal for groups or families. After a hard day of skiing, relax your bones in the lodge's outdoor Jacuzzi, then kick back for a game of backgammon in the cozy Fireside Room. Skiers are pampered with their own ski lockers; all guests enjoy free covered parking and a continental breakfast. Other perks include free shuttle service right outside the front door, and Mammoth's best restaurant, Nevados (see review), is within easy walking distance. *$–$$; AE, DIS, MC, V; checks OK; www.sierralodge.com; at Sierra St.*

Tamarack Lodge Resort / ★★

TWIN LAKE RD, MAMMOTH LAKES; 760/934-2442 OR 800/MAMMOTH

The 6-acre Tamarack Lodge sits at an elevation of 8,600 feet on the edge of Twin Lake, and come summer or winter, it's an extremely romantic retreat. The resort offers 11 lodge rooms (some with shared baths) and 27 cabins that come in a variety of configurations—from studios to two-bedroom/two-bathroom suites. All have kitchens, private bathrooms, heat, and telephones. The best units are the lakefront cabins, so be sure to request one with a lake view. The rustic Lakefront Restaurant offers the most romantic dinner setting in Mammoth Lakes. Its seasonally changing menu may feature such well-prepared fare as grilled medallions of elk fillet with a blueberry–juniper berry sauce and fresh sea scallops in a caper, chardonnay, and tarragon beurre blanc. In the winter, the lodge opens the Tamarack Cross-Country Ski Center, with 25 miles of groomed trails, lessons, rentals, and tours. *$$–$$$; AE, MC, V; checks OK; www.tamaracklodge.com; off Lake Mary Rd, 2½ miles above town.*

Convict Lake

RESTAURANTS

The Restaurant at Convict Lake / ★★★

CONVICT LAKE; 760/934-3803

The anglers who toss their lines into Convict Lake have kept this restaurant to themselves for many years. Their secret, however, is yet another big one that got away, as others have begun to journey to this glorious lakeside spot for a meal. Some patrons make a meal out of the appetizers at the bar, while others settle into the cozy booths in the elegant dining area. Popular entrées from the seasonal menu include local Alpers Ranch rainbow trout and duck confit flavored with sun-dried cherry sauce and garnished with candied orange zest. For dessert try the tasty meringue topped with kiwifruit and whipped cream or the bananas Foster flambé. *$$$; AE, DIS, MC, V; checks OK; dinner every day; full bar; reservations recommended; www.convictlake.com; from Hwy 395 take the Convict Lake exit; 3½ miles south of Mammoth Lakes.* ♿

IT TAKES GREEN TO KEEP TAHOE BLUE

By the time explorers Kit Carson and John Frémont ventured upon the brilliant blue waters of Da-ow-wa-ga ("edge of the lake"), what we now call Lake Tahoe had been a gathering place and spiritual site of the Washoe Indians for centuries. Fortune seekers soon followed the explorers, first for gold and silver, later for timber. Then wealthy San Franciscans in a quest for vacation sites fell in love with the lake, and hotels and gambling halls sprang up to shelter and entertain them. Tourism boomed. The 1960 Olympics at Squaw Valley revealed a first-class skiing area to the whole world. Today the lake is the focus of more than 20 million annual visitors—as many as 200,000 on summer weekends.

All this adoration takes its toll. One of the clearest and deepest lakes in the world, Tahoe has seen its famous transparency rise from 105 feet to around 70 feet. Algae coats the shoreline rocks in the spring. Wood-burning fireplaces, automobile exhaust, outboard motors, golf course fertilizers—all these by-products of human activity have an impact on the lake. If current levels of pollution continue, scientists say, within 30 years the lake will have lost half its transparency, changing color from blue to green. Local wildlife and forests are also suffering from urbanization. That's the bad news.

The good news is that the pitched warfare between environmentalists and businesses, developers, and property owners has abated, and a cooperative

Skiing the Sierra Nevada

When the Golden State's denizens gear up for ski season, they all usually have one destination in mind: **LAKE TAHOE**, the premier winter playground for deranged daredevils and cautious snowplowers alike. Whether you're a 6-year-old hotshot schussing down chutes, a 60-year-old granddaddy trekking through cross-country tracks, or someone in between, the Tahoe region will surely please you. A smorgasbord of downhill slopes encircles the famous twinkling alpine lake, while the cross-country ski trails are some of the most scenic and challenging in the country.

Top of the **CROSS-COUNTRY FAVORITES** list is the North Shore's **ROYAL GORGE** (Soda Springs exit off I-80; 800/500-3871 or 800/666-3871 in Northern California; www.royalgorge.com), the largest cross-country ski resort in North America: 200 miles of trails for skiers of all levels, 9,172 acres of skiable terrain, an average annual snowfall of more than 650 inches, 10 warming huts (for defrosting those frozen fingers and toes), and two lodges. More experienced Nordic skiers should head over to **EAGLE MOUNTAIN** (from I-80, exit at Yuba Gap, turn right, and follow the signs; 530/389-2254 or 800/391-2254), one of the area's best-kept secrets, which offers 47 miles of challenging trails with fantastic Sierra vistas. The South Shore's choicest cross-country tracks are at Sorensen's Resort in public-private partnership to preserve the lake and its environs seems to be genuinely under way. Up to $20 million in federal and state funds are being used for restoration and conservation. In addition to the nature front, cooperative efforts are manifesting themselves in a cleanup of the tackier urban areas. Low-rent motels, T-shirt stores, and souvenir shops in the commercial strip at the north end of South Lake Tahoe, for instance, are already being bulldozed out of existence and replaced by upscale hotels and restaurants, an ice skating rink, and a major shopping mall. While this may not seem like the stuff of a nature lover's dreams, the new development has a silver lining. Previously, 95 percent of the ground in the commercial areas was covered in concrete, funneling polluted snowmelt and rainwater straight into the lake. All newly redeveloped areas will have holding and treatment ponds to clean up the runoff and must preserve the surrounding forests. In South Lake Tahoe, Heavenly's central ski gondola and a high-tech bus system, two eco-friendly methods of luring people out of their cars, are already in use.

Perhaps the most visible sign of changing attitudes is the prevalence of Keep Tahoe Blue bumper stickers. At one time considered anti-progress, the signs could get your car defaced. Now they are everywhere. Admirers of one of the world's natural wonders are at last united in their efforts to save the lake—and it's working. The latest report is that the clarity of Lake Tahoe is improving.

HOPE VALLEY, and they're open to the public at no charge. You'll find more than 60 miles of trails winding through the **TOIYABE NATIONAL FOREST**—plenty of room to master that telemark turn and escape the Tahoe crowds. Rentals, lessons, tours, and trail maps are available at the **HOPE VALLEY OUTDOOR CENTER** (from Hwy 50 in Myers, take Hwy 89 south over the Luther Pass to the Hwy 88/89 intersection, turn left, and continue to 14655 Hwy 88; 530/694-2266; www.hopevalleyoutdoors.com), located 300 yards east of Sorensen's Resort. Farther south is the **BEAR VALLEY CROSS-COUNTRY** area (off Hwy 4; 209/753-2834; www.bearvalleyxc.com), with 43 miles of groomed Nordic track—one of the largest track systems in the United States. **YOSEMITE CROSS-COUNTRY CENTER** (209/372-8444) at **BADGER PASS SKI AREA** (off SR 41) offers rentals, lessons, and excursions on 90 miles of groomed trails (there's a total of 350 miles of cross-country trails in the park). There are also two major cross-country ski centers at **MAMMOTH MOUNTAIN SKI AREA** (off Hwy 395), where L.A. folk flock on winter weekends; for more information, call the Mammoth Lakes Visitors Bureau (760/934-2712 or 800/367-6572).

For **DOWNHILL** thrill seekers, Lake Tahoe offers a plethora of first-rate resorts that cater to every age, ability, and whim. Families fare best at **NORTHSTAR**, while serious skiers find the most challenging terrain at **SQUAW VALLEY USA**,

KIRKWOOD, **HEAVENLY SKI RESORT**, and **ALPINE MEADOWS**. Wherever you're staying, be sure to inquire about ski-package deals. Although most Northern Californians rarely tote their skis beyond Tahoe, a host of top-notch ski resorts dot the landscape south of the lake, including one of the state's best: **MAMMOTH MOUNTAIN SKI AREA**. Aside from Mammoth, these south-of-Tahoe ski spots are often less crowded and less expensive than their lakeside counterparts. Here's a roundup of the Sierra's major downhill ski areas, from the outer reaches of North Lake Tahoe to as far south as Badger Pass, just outside Yosemite National Park.

Lake Tahoe Ski Resorts

ALPINE MEADOWS (off Hwy 89; 530/583-4232 or 800/949-3296; www.skialpine.com). A favorite among locals, Alpine has runs on a par with Squaw Valley's best—but all you really need to know is that, as most of the other ski resorts are raising their lift ticket prices, Alpine Meadows is lowering theirs. Highlights include an excellent snowboarding park and superpipe, snow play areas, a family ski zone, unique kids' programs, and plenty of black diamond runs. Alpine Meadows also offers Beds & Boards ski-lodging packages, which are outstanding values.

BOREAL (off I-80; 530/426-3666; www.skiboreal.com). Small, easy to ski, and easy to get to (right off I-80 well before the Lake Tahoe exit), Boreal is a good beginner's resort and, with eight terrain parks offering slide rails, ride pipes, and plenty of big-air opportunities, it's also a mecca for snowboarders. This is one of the few places in the Lake Tahoe area that offers night skiing (open until 9pm) and, because of its extensive snowmaking equipment, it's usually one of the first ski areas to open each season.

DIAMOND PEAK (from Hwy 28, exit on Country Club Dr, turn right on Sky Wy, and drive to Incline Village; 775/832-1177; www.diamondpeak.com). Located in Incline Village on the Nevada side of Tahoe's North Shore, this small, family-oriented ski resort guarantees good skiing—if you don't like the conditions, you can turn in your ticket within the first hour for a full refund. The resort has spectacular lake views and excellent kids' programs, including a snowboard park and sledding area.

DONNER SKI RANCH (Soda Springs exit off I-80; 530/426-3635; www.donnerskiranch.com). Just up the road from Sugar Bowl is Donner, where a ski pass costs about half of what you'd pay at neighboring resorts. And despite its small size, this unpretentious ski area has a lot to offer skiers of all levels: tree skiing, groomed trails, and a few steeps and jumps, not to mention convenient parking and a cozy, down-home lodge.

GRANLIBAKKEN (off Hwy 89 at the junction of Hwy 28; 800/543-3221; www.granlibakken.com). Tiny and mainly for tots, this is a great place to teach kids the fundamentals. A rental shop, ski school, snow play area, warming hut, and snack bar are all on the premises. And later, when you'll surely need a drink, you won't have far to go to find the Tahoe City nightspots.

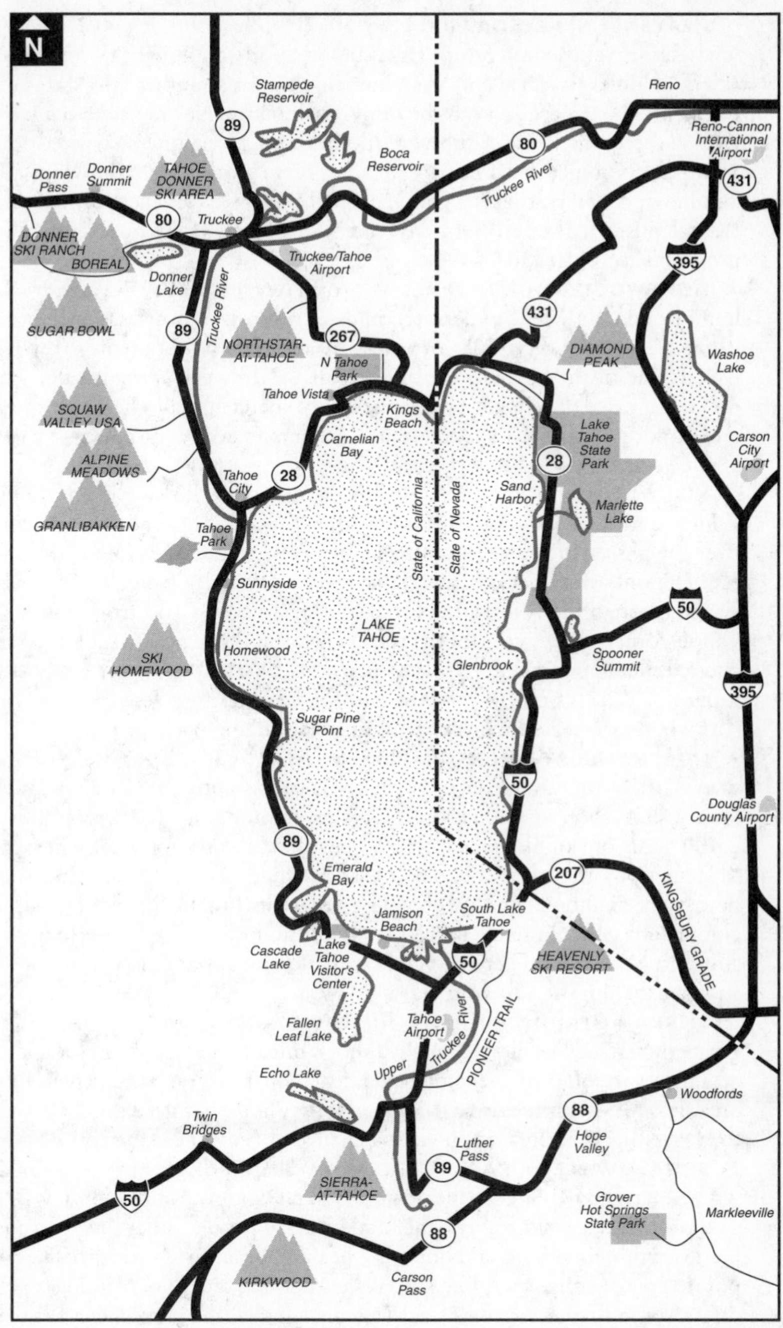

Lake Tahoe Ski Resorts

HEAVENLY SKI RESORT (off Hwy 50; 702/586-7000 or 800/2-HEAVEN; www.skiheavenly.com). South Lake Tahoe's pride and joy has something for skiers of all levels. Heavenly is so immense that it straddles two states (California and Nevada); those in the know park on the Nevada side to avoid the weekend crowds. With a snowboard park and specially constructed terrain features, combined with nearby arcades, recreation centers, bowling alleys, and movie theaters, this is a good choice if you have teenagers or like to play the casinos. Heavenly offers day care for infants, child care, and full-day programs for older kids.

HOMEWOOD MOUNTAIN RESORT (off Hwy 89; 530/525-2992; www.ski homewood.com). This underrated midsize resort is a locals' favorite because it has a little of everything for skiers of all levels (without the crowds), as well as one of the best views of Lake Tahoe. Midweek specials often knock down the price of a ticket by as much as 50 percent (call ahead for quotes), and children under 10 ski free when accompanied by an adult—easily the best deal around.

KIRKWOOD (off Hwy 88; 209/258-6000; www.kirkwood.com). When skiing conditions just don't get any better, Tahoe locals make the pilgrimage over the passes to where the snow is the deepest and the skiing is the sweetest. The only drawback is that Kirkwood is 30 miles south of South Lake Tahoe (though the resort offers free shuttle service to and from South Lake Tahoe); otherwise, it's one of the top ski areas in the region, with lots of snow and excellent spring skiing. The **KIRKWOOD CROSS-COUNTRY SKI CENTER** (209/258-7248) is one of the best in the state and offers lessons for all ages. Kirkwood also sells some very tempting ski-lodging packages.

NORTHSTAR-AT-TAHOE (off Hwy 267; 530/562-1010 or 800/466-6784; www.northstarattahoe.com). Northstar is consistently rated one of the best family ski resorts in the nation thanks to its numerous kids' programs and 2,400 acres of skiable terrain. It also has the dubious honor of being called "Flatstar" by the locals because of its penchant for grooming, but several new black diamond runs are starting to erase its low-thrills reputation. It's a completely self-contained ski resort (you'll find everything from lodgings to stores to a gas station here), so you can park your car and leave it in the same spot for the duration of your stay.

SIERRA-AT-TAHOE (off Hwy 50; 530/659-7453; www.sierratahoe.com). Formerly named Sierra Ski Ranch, Tahoe's third-largest ski area is a good all-around resort, offering a slightly better deal than most comparable places in the area. It's not worth the drive from the North Shore, but it's a good alternative to Heavenly Ski Resort if you want a change of venue near the South Shore.

SQUAW VALLEY USA (off Hwy 89; 530/583-6985 or 800/403-0206; www.squaw.com). Site of the 1960 Winter Olympic Games, Squaw is one of the world's top ski resorts, the kind of place people either love (because it has everything a skier could hope for) or hate (because it's gone the megacorporate route with Aspen-like ski villages and expensive everything). Squaw offers some of the country's most challenging terrain, excellent ski-school programs for kids and teens, top-of-the-line chairlifts, night skiing from

4 to 9pm, and a snowboard park, plus a variety of nonskiing activities including ice skating, swimming, and even bungee jumping.

SUGAR BOWL (Soda Springs exit off I-80; 530/426-9000; www.sugarbowl.com). Here's another good all-around midsize ski resort, with about 50 runs on 1,500 skiable acres. Sugar Bowl's most popular feature, however, is its accessibility—it's the closest resort from the valley off Interstate 80, about 40 minutes closer than Squaw Valley USA (and several bucks less a pass, thank you). Whether it's worth the drive from the North Shore, however, is questionable.

TAHOE DONNER SKI AREA (from I-80, take the Donner State Park exit, turn left on Donner Pass Rd, and go left on Northwoods Blvd; 530/587-9425; www.tahoedonner.com). If you're a beginner to intermediate skier and are staying on the North Shore, Tahoe Donner is a viable option, offering short lift lines, no car traffic, and relatively low prices.

South-of-Tahoe Ski Resorts

BADGER PASS SKI AREA (off SR 41; 209/372-8430; www.yosemitepark.com). Unpretentious, friendly, and affordable, Badger Pass—located 23 miles from Yosemite Valley inside Yosemite National Park—keeps its predominantly intermediate ski and snowboard runs well manicured. Established in 1935, it's California's oldest operating ski area, and it offers some unique family activities, such as daily snowshoe walks led by a ranger-naturalist, excellent cross-country skiing, tubing, and ice skating in the shadow of Half Dome.

BEAR VALLEY MOUNTAIN RESORT COMPANY (off Hwy 4; 209/753-2301; www.bearvalley.com). Nestled in the small town of Bear Valley, this is one of the undiscovered gems of downhill skiing in Northern California. The eighth-largest largest ski area in the state, it has a network of 60 trails for skiers of all levels, serviced by 11 lifts that can accommodate 12,000 skiers per hour. Considering the relatively inexpensive lift tickets and the diversity of the terrain, Bear Valley offers one of the best deals in the state.

DODGE RIDGE SKI AREA (off SR 108; 209/965-3474; www.dodgeridge.com). This small ski resort in the tiny town of Pinecrest has a decades-long reputation as a friendly, low-key ski area that's short on frills but high on family conveniences, such as a top-ranked children's ski school. Its lift lines are often short, and Dodge Ridge is the closest ski resort to the Bay Area (it's just above Sonora and Columbia). More advanced skiers, however, would be happier driving the few extra miles to Bear Valley for more challenging terrain.

JUNE MOUNTAIN (on June Lake Loop off Hwy 395; 760/648-7733 or 888/JUNEMTN; www.junemountain.com). Purchased by Mammoth Mountain Ski Area owner Dave McCoy in 1986, June Mountain offers skiers a calmer and less crowded ski experience than its colossal cousin across the valley. It may be about one-fifth the size of Mammoth, but June also offers great skiing—wide bowls, steep chutes, forested trails—with the added attraction of a spectacular Sierra view from its two peaks: 10,050-foot Rainbow Summit and 10,135-foot June Mountain Summit.

MAMMOTH MOUNTAIN SKI AREA (off Hwy 395; for ski-resort information, call the Mammoth Lakes Visitors Bureau at 760/934-8006 or 800/MAMMOTH; www.mammothmountain.com). Mammoth vies with Heavenly for the title of largest ski resort in the state, and it's L.A.'s prime weekend ski destination. What makes it so great? The numbers speak for themselves: 8 to 12 consistent feet of snowpack, 27 chairlifts, 150 runs, 3,100 vertical feet, an average of 300 sunny skies per year, and 3,500 acres of skiable terrain.

GOLD COUNTRY

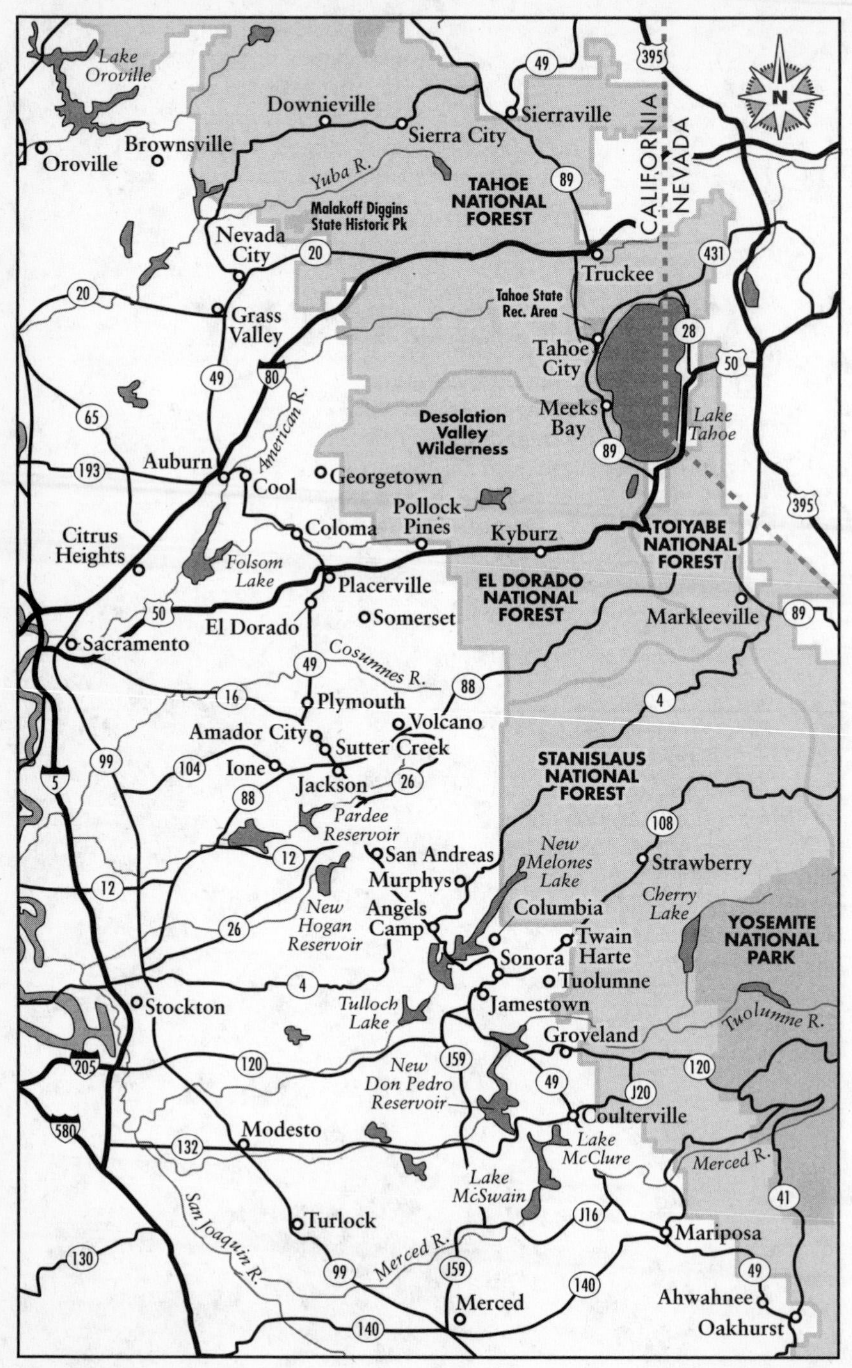

Lake Oroville
Oroville
Brownsville
Downieville
Sierra City
Sierraville
Yuba R.
TAHOE NATIONAL FOREST
Malakoff Diggins State Historic Pk
CALIFORNIA
NEVADA
N
Nevada City
Truckee
Tahoe State Rec. Area
Grass Valley
Tahoe City
Meeks Bay
Lake Tahoe
American R.
Desolation Valley Wilderness
Auburn
Cool
Georgetown
Pollock Pines
Citrus Heights
Coloma
Kyburz
TOIYABE NATIONAL FOREST
Folsom Lake
Placerville
EL DORADO NATIONAL FOREST
El Dorado
Somerset
Markleeville
Sacramento
Cosumnes R.
Plymouth
Volcano
Amador City
Sutter Creek
Ione
Jackson
STANISLAUS NATIONAL FOREST
Pardee Reservoir
San Andreas
New Melones Lake
Strawberry
Murphys
Cherry Lake
New Hogan Reservoir
Angels Camp
Columbia
YOSEMITE NATIONAL PARK
Twain Harte
Sonora
Tuolumne
Stockton
Tulloch Lake
Jamestown
Tuolumne R.
Groveland
New Don Pedro Reservoir
Coulterville
Lake McClure
Modesto
Merced R.
Lake McSwain
San Joaquin R.
Turlock
Mariposa
Merced R.
Ahwahnee
Merced
Oakhurst

GOLD COUNTRY

On the morning of January 24, 1848, a carpenter named James Marshall was working on John Sutter's mill in Coloma when he stumbled upon a gold nugget in the south fork of the American River. Despite Sutter's efforts to keep the find a secret, word leaked out that the hills of California were littered with gold.

By 1849, word had spread throughout the United States, Europe, and other corners of the globe that gold miners in California were becoming millionaires overnight. In just one year, more than 80,000 eager souls stampeded across water and land to reach the hilly terrain now known as the Gold Country and the mother lode. By 1852, more than 200,000 men were working the mines. Many of the forty-niners had to fight for their claims to the land, claims that left the average miner with little more than dirt and grime in his pocket. Crime and starvation were rampant, and when the exhausted miners put away their picks and pans for the night, most sought comfort in drinking, gambling, and prostitutes. It was a wild and heady time that brought riches to relatively few but changed the Golden State forever.

During the next 50 years, 125 million ounces of gold were mined from the Sierra foothills, an amount worth a staggering $50 billion today. You can follow in the miners' footsteps (geographically, at least) by cruising along the aptly numbered Highway 49, the zigzagging, 321-mile gold rush road that links many of the mining towns. Yep, there's still many a precious nugget in them thar hills and cricks, and you can hire a prospector to show you how and where to try your luck. But spend any time in the Sierra foothills and you'll soon discover that the real gold lies in the histories of the tiny towns that characterize this region and in the grassy foothills that turn golden beneath the summer sun.

ACCESS AND INFORMATION

Today, the Gold Country is truly a region for all seasons, with wineries, antique shops, historic parks, caverns, and museums open throughout the year. Late spring and early summer bring explosions of wildflowers and rafters heading down the American, Merced, Tuolumne, and Yuba rivers. The crisp air of autumn ushers in apple and grape harvests and vibrantly hued leaves on the Chinese pistache, dogwood, and maple trees. During the winter, when the Sacramento and San Joaquin valleys are shrouded in fog, the sun is often shining in the Gold Country, and the region is only a short drive away from most local ski resorts. You'll want an air-conditioned room on the hottest summer days and tire chains in the winter if you're heading up to Kyburz or Sierra City.

If, like most visitors to the area, you decide to drive, there are several ways to enter the region. With **INTERSTATE 5** or **HIGHWAY 99** as your motoring-off point, you will find a slew of highways and county roads (marked with a *J*) running east toward **HIGHWAY 49**. A California or Gold Country region map is your best bet for finding the quickest route, as well as for deciphering all those tempting side roads that pop up along the way.

Though the easiest way to explore the towns on and off Highway 49 is by car or motorcycle, there are a few other ways to reach the area. **AMTRAK'S**

CAPITOL CORRIDOR (877/974-3322; www.capitolcorridor.org) runs a daily train from the Bay Area to Sacramento, but the only stop it makes in the Gold Country is the town of Auburn.

Nine noncommercial small-passenger and private plane airports dot the Gold Country from Nevada City to Mariposa. Check your **AOPA DIRECTORY** or **WESTERN FLIGHT GUIDE** (or even a California road map) for locations. **COLUMBIA AIRPORT** (10767 Airport Rd, Columbia; 209/533-5685) is an easy half-mile walk away from Columbia State Historic Park, and you can rent a car at **CALAVERAS COUNTY AIRPORT** (3600 Carol Kennedy, San Andreas; 209/736-2501) for a few hours on weekdays if you let them know ahead of time. Staff at most of the other airports can help you arrange for a taxi or rental car (best to call ahead) if you don't want to walk the 2 to 5 miles into town.

Northern Gold Country

You'll find some of the most authentically preserved towns in the northern Gold Country, including Grass Valley, where more than a billion dollars in gold was extracted, and Nevada City, former home of one of the region's more famous miners, President Herbert Hoover. The farther east you travel in the Gold Country, the closer you move toward the Sierra Nevada mountains. In towns like Downieville, Sierra City, Kyburz, and Twain Harte, the Gold Country foothills begin to lose their gentle climb; slopes get steeper, and oak trees fade into forests of fir and pine.

Sierra City

Upon entering Sierra City, the first thing all visitors do is tilt their heads back to take in the magnificent view of the towering **SIERRA BUTTES**. Don't worry if you forgot your binoculars: just about every restaurant and lodging in town has a telescope pointing straight up at these majestic mountains. Black bears lumber through this little town on a daily basis, so unless you are willing to sacrifice a rear window, be careful not to leave any food in your vehicle. Dozens of nearby hiking and cross-country ski trails wind through **TAHOE NATIONAL FOREST** to more than 30 mountain lakes, which offer great trout fishing. Local activities include mountain biking, horseback riding, kayaking, snowmobiling, and enjoying the pristine scenery. For more information about Sierra City, log onto www.sierracity.com.

RESTAURANTS

Herrington's Sierra Pines Resort / ★★

104 MAIN ST, SIERRA CITY; 530/862-1151 OR 800/682-9848

Trout amandine (made with rainbow trout straight from the resort's pond) is the specialty at this cozy, log- and wood-paneled dining room situated on the north fork of the Yuba River. The dinner menu also offers New York steaks, charbroiled center-cut pork chops, clam linguine, honey-dipped deep-fried chicken, and other high-calorie dishes that'll satisfy a mountain man's appetite. The Saturday night special is slow-roasted prime rib au jus, and all entrées come with a hot loaf of house-baked bread. The lodge serves breakfast as well: pork chops and eggs with biscuits and gravy should keep you going until dinner. From mid-April to mid-November, the pet-friendly resort also offers 21 motel-style units with covered decks, most with views of the Yuba River. *$$; DIS, MC, V; checks OK; breakfast, dinner every day (closed mid-Oct–mid-May); full bar; reservations recommended; www.herringtonssierrapines.com; south side of Hwy 49 at the west end of town.*

Mountain Creek Restaurant & the Buckhorn Tavern / ★★

225 MAIN ST, SIERRA CITY; 530/862-1171

This classic 1889 tavern is the most popular bar and restaurant in Sierra City, particularly when the 49ers are playing. It's also the only restaurant in California we know of that has creek-side dining on a terraced garden patio. On a warm summer evening it's the perfect setting for digging into a New York steak, charbroiled salmon, or barbecued ribs. Daily specials are always of the meat-and-potatoes variety and range from braised Bavarian pork to roasted leg of lamb and bacon-wrapped filet mignon. On summer Saturdays they host barbecues in the garden. The days of operation vary seasonally, so be sure to call ahead. *$$; MC, V; checks OK; breakfast, lunch Wed–Sun, dinner Wed–Mon; full bar; no reservations; www.mountaincreekrestaurant.com; downtown.*

LODGINGS

High Country Inn / ★★★

100 GREENE RD, SIERRA CITY; 530/862-1530 OR 800/862-1530

The highlights of the High Country Inn are the spectacular view of the Sierra Buttes and the grove of aspens fluttering in the breeze along the north fork of the Yuba River. The B and B's four individually decorated guest rooms come with king or queen beds, antique furnishings, and beautiful views of the mountains, river, and private trout pond. The best and largest room is the Sierra Buttes Suite, which encompasses the entire second floor and has a king-size bed and fireplace (the bathroom is almost a suite of its own, with a 6½-foot-long 1846 bathtub and a dressing room complete with terry-cloth robes). Families often opt for the spacious Howard Creek Room because it has both a king-size and a daybed, as well as space for a roll-away. Room rates include a full country breakfast in addition to the trays of coffee and tea that are placed outside each room by 7am. *$$$; AE, DIS, MC, V; checks OK; www.hicountryinn.com; 5 miles east of town, on the south side of Hwy 49 and Gold Lake Rd.*

GOLD COUNTRY THREE-DAY TOUR

DAY ONE: *The northern highlights.* Get on the road early, drive north on Highway 49 to Nevada City, and check in at the **BELLA ROSA INN**. Have the innkeeper make dinner reservations for you at the **CITRONÉE BISTRO & WINE BAR** or **NEW MOON CAFE**. Have an alfresco lunch at the **COUNTRY ROSE CAFE**, then walk over to the chamber of commerce and pick up a free walking-tour map. After seeing the highlights, drive north on Highway 49 to **DOWNIEVILLE**, one of the most scenic little mountain towns in California. Take a guided tour of the **DOWNIEVILLE MUSEUM**, then head back toward Nevada City to the 3,000-acre **MALAKOFF DIGGINS STATE HISTORIC PARK**. After an early dinner, return to the Bella Rosa Inn and relax with a good book in the outdoor hot tub (the Gold Country's warm summer nights are wonderful).

DAY TWO: *Laughter to the rafters.* After a gourmet breakfast at the Bella Rosa, drive south on Highway 49 to the **MARSHALL GOLD DISCOVERY STATE HISTORIC PARK** in Coloma. Spend an hour wandering through the historic buildings and the site where gold was first discovered or, better yet, book a trip with **WHITE WATER CONNECTION** and spend the day white-water rafting down the south fork of the American River. You'll be plenty hungry afterward, so hop in the car and have an early dinner at either **ZACHARY JACQUES** in Placerville or **POOR RED'S** in El Dorado. After dinner, check in to the **SHAFSKY HOUSE** and relax.

Downieville

This scenic little mountain town at the junction of the Yuba and Downie rivers hasn't changed much since the 1850s: venerable buildings still line the boardwalks along crooked Main Street, and trim homes are cut into the canyon walls above. Downieville's population hovers around 350 (closer to 500 in the summer), though during its heyday 5,000 prospectors panned the streams and worked the mines here. The lusty gold camp even had the dubious distinction of being the only place in California where a woman was lynched.

A former gold rush–era Chinese goods store houses the **DOWNIEVILLE MUSEUM** (330 Main St; open 11am–4pm Wed–Fri, 10am–4pm Sat–Sun, May–Oct). For guided tours of the museum call 530/289-3423. The **SIERRA COUNTY COURTHOUSE** (100 Courthouse Sq; 530/289-3698) displays gold dug out of the rich Ruby Mine, and next door stands the only original gallows in the Gold Country. For more gold rush history and lore, check out the **SIERRA COUNTY HISTORICAL PARK** (530/862-1310) on Highway 99, 1 mile north of Sierra City, where the restored Kentucky Mine and a stamp mill still stand. The park is open Wednesday through Sunday, Memorial Day through September, and on weekends in October, weather permitting.

DAY THREE: *South to Sutter Creek.* After breakfast at the Shafsky House, take a leisurely drive south on Highway 49 for a day of antiquing in **AMADOR CITY** and **SUTTER CREEK**. Be sure to stop at the **SUTTER GOLD MINE** and take a guided tour. Drop off your luggage at **THE FOXES IN SUTTER CREEK BED & BREAKFAST INN**, then walk down the street to **SUSAN'S PLACE** (15 Eureka St; 209/267-0945; www.susansplace.com) for lunch. Next, take the scenic 12-mile Sutter Creek–Volcano Road into **VOLCANO** and have a cocktail at the **ST. GEORGE HOTEL'S WHISKEY FLAT SALOON**. If you're traveling between mid-March and mid-April, drive 3 miles north on Ram's Horn Grade to **DAFFODIL HILL** to admire the half million daffodils in bloom on this 4-acre ranch (follow the signs). If there's time on the way back, make a short stop at **INDIAN GRINDING ROCK STATE HISTORIC PARK**, and take a moment to stretch your legs on the half-mile nature trail where the Miwok once walked, hundreds of years before anyone in the region even cared about that shiny stuff shimmering in the creeks. Head nine miles north of Sutter Creek to **RESTAURANT TASTE** (9402 Main St; 209/245-DINE; www.restauranttaste.com) in Plymouth, a true culinary experience, for dinner (and breakfast in bed at the Foxes the following morning). Spend the rest of the next day touring the charming towns of **ANGELS CAMP**, **MURPHYS**, **SONORA**, and **JAMESTOWN**. Now that's a Gold Country vacation.

For local news and current Downieville events, pick up a copy of the **MOUNTAIN MESSENGER** (313 Main St; 530/289-3242), California's oldest weekly newspaper, published since 1853. To tour this scenic area by mountain bike, visit the friendly people at **YUBA EXPEDITIONS** (208 Main St; 530/289-3010; www.yubaexpeditions.com). They rent demo bikes, shuttle mountain bikers to the top of the mountain, and offer guided mountain-biking trips.

Brownsville

If you're driving anywhere near this remote region of the Gold Country, consider making a reservation for a tour of the **RENAISSANCE VINEYARD & WINERY** (12585 Rices Crossing Rd, Oregon House; 800/655-3277; www.renaissancewinery.com; 7 miles south of Brownsville, call for directions), a spectacular 365-acre winery with rose gardens fit for a queen's palace. Located in the nearby village of Oregon House, Renaissance is at an elevation of 2,300 feet and is one of the largest mountain vineyards in North America. The visitors' schedule is subject to change, but tastings are available in the Lakeside Tasting Room (11am–3pm Mon–Sat; 530/575-1254); appointments are highly suggested, even if you just want to smell the roses. The

Wine & Roses Tasting is a fun activity for a group (minimum of four people required), as participants receive an estate- or reserve-level wine tasting paired with a 45-minute tour of the garden, which includes more than 300 varieties of roses. You may bring your own picnic lunch or purchase one in advance from the tasting room.

For a glimpse of life in the 1800s, visit the **YUBA FEATHER MUSEUM** (19096 New York Flat Rd, Forbestown; 530/675-1025), just 15 minutes outside of Brownsville. The museum features more than 3,000 photographs and life-size exhibits, including a schoolhouse, barbershop, jail, Native American Maidu village, and Chinese laundry. This miniature town of yesteryear is open only on weekends from noon to 4pm, Labor Day through Memorial Day.

Nevada City

Established in 1849 when miners found gold in Deer Creek, Nevada City occupies one of the most picturesque sites in the Sierra foothills. When the sugar maples blaze in autumn, the town resembles a small New England village, making it hard to believe this was once the third-largest city in California. This is also B and B heaven, and with so many beautifully restored houses to choose from, you'll have a tough time selecting a favorite. To understand the lay of the land, put on your walking shoes and pick up a free walking-tour map at the **CHAMBER OF COMMERCE** (132 Main St at Coyote St; 530/265-2692 or 800/655-NJOY; www.nevadacitychamber.com). Town highlights include the **NATIONAL HOTEL**, where the cozy gold rush–era bar is ideal for a cocktail or two, and the white, cupola-topped **FIREHOUSE NUMBER 1 MUSEUM** (214 Main St at Commercial St; 530/265-5468), which features gold rush memorabilia, rare Indian baskets, a fine Chinese altar from a local 1860s joss house, and relics from the infamous and ill-fated Donner Party. The museum is open from 1 to 4pm daily in summer and from 11:30am to 4pm Saturday and Sunday, May through October.

North of Nevada City is the 3,000-acre **MALAKOFF DIGGINS STATE HISTORIC PARK** (530/265-2740), home of the world's largest hydraulic gold mine and a monument to mining's devastating environmental results. During the gold rush days, nearly half a mountain was washed away with powerful jets of pressurized water, leaving behind a 600-foot-deep canyon of minaret-shaped, rust-colored rocks—eerily beautiful to some but an eyesore to most. Inside the park is the semirestored mining town of North Bloomfield, where you can hike along a 3-mile loop trail that features hydraulic mining memorabilia. The easiest way to reach the park is to drive north on Highway 49, 5 miles past the Yuba River, turn right on Tyler-Foote Crossing, then continue 14 miles up to the park.

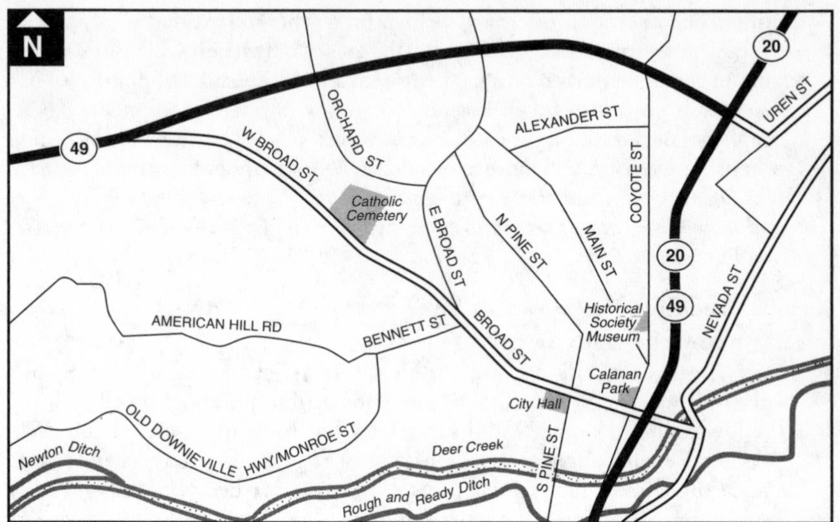

Nevada City

RESTAURANTS

Citronée Bistro & Wine Bar / ★★★

320 BROAD ST, NEVADA CITY; 530/265-5697

Whether you are seated in the bistrolike room upstairs or in the more intimate back room downstairs, you will soon understand why this Nevada City restaurant was recommended by the *New York Times*. The restaurant offers American regional cuisine with Mediterranean, Mexican, and Asian influences, with a full dinner menu and a tapas/grazing menu for the less ravenous. A recommended starter for the evening menu is the seared ahi appetizer with yuzu vinaigrette, carrot brunoise, and white truffle oil, topped with shaved fennel. Entrées include sautéed black cod with citrus quinoa, sweet onion tart, and broken herb vinaigrette, and braised rabbit with cognac, orange, and dried prunes with creamy pappardelle. *Wine Spectator* magazine once bestowed upon Citronée an award of excellence for its selection of more than 150 wines. Bring your own wine for a $20 corkage charge, or purchase a bottle at the attached store and have the fee waived. *$$$; AE, MC, V; local checks only; lunch Mon–Fri, dinner Wed–Mon; beer and wine; reservations recommended; www.citroneebistro.com; across from City Hall.*

Country Rose Cafe / ★★

300 COMMERCIAL ST, NEVADA CITY; 530/265-6248

Within this tall, stately brick building, you'll find chef-owner Michael Johns cooking some mighty fine French country fare. After seating you, one of the cheerful waitstaff lugs over a large chalkboard that lists the day's specials, which are mostly French with a smattering of Italian, Mexican, and American dishes. The afternoon offerings, written on a white board that's propped on the table for your perusal, usually include great sandwiches, such as the savory salmon-cucumber served on a baguette with an herb spread. For dinner, Johns's specialty is swordfish oscar. Fortunately, sunny days are in abundance here, enabling diners to sit on the café's pretty, walled-in garden patio. The wine and beer lists are terrific, and more than a dozen wines are poured by the glass. *$$$; AE, DC, MC, V; local checks only; lunch, dinner Tues–Sun, brunch Sun; beer and wine; reservations recommended; near the center of town at Commercial and Pine sts.* ♿

Kirby's Creekside Restaurant & Bar / ★★

101 BROAD ST, NEVADA CITY; 530/265-3445

Deer Creek calmly flows underneath the large, sun-filled deck at Kirby's Creekside, one of Nevada City's most popular restaurants. If possible, forgo the low-ceilinged dining room for a far more romantic table on the deck. The lunch menu offers a large selection of salads and sandwiches, as well as heartier entrées such as meat loaf with garlic mashed potatoes and daily seafood specials. Dinner is a more elaborate affair, kicked off with appetizers like marinated portobello mushrooms served with roasted tomato aioli. For your next course, select from one of a half dozen pasta dishes and entrées, such as stuffed pork loin in crème de cassis sauce. Prix-fixe multicourse dinners are also available, and children can choose from the kids' menu. Kirby's takes its wine list as seriously as its food and maintains a very good selection. The wine and beer bar, located on the main floor, offers live music Tuesday through Saturday. The main restaurant is downstairs, but dinner can also be served at the bar. *$$–$$$; AE, DIS, MC, V; checks OK; lunch, dinner every day; beer and wine; reservations recommended; west side of Hwy 49 at Broad and Sacramento sts.* ♿

New Moon Cafe / ★★★

203 YORK ST, NEVADA CITY; 530/265-6399

Set inside a cedar cabin lined with glass windows and decorated with Mediterranean touches and large paintings from local artists, this restaurant is popular with locals and tourists alike. But it isn't just the pleasant ambience that keeps folks coming back. Everything, from the organic-grain bread to the handmade ravioli, is made from scratch. Whenever possible, the food is purchased locally, and the meat dishes, such as the Muscovy duck breast, pan roasted with local blackberry-syrah sauce and corn cake, are always free-range and antibiotic free. Five to seven fresh vegetables are served with every entrée, including the vegetarian wild mushroom lasagne, made with New Moon's own fresh pasta, smoked mozzarella, caramelized onions, green olives, roast garlic, spinach, tomato, and ricotta in an individual ramekin. *$$$; DC, MC, V; checks OK; lunch Tues–Fri, dinner Tues–Sun; beer and wine; reservations recommended; www.thenewmooncafe.com; 1 block from Broad St.* ♿

LODGINGS

Bella Rosa Inn / ★★★

517 W BROAD ST, NEVADA CITY; 866/696-0555

Bella Rosa opened in 2007 and brought a much-needed breath of fresh air to the area's B and B scene. Owners Gina and Ben purchased the stately historic home—once owned by the Downeys, a prominent mining family—and turned it into a romantic weekend getaway spot for couples, adding lavish touches like a sauna (complete with television and iPod hookup), an outdoor hot tub, and an on-call massage therapist. Though on the smaller side, the six luxurious guest rooms feature flat-screen TVs, chandeliers, wireless Internet access, hairdryers, robes, and slippers. Tea and an impressive breakfast spread are served on the outside patios; complimentary drinks are doled out in the upstairs sunroom. The seasoned innkeeper, Diane, willingly cooks up meals that cater to guests with specific dietary needs, such as vegetarians, dieters, and those who don't eat carbs. And a bedtime chocolate and liquor are left behind for your nighttime pleasure. A bonus history lesson: the story goes that the building was once a brothel, and the upstairs hallway was curved so men could peek around the wall and see who was coming as they snuck out after a "visit." A two-night minimum stay is enforced on weekends. *$$; AE, MC, V; checks OK; www.bellarosainn.net; at Bennett St.*

Deer Creek Inn Bed & Breakfast / ★★★

116 NEVADA ST, NEVADA CITY; 530/265-0363 OR 800/655-0363

Perched on the banks of Deer Creek, which was famous in the gold rush days as a "pound-a-day" source for gold panners, this three-story Queen Anne Victorian has been completely restored and attractively decorated as a bed-and-breakfast. The six guest rooms have either king- or queen-size four-poster or canopy beds with down comforters, private baths with marble or claw-foot tubs, and verandas or patios facing the creek or town. Charming Winifred's Room has been the site of at least a half dozen marriage proposals (perhaps it's the romantic veranda overlooking the creek that inspires couples to commit). In the morning, guests feast on a gourmet breakfast served on the deck overlooking the creek and rose garden or in the formal dining room. Wine and hors d'oeuvres are served each evening. *$$$; AE, MC, V; checks OK; www.deercreekinn.com; at Nevada and Broad sts.*

Emma Nevada House / ★★★☆

528 E BROAD ST, NEVADA CITY; 530/265-4415 OR 800/916-3662

Built in 1856, the immaculately restored Emma Nevada House (the childhood home and namesake of 19th-century opera star Emma Nevada) is one of the finest bed-and-breakfast inns in the Gold Country. On summer days you can't help but relax and enjoy the warm sunshine on the inn's deck and wraparound porch. Many of the home's antique fixtures, such as the gas-lit chandeliers, claw-foot bathtubs, transoms, and doors, have been refurbished and modernized, and the six guest rooms all have private baths and queen-size beds.

One of the preferred units is Nightingale's Bower, a room on the main floor with bay windows, a fireplace, elegant Italian bedding, and a Jacuzzi. Another popular choice for honeymooners is the romantic Empress Chamber, with its large wall of windows, soothing ivory and burgundy tones, and Jacuzzi tub for two. A full breakfast of fresh fruit, juices, muffins or scones, and an entrée such as onion-caraway quiche, pumpkin waffles, or Emma's special cobbler, is served in the dining room or sunroom overlooking the garden. The shops and restaurants of Nevada City's Historic District are only a short walk away. *$$$; AE, DC, MC, V; checks OK; www.emmanevadahouse.com; right fork of the Y at the top of Broad St.*

National Hotel / ★

211 BROAD ST, NEVADA CITY; 530/265-4551

The grand old National Hotel is truly a California institution. It opened in the mid-1850s and is the oldest continuously operating hotel west of the Rockies. It's located near what was once the center of the town's red-light district, and the lobby is full of mementos from that era. Sure, the place shows its age, and the decor (particularly the carpets) is a mishmash of every era from the 1850s to the 1950s. But, hey, such color keeps away the fastidious and faint of heart. The 42 guest rooms are furnished with antiques, and all but eight units have private bathrooms. The hotel also has a swimming pool filled with cool mountain water and a Victorian-era dining room serving traditional American fare—such as prime rib, steak, and lobster tail—as well as homemade desserts. The hotel features live music on Fridays and Saturdays and a popular Sunday brunch. *$$; AE, MC, V; local checks only; www.thenationalhotel.com; located at the center of town.* ♿

The Parsonage Bed & Breakfast Inn / ★★

427 BROAD ST, NEVADA CITY; 530/265-9478

Once home to the ministers of the Nevada City Methodist Church, the Parsonage is quiet, unassuming, and an essential stop for California history buffs. Owned and operated by a great-granddaughter of California pioneer Ezra Dane, the place is something of a living museum. Deborah Dane lovingly maintains the home, which is decorated with collections from three generations of Californians—everything from a Sheraton dining room set to Chinese rice-paper-and-silk peacock screens. All six guest rooms have private baths and are furnished with the family's museum-quality heritage antiques. A full breakfast is served each morning. *$$; DIS, MC, V; no checks; www.theparsonage.net; in historic downtown.*

Piety Hill Cottages / ★★★

523 SACRAMENTO ST, NEVADA CITY; 800/443-2245

Originally built in 1933 as an auto court, Piety Hill Cottages has been imaginatively and charmingly restored and redecorated by owners-innkeepers Joan and Steve Oas. The inn consists of nine cottages clustered around a grassy, tree-shaded courtyard and garden. Each of the one-, two-, and three-room cottages has a kitchenette stocked with complimentary hot and cold beverages, at least one king- or queen-size bed, a private bath, cable TV, and air-conditioning. One unit also has a wood-burning stove; several have garages. Each morning, the innkeepers deliver a breakfast basket filled with juice, fresh fruit, and lemon poppy seed bread or orange sourdough French toast. Guests are free to linger in the lodge-style living room, soak in the gazebo-sheltered spa (available spring through fall) nestled among cedars, and barbecue on the outdoor grills. The larger cottages may be rented by the week in the summer, *$$–$$$; AE, MC, V; checks OK; www.pietyhillcottages.com; 2 blocks southeast of Hwy 49.*

The Red Castle Historic Lodging / ★★★½

109 PROSPECT ST, NEVADA CITY; 530/265-5135 OR 800/761-4766

A towering, four-story red brick manse detailed with lacy white icicle trim, the Red Castle is a Gothic Revival gem. Located on a quiet tree-lined street and surrounded by terraced gardens, the B and B still boasts much of its original woodwork, plaster moldings, ceiling medallions, and handmade glass from the 1860s. The seven high-ceilinged guest rooms (three are suites) have either a private or shared veranda that overlooks the rose garden, and all have private bathrooms that have been restyled in gold rush–era fashion. The oft-photographed Garden Room on the mansion's entry level is furnished with a canopy bed, fringed and tasseled vintage portieres, French doors, dramatic contrasting wallpaper and carpet, and two mannequin arms in the bathroom that reach out for your towels. Smaller quarters are upstairs on the former nursery floor, but climb a bit higher and you'll find the three-room Garret Suite, where the private veranda provides a superb view of Nevada City. The Red Castle's ever-changing five-course buffet breakfast (prepared by an in-house chef) is a feast, and the afternoon tea is a great way to meet the other guests. *$$$; MC, V; checks OK; www.redcastleinn.com; at Nile St.*

Grass Valley

Once known for rich quartz mines, Cornish pasties, and gold rush entertainers like Lola Montez and Lotta Crabtree, Grass Valley has a historic and slightly scruffy downtown that's a pleasure to explore, as well as elegant bed-and-breakfasts and good restaurants. Stop at the **CHAMBER OF COMMERCE** (248 Mill St; 530/273-4667 or 800/655-4667; www.grassvalleychamber.com), site of the Lola Montez home, for a free walking-tour map of the town and two terrific brochures listing more than two dozen scenic walking, hiking, and mountain-biking trails. As you tour the town, be sure to stop at the 10-ton Pelton Waterwheel (at 30 feet in diameter, it's the world's largest) on display at the exemplary **NORTH STAR MUSEUM AND PELTON WHEEL EXHIBIT** (south end of Mill St at McCourtney Rd; 530/273-4255). The museum building, open daily May through October, was once the powerhouse for the North Star Mine. Part of the park is wheelchair accessible.

Every second weekend in June, the area hosts the annual Father's Day Bluegrass Festival (www.fathersdayfestival.com), which brings some of the country's best folk acts to Grass Valley. Pack a chair, an umbrella, and a picnic lunch; the heavily wooded grounds provide the perfect shady venue for a Saturday family outing.

Just outside of town is the 785-acre **EMPIRE MINE STATE HISTORIC PARK** (10791 E Empire St; 530/273-8522; www.cal-parks.ca.gov), the oldest, largest, deepest, and richest gold mine in California. Its underground passages once extended 367 miles, descended 11,007 feet into the ground, and produced an estimated 5.8 million ounces of gold between 1850 and 1956, when it finally closed. A museum occupies a former stable, and the impressive granite and red brick **EMPIRE COTTAGE**, designed by San Francisco architect Willis Polk in 1897 for the mine's owner, is a prime example of what all that gold dust could buy. For the most part, the park is wheelchair accessible, and dogs on leashes are permitted. From March to November, tours are given daily, and a mining movie is shown.

After touring Grass Valley, head about 5 miles west on Highway 20 for a pleasant side trip to the tiny town of **ROUGH AND READY**, which once chose to secede from the Union rather than pay a mining tax. Then continue on Highway 20 for another couple of miles and turn north on Pleasant Valley Road; 15 miles up the road is **BRIDGEPORT**, home of California's longest covered bridge. Built in 1862, the bridge provides a good spot to dangle your fishing line.

RESTAURANTS

Tofanelli's / ★★

302 W MAIN ST, GRASS VALLEY; 530/272-1468

Tofanelli's is one of Grass Valley's cultural and culinary meeting places. The restaurant consists of a bright, cheery trio of dining areas—atrium, outdoor patio, and dining room—separated by exposed brick walls and decorated with prints and paintings. When the locals convene here for lunch, they often order the restaurant's famous veggie burger. The tostadas also make a very good midday meal, including the version topped with marinated chicken breast (or tofu), brown rice, the house pinto beans, greens, carrots, and tomatoes. Tofanelli's whips up several vegetarian dishes, but the kitchen can also turn out a mean hamburger and Reuben sandwich. Each week the chefs prepare a new dinner menu, which might feature Brie chicken breast with pesto, red peppers, and garlic, or the popular house lasagne with three cheeses, fresh spinach, and house-made marinara. *$; AE, MC, V; breakfast, lunch, dinner every day; full bar; reservations required for parties of 6 or more; www.tofanellis.com; next to the Holbrooke Hotel.* ♿

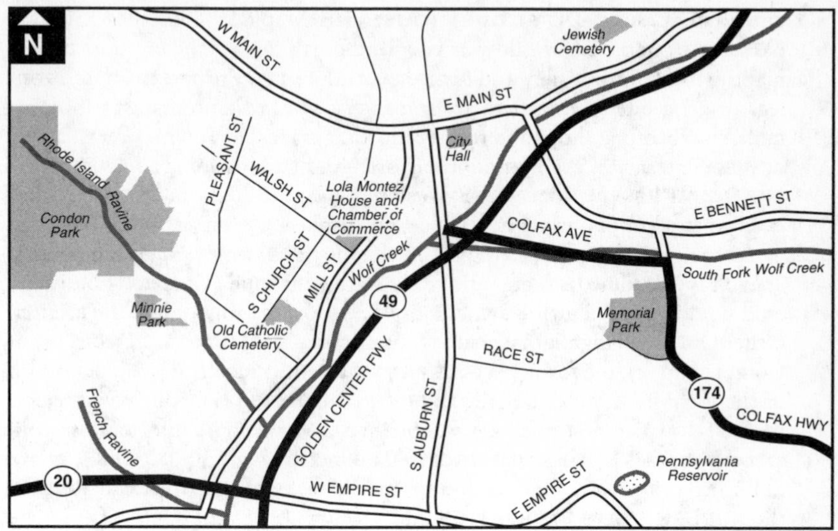

Grass Valley

LODGINGS

The Holbrooke Hotel / ★★★

212 W MAIN ST, GRASS VALLEY; 530/273-1353 OR 800/933-7077

Mark Twain slept at this Victorian-era white-clapboard building, the oldest and most historic hotel in town. So did entertainers Lola Montez and Lotta Crabtree, as well as the notorious gentleman-bandit Black Bart. But don't be intimidated; despite its rugged gold rush grandeur, the 147-year-old Holbrooke Hotel is a relaxed and accommodating establishment. Many of the 28 guest rooms have private balconies, and all contain gold rush–era furniture and antiques, cable TVs tucked away in armoires, wireless Internet, hair dryers, coffeemakers, and contemporary bathrooms (most with claw-foot bathtubs). The best rooms are the larger Veranda rooms that face Main Street and have access to the balconies. A continental breakfast is served in the library. The hotel's restaurant offers upscale American fare, and the Holbrooke's Golden Gate Saloon is the best bar on Main Street, so light sleepers should request a suite far from the libations. *$$; AE, DC, DIS, MC, V; checks OK; www.holbrooke.com; between S Church and Mill sts.* ♿

Auburn

The Gold Country's largest town, Auburn is sprawled on a bluff overlooking the American River and has been the seat of Placer County since 1850. Nowadays, Auburn serves mainly as a pit stop for vacationers headed to Lake Tahoe. Its few noteworthy sights, including **OLD TOWN** and the impressively domed **PLACER COUNTY COURTHOUSE** (101 Maple St; 530/889-6550), are best seen from the car window as you head north toward the far more congenial towns of Grass Valley and Nevada City. But if you're here to stretch your legs or get a bite to eat (there are some very good restaurants), stroll by the numerous bustling shops and restaurants that grace Old Town's streets. Many of these enterprises are housed in historic gold rush buildings, including the **SHANGHAI RESTAURANT** (289 Washington St; 530/823-2613), which has been open continuously since 1906 and displays a wonderful collection of memorabilia in its bar (where part of the movie *Phenomenon*, starring John Travolta, was filmed). A gigantic stone statue of Claude Chana, who discovered gold in the Auburn Ravine in 1848, marks the town's historic section. Other Old Town highlights include the whimsical **FIREHOUSE** (Lincoln Wy at Commercial St), the former **WELLS FARGO BANK** (Lincoln Wy, 1 block south of the firehouse), built in 1852, and the **POST OFFICE** (Lincoln Wy at Sacramento St), which first opened its doors in 1849. For more information, contact the **CHAMBER OF COMMERCE** (601 Lincoln Wy; 530/885-5616; www.auburnchamber.net). The north and middle forks of the American River in the **AUBURN STATE RECREATION AREA** (Hwy 49, 1 mile south of Auburn; 530/885-4527) are popular destinations for gold panners, swimmers, picnickers, and rafters. The recreation area also has great camping sites, hiking trails, equestrian trails, and mountain-biking routes.

RESTAURANTS

Bootlegger's Old Town Tavern & Grill / ★✯

210 WASHINGTON ST, AUBURN; 530/889-2229

Located in a handsome old brick building in the heart of Auburn's historic center, Bootlegger's offers a large, eclectic seasonal menu that's chock-full of tempting choices. Two lunchtime winners are the spicy Creole chicken gumbo and the fish tacos—marinated white fish on white corn tortillas with Jack cheese, napa cabbage, and a jalapeño cilantro aioli, topped with pico de gallo. For dinner, choose from an expansive menu of pastas, grilled steak, ribs, lamb, or chicken. *$$; AE, DIS, MC, V; checks OK; lunch Tues–Sat, dinner Tues–Sun; beer and wine; reservations recommended; www.bootleggersauburn.com; in Old Town.* ♿

Latitudes / ★★

130 MAPLE ST, AUBURN; 530/885-9535

Latitudes, which chef-owners Pat and Pete Enochs call their "world kitchen," is located in a pretty Victorian building just above Auburn's Old Town. Every month the menu takes on the cuisine of a foreign country (for example, German Cuisine month will likely feature plenty of schnitzel, sauerbraten, and German Oktoberfest sausage). The lunch menu includes a terrific tofu Florentine (grilled with cashews, green onions, and spinach) and a tenderloin fajita (pepper-coated strips grilled with vegetables and red wine, served in a sun-dried tomato tortilla with lettuce and Caesar dressing). Dinner is equally rewarding, with fresh Atlantic salmon, gingered prawns, East Indian curried tofu, and a fork-tender filet mignon. The extensive wine and beer lists feature brands from around the world. And as if the great food weren't enough, Latitudes often has live music in its downstairs bar on Fridays and Saturdays. *$$; AE, DIS, MC, V; local checks only; lunch Wed–Sat, dinner Wed–Sun, brunch Sun; full bar; reservations recommended; www.latitudesrestaurant.com; across from the courthouse.* ♿

Le Bilig / ★★★

11750 ATWOOD RD, AUBURN; 530/888-1491

Husband-and-wife team Marc and Monica Deconinck created this intimate French bistro. Marc, an accomplished chef from Lille in northern France, specializes in hearty, rustic French comfort food—not unctuous, sauced French fare or prissy nouvelle cuisine. In winter, Deconinck might be dishing out a definitive French onion soup or ham hocks with lentils; in early spring, look for his lamb shanks roasted with fennel and thyme-infused tomatoes. A few house specialties are served nearly year-round, like Brittany-style whole wheat or buckwheat crepes prepared in a *bilig* (French cast-iron crepe pan) with savory fillings like poached fresh salmon. The wine list has some rarities and bargains, including reasonably priced French bottles from the '70s and '80s and local wines from El Dorado and Amador counties. *$$$; MC, V; checks OK; dinner Wed–Sat; beer and wine; reservations recommended; www.lebiligkitchen.com; off Hwy 49, 1 block west of the Bel Air Shopping Center, at the north end of town.*

Georgetown

When the tent city located here burned in 1852, this mountain town was rebuilt with much wider streets, which are now graced by a few noteworthy old buildings: **IOOF HALL** (at Main St and Hwy 193), the **GEORGETOWN HOTEL** (6260 Main St), and the **AMERICAN RIVER INN** (see review), which had a previous life as a boardinghouse. In the spring, spectacular displays of wild Scotch broom cover the Georgetown hillsides. At first glance there isn't much to do in this town; and after you've examined the **SIGNPOST FOREST** pointing the way to at least a dozen destinations out of town (feel free to put up your own) and sipped on a beverage at the karaoke bar in the Georgetown Hotel, you'll realize there isn't much to do at second glance either. But that's what your car is for, and if you want to experience small-town life in the Sierra foothills or, like Garbo, you just want to be alone, Georgetown is the place to be.

LODGINGS

American River Inn / ★★

CORNER OF MAIN AND ORLEANS STS, GEORGETOWN; 530/333-4499 OR 800/245-6566

This hotel-built-from-gold originally served as a stagecoach stop and boardinghouse for miners, and today's innkeepers, Will and Maria Collin, have done an exemplary job of maintaining the inn's 13 guest rooms, each replete with Victorian flourishes and antiques, feather beds, and down comforters; a few share bathrooms. Make your way past the ceramic masks, teddy bears, and Elvis jigsaw puzzles spilling out into the hallway from the gift shop to find the individually decorated guest rooms; they vary dramatically in price, decor, and amenities, so be sure to ask the innkeepers which room is best for you. The inn has a pool and a 50-jet, 8-person hot tub surrounded by a Victorian garden, as well as mountain bikes, a putting green, horseshoes, table tennis, badminton, a driving range, and a croquet ground. Rates include a full breakfast for two and wine and hors d'oeuvres each afternoon. If you arrive in Georgetown by plane, take advantage of the inn's free airport limo. *$$; AE, DIS, MC, V; checks OK; www.americanriverinn.com; corner of Main and Orleans sts.* ♿

Coloma

As every Sacramento schoolchild knows (or should know), the gold rush began here when carpenter James Marshall found traces of the precious metal on January 24, 1848, at the sawmill he and John Sutter owned. A full-scale working replica of the famous sawmill and other gold-related exhibits are displayed at **MARSHALL GOLD DISCOVERY STATE HISTORIC PARK** (Hwy 49; 530/622-3470; www.coloma.com/gold), a 280-acre expanse of shaded lawns and picnic tables that extends through three-quarters of the town. Stop at the park's small **GOLD DISCOVERY MUSEUM** for a look at Native American artifacts and James Marshall memorabilia, and pick up the self-guided tour pamphlet outlining the park's highlights.

Coloma is thick with tourists and river rafters on summer weekends, so try to plan your visit during the week, when you can picnic in peace and float down the **AMERICAN RIVER** without fear of colliding with others. To plan your river rafting trip, contact **WHITE WATER CONNECTION** in Coloma (530/622-6446 or 800/336-7238; www.whitewaterconnection.com), which offers half- to two-day trips down the rapids of the American River. For a mellower but no less dramatic experience, attend an audience-participation melodrama at the **OLDE COLOMA THEATER** (380 Monument Blvd; 530/626-5282; www.oldecolomatheatre.com). Popcorn throwing and booing are required.

LODGINGS

Coloma Country Inn / ★★★

345 HIGH ST, COLOMA; 530/622-6919

This winsome six-room B and B is set on 5 private acres in the heart of the Marshall Gold Discovery State Historic Park. The gray and white 1852 clapboard farmhouse provides a tranquil retreat from the summer crowds. Each of the rooms are individually decorated with turn-of-the-century antiques, handmade quilts, and fresh flowers. The Rose Room has both a private bath and a patio, while the Eastlake Room comes with a private balcony and a view of the garden, as well as a private bath. Families might prefer the detached Cottage Suite in the 1888 Carriage House, which comes with a queen-size bed and a daybed fitted with a trundle, which can be used to make a king-size bed. The suite also has a kitchenette, a sitting area, and a private courtyard. Every day ends in a most civilized manner, with iced tea and homemade cookies in the garden gazebo. The entire inn can be rented out for special occasions. *$$–$$$; AE, DIS, MC, V; checks OK; www.colomacountryinn.com; in Marshall Gold Discovery State Historic Park.*

El Dorado

Three miles south of Placerville on Highway 49 sits the small town of El Dorado, whose denizens tolerate but in no way cultivate tourism. In fact, most travelers pass right on through—except for those who know about **POOR RED'S** (see review), a bar and restaurant that may not look like much from the outside (or the inside, for that matter) but is known throughout the land for its famous cocktail.

RESTAURANTS

Poor Red's / ★

6221 PLEASANT VALLEY RD, EL DORADO; 530/622-2901

It's not often that a small-town bar garners an international reputation, but this Cheers of the Gold Country has had its name translated into more tongues than a Robert Ludlum novel. It all started one night when the proud owners of a new gold-hued Cadillac asked the bartender to whip up a commemorative drink to celebrate their purchase. Grabbing the only thing behind the bar that was gold-colored (Galliano liqueur), the bartender dusted off the bottle, added a shot of this and a jigger of that, and—eureka!—the frothy Golden Cadillac was born. By alchemic accident, this tiny Golden State saloon soon became the largest user of Galliano in North America. Legend has it that during Poor Red's, er, golden era, dozens of bottles were emptied every day as celebrities, dignitaries, and plain folks all queued up at the door for a chance to squeeze inside. *$; AE, DC, DIS, MC, V; checks OK; lunch Mon–Fri, dinner every day; full bar; no reservations; downtown.*

Placerville

One of the first camps settled by miners who branched out from Coloma, Placerville was dubbed Dry Diggins because of a lack of water. Its name was changed to Hangtown in 1849 after a series of grisly lynchings; it became Placerville in 1854 to satisfy local pride. Among the town's historical highlights are the no-longer-occupied brick-and-stone **CITY HALL** (487 Main St, though the new headquarters is at 3101 Center St), which was built in 1860 and originally served as the town's firehouse, and the **HISTORIC SODA WORKS** building, home of the 150-foot gold mine. Another noteworthy edifice is the **HISTORIC CARY HOUSE HOTEL** (see review), where Mark Twain once lodged. Across the street, note the dangling dummy that marks the location of the town's infamous hanging tree. If you get a sudden longing for the *Wall Street Journal* or the *New York Times*, step into **PLACERVILLE NEWS** (409 Main St; 530/622-4510). The store has been run by the same family since 1912. Just a few doors down is **PLACERVILLE HARDWARE** (441 Main St; 530/622-1151), established in 1852. A single brass tack marks each foot along a section of the 100-foot-long store (two tacks mark every 5 feet), which is handy for measuring lumber or lengths of rope, and may just explain the origin of the expression "getting down to brass tacks."

A mile north of downtown Placerville is **GOLD BUG PARK**, home of the city-owned **GOLD BUG MINE** (Bedford Ave; 530/642-5207; www.goldbugpark.org). Tours of the mine lead you deep into the cool, lighted shafts. **EL DORADO COUNTY HISTORICAL MUSEUM** (104 Placerville Dr; 530/621-5865; www.co.el-dorado.ca.us/museum), adjacent to the county fairgrounds, is open Wednesday through Sunday and showcases Pony Express paraphernalia, an original Studebaker wheelbarrow, a replica of a 19th-century general store, and a restored Concord stagecoach, plus other mining-era relics.

Every autumn, droves of people—about half a million each year—come to a small ridge just east of Placerville called **APPLE HILL ORCHARDS** (from Hwy 50, take the Carson Rd exit and follow the signs; www.applehill.com). What's the attraction? Why, apples, of course. Baked, fried, buttered, canned, candied, and caramelized apples, to name just a few variations. Dozens of vendors sell their special apple concoctions, and in September and October (peak apple harvest season), if you don't mind the crowds, it's definitely worth a stop.

RESTAURANTS

Sweetie Pie's / ★★

577 MAIN ST, PLACERVILLE; 530/642-0128

If you're passing through Placerville on your way to Tahoe and want to stop for breakfast or lunch, this little café and bakery on Main Street is the place to go. A bowl of freshly made soup served with house-baked sourdough bread makes a great light meal. Or you might fancy a slice of vegetable quiche with a freshly tossed garden salad. Whatever you choose, save room for the pie. Better yet, eat dessert first—it's that good. Don't miss the thick, rich olallieberry pie or the rhubarb pie filled with tart chunks of the real thing. Other sweet-tooth temptations include cream pies and cinnamon and pecan rolls. Should you need more than a sugar rush to get you pumped, various coffee drinks are offered as well. Breakfasts at Sweetie Pie's can be rich and filling: waffles, pancakes, egg dishes, and biscuits topped with a spicy sausage gravy (and, of course, a pie to go). *$; MC, V; checks OK; breakfast, lunch every day; beer and wine; no reservations on weekends; www.sweetiepies.biz; across from the Historic Soda Works building.* ♿

Zachary Jacques / ★★★

1821 PLEASANT VALLEY RD, PLACERVILLE; 530/626-8045

For more than 15 years Zachary Jacques has been one of Placerville's best restaurants. The cozy, faux-French rural decor is a suitable setting for French country cuisine. The seasonal menus—both à la carte and prix fixe—feature such provincial classics as Burgundy-style escargots with garlic butter and parsley to *saumon en croûte*, a fresh fillet of king salmon baked in puff pastry with basil and mushrooms. On Saturday there's live music by a local group, and a Twilight Menu is served from 4 to 6pm Wednesday through Friday. Finding the perfect bottle of wine to accompany your order is never a problem: the wine list, which received an award of excellence from the highly respected *Wine Spectator* magazine, features more than 300 French and American labels. *$$$; AE, MC, V; no checks; dinner Wed–Sun; beer and wine; reservations recommended; www.zacharyjacques.com; 3 miles east of Diamond Springs.* ♿

LODGINGS

Historic Cary House Hotel / ★★☆

300 MAIN ST, PLACERVILLE; 530/622-4271

Originally built in 1857, the Cary House is a historically significant Victorian inn centrally located on Main Street. The four-story brick building was the headquarters of the Wells Fargo stage lines during the gold rush, and according to local lore, a total of $90 million worth of bullion was dumped on the hotel's porch before being transported to the U.S. Mint in San Francisco. Years later, newspaper editor Horace Greeley used the balcony above the porch to make his "Go West, young man" presidential campaign speech to miners. All 38 of the individually decorated guest rooms have vintage furnishings along with modern comforts such as wireless Internet, air-conditioning, private baths, TVs, and phones; many units have kitchenettes as well. A complimentary continental breakfast is served in the pantry. *$$$; AE, DIS, MC, V; no checks; www.caryhouse.com; between Bedford and Spring sts.*

The Shafsky House / ★★

2942 COLOMA ST, PLACERVILLE; 530/642-2776

Cool refreshments and pairs of slippers await new arrivals as they step out of their shoes and into the early 1900s at this absolutely charming 1902 Queen Anne Victorian. Lining the walls of the stairway to the second floor are photographs of the Shafsky family, including Albert Shafsky, who came to the United States from Moldavia in the late 1800s, and his daughter Alberta Shafsky. Uniquely decorated with period antiques, the three guest rooms come with private baths and king- or queen-size beds (with feather beds and goose-down comforters in the winter months). Room rates include a fantastic gourmet breakfast of cranberry banana nut bread, oven-baked apple pancakes, and other Shafsky House specialties served on china in the elegant dining room. *$$; DIS, MC, V; local checks only; www.shafsky.com; 1 block north of Hwy 50, at the corner of Spring and Coloma sts.*

Kyburz

LODGINGS

Strawberry Lodge / ★★

17510 HWY 50, KYBURZ; 530/659-7200

Wedged between the giant conifers and granite headwalls of Lake Tahoe's southwestern rim, the barnlike Strawberry Lodge has been the headquarters for year-round outdoor activities for more than a century. Named for the wild strawberry patches that once covered the area, the lodge has 44 rooms (most with private baths) that often get booked up during the peak months of summer and winter (the place does a fierce wedding business). The rooms overlooking the river are the quietest. In the newer section (built in 1997), the rooms feature cabin-style log furniture and private baths. The rooms in Annex Lodge (across the highway) vary in size, also come with private baths, and are among the least expensive. Families or small groups might prefer the Hawks Nest in the newer wing of the lodge, with two queen-size beds and a single. The Strawberry Lodge's dining room serves breakfast, lunch, and dinner. The lodge also has a full-service bar and a large patio with beautiful views of the Sierra Nevada mountains. *$$; AE, MC, V; no checks; www.strawberrylodge.com; 43 miles east of Placerville, 9 miles east of Kyburz.*

Fair Play

LODGINGS

Fitzpatrick Winery and Lodge / ★★

7740 FAIR PLAY RD, FAIR PLAY; 530/620-3248 OR 800/245-9166

If you've never experienced true Irish hospitality, reserve a night at Brian and Diana Fitzpatrick's country-style winery and lodge. Sitting atop a hill with a commanding 360-degree view of the countryside, their 40-acre retreat has five sun-filled guest rooms, all with a combination of antique and modern furnishings, oodles of exposed wood (the rustic Log Suite is our favorite), and private baths. Guests may also dive into the 82-foot lap pool, take a soak in the spa, relax by the fire in the great room, or bask in the sun at tables on the expanded deck, where chefs cook meats and breads in the outdoor wood-fired oven. A full breakfast and complimentary glasses of the Fitzpatricks' wine are included in the room rate. On Friday nights during the extended evenings of daylight savings time, the Fitzpatricks serve pizza, salad, cheesecake, and, of course, handcrafted, organically grown wine. *$$–$$$; AE, DC, DIS, MC, V; checks OK; www.fitzpatrickwinery.com; off Mount Aukum Rd, 6 miles southeast of town.* ♿

Southern Gold Country

Placerville may be the center of the Gold Country, but it's not the prettiest town by a long shot. Rather, the gold rush towns a few miles to the south (Amador City, Sutter Creek, and Jackson) are far more visually appealing destinations. The rolling hills and majestic oaks of the southern Gold Country are honeycombed with mysterious caverns and abandoned mines, including the deepest gold mines on the continent. The mining boom went bust by 1860, and most of the gold rush towns were abandoned by the 1870s, but some towns have survived by mining for tourist dollars. Along with sightseeing and B and B hopping, most visitors journey to this area for the fishing, camping, hiking, rafting, and mountain biking. And yes, some diehards still come just to pan for gold.

The first town you'll pass heading south is Plymouth, the starting point of the **AMADOR COUNTRY WINERIES** (209/267-2297; www.amadorwine.com), located along the Shenandoah Valley Road. The town's **POKERVILLE MARKET** (18170 Hwy 49; 209/245-6986) carries almost all of the wines produced in the area and sells them at low prices. If you are planning to visit the wineries, the market's deli is a great place to pick up a picnic lunch to take with you.

For more information about the southern Gold Country, contact the **AMADOR COUNTY CHAMBER OF COMMERCE** (209/223-0350; www.amadorcounty chamber.com).

Amador City

Once a bustling mining town, Amador City is now the smallest incorporated city in California. Lined with false-fronted antique and specialty boutiques—handcrafted furniture, gold rush memorabilia, rare books, Native American crafts—this block-long nonmetropolis is a good place to stop, stretch your legs, and window-shop along the boardwalk. Parking can be difficult, particularly on summer weekends.

RESTAURANTS

Imperial Hotel Restaurant / ★★★

14202 HWY 49, AMADOR CITY; 209/267-9172 OR 800/242-5594

This elegant restaurant in the Imperial Hotel has earned a solid reputation for serving superb California-Mediterranean cuisine in a relaxed setting.

The menu changes seasonally (and, apparently, so do the chefs). A fall menu might include a smoked pork chop with fig and onion confit or a pan-broiled rib eye with a provençal herb crust. Fresh seafood is offered nightly, such as lemon-baked sea bass wrapped in parchment and served with a wilted spinach salad. The dessert selection is impressive as well: crème brûlée, custom-made ice cream, and a selection of cakes and tortes. On warm summer evenings, be sure to request a table on the back patio. *$$$; AE, DIS, MC, V; checks OK; dinner Wed–Sun, brunch Mother's Day and Easter; full bar; reservations recommended; www.imperialamador.com; downtown.* ♿

LODGINGS

Imperial Hotel / ★★★

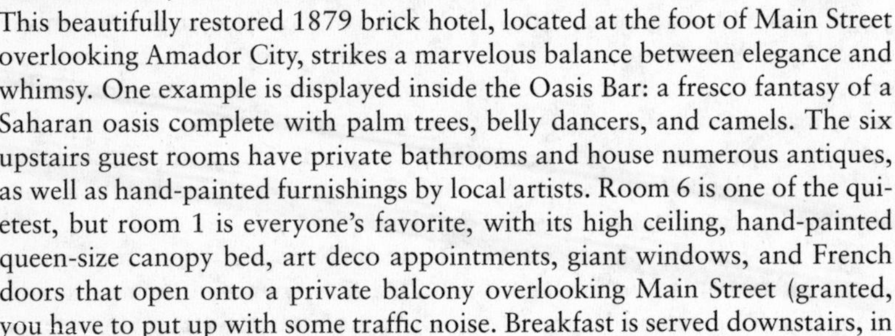

14202 HWY 49, AMADOR CITY; 209/267-9172 OR 800/242-5594

This beautifully restored 1879 brick hotel, located at the foot of Main Street overlooking Amador City, strikes a marvelous balance between elegance and whimsy. One example is displayed inside the Oasis Bar: a fresco fantasy of a Saharan oasis complete with palm trees, belly dancers, and camels. The six upstairs guest rooms have private bathrooms and house numerous antiques, as well as hand-painted furnishings by local artists. Room 6 is one of the quietest, but room 1 is everyone's favorite, with its high ceiling, hand-painted queen-size canopy bed, art deco appointments, giant windows, and French doors that open onto a private balcony overlooking Main Street (granted, you have to put up with some traffic noise. Breakfast is served downstairs, in your room, or on the patio or balcony. *$$; AE, DIS, MC, V; checks OK; www.imperialamador.com; downtown.*

Sutter Creek

"Big Four" railroad baron Leland Stanford made his millions at Sutter Creek's Lincoln Mine, then used his windfall to invest in the Transcontinental Railroad and fund his successful campaign to become governor of California. Sutter Creek is the self-proclaimed "nicest little town in the mother lode" and was named after sawmill owner John Sutter. It boasts some beautiful 19th-century buildings, including the landmark **KNIGHT'S FOUNDRY HISTORIC WATER-POWERED IRON WORKS** (81 Eureka St; 209/267-5967; www.knightfoundry.org), the last water-powered foundry and machine shop in the nation, and the **DOWNS MANSION** (Spanish St, across from the Immaculate Conception Church), the former home of the foreman at Leland Stanford's mine. Also worth exploring is the **SUTTER GOLD MINE** (13660 Hwy 49, ½ mile south of Amador City; 209/736-2708 or 866/762-2837; www.suttergold.com; open 9am–5pm every day in summer, 10am–5pm every day Oct–May), where you can take a guided tour into the bowels of a modern hard-rock gold mine, then pan for real gold using gold pans or sluice boxes (a few bucks buys you a bag of ore sold at the gift shop, and the bag is guaranteed to hold either gold or gemstones). It's a great way to learn about geology and the history of mining technology, and kids get a kick out of panning for real gold.

LODGINGS

Eureka Street Inn Bed and Breakfast / ★★

55 EUREKA ST, SUTTER CREEK; 209/267-5500 OR 800/399-2389
Chuck and Sandy Anderson have been making new friends as innkeepers of this quaint Craftsman-style inn since 1999. Step into the living room, with its overstuffed leather sofa and stained-glass windows, and you'll instantly feel at home. The downstairs common areas are comfortable and cozy, and the four guest rooms on the second floor are bright, cheerful, and tastefully decorated with gold rush–era antiques; all have private bathrooms, gas fireplaces or stoves, and air-conditioning (a must in midsummer). Chuck is in charge of the gourmet breakfasts—eggs Benedict on artichoke hearts, cheese blintzes, French toast, and poached pears—served in the formal dining room. *$$; DIS, MC, V; checks OK; may be closed last 2 weeks of Dec and all of Jan; www.eurekastreetinn.com; 1½ blocks off Main St, near the foundry.*

The Foxes in Sutter Creek Bed and Breakfast Inn / ★★★

77 MAIN ST, SUTTER CREEK; 209/267-5882 OR 800/987-3344
This is, without question, one of the finest B and Bs in the Gold Country. An immaculate garden fronts the gold rush–era foundation, and from there it only gets better. Each of the seven guest rooms is beautifully furnished with antiques, including a massive, elaborate Victorian headboard and an armoire that seems too priceless to actually use. All of the rooms have private baths, and five have fireplaces. What helps account for this B and B's popularity is the hearty breakfast spread, delivered on a silver platter with the morning paper to your room or the garden gazebo (why can't life always be like this?). Located on Main Street, the inn is only steps away from Sutter Creek's shops and restaurants. Reserve early to avoid a two-month wait for weekend stays during peak seasons. *$$$; DIS, MC, V; checks OK; www.foxesinn.com; downtown.*

Grey Gables Inn / ★★☆

161 HANFORD ST, SUTTER CREEK; 209/267-1039 OR 800/473-9422
Surrounded by terraces of colorful and meticulously manicured gardens, this adorable three-story Victorian retreat offers eight carpeted guest rooms named after British poets and writers. Our favorite, the Byron Room, is bedecked in hues of deep green and Normandy rose, which pair well with the dark-wood furnishings and Renaissance Revival bed. Aside from the king-size bed in the Brontë Room, all of the boudoirs have queen-size beds, gas-log fireplaces, large armoires, air-conditioning, and private baths (a few with claw-foot tubs). A bounteous breakfast, delivered on fine English bone china, is served either in the formal dining room or in your room. And in true English fashion, there is an informal tea every afternoon from 3 to 4pm; wine and cheese is served daily from 6 to 7pm. The only drawback to this English

PURPLE GOLD: THERE'S WINE IN THEM THAR HILLS

During the gold rush, dozens of wineries existed in the Sierra foothills, started mainly by Italian immigrants. Sadly, the end of the mining boom and the beginning of Prohibition brought a severe wine-making drought to the region. Today, however, there are more than 60 wineries in the area (from Mariposa to Nevada County) producing, naturally enough, gold medal–winning wines. Most are small, family-owned establishments offering free public tours, tastings, and picnic sites.

Thirty-two varietals flourish within the microclimates of the foothills, resulting in everything from rich, spicy zinfandels to full-bodied chardonnays and fruity rieslings. Fortunately, wine enthusiasts don't have to travel all over the counties and down isolated roads to taste them. Most of the **AMADOR COUNTY WINERIES** (209/245-6992; www.amadorwine.com) are situated along the Shenandoah Valley Road out of Plymouth. The 9 wineries in **CALAVERAS COUNTY** (866/806-9463 or 209/728-9467; www.calaveraswines.org) are within a 3-mile radius of the town of Murphys, and there are 24 tasting rooms in all. The majority of wineries in **EL DORADO COUNTY** (800/306-3956; www.eldoradowines.org) are around the Apple Hill area and between the towns of Fair Play and Mount Akum. A map to all the region's wineries can be found in the **VINE TIMES** (www.thevinetimes.com), a complimentary wine newspaper, and county winery maps can be picked up in visitor centers and most lodgings. Many of the wineries are open daily and most offer free wine tastings.

While the quaint factor of the tasting rooms has little effect on how a wine tastes, the atmosphere adds to the wine taster's experience. Listed below are just a few among the more interesting to see.

Eden is that the house abuts heavily traveled Highway 49 (though the rooms are soundproof). On the plus side, Sutter Creek's shops and restaurants are only a short walk away. *$$$; AE, DIS, MC, V; checks OK; www.greygables.com; on Hwy 49, at the north end of town.* ♿

Jackson

Just beyond an enormous Georgia-Pacific lumber mill lies Jackson, the seat of Amador County. Jackson hides most of its rowdy past behind modern facades, but old-timers know the town (once called "little Reno") as the last place in California to outlaw prostitution. For a trip back in time, take a gander at the **NATIONAL HOTEL** (2 Water St; 209/223-0500), which has been in continuous operation since 1862 and has built up quite a guest list: Will Rogers, John Wayne, Leland Stanford, and almost every other 19th-century

BOEGER (1709 Carson Rd, Placerville; 530/622-8094; www.boegerwinery.com). Started by the Lamardo Fossati family in 1850, this winery is surrounded by both vineyards and pear orchards—a perfect picnic spot. Try the barbera served in the 1857 Swiss-Italian stone wine cellar and tasting room.

SIERRA VISTA (4560 Cabernet Wy, end of Leisure Ln, Placerville; 530/622-7221; www.sierravistawinery.com). Taste the flagship Rhône-style wines of this family-operated winery while gazing at the magnificent view of the snowcapped Sierra Nevada mountains. Picnic tables rest on the shaded lawn, circled by a flower garden. Winery tours are available by appointment.

STEVENOT (2690 San Domingo Rd, Murphys; 209/728-0638; www.stevenotwinery.com). Guests can sip the winery's signature chardonnay in the 1887 Shaw ranch house. Grapevines grow so close to the building, you'll be tempted to pick the grapes yourself. During the summer, Shakespearean plays are performed on the pretty lawn.

STORY WINERY (10525 Bell Rd, Plymouth; 209/245-6208; www.zin.com). Hundred-year-old Mission grapevines grow in the vineyards of this family-operated winery that produces Mission, zinfandel, and chenin blanc wines. The cabinlike tasting room and picnic area are dramatically perched above the Cosumnes River, offering visitors an exciting view of the canyon.

VILLA TOSCANO (10600 Shenandoah School House Rd; 209/245-3800; www.villatoscano.com). The faux red-clay tasting room rises above the formal grounds of this Tuscan-style villa with two koi ponds, roses, and round mosaic café tables. This newer vineyard produces barbera and sangiovese, among other wines.

California governor. Ragtime tunes and classic oldie sing-alongs are played on the grand piano, and guests register for the spartan rooms with the bartender through a wooden cage at the back of the saloon.

Gold rush buffs shouldn't miss the **AMADOR COUNTY MUSEUM** (225 Church St; 209/223-6375; open Wed–Sun; tours 11am–3pm Sat–Sun), which has scale models of the local Kennedy and Argonaut hard-rock mines, among the deepest and richest in the nation (this is also where Will Rogers filmed *Boys Will Be Boys* in 1920).

There's also **KENNEDY TAILING WHEELS PARK** (take Main St to Jackson Gate Rd, just north of Jackson; no phone), site of the Kennedy and Argonaut mines, the mother lode's deepest. Though these mines have been closed for decades, their head frames and huge tailing wheels (some are 58 feet in diameter) remain to help show how waste from the mines was conveyed over the hills to a settling pond.

A few miles south of Jackson is the "Historic 49" turnoff to **MOKELUMNE HILL**, a town once so rich with gold that claims were limited in size to 16 square feet and the hill was covered with tents and shacks of wood and tar paper. Although there's little going on these days in this sleepy, block-long town (try to imagine a past population of 15,000, including an old French quarter and a Chinatown), it's still a pleasant 15-minute drive through Mokelumne's green pastures, along its historic but minuscule Main Street, past the Protestant, Jewish, and Catholic cemeteries of its former residents, and back onto the highway.

If all this touring has given you a forty-niner-size appetite, indulge in a messy Moo-Burger and shake at **MEL AND FAYE'S DINER** (205 Hwy 49, Jackson; 209/223-0853; www.melandfayesdiner.com), a local landmark since 1956.

RESTAURANTS

Upstairs Restaurant & Streetside Bistro / ★★

164 MAIN ST, JACKSON; 209/223-3342

Chef Layne McCollum, who learned his trade at the California Culinary Academy, presides over this two-story restaurant housed in a handsome gold rush–era building made of exposed brick and petrified wood. The bright, cheery Streetside Bistro offers quiche, soups, salads, and gourmet sandwiches such as smoked pork loin with red chile pesto for lunch. For dinner, take the stairway to the Upstairs Restaurant, a long, narrow room of exposed brick and glass furnished with white-linen-topped tables graced with fresh flowers and oil lamps. McCollum's small, contemporary American menu changes weekly, though you might encounter pasta puttanesca prepared with tomato-basil fettuccine, smoked vegetables grilled with pesto, or grilled boneless breast of duck topped with blackberry-ginger sauce. A prix-fixe five-course special is offered on every menu. *$$$; AE, DIS, MC, V; checks OK; lunch, dinner Wed–Sun; beer and wine; reservations recommended; downtown.*

Volcano

This tiny town with fewer than 100 residents is so wonderfully authentic that it borders on decrepit (it doesn't get more gold rush–genuine than this). During the heady mining days, this unusually sophisticated town built the state's first library and its first astronomical observatory. Nowadays you can see some preserved buildings and artifacts, including a Civil War cannon. The town got its name in 1848 when miners mistook the enormous, craggy boulders in the center of town for volcanic rock. An outdoor amphitheater, hidden behind stone facades along Main Street, is the site of popular summer theatricals performed by the **VOLCANO THEATRE COMPANY** (on Main St, 1 block N of the St. George Hotel; www.volcanotheatre.org). Watching a play under the stars is a wonderful Gold Country experience; purchase tickets online at www.highsierratickets.com or call 209/296-5495. And at nearby **INDIAN GRINDING ROCK STATE HISTORIC PARK** (located 1 mile south of Volcano off Pine Grove/Volcano Rd; 209/296-7488), you'll find 3,000-year-old petroglyphs and an enormous limestone outcropping—the largest of its kind in America—dotted with thousands of holes created by generations of native Miwoks, who ground their acorn meal on the rock here. The park also has a fine Indian artifacts museum and a replica of a Miwok ceremonial roundhouse. After touring the town, take the side trip up winding Ram's Horn Grade to cool off in the funky, friendly bar at the **ST. GEORGE HOTEL** (see review). Or, from mid-March through mid-April, picnic amid the nearly half-million daffodils (more than 100 varieties) in bloom on **DAFFODIL HILL**, a 4-acre ranch 3 miles north of Volcano (follow the signs on Ram's Horn Grade; 209/296-7048; www.comspark.com/daffodilhill). Entrance to the ranch is free, but donations are accepted.

RESTAURANTS

The St. George Hotel Restaurant / ★★★

16104 MAIN ST, VOLCANO; 209/296-4458

Voted the number-one restaurant in Amador County by readers of the *Amador Ledger Dispatch*, the St. George's seasonally changing menu offers some of the finest cuisine in the region. Whenever possible, the kitchen staff uses locally grown produce and herbs from the St. George Hotel's garden. Be sure to start the feast with the St. George ravioli appetizer: crisp wontons layered with sautéed mushrooms and spinach over a chicken and sun-dried tomato galantine, resting on a bed of roasted red pepper pesto and braised leek sauce. Locals drive in from Jackson for lamb and fish entrées like the South of the Border grilled salmon topped with mango. For those who long for that traditional slab of meat, there's always the saffron-infused roasted rack of lamb. Choosing from the dessert menu isn't easy, but the frozen chocolate nut mousse with macadamia nut filling and Oreo cookie crust is definitely something to sigh over. *$$$; AE, MC, V; checks OK; dinner Thurs–Sun, brunch Sun; full bar; reservations recommended; www.stgeorgehotel.com; downtown.*

LODGINGS

The St. George Hotel / ★★

16104 MAIN ST, VOLCANO; 209/296-4458

In its heyday in the 1860s, the burgeoning village of Volcano offered a tired miner his choice of 17 hotels. Those whose pockets held the largest nuggets chose the St. George. Wrapped with balconies and entwined with Virginia creeper, it's still a gold mine for anyone spending an evening in this little town. The owners have recaptured some of the hotel's original charm: the restaurant is delightful, the parlor and grounds exquisite (think weddings), and the Bungalow Rooms in the modernized annex are bright and comfortable. The 12 guest rooms in the main building are by far the most interesting. Each room

THE HEROES AND VILLAINS OF THE GOLD RUSH ERA

Gold! From Sutter's Mill the word spread like wildfire, bringing hordes of fortune seekers and adventurers from around the globe to the Sierra foothills. But who would write their stories? Who would entertain them? And who would rob them of their gold?

It was "The Celebrated Jumping Frog of Calaveras County" that first brought international fame to **MARK TWAIN**—and he heard the story while drinking in a saloon in Angels Camp. Between writing for newspapers in San Francisco and Carson City, Nevada, Twain hung out with his mining buddies on Mokelumne Hill near Jackson. This author and humorist has since become the George Washington of the Sierra foothills, with seemingly every third lodging claiming "Mark Twain slept here."

Once mistress to Czar Nicholas I and the lunatic King Ludwig I of Bavaria, the beautiful and voluptuous **LOLA MONTEZ** arrived in Grass Valley on the arm of her second husband. But after she threw him out, she returned to doing what she thought she knew best: the Spider Dance. Wearing a scandalous knee-length skirt covered with cork tarantulas, Lola could always pack a theater—at least for one night. Despite her lack of talent, Lola took her act on the road, where the miners she entertained in the camps loved her—and Lola, in turn, loved them back.

Whatever Lola Montez lacked in talent, her Grass Valley neighbor **LOTTA CRABTREE** had in spades. Pushed by her mother, the gifted little girl performed in mining camps throughout the Sierras before moving to Boston, where

is decorated with antiques and personal effects donated by admired friends and relatives. The rooms in back have garden views and are perfect for morning people who like to rise with the sun. Otherwise, your best bet is to ask for a balcony room in front. On the downside, all rooms in the main lodge share a total of five bathrooms. A continental breakfast, served in the large downstairs parlor, can also be enjoyed in the garden. *$$; AE, MC, V; checks OK; open Wed–Sun; www.stgeorgehotel.com; downtown.* ♿

Angels Camp

Cruise right through the overcommercialized and truly uninspiring town of San Andreas and you'll eventually pull into Angels Camp, made famous by Mark Twain's short story "The Celebrated Jumping Frog of Calaveras County." Every year on the third weekend in May, thousands of frog fans flock to the **CALAVERAS COUNTY FAIR** (at the county fairgrounds, 2 miles south of town; 209/736-2561; www.frogtown.org) to witness the **JUMPING FROG JUBILEE**, one of the premier frog-jumping contests in the world and a truly "ribbiting" she became a famous actress and the first female millionaire in the country.

Famous for saying "please" when he pointed his (empty) double-barreled shotgun at Wells Fargo stagecoach drivers and demanded their strongboxes full of gold, **BLACK BART**—the "gentleman bandit"—never stole from the passengers riding the stage. Much of his success as a thief can be attributed to his skill as a backwoodsman and to his double life as a distinguished gentleman living in San Francisco, where he was known only as Charles E. Bolton.

The murderous activities attributed to outlaw **JOAQUIN MURIETA** may have been the work of as many as five different Joaquins. More myth than man, and much romanticized in an 1854 biography, the name Murieta was soon whispered fearfully by miners and printed in newspapers throughout California whenever gold was missing and bodies were found. Eventually killed by the California Rangers, Murieta had his head lopped off and placed in a jar. For years it toured the West via local fairs and celebrations, where for a dollar you could see what was left of the notorious bandit king. But was it Murieta's head, or that of another Joaquin?

The foothills are filled with stories of gold rush heroes whose fame may not have crossed the Sierra Nevada—like one-eyed **CHARLEY PARKER**, the woman who handled the reins of Wells Fargo stagecoaches in the guise of a man, and **SNOWSHOE THOMPSON**, who carried the miners' mail to Nevada and back over the snow-covered Sierras. Theirs are the stories that make up the lore of this region, and they can be heard in every town along the forty-niner trail.

competition. The festival, started in 1928 to mark the paving of the town's streets, also features livestock exhibitions, pageants, cook-offs, arm-wrestling tournaments, carnival rides, live music, a rodeo, and—for those who forgot to bring one—frogs for rent. The record, by the way, is 21 feet, 5¾ inches, jumped in 1986 by Rosie the Ribbiter, beating the old world record by 4½ inches.

RESTAURANTS

CAMPS / ★★★

676 MCCAULEY RANCH RD, ANGELS CAMP; 209/729-8181

A bit hard to find, CAMPS is ensconced within the sprawling Greenhorn Creek golf resort on the western fringes of Angels Camp. With outer walls of locally mined rhyolite designed to blend into the natural surroundings, the restaurant's earth tones and wicker-and-wood furniture offer a relaxing atmosphere where you can contemplate the many problems with your golf swing. The best seats in the house are on the spacious veranda overlooking the course, a fine venue for the traditional California cuisine. The menu changes frequently, but you can count on a variety of cuts of certified Angus beef, fresh fish, and organically grown vegetables. Finding the right wine to pair with your meal shouldn't be a problem, as the wine list has been given *Wine Spectator*'s Award of Excellence multiple times. *$$$; AE, MC, V; checks OK; lunch, dinner Wed–Sun, brunch Sun; full bar; reservations recommended; www.greenhorncreek.com; ½ mile west on Hwy 4, from north junction of Hwys 4 and 49.* ♿

Murphys

Gingerbread Victorian homes behind white picket fences and tall locust trees border the streets in Murphys, a former trading post set up by brothers Dan and John Murphy in cooperation with local Native Americans (John married the chief's daughter). It's worth taking the detour off Highway 49 just to stroll down the tree-lined Main Street—or, better yet, to sample the region's brews at **MURPHY'S BREWING COMPANY** in Murphys Historic Hotel & Lodge (see review). Most of the **CALAVERAS WINERIES** (209/728-9467 or 866/806-9463; www.calaveraswines.org) have tasting rooms right in the heart of town. Peer below the foundations of **MURPHYS CREEK ANTIQUES** next to the hotel to find the cavelike interior of the tasting room at **ZUCCA** (209/736-2949; www.zuccawines.com). Just a few steps farther and you'll find **MALVADINO'S** (209/754-1002). Pick up a map in town to visit the wineries located just outside the city.

Eighteen miles northeast of Murphys on Highway 4 is **CALAVERAS BIG TREES STATE PARK** (209/795-3840; www.bigtrees.org), where you can see giant sequoias that are among the biggest and oldest living things on earth. It's also a popular summer retreat for camping, swimming, hiking, and fishing along the Stanislaus River. In the mid-1800s gold prospectors discovered many of the area's numerous caverns, some of which can now be toured: **MERCER CAVERNS** (209/728-2101; www.mercercaverns.com), which has crystalline stalactites and stalagmites in a series of descending chambers; **MOANING CAVERN** (209/736-2708; www.caverntours.com), where a 100-foot stairway spirals down into a limestone chamber so huge it could house the Statue of Liberty (it's also a great place to try out your rappelling skills); and **CALIFORNIA CAVERNS** (209/736-2708; www.caverntours.com), the West's first commercially developed cave and the largest single cave system in Northern California. It has yet to be fully explored.

RESTAURANTS

Grounds / ★★

402 MAIN ST, MURPHYS; 209/728-8663

River Klass, a gregarious transplant from the East Coast, opened this hugely popular coffeehouse and café in 1993. It was quickly nicknamed the Rude Boy Café because of Klass's acerbic wit, but all you're likely to encounter is a cheerful staff and a room full of locals who are addicted to the potato pancakes (served with every made-to-order omelet), freshly baked breads, free-range egg dishes, and rich coffee. Lunch favorites include the grilled eggplant sandwich stuffed with smoked mozzarella and fresh basil, and the sausage sandwich on house-baked bread. The dinner menu, which changes about twice a week, offers everything from grilled halibut served with rock shrimp and spinach dumplings to fettuccine topped with sautéed shrimp, halibut, and mussels in a garlic cream sauce. *$$; AE, DIS, MC, V; checks OK; breakfast, lunch every day, dinner Wed–Sun; full bar; reservations recommended; east side of street, center of town.* ♿

LODGINGS

Dunbar House, 1880 / ★★★

271 JONES ST, MURPHYS; 209/728-2897 OR 800/692-6006

Without question, Dunbar House is among the finest B and Bs in the Gold Country. Century-old gardens adorn this lovely Italianate home built in 1880 by Willis Dunbar, a superintendent for the Utica Water Company, for his bride. The lush grounds are complemented by a two-person hammock, a gazebo, a rose garden with benches, and a swing. All five guest rooms are furnished with gas-burning fireplaces, heirloom antiques, down pillows and comforters, 350-thread-count Egyptian cotton bed linens, thick cotton towels imported from England, and vases of fresh flowers. The Cedar Room offers a private sunporch and a two-person whirlpool bath, while the two-room Sugar Pine Suite comes with English towel warmers and a balcony perched among the elm trees. For breakfast, fresh juices, coffee, house-made pastries, and a main dish such as a fabulous crab and cheese English muffin are served in your room, at the dining room table, or in the gorgeous garden. *$$$–$$$$; AE, MC, V; checks OK; www.dunbarhouse.com; just off Main St at south end of town.*

Murphys Historic Hotel & Lodge / ★

457 MAIN ST, MURPHYS; 209/728-3444 OR 800/532-7684

When this hotel opened in 1856, who could have known what kind of characters would pass through its doors? The illustrious guest register includes Ulysses S. Grant, Mark Twain, Horatio Alger, Susan B. Anthony, and Black Bart, to name just a few. Although its days of housing dignitaries are long past, this national- and state-registered landmark still maintains its hold as the town's social center. Any time of day or night you'll find a few locals here at the old-fashioned saloon, hunched over stools, voicing their opinions and politely ignoring the tourists who stop in for a beer. The main building has nine historic guest rooms that reflect a turn-of-the-century lifestyle (that is, thin walls and no phones, televisions, or private baths), while the newer building offers 20 modern rooms with private bathrooms and hair dryers. In the dining area—open for breakfast, lunch, and dinner—you'll find huge platters of chicken, beef, seafood, and pasta, but the lackluster service and mediocre cuisine usually discourage most visitors from coming back (especially with the estimable Grounds restaurant just down the street). *$$; AE, DC, DIS, MC, V; checks OK; www.murphyshotel.com; downtown.* ♿

The Victoria Inn / ★★

402 MAIN ST, MURPHYS; 209/728-8933

A town in need of more luxury accommodations, Murphys hadn't celebrated the opening of a new inn in more than a century until 1993, when this two-story shingle-and-rock charmer opened its doors on Main Street. Each of the 14 individually decorated guest rooms has an eclectic mix of Victorian and modern amenities: fireplaces or woodstoves, claw-foot tubs or spas, and brass or antique beds. The two best rooms for romance are the Wisteria, with its king-size bed, fireplace, wet bar, spa tub for two, and private porch overlooking the garden, and the Anniversary Suite, which features a private balcony, a wet bar, a double-sided fireplace, a king-size sleigh bed, and an enormous spa tub. You'll like the location right on the lively section of Main Street. *$$$–$$$$; DIS, MC, V; checks OK; www.victoriainn-murphys.com; in the Miner's Exchange Complex.* ♿

Columbia

Some mighty fortunate forty-niners unearthed a staggering $87 million in gold in this former boisterous mining town, once the state's second-largest city (it was only two votes shy of becoming the state capital over Sacramento). But by the late 1850s, when the gold no longer panned out, Columbia's population of 15,000 had nearly vanished. In 1945 the entire town was turned into **COLUMBIA STATE HISTORIC PARK** (209/532-4301 or 209/532-0150). This is the mother lode's best-preserved park, filled with Western-style Victorian hotels and saloons, a newspaper office, a working blacksmith's forge, stagecoaches, and numerous other relics of California's early mining days. Follow the free, short, self-guided park tour, and don't miss the **WELLS FARGO EXPRESS OFFICE**, a former stagecoach center, and the restored **COLUMBIA SCHOOLHOUSE**, in use until 1937. Big-time gold rush buffs who want more local history should pick up the inexpensive walking-tour booklet at the visitor center or sign up for a 45-minute guided mine tour. For a more leisurely view of the park, hop aboard one of the horse-drawn stagecoaches. And to learn how to pan for gold, stop by **HIDDEN TREASURE GOLD MINE TOURS** (209/532-9693) at the corner of Main and Stage streets.

RESTAURANTS

The City Hotel Restaurant / ★★

MAIN ST, COLUMBIA; 209/532-1479 OR 800/532-1479

The City Hotel Restaurant is a rarity—a culinary palace in the heart of a state park. Inside, it's decked out with red velvet drapes, oil paintings, and antique furniture topped with crisp linens and flowers. The restaurant and hotel are a hotel-hospitality training center for nearby Columbia College, and the students assist the staff here. If this is Hotel Hospitality 101, these are 4.0 students—the serving staff even dresses in period costumes. You may order from the small prix-fixe or à la carte menus featuring dishes like grilled tournedos of beef tenderloin with potato and blue cheese twice-baked soufflé, or pan-seared fillet of salmon over stir-fried vegetables with shiitake mushroom compote. For dessert, diners who can wait 30 minutes will be justly rewarded with a lemon soufflé crowned with Grand Marnier sauce. California vintages feature prominently on the wine list. While you wait for your dinner table, spend some time in What Cheer, the hotel's saloon. *$$$; AE, DIS, MC, V; checks OK; dinner Tues–Sun, brunch Sun; full bar; reservations required Fri-Sat, recommended Sun-Thurs; www.cityhotel.com; between Jackson and State sts.*

LODGINGS

City Hotel / ★★

MAIN ST, COLUMBIA; 209/532-1479 OR 800/532-1479
City folk who frequented this opulent hotel in 1856 called it the Gem of the Southern Mines. Predictably, the building has gone through several incarnations since then, but when the town was turned into a state historic park in 1945, visitors once again returned to this venerable landmark. In the '70s, nearby Columbia College obtained grant money to renovate the structure and turn it into a hotel-hospitality training center, and now students assist the staff here. The lobby is fitted with period settees and marble-topped tables, and 6 of the 10 high-ceilinged rooms face a central parlor, where you can relax and read the newspaper or chat with fellow guests. Rooms 1 and 2 are the largest and have balconies overlooking Main Street. All of the rooms are nicely furnished with Renaissance Revival beds and antiques, but they also only have half baths—the showers are down the hall (the hotel provides comfy robes, slippers, and wicker baskets full of toiletries to ease the trip). *$$; AE, DIS, MC, V; checks OK; www.cityhotel.com; between Jackson and State sts.*

Twain Harte

LODGINGS

McCaffrey House Bed & Breakfast Inn / ★★★☆

23251 HWY 108, TWAIN HARTE; 209/586-0757 OR 888/586-0757
Located in the Stanislaus National Forest, this gorgeous, sprawling three-story country home was built specifically as a B and B, and it's one of the top 10 in the Gold Country. Each of the eight immaculate guest rooms has its own bath with a shower and tub, a hair dryer, an individually controlled thermostat, access to a library of 400 movies, a private phone, and wireless Internet. All but two units have private decks. But it's the details that make the difference: a nearby creek to lull you to sleep, a forest view from your deck, queen-size quilts handmade by the Amish of Pennsylvania, a black iron stove in every room, exceptional gallery-quality art adorning the walls, TVs with

VCRs stored in pine wood armoires, a library of paperbacks, an outdoor hot tub perfectly situated to watch the full moon passing overhead—and more. In the summer, breakfast and hors d'oeuvres, wine, and sparkling cider are served on the huge redwood deck, which surrounds the house and overlooks the verdant hollow. Owners Michael and Stephanie McCaffrey and their gaggle of pets are all incredibly friendly—reason enough to return again and again. *$$$; AE, MC, V; checks OK; www.mccaffreyhouse.com; 11 miles east of Sonora.*

Sonora

When the traffic starts to crawl along Highway 49, you're probably closing in on Sonora. In forty-niner days, Sonora competed with Columbia for the title of wealthiest city in the southern mother lode. Today, it is the Gold Country's largest and most crowded town and the Tuolumne County seat, with dozens of stores and small cafés lining the main thoroughfare. If you have time to spare, search for a parking space along Washington Street (no easy feat on weekends) or park in one of the lots a block east of Washington on Stewart Street, and take a look at the well-preserved 19th-century **ST. JAMES EPISCOPAL CHURCH** at the top of Washington Street and the **TUOLUMNE COUNTY MUSEUM AND HISTORY CENTER** (158 W Bradford St; 209/532-1317) located in the century-old jail. If you have yet more time to kill, take a leisurely drive along the picturesque **DETOUR ROUTE 108**, which heads west into the Sierra Nevada over **SONORA PASS** and through several scenic alpine communities.

RESTAURANTS

Banny's / ★★

83 S STEWART ST, SONORA; 209/533-4709

Banny's decor may be simple, but chef-owner Rob Bannworth's menu is quite sophisticated. He's a passionate cook who takes his sauces seriously, and you certainly can't complain about the reasonable prices for entrées such as the house favorite, garlic fettuccine rolled fresh daily. With dishes ranging from $11 to $20, you'll spend only about half of what you'd have to shell out in the Bay Area for fare of equal quality. Please note that service can be slow at times, so we don't recommend dining here if you're in a hurry. *$$; DIS, MC, V; checks OK; lunch Mon–Sat, dinner every day; beer and wine; reservations recommended; www.bannyscafe.com; in Old Town.*

LODGINGS

Barretta Gardens Inn / ★★

700 S BARRETTA ST, SONORA; 209/532-6039 OR 800/206-3333

There is always something blooming in the expansive gardens of native flowering shrubs surrounding this small country inn, which is perched on a hillside southeast of downtown Sonora. The wraparound porch is perfect for curling up with a good book (or your honey) in spring or autumn. Winter conversation takes place on soft sofas around the fireplace in the comfortable living room. The inn has eight individually decorated guest rooms; all of them come with fresh flowers, TVs and VCRs (and a library of 250 movies), soft, terry-lined bathrobes, and small refrigerators stocked with beverages. Coffee, tea, and juice are delivered to your room at your convenience in the morning. The parlor boasts a cozy fireplace, and there is a hot tub located outside. Breakfast entails fresh fruit, omelets, pancakes, Numi organic tea, and the like. *$$–$$$; AE, MC, V; checks OK; www.barrettagardens.com; a few blocks east of Washington St.*

Jamestown

Jamestown has been preoccupied with gold since the first fleck was taken out of Woods Creek in 1848; a marker even commemorates the discovery of a 75-pound nugget. For a fee, you can pan for gold in troughs on Main Street or go prospecting with a guide. But gold isn't Jamestown's only claim to fame. For decades, this four-block-long town lined with picturesque buildings has been Hollywood's favorite Western movie set: scenes from famous flicks like *Butch Cassidy and the Sundance Kid* were shot here, and vintage railway cars and steam locomotives used in TV classics like *Little House on the Prairie*, *Bonanza*, and *High Noon* are on display at the **RAILTOWN 1897 STATE HISTORIC PARK** (5th Ave at Reservoir Rd, near the center of town; 209/984-3953; www.csrmf.org/railtown). You can view the vehicles at the roundhouse daily or ride the rails on weekends from April through October and during holiday events, such as the Santa Train ride in December.

LODGINGS

The Historic National Hotel & Restaurant / ★★

18183 MAIN ST, JAMESTOWN; 209/984-3446 OR 800/894-3446

The ongoing restoration, which began in 1974, of the 1859 National Hotel was so impressive that both the Tuolumne Visitors Bureau and the Tuolumne County Lodging Association bestowed awards for its new look. Inside the nine guest rooms, 19th-century details (handmade quilts, lace curtains, brass beds) blend with 20th-century comforts (private bathrooms). The original gold rush saloon, with its handsome redwood bar, is the best place in town to eavesdrop on local gossip. A generous continental breakfast includes cereal, house-made muffins, hard-boiled eggs, fresh fruit, fresh-squeezed juices, coffee and tea, and the morning paper. Brunch, lunch, and dinner are served to the public in the handsome, old-fashioned dining room, replete with antiques, old photos, and gold rush memorabilia. You'll find an extensive array of hearty steak, prime rib, chicken, seafood, and pasta dishes, as well as house-made desserts and numerous fine wines from their award-winning wine list.

On sunny days or warm summer nights, ask for a table in the Garden Courtyard, draped by vines from a century-old grape arbor. *$$; AE, DC, DIS, MC, V; checks OK; www.national-hotel.com; downtown.*

Jamestown Hotel & Restaurant / ★★

18153 MAIN ST, JAMESTOWN; 209/984-3902 OR 800/205-4901

Built at the turn of the last century and converted into a hospital in the 1920s, this two-story brick charmer with its Western facade and wood veranda was eventually transformed into one of the most authentic gold rush–era hotels in the Gold Country. The eight engaging guest rooms—named after female gold rush personalities—are filled with antiques and luxuriously appointed with either claw-foot or whirlpool tubs, air-conditioning, hair dryers, and Turkish cotton bathrobes. The romantic Lotta Crabtree Suite is furnished with lots of wicker, floral fabrics, a beautiful wrought-iron queen-size bed, and a claw-foot tub. A separate sitting room and claw-foot tub are part of the fiery Lola Montez Suite, which is rumored to be haunted by the countess herself (more likely a ghostly impersonator, as no one can confirm that the lady ever stayed at the hotel). A full breakfast is included in the room rate. Downstairs is a classic Western-style bar that's worth a gander even if you're just passing through. *$$; AE, DC, DIS, MC, V; no checks; www.jamestownhotel.com; downtown.* ♿

Mariposa

The town clock in the two-story **MARIPOSA COUNTY COURTHOUSE** (Bullion St between 9th and 10th sts) has been marking time since 1866. Another town landmark is **ST. JOSEPH'S CATHOLIC CHURCH** (4985 Bullion St), built in 1863; and behind it lies the entrance to the **MARIPOSA MINE**, discovered by Kit Carson in 1849 and later purchased by John C. Frémont, who owned most of the land around these parts.

Two miles south of Mariposa at the Mariposa County Fairgrounds is the **CALIFORNIA STATE MINING AND MINERAL MUSEUM** (5007 Fairgrounds Rd; 209/742-7625), a state geology center with one of the country's finest collections of gems and minerals. One wing showcases 20,000 glittering gems and minerals; another holds artifacts and photos that tell California's mining story.

A side trip off Highway 49 leads to **HORNITOS** (Spanish for "little ovens"), a name that refers to the shape of the tombs on Boot Hill. This formerly lawless burg is nearly a ghost town, though it was once a favorite haunt of Gold Country bandito Joaquin Murieta, whose pickled head was turned over to state authorities in a glass jar for a $1,000 reward in 1853. Weathered old buildings (saloons, fandango halls, and gambling dens) stand around the plaza, some flaunting bullet holes from bygone battles.

RESTAURANTS

Charles Street Dinner House / ★★

5043 CHARLES ST, MARIPOSA; 209/966-2366

This going-on-30-year-old landmark isn't as formal as its name might suggest. Rather, it's a place where the Old West reigns over decor, food, and service. The waitstaff are dressed in period costume and look as though they just stepped out of the historic photos on the wall. Although the culinary offerings—steaks, chops, chicken, fresh seafood—are fairly common fare, they are skillfully prepared and well presented. Dinner specials might include broiled chicken breast, rack of lamb, duck, lobster, scampi, or prime rib, and all dinners are served with soup and salad. The 2,000-bottle wine cellar offers an impressive array of vintages. *$$; AE, DIS, MC, V; local checks only; dinner Wed–Sun; beer and wine; reservations recommended; www.charlesstreetdinnerhouse.com; Hwy 140 and 7th St.*

Ocean Sierra / ★★

3292 E WESTFALL RD, MARIPOSA; 209/742-7050

This little cabin in the woods is home to some of the best cuisine in the county. Dinner begins with a soup (the spicy gazpacho is fantastic) and a green salad served with a chilled fork. Entrées include lemon-grilled prawns, New York pepper steak, a savory vegetarian stir-fry, and Australian lobster. Complete your meal with homemade ice cream, the oh-so-tasty So Slim Key Lime Cheesecake, or other desserts of the day. The restaurant, with its high pine ceiling, chipped-wood walls, brick fireplace, and white linen tablecloths, has the feel of a French mountain inn. Even the deer come by at dusk to graze on the lawn. *$$$; DIS, MC, V; checks OK; dinner Fri–Sun; beer and wine; reservations recommended; at Triangle and E Westfall rds.*

LODGINGS

Meadow Creek Ranch / ★★

2669 TRIANGLE RD, MARIPOSA; 209/966-3843 OR 800/853-2057

A stage stop in the 1850s, this refurbished ranch house is one of the most secluded bed-and-breakfasts in the Gold Country—a good choice for those looking for romantic solitude. There are only two guest rooms, each decorated in Early American style. The Garden Gate Room, located in an annex to the main house with a private entrance, offers a queen-size bed, twin bed in the alcove, sitting area, private bath with soaking tub, and patio that overlooks the meadow. The cozy Country Cottage Room is a converted chicken coop—stay with us here—that has been beautifully decorated in mahogany and has a queen-size bed imported from Austria, a private bath with a clawfoot tub, and a sitting area. Both rooms have wireless Internet. A hearty breakfast is served family-style in the ranch house's spacious dining room. *$$; AE, DIS, MC, V; checks OK; www.meadowcreekranchinn.com; about 11½ miles south of Mariposa on Hwy 49.* ♿

Oakhurst

RESTAURANTS

Erna's Elderberry House / ★★★★

48688 VICTORIA LN, OAKHURST; 559/683-6800

Vienna-born Erna Kubin-Clanin selected this Oakhurst hillside in 1984 as the site for her now-famous restaurant and Château du Sureau (see review). The location is reminiscent of a corner of Provence, and, indeed, after indulging in one of her meals, you'll think you've been transported to some European gastronomical paradise. Ever since the *New York Times* praised Erna's Elderberry House as "one of the most elegant and stylish restaurants in the nation," epicureans from around the world have made the pilgrimage to the elaborate, Mediterranean-style dining room ensconced among pine trees and elderberry bushes. The prix-fixe dinner is a six-course affair that changes daily. A meal might begin with a grilled vegetable and goat cheese terrine, followed by chilled Yukon gold potato soup, then onto the main courses: Dungeness crab sandwich served with yucca root cake, avocado, and saffron aioli; foie gras apricot spaetzle; or curry-roasted pork tenderloin. The sweet finale might be a caramelized banana-chocolate tart. If you prefer a more casual meal, the château's Restaurant-Cellar Bar offers a small bistro-style menu. *$$$$; AE, DIS, MC, V; no checks; dinner every day, brunch Sun; full bar; reservations recommended; www.elderberryhouse.com; off Hwy 41, just west of town.* ♿

LODGINGS

Château du Sureau / ★★★★

48688 VICTORIA LN, OAKHURST; 559/683-6860

In 1991, when the opulent Château du Sureau was completed (*sureau* is French for "elderberry"), Erna Kubin-Clanin was able to offer her guests a magnificent place to stay after indulging in the exquisite cuisine of her Elderberry House (see review). Erna's desire for perfection doesn't stop in the kitchen, as you'll instantly notice once you see the château's massive chandeliers and 19th-century paintings, the cathedral windows framing grand Sierra views, and the imported tiles that complement the limestone in the baths. The 10 guest rooms come replete with goose-down comforters, canopy beds, antiques, Provençal fabrics, tapestries, fresh flowers, fireplaces, and CD sound systems. The elegant Thyme Room is designed to easily accommodate wheelchairs; the Mint Room has a private entrance; and the Saffron Room has a breathtaking Napoleon III–era bedroom set made of ebony and inlaid ivory. A European-style breakfast is served in the cozy breakfast room or alfresco on the patio. Elsewhere on the grounds lie a fountain, a swimming pool, and a giant outdoor chess court with 3-foot-tall pieces. There's even a tiny chapel where wedding bells occasionally ring. The château's pièce de résistance is the Villa Sureau, a private two-bedroom, two-bath guest residence, featuring a salon, a library, and authentic antique furnishings and original artwork from the early 19th century. Outside the villa is a private Roman spa, where you can soak under the stars or receive a massage. *$$$$; AE, MC, V; no checks; www.chateaudusureau.com; off Hwy 41, just west of town.* ♿

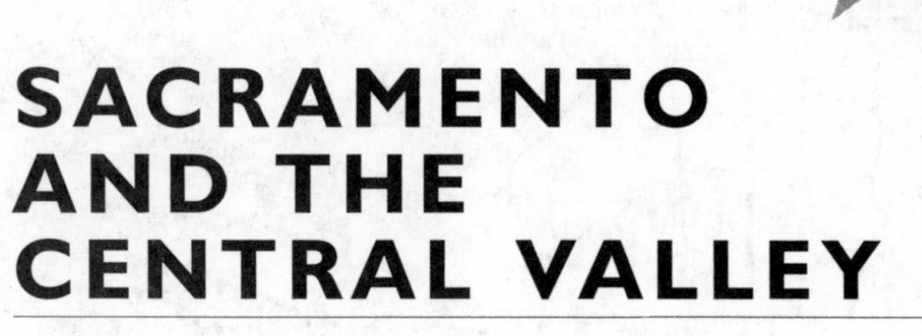

SACRAMENTO AND THE CENTRAL VALLEY

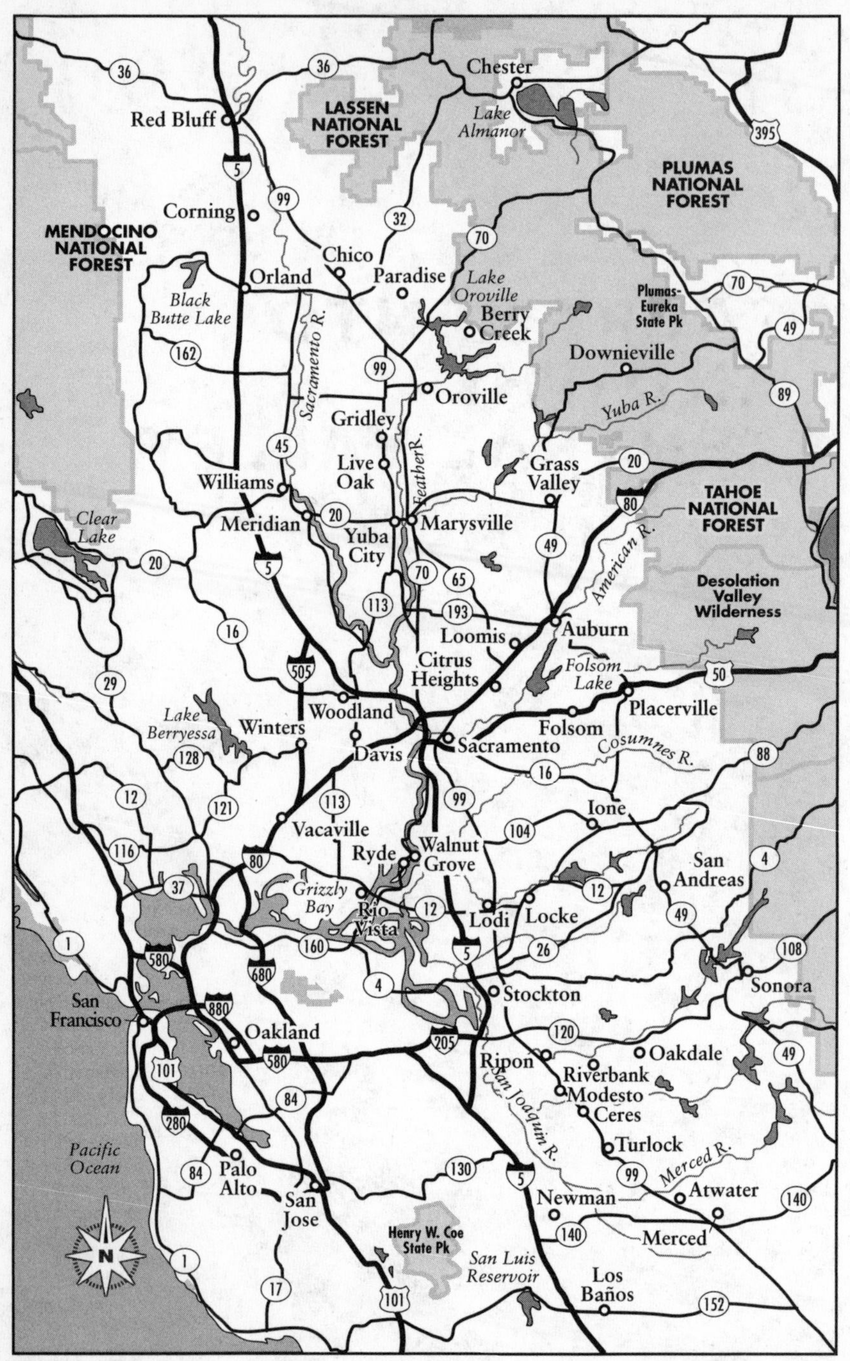

Chester
Lake Almanor
LASSEN NATIONAL FOREST
Red Bluff
PLUMAS NATIONAL FOREST
Corning
MENDOCINO NATIONAL FOREST
Chico
Orland
Paradise
Lake Oroville
Berry Creek
Black Butte Lake
Plumas-Eureka State Pk
Downieville
Oroville
Sacramento R.
Gridley
Yuba R.
Live Oak
Feather R.
Grass Valley
Williams
TAHOE NATIONAL FOREST
Meridian
Marysville
Clear Lake
Yuba City
American R.
Desolation Valley Wilderness
Loomis
Auburn
Citrus Heights
Folsom Lake
Placerville
Woodland
Lake Berryessa
Winters
Folsom
Davis
Sacramento
Cosumnes R.
Vacaville
Ione
Ryde
Walnut Grove
San Andreas
Grizzly Bay
Rio Vista
Lodi
Locke
Stockton
Sonora
San Francisco
Oakland
Ripon
Oakdale
Riverbank
Modesto
Ceres
San Joaquin R.
Pacific Ocean
Turlock
Palo Alto
Merced R.
San Jose
Atwater
Newman
Merced
Henry W. Coe State Pk
San Luis Reservoir
Los Baños

SACRAMENTO AND THE CENTRAL VALLEY

Here's a bit of trivia you probably didn't know: California's Central Valley is the largest expanse of flatland west of the Continental Divide—nearly 300 miles long and 50 miles wide. Stretching from Los Banos in the south to Red Bluff in the north, this mighty plain is bordered by the Sierra Nevada Mountains on the eastern flank and the Coast Ranges to the west. At the heart lies the capital city, Sacramento, the legislative pulse of the state. For the most part, the Central Valley is slightly above sea level, with the exception of the Sutter Buttes (the world's smallest mountain range), located just north of Sacramento, and the Sacramento River Delta, which is largely below sea level. Like a huge patchwork quilt, the Central Valley encompasses miles of farmland, orchards, and vineyards, stitched with irrigation canals, lakes, and rivers.

ACCESS AND INFORMATION

INTERSTATE 5 and **HIGHWAY 99** are the primary north-south routes through the Central Valley. Among the many east-west arteries are **HIGHWAY 152** between Los Banos and Merced, and **HIGHWAY 132** between the Altamont Pass and Modesto in the south, while to the north, **HIGHWAY 20** serves as an artery from the foothills near Grass Valley to Clear Lake. Interstate 5 provides easy access to **SACRAMENTO INTERNATIONAL AIRPORT (SMF)**, while **INTERSTATE 80** will take you east to the Reno/Lake Tahoe region or west to San Francisco. Through the Delta, **HIGHWAY 12** is the major thoroughfare from 99 or Interstate 5, and from Sacramento, **HIGHWAY 160** winds along the Sacramento River, across drawbridges and swing bridges, and is by far the most scenic. There is no public transportation system for the region (only within the cities), so it is best to explore this area by car. However, take notice that the Central Valley is often blanketed with thick fog during the winter months (December through February is the worst). Driving can be hazardous, and often flights are delayed at Sacramento's International Airport due to poor visibility. Always call the airline to confirm schedules, and for news on current road conditions throughout the Central Valley and the state, visit www.dot.ca.gov or call 800/427-ROAD.

Stockton and the South Central Valley

The communities between Los Banos and Stockton—some tiny, some rapidly developing (like Modesto)—are worth exploring. This region of the Central Valley can be defined as the east-west midway point between Yosemite National Park and the San Francisco Bay Area. Closer inspection, however, finds this agriculturally abundant area rich in history, cultural diversity, and small-town flavor.

Merced

Merced has claimed the title "Gateway to Yosemite" for more than a century, and the majority of its visitors are San Francisco Bay Area residents just passing through. Those who stop long enough to look around usually end up at **APPLEGATE PARK** (between M and R sts), a 23-acre greenbelt with more than 60 varieties of trees, an immaculate rose garden, a small, free zoo, and, in the summer, amusement rides to whirl and twirl you and the kids. On Thursday evenings, local farmers sell their fresh produce from 6 to 9pm on **MAIN STREET** (between N and K sts), a good place to buy picnic basket ingredients. One of the more interesting sights in the area is the **MERCED COUNTY COURTHOUSE MUSEUM** (21st and N sts; 209/723-2401; www.mercedmuseum.org), the pride and joy of Merced and a monument to the early settlers of the great Central Valley.

RESTAURANTS

Branding Iron Restaurant / ★★

640 W 16TH ST, MERCED; 209/722-1822

This paean to the American Beef Council has satiated Mercedites for nearly half a century; it's a classic small-town steak house with the brains to keep things steady and unchanging. The owners have added to the Branding Iron's Old West ambience by decorating its rough-hewn redwood walls with registered livestock brands from all over California. Dinner begins with soup and salad, followed by such carnivorous delights as a thick cut of choice prime rib seasoned with coarse-ground pepper, garlic, rosemary, and thyme, and a large baked potato with all the fixin's. If your stomach (or waistline) will allow it, finish the evening with a sweet treat from the well-stocked dessert tray. *$$; AE, MC, V; local checks only; lunch Mon–Fri, dinner every day; full bar; reservations recommended; www.thebrandingiron-merced.com; at W 16th and M sts.* ♿

Turlock

RESTAURANTS

El Jardín / ★★

409 E OLIVE ST, TURLOCK; 209/632-0932

True to its name, El Jardín has a fragrant, colorful flower garden surrounded by several outdoor tables—the place to sit when the weather is mild. The authentic south-of-the-border fare—all offered at south-of-the-border prices—includes such house specials as the Milanesa breaded beef fillet with fresh green salsa and the tender and tasty *pollo a la parilla* (grilled chicken breast). For *los niños* there are kid-size enchiladas, quesadillas, taquitos, burritos, and tostadas served with rice and beans. *$; V; no checks; lunch, dinner* *every day; beer and wine; reservations recommended; 1 block west of Golden State Blvd, 1 block north of Main St.* ♿

Modesto

RESTAURANTS

Hazel's / ★★

431 12TH ST, MODESTO; 209/578-3463

This popular continental restaurant has been around nearly half a century and is a favorite romantic weekend retreat for both residents and visitors in the Modesto area. The current owners maintain original owner Hazel Saylor's time-honored menu, featuring dishes as simple as liver and onions topped with sautéed mushrooms and as deluxe as the Australian lobster tail. Hazel's version of cannelloni, stuffed with seasoned veal, chicken, and mushrooms, is still a lunchtime favorite. The wine list is well edited and reasonably priced, with several selections available by the glass. *$$–$$$; AE, DC, DIS, MC, V; local checks only; lunch Tues–Fri, dinner Tues–Sat; full bar; reservations recommended; www.hazelsmodesto.com; corner of 12th and E sts.* ♿

Tresetti's World Caffe / ★★

927 11TH ST, MODESTO; 209/572-2990

Located a few blocks from city hall, this popular hangout attracts a steady gaggle of lawyers, lobbyists, politicians, and other professionals who congregate at the stylish galvanized steel and polished-wood wine bar. The adjacent high-ceilinged dining room is equally chic, with its burgundy drapes, matching cement floor, pale yellow walls, glass facade overlooking downtown Modesto, and only a dozen tables. The chef focuses on classic dishes from around the world. Offerings range from baked Moroccan chicken with currant couscous and a curry-lime yogurt, to potato-encrusted Australian lamb loin with Shiraz balsamic demi-glace and a cilantro-lime-Dijon aioli on roasted garlic mashed potatoes. Tresetti's also has a large assortment of single-malt whiskeys and ports. *$$; AE, DC, DIS, MC, V; checks OK; lunch, dinner Mon–Sat; full bar; reservations recommended; www.tresetti.com; corner of 11th and J sts.* ♿

LODGINGS

Doubletree Hotel Modesto / ★

1150 9TH ST, MODESTO; 209/526-6000 OR 800/222-TREE

Towering 14 stories above the Modesto landscape, the Doubletree is the Central Valley's premier business and luxury accommodation. Guests are pampered with such amenities as a spa, sauna, sundeck, heated outdoor pool, weight room, restaurant, two bars, and extensive conference facilities. Each of the 258 comfortable guest rooms (including 6 suites) are equipped with a TV, three telephones with a fax/PC data port and direct inward dialing, a king- or queen-size bed, a separate desk and table, a coffeemaker, an iron and ironing board, and a hair dryer. A free shuttle will whisk you to the Modesto airport; if you have your own wheels, take advantage of the free parking in the sheltered lot. *$$$; AE, DC, DIS, MC, V; checks OK; www.doubletreehotels.com; at K St.* ♿

Oakdale

Sitting on Highway 120, en route to Yosemite, this "Cowboy Capital of the World" is the home of the **OAKDALE COWBOY MUSEUM** (355 East F St; 209/847-5163; www.oakdalecowboymuseum.org), which houses items from world-renowned rodeo champions. Succulent lovers—and who isn't?—shouldn't miss **POOT'S HOUSE OF CACTUS** (on the way to Oakdale, 5 miles east of Hwy 99; 17229 E Hwy 120; 209/599-7241), a bristling collection of cactus and unusual plants from around the world. Another town highlight is the **SATURDAY OAKDALE LIVESTOCK AUCTION** (6001 Albers Rd; 209/847-1033). Just be careful not to scratch your nose—you could become the dumbstruck new owner of a 600-pound Black Angus.

RESTAURANTS

H-B Saloon and Bachi's Family Restaurant / ★

401 EAST F ST, OAKDALE; 209/847-2985

For a real Central Valley experience, don your cowboy boots and ten-gallon hat and head for the H-B Saloon, a decidedly funky old bar and restaurant festooned with faded photos of ranches and rodeos, mounted game, old-fashioned tack, branded wainscoting, and other mementos of ranching life. During any time of the day or night you'll find aging cattlemen in baseball caps and cowboy hats playing shuffleboard or poker in the saloon, drinking cheap beers, listening to Johnny Cash on the jukebox, and doing their best to ignore the occasional wayward tourist. Dinner, served family-style in the adjacent Bachi's Restaurant, will satisfy even the hungriest cowboy: choose from rib-eye steak, pork chops, lamb chops, chicken, baby back ribs, halibut, and prime rib. Each inexpensive meal includes red wine, soup, salad, French fries, bread, beans, and potato salad. *$; AE, DIS, MC, V; local checks only; lunch Mon–Fri, dinner Wed–Sat; full bar; no reservations; next to the Hershey Visitors Center.* ♿

Stockton

The birthplace of Caterpillar tractor inventor Benjamin Holt and heartthrob rock star Chris Isaak, and summer home of the San Francisco 49ers, Stockton used to be a simple blue-collar town. In 1999, it was chosen as an All-American City by the National Civic League. A multicultural blend of European, Mexican, and Asian immigrants who own businesses and provide services and labor in this agriculturally abundant region make diversity a watchword here. Some 75 languages are spoken within the city limits.

For a taste of regional history and fine art, a visit to the **HAGGIN MUSEUM** (1201 N Pershing Ave; 209/940-6300; www.hagginmuseum.org) is a must. Maestro Peter Jaffe conducts the innovative **STOCKTON SYMPHONY** (46 W Fremont St; 209/951-0196; www.stocktonsymphony.org) along with high-caliber guest artists. The **STOCKTON CIVIC THEATRE** (2312 Rose Marie Ln; 209/473-2424; www.sctlivetheatre.org) puts on affordable, quality productions, and the historic **FOX THEATRE** (242 E Main; 209/462-2694; www.stocktongov.com/foxtheatre/) is the place to see big-name performers.

On those scorching summer days, what better way to cool off than a trip to the **OAK PARK ICE ARENA** (3545 Alvarado St; 209/937-7433). **THE CHILDREN'S MUSEUM OF STOCKTON** (402 W Weber Ave; 209/465-4386; www.stocktongov.com/childrensmuseum/) is a hands-on discovery and learning center for kids as well as parents. **MICKE GROVE PARK & ZOO** (take the Eight-Mile Rd exit from Hwy 99; 11793 N Micke Grove Rd; 209/331-7400; www.mgzoo.com) is shaded by huge oak trees—a great place to picnic. It also features a zoo known for its endangered species breeding program, a golf course, a driving range, Japanese gardens, and a small amusement park for the younger ones. For a rundown on the agricultural history of the San Joaquin Valley, check out the **SAN JOAQUIN COUNTY HISTORICAL MUSEUM** (located inside Micke Grove Park; 209/331-2055; www.sanjoaquinhistory.org).

From May through October the **STOCKTON CERTIFIED FARMERS MARKETS** (209/943-1830; www.stocktonfarmersmarket.org) offer superb local produce and are held Thursday through Sunday mornings at various locations around town. And speaking of produce, the annual **STOCKTON ASPARAGUS FESTIVAL** (Oak Grove Regional Park, Eight-Mile Rd exit off I-5; 209/644-3740; www.asparagusfest.com), held every fourth weekend in April, has grown into one of the most popular food and entertainment events in Northern California. This three-day festival features more than 50 entertainers, gourmet asparagus dishes, a wine and beer pavilion, a classic car show, a 5K run, and more, all celebrating—you guessed it—asparagus. For more information on this event or other activities in the Stockton area, call the **STOCKTON CONFERENCE AND VISITORS BUREAU** (445 W Weber Ave; 877/778-6258; www.visitstockton.org).

RESTAURANTS

Bobs at the Marina / ★★☆

6639 EMBARCADERO, STOCKTON; 209/957-3279

It's hard to find a decent brunch in Stockton—everything seems to be chain restaurants or cheap Mexican places. Though it feels more like a diner or fast-food joint—orders are placed at the counter, your name is announced over the loudspeaker—Bobs at the Marina is down-home country cooking at its finest. There's no pretense here: Everything is served with paper plates and cups and plastic silverware. You can get a tasty, mammoth hamburger for under five bucks, and a full breakfast—like a chorizo omelet and browned potatoes or a breakfast burrito and hash browns—for just a dollar and a half more. And the fresh blueberry hotcakes taste just like the ones your momma used to make. Most patrons sit at tables on the spacious outdoor patio, as the inside is tiny and often packed to the gills. *$; cash only; breakfast, lunch every day; beer and wine; no reservations; www.bobsatthemarina.com; on the marina.* ♿

Ernie's on the Brick Walk / ★★

296 LINCOLN CENTER N, STOCKTON; 209/951-3311

In 1994, chef-owner Warren K. Ito moved his Ernie's Pasta Barn from the country northeast of Stockton to this brick walk location, tucked among the coffeehouses and gift shops of Lincoln Center North. Ernie's concise menu still reflects quality as opposed to quantity (that applies to portions as well). For starters try the polenta Castello, topped with melted blue cheese, sautéed mushrooms, and marsala sauce. The mixed mushroom fusilli is tossed with a light roasted garlic–cream sauce with shiitake, oyster, portobello, and porcini mushrooms. If you're craving something more filling, try the New Zealand lamb chops with kalamata olive and rosemary soubise. The restaurant also offers nightly specials and an impressive wine list with the largest selection of ports in the area. *$$; AE, DIS, MC, V; no checks; lunch Mon–Fri, dinner every day; full bar; reservations recommended; center of Lincoln Center N at Benjamin Holt Dr.* ♿

Garlic Brothers / ★★

6629 EMBARCADERO DR, STOCKTON; 209/474-6585

As if the name alone weren't enough to draw you into this chill lair, the Keith Haring–like local artwork just might. Similarly, the chairs are classroom-style in primary colors, and many of the pieces that adorn the walls are made or curated by owner-artist Greg Risso. Locals don't necessarily come here for the food—while fine, it's nothing spectacular—but rather the laid-back vibe, live music, and waterfront location. Food is standard bar fare; you'll see the word "fried" often on the menu, and garlic, clearly, has a heavy presence. Garlic Brothers does pizza particularly well with its Italian-style oven, and Tuesday is half-price pizza night. Order an inventive pie, like the Mona Lisa, which has olives, sun-dried tomatoes, roasted garlic, and Italian sausage. *$$; AE, DIS, MC, V; checks OK; lunch Tues–Sun, dinner every day; full bar; reservations recommended; on the marina.* ♿

LODGINGS

Sheraton Stockton Hotel at Regent Pointe / ★★★

110 W FREMONT ST, STOCKTON; 209/944-1140

You wouldn't know this was part of a major hotel chain were it not for the sign out front. As part of an effort to revitalize the downtown, Sheraton Stockton, located on McLeod Lake, opened its doors in 2008 with a soothing nautical theme, luxury rooms, and a chic lounge, Hippo Bar, on the lobby level. With wooden floors, navy blue curtains and bed skirts, blue-and-white–striped furniture, and yellow accent walls, you'll forget you're in a hotel and think you've woken up aboard a sailboat instead. The 179 guest rooms proffer views of the Delta waterways, as well as beds that feel like they're made of clouds, flat-screen TVs, CD-player alarms, wireless Internet, coffeemakers, irons, and Bliss bath products. Other perks include a fitness center and an outdoor pool. An added bonus: the Sheraton is located next to the Stockton Arena and just a couple of blocks from the Bob Hope Theatre—which hosts an array of musical and comedic revues—and the main downtown drag. *$$$; AE, DIS, MC, V; checks OK; www.sheratonstockton.com; at N Commerce St.* ♿

Lodi

For more than a century, vineyards have thrived in Lodi. Situated just east of the fertile Sacramento River Delta and west of the Sierra Nevada foothills and sandwiched among the cherry orchards, with alluvial soil, abundant water, warm days, and cool nights (because of the Delta breezes), Lodi is geographically ideal for growing wine grapes. Check out the **LODI GRAPE FESTIVAL AND HARVEST FAIR** (209/369-2771; www.grapefestival.com), held each second or third weekend in September. The **DISCOVER LODI! WINE AND VISITORS CENTER** (2545 W Turner Rd; 209/365-0621; www.lodiwine.com) is a great place to pick up a map and learn more about Lodi-area wines and wineries.

RESTAURANTS

Rosewood Bar & Grill / ★★½

28 S SCHOOL ST, LODI; 209/369-0470

Talented chef John Hitchcock, formerly of Wine and Roses Country Inn (see review) and a graduate of the world-renowned Culinary Institute of America, consistently presents delectable creations with attention to detail at the three-year-old Rosewood, which is owned by the Wine and Roses proprietors and is slightly more casual. Service is speedy and the waitstaff friendly. Start with an apple salad with candied walnuts and crumbled blue cheese, follow with the chicken piccata or shrimp penne, and finish with old-fashioned apple pie. The upside is that it's pretty easy to get a table here most nights (even on weekends); the downside is no matter how crowded the restaurant, the acoustics from the adjoining bar make it noisy. *$$–$$$; AE, DC, DIS, MC, V; no checks; dinner every day; reservations recommended; rosewoodbarandgrill.com; at Oak St.* ♿

THE LODI ON WINES

If it's good wine you're seeking, spend some time visiting Lodi's wineries. You'll learn a little history while you swirl and sip.

DELICATO WINERY (12001 Hwy 99, Manteca; 800/924-2024; www.delicato.com). Established in 1924 by Gaspare Indelicato, this large vineyard and winery is presently run by Gaspare's three sons. Delicato has a busy gift shop and tasting room filled with cutesy merchandise and medal-draped bottles displaying awards from various wine competitions. Tasting 9am–5:30pm, tours at 11am every day.

THE LUCAS WINERY (18196 N Davis Rd, Lodi; 209/368-2006; www.lucaswinery.com). This charming winery was built specifically for the gentle handling of classic, old-vine zinfandel wine grapes from the famous Zinstar vineyards. The trendy tasting room (a former tractor barn) sits next to a climate-controlled, gravel-floored aging room known as the Grand Chai (French for "barrel room"). Tasting and short tour noon–4:30pm Thurs–Sun.

MICHAEL DAVID VINEYARDS (4580 W Hwy 12, Lodi; 209/368-7384; www.lodivineyards.com). These award-winning wines are available to sample at the Phillips Farm Produce Market, packed full of fresh asparagus, sweet corn, cherries, and whatever else is in season. A branch of Phillips Farms, Michael David specializes in Rhône varietals and blends. The small café serves burgers made with Phillips's own range-fed beef, along with killer fresh-fruit milk shakes and pies. Tasting 10am–5pm every day, tours by appointment only.

Wine and Roses Country Inn / ★★★

2505 W TURNER RD, LODI; 209/334-6988

The landscaping at this 1902 homestead estate (listed with the San Joaquin County Historical Society) is simply stunning, and the food itself leaves little to be desired. For lunch, try the classic Caesar salad or the grilled boneless quail with warm poblano peppers and sweet corn salad. The dinner menu will tempt you with grilled New York steak with truffle mashed potatoes, haricots verts, and Madeira sauce, or grilled hen duck breast, marinated and served with Asian greens, five-spice sauce, jasmine rice, and crispy duck spring rolls. Order a bottle of one of the increasingly popular Lodi wines to round out the meal. Be sure to leave room for dessert, such as the Madagascar vanilla poached pear wrapped in puff pastry with vanilla-bean crème anglaise and a port wine reduction. *$$; AE, DC, DIS, MC, V; checks OK; lunch, dinner every day, brunch Sat–Sun; full bar; reservations required; www.winerose.com; 5 miles east of I-5, 2 miles west of Hwy 99, at Turner and Lower Sacramento rds.* ♿

OAK RIDGE WINERY (6100 E Hwy 12, Lodi; 209/369-4758; www.oakridgewinery.com). This winery was founded in 1934, just after the repeal of Prohibition. Step inside the 50,000-gallon redwood-barrel tasting room and sample their reds and whites. Picnic tables are available, surrounded by colorful gardens. Tasting 11am–4pm Thurs–Sun, tours by appointment only.

PEIRANO ESTATE (21831 N Hwy 99, Acampo; 209/369-9463; www.peirano.com). Conveniently located on the Highway 99 frontage road, Peirano owns the largest single block of head-trained, natural-rooted zinfandel remaining in the country. The cheerful tasting room is actually the remodeled Peirano Estate farmhouse, built in 1904. Enjoy a picnic among the 90-year-old vines or browse the gift shop while you sample the popular wines. Tasting 11am–5pm Thurs–Mon.

THE VAN RUITEN FAMILY WINERY (340 W Hwy 12, Lodi; 209/334-5722; www.vrwinery.com). In 1998, John Van Ruiten and his family, generations-old Lodi-area grape growers, created this state-of-the-art winery. Surrounded by vineyards and featuring a glass-fronted, two-story tasting room, Van Ruiten offers one of the first cab-shiraz blends produced in this country along with old-vine zins and a chardonnay. Tasting 11am–5pm Tues–Sun, tours by appointment only.

WOODBRIDGE BY ROBERT MONDAVI (5950 E Woodbridge Rd, Acampo; 209/365-8139; www.woodbridgewines.com). The late Robert Mondavi was raised among the vineyards of Lodi. In 1979 he established Woodbridge, just northeast of town. Here the winemakers produce cabernet sauvignon, chardonnay, merlot, muscat, sauvignon blanc, white zinfandel, and a specialty dessert wine called Portacinco. Tasting and retail sales 10:30am–4:30pm every day, tours 9:30am and 1:30pm.

LODGINGS

Wine and Roses Country Inn / ★★★

2505 W TURNER RD, LODI; 209/334-6988

Martha Stewart and Lady Margaret Thatcher, the former British prime minister, are among the guests who've signed the register at this tasteful country inn situated on 5 acres of towering 100-year-old deodar cedars, cherry trees, and beautifully landscaped gardens. The 1902 estate, owned and operated by Del and Sherri Smith and their partners Russ and Kathryn Munson, underwent a $5 million project a few years back that added 36 rooms, each with a private courtyard entry, spa tub, fireplace, large television, garden veranda, and room service; two 5,000-square-foot banquet facilities; a spa and therapy center; a flower shop; a pool; a Jacuzzi; a large catering kitchen; and a small café. The 10 original rooms have queen-size beds, turn-of-the-century decor, and handmade comforters. In the rose-toned sitting room, camelback couches and wing chairs are clustered around a wide fireplace that's always ablaze in the winter. Guests are treated to evening wine and a gourmet breakfast served in the popular restaurant (see review), located on the ground floor. *$$–$$$; AE, DC, DIS, MC, V; checks OK; www.winerose.com; 5 miles east of I-5, 2 miles west of Hwy 99; at Turner and Lower Sacramento rds.* ♿

Sacramento and the Delta Region

Five rivers, 57 islands, and 1,000 miles of navigable waterways make up the Sacramento River Delta, which is easily mistaken at high tide for a vast inland lake. It's the largest estuary on the West Coast, touching six counties and containing half the freshwater runoff in California. After the completion of the Transcontinental Railroad in 1869, a workforce of some 10,000 Chinese laborers began work on the levee system, reclaiming the fertile farmland. Today's Delta is dotted with old-fashioned island towns—from Rio Vista to the tiny hamlets just south of Sacramento—connected by drawbridges, ferries, and winding levee roads. For a true Delta experience, rent a houseboat and cruise this labyrinth of waterways for a few days. Houseboat, ski-boat, and wave-runner rentals are available several miles north of Stockton at **HERMAN AND HELEN'S MARINA** (off I-5, at the west end of Eight-Mile Rd; 209/951-4634; www.houseboats.com) and **PARADISE POINT MARINA** (8095 Rio Blanco; 209/952-1000 or 800/752-9669; www.paradisepointmarina.com). If you'd rather explore by car, keep in mind that many folks miss the beauty of the Delta as they speed along the rivers of highway that bisect this unique and delicate ecosystem. Slow down, relax a bit, and get on "Delta time."

Rio Vista

This slow-paced Delta town, located at the junction of Highways 12 and 160, is considered by many to be the heart of the Delta. With a population of 5,000, its residents include speed demon Craig Breedlove—former land-speed record holder—and Dennis Hope of Lunar Embassy–Celestial Property Sales, who can sell you a piece of property anywhere in the universe. There's not much to do in town—the river is the main attraction here—although you might check out the **RIO VISTA MUSEUM** (16 N Front St; 707/374-5169; open weekends only) for a rundown on the history of farming and dredging in the area. Even if you don't have the nerve to eat at **FOSTER'S BIGHORN** (143 Main St; 707/374-2511; www.fostersbighorn.com), it's worth a peek. This stuffy bar and restaurant displays some 300 wild game trophies from Bill Foster's private collection, including a full-grown bull elephant—complete with ivory tusks—and a giraffe (who could shoot a giraffe?). **HUMPHREY** the wayward humpback whale cruised this part of the river back in 1985 (good thing Foster was already dead), and there's a stone monument to Humphrey on the waterfront, adjacent to **CITY HALL** (1 Main St; 707/374-6451).

Isleton

Once the asparagus capital of the world and an original stop for the *Delta King* river boat, Isleton today is known as Crawdad Town USA—home of the **CRAWDAD FESTIVAL** (www.crawdadfestival.org) each Father's Day weekend. This sleepy little town on Highway 160 has a sense of humor (the local bait shop is the "Master-Baiter") and a Chinatown, where decrepit buildings stand beside refurbished ones.

Walnut Grove

RESTAURANTS

Orilla del Rio / ★★

14133 MARKET ST, WALNUT GROVE; 916/776-2007

This family-owned restaurant pumps out the best Mexican food in the Delta. Meals seem to be health conscious, so if you order wisely, your cholesterol count won't skyrocket too seriously. Try the chile-lime chicken wings for starters and the alligator tacos for something totally different. The chile verde, made with lean pork, is very good. A variety of house-made salsas are always available at the salsa bar, and if you're really not watching that cholesterol, finish off your meal with an order of the delightfully rich flan. *$; no credit cards; checks OK; breakfast Sat–Sun, lunch, dinner Tues–Sun; beer and wine; no reservations; 1 block east of Hwy 160.* ♿

Ryde

LODGINGS

The Ryde Hotel / ★★

14340 HWY 160, RYDE; 916/776-1318 OR 888/717-RYDE

Originally built as a boardinghouse, this four-story peach stucco inn on the banks of the Sacramento River became famous as a speakeasy during Prohibition, when steamers and paddleboats brought crowds of city folk in search of jazz and illicit liquor. The Ryde attracted movie stars, politicians, and presidents: Herbert Hoover announced his candidacy here in 1940. In 1997, the hotel changed hands and underwent major renovations. The owners have managed to maintain the original historic design while integrating modern amenities. The hotel now has 42 guest rooms decorated in a 1920s art deco style with a mauve, gray, and black color scheme. Two golf suites face the executive nine-hole golf course, which winds through a stately pear orchard. Some of the rooms exemplify the original European-style accommodations, with shared bathroom facilities. Continental breakfast is included and is served in the salon or outside on one of the patios, and the restaurant's Sunday champagne buffet brunch ($26.95 for adults, half price for children) is wildly popular. Hotel guests may arrive by car or tie their vessels at the private boat dock. *$$–$$$; MC, V; checks OK; www.rydehotel.com; 3 miles south of Walnut Grove.*

Locke

The town of Locke was established in 1915, soon after a devastating fire destroyed the neighboring Chinese community of Walnut Grove. Since Asian Americans at that time couldn't legally own property, a committee of Chinese merchants led by (Charlie) Lee Bing approached landowner George Locke and persuaded him to allow a new community to be built on his land. Chinese architects designed Lockeport, which became Locke as it exists today. At one time this hamlet claimed more than 600 permanent residents. Businesses flourished, including illicit activities that thrived in the form of gambling houses, brothels, speakeasies, and opium dens.

Locke was also the educational center for the region. The **JOE SHOONG CHINESE SCHOOL** was built in 1926, with funding from Joe Shoong, the millionaire who founded National Dollar Stores. Shoong endorsed Chinese language, art, and culture in schools built specifically for Chinese youth. Located at the north end of town, at the corner of Main and Locke streets, the school is now a museum and open for public viewing. Next door, **YUEN CHONG MARKET** (916/776-1818), established in 1916 by a Chinese cooperative, stocks a wide selection of cold drinks. Today, you can wander Locke's Main Street and easily imagine what it must have been like in the days of Prohibition. Notice the worn wooden sidewalks; like the town, they seem warped in time. Visit **AL THE WOP'S** (see review), Lee Bing's original restaurant. For information about a guided tour of Locke, given by a resident historian, stop in at **LOCKE ART CENTER** (916/776-1661).

RESTAURANTS

Al the Wop's / ★

13936 MAIN ST, LOCKE; 916/776-1800

Al Adami bought this former Chinese restaurant in 1934. When Al died in 1961, his bartender, Ralph Santos Sr., took over this venerable and legendary Delta institution. In 1981 Ralph was succeeded by his son, who changed the name of this restaurant to Al's Place—a more politically correct moniker. Alas, the name change didn't go over too well, in part because people drove the phone company crazy asking for "Al the Wop's" and got very surly when the name didn't come up in the database. In 1995, Ralph's nephews, Lorenzo and Steve Giannetti, took over the place and, by popular demand, reinstated the old name. The low-ceilinged dining room in the back of the building is furnished with long tables and benches—just as it was in the '30s. The food is simple but adequate, and the assorted tourists, boaters, and local characters who hang out here like it that way. Fridays, Saturdays, and Sundays are steak and lobster nights; otherwise, Al's dinners are limited to chicken and New York steaks (12 or 18 ounces) served with a side of spaghetti or French fries and maybe a bowl of homemade minestrone. *$; no credit cards; checks OK; lunch, dinner every day; full bar; no reservations; middle of Main St.*

Lockeford

LODGINGS

The Inn at Locke House / ★★★★

19960 ELLIOTT RD, LOCKEFORD; 209/727-5715

You've never met two nicer B and B owners than Lani and Richard Eklund, who run the inn with their daughter, Kerri, and came to town from Virginia to save the ancestral home of the Locke family. After one serious renovation, the Eklunds turned the house, originally built in the 1860s with nine bedrooms to accommodate Dr. Dean Jewett Locke's 13 children and wife, into four bed-and-bath rooms with old-fashioned claw-foot tubs, custom-made armoires, televisions, fireplaces, hair dryers, CD players, and antique beds. Other on-site amenities include wireless Internet, a DVD player, a VCR, board games, and washer and dryer. On the other side of the kitchen is the Water Tower Suite, which is massive and boasts a four-poster canopy queen bed, sitting area, satellite TV, and spiral staircase that leads up to a sunroom. In the downstairs of the main house, there are parlors (complete with pianos) and a dining room for guest use. Many of the house's accoutrements—pews, lithographs, poor box, hat rack—are still intact from the 1800s and early 1900s. Lani cooks up one mean multicourse breakfast that will take care of your need to eat for the remainder of the day; eggs Benedict and orange French toast with toasted walnuts and seasonal berries are her specialties. After you eat, ask Lani and Richard for the full tour of the lush grounds. *$$–$$$; AE, DIS, MC, V; checks OK; www.theinnatlockehouse.com; just off Main St (Highways 88 or 12).*

Sacramento

Heart of the Central Valley and capital city of the state, Sacramento has long been regarded as the second-class stepsister of San Francisco. But with its increasing number of skyscrapers, upscale restaurants, and swanky hotels (as well as the NBA's Sacramento Kings, the women's NBA Sacramento Monarchs, and Class AAA baseball's Rivercats), California's capital city is no longer the sleepy little valley town folks whiz through on their way to Lake Tahoe. Located 90 miles northeast of the Bay Area, the city is best known for its dual status as the seat of state government and the epicenter of California's biggest industry—agriculture. But disregard any disparaging words you may have heard about this fertile hot spot: there are no cows (or even cowboy hats) within city limits, and most of the city slickers don't pick tomatoes for a living.

A former gold rush boomtown, Sacramento sprang up where the American and Sacramento Rivers meet—a tourist area now known as **OLD SACRAMENTO**. In 1839 Swiss immigrant John Sutter traversed both waterways, built his famous fort, and established his colony called New Helvetia (New Switzerland). But his hopes that the thriving colony would evolve into his own vast empire were dashed when gold was discovered up near his sawmill in 1848. Sutter's colonists deserted New Helvetia to search for the precious nuggets, and as word of the discovery spread, thousands more wound their way to the hills above Sacramento to seek their fortunes. Ironically, Sutter himself never prospered from the gold rush, and he died a bitter, penniless man.

Today, Sacramento is home to more than a million people, many of whom play politics with the capital crowd or practice law. They dote on their spectacular Victorian homes and fine Craftsman-style bungalows, and are justly proud of the tree-lined streets and thick carpets of grass that surround their houses and parks.

In the scorching summer months, when thermometers often soar above three digits for days, many folks beat the heat by diving into swimming pools, chugging around the Delta on a houseboat, or floating down the American River in a raft or an inner tube. Once the sun sets, however, things usually cool off dramatically. Winters are punctuated by the famous tulle fog—so thick it can block the sun for weeks at a time. But as all ski buffs know, Sacramentans get the jump on their Bay Area neighbors racing to the snowy slopes of Tahoe, thanks to the city's proximity to the Sierra Nevada.

ACCESS AND INFORMATION

Conveniently located just 15 minutes north of downtown, the **SACRAMENTO INTERNATIONAL AIRPORT (SMF)** (6900 Airport Boulevard; 916/ 874-0719; www.sacairports.org) is easily accessible from Interstate 5. **SUPERSHUTTLE SACRAMENTO** (www.supershuttle.com; 800/BLUE-VAN) provides door-to-door service, while taxis and vans are available 24 hours a day from **SACRAMENTO INDEPENDENT TAXI** (916/457-4862) and **YELLOW CAB** (916/464-0777). **AMTRAK'S CAPITOL ROUTES** (5th and I sts; 800/872-7245; www.amtrak.com) connect Sacramento and the Bay Area several times a day. City bus and light rail service is operated by **SACRAMENTO REGIONAL TRANSIT DISTRICT** (916/321-BUSS), and the **GREYHOUND TERMINAL** (7th and L sts; 916/444-6858) is open 24 hours and can connect you to just about anywhere. By car, **INTERSTATE 5** and **US HIGHWAY 99** reach Sacramento on the north-south route; **INTERSTATE 80** is a direct route from the Bay Area, and **US HIGHWAY 50** will get you there from Lake Tahoe and Reno. Once downtown, it's nice to know that the "lettered" city streets (C–Z) run from north to south, with M Street also being known as Capitol, and the "numbered" streets (2nd–29th) run west to east, with First Street referred to as Front Street due to its location on the waterfront. Parking can be a challenge along the streets, so look for the large public lots, which usually have spaces available. For more information, contact the **SACRAMENTO CONVENTION AND VISITORS**

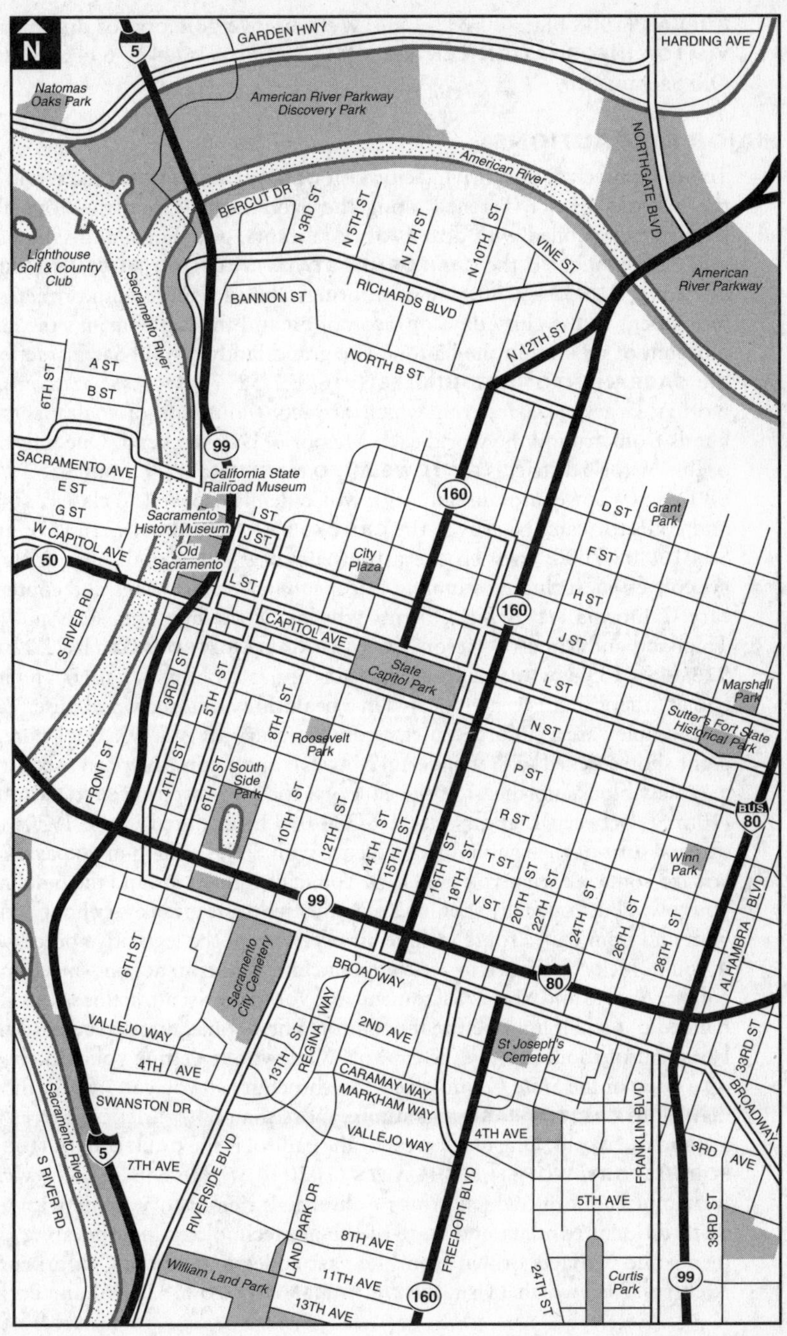
N
GARDEN HWY
HARDING AVE
Natomas Oaks Park
American River Parkway Discovery Park
American River
NORTHGATE BLVD
Lighthouse Golf & Country Club
Sacramento River
BERCUT DR
N 3RD ST
N 5TH ST
N 7TH ST
N 10TH ST
VINE ST
American River Parkway
BANNON ST
RICHARDS BLVD
N 12TH ST
NORTH B ST
A ST
B ST
6TH ST
SACRAMENTO AVE
California State Railroad Museum
E ST
G ST
Sacramento History Museum
I ST
J ST
W CAPITOL AVE
Old Sacramento
City Plaza
L ST
D ST
Grant Park
F ST
H ST
CAPITOL AVE
J ST
State Capitol Park
L ST
Marshall Park
S RIVER RD
3RD ST
5TH ST
8TH ST
Roosevelt Park
N ST
Sutter's Fort State Historical Park
FRONT ST
4TH ST
6TH ST
South Side Park
10TH ST
12TH ST
14TH ST
15TH ST
16TH ST
18TH ST
P ST
R ST
T ST
V ST
20TH ST
22TH ST
24TH ST
26TH ST
28TH ST
Winn Park
ALHAMBRA BLVD
6TH ST
Sacramento City Cemetery
BROADWAY
VALLEJO WAY
13TH ST
REGINA WAY
2ND AVE
St Joseph's Cemetery
33RD ST
BROADWAY
4TH AVE
CARAMAY WAY
MARKHAM WAY
SWANSTON DR
VALLEJO WAY
4TH AVE
FRANKLIN BLVD
3RD AVE
7TH AVE
RIVERSIDE BLVD
LAND PARK DR
FREEPORT BLVD
5TH AVE
33RD ST
S RIVER RD
8TH AVE
William Land Park
11TH AVE
13TH AVE
24TH ST
Curtis Park
5
99
50
160
80
BUS 80

Sacramento

BUREAU (1608 I St; 800/292-2334; wwwdiscovergold.org) or drop in at the **VISITOR INFORMATION CENTER** (1002 2nd St; 916/442-7644), located in Old Sacramento.

MAJOR ATTRACTIONS

To best appreciate this thriving city, visit **OLD SACRAMENTO** (a.k.a. Old Sac), the historic district. Perched along the Sacramento River, this four-block-long stretch is filled with dozens of restaurants, gift shops, and saloons. An Old Sac highlight is the **CALIFORNIA STATE RAILROAD MUSEUM** (111 I St at 2nd St; 916/323-9280; www.californiastaterailroadmuseum.org), a grand monument to the glory days of locomotion and the Big Four; it's the largest museum of its kind in the nation. The granddaddy of Old Sac attractions is the **SACRAMENTO JAZZ JUBILEE** (916/372-5277; www.sacjazz.com), the world's largest jazz festival, which attracts thousands of toe-tappers and bands from around the world each Memorial Day weekend. One mile south of this historic district is the **TOWE AUTO MUSEUM** (2200 Front St; 916/442-6802; www.toweautomuseum.org), which displays over 150 classic, vintage, and collector cars. Nearby is the **CROCKER ART MUSEUM** (216 O St at 3rd St; 916/808-7000; www.crockerartmuseum.org), home of the region's largest art collection, including stunning European master drawings and contemporary California art by local talents who made the big time, such as Wayne Thiebaud and Robert Arneson. **LA RAZA GALLERIA POSADA** (1022 22nd St; 916/446-5133; www.larazagaleriaposada.org) is a Chicano, Latino, and indigenous American arts center located in a beautifully restored warehouse. Within this complex are a cultural center, a contemporary art gallery, a bookstore, and a gift shop stocked with wonderful Mexican and Latin American folk art.

A few blocks northeast of the gallery is the awe-inspiring **STATE CAPITOL** (10th St, between L and N sts; 916/324-0333;), restored in the 1970s to its original turn-of-the-century magnificence with $67.8 million in taxpayers' dollars (so come see what you paid for). You may wander around the building on your own, but you really shouldn't miss the free tours given every hour between 9am and 4pm daily. Tours include an overview of the legislative process and, if you're lucky, a chance to see the political hotshots in action—including, of course, Arnold and Maria, Sacramento's favorite tourist attractions. Tickets are handed out a half hour before the tour on a first-come, first-served basis in the basement of room B-27 in the capitol. While you're getting your tickets, pick up a copy of the *State Capitol Tree Tour* brochure so you can saunter through marvelous **CAPITOL PARK** and admire more than 340 varieties of trees from around the world. One block west of the capitol is the **CALIFORNIA MUSEUM FOR HISTORY, WOMEN & THE ARTS** (1020 O St; 916/653-7524; www.californiamuseum.org), which brings California's rich history to life with a mix of traditional exhibits and state-of-the-art technology incorporating documents and artifacts drawn from the vast collections of the California State Archives. Also worth a visit, the **SACRAMENTO ZOO** (3930 W Land Park Dr;

916/264-5888; www.saczoo.com) houses 400 animals, including more than 40 endangered or threatened species.

If you're a big history buff, step back in time by strolling through **SUTTER'S FORT** (between K and L sts at 27th; 916/445-4422), where you can view the restored, self-contained community that Sutter built in the wilderness in 1839. On the same grounds is the **CALIFORNIA STATE INDIAN MUSEUM** (2618 K St; 916/324-0971), with artifacts from more than 100 California Indian tribes, including one of the finest basket collections in the nation. Of special interest is a display about Ishi, the last of the Yahi Indians, who managed to remain hidden from Western civilization until 1911, when he was discovered in Northern California.

PERFORMING ARTS

The **SACRAMENTO CONVENTION CENTER** (1400 J St; 916/264-5291; www.sacramentoconventioncenter.com) has information on the **SACRAMENTO PHILHARMONIC** (3418 3rd Ave; 916/732-9045; www.sacphil.org) and other big-name jazz and classical performers. Just up the road is the **CREST THEATER** (1013 K St; 916/442-7378; www.thecrest.com), a refurbished art deco palace that hosts rock, folk, reggae, and world-beat concerts and runs classic and independent films.

Sacramento has a thriving live theater scene, and two top venues are the **SACRAMENTO THEATER COMPANY** (1419 H St; 916/446-7501; www.sactheatre.org) and the **B STREET THEATRE** (2711 B St; 916/443-5300; www.bstreettheatre.org), co-founded by actor Timothy Busfield (of the TV show *thirtysomething*) and his brother Buck. They've also recently launched the **CALIFORNIA CHILDREN'S THEATRE**, which has received raves from kids and parents alike. The **CALIFORNIA MUSICAL THEATRE** (1419 H St; 916/557-1999; www.californiamusicaltheatre.com) hosts one of the city's most popular summer pastimes, the **MUSIC CIRCUS**, an annual festival of Broadway musicals presented in the impressive new Wells Fargo Pavilion. This 50-year-old summer musical tradition revives the music of Cole Porter, the Gershwins, and Stephen Sondheim using professional casts from Broadway and Hollywood. Equally if not more popular, the **SACRAMENTO LIGHT OPERA ASSOCIATION**'s Broadway Series runs from September through June, featuring as many as nine Broadway shows and giving Sacramento top-notch performances year-round.

RECREATION

Sacramento's two most notable natural attractions are its two rivers: the bustling boat-filled **SACRAMENTO RIVER** and the raft-filled **AMERICAN RIVER**. For cyclists and joggers, nothing beats the **AMERICAN RIVER PARKWAY**, a 5,000-acre nature preserve with a 22-mile-long pothole-free bike trail, which starts in Old Sac and follows the water all the way to the town of Folsom. You can rent a bike for a day at **CITY BICYCLE WORKS** (2419 K St; 916/447-2453; www.citybicycleworks.com). In the sweltering Sacramento summers

SACRAMENTO AREA THREE-DAY TOUR

DAY ONE: *Just like old times.* After breakfast at the **FOX & GOOSE**, start your first day in **OLD SACRAMENTO** with a stop at the visitor information center on Second Street; pick up a map of attractions. Spend some time exploring the **CALIFORNIA STATE RAILROAD MUSEUM**, for an understanding of how the railroads shaped California history. Browse the rest of Old Sacramento by foot, or consider a paddle wheel sightseeing cruise aboard either the historic **SPIRIT OF SACRAMENTO** or the **MATTHEW MCKINLEY** (916/552-2933 or 800/433-0263). Wander over to the **RIO CITY CAFE** for lunch with a view of the river on the deck, weather permitting. If you're ready for more history, don't miss the **CROCKER ART MUSEUM**, or if you've got small kids along, visit the **SACRAMENTO ZOO** and the adjacent **FAIRY TALE TOWN AND FUNDERLAND** amusement park. When you're ready to kick back, board the **DELTA KING** and head for the fourth-floor lounge for an early-evening aperitif and view of the sunset. Lodging at the centrally located **STERLING HOTEL** is highly recommended. Enjoy tonight's dinner at **PARAGARY'S BAR AND OVEN**.

DAY TWO: *State of the arts.* Begin today with breakfast and people watching at the **TOWER CAFE** (1518 Broadway; 916/441-0222). You may be interested to know you're sitting in the birthplace of Tower Records. Choose a table on the green outdoor patio, space and weather permitting. Then head over to **SUTTER'S FORT** and the **CALIFORNIA STATE INDIAN MUSEUM**. Arrive at the **PAVILIONS** mall before the lunch crowd for a remarkable deli experience at **DAVID BERKLEY**. Dine there and browse the small but interesting shopping center, or pack a picnic and head for **CAPITOL PARK** for lunch under the huge trees.

many locals and visitors alike abandon their bikes for a leisurely raft trip down the American River with **AMERICAN RIVER RAFT RENTALS** (11257 S Bridge St, Rancho Cordova; 916/635-6400; www.raftrentals.com) or head for **SIX FLAGS DISCOVERY KINGDOM** in nearby Vallejo (1001 Fairgrounds Dr; 707/643-6722; www.sixflags.com). **SHADOW GLEN RIDING STABLES** (4854 Main Ave, Orangevale; 916/989-1826; www.shadowglenstables.com) offers hourly horseback riding and guided trail rides around Folsom Lake from April to November, and the **ICELAND ICE SKATING RINK** (1430 Del Paso Blvd; 916/925-3121; www.icelandsacramento.com) provides a cool indoor alternative. If you're cruising through town during the last two weeks of August, set aside a day or night to visit the **CALIFORNIA STATE FAIR** (1600 Exposition Blvd off the I-80/Capital City Fwy; 916/263-FAIR; www.bigfun.org), Sacramento's grandest party. The carnival area is predictably cheesy, but the livestock exhibits and wine tasting are worth the admission price.

From here, take the **STATE CAPITOL TOUR** (free) then walk to the poignant **CALIFORNIA VIETNAM VETERANS MEMORIAL** (www.cavietnammemorial.com). For dinner with music (Spanish classical and flamenco guitar), try **TAPA THE WORLD**, or for a wonderfully elegant and exotic meal, try Sacramento's famous **LEMON GRASS**, before catching some zzzz's back at the Sterling.

DAY THREE: *Cruisin' country roads.* After breakfast at **33RD STREET BISTRO**, leave the city for a tour of the rural levee roads of the Sacramento River Delta and the century-old vineyards of **LODI**. From Sacramento, take scenic Highway 160S through Freeport and Hood. Explore the tiny town of Locke, built by Chinese immigrants in 1915. Have lunch at the popular **ORILLA DEL RIO** in Walnut Grove. Cross the Sacramento River just past town and head south. Stop by the **RYDE HOTEL**, a former boardinghouse and speakeasy, for a bit, then head west toward the **GRAND ISLAND MANSION** (13415 Grand Island Rd, Walnut Grove; 916/775-1706; www.grandislandmansion.com), a 1917 Italian Renaissance–style inn with lush gardens. Just south of the mansion, hop on the **J-MACK FERRY** (free) and cross **STEAMBOAT SLOUGH**. Turn left and follow the water to the next ferry crossing—the **REAL MCCOY**. This ferry (also free) takes you across **CACHE SLOUGH**, where you disembark just a few miles from the town of Rio Vista. On Highway 12, head east toward Lodi, driving over drawbridges and through patchworks of sunflowers, vineyards, and corn. Between Interstate 5 and Lodi, stop in at the **VAN RUITEN FAMILY WINERY** (340 W Hwy 12; 209/334-5722; www.vrwinery.com) to sample or purchase some of Lodi's respected and popular varietals. Finish the long day with a relaxing dinner and pampered lodging at Lodi's **WINE AND ROSES COUNTRY INN**.

RESTAURANTS

Biba / ★★★★

2801 CAPITOL AVE, SACRAMENTO; 916/455-2422

Biba is a study in understated neo-deco design, the sort of place where you'd expect precious, trendy foods to dominate the menu. Fortunately, they don't. Bologna-born chef-owner Biba Caggiano is a traditionalist to the core, and what comes out of her kitchen is exactly what she learned at her mother's elbow: classical Italian cooking based on the finest ingredients available and a painstaking attention to detail. The menu changes seasonally, but expect to find such entrées as grilled shrimp wrapped in basil and Parma ham, shiitake ravioli with pancetta and sage, and handmade garganelli pasta in a slowly simmered bolognese meat ragù. As if all that weren't enough, the long list of domestic and Italian wines should please even the snootiest connoisseur. In addition to running one of the region's finest restaurants, Biba has written more than a half dozen books on Italian cooking, filled with recipes from the homes, trattorias, and restaurants of Emilia Romagna. *$$$; AE, DC, MC, V; no checks; lunch Mon–Fri, dinner Mon–Sat; full bar; reservations recommended; www.biba-restaurant.com; at 28th St.* ♿

Café Bernardo / ★★☆

1431 R ST, SACRAMENTO; 916/930-9191

Popular with the dog-walking set, who like to dine on the roomy patio while their pooches lounge nearby, this European-style café is bustling on the weekends, when Sacramentans flock here for one of the best brunches in town. And there's no waiting around for a server to attend to you—simply place your order at the counter, take a number, and find a place to sit; a busboy will deliver the goods. The menu has all the normal brunch favorites with a twist—like Amaretto French toast; malted Belgian waffles; and Eggs Bernardo, two poached eggs doused in house-made hollandaise sauce on toasted rosemary bread. Lunch and dinner is standard café fare: salads, sandwiches, burgers, and pizzettas. Chef Jason Boggs also serves up vegetarian options like a tofu scramble and a mushroom-patty sandwich. There's a second branch on Capitol Avenue and a third out in Davis. *$$; AE, DC, DIS, MC, V; checks OK; breakfast, lunch, dinner every day; no reservations; www.cafebernardo.com; at 15th St.* ♿

David Berkley / ★★★

515 PAVILIONS LN, SACRAMENTO; 916/929-4422

Located in the Pavilions, Sacramento's upscale shopping center, David Berkley is essentially a delicatessen—but, wow, what a deli! Just about everything served here is perfect. There's one of the region's best selections of wine and beer, and the deli section offers nearly two dozen different salads every day, including several low-fat options. Try sinking your teeth into the savory smoked-chicken salad; the wild rice and pear salad; or the luscious shrimp, avocado, cucumber, and fresh dill combination. A takeout meal, which changes weekly, might include a salad of jicama and orange slices tossed with a citrus vinaigrette; a thick, grilled New York steak crusted with Dijon mustard and horseradish; herbed mashed potatoes; and sautéed baby vegetables. Finish your feast with a decadent cheesecake or tart. Arrive early if you're planning to eat here, since seating is limited (most tables are outdoors) and this place packs 'em in. *$$; AE, MC, V; checks OK; lunch every day; beer and wine; no reservations; www.dberkley.com; in the Pavilions shopping center, on the north side of Fair Oaks Blvd, between Howe and Fulton aves.* ♿

Dos Coyotes Border Cafe / ★★

1735 ARDEN WY, STE 230, SACRAMENTO; 916/927-0377

With its leaping lizards and chile pepper decor, this Arden Fair branch of the popular eatery in Davis is always hopping, serving up consistently fresh and creative fare like mango-charbroiled chicken quesadillas or paella burritos. For a full review, see the Restaurants section of Davis. *$; AE, MC, V; no checks; lunch, dinner every day; beer and wine; no reservations; at Market Square in the Arden Fair shopping mall.* ♿

Fox & Goose Pub and Restaurant / ★★

1001 R ST, SACRAMENTO; 916/443-8825

You'll see chaps chugging down pints of bitter and having a jolly good time over a game of darts at this bustling British pub, almost as genuine as any neighborhood spot you're likely to find in the United Kingdom. Owned by Allyson Dalton, daughter of the original founders, the Fox & Goose is a River City institution, offering a wee bit of everything—beer, breakfast, lunch, and live music—and doing it all wonderfully. There are more than 15 beers on tap, including brews from England, Ireland, and Scotland. For breakfast, choose from a variety of omelets as well as kippers (Atlantic herring), grilled tomatoes, crumpets, and such authentic English treats as bangers and mash; or you can take the California-cuisine route and order the vegetarian pub grill (scrambled tofu mixed with pesto and red onions or curry and green onions). The Fox & Goose is famous for its burnt cream—a rich, velvety custard topped with caramelized brown sugar—but the other desserts are equally delectable. Be forewarned: This is a popular pub and reservations are not accepted, so arrive a little early, particularly for lunch. At night the place swings to folk, jazz, and bluegrass tunes. *$; AE, MC, V; local checks only; breakfast, lunch every day, dinner Mon–Sat; beer and wine; no reservations; www.foxandgoose.com; at 12th St, just south of the capitol.* ♿

Lemon Grass / ★★★★

601 MUNROE ST, SACRAMENTO; 916/486-4891

This elegant restaurant, offering a unique blend of Vietnamese and Thai cooking, keeps getting better and better and is approaching nirvana. Owner Mai Pham uses local organically grown produce whenever possible, fresh seafood, Petaluma free-range chicken, and little or no oil in many of her culinary masterpieces. The Siamese Seafood Feast, a Thai bouillabaisse, comes bubbling with fresh clams, sea scallops, mussels, and prawns in a spicy, hot-and-sour broth infused with lemongrass, galangal (Thai ginger), kaffir lime leaves, and chiles. The wide-ranging dessert menu features such delicacies as Saigon by Night, a blend of Vietnamese espresso, hazelnut syrup, whipped cream, and vanilla ice cream; and a banana cheesecake topped with a scoop of coconut sorbet. Mai, a best-selling author, has been featured in *Martha Stewart Living* magazine and on National Public Radio's program *Fresh Air*. *$$; AE, DC, MC, V; no checks; breakfast, lunch every day, dinner Mon–Fri; full bar; reservations recommended; www.lemongrassrestaurant.com; just north of Fair Oaks Blvd, near Loehmann's Plaza shopping center.* ♿

Mulvaney's B&L / ★★★★

1215 19TH ST, STE 100, SACRAMENTO; 915/441-6022

Sacramento's once-barren downtown area has recently seen a culinary resurgence, and Mulvaney's B&L, which opened in 2006, proudly leads the pack. The B&L stands for Building & Loan, a nod to the Jimmy Stewart film *It's a Wonderful Life*. Chef Patrick Mulvaney is often behind the counter of the open kitchen preparing your dinner, but during his downtime, he's known to flit around mingling with guests. The menu is printed daily, though some dishes are so well received they appear time and time again. A meal could begin with Mulvaney's signature house-smoked salmon on Irish brown bread, followed by sweet yellow corn and ricotta ravioli with brown butter, before the pièce de résistance, the grilled Hawaiian ahi with sesame and soy, arrives. And you can't leave without sampling the most popular dessert on the menu, the Valhrona Ding Dong, comprising devil's food cake, mousse, and ganache. The inside seats 35, but there's a very lovely, well-landscaped patio out back; heat lamps are provided on chilly evenings. Mulvaney is also developing the building next door—accessed via the patio—into a bar and event space. Although this is a "grown-up" restaurant, the staff is more than happy to create children's meals for the kiddies. *$$$–$$$$; AE, DC, DIS, MC, V; checks OK; dinner Wed–Sat; full bar; reservations recommended; www.culinaryspecialists.com/mulvaneybl.htm; at L St.* ♿

Paragary's Bar and Oven / ★★★★

1401 28TH ST, SACRAMENTO; 916/457-5737

Part of the Randy Paragary empire, each of Central Valley's Paragary Restaurant Group entities has different and wonderfully imaginative menus that change frequently and feature produce from the restaurant's own garden. This one is well known for zesty pizzas cooked in wood-burning ovens, mesquite-grilled entrées with a strong Italian accent, and freshly made pastas and desserts. Recent offerings included a salad of sliced mushrooms with Jarlsberg cheese, parsley, lemon, and olive oil; a pizza with Italian sausage, cilantro pesto, sautéed red onions, and sweet peppers with mozzarella; and a Niman Ranch pork chop with fresh corn polenta, cornmeal-crusted zucchini, and sweet onion jam. *$$$; AE, DC, MC, V; no checks; lunch Mon–Fri, dinner every day; full bar; reservations recommended; www.paragarys.com; at N St.* ♿

Rio City Cafe / ★

1110 FRONT ST, SACRAMENTO; 916/442-8226

Located on the Sacramento River smack-dab in the middle of Old Sac, the city's premier tourist attraction, the Rio City Cafe has a commanding view up and down this Old Man River. The pleasantly light, airy, and attractive dining room also offers a view of the glassed-in kitchen so you can watch the cooks as they sauté and grill the evening's entrées. The fare here is primarily Southwestern with a dash of California. For lunch, expect a large variety of soups, salads, and sandwiches; the dinner entrées change as regularly as the Delta tides. Rio's extensive wine list features a thoughtful collection of California vintages. *$$; AE, DC, DIS, MC, V; no checks; brunch, lunch, dinner every day; full bar; reservations recommended; www.riocitycafe.com; between J and K sts.* ♿

Tapa the World / ★★

2115 J ST, SACRAMENTO; 916/442-4353

Choose from a wide selection of flavorful tapas at this extremely popular dinner house, one of the few in Sacramento that serves from noon until midnight. Try one of the paellas—the deep-dish saffron-simmered rice feasts—available in *mariscos* (seafood), *mixta* (chicken, seafood, and chorizo), or vegetarian versions. Or try the *lomo de cordero*, marinated grilled lamb loin served with wild mushroom rice and three specialty sauces—rioja wine, avocado, and balsamic. The menu also features a braised tri-tip dinner, a nightly grilled venison special, and oh-so-delicious Kobe beef. The wine list offers numerous Spain and California varietals to complement your meal. And don't miss the Chocolate Addiction, a double-layered chocolate mousse cake topped with a warm simmered and reduced sangría and fresh strawberries. Tapa your feet to the live Spanish and flamenco guitar performances every night of the week. *$$; AE, DIS, MC, V; no checks; lunch, dinner every day; full bar; no reservations; www.tapatheworld.com; between 21st and 22nd sts.* ♿

33rd Street Bistro / ★★

3301 FOLSOM BLVD, SACRAMENTO; 916/455-2233

The 33rd Street Bistro was a huge success right from the start, and it just keeps getting better. Chef-owner Fred Haines has combined a casual, trendy ambience—a handsome red brick wall, high ceilings, and vibrant oversize paintings of vegetables—with terrific food at reasonable prices. You can order the excellent salads in a large or "lite" size, including a knockout Mediterranean salad tossed with wood-roasted chicken, sweet red peppers, red onions, white beans, and feta. The entrées, called "large plates," usually include your choice of salmon, chicken, or pork and are served with grilled or sautéed seasonal vegetables. The daily soups are always outstanding, and so are the seasonal desserts. Expect a crowd during peak dining hours. *$$; AE, MC, V; checks OK; breakfast, lunch, dinner every day; full bar; no reservations; www.33rdstreetbistro.com; at 33rd St.* ♿

The Waterboy / ★★★★

2000 CAPITOL AVE, SACRAMENTO; 916/498-9891

Chef-owner Rick Mahan insists on fresh, high-quality ingredients like naturally raised beef from Niman Ranch and lamb from James Ranch, organic produce from Full Belly Farms and Live Oak Farm, and outstanding breads from Grateful Bread. Named after the Celtic rock band the Waterboys, this midtown restaurant is a bright and cheery gem, serving bold and imaginative dishes inspired by recipes from southern France and northern Italy. The menu changes monthly to stay in sync with the seasons. A recent dinner menu included handmade potato gnocchi with pesto and vine-ripe cherry tomatoes;

carnaroli risotto with oxtails, porcini mushrooms, tomatoes, Parmigiano-Reggiano and sage; and a sweet corn soup. If there's room for dessert, don't miss Edie Stewart's heavenly creations, like the warm fruit crostada with vanilla-bean ice cream and caramel. The wine list promotes fine California varietals and ports with choices available by the bottle, glass, or half glass. *$$–$$$; AE, DC, DIS, MC, V; no checks; lunch Mon–Fri, dinner every day; beer and wine; reservations recommended; www.waterboyrestaurant.com; at 20th St and Capitol Ave.* ♿

Zinfandel Grille / ★★★

2384 FAIR OAKS BLVD, SACRAMENTO; 916/485-7100

There are two Zinfandel Grilles—the original on Fair Oaks Boulevard, a second in Folsom (see review in the Restaurants section of Folsom)—a proliferation due to their history of consistently good and imaginative food. The menu (which changes every two months) still shines with the creative talents of the staff, who continue to please with entrées like the four-mushroom lasagne (porcini, oyster, cremini, and shiitake) with beautifully blended flavors and béchamel sauce; or the grilled, spice-crusted pork tenderloin with Anaheim chiles and zucchini, cilantro pesto, and fried polenta. And you must try one (or more) of the award-winning desserts—seasonal crème brûlée, tiramisu, and Boston cream pie. *$$$; AE, MC, V; no checks; lunch Mon–Fri, dinner every day; full bar; reservations recommended; www.zinfandelgrillesacramento.com; between Howe and Fulton aves.* ♿

LODGINGS

Amber House / ★★★

1315 22ND ST, SACRAMENTO; 916/444-8085 OR 800/755-6526

Amber House is actually two restored historic homes—a 1905 Craftsman and an 1895 Colonial Revival—set across the street from each other. The 10 guest rooms, named after artists, writers, and musicians, have private Italian-marble-tiled baths stocked with plush robes, flat-screen HD TVs with DVD players, CD players, free wireless Internet, phones with voice mail, Frette linens, and irons and boards. Some have iPod docks, and others have fireplaces. Seven rooms have Jacuzzis for two; the other three have antique soaking tubs. The Mozart and Vivaldi suites house private patios. Guests may enjoy their gourmet breakfast at whatever time they wish, served in their room, the dining room, or in one of the inn's gardens. Amber House is located on a quiet, shady street eight blocks from the capitol and is within easy walking distance of half a dozen of Sacramento's finest restaurants. *$$; AE, DC, DIS, MC, V; no checks; www.amberhouse.com; between Capitol Ave and N St.*

The Citizen Hotel / ★★★

926 J STREET, SACRAMENTO; 916/447-2700

If you are looking for more than just a room, Joie de Vie's newest boutique hotel located in downtown Sacramento is your best bet. About 200 uniquely decorated rooms make up this 1920s swanky hotel where you feel like you have been transported to another time. The Citizen's attention to detail runs throughout the single rooms and suites accented with top-of-the-line linens, robes, and bath essentials. All rooms offer flat-screen TVs, iPod docks, and Wi-Fi. The Grange restaurant located on the first floor of the hotel offers patrons a superior dining experience as well as a place to see the "who's who" of Sacramento. Grange fare is also available via room service. In addition, guests will appreciate the hotel's proximity to many downtown Sacramento attractions. *$$$; AE, DC, DIS, MC, V; www.citizenhotel.com; at 9th.* ♿

Hyatt Regency Sacramento / ★★★

1209 L ST, SACRAMENTO; 916/443-1234 OR 800/233-1234

The Hyatt and the nearby Sheraton Grand Sacramento (see review) are the only lodgings in Sacramento that truly feel like big-city hotels. Rooms, 375 square feet in size, are pretty run-of-the-mill with free wireless Internet, a minibar, a coffeemaker, satellite TV, a clock radio, and a morning newspaper. The Hyatt boasts a vaulted marble entryway; a sumptuous, light-filled atrium lounge; 500 beautifully appointed rooms with pretty views of palm-tree-lined Capitol Park; and excellent service. There are two fine restaurants within the hotel: Dawson's American Bistro and Vines, an all-seasons café featuring local produce. The outstanding artwork displayed throughout the hotel—murals, paintings, and wrought-iron railings and banisters—are by local artists. *$$$; AE, DC, DIS, MC, V; checks OK; www.sacramento.hyatt.com; at 12th St, across from the capitol.* ♿

Le Rivage / ★★★☆

4350 RIVERSIDE BLVD, SACRAMENTO; 916/443-8400 OR 888/760-5944

Surprisingly, not many Sacramento residents seem to know about this sprawling five-star hotel—perhaps because it's in a residential neighborhood right by the river and not the easiest place to find. The 101 rooms feature claw-foot tubs, wireless Internet, flat-screen televisions, refrigerators, safes, iPod clock radios, coffeemakers, hair dryers, and magnified makeup mirrors. Some rooms have private balconies, fireplaces, and Jacuzzis. There's also a fabulous spa, a fitness center, an outdoor pool and whirlpool, and bocce ball courts on-site. You can rent mountain bikes and Jet Skis seasonally, and there's even a riverfront bicycle trail. Those with boats can pull right up to the hotel off the Sacramento River and dock there. If you arrive by car you'll almost be forced to use the valet (despite the many vacant parking lots), which is a $21 charge. Many nights, there's live jazz in the lobby bar area. The Governator has been known to dine at the adjoining restaurant, Scott's Seafood on the River. *$$$–$$$$; AE, DIS, MC, V; checks OK; www.lerivagehotel.com; follow Riverside Blvd south, under I-5.* ♿

Sheraton Grand Sacramento Hotel / ★★★

1230 J ST, SACRAMENTO; 916/447-1700 OR 800/325-3535

Yet another player in downtown Sacramento's glitzy and glamorous overhaul, this 26-floor conversion of a the historic Public Market Building (designed in 1923 by renowned architect Julia Morgan) is a charmer. It's close to everything: the Sacramento Convention Center, the State Capitol complex, and some good restaurants and hot night spots (yes, you Bay Area snobs, hot night spots in Sacramento!). The Public Market Bar has become one of the places trendy folks gather after work. The 503 attractive guest rooms offer all the standard luxury amenities, plus one you won't find at almost any other major hotel—Sheraton's own Sweet Sleeper dog beds. The hotel has two restaurants: the Morgan Central Valley Bistro, with a splendid view of the soaring atrium, open for breakfast, lunch, and dinner; and the more casual Glides Market Café, open until 3pm, with indoor and outdoor seating and wireless access in case your date is a laptop. *$$$; AE, DC, DIS, MC, V; checks OK; www.starwood.com/sheraton; on J St between 12th and 13th sts.* ♿

Sterling Hotel / ★★★

1300 H ST, SACRAMENTO; 916/448-1300

This striking turn-of-the-century Victorian inn with its beautiful garden and manicured lawn immediately draws the attention of all who pass by. Inside, it's a sleek luxury hotel aimed at the upper echelon of corporate travelers. The interior is awash in Asian-influenced, neo-deco flourishes, and the artwork has a decidedly Zen twist. Even the impressive elevator is a sight to behold. The 17 guest rooms are large, airy, and spotless; each has a marble bathroom equipped with a Jacuzzi (some nearly the size of a small swimming pool), replicas of antique furniture, big CEO-style desks, voice mail and data ports, and numerous brass fixtures. Chanterelle, the hotel's small but highly regarded restaurant, is located on the ground floor with a charming patio for fair-weather dining. *$$$; AE, DC, MC, V; checks OK in advance; www.sterlinghotel.com; at 13th St.* ♿

Northern Central Valley

Leaving the urban, political sprawl of Sacramento, the Northern Central Valley opens into a patchwork of farmland and orchards, stitched together by country roads and small towns. From historic Sutter Street in Folsom to the charming college town of Chico, with its abundance of outdoor-activity options, this region of the Golden State has something for everyone.

Folsom

RESTAURANTS

Zinfandel Grille / ★★★

705 GOLD LAKE DR, FOLSOM; 916/985-3321

Located near Lake Natoma, this branch of the well-liked restaurant in Sacramento is very popular, even at lunchtime, so reservations are strongly advised. On par with the other fine dining establishments in Folsom, the Zinfandel serves such culinary delights as grilled portobello mushrooms and sweet onion risotto–fontina cake with a balsamic vinegar sauce for starters, followed by main courses such as spinach linguine with smoked salmon and mussels with leeks, fresh dill, shallots, and a touch of vermouth. For a full review, see the Restaurants section of Sacramento, home of the main location. *$$$; AE, MC, V; no checks; lunch, dinner every day; full bar; reservations recommended; in the Lakes shopping center.* ♿

Loomis

LODGINGS

The Flower Farm Inn / ★★★

4150 AUBURN–FOLSOM RD, LOOMIS; 916/652-4200

Set in a bucolic countryside and oozing charm from every 100-year-old board, the Old Flower Farm looks out over (what else?) a flower farm. With its century-old architecture lovingly painted and restored, it looks like a cover shot for *Sunset* magazine. And inside it's even more impressive. The seven rooms named after flowers each have a queen-size bed topped with an overstuffed down comforter and a private bath with a claw-foot tub and shower (complete with fresh-cut flowers, candles, and organic bath products). The private Hibiscus Cottage is a favorite of honeymooners, with its spa tub for two, vanity alcove, and lovely antique furniture. The swimming pool beckons on hot summer days, and Folsom Lake, a mecca for boaters and anglers, is only a five-minute drive away. Breakfasts are healthy and hearty, served with fresh fruit, homemade jams, and juices made from the farm's own fruit. *$$–$$$; AE, MC, V; checks OK; www.flowerfarminn.com; halfway between the towns of Auburn and Folsom, at Horseshoe Bar.*

Davis

The **UNIVERSITY OF CALIFORNIA AT DAVIS (UCD)** is this little city's claim to fame, particularly the college's respected veterinary science and enology schools. A former farming town, Davis is also famous for its city officials who pride themselves on finding more ecological ways of living on the planet. For example, to encourage people to cut down on fuel consumption, the city has built 67 miles of bike lanes and trails. The urban-village atmosphere of downtown Davis draws shoppers, diners, and browsers to its charming streets. Great minds of Davis get their world-shaking ideas while sipping espresso at **MISHKA'S CAFE** (514-B 2nd St; 530/759-0811; www.mishkascafe.com); they spend hours studying the works of other great minds at the **AVID READER** (617 2nd St; 530/758-4040); and they take out their aggressions by climbing the walls (literally) at **ROCKNASIUM** (720 Olive Dr; 530/757-2902; www.rocknasium.com). The $57 million **MONDAVI CENTER FOR THE PERFORMING ARTS** (at the southwest corner of UCD, I-80 exit UCD/Mondavi Center; 530/754-ARTS or 866/754-ARTS; www.mondaviarts.org) is the premier performance venue in the Sacramento Valley, with two theaters featuring world-famous personalities, musicians, dancers, and performance artists. Davis boasts one of the most appealing **FARMERS MARKETS** (Central Park, 3rd and B sts; Sat mornings and Wed evenings) in the nation, with lots of produce for purchase—mostly organic, naturally—and other gourmet foods prepared on the spot, as well as musicians and stuff for kids. Or, if you've always wanted to jump out of an airplane, try **SKYDANCE SKYDIVING** (Yolo County Airport; 800/759-3483; www.skydanceskydiving.net). For more information on what to see and do in Davis, call the **DAVIS CONFERENCE AND VISITORS BUREAU** (877/71DAVIS; www.davisvisitor.org).

RESTAURANTS

Dos Coyotes Border Cafe / ★★

1411 W COVELL BLVD #108, DAVIS; 530/753-0922
2191 COWELL BLVD #A, DAVIS; 530/758-1400

This distant outpost of Southwestern cuisine is one of the hottest restaurants in Davis. The crowds come for the fresh, consistently good food, such as the house-made salsas (help yourself to the salsa bar), shrimp tacos, and ranchero burritos with marinated steak, chicken, or vegetarian fillings. Equally good are the more unconventional offerings, such as the mahimahi taco or the Yucatan salad with marinated, charbroiled chicken breast, black beans, red onion, carrots, cabbage, sweet peppers, and corn served on a flour tortilla. Owner Bobby Coyote has turned his café into a howling success—even the branch in Sacramento (1735 Arden Wy; 916/927-0377) attracts crowds. *$; AE, MC, V; no checks; lunch, dinner every day; beer and wine; no reservations; www.doscoyotes.net; in the Marketplace shopping center, just east of Hwy 113.* ♿

LODGINGS

Hotel Palm Court / ★★

234 D ST, DAVIS; 530/753-7100 OR 800/528-1234

This chic, unobtrusive jewel is reminiscent of a fine little boutique hotel (you'd never guess it's owned by Best Western). The lobby is small and intimate with a

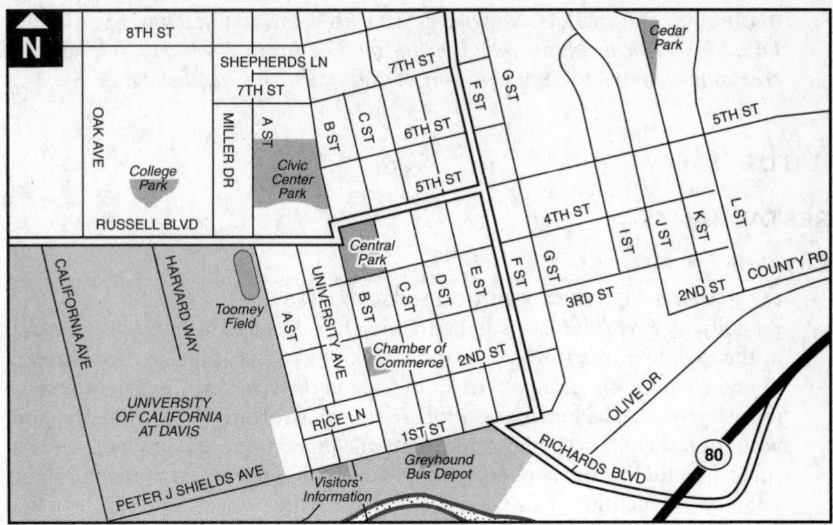

Davis

kind of Raffles Hotel look—English with a dash of East Indian. The 27 suites (all for nonsmokers) have lots of goodies for the serious traveler, including two TVs and telephones in every room, office desks, sofa beds (in addition to the beds in the adjoining rooms), irons and ironing boards, and hair dryers. The East Indian–English flair continues in the room decor, with dark wooden blinds; Regency furnishings in hues of rust, maroon, and gold; and handsome armoires that conceal TVs, honor bars, and refrigerators. The two Palm suites are the ritziest, with fireplaces, marble bathrooms with whirlpool baths, and full-length balconies. *$$; AE, DC, DIS, MC, V; no checks; www.bwpalmcourt.com; at 3rd St.* ♿

Woodland

RESTAURANTS

Morrison's Upstairs / ★★

428½ 1ST ST, WOODLAND; 530/666-6176

Tucked into the attic of one of Woodland's most striking buildings, an 1891 Queen Anne Victorian that was originally a luxury apartment house, Morrison's Upstairs combines old-fashioned elegance with a predinner aerobic workout; guests must climb three flights of stairs to reach the dining room. (The elevator is an option for those who are easily winded.) Favorite entrées include an abundance of creatively prepared fresh fish dishes, plump beer-batter prawns, fettuccine with prawns in a Parmesan cream sauce, perfectly cooked prime rib, and steak Morrison—a 12-ounce prime-cut New York strip smothered with mushrooms and shallots. Morrison's wine list is the best in town. *$$; AE, DC, DIS, MC, V; local checks only; lunch Mon–Fri, dinner every day; full bar; reservations recommended; www.morrisonsupstairs.com; at Bush St.* ♿

Yuba City

RESTAURANTS

City Cafe / ★★

667 PLUMAS ST, STE C, YUBA CITY; 530/671-1501

By golly, sleepy Yuba City's gone trendy with this chic little café smack-dab in the middle of the town's historic section. Take a seat inside the bistrolike dining room (a bit cramped) or sit outside in the courtyard, where you have more legroom. The lunch menu focuses on an assortment of panini prepared with focaccia and herb mayo, including the popular grilled eggplant, sautéed spinach, mild banana pepper, and feta sandwich. Dinner is a more ambitious affair, with such items as Cajun jambalaya with prawns, chicken, smoked ham, and sausage in a tomato broth over rice, and charbroiled fillet steak in a cherry pepper and miso demi-glace served with grilled bok choy and mashed potatoes. City Cafe has a good selection of beer and wine, with many wines available by the glass. *$$–$$$; DIS, MC, V; no checks; lunch Mon–Fri, dinner Tues–Sat; full bar; reservations recommended; at Colusa Hwy.* ♿

Ruthy's Bar and Oven / ★★

229 CLARK AVE, YUBA CITY; 530/674-2611

If you're a big breakfast eater, make a beeline to Ruthy's. You'll find such belly-packing fare as French toast made with Ruthy's own cinnamon-raisin bread, terrific whole wheat and buttermilk pancakes, and creative egg dishes such as the omelet stuffed with Monterey Jack cheese and prawns sautéed in garlic-herb butter. For lunch, head straight for the salad bar or order a sandwich served on house-made bread. Dinner is more elaborate, with interesting appetizers like little chicken quesadillas, tiny New Zealand clams steamed in a garlic and white wine sauce, and spicy Cajun prawns in a garlic red pepper sauce. Entrées vary from house-made fettuccine tossed with house-smoked salmon to a spicy chicken stir-fry. *$$; AE, DIS, MC, V; checks OK; breakfast Sat–Sun, lunch, dinner Tues–Sat; full bar; no reservations; in the Hillcrest Plaza mini-mall, south of Franklin Rd.* ♿

LODGINGS

Harkey House / ★★

212 C ST, YUBA CITY; 530/674-1942

Sitting just a few hundred feet from the Yuba River, this cream-colored 1874 Victorian Gothic B and B trimmed in gold offers four guest rooms with private baths, a cottage, and diversions such as a spa, a chess table, and an antique Chickering piano. Outside there is a garden with a swimming pool, deck furniture, and a hammock. The spacious Camilla's Cottage has a fireplace, French hutch, marble table, TV-VCR-CD player, small kitchen, two-person shower, and oriental rugs. The soft green Empress Room features a gas fireplace, antique kimono, and water fountain. In the solarium-style dining area guests are treated to a full breakfast, which might include Belgian waffles, zucchini croquettes, Canadian bacon, fresh fruit, and scones. *$$; AE, DIS, MC, V; checks OK; www.harkeyhouse.com; in Old Town, across from the courthouse.*

Marysville

RESTAURANTS

Silver Dollar Saloon / ★

330 1ST ST, MARYSVILLE; 530/743-0507

As you amble up to the Silver Dollar Saloon, be sure to pay your respects to the massive wooden cowboy standing guard at the entrance. This restaurant and saloon is a lively relic of Marysville's frontier past, with Western memorabilia scattered throughout the building. The menu features terrific grilled steaks and steak sandwiches, grilled chicken, hot pastrami sandwiches, and delectable barbecued ribs. For those craving a lighter meal, they also serve up some tasty grilled vegetables, and to give the place a hint of multiculturalism, the Honolulu-born owner has added some Hawaiian specialties. On Friday and Saturday nights the place is packed with cowpokes tappin' their boots to the country music mixed by a DJ. *$; MC, V; no checks; lunch, dinner Mon–Sat; full bar; no reservations; www.silverdollarsteaks.com; in Old Town, between C and D sts.* ♿

Williams

LODGINGS

Wilbur Hot Springs / ★★

3375 WILBUR SPRINGS RD, WILBUR SPRINGS; 530/473-2306

This sanctuary was named after Ezekial Wilbur, who, with a partner in the 1860s, purchased 640 acres along Sulfur Creek to mine copper. When the mining venture failed, Wilbur bought out his partner, built a small hotel, and opened Wilbur Hot Springs. Today Wilbur sits 22 miles west of Williams, on private property within a 15,000-acre nature preserve. You'll find no electricity here—the hotel is softly lit with solar power and warmed by gas fireplaces. There are 17 private guest rooms (toilets are located, European-style, throughout the hotel), a spacious suite with private bath and kitchen, and a comfortable 11-bed bunk room. Since there is no restaurant, guests bring their own groceries and use the well-equipped commercial kitchen, where dry spices, cookware, utensils, dishes, and refrigeration and freezer storage are supplied. The hot springs area (the highlight of your stay) is dimly lit with Japanese lanterns and sheltered by a cedar A-frame bathhouse where clothing is optional and noise is a no-no. Guests have 24-hour access to the hot springs. A spacious redwood deck surrounds the bathhouse and leads to an 80°F outdoor pool, a dry sauna, and private outdoor showers. *$$–$$$; MC, V; checks OK; www.wilburhotsprings.com; from I-5, take Hwy 20 W, go north on Bear Valley Rd (4 miles), turn left onto Wilbur Springs Rd at the Wilbur Silver Bridge, drive 1 mile, and enter gate.*

Oroville

Oroville has been largely, and undeservedly, overlooked by tourists. This historic gold rush town is the site of the second major gold discovery after Coloma and the center of a rich agricultural industry (specializing in cattle, citrus, nuts, and olives). The **OROVILLE CHINESE TEMPLE AND GARDEN** (1500 Broderick St; 530/538-2496) was built in 1863 to serve the 10,000 Chinese who worked the mines here. It has an extensive collection of tapestries, costumes, and puppets used in Chinese opera, and its lovely gardens, planted exclusively with plants from China, offer a great place for meditation. The 770-foot-tall **OROVILLE DAM** (from Hwy 70, head east on Oroville Dam Blvd) is the tallest earthen dam in the country, and **LAKE OROVILLE** (530/538-2219) is regularly rated as one of the best bass fishing spots in the United States. It is also a house boaters' paradise, with 24 square miles of surface area and 167 miles of shoreline. Just south of the dam you can rent a houseboat, ski boat, or wave-runner and find out where to reel in the big ones by visiting the folks at **BIDWELL CANYON MARINA** (801 Bidwell Canyon Rd; 530/589-3165; www.gobidwell.com). The 640-foot-high **FEATHER FALLS**, the sixth-tallest waterfall in the country, is a worthy side trip if you're up for a moderately strenuous hike. Your reward: spectacular views of the falls, the Sacramento Valley, and the Coast Range; for directions and details, call the **OROVILLE AREA CHAMBER OF COMMERCE** (530/538-2542; www.orovilleareachamber.net).

Berry Creek

LODGINGS

Lake Oroville Bed and Breakfast / ★★★

240 SUNDAY DR, BERRY CREEK; 530/589-0700 OR 800/455-LAKE

"Silent, upon a peak in Darien. . . ." With apologies to Mr. Keats, make that "upon the outskirts of Oroville" and you have a pretty fair description of the Lake Oroville Bed and Breakfast, sitting in lonely yellow splendor on 40 acres high above the lake, with views in every direction. Built in 1992, the B and B has six guest bedrooms with private entrances and baths, and five

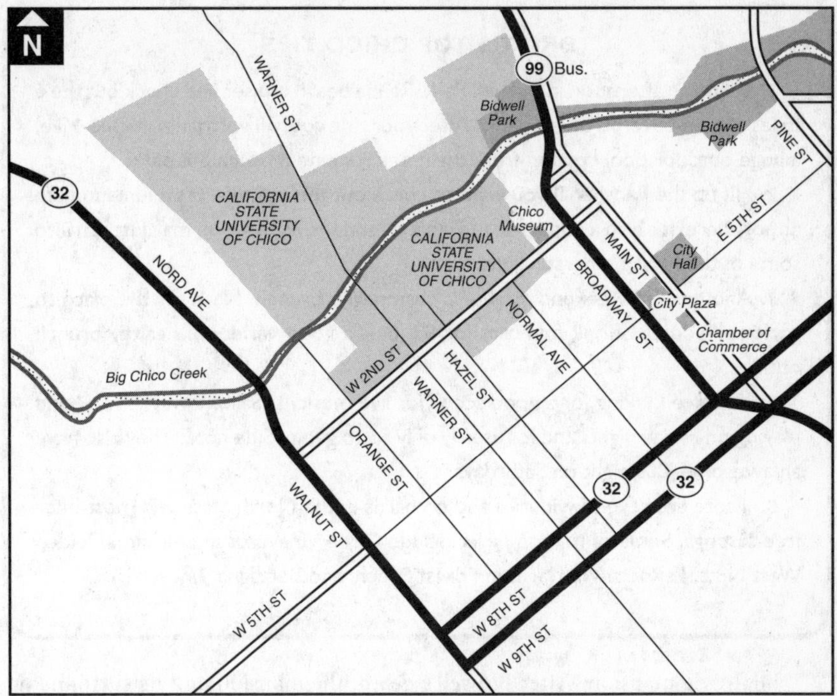

Chico

of them have whirlpool tubs. The Rose Petal Room is appropriately covered with rose-print wallpaper, and a white Battenberg bedspread is draped over the king-size bed, from which you have a view of the lake, as you do from the Victorian Room. The Monet Room, Max's Room, the Arbor Room, and the Vine Room all have queen-size beds and views of the surrounding woods. Breakfast is a hearty affair, with a choice of quiche, eggs Benedict, crepes, waffles, or French toast. There's even a small playroom for children, and many family reunions and other group events are hosted here, too. A gas grill is available for guests who get so downright relaxed they'd rather barbecue than drive into town for dinner. Pets are welcome. *$$; AE, DIS, MC, V; checks OK; www.lakeorovillebedandbreakfast.com; from Hwy 70 take Oroville Dam Blvd/Hwy 162 east for 1.7 miles, turn right at Olive Hwy, continue for 13½ miles, then turn left at Bell Ranch Rd, bear right, and go ½ mile to Sunday Dr.* ♿

Chico

This charming little city was founded in 1860 by John Bidwell, a member of the first wagon-train expedition to reach California. After he struck gold near Oroville and purchased land along Chico Creek, he built a three-story Italian

BRITT'S TOP CHICO TIPS

1. Spend an afternoon in Bidwell Park. Rent a beach cruiser and check out the 6 miles of tree-covered paved paths. After your ride cool off with a dip in One-Mile, a huge outdoor pool created from the creek running through the park.

2. Hit up the Banshee if you want to check out the nightlife. It's a fun, intimate atmosphere. It's also a good place to start or end the night—you may just run into some of the local TV personalities.

3. Another fun weekend activity is champagne brunch. Nash's is the place to go for all-you-can-drink mimosas for $3, plus a good variety of healthy brunch options.

4. If you're looking for a good scene for live music, LaSalles always has a band playing on Friday nights and it's usually only $5 to get in. Side note: They also have an awesome '80s night on Saturdays.

5. There are several wineries and orchards in the North State and most offer free tastings. Some of my top picks include Gayle Vineyards in Durham, Golden West Nuts, LaRocca Vineyards in Forest Ranch, and Bertagna Vineyards.

villa–style mansion. After Bidwell's death, the mansion and its surrounding grounds were donated for the establishment of a Christian school and later became **CALIFORNIA STATE UNIVERSITY–CHICO (CHICO STATE)**. Today, **BIDWELL MANSION STATE HISTORIC PARK** stands adjacent to the beautifully landscaped campus grounds surrounded by hundreds of varieties of trees Bidwell introduced to the area. Across town, **BIDWELL PARK** is a 3,600-acre playground for outdoor enthusiasts, with swimming holes; hiking, biking, and equestrian trails; picnic areas; and facilities for organized sports. These days, Chico State, once known as the nation's number-one party school, has a new designation as the nation's number-one bike town, with user-friendly bike paths leading in and out of town. **UPPER BIDWELL PARK** has become somewhat of a mecca for mountain bikers.

To find out what's going on around town, settle in at one of the espresso bars and thumb through the **CHICO NEWS AND REVIEW** (353 E 2nd St; 530/894-2300; www.newsreview.com), the city's fine alternative-press newspaper. Or simply relax à la Chico by observing the brewing-to-bottling process and sampling the award-winning ales and lagers at **SIERRA NEVADA BREWING COMPANY** (1075 E 20th St; 530/893-3520; www.sierra-nevada.com); free tours are offered daily.

6. Tubing down the Sacramento River is a popular summertime activity. Gas stations sell tubes—just take 5th Street down to Scotty's Landing and follow the crowd.

7. Need some downtime? Bidwell Perk is an adorable local coffee shop off the beaten path that has a relaxing atmosphere and delicious coffee.

8. Just an hour to the east of Chico is Lake Almanor. It's a perfect mountain getaway and a great place to wakeboard in the summer.

9. Take a tour of the Sierra Nevada Brewery. It's one of the coolest establishments in Chico. Save room for a pale ale draft and pretty much anything on their elaborate menu.

10. Head to downtown on a weekend. Meters are free and there's an awesome farmers market every Saturday. Plus, boutique shopping in downtown is a fun way to spend an afternoon. I love LuLu's for clothing; they have cute stuff at great prices. Bird in Hand is a great artsy store and oddly enough the National Yo-Yo Museum is located in the back.

Britt Carlson is a reporter and anchor for KHSL-TV in Chico who's always searching for new, fun activities in the North State.

RESTAURANTS

The Albatross / ★★

3312 THE ESPLANADE, CHICO; 530/345-6037

Set in a neighborhood of old mansions, the Albatross was a private home before it was converted into a dinner house with several small, casual dining rooms and a wonderfully landscaped garden patio. The service is excellent, and despite the waitstaff's aloha attire and the restaurant's tropical decor, you won't find any pounded taro root or papaya salsa on the menu. What you will find is well-prepared mahimahi, fresh salmon topped with champagne butter, and blackened swordfish, as well as steak and slow-roasted prime rib. All the entrées come with steaming-hot sourdough and squaw bread, choice of potato, and unlimited trips to the first-rate salad bar. Top off your meal with the ultrarich Island Pie: macadamia nut ice cream piled onto a cookie-crumb crust and smothered with fudge, whipped cream, and a sprinkling of almonds. *$$; AE, MC, V; checks OK; lunch Mon–Fri, dinner every day; full bar; reservations recommended; www.thealbatross.com; north of downtown.* ♿

The Black Crow Grill and Taproom / ★★★

209 SALEM ST, CHICO; 530/892-1392

This popular downtown restaurant has reasonably priced meals, good service, and a lively atmosphere. Check the daily specials menu, which features a choice of wines, starters, entrées, and desserts. Try the Fuji apple salad with organic baby greens, blue cheese, currants, and caramelized walnuts with aged balsamic vinaigrette for a start. Entrées include house-made linguine with bay scallops, corn, roasted tomato, and a white wine–artichoke basil pesto sauce; lemon roasted half chicken served with garlic mashed potatoes and herbed pan gravy; and pan-roasted Atlantic salmon, seared and smothered with an orange stone-ground-mustard butter sauce. And if it's on the menu, don't miss their creamy lemon brûlée, a perfect end to a satisfying meal. *$$; AE, MC, V; checks OK; lunch, dinner Mon–Sat, brunch Sat–Sun; full bar; reservations recommended; www.theblackcrow.com; corner of 2nd and Salem sts.* ♿

LODGINGS

Johnson's Country Inn / ★★★★

3935 MOOREHEAD AVE, CHICO; 530/345-7829 OR 866/872-7780

Set in the heart of a picture-perfect almond orchard, this Victorian-style farmhouse is an ideal place for a wedding, an anniversary, or simply a peaceful retreat—and you'd never notice that it's only five minutes from downtown Chico. Built specifically as a B and B in 1992, the inn has four guest rooms, all with private baths. The Icart Room is furnished in a French country–style in shades of green, blue, and rose (and it's wheelchair accessible). The Jarrett Room is decorated in soft greens and blues and has a view of the orchard from an upstairs window. The Sexton Room is decked out in floral hues of rose, beige, and blue with furnishings designed by William Morris, the famous pre-Raphaelite English artist and poet. The romantic Harrison Room has an 1860s Victorian double bed, a fireplace, and a private Jacuzzi. Owners David and Joan Johnson deliver a coffee and juice tray in the morning then later bring an ample country breakfast, including locally made apple sausages, peach French toast, frittata, and almond coffee cakes (you can guess where the almonds come from—as do many of the fresh fruits and herbs in season). Wine is provided each afternoon to allow guests to decompress from a hard day on the croquet court; sip it while swinging in the outdoor hammock or in front of the fireplace in the library. *$$; AE, MC, V; checks OK; www.chico.com/johnsonsinn; travel west on W 5th St for 1 mile, past Walnut to Moorhead Ave.* ♿

Red Bluff

LODGINGS

Jeter Victorian Inn / ★★

1107 JEFFERSON ST, RED BLUFF; 530/527-7574

If you're a fan of true Victoriana, this is your place. Completely furnished in authentic antiques, this warm and appealing bed-and-breakfast features five guest rooms filled with the period art and furniture that owner Mary

Dunlap has collected for more than 50 years. The inn is on a quiet, tree-lined street, in a lovely garden setting, where, weather permitting, bountiful breakfasts are served alfresco. Red Bluff is noted for its antique shops and Victorian-era museums. Spending the night in one is even better. *$$; MC, V; checks OK; www.jetervictorianinn.com; corner of Union and Jefferson sts, 2 blocks east of Union.*

Index

C

D

E

H

M

N

O

Q

R

Q

R

S

T

U

V

W

Best Places Northern California Report Form

Based on my personal experience, I wish to nominate the following restaurant, place of lodging, shop, nightclub, sight, or other as a "Best Place"; or confirm/correct/disagree with the current review.

(Please include address and telephone number of establishment, if convenient.)

REPORT

Please describe food, service, style, comfort, value, date of visit, and other aspects of your experience; continue on another piece of paper if necessary.

I am not associated, directly or indirectly, with the management or ownership of this establishment.

SIGNED

ADDRESS

PHONE **DATE**

Please address to *Best Places Northern California* and send to:

SASQUATCH BOOKS
119 SOUTH MAIN STREET, SUITE 400
SEATTLE, WA 98104

Feel free to e-mail feedback as well: **BPFEEDBACK@SASQUATCHBOOKS.COM**